The Fleischmann Report

Volume I

The Fleischmann Report

On the Quality, Cost, and Financing of Elementary and Secondary Education in New York State

THE VIKING PRESS
NEW YORK

All rights reserved

Published in 1973 in a hardbound and paperbound edition by
The Viking Press, Inc.
625 Madison Avenue, New York, N.Y. 10022

Published simultaneously in Canada by
The Macmillan Company of Canada Limited

SBN 670–31778–0 (hardbound)
    670–00369–7 (paperbound)

Library of Congress catalog card number: 72–81121

Printed in U.S.A. by The Colonial Press Inc.

Foreword

This Commission was appointed late in 1969 by joint action of Governor Rockefeller and the Board of Regents of the State of New York. Earlier that year the Legislature had made an initial appropriation to finance such a Commission. In succeeding years, the Commission has continued to receive not only generous financial support in difficult economic circumstances, but, of equal importance, the invaluable assistance and experienced counsel of its three sponsors. On behalf of the Commission, I express our gratitude for all of this help, unstintingly and (so we felt) enthusiastically given. It seemed to us that this broad public support for the work of the Commission was a clear expression of the faith which the citizens of this state continue to manifest: better education for everyone offers the best chance for major improvement in the quality of American life in the years ahead. The members of the Commission share that faith and consider themselves to have been privileged to participate in this great undertaking.

The mission of this Commission is to report on the quality, cost and financing of elementary and secondary education in New York State, and to make recommendations for the improvement of performance in all these dimensions. The mission which has been given to us indicates clearly that those who created the Commission envisaged perhaps the most comprehensive report on primary and secondary education ever authorized by a single state. The members of the Commission have accepted this ambitious purpose. The people of New York State will judge how far we have succeeded in carrying out our formidable undertaking.

The intensive study which we have conducted over the last two years demonstrates to us the wisdom of reviewing the three subjects—quality, cost and financing of education—in a single endeavor. It is now clear to all of us that quality, cost and financing are inextricably interrelated. Quality cannot be considered in a vacuum, since a price must be paid for it; both quality and permissible cost are in turn affected by the equity and the productiveness of the means that are selected to finance the educational programs.

In the balance of the report, it will be observed that we have added two other general subjects for analysis, namely, governance and organization. These cut across considerations of quality, cost and financing, and consideration of these subjects is essential if proposals for substantive change are to achieve their maximum benefits.

The same two years of study have impressed the Commission increasingly as each day has gone by with the vast scope of the inquiry which has been entrusted to us, and with the impossibility of a wholly satisfactory solution for some of the most pressing problems of American education. The Commission soon became aware of the necessity for setting down a rule of self-limitation. The problems of American education are aspects of the problems of American life. In this nation we face a breathtaking pace of change in the condition of life; a shift from traditional mores and disciplines to new, more fluid and experimental codes; a lack of agreement on national priorities. We confront poverty and a housing shortage, the financial drain of the war in Vietnam and the on-going arms race, the spread of violence and drug addiction as supposed solutions to, or escapes from, an unhappy reality. And all of this is taking place while unprecedented changes in knowledge and communications occur almost daily—changes at once disturbing and promising which have expanded the limits of man's physical activities beyond the moon.

Clearly no one Commission can responsibly attempt the solution of all of these problems. While the problems of education cannot be wholly separated from the larger problems of American society and the world of today, we have decided that an attempt to prescribe for the totality of our social ills would dilute our proposals for improvements of the educational system as such. Our report reflects this decision. Thus, for example, while the phenomenon of violence in the schools has an obvious and pressing relevance to urban educational problems, it is here considered only in relation to education but is not given major attention. This matter is now under investigation by other qualified groups and individuals; we have felt it wise to concentrate our efforts essentially on problems distinctive to education. We have deliberately not attempted to solve great problems which impinge on our field but which appear to be incapable of solution in a purely educational context.

While some of the Commission members are or have been professional educators, others (including the Chairman) lacked that experience. Not only have these latter had little precise knowledge of education, but we have discovered that we had a substantial number of misconceptions about it. In particular, it came as a surprise to learn how little hard knowledge exists in the field of education—and specifically with respect to the manner in which education of high quality can be produced. As examples, there is no broad agreement among educators as to what method of teaching reading is most effective (though all are agreed that all but a very few children can be taught to read adequately); there is no agreement as to the optimum size of a class in primary or secondary schools; a continuous controversy drags on as to the merits of "open" schools as against their more formal counterparts; last but hardly least, there is not even a consensus as to what the "goals" or "objectives" of education should be. These matters have been subject to debate for decades, in some cases for centuries, but disagreements persist.

Millions of dollars have been spent on educational research and it is important to understand the reasons for the lack of agreement on basic principles. One reason is that education touches on the goals of human life and society, matters on which disagreement is to be expected. Another is that there have been very few *comprehensive* research projects directed at major educational problems. Such projects take years to conduct, or cost vast sums of money, or both. And because the innumerable conditions to be controlled are almost beyond control, results are seldom decisive. An example is the 1966 Coleman Report, *Equal Educational Opportunity,* thought by many to be one of the great American education research projects. Despite its reputation, controversy now rages among educators as to the adequacy of the methodology and the validity of the conclusions. In our society we have not reached the necessary threshold of commitment to lengthy and expensive study of human behavior which might conceivably permit commissions such as ours to base recommendations upon more conclusive scientific findings.

With this history in mind, it was apparent that we had neither time nor resources available to permit us to conduct broad independent research which would add substantially to the fund of new and proven knowledge and provide needed breakthroughs in the field of education. This was all the more obvious because of the number and variety of subjects upon which we were asked to express our considered judgment.

Accordingly, we came to recognize that our task was not unlike that of a royal commission in Great Britain—to gather all available data in the field; to expose ourselves to a cross-section of expert opinion; to analyze and systematize it; to fill in interstices by additional research projects, often of a very substantial nature, presenting available and some new data in new relationships; to identify the problems, and to examine alternative solutions. Then—most difficult of all—our task was to recommend the best or (sometimes) the least disastrous solution upon the basis of the frequently inadequate data available. This, as we came to see, was just the task which governors, legislators, Regents, and decision-makers face every day in every important concern of life. If our conclusions have merit, it is because we had resources not available to decision-makers in general—first, two years of concentrated study; second, the dedicated guidance of a staff of distinguished educators; third, continuous counsel from the educational community as a whole; and fourth, the financial resources to carry on the specific research projects essential to a sound evaluation.

In addition to our discovery of great gaps in the basic information available in major fields of educational policy, we must record one other major problem which plagued us. We gave much study to what may currently be the most difficult educational problem of all, namely, how to match limited resources (particularly in years of fiscal crisis for New York State), with constantly increasing demands upon the educational dollar, many of these demands justified and even essential if good education is to be available equally for all the children of this state. The historical evolution of the problem is clear. New York State, like most of the states of the Union, has experienced a rapid increase in the number of students in the past quarter-century. Salaries, wages and benefits of teachers, administrators and other school workers account for approximately 84 per cent of educational operating expenditures. Such remuneration also increased rapidly during the same period; these workers, like others, suffered from the on-going inflation which still grips the nation.

Even now, after this vast acceleration of educational expenditure, we are faced with legitimate demands for increased personnel to meet the state's obligation to underprivileged and handicapped children. Simultaneously, the state must consider major new expenditures, either for aid to parochial schools which are in a financial crisis or, alternatively, for the education of students who may be forced to transfer into the public schools. The hope held by many of our citizens that advances in technology can reduce or limit teacher expenditures, we have found to our sorrow, is only a hope. Technology is not sufficiently advanced to contribute substantially to the solution of educational problems during the present decade, though with the support of large developmental expenditures which ought to be made by the Federal Government, it can unquestionably do so thereafter.

On the brighter side, birthrate statistics point finally to a leveling off, and perhaps even a slight decline in student enrollment over the coming decade. Consequently, the need for an ever-increasing number of new teachers should diminish.

In this report, we have confronted the pervasive problem of increasing cost in a variety of ways. We discuss, for example, greater use of trained paraprofessionals in the schools in the many situations where this seems appropriate. We have studied our public employees' pension system as it affects present and future employees. We review the justification for maintenance of the very large number of non-teaching educational personnel generally designated as administrators; this is a category in which New York is consistently the leader of the nation in per-pupil expenditure. We have proposed cost-saving techniques in the provision of supplies and non-educational services and in the use of physical facilities; in particular, we propose enabling legislation to permit school districts to adopt a continuous learning year. Most important of all, we have attempted to take advantage of the leveling off of the student population which is now taking place. We believe that all of this should result in the state's ability to control increasing educational expenditures more successfully than in the past.

A word about certain characteristics of our report. The substance of our recommendations has necessarily been profoundly influenced by a series of judicial decisions of great importance; the most significant of these have been handed down during the past year, and some of them are still on appeal to higher tribunals. They bear upon such vital subjects as the financing of education as it affects equality of educational opportunity; racial segregation; aid to parochial schools; and special obligations of the state with respect to certain handicapped children. Some of these have literally been landmark opinions which, if upheld, would drastically limit the options of New York State in these areas. The lawyers on the Commission and staff have appraised these decisions to the best of their professional ability. It has been our general purpose to propose changes in New York's educational system which would be essential if the state is to meet judicial standards which we believe to be sound in principle and constitutionally valid. In our view it is better for New York to adopt a plan which meets constitutional criticism of the kind now emerging, rather than be forced to alter its educational system in haste as a consequence of judicial mandate.

It should be observed that the Chairman, at least, has nursed a deep aversion to commission reports which mainly recommend further study of the subjects the commission was created to study. We have tried to keep such recommendations to a minimum, but we could not entirely eliminate them. Great problems of life require endless difficult reappraisals.

In making our recommendations, it has been our constant endeavor to be as precise as possible. It has been our conviction that our report will be little noted nor long remembered unless it is very specific indeed and makes concrete legislative and administrative proposals which, if approved by the public, will be adopted and put into effect over the next few years. This, in our judgment, is the most frequent shortcoming of educational studies of this sort, and we have tried to avoid it. Dr. Allan Sproul had this to say about a report on "Education for the Urban-Disadvantaged" by the Research and Policy Committee of the Committee for Economic Development (of which he was a member):

There are a lot of raisins in this pudding but they are encased in a melange of noble intention and good advice without adequate consideration of the priorities or means. Whatever the educational value of the statement may be in the area in which many studies have been and are being made, the thrust towards effective action is diffuse and weak.

It is our hope that no such criticism can fairly be leveled at this report.

The five broad categories of problems which we have studied call for different types of solutions. Thus, in areas of cost, financing, governance and organization, we have not hesitated to recommend far-reaching legislative changes which we have thought necessary. When such problems could be solved without legislative change, we have suggested appropriate administrative measures.

Obviously, while we expect the recommended changes in cost, financing, governance and organization to have important beneficial consequences on the quality of education, this is a long-range project and improvement cannot wait. Therefore, while we have not intended to write a textbook on pedagogy, we have reviewed most of the controversial issues of educational policy and practice, and have given our views with respect to what our educational goals should be and how we can approach them. Sometimes, but not usually, this has meant changes in statutes or administrative regulations. More often, however, we have simply expressed what we hope is the best informed opinion on such subjects as how to improve reading skills with the greatest speed. In such areas, to borrow Commissioner Nyquist's happy phrase, we hope simply to qualify as "forward-looking, perceptive and artful navigators of areas of ignorance."

Finally, the Commission set another ground rule for itself. Wherever possible, each recommendation has a price tag attached to it. Because of the possibility of continued inflation, this could be no more than a sketchy estimate in cases where a proposed program would take shape over the next decade. In addition, we have given our own view as to the most effective, equitable and socially desirable manner to meet additional financial requirements. It will be noted that we have followed this rule even to the extent of proposing alternative methods of financing. We did this because, while it is the unanimous view of the Commission that a much larger share of the cost of public education ought to be borne by the Federal Government, there is no assurance that this is going to happen.

We followed this course for at least three reasons: (1) All of us are surfeited with reports at the national and state levels which urge the adoption of grandiose and often desirable programs without pricing them or even suggesting where the money is to come from; (2) we thought such an effort was certainly within our mandate; and (3) while not always limiting ourselves to what appeared clearly feasible from a legislative standpoint (since not all of us could claim expertise in such prognostications), it seemed probable that the Governor, the Legislature, the Regents, and the public at large, would all give more serious consideration to particular proposals as well as to the over-all program if they were advised as to the probable financial and tax consequences of their acceptance. We thought this quite indispensable at a time like the present, when New York State faces an economic crisis as grave as any in our history. We understand that one consequence of this crisis may well be to postpone improvements involving expenditures which otherwise would be clearly justified and essential.

It should be remembered, however, that changes of the magnitude we have suggested cannot be accomplished in a single year. We therefore hope that if our proposals meet general approval, the Legislature will act during the 1972 session to create the legal framework necessary for the reorganization to be accomplished in a succeeding year. In the same way, we hope that school boards, administrators and teachers will take steps immediately to bring about recommended changes in areas of their responsibility since many of them require little or no increase in current expenditures.

In a field so complex and difficult no one can be certain of the validity of his own conclusions. Particularly is this so when controversial matters inevitably evoke opposing views. As Chairman, however, I am perhaps particularly aware of the high competence and dedication of my fellow Commissioners and our indefatigable staff. It is, of course, the hope of all of us that our recommendations will become effective during the years ahead but regardless of what occurs, the Commission, I believe, will leave a priceless legacy of study, analysis and research which will be useful for decades to come. I therefore commend the report to the serious consideration of the people of the State of New York.

MANLY FLEISCHMANN
Chairman

NOTE ON FORMAT   Separate statements by one or more Commissioners, whether concurring or dissenting, are printed at the ends of the relevant chapters. Other appendices follow those sections.

Contents

3 FEDERAL AID TO EDUCATION 209

Why Federal Government Participation? 209
The Future Federal Role, 212
Summary, 219
Appendix:

4 RACIAL AND ETHNIC INTEGRATION IN THE PUBLIC SCHOOLS 225

Appendices:

5 AID TO NONPUBLIC SCHOOLS 387

Appendices:

Subsequent chapters of the Fleischmann report will be published in two volumes in 1973.

The Fleischmann Report

1

The State of Education in New York

The public school system in New York State has undergone massive expansion in the past quarter century, almost doubling its student body since 1945—from 1,783,325 to 3,489,245 in 1970.[1] The major priority has been to find the resources and build the schools to take care of rising numbers. This job is largely finished; even high estimates of pupil enrollment for the coming decade show only a small increase compared to the past rate of growth. Conservative projections show that the size of public school enrollment in 1980 could actually be smaller than it is today.

Fiscal and administrative energies can therefore be turned in other directions in the coming decade: achieving equity in financing and programming, improving the quality of teaching and raising the level of pupil performance. This report will propose specific steps to be taken toward these goals. But first we must make as accurate an assessment as we can of the present state of education in New York State.

How many students are there? How many teachers? How much money is now spent on education and where is the money going? What kind of student is benefiting most from the educational system? Which students are benefiting least? Is quality adequate? How effective is school management? Can resources be used more efficiently and economically?

Three major findings deserve emphasis before we present detailed data in response to these questions:

1. First, New York State has made a notable effort over the last several decades to improve the quality of its schools. Enrollments have been

3

growing, but so have expenditures and staff. Many of its students have succeeded in national competition. By now, the resources of New York State's educational system are second to no other state. According to most of the traditional indicators of quality—ratio of staff to students, teacher salaries, expenditures per student—New York ranks at or near the top of the nation. The record of the past is reason for high hopes for the future.

2. The biggest problem in the state is the high correlation between school success or failure and the student's socio-economic and racial origins. The higher on the socio-economic scale a child is, the more likely he is to succeed in school. While children from affluent backgrounds score well on standardized tests, graduate from high school and attend college, children from low-income and minority backgrounds fail in school in numbers which far exceed their proportion of the state's total population. In spite of high expenditures and quality improvements, New York State is not providing equality of educational opportunity to its students as long as the pattern of school success and school failure remains closely tied to a child's social origins.

3. Certain educational problems are not getting the attention they deserve —the problems of racial and ethnic imbalance, non-English-speaking students, handicapped students and drug abuse. These areas will be considered at length in separate chapters.

Our detailed report on the state of education follows, beginning with an analysis of enrollment trends and an evaluation of school system resources, then moving on to a discussion of the relationship between socio-economic status and school achievement.

ENROLLMENT TRENDS

Growth of Student Body Since 1930

In 1930, enrollment in New York State public schools was 2.10 million. By 1945, following the Depression and World War II, the number had dropped to 1.78 million. From then on enrollment grew steadily, exceeding 2.77 million in 1960 and rising to 3.49 million in 1970—nearly doubling in size over 25 years. (Table 1.1.) In 1970–71, there were an additional 784,058 students, representing 18.3 per cent of the school-age population of the state, enrolled in nonpublic schools.[2] (Table 1.2.)

Future Enrollment

Figures 1.1, 1.2 and 1.3 depict actual public school enrollments in New York State from 1930 to 1970 and three versions of projected enrollments

TABLE 1.1

Fall Enrollment in Public Elementary and Secondary Schools, 1930–31 to 1970–71

School Year	Entire State Fall Enrollment	Upstate Fall Enrollment	New York City Fall Enrollment
1930–31	2,098,892	1,033,496	1,065,396
1935–36	2,199,336	1,078,087	1,121,249
1940–41	2,083,651	1,024,882	1,058,769
1945–46	1,783,325	940,231	843,094
1950–51	1,933,907	1,408,699	885,208
1956–57	2,420,170	1,492,172	927,998
1957–58	2,527,850	1,577,613	950,237
1958–59	2,622,602	1,654,738	967,864
1959–60	2,697,676	1,720,145	977,531
1960–61	2,770,824	1,784,127	986,697
1961–62	2,856,168	1,851,899	1,004,269
1962–63	2,960,568	1,933,140	1,027,428
1963–64	3,051,006	2,005,452	1,045,554
1964–65	3,121,717	2,067,516	1,054,201
1965–66	3,176,574	2,116,520	1,060,054
1966–67	3,248,879	2,171,034	1,077,845
1967–68	3,325,477	2,225,255	1,100,222
1968–69	3,397,413	2,280,702	1,116,711
1969–70	3,442,809	2,328,783	1,113,826
1970–71	3,489,245	2,353,947	1,135,298

Notes on sources for tables and figures begin on page 465.

to 1980 for New York State, Upstate New York and New York City, respectively.[3] All three projections were derived from population forecasts prepared by the State Office of Planning Services (OPS) based on 1970 Census data. All three share common assumptions about student promotion, repetition and dropout rates over the coming decade. The dropout rate, for example, is estimated to decline by 40 per cent. Such a prediction is dependent upon the ability of schools to adapt to the needs of a wider range of students than they have been able to do in the past. A 40 per cent reduction in the dropout rate will be necessary if the state population is to have the same level of educational attainment as the nation as a whole by 1980, and to meet the rising educational requirements of employers.[4]

The difference between each of these three projections of public school enrollment is their respective assumptions about the future of nonpublic

TABLE 1.2

Fall Enrollment in Nonpublic Schools, Selected Years,
1935–36 to 1970–71

Year	Total
1935–36	309,059
1940–41	410,809
1945–46	458,865
1950–51	542,212
1955–56	708,519
1960–61	841,345
1967–68	884,111
1968–69	872,717
1969–70	841,378[a]
1970–71	784,058

[a] Estimated.

school enrollments. The best estimate, the middle projection, anticipates an average annual decline over the decade of 6 per cent in nonpublic, largely Catholic, school enrollments.[5] This projection assumes that Catholic school enrollment will decline by 55 per cent during the present decade. Such a decrease was predicted on the basis of declining birth rates, changing educational preferences among Catholics and rising costs in Catholic schools.[6]

The other two projections represent the extremes of change possible in nonpublic school enrollments. One, the lowest, assumes that Catholic school populations will decline no faster than the declination rate between 1968–69 and 1969–70.

The third projection, the highest, is based on a precipitate decline of enrollment in nonpublic schools. It assumes that Catholic elementary schools would close entirely and that enrollments in Catholic secondary schools would decline by 50 per cent by the end of the decade.*

Figures 1.1 and 1.2 indicate that for New York State as a whole, and for the non-urban areas of the state, the rapid growth in *public* school en-

---

* It should be noted that some members of the Commission believe that new means of aid to assist parents who wish to send their children to nonpublic schools can and should be found. Should this approach be taken by the State Legislature, some Commissioners feel that the best estimate for nonpublic school enrollments might be the lower projection, i.e., continuation of the 1968–69 and 1969–70 trends; the rate of change in the enrollment in public schools would correspondingly be affected, and, consequently, the enrollment projections used for purposes of this study would have to be adjusted.

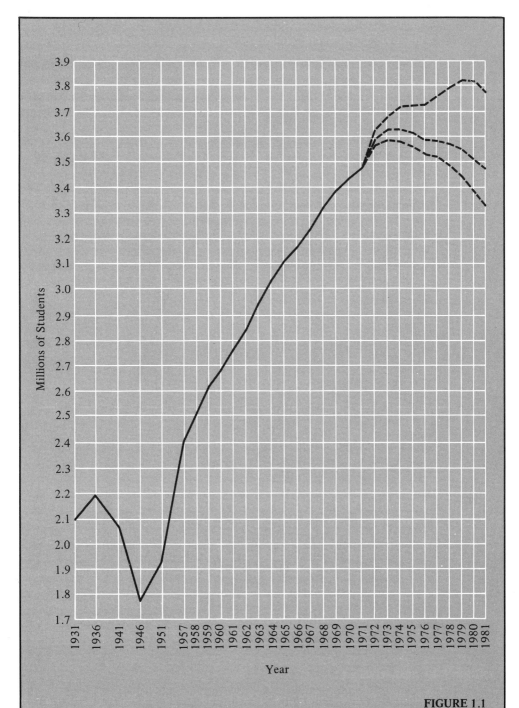

FIGURE 1.1

Fall Enrollment in Public Elementary and Secondary Schools in New York State from
Year Ending June 30, 1931–1971. With High, Medium and Low Projections to Year
Ending June 30, 1981. (In millions.)

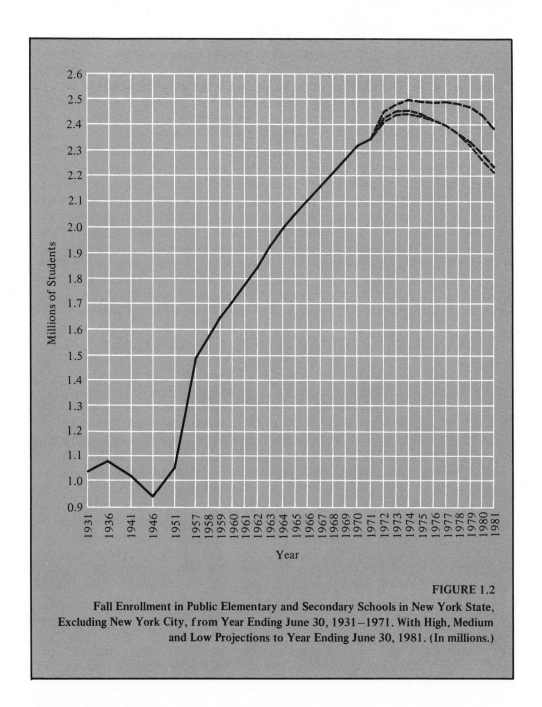

FIGURE 1.2

Fall Enrollment in Public Elementary and Secondary Schools in New York State, Excluding New York City, from Year Ending June 30, 1931–1971. With High, Medium and Low Projections to Year Ending June 30, 1981. (In millions.)

rollments has come to an end, at least for the next decade or two. Even based on the high projection in which public schools would absorb almost all nonpublic school students by 1980, public school enrollments would increase statewide by only 250,000 students over the present level. Most

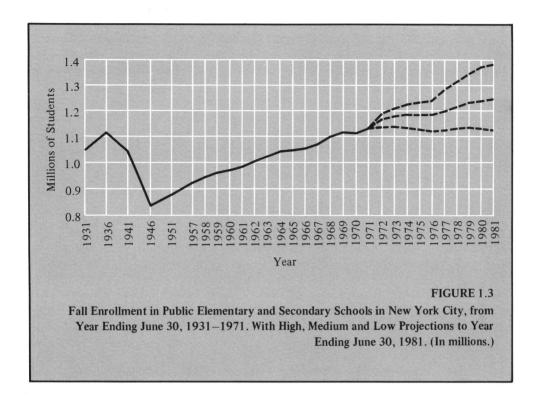

FIGURE 1.3

Fall Enrollment in Public Elementary and Secondary Schools in New York City, from Year Ending June 30, 1931–1971. With High, Medium and Low Projections to Year Ending June 30, 1981. (In millions.)

of this increase would occur in heavily urbanized school districts. (See Figure 1.3 for New York City rates.) Under the more conservative assumptions of moderate declines in nonpublic school enrollments (medium projection) or no decline at all (low projection), public school enrollment in 1980 would actually be lower than it is today.

An examination of these regional predictions makes it possible to show more precisely where future gains and losses in enrollment are most likely to occur. Table 1.3 presents the three types of pupil enrollment projections by geographic region. According to the low projections, enrollment in most regions can be expected to decline in the next 10 years. The only exceptions are New York City, the mid-Hudson region and the Rochester region. Under the medium projections, the Capital District region (Albany) and the Syracuse region would also be expected to realize slight increases in public school enrollments; under the high projections, enrollment in the Rockland-Westchester region would increase. The remaining six regions would still experience a decrease.

In short, at least for the next decade or two, New York State will not face the rapid expansion of pupil population that characterized the last 25 years. The consequences are important. Once inflation is taken into account, the major part of future increments in financial resources available

TABLE 1.3

**Percentage Change in K-12 Public Enrollments,
1969–70 to 1980–81**

Regions	Run #1, Low Projection	Run #2, Medium Projection	Run #3, High Projection
New York City	.6%	10%	23%
Long Island	− 8	− 8	− 2
Rockland- 　Westchester	− 8	− 7	4
Mid-Hudson	20	21	25
Capital District 　Albany (core)	− 1 − 8	1 − 2	10 15
Northern	−15	−14	−11
Mohawk Valley	− 7	− 4	0
Binghamton 　Broome (core)	−13 −17	−13 −17	−10 −11
Syracuse 　Onondaga (core)	− 1 − 1	.6 2	6 9
Rochester 　Monroe (core)	1 8	3 11	10 21
Elmira	−11	−10	− 9
Buffalo 　Erie (core)	−12 − 9	−12 − 9	− 1 5

for education can go toward improvements in the quality of New York State's educational system.

The section which follows analyzes past and present utilization of resources in terms of both personnel and dollar expenditure.

EDUCATIONAL RESOURCES IN THE STATE

Personnel

The size of the educational labor force has increased even more rapidly than enrollment. In 1930, there were 77,931 educational professionals in

New York State (teachers, principals, superintendents and other administrators).[7] Forty years later the number had grown to 213,492.[8] (Figure 1.4.)

More significant than the number of educational professionals in the

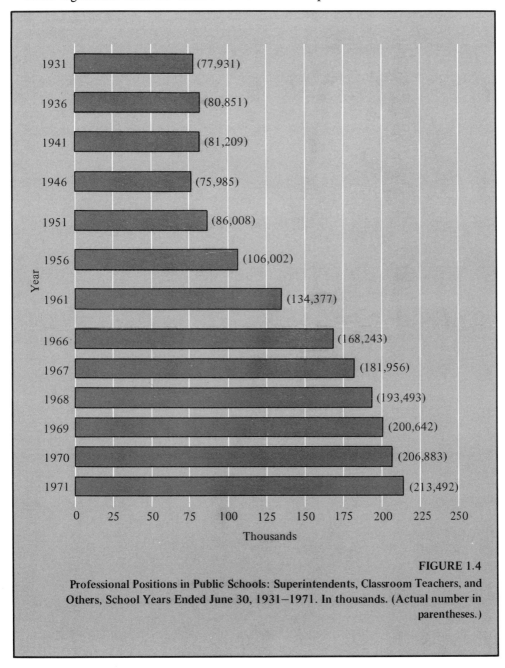

FIGURE 1.4

Professional Positions in Public Schools: Superintendents, Classroom Teachers, and Others, School Years Ended June 30, 1931–1971. In thousands. (Actual number in parentheses.)

schools of New York State is the ratio of staff to students. In the fall of 1969, the lowest pupil/teacher ratio in the United States was 18.7-to-1 in South Dakota; the highest was 26.6-to-1 in Utah. New York ranked tenth with a ratio of 20.4-to-1.

Within New York State, the pupil-to-professional educator (including all certificated teachers and administrators) ratio has been decreasing during the past several decades as the growth in staff exceeded the growth in pupil population. The greatest growth in professional staff occurred during the past 15 years. In 1955, there were approximately 100,000 educational professionals in the state; since 1955 the number has doubled. At present there are approximately 61 professional staff members for every 1,000 students in the state (in 1930, the ratio was 37 staff members to every 1,000 students.)[9] (Table 1.4.) It is to be noted that among highly industrialized states such as Michigan, California and Illinois, New York has the lowest pupil/educator ratio.[10]

The state has made a massive investment in reducing class size in order to raise quality. Unfortunately, however, pupil-to-professional educator

TABLE 1.4

Professional Staff per 1,000 Public School Students, Selected School Years ending June 30, 1931–1971

Year	Professional Staff/Student Ratio
1931	37.1
1936	36.8
1941	39.0
1946	42.6
1951	44.5
1957	46.3
1961	48.5
1966	53.0
1967	56.0
1968	58.2
1969	59.1
1970	60.1
1971	61.2

ratios vary widely from school district to school district. Personnel resources are not being applied equally throughout the state.

Even though more men have entered the teaching force in recent years, teaching remains a largely female profession; however, the number of women in administrative and supervisory positions is alarmingly low. For example, in 1970, there was only one female state district superintendent, though 60 per cent of the classroom teachers were female. (The subject of job discrimination in education is dealt with in more detail in our chapter on Educators and Educational Policy.)

Average teachers' salaries in New York are the highest in the nation, with the exception of Alaska, where pay scales reflect a substantially higher cost of living. In 1970, a New York State teacher received an average salary of $11,100; the national average for the same year was $9,265.[11] This average does not include pensions or fringe benefits, which are generous in New York and probably enhance the already favored position of the New York teacher.

As with pupil-to-professional ratios, salaries are not consistent throughout the state. Because of present school finance inequities, some districts are able to offer very high salaries to teachers while other districts do not have enough money to compete successfully for well-trained personnel. (Subsequent chapters on School Finance and Educators and Educational Policy discuss these specific problems.)

District Organization

School district organization is not directly related to what goes on in the classrooms, but it certainly influences how the educational system is managed. Two important facts stand out: First, the range in size of districts is astonishing. For instance, New York City is the nation's largest school district, with more than 1.1 million enrolled students. At the same time, there are several school districts in the state that operate no schools at all. Second, as the educational system in New York grew over the past several decades, the number of school districts decreased. As shown in Figure 1.5, there were over 9,000 school districts in New York in 1930; by 1970 the number had decreased to approximately 760.[12] This consolidation movement has increased both the efficiency and effectiveness of the educational system. However, further improvement is still possible and desirable. The Commission believes that some existing school districts have pupil enrollment which is too low to justify their continuance as separate operating districts. (In the chapter on Governance this problem will be discussed.)

Expenditures

Given the growth in pupil enrollment and staff size during the past decades, it is logical to assume that public school expenditures have increased, and,

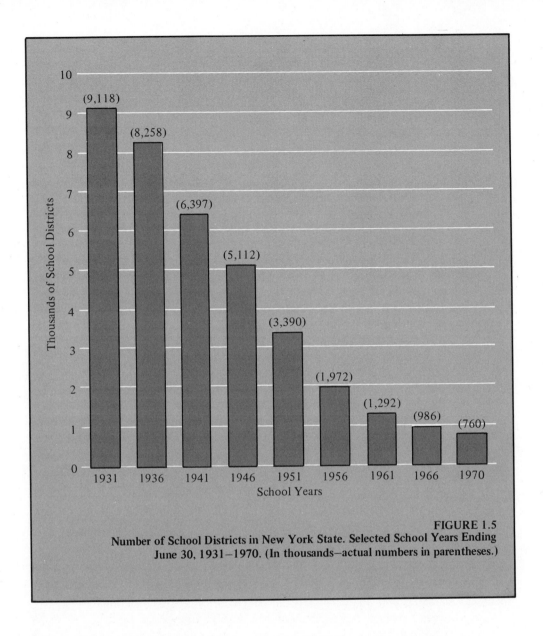

FIGURE 1.5
Number of School Districts in New York State. Selected School Years Ending
June 30, 1931–1970. (In thousands—actual numbers in parentheses.)

in fact, in the years since 1930 dollar expenditures have increased more
than tenfold. In 1930, the total general fund expenses for the public schools
were approximately $319 million.* Figure 1.6 shows that by 1970, the
figure exceeded $4 billion. The greatest increase has occurred over the past

---

* General fund expenses do *not* include Trust and Agency Fund, School Store Fund,
School Lunch Fund, Federal Aid Fund and Capital Fund.

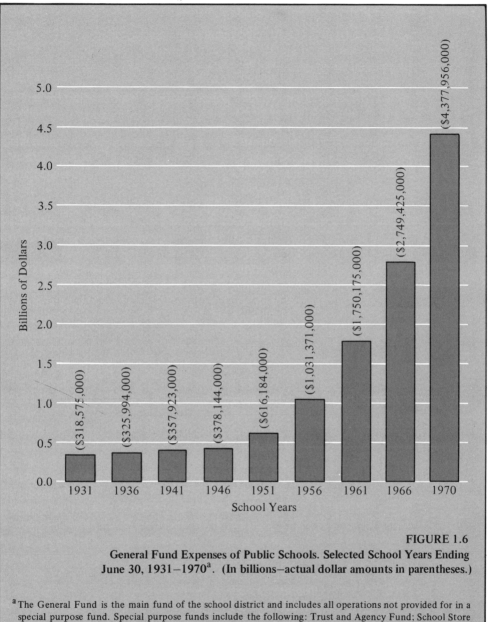

FIGURE 1.6

General Fund Expenses of Public Schools. Selected School Years Ending June 30, 1931–1970[a]. (In billions—actual dollar amounts in parentheses.)

[a] The General Fund is the main fund of the school district and includes all operations not provided for in a special purpose fund. Special purpose funds include the following: Trust and Agency Fund; School Store Fund; School Lunch Fund; Federal Aid Fund; and Capital Fund. The Federal Aid Fund is used to account for special projects or programs supported in whole or in part with Federal funds.

15 years. In 1956, total public school expenditures were slightly higher than $1 billion.[13]

Of course, a substantial portion of the increase is accounted for by the expansion of school enrollments—more dollars are needed to educate more students. Per-pupil expenditures, which measure the amount of money spent on each pupil and therefore take account of enrollment increases, also increased from $167 in 1930–31 to $1,305 for 1970–71.[14] (Table 1.5.) Some of this increase reflects inflation—the declining buying power of the dollar—rather than a real growth in expenditures. When per-pupil general fund expenditures are expressed in "constant dollars," * the rise is not as great. Between 1945 and 1970, per-pupil expenditures in constant dollars increased from $477.66 (in 1945–46) to $818.35 (in 1970–71).[15] This is an increase of 71.3 per cent. (Table 1.6.) Over the same span of years public school enrollments increased 95.7 per cent, professional staff grew 181.0 per cent, and the staff ratio per 1,000 pupils increased 43.7 per cent.**

New York State's taxpayers have borne almost all of these expenditure increases. Figure 1.7 illustrates the tremendous growth in local property tax revenues over the past four decades. The local tax contribution to public education in 1931 was approximately $264 million. By 1969, this had grown to almost $2 billion. Similarly, the state's contribution increased in that same time period from less than $100 million to almost $2 billion.[16] (Figure 1.8.)

New York State's reliance on state and local tax levies to support education reflects the Federal Government's small contribution to education. Even though the Federal contribution has increased over the past five years (Table 1.7) in 1969, Federal funds still accounted for only 5.7 per cent of New York's total public school revenues—$261 million.[17]

COMPARATIVE ANALYSIS OF NEW YORK STATE EXPENDITURES New York has a well-founded reputation for high spending in public education. In 1967–68, the latest year for which official, detailed data on educational spending for all states are available, New York spent 53 per cent more

---

* The term "constant dollars" refers to a means of measuring the buying power of the dollar from year to year, taking account of the effect of inflation.
** Throughout this chapter, we compare data from 1930 (or 1931) and 1970 (or 1969). In this case, for the following technical and statistical reasons, the comparisons are made for the years 1945 to 1970:

1. Any discussion of constant dollars (using a price index to deflate costs) assumes that patterns of consumption remain constant over the period in question. However, it cannot be assumed that consumption patterns remained constant for the 40 years between 1930 and 1970.
2. In general, price indices do not deal carefully with changes in quality. For example, a price index of education must assume that the beginning salary for teachers attracted the same quality of teacher in 1930 as it does in 1970. Such an index does not recognize changes in education or preparation of teachers.

TABLE 1.5

General Fund Expenditures per Pupil in Average Daily Attendance
in Public Schools,[a] School Years ending June 30, 1931–1971

Year	Total	Year	Total
1931	$166.86	1951	$357.25
1932	172.48	1952	387.67
1933	160.71	1953	401.99
1934	153.82	1954	419.21
1935	156.95	1955	455.88
1936	163.23	1956	487.76
1937	167.54	1957	531.58
1938	178.37	1958	587.49
1939	177.35	1959	616.20
1940	185.93	1960	647.92
1941	191.82	1961	680.33
1942	199.97	1962	724.11
1943	210.29	1963	790.60
1944	218.94	1964	834.36
1945	225.05	1965	890.14
1946	243.13	1966[b]	954.76
1947	266.72	1967[b]	1,065.05
1948	293.54	1968[b]	1,149.35
1949	319.19	1969[b]	1,302.52
1950	331.33	1970[b]	1,305.26
		1971[b]	1,500.00 (estimated including federal aid)

[a] Average daily attendance is the average number of pupils present on each regular school day in elementary and secondary grades during a given period. The average is determined by dividing the total number of attendance days of all pupils by the number of days school was in session.

[b] Expenditures per pupil are reported for the General Fund only. The General Fund is the main fund of the school district and includes all operations not provided for in a special purpose fund. Special purpose funds include the following: Trust and Agency Fund; School Store Fund; School Lunch Fund; Federal Aid Fund; and Capital Fund. The Federal Aid Fund is used to account for special projects or programs supported in whole or in part with Federal funds. Expenditures from the Federal Aid Fund increase the total per-pupil expenditures by the following amounts: 1966: $16.98; 1967: $48.88; 1968: $49.99; 1969: $49.39; 1970: $50.75.

than the national average expenditures per public school student.[18] Comparing New York State to the national average is not really very revealing, however, because that average includes both rich and poor states; it is, therefore, better to compare New York to other relatively rich or heavily

TABLE 1.6

General Fund Per-Pupil Expenditures, in Constant 1958 Dollars[a]
Selected School Years ending June 30, 1946–70

Year	Total
1946	$477.66
1951	483.42
1956	541.35
1961	631.69
1966	754.75
1970	818.35

[a] Dollars are expressed in 1958 constant dollars, using the implicit price deflator for state and local government purchases: *Survey of Current Business*, August, 1965 and 1970.

industrialized states. Table 1.8 shows how spending on public schools in New York compares with spending in California, Connecticut, Illinois, New Jersey and Pennsylvania. With the exception of Pennsylvania, which is the largest industrialized state in New York's general geographic region, all of these states rank far above national average income per capita. (For 1970, the relevant personal income per capita figures are as follows: United States average, $3,910; New York, $4,797; New Jersey, $4,539; Illinois, $4,516; California, $4,469; Pennsylvania, $3,893.)[19]

In *absolute terms* New York spends more on instruction per student than the five other comparable states; specifically, in 1967–68, New York was spending $619 per student on instruction while Connecticut[20] was spending $503 and California $485. (Table 1.8.) New York is also spending a great deal more on Fixed Charges and Other Services.

Table 1.9 suggests why New York's instructional expenditures are so high. One factor is teachers' salaries, which are high in New York State (although they are not much higher than salaries in other comparable states). Another important factor is staffing patterns. In 1967–68 New York enrolled 7.4 per cent of all United States students, but employed 9.3 per cent of the nation's public school instructional staff. In contrast, California had a larger share of the nation's students than it did of instructional staff (10.0 per cent of the students, 9.1 per cent of the staff). Furthermore, New York employs an unusually high number of educational professionals who do not carry full-time teaching responsibilities. In fact, New York engaged 13.3 per cent of the nation's non-teaching educational specialists in 1967–68. This is roughly twice the proportion one might expect on the basis of the size of New York's school population.[21]

The unusually high expenditures under the category of fixed charges in

TABLE 1.7

Local Tax Levy, State Aid and Federal Aid Paid—Relationship of Each to Total for Selected Years (in millions and per cents of total revenue)

School Year	Local Tax Levy[a]	Per Cent	State Aid	Per Cent	Federal Aid Paid	Per Cent	Total
1950–51	$ 345	57.7	$ 247	41.3	$ 6	1.0	$ 598
1960–61	963	55.4	748	43.0	28	1.6	1,739
1962–63	1,161	54.3	944	44.2	31	1.5	2,136
1964–65	1,408	55.9	1,077	42.7	35	1.4	2,500
1965–66	1,486	51.9	1,272	44.4	104	3.6	2,862
1966–67	1,605	49.5	1,460	45.0	178[b]	5.5	3,243
1967–68	1,760	50.2	1,638	46.8	105[b]	3.0	3,503
1968–69	1,957	47.8	1,997	48.8	139[b]	3.4	4,093
1969–70	2,197	48.8	2,048	45.5	261[b]	5.7	4,506

[a] As reported in *Analysis of School Finances, New York State School Districts*, Bureau of Educational Finance Research, New York State Education Department, for years 1960–61 through 1968–69, and *Statistics for Schools, Year 1950–51*, New York State Education Department Annual Report.
[b] Includes federal aid to school districts, Boards of Cooperative Educational Services, County Vocational Education Boards and Elementary and Secondary Education Act of 1965, Title III.

New York is apparently related to comparatively generous pension programs. Most recent comparative data available on this point are for the year 1965–66. In that year, expenditures for retirement and social security (converted to a per-student basis) were as follows: New York, $94; New Jersey, $58; Pennsylvania, $42; California, $31; Connecticut, $31; Illinois, $31.22.[22] Because of strength of teacher bargaining in New York and because of interest that teachers have recently expressed in retirement plans, especially in New York City, it is possible that the gap between New York and other leading states has widened from 1965–66 to the present. (See chapter on Educators and Educational Policy.)

As for high expenditures in the category of Other Services, the chief factor appears to be student transportation. In 1965–66, New York was spending $38 per pupil, while Connecticut was spending $21. The other states in our comparative group were all spending less than $21 per student on transportation.[23]

From the preceding discussion, it would appear that New York is leading all comparable states in expenditures. However, expenditure comparisons among states cannot be perfectly accurate because states differ both in the programs they offer in public schools and in their accounting practices.

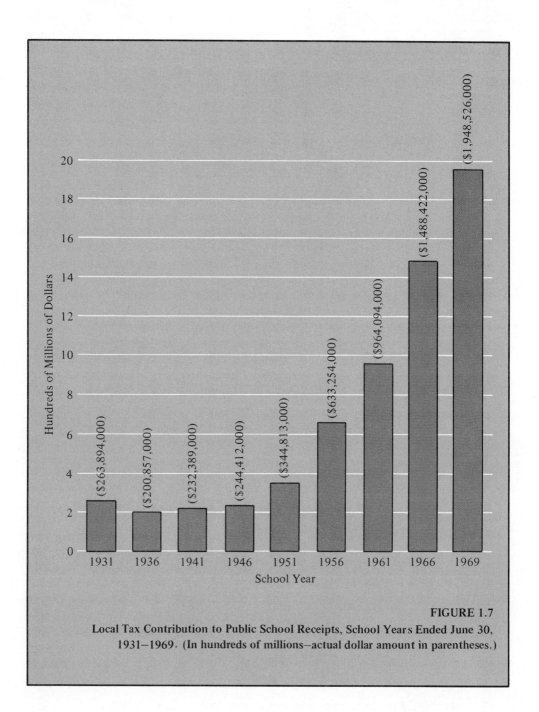

FIGURE 1.7

Local Tax Contribution to Public School Receipts, School Years Ended June 30, 1931–1969. (In hundreds of millions—actual dollar amount in parentheses.)

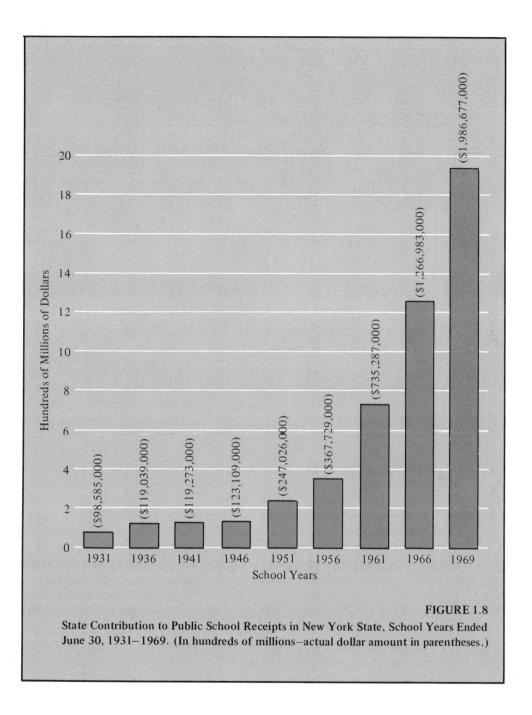

FIGURE 1.8

State Contribution to Public School Receipts in New York State, School Years Ended June 30, 1931–1969. (In hundreds of millions—actual dollar amount in parentheses.)

TABLE 1.8

Public School Expenditures per Enrolled Student, United States, New York and Selected States, 1967–68

Areas	Total Expend- itures	Total Current Expenses[a]	Admin- istration	Instruc- tion	Opera- tion of Plant	Mainte- nance of Plant	Fixed Charges	Other Services	Other Pro- grams	Capital Outlay	Interest
United States	737	601	28	411	46	18	53	45	19	95	22
New York State	1,130	976	48	619	66	23	134	85	21	97	35
California	906	676	39	485	52	23	47	30	85	113	31
Connecticut	790	707	29	503	55	17	53	50	5	54	25
Illinois	769	645	34	440	64	20	47	40	10	94	20
New Jersey	869	700	27	464	55	21	85	48	12	130	27
Pennsylvania	777	627	33	413	50	18	62	50	12	92	46

[a] Total current expenses of full-time elementary and secondary day schools.

TABLE 1.9

Data on Staffing Patterns, United States, New York and Selected States

Region or State	Enrollment 1967–68	Share of Total	Instructional Staff 1967–68	Share of Total	Classroom Teachers 1967–68	Share of Total	Average Annual Salary of Instructional Staff, 1969–70
United States	44,742,341	100.0	2,071,246	100.0	1,863,967	100.0	$ 8,840
New York State	3,325,477	7.4	191,818	9.3	164,288	8.8	10,200
California	4,466,266	10.0	188,816	9.1	171,102	9.2	9,980
Connecticut	628,252	1.4	31,272	1.5	28,557	1.5	9,400
Illinois	2,215,328	5.0	109,426	5.3	98,918	5.3	9,950
New Jersey	1,452,457	3.3	72,262	3.5	65,900	3.5	9,500
Pennsylvania	2,310,486	5.2	101,476	4.9	92,818	5.0	9,000

TABLE 1.10

State/Local Expenditures on Vocational Education, 1969

	Enrollment	Share of Total	Expenditures on Vocational Education	Share of Total
United States	45,618,578	100.0	1,114,080,000	100.0
New York	3,513,432	7.7	216,909,000	19.5
California	4,597,700	10.1	62,864,000	5.6
Connecticut	646,393	1.4	20,568,000	1.9
Illinois	2,324,516	5.1	28,765,000	2.6
New Jersey	1,454,378	3.2	25,896,000	2.3
Pennsylvania	2,317,500	5.1	87,602,000	7.9

For example, on the basis of 1969 data in Table 1.10, it would appear that New York State's local-state expenditure on vocational education equalled nearly 20 per cent of the national total, while the state had a student population of only 7.7 per cent of the national total. At the same time, it would appear that California accounted for only 5.6 per cent of the nation's vocational expenditures from state-local funds while having roughly 10 per cent of total student enrollment in the nation. This kind of comparison is misleading, however, for in California most vocational programs are found in junior colleges and in other institutions that are classified as higher education. In New York, on the other hand, vocational education is still primarily a responsibility of the secondary schools. The expenditures, therefore, appear in the elementary-secondary account in New York and in the higher education account in California.[24]

Nevertheless, even the rough comparisons that we can make from available data raise some important questions: Are the relatively large numbers of non-teaching professionals in New York effectively deployed? Is it desirable to try to control the high costs of providing pensions for teachers? Both of these expenditure items represent, in some sense at least, using resources for school services other than teaching.

Since 1945, the tremendous growth in the student population has made heavy demands on the state's education resources, both human and fiscal. That growth has already begun to level off, a trend that is expected to continue for at least 20 years. The Commission, therefore, believes that educational priorities may now be reordered. Our analysis of the *outcomes* of education in the state which follows (using test scores, dropout rates and

graduation patterns, and post-secondary school attendance as measures of
school system performance) reveals that it is time to focus resources on
areas that will bring higher returns in performance for *all* pupils.

SCHOOL PERFORMANCE

The most striking fact that emerged from our studies of school performance
in New York State is the high correlation shown between school success
and the socio-economic origin of pupils. This is true at all levels of the
performance scale. Students whose parents have high incomes and are
highly educated tend to do well on all measures of school success (length
of time in school, test scores, post-secondary school attendance and occupational success); students on the bottom of the scale tend to do poorly on
these same measures; and students from middle-level socio-economic backgrounds tend to perform somewhere in the middle.

The close parallel between school success and the child's socio-economic origin suggests that something is wrong with the way our educational system operates. The Commission is well aware that innate learning
ability varies widely from student to student, but it has seen no persuasive
evidence that such innate ability correlates with family income, race, sex,
parental occupation or ethnicity. In theory, therefore, differences in average
group levels of performance should be insignificant. In fact, they are not:
Equality in educational opportunity does not exist for the students of New
York State. We conclude that in schools in which differences in the average
performance levels of social class, racial and geographic groups exist, public policy should be directed toward their elimination.

Removing these inequities deserves top priority, even though New York
State students, when compared to the rest of the nation, rank at or near
the top on most measures of student performance. When viewed over time,
most aggregate measures of student performance show an improvement.
More students in New York State graduate from high school and go on to
college than ever before. This has meant that more children from lower
socio-economic status (SES) backgrounds finish high school and attend
college. What has not improved is their standing relative to their peers from
more affluent backgrounds. The problem is particularly distressing because
a large proportion of the low-SES children in the state come from certain
geographical regions and racial and ethnic groups.

The results of our studies of pupil performance may be summarized in
four findings, on which we provide detailed data in the following pages:

1. New York State students, compared to students in other states, rank
    at or near the top in most measures of pupil performance.
2. Within New York State there is a significant and consistent relation be-
    tween test scores or class rank and socio-economic status.

3. Dropout, high school graduation, college attendance and employment rates vary significantly among socio-economic, racial and regional groups.
4. Students who go to college are unevenly distributed on the basis of race and SES according to the type of college they attend.

Achievement Data: National Comparisons

Results from four tests (Scholastic Aptitude Test, National Merit Scholarship Qualifying Test, the Pupil Evaluation Program and the Regents Scholarship and College Qualification Test) are used to examine pupil achievement nationally and performance variation within New York State.

SCHOLASTIC APTITUDE TESTS   The Scholastic Aptitude Tests (SAT's) are administered nationally to college-bound students. Most students take them in December of their senior year, although a number of students take the tests in the spring of their junior year. The tests are composed of two sections—verbal and quantitative ability. The highest score a student can receive on each section is 800. Table 1.11 compares average New York State and national performance for 1968–69. During that year, New York State students performed above the national mean on both the verbal and quantitative sections of the SAT's.

It must be remembered that SAT's are given to *college-bound* students. Therefore, if New York State encourages students of lower ability to go to college, and they take SAT's, the New York mean SAT scores will be lower than they might have been if only the students who had shown high ability took the tests. Thus, it is not simple to draw conclusions from the preceding data. A school system that encourages lower ability students to take these tests and apply to college may be performing better in terms of one objec-

TABLE 1.11

Comparison of National and New York State SAT Norms, 1968–69

| | NUMBER OF STUDENTS | | AVERAGE | |
	U.S.	N.Y.	U.S.	N.Y.
Senior Boys: Verbal	498,462	65,978	457	470
Senior Girls: Verbal	415,925	55,221	464	476
Senior Boys: Math	498,462	65,970	510	525
Senior Girls: Math	415,925	55,208	465	481

tive of the schools than a higher-scoring school system which provides less encouragement to lower-ability students.

NATIONAL MERIT SCHOLARSHIP QUALIFYING TESTS. National Merit Scholarship Qualifying Tests (NMSQT's), like SAT's, are administered to college-bound students throughout the country. According to their scores on this aptitude test, students are rated "commended students," Merit Finalists, or Merit Scholars. Only a portion of Merit Scholars receive actual financial aid, but all students who do well on this test are highly regarded by school principals and college admissions officers. The number of Merit Scholarships awarded in any one state is fixed in accord with the number and characteristics of that state's student population. Therefore, the *number* of scholarships awarded in New York State reveals little about the test performance of students in New York State relative to that of students in other states. However, it is important to note the distribution of New York State NMSQT scores compared to the nationwide distribution of scores; this comparison provides an approximate idea of how New York State's students perform.

In 1968–69, the highest possible NMSQT score was 166. In Table 1.12 the percentage of students in New York scoring below a specified point is compared to the national percentages.

New York State scores are consistently two points higher than the na-

TABLE 1.12

Percentiles for NMSQT Scores of United States and New York State Students

Percentage Receiving Lower Scores	SCORES	
	U.S.	N.Y.
99	145–163	147–163
98	142–144	144–146
97	140–141	142–143
96	139	140–141
95	137–138	139
94	136	138
93	134–135	136–137
92	133	135
91	132	134
90	131	133
50	105	107

tional scores within each percentile level. Since the cut-off point for those students receiving high honors (finalist or scholar status) is not determined on a national basis, it is not possible to compare New York State's cut-off point (147) to the national norm. However, all who scored 134 or above throughout the United States were named "commended students." Nationally, 7 per cent of all students taking the tests were so designated, while in New York State 9 per cent ranked as "commended students."

It is worth emphasizing again that both SAT's and NMSQT's are administered to the *college-bound* population of a school. These students have already gone through a process of selection that virtually assures they will perform better on these standardized tests than would their non-college-bound peers. Therefore, all these test results can show is that the college-bound population of New York State is somewhat better prepared and higher achieving than the college-bound population of the rest of the country. These results say nothing about how New York State schools are preparing all other students in the state.

The test results discussed above show that New York State students compare favorably to students across the country. The results from two other tests—the Pupil Evaluation Program (PEP) and the Regents Scholarship and College Qualification Test (RSCQT)—show performance variations of students within New York State. From these tests, it is clear that there are substantial variations in achievement among socio-economic, geographic and racial groups in New York State.

Socio-Economic Disparities in Student Achievement

Many studies have shown the relationship between certain socio-economic measures and achievement in school. One study undertaken for the Commission by Walter I. Garms examined the relationship between various socio-economic measures and the percentage of children having abnormally low reading and arithmetic achievement in the third grade of 301 schools in New York State in 1970.[25] Using 39 socio-economic variables, it was possible to predict approximately 65 per cent of the variation among schools in "per cent below minimum competence in reading" and "per cent below minimum competence in arithmetic."

According to this study, 58 per cent of the variance in student achievement was predicted by three socio-economic factors—broken homes, over-crowded housing and education of the head of household. Using a large representative sample, Garms found racial and ethnic variables to be of much less importance than these socio-economic indicators. When the racial and ethnic variables were introduced into the analysis, they accounted for less than an additional 2 per cent of the variation in student achievement. This suggests that the high failure rate of blacks and Puerto Ricans, for example, is more a consequence of their disproportionate membership in lower socio-economic classes than an independent function of cultural disadvantage related to race or ethnicity.

The results of the Pupil Evaluation Program (PEP) batteries and of the Regents Scholarship and College Qualification Test (RSCQT), and class rank in high school, demonstrate further that socio-economic factors are related to achievement in New York State.

PUPIL EVALUATION PROGRAM   The Pupil Evaluation Program (PEP) was originated in New York State in 1965. Because the tests are standardized within New York's borders, they can be used to measure differences in performance among different student populations within the state, something that cannot be done with either SAT's or NMSQT's.

PEP tests are given to all New York State students in both public and nonpublic schools in the third, sixth and ninth grades. (Initially, a first grade preparedness test was also given, but it was subsequently dropped from the test battery because of its inaccuracy.) The tests focus upon achievement in reading and mathematics. For each of the tests at each grade level a judgment is made as to what score represents a minimum competence level. This level refers to the number of items a student must miss before the results suggest the need for compensatory help beyond that normally available in the classroom. In 1966, when the norms were first developed for the third and sixth grade tests,* the number of children scoring at the minimal competence level was set to correspond to the percentile closest to the third stanine division of the distributions, which happened to be the 23rd percentile. Therefore, by definition, in 1966 23 per cent of the third and sixth graders tested fell below the minimum competence level.

One of the most striking phenomena in the PEP score data is that over time more and more children throughout the state are falling below the minimum competence level in both reading and mathematics. Also, as students progress from third to sixth grade, more of them fall below minimum competence. The most dramatic increase in the number of students falling below minimum competence is found in sixth grade. (See Tables 1.13 and 1.14.) In 1970, 26.9 per cent of the sixth graders tested fell below minimum competence in reading and 28.9 per cent were below the norm in mathematics.

PEP score data also reveal strong geographic patterns of success and failure. Table 1.15 shows that the degree of reading failure in the large cities of the state is dangerously high. This is especially true in New York City where more than one out of every three third, sixth and ninth grade students scored below the minimum competence level. By contrast, in "village" districts, the category into which most wealthy suburban schools fall, the comparable statistic is only one out of every nine students.

---

* No norms were developed for the ninth grade tests.

TABLE 1.13

Percentages of Students Tested in the New York State Pupil Evaluation
Program Falling below Minimum Competence Levels in Reading, Fall, 1966–70

Grade	1966	1967	1968	1969	1970
3	23.0	23.1	22.5	23.1	23.9
6	23.0	23.6	23.6	25.3	26.9
9	20.8	21.8	22.8	22.0	23.2

These figures are disturbing for two reasons. In the first place, they show
that over one quarter of the students tested fall below the minimum competence level. Failure of this magnitude not only places limits on the future
of individual students, but also detracts greatly from New York State's social
environment and economic productivity.

Second, the uneven geographic distribution of failure indicates that
children in the state's large cities bear the heaviest burden of school failure.
And, on the whole, low-income and minority-group students are concentrated in large cities throughout the state. These are the very children for
whom school is expected above all to serve as an avenue to a happy and
productive life. But, if children are not able to read or cipher, the road out
of poverty is effectively closed.

THE REGENTS SCHOLARSHIP AND COLLEGE QUALIFICATION TEST   Like
the PEP tests, the Regents Scholarship and College Qualification Test
(RSCQT) is given only in New York State. Unlike PEP, the RSCQT is

TABLE 1.14

Percentages of Students Tested in the New York State Pupil Evaluation
Program Falling below Minimum Competence Levels in
Mathematics, Fall, 1966–70

Grade	1966	1967	1968	1969	1970
3	23.0	22.0	20.1	19.5	18.8
6	23.0	25.1	25.4	26.8	28.9
9	20.7	23.8	25.5	25.4	27.0

TABLE 1.15

Per Cent of Public and Nonpublic School Students in Grades 3, 6 and 9 below
Minimum Competence in Reading and Arithmetic in New York State, 1969–70

Community Type	Per Cent of All Pupils Below Minimum Competence, Within Community Types	Per Cent of All Pupils in State Below Minimum Competence	Per Cent of State Enrollment in Grades 3, 6 and 9
New York City	39	55	35.8
Other Large Cities	27	8	7.3
Medium Sized Cities	19	2	2.6
Small Cities	18	5	6.2
Villages	13	21	35.3
Large Rural Districts	16	6	8.8
Small Rural Districts	16	3	4.0
Entire State	24	100	100.0

administered annually to *college-bound* high school seniors who elect to
take it. Therefore, when discussing RSCQT scores, we must remember that
the students who choose to take this test are likely to score higher than a
representative sample of all New York State students.

A study conducted by the State Education Department's Office of Planning in Higher Education provides data on the relationship between socio-
economic status (SES), scores on the RSCQT and class rank.[26] Data were
obtained from a random sample of 101 public secondary schools in the
state. A sociological scale was used to categorize students into five SES
categories. SES Class I is the highest and SES Class V is the lowest.

The study revealed a substantial positive relationship between SES and
test performance on the RSCQT. Moreover, the relationship between SES
and over-all student achievement is undoubtedly stronger than this study
reveals because, as with SAT's and NMSQT's, only students with college
aspirations take the RSCQT, and these students already constitute a fairly
high SES group.

Table 1.16 illustrates the relation between a student's SES and his score
on the RSCQT. The percentage of students who score in the upper quarter
of the RSCQT increases consistently as SES rank rises. The relation between rising RSCQT score and ascending SES rank holds across each
quarter of RSCQT scores. Fifty per cent of the students in the highest SES
group scored in the upper quarter on the RSCQT, as compared to only 13

TABLE 1.16

Performance Differences by Socio-Economic Status on RSCQT
(SES I to SES V; highest to lowest)

RSCQT Scores	SES I	SES II	SES III	SES IV	SES V
Upper Quarter	50%	37%	31%	21%	13%
Upper Half	26	30	27	23	18
Lower Half	17	22	25	26	27
Lower Quarter	7	12	17	30	42
Total	100	100	100	100	100

per cent from the lowest SES group. Only 7 per cent of the students from the first SES group scored in the bottom quarter on the RSCQT, contrasted with 42 per cent from the lowest SES group.

There is also a strong correlation between high school class rank and SES as illustrated by Table 1.17. Invariably students from high SES backgrounds rank at the top of their high school class in greater numbers than their counterparts from low SES backgrounds.

TABLE 1.17

High School Class Rank by Socio-Economic Status (SES)
(SES I to SES V; highest to lowest)

Class Rank	SES I	SES II	SES III	SES IV	SES V	Total Respondents
Top Quartile	46.6%	31.9%	28.5%	22.4%	17.3%	25.5%
2nd Quartile	21.2	25.2	22.6	21.7	21.3	22.2
3rd Quartile	9.9	20.3	18.8	22.7	20.2	20.0
Bottom Quartile	6.7	9.5	12.8	17.8	21.6	15.8
No Response	15.5	13.1	17.2	15.4	19.6	16.5
Total	100.0	100.0	100.0	100.0	100.0	100.0

Dropout Rates and High School Graduation Patterns

Elementary and secondary education is essentially a universal activity for New York State youth between the ages of five and 17. In 1965, for example, 96.3 per cent of the population in this age group was enrolled in public or private schools.[27] A substantial number of students, however, continue to drop out of high school after they pass the age of 16.

One measure of the number of students who fail to complete high school is "holding power." Holding power represents the high school graduates in a given year as a percentage of those students who entered ninth grade four years earlier. Hence, it shows how well high schools are able to "hold" their students. In 1931, only 32.4 per cent of the students in New York who had entered public high school four years earlier graduated from high school. (Figure 1.9.) This holding-power statistic increased dramatically until 1963 when it stabilized at between 74 and 77 per cent.

It seems, then, that New York State high schools are holding more students today than they did forty years ago. A closer look at the statistics, however, reveals that certain groups of students may be staying in school longer, but others are dropping out at an alarming rate. First, as Table 1.18 shows, there are substantial geographic disparities in holding-power and dropout rates. In 1968–69, three wealthy suburban counties, Nassau, Rockland and Westchester, had high school graduating classes that were 90 per cent of their ninth grade enrollments four years earlier. By contrast, only 55 per cent of ninth graders in New York City were graduated from high school four years later. In other large cities, dropout rates are relatively higher than in suburban counties.

Also, if a student in New York State is black or Spanish-speaking, he is more likely to drop out of high school before graduation. There are no holding power statistics through graduation for various racial and ethnic groups, but statistics showing entrance in 12th grade can be used for the same purpose.*

As Table 1.19 indicates, slightly less than 80 per cent of all New York State ninth grade public school students in 1967 entered grade 12 in the fall of 1970. However, entrance rates are significantly higher for white students (designated as "Other" on Table 1.19) than they are for minority-group students. While 86.5 per cent of the white pupils in the state progressed from ninth to 12th grade, only 56.1 per cent of the black students and 47.5 per cent of the Spanish-surnamed students progressed similarly.

---

* There are several cautions to bear in mind in examining this minority dropout data, but in every case they operate to underestimate the extent of the minority dropout pattern. The data in Table 1.19 do not represent a true cohort, since the individual students were not identified and followed over the four-year period. Instead, there is an assumption of zero net-migration within each of the categories. The assumption of zero net-migration is more defensible with larger geographic (or ethnic) groupings than with the smaller ones. Therefore, the holding-power figures for the total state are more precise than those for the other three categories. If any bias does exist, however, it exists in presenting conservative comparisons among the ethnic groups. True cohort data would likely show an even larger discrepancy in holding power between minority and non-minority groups, since the minority population of our urban centers—where holding power is the weakest—has been increasing rapidly in proportion to the non-minority population.

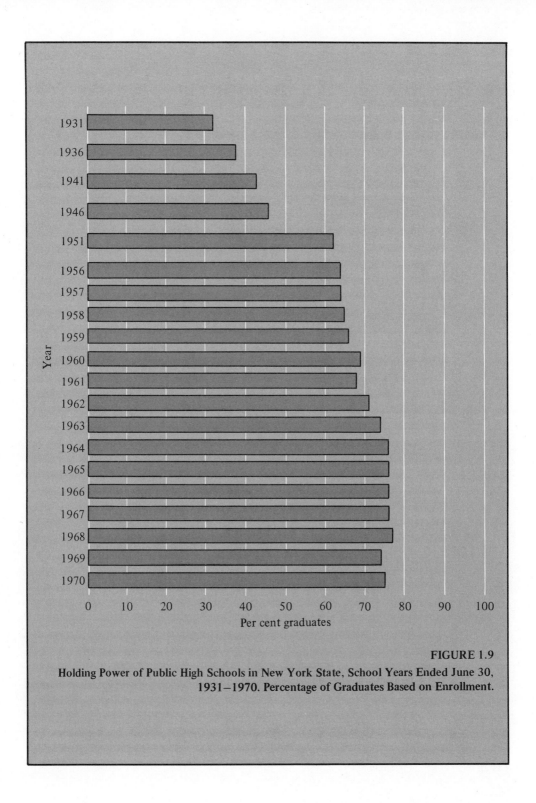

FIGURE 1.9

Holding Power of Public High Schools in New York State, School Years Ended June 30, 1931–1970. Percentage of Graduates Based on Enrollment.

TABLE 1.18

Holding Power of Public High Schools (Day High School Graduates and
Ninth Grade Enrollment 4 Years Earlier), School Year Ended June 30, 1969

County	Ninth Grade Enrollment 1965–1966	Number of Day Graduates	Graduates as a Per Cent of Enrollment
New York State	248,501	182,758	74
New York City	87,977	48,111	55
Rest of State	160,524	134,647	84
Albany	3,234	2,756	85
Allegany	834	691	83
Broome	3,837	3,154	82
Cattaraugus	1,582	1,351	85
Cayuga	1,257	991	79
Chautauqua	2,764	2,240	81
Chemung	1,737	1,391	80
Chenango	875	787	90
Clinton	1,047	848	81
Columbia	838	620	74
Cortland	709	583	82
Delaware	840	662	79
Dutchess	2,920	2,304	79
Erie	15,108	12,291	81
Essex	611	434	71
Franklin	796	692	87
Fulton	950	735	77
Genesee	1,073	831	77
Greene	487	380	78
Hamilton	90	66	73
Herkimer	1,214	1,020	84
Jefferson	1,567	1,160	74
Lewis	562	459	82
Livingston	893	686	77
Madison	1,191	951	80
Monroe	8,782	7,586	86
Montgomery	917	778	85
Nassau	28,401	25,312	89
Niagara	4,313	3,260	76
Oneida	3,986	3,201	80
Onondaga (Continued)	6,308	5,157	82

TABLE 1.18 (*Continued*)

County	Ninth Grade Enrollment 1965–1966	Number of Day Graduates	Graduates as a Per Cent of Enrollment
Ontario	1,291	1,014	79
Orange	3,264	2,564	79
Orleans	692	520	75
Oswego	1,880	1,414	75
Otsego	938	765	82
Putnam	651	490	75
Rensselaer	1,800	1,425	79
Rockland	2,813	2,539	90
St. Lawrence	2,070	1,742	84
Saratoga	1,822	1,579	87
Schenectady	2,241	2,016	90
Schoharie	439	374	85
Schuyler	256	194	76
Seneca	619	470	76
Steuben	2,113	1,689	80
Suffolk	16,237	13,859	85
Sullivan	901	705	78
Tioga	796	647	81
Tompkins	1,083	903	83
Ulster	2,139	1,699	79
Warren	868	660	77
Washington	982	739	75
Wayne	1,453	1,069	74
Westchester	12,291	11,446	93
Wyoming	727	481	66
Yates	435	267	61

Over-all, nearly one-half (47 per cent) of New York State's minority students who entered ninth grade in the fall of 1967 failed to reach the 12th grade four years later.

In New York City and the other Big Six cities the situation is even more distressing. In these cities, holding-power rates for *all* students—white and minority-group members—are lower than for the state as a whole. Nearly 90 per cent of the white students outside the Big Six cities reached 12th grade. In Albany, Buffalo, Rochester, Syracuse and Yonkers, 84.4 per cent

TABLE 1.19

Enrollment Distribution and Holding Power[a] of Public School Students
by Racial/Ethnic Origin, New York State, Fall, 1967 to Fall, 1970

Location/Racial-Ethnic Origin	ENROLLMENT				PER CENT DISTRIBUTION				Per Cent Holding Power[a]
	Grade 9[b] (1967)	Grade 10 (1968)	Grade 11 (1969)	Grade 12 (1970)	Grade 9 (1967)	Grade 10 (1968)	Grade 11 (1969)	Grade 12 (1970)	
New York City									
Black	25,574	24,988	21,053	13,069	28.6	27.2	27.8	23.4	51.1
SSA[c]	18,331	17,158	12,118	8,212	20.5	18.7	16.0	14.7	44.8
Other	45,515	49,722	42,666	34,635	50.9	54.1	56.2	61.9	76.1
Total	89,420	91,868	75,837	55,916	100.0	100.0	100.0	100.0	62.5
Other Big 6 Cities[d]									
Black	3,420	2,944	2,406	2,108	25.1	21.6	20.5	19.7	61.6
SSA	204	199	179	125	1.5	1.5	1.5	1.2	61.3
Other	10,001	10,466	9,146	8,445	73.4	76.9	78.0	79.1	84.4
Total	13,625	13,609	11,731	10,678	100.0	100.0	100.0	100.0	78.4
Rest of State									
Black	4,971	5,064	4,394	3,867	3.2	3.3	3.1	2.8	77.8
SSA	1,021	823	885	961	0.7	0.5	0.6	0.7	94.1
Other	148,274	145,986	138,461	133,270	96.1	96.2	96.3	96.5	89.9
Total	154,266	151,873	143,740	138,098	100.0	100.0	100.0	100.0	89.5
Total State									
Black	33,965	32,996	27,853	19,044	13.2	12.8	12.0	9.3	56.1
SSA	19,556	18,180	13,182	9,298	7.6	7.1	5.7	4.5	47.5
Other	203,790	206,174	190,273	176,350	79.2	80.1	82.3	86.2	86.5
Total	257,311	257,350	231,308	204,692	100.0	100.0	100.0	100.0	79.6

[a] Holding Power = Grade 12 Enrollment, Fall, 1970, through Grade 9 Enrollment, Fall, 1967.
[b] Estimated.
[c] Spanish-Surnamed Americans.
[d] Includes Albany, Buffalo, Syracuse, Rochester, Yonkers.

of the white students reached 12th grade. And, in New York City only 76.1 per cent of the white students reached 12th grade.

In these same cities, the holding-power statistics for minority-group students are even lower. Only 51.1 per cent of the blacks and 44.8 per cent of the Spanish-surnamed students who entered ninth grade in New York City in 1967 were still enrolled four years later. In the remaining Big Six cities, 61 per cent of the minority-group students in ninth grade entered grade 12 four years later.

TABLE 1.20

College Application Rates by Socio-Economic Status

	Average Number of Applications Submitted	Per Cent of Respondents Submitting Applications
SES I	3.3	95.4
SES II	2.9	93.8
SES III	2.3	84.9
SES IV	1.7	73.8
SES V	1.4	66.1
Total Phase I Sample	2.0	78.5

For New York State as a whole, 53,000 pupils—more than the entire school population of the City of Rochester—enrolled in the ninth grade in 1967, dropped out of school before entering the 12th grade. Of those 53,000 dropouts, 25,000 were members of minority groups. While minority-group members represented only 21 per cent of the state's ninth grade enrollment, they comprised 48 per cent of those who failed to remain in school until the 12th grade. Nonetheless, the absolute number of white dropouts exceeded the number of minority-group dropouts by 3,000 pupils.

These data on student performance show that a pattern of failure begins early for children of low-income families, particularly those in the large cities of the state. These children are more likely to do poorly on standardized tests and fail to graduate from high school (or even enter 12th grade) than children from higher-income families. Among students who do graduate from high school, it appears that social class and college attendance are similarly related. The percentage of high school seniors who submit college applications increases as socio-economic status increases. Students from the highest SES group applied to college at a rate 45 per cent greater than students from the lowest SES group. (Table 1.20.)

Post-Secondary School Attendance

In 1955, 43 per cent of the graduates of New York State's public and private high schools entered degree-granting post-secondary institutions. In 1970, 66 per cent of all public and nonpublic high school graduates enrolled in such institutions, and 71 per cent pursued some form of post-secondary education.[28]

Post-secondary school attendance figures are not compiled state-by-state;

consequently, we cannot make precise comparisons between New York and other states. However, we do know that in the nation as a whole, 60 per cent of all high school graduates enter college. According to this national standard, then, New York appears to be faring well.

Between the fall of 1964 and the fall of 1970, the number of public and nonpublic high school graduates from New York State attending post-secondary institutions increased from 61 per cent to 71 per cent. The percentage of New York State high school graduates who entered two-year colleges grew from 13 per cent in 1964 to 24 per cent in 1970 and accounted for most of the increase. (Table 1.21.)

POST-SECONDARY SCHOOL ENROLLMENT AND SES   Despite the substantial increase in college enrollments, the relationship between a student's social class origins and his educational attainment, which is so crucial in elementary and secondary school, continues to be influential at the post-secondary level. This is a result of a multiple sorting process which has already occurred at lower educational levels. Further stratification takes place within the post-secondary system.

In recent years, larger proportions of students from low SES backgrounds have been going on to post-secondary educational institutions. While the percentage of lower-class students who attend college has increased, this expansion of college enrollment has not necessarily improved their position relative to high-status groups. In fact, an elaborate in-college stratification system has developed. Lower SES students are confined to predominantly low-prestige institutions and they usually prepare for lower-status occupations. Though more children finish high school and go on to college, which school they attend is to a large extent influenced by their social position.

The Commission contracted with the American Council of Education (ACE) to provide data on college freshmen from New York State.[29] The results of the study indicate that there is a strong relationship between the type of college a student attends and his social origins.

The Council conducts a large-scale annual survey that presents national data on the characteristics of students entering college for the first time as full-time freshmen. From the 1969 sample the responses of 25,000 New York State students were extracted. A weighting procedure was used to estimate the attendance patterns of the entire state population. Analysis related socio-economic characteristics of students (race, sex, family income, high school grade point average, father's education, type of high school attended and type of home town) to type of post-secondary institution attended, students' degree plans, the selectivity of the institution and source of student finances. This study presents an accurate profile of students from New York State who attended institutions of higher education, both in-state and out-of-state.

In the fall of 1969, 57.6 per cent of the students from New York State entering college for the first time were male and 42.3 per cent were female.

TABLE 1.21

Trends in College-Going Rates, New York State, 1964–70

Entering Post-Secondary Education in the Fall of	PER CENT OF GRADUATES OF PUBLIC HIGH SCHOOLS ENTERING			PER CENT OF GRADUATES OF NONPUBLIC HIGH SCHOOLS ENTERING			PER CENT OF ALL GRADUATES ENTERING			
	Degree-Granting Institutions		Other Post-Secondary	Degree-Granting Institutions		Other Post-Secondary	Degree-Granting Institutions		Other Post-Secondary	Total Post-Secondary
	4-Year	2-Year		4-Year	2-Year		4-Year	2-Year		
1964	37	14	7	55	12	7	41	13	7	61
1965	36	16	8	56	13	7	38	15	7	60
1966	32	18	8	53	19	7	35	18	8	61
1967	35	19	7	56	17	7	39	19	7	65
1968	37	21	7	56	18	7	40	20	7	67
1969	37	22	7	57	19	6	41	22	6	69
1970	38	25	5	58	21	5	42	24	5	71

White students comprised 94.1 per cent of the total, and non-white students 5.9 per cent. Fifty-eight per cent of the students attended four-year colleges and 42.5 per cent attended two-year colleges. Sixty-six per cent were enrolled at public universities and 34.5 per cent attended private universities.

Twelve per cent of the students enrolled in college were from families earning less than $6,000; 30 per cent were from families earning from $6,000 to $9,999; 29.6 per cent from families earning $10,000 to $14,999; and 26.8 per cent were from families with earnings of $15,000 or more. (Table 1.22.) The majority of college students from New York were from families whose annual income exceeded $10,000. It was not possible to compare this income distribution to a statewide income distribution because 1960 figures were already out of date and 1970 figures were not available at the time of this study. Nevertheless, it does appear that the college population of New York State, like the college population of the nation, is primarily from high-income groups.

Family background is also important in determining the type of institution a student attends. Students entering college in the fall of 1969 were more likely to attend a two-year rather than a four-year college if they were from a low-income family or if their father had a relatively low level of educational attainment. Fifty-four per cent of entering freshmen whose combined family income was under $6,000 entered two-year colleges, and 45.5 per cent entered four-year colleges. In contrast, only 28.8 per cent of students whose family income was over $15,000 entered two-year colleges and 71.2 per cent entered four-year colleges. (Table 1.22.) A similar pattern based on father's education was apparent. (Table 1.23.)

In addition to illustrating the relationship between family income and college attendance and type of institution selected, the ACE data demonstrated that family income level is also related to the prestige of the college that a student attends. Moreover, all these relationships hold not only for family income level, but also for father's education level. As one might expect, the greater a father's post-secondary schooling, the greater the probability that his child will go to college. And, as the level of the father's post-secondary education increases, it becomes more likely that his child's post-secondary education will also increase.

Figures suggest that while most children are receiving more education than did their fathers (60 per cent of the college population came from homes where the father did not attend college), the relative standing of students is not changing greatly. Children of the least educated fathers are receiving less education than the children of more highly educated fathers. If they attend college, these students are likely to attend two-year and/or public institutions.

The connection between parents' education and income levels and students' post-secondary school activities is not new. In 1938 the *Regents Inquiry* noted variations by race and social class in high school graduation

TABLE 1.22

College Attendance by Parental Income and College Type
New York State Freshmen, 1969

COMPOSITION OF INSTITUTIONS BY PARENTAL INCOME

	Less than $6,000	$6,000– 9,999	$10,000– 14,999	$15,000 Plus	Total
Per Cent of Total Sample	12.3	31.3	29.6	26.8	100.0
Private University	4.2	11.6	22.1	62.1	100.0
Public University	4.4	13.2	22.3	60.1	100.0
Private 4-Year College	8.8	21.9	27.9	41.3	99.9[a]
Public 4-Year College	11.7	36.5	32.1	19.6	99.9[a]
Private 2-Year College	13.5	29.5	31.5	25.6	100.1[a]
Public 2-Year College	16.8	38.0	29.7	15.5	100.0

PER CENT OF INCOME CLASSES IN TYPES OF POST-SECONDARY INSTITUTIONS

	Private Univ.	Public Univ.	Private 4-Year	Public 4-Year	Private 2-Year	Public 2-Year	Total
Per Cent of College Population in Institutional Type	4.6	4.7	17.7	31.0	11.9	30.2	100.1[a]
Less than $6,000	1.6	1.6	12.7	29.6	13.0	41.4	99.9[a]
$6,000–$9,999	1.7	1.9	12.4	36.1	11.2	36.7	100.0
$10,000–$14,999	3.5	3.5	16.7	33.5	12.6	30.3	100.1[a]
$15,000 Plus	10.8	10.3	27.3	22.7	11.3	17.5	99.9[a]

[a] Figures may not total exactly 100 per cent because of rounding.

and college attendance. The study noted variations in school persistence levels and college attendance by family financial level, race, language spoken in the home and parental occupation. It concluded from these results that:

These differences possess far more than statistical significance; they are challenging our whole educational and social plan, for they show clearly that

TABLE 1.23

College Attendance by Father's Education and College Type, New York State Freshmen, 1969

COMPOSITION OF INSTITUTIONS BY FATHER'S EDUCATION

	Less than H.S.	H.S. Degree	Some College	College Degree or More	Total
Per Cent of Total Sample	27.2	32.8	16.4	23.7	100.1[a]
Private University	9.3	20.6	18.9	51.2	100.0
Public University	9.4	20.1	18.8	51.6	99.9[a]
Private 4-Year College	18.2	26.1	17.7	38.0	100.0
Public 4-Year College	27.0	35.4	17.3	20.3	100.0
Private 2-Year College	34.2	32.6	15.1	18.1	100.0
Public 2-Year College	35.3	38.0	14.5	12.3	100.1[a]

PER CENT OF EDUCATIONAL CLASSES IN TYPES OF POST-SECONDARY INSTITUTIONS

	Private Univ.	Public Univ.	Private 4-Year	Public 4-Year	Private 2-Year	Public 2-Year	Total
Per Cent of College Population in Institutional Type	4.8	4.6	17.8	30.2	11.9	30.6	99.9[a]
Less than H.S.	1.7	1.7	11.9	30.1	15.0	39.7	100.1[a]
H.S. Degree	3.0	2.8	14.2	32.6	11.9	35.5	100.0
Some College	5.6	5.3	19.2	31.9	11.0	27.1	100.1[a]
College Degree or More	10.4	10.1	28.5	26.0	9.1	15.9	100.0

[a] Figures may not total exactly 100 per cent because of rounding.

retention in school has varied with the assets or the advantages of pupils. While encouraging variations occur occasionally, the great mass of adolescent boys and girls seem destined to maintain in their generation the economic hierarchy established for the preceding one. . . . It is incumbent upon the school, however, as the only agency in society actively in touch with

TABLE 1.24

Number of High School Graduates by I.Q. and According to Family Income,
and Percentage Planning to Continue Their Education, 1953

Ability	INCOME UNDER $4,000		INCOME $4,000–7,999		INCOME $8,000 AND OVER	
	Number	Per Cent	Number	Per Cent	Number	Per Cent
I.Q. 130 and Over	252	77	268	79	192	96
I.Q. 120–129	974	61	988	72	466	95
I.Q. 110–119	2,261	49	1,925	58	662	89

all boys and girls, to make certain that the accident of birth has not robbed able young people of the opportunity to rise above home limitations.[30]

The study also noted that low economic status tended to be associated with low scholastic achievement, but this did not account for all the variation in school performance:

. . . of all the pupils indicating choice that will involve no college study, from a fifth to a fourth are clearly superior in intelligence to the average student specifying some professional goal.[31]

A New York State Education Department study, *Crucial Questions about Higher Education,* revealed that the same problems existed 17 years later. In 1955, 48 per cent of those planning to continue their education were children of men who had some post-secondary education; 24 per cent were the children of college graduates. Only 13 per cent of the youth not continuing their education were the children of college graduates.[32]

A comparison between all high school graduates continuing their education full-time and all graduates whose I.Q.'s were 110 or higher showed that "family income exerts a greater influence upon the decision to pursue higher education than does the ability of high school graduates as indicated by I.Q." [32] (Table 1.24.)

In 1938 and 1955, family characteristics were highly correlated with college-going patterns for New York State students. In 1969, students from high-income families were more likely to attend four-year private colleges, and go to school out-of-state. During the past thirty years, only slight progress has been made in severing the connection between socio-economic status and post-secondary school attendance.

Education and Unemployment

All high school graduates in New York State, of course, do not go on to college. Many seek employment directly after high school. One of the goals stated for education is that it should prepare students for productive employment. Schools, it should be emphasized, are not responsible for employment conditions within a state. Investment rates, tax structures and the health of the national economy play a role in determining how many jobs will be available in a state and who will be able to fill them. Moreover, because migration among states is relatively high, not all the employees of any given state are graduates of its school system. Nevertheless, though it is not the only influence, school training does have a bearing upon the employability of an individual.

Table 1.25 notes employment and unemployment figures for the United States, New York, California and Illinois. Within each state, the figures are subdivided by race, age, and sex of worker.

New York falls below the national average and the average for both

TABLE 1.25

| | CIVILIAN LABOR FORCE PARTICIPATION RATE | | | | UNEMPLOYMENT RATE | | | |
	U.S.	N.Y.	Calif.	Ill.	U.S.	N.Y.	Calif.	Ill.
Total	60.4	57.9	60.4	62.0	4.9	4.5	7.2	3.6
White	60.2	57.5	60.1	62.4	4.5	4.3	7.0	3.4
Men, 20+ years	82.8	80.4	82.9	84.6	3.2	3.4	5.6	2.2
Women, 20+ years	42.4	40.3	42.0	43.9	4.4	4.4	6.4	3.3
Both sexes, 16–19 years	51.4	42.3	50.3	57.0	13.5	12.4	18.5	10.8
Other[a]	61.8	61.7	63.3	59.0	8.2	5.6	9.1	5.9
Men, 20+ years	81.4	84.8	81.3	82.7	5.6	4.9	6.3	4.7
Women, 20+ years	51.8	50.7	53.7	47.7	6.9	3.8	6.9	3.0
Both sexes, 16–20 years	40.5	35.3	39.4	—	29.1	22.2	40.7	—

[a] For purposes of this chart, "Other" is defined to include blacks, Spanish-surnamed Americans, American Indians, and Orientals.

Illinois and California on the civilian labor force participation rate.* However, unemployment in New York State appears to be lower than in the nation as a whole, and in California.

As is the case for the country as a whole, unemployment in New York State tends to hit minority groups the hardest. Except among females 20 years and older, unemployment for minority-group members in New York State is higher in every category than for whites. For example, a minority-group boy or girl between 16 and 19 is almost twice as likely to be unemployed as a similar white youth. This fact undoubtedly reflects discriminatory hiring practices. In addition, it reflects the low-achievement scores and high dropout rates of minority-group students.

STUDENT AND TEACHER OPINIONS

Another way to judge the success of an educational system is to examine how it is viewed by the people within it. While this is a qualitative measure, as opposed to a quantitative one such as test scores or incidence of dropouts, it is still valid. Any school will be more effective in achieving its basic goals when its students have positive feelings about the school, the teachers and the curriculum, and when the teachers have positive attitudes about their jobs and their students.

The Students' View

The Commission heard intelligent and informative testimony from many high school students and from first-year college students whose memories of high school were still clearly in mind. The Commission also contracted for a survey of student and teacher opinion in the high schools of New York State.[34] The survey sampled opinions of students and teachers in 15 New York State high schools—five in New York City, four in large upstate cities, and the rest in smaller localities. The schools varied in size as well as in social and ethnic composition. While the study does not provide a statistically accurate profile of *all* student and teacher opinion, it does present an overview of how students and teachers feel about their schools—and each other.

More than 66 per cent of the students sampled indicated that they did not enjoy school. Responses also revealed tension in student-teacher relations. Students generally felt that teachers did not help them to do their best, did not understand their problems, did not help them to improve their skills and were not concerned with their future. More than simply not enjoying school, many students indicated that their school experience was actually painful.

---

* This is true for every category except "Other" males, 20 years and older.

Students felt that administrators were not sufficiently accessible. They reported that the proliferation of school rules was oppressive and, more importantly, that enforcement of discipline was unfair, arbitrary or discriminatory. When school administrators failed to respond to their complaints, they felt tension and conflict resulted.

Race relations emerged as another major area of concern. Minority students were acutely conscious of what they perceived as "overt racism" in the schools. More than half the black students in the sample felt they were being excluded from school activities because of race, and both black and Puerto Rican students felt that school regulations were applied more harshly to them.

In general, white students and teachers appeared to be unaware of the problems minority students cited. In contrast to the feelings of more than half of the black students, only 11 per cent of the white students felt that blacks were excluded from school activities because of race. White teachers seemed to feel that black students had more than their share of influence, and also commented frequently that blacks exhibited racism toward them.

Teachers' perceptions of the school situation were substantially different from those of students. Teachers appeared largely unaware of the negative feelings of their students. When asked to rate school morale as "positive," "average" or "negative," 52 per cent of students picked "negative" while 64 per cent of the teachers picked "positive." Asked to assign the same ratings to the over-all educational process, 52 per cent of the teachers chose "positive" compared with only 28 per cent of the students. (For additional comparisons, see Table 1.26.)

Student dissatisfaction of this magnitude is a real cause for concern. Elsewhere in this report we consider measures designed to foster increased student participation in the educational process, and to develop a curriculum which actively engages student interest.

Teacher Opinions

In some ways, teacher attitudes resembled those of students. Both groups placed high priority on self-understanding and working for change within social institutions. Students and teachers also agreed on certain goals related to the process of education: Both groups desired a student-focused learning environment and a liberal orientation emphasizing student participation.

Perhaps more surprising than teacher-student agreement was the level of agreement among teachers, regardless of differences in age, sex, type of school or teaching experience. At first glance, the level of consensus on basic issues indicated an impressive foundation for a working organization. Further analysis, however, revealed that such agreement may be a result of

TABLE 1.26

How Teachers Treat Students

	TEACHER		STUDENT	
	Negative	Positive	Negative	Positive
Treat students as responsible	10.4%	52.4%	34.9%	37.0%
Listen to students' opinions	15.3	46.6	42.1	31.2
Understand student problems	21.8	41.7	52.7	21.0
Help students develop skills	12.9	49.6	43.0	29.2
Help students do best	8.9	55.1	40.1	29.9
Concerned about students' future	10.4	60.2	42.1	32.0

How Students Treat Teachers

	TEACHER		STUDENT	
	Negative	Positive	Negative	Positive
Students respect teachers	13.8%	52.8%	36.5%	29.2%
Students listen to teachers' opinions	18.3	39.6	35.3	28.9
Students help teacher do best	23.8	32.3	46.8	18.1
Students understand teachers' problems	63.3	9.3	61.7	14.9
Students can disagree with teachers	7.0	72.7	48.0	29.9

an atmosphere that encourages teachers to profess certain abstract progressive beliefs while establishing role requirements that make attainment of their ideals very difficult. Teachers are understandably torn between their own educational ideals and the everyday demands made on them to maintain order and control.

Generally, teachers wanted to change schools in ways that were opposed to the desires of students. They wanted to increase the level of discipline, while students wanted to decrease it. Teachers' attitudes were further clarified by their responses to the question of who had influence in school; their answers revealed that teachers felt impotent.

The study also found that teachers have difficulty identifying with a "coherent role group." Part of this difficulty results from structuring the school into a series of classrooms, each monitored by one teacher, with little chance of communication and discussion among colleagues.

Fifty-two per cent of the teachers sampled felt that they thought of students as "responsible." Forty-seven per cent felt that they listened to students' opinions, and 50 per cent felt that they helped students to do their best. Teachers as a group had more positive feelings about the student-teacher relationship than the students had. Fifty-three per cent of the teachers felt that students respected them, while only 30 per cent of the students noted that they had respect for their teachers. Seventy-three per cent of the teachers saw students as being relatively free to criticize them, but only 30 per cent of the students felt able to criticize.

These findings indicate an obvious lack of communication between teachers and students, as well as among teachers. Forty-two per cent of the teachers felt they understood the problems of being a student, but 53 per cent of the students disagreed. Both students and teachers agreed that students did not understand the special problems of being a teacher.

SPECIAL PROBLEMS IN NEW YORK STATE SCHOOLS

Measuring school performance can help identify those students who need special attention and to whom additional resources should be directed. However, it is equally important to identify specific problem areas in education throughout New York State, areas to which the allocation of increased resources could have a significant impact. In the years since the last intensive examination of elementary and secondary education in New York State, the *Regents Inquiry* in 1938, a number of social problems have developed.

Four such areas in which the schools should have significant impact are racial and ethnic integration, the education of non-English-speaking students, the needs of handicapped students and the problem of drug abuse. These problem areas, which are discussed in separate chapters, are summarized below.

Racial and Ethnic Imbalance

New York is experiencing rapidly growing racial and ethnic separation in its schools. Over 93 per cent of New York's public school students are being educated in 676 school districts that are "segregated." ("Segregated" is defined in the chapter on Racial and Ethnic Integration.) The Commission is particularly disturbed by the fact that, despite the good intentions and hard work of a number of state officials and the leadership of the Board of Regents, the situation is deteriorating. As we show in our chapter on Racial and Ethnic Integration in the Public Schools, there is more racial separation in New York's schools today than there was in 1954 at the time of the United States Supreme Court's landmark decision. While racial segregation in the Southern states has declined dramatically, New York continues to experience increasing racial separation.

Non-English-Speaking Students

In the decade between 1960 and 1970, the number of Puerto Rican immigrants to New York State—mainly to New York City—was close to one million. The number of Spanish-surnamed American students in New York City public schools alone now stands at 290,000, approximately 135,000 of whom are unable to speak English with sufficient fluency to benefit from regular classroom instruction. Another 18,000 students of Chinese, Italian, French and other backgrounds also cannot speak English. Despite this situation, bilingual education programs reach only 4,000 students in New York City. It is no wonder that Puerto Rican students are scoring poorly on standardized tests, dropping out of school at an extraordinary rate (52 per cent between 10th and 12th grades), failing to take advantage of post-secondary school opportunities, and finding it very difficult to compete in the job market.

Handicapped Students

Nearly one out of every 10 students in New York State is affected by some sort of physical, mental or emotional condition which impairs his or her ability to benefit from a regular school program. Nevertheless, it is estimated that New York today is providing appropriate school services to only 53 per cent of these children. There are approximately 215,000 handicapped youngsters for whom no appropriate school services are available.

Drug Abuse

It is difficult to pinpoint the causes behind the rapidly increasing problem of drug abuse in New York State. Studies conducted for the Commission reveal that one high school student in four in New York State routinely takes some form of psychoactive drug. In New York City, the figure is one high school student in two. In spite of the magnitude of this problem, in 1970 New York State appropriated only $20 million for school-related drug education programs. And the lack of planning and coordination of drug abuse programs is even more serious than the limited size of the budget.

THEMES OF THE REPORT

After reviewing the present state of education in New York State, the Commission concludes that the schools should strive to achieve four goals—equality, excellence, efficiency and flexibility.

We agree with John W. Gardner, former Secretary of Health, Education and Welfare, that equality and excellence are not antithetical goals, and we think that the schools of New York State can and must strive for both. A far greater effort must be made to reduce the school-related inequities among different social groups in New York State. At the same time, the educational system has to improve to provide *higher quality* education to all students.

The educational system of the state must also become more efficient. Certainly the fact that large numbers of children do not learn to read or write or cipher satisfactorily is evidence that the schools have a long way to go before they can be said to be efficient at their basic job. It is unfortunate also that many gifted and talented students do not find enough challenge in their schools. Equally disturbing to the Commission is the fact that substantial increases in costs per pupil in recent years have not been accompanied by comparable improvement in school performance. Consequently, the Commission concludes that efforts must be made to increase productivity within the system. It believes that such increased efficiency can be obtained by better deployment of educational personnel, revision of salary and pension arrangements, accountability and monitoring systems for schools and more rapid development of educational technology.

Another conclusion of the Commission is that there is need for more responsiveness and flexibility in the educational system. Witness after witness at public hearings emphasized that schooling throughout New York State is too rigid and inflexible. These charges are of concern to the Commission for three reasons:

1. In most communities, the clients—parents, students and local citizens—feel that they have little influence over what happens in their schools. This is not a healthy condition for learning, and schools will have to find ways to become more sensitive to their needs and wishes. Proposals in the chapter on Governance should contribute toward developing a better relationship between the schools and the various publics they serve.

2. The standardization of most educational practices implies that we have discovered "the best" way to teach and the "most effective" way to organize schools under all circumstances. In truth, we often do not know which methods are the best or which organizational strategies are the most effective. The Commission believes that the urgent educational strategy today is to encourage diversity and to allow competent instructors considerable discretion in the way in which they teach. This is not to say there should be no accountability in accordance with basic educational standards. Instead, it is to emphasize standardization of the *outcomes* of education—all children should know how to solve problems and make decisions, and should be able to read and work well with numbers—and not necessarily standardization of the *processes* by which these outcomes are achieved. For this reason, schools should be encouraged to innovate freely and to report the results of such innovations. Without a substantial period of experimentation and dissemination of findings, we can never hope to determine which methods are truly the best ones to follow.
3. The Commission fears that without flexibility the schools will be ill-prepared to meet future challenges. Thirty years ago, no one could have predicted today's technological advances or the social problems that now affect American life. The present rapid rate of change is going to persist, and the educational system will have to continue adjusting to it. Such adjustment will be substantially easier if there is constant effort to evaluate results and seek better methods.

The Commission is well aware that the schools cannot solve all the problems of the society. Pupils are profoundly affected by family and social circumstances, and the schools cannot be expected to achieve equal educational performance without the support of other social forces. But this fact is not an excuse for inaction. Continuous effort and flexibility of method can lead to far better results than those reported in this chapter.

School Finance: Toward Equality of Opportunity

EQUALITY: THE PROBLEM OF DEFINITION

"Equality" is a difficult word to define. Though it carries a favorable connotation, it is ambiguous and encompasses many complicated concepts.

Dictionaries offer little help in defining the word. Webster defines *equality* as the "condition of being equal." Equal is given six definitions: of the two that seem most appropriate for our purposes, one, "characterized by justice, fair" is labeled *archaic;* the other, "uniform, equable" is labeled *obsolete.* Philosophers, statesmen and men in the street have argued for centuries about its meaning, and how it might be achieved by law, by custom or by force of public opinion.

It is impossible to arrive at a definition of equality which is suitable for all purposes; instead, we shall attempt to describe "equality" as it relates to educational opportunity.

Financial equality in education is the concern of this chapter. What is meant by equality in raising educational revenues? What is meant by equality in distributing those revenues throughout the state? How does such equality, or inequality, affect our educational efforts? How far from the goal of equality are we in New York State today, and, finally, what can and should be done about it?

Because of the lack of experimentally proven data on the learning process, it is currently fashionable in academic circles to assert that more money for schools does not necessarily mean better education.* In a very

---

* Such an interpretation was commonly drawn from James S. Coleman, *et al., Equality of Educational Opportunity* (Washington, D.C.: Government Printing Office, 1966). Other studies have cast doubt on the validity of the interpretation; cf. James W. Guthrie, *et al., Schools and Inequality* (Cambridge, Mass.: MIT Press, 1971).

narrow sense this may be true. For example, it has never been proven that a student/teacher ratio of 28 to one necessarily provides better education than a ratio of 30 to one for normal children. But if it is true that minor variations in student/teacher ratios are not highly significant for normal pupils, it is even clearer that substantial differences in student/teacher ratios are of controlling importance in the education of handicapped children. Here the effective ratio is not 30 to one but often five to one. The expense of employing additional teachers for these children cannot be avoided unless we are to relegate a sizable percentage of our present school population to a hopelessly inferior status for the rest of their lives. Apart from these extreme situations, experience tells us that the amount of money expended does make a meaningful difference in the quality of education. Notably, the current trend of judicial opinion to the effect that grossly unequal expenditures per pupil within a state violate the Federal Constitution is based on the assumption that educational expenditures and quality are related.*

---

* On August 30, 1971, the California Supreme Court, in *Serrano* v. *Priest* (5 Cal. 3d 584, 487 P. 2d 1241 [Cal. Sup. Ct., 1971]), by a majority of 6–1, announced a decision that seems likely to be of landmark significance. While the judgment did not terminate the litigation, the Court tentatively concluded that the state's system of public school finance denies children the equal protection guaranteed under the 14th Amendment, because it produces substantial disparities among school districts in the amount of revenue available for education. While this decision has no immediate legal impact outside California, if its analysis is substantially correct, the public school finance systems in the great preponderance of states, including New York, are unconstitutional as well.

In California, as in most states, public elementary and secondary schools depend in large part on funds generated from local property taxes. Because taxable real property valuation on a per-pupil basis varies widely from district to district, receipts from local property taxes per pupil vary widely as well. Although California, again like most states, provides aid from general state revenue sources to school districts pursuant to a formula that purports to equalize inter-district disparities, such disparities continue to exist. Addressing itself to this phenomenon, the Court observed:

> Affluent districts can have their cake and eat it too; they can provide a high quality education for their children while paying lower taxes. Poor districts, by contrast, have no cake at all. [487 P. 2d at 1251–2.]

In this context the Court declared:

> We have determined that this funding scheme invidiously discriminates against the poor because it makes the quality of a child's education a function of the wealth of his parents and neighbors. Recognizing as we must that the right to an education is a fundamental interest which cannot be conditioned on wealth, we can discern no compelling state purpose necessitating the present method of financing. [*Ibid.*, p. 1244.]

Another recent decision in the United States District Court of Minnesota, *Van Dusartz* v. *Hatfield*, came to the same conclusion regarding educational finance in that state. As to the relation between cost and quality, the Court stated:

> . . . the Legislature would seem to have foreclosed this issue to the state by establishing a system encouraging variation in spending; it would be high irony for the state to argue that large portions of the educational budget authorized by law are in effect thrown away. [334 F. Supp. 870, 873–4 (D. Minn., 1971).]

Also, in December 1971, in *Rodriquez* v. *San Antonio Independent School District*, a

Thus, while equality of expenditure in accordance with some reasonable educational standard may not inevitably result in higher quality education, we feel that such equality is the essential first step toward achieving that goal. Without that equality, large numbers of children in districts lacking in financial resources are doomed to inferior educational achievement. Society is fated to assume the ever-increasing burden of supporting those who cannot make their own way in the world. Inequality and inequity in financing, both in raising and in distributing resources, is the key log jam which must be removed before the movement toward higher levels of educational achievement can be resumed.

This brings us to a closer scrutiny of the basic elements of educational equality and a consideration of the ways in which revenues ought to be raised and distributed for educational purposes to ensure such equality.

Raising Educational Revenues

The Commission believes that the responsibility for raising educational revenues belongs to the state. The state's responsibility can no longer be avoided by leaving the decision of how, and how much, revenue is to be raised to each school district.

This position is not inconsistent with the Commission's desire to *strengthen* local control over many educational matters.* Centralization and decentralization are not mutually contradictory concepts; it is clearly possible to have centralized financing and decentralized policymaking. The Commission strongly urges that greater decision-making power be granted to the local school, since it is the school, not the school district, that is the basic educational unit and the natural center for both performance and fiscal accountability. Local boards of education, too, should have more power to shape the ends of education in their districts under state assumption of educational financing, since the boards of education will have to spend less of their time in finding necessary resources, and will have more time to concentrate on purely educational concerns.

—Full state funding of education can be accomplished by means of any form of taxation—real property tax, income tax, sales tax, or any combination thereof, provided it is fairly administered throughout the state. How-

---

three-judge panel of the United States District Court, Western District of Texas, ruled that the method of financing elementary and secondary education in that state violates the 14th Amendment. The Court's decision was based on the same reasoning expressed in the *Serrano* decision. The Court granted state officials a period of two years in which to devise a plan to reallocate school funds to assure that children's educational opportunities are not a function of wealth other than the wealth of the state as a whole. The case has been appealed to the United States Supreme Court.

* For further analysis of the local control issue see the later section of this chapter, "Analysis of Arguments Against Full State Funding," and the chapter on Governance.

ever, it is clear that the ever-increasing demands of public services require that taxes must be largely raised from those who have the wealth.

—Assumption of all educational costs by the state (full state funding) is not mandatory to achieve equalization of expenditure among school districts, although it is preferred to other possible methods (see below). However, if the state does not assume the cost, it must provide an equalizing formula which will assure that a homeowner at one end of the state is not taxed for a *given quality of education* at a different rate or on different principles than a similar homeowner in another locality.

—Full state funding does not of itself require an increase in total educational expenditures. The state could, if it wished, raise exactly the same amount of money by state taxation that is now raised by the combination of local and state taxation. It would then redistribute this fund among the school districts in accordance with a formula that is fair and equitable to the children of every district. This would mean that poor districts would be "leveled up" and rich districts would be "leveled down." However, leveling down educational expenditures in any district is not a simple task and may involve problems of a legal nature because high spending districts have fixed costs often based on contractual obligation. Thus, as a practical matter, full state funding is almost certain to produce more leveling up than down; this in turn makes it probable that one consequence of state assumption means higher over-all educational expenditure.

—Full state funding makes possible, though it does not automatically provide, more effective controls over expenditures. It permits the state to invest in improvement in quality at a rate consonant with the growth of the over-all economy of the state. It eliminates the present competition among wealthy districts for the most elaborate schoolhouse and similar luxuries.

Distributing School Revenues

While an equitable distribution plan requires that educational expenditures for any child be a product of the state's total wealth rather than the wealth of a single school district, neither legal nor moral principles require identical educational expenditures for each child in the state. Such a distribution would in fact *deprive* handicapped children of equality of educational opportunity. Guiding principles for distribution of funds should be need and capacity to learn. Sufficient funds should be provided so that each educable child can attain a minimum but reasonably high level of educational achievement which will permit him to become a useful, self-supporting individual. Equitable distribution should provide children who can benefit from continued learning with further education that equips them for positions of leadership. Finally, special provisions should be made for the particularly gifted whose contributions to the nation can be expected to be maximized if their talents are recognized and nurtured.

The fundamental dilemma in school finance stems from the historic and fundamental paradox in our nation: the frequent conflict between equality and individual freedom. Thus, the principle of equality in school finance requires that resources of the state raised by taxation for education be used to support equal educational opportunities for all of the children of the state, a principle affirmed in *Serrano v. Priest* (*supra*). As long as individual children, rather than school districts, are entitled to equal protection under the laws of the state, the state cannot permit individual districts to tap a portion of the state's wealth for educational increments or "add-ons" for their children while children elsewhere are deprived of similar increments by reason of either the relative low wealth or relative lack of concern for education of the district in which they happen to reside. As long as funds are not state-generated, on the other hand, neither can the state use its power to deny *individuals* the right to invest more in education than the state provides.

Any phased change in the direction of greater educational equality would surely win judicial approval if it were appropriate to the existing situation. Thus, temporary "save harmless" provisions insuring that no district receives less under a new system than it had been receiving previously, though theoretically unequal are common and can be designed to minimize the likelihood of judicial modification.

EQUALITY AS AFFECTED BY THE RELATION BETWEEN SYSTEMS OF REVENUE RAISING AND DISTRIBUTION

It is repugnant to the idea of equal educational opportunity that the quality of a child's education, insofar as that education is provided through public funds, is determined by accidents of birth, wealth, or geography; that a child who lives in a poor district is, by reason of that fact alone, entitled to lower public investment in his education than a child in a rich district. It is unconscionable that a poor man in a poor district must often pay local taxes at higher rates for the inferior education of his child than the man of means in a rich district pays for the superior education of his child. Yet, incredibly, that is the situation today in most of the 50 states, and that is the case in New York.

The New York State school system does not provide educational equality. In fact, its structure insures the continuance of basic inequality in educational revenue raising and expenditure.

It is not necessary here to review in detail the elements of the state distribution formula designed to minimize some of the inequities arising out of differences in true value of taxable property among districts.* Suffice it to say that expenditures per pupil throughout the state tend to

---

* Appendix 2A offers information on the various education grants of New York State. Appendix 2B gives details about education finance in the districts of Long Island.

vary directly with the value of taxable property and that the state aid formula does not in fact eliminate large discrepancies in per-pupil expenditure.

Two Long Island districts strikingly illustrate the disparities that now exist and must be eliminated. They are by no means unique; similar disparities exist in every region of the state. An examination of the figures for 1968–69[1] for two Long Island school districts within 10 miles of each other—Great Neck and Levittown—illustrates the deficiencies of state aid.

	Per Pupil Enrolled
GREAT NECK: (Student Enrollment: 9,869)	
Revenue from Local Property Tax	$1,684.07
Revenue from Tuition and Other Local Sources	29.29
Revenue from State Sources	364.16
Revenue from Federal Sources	— 0 —
Total Expenditure	$2,077.52

True Value Assessed Property: $64,400 per pupil
Tax Rate: $2.72 per $100

LEVITTOWN: (Student Enrollment: 17,280)	
Revenue from Local Property Tax	$ 410.31
Revenue from Tuition and Other Local Sources	13.87
Revenue from State Sources	764.48
Revenue from Federal Sources	.71
Total Expenditure	$1,189.37

True Value Assessed Property: $16,200 per pupil
Tax Rate: $2.72 per $100

After payment of state aid designed to equalize expenditures per pupil, the Great Neck student has about 80 per cent more money spent on his education than does the Levittown student. How can this be?

Levittown receives more money from the state than does Great Neck. But the amount of state aid in question does not begin to equalize the school revenues in these two districts. The aid money granted to Levittown approaches the maximum amount of state aid available to a district—$400 more per pupil than Great Neck—but at the same time, Great Neck can generate almost $1,300 more per pupil in local property taxes than can Levittown.

It might be assumed that Levittown is not taxing itself enough for educational services because the residents do not care about their schools. In fact, Levittown taxes itself at the rate of $2.72 per $100 of true value, a rate that is *precisely* the same as that of Great Neck, and *higher* than the Long Island regional average of $2.29 per $100 of true value. However, the true value of assessed property in Levittown is very low: $16,200 per pupil as compared to the regional average of $30,500 per pupil. Even though Levittown taxes itself at a high rate, the property will never generate the kind of educational revenue which is generated at the same rate in Great Neck, where the true value of assessed property is $64,400 per pupil. *In fact, in Great Neck, the revenue from local property taxes alone is greater than the average revenue per pupil throughout Long Island from all sources (state, federal, local property tax, tuition, and other revenue sources).*

Despite gross inequities in local tax capacity, Great Neck receives money from the state under the "flat grant" provision of the state aid formula which assures that every district in New York, *no matter how wealthy,* receives a minimum grant (in 1968–69, $274; today, $310) from the state.* Rich districts, in effect, receive a windfall since many school districts would not be entitled to this amount if the aid formula did not contain a flat grant provision.

Another structural limitation of the state formula, perhaps even more damaging than the minimum grant provision, is the state aid ceiling which is the maximum expenditure level to which the formula will be applied. Thus, a district can receive state aid only up to a given level of support above which any revenue has to be generated wholly within the district itself. The ceiling in 1968–69 was $760; since 1970–71 it has been $860. On Long Island, in 1968–69, no district was spending below the ceiling; therefore, all 131 districts in the region were paying their own way on expenditures above $760. Unless the ceiling is placed at a level sufficiently high to bring the expenditure level of the poorest district to that of the richest district in the state, there will not be full equalizing, and until the ceiling is well above the median, a condition of equalization cannot even be approached.

Moreover, the current aid formula provides that the state shall allocate only 90 per cent of the ceiling, or $684 per pupil in 1968–69. Under the formula, even if the low fiscal capacity of a poor district were such that it would be entitled to an aid ratio higher than 90 per cent, the state would not allocate the additional 10 per cent aid.

Obviously, the student in Levittown is educationally disadvantaged compared to the student in Great Neck. The head of a household in Levittown is similarly economically disadvantaged. While there are no accurate figures, the typical household income in Levittown is considerably less than in Great Neck. Since in 1968–69 the school property tax rate was precisely

---

* Additional state aid to a wealthy district like Great Neck can come in the form of growth aid, size correction aid, transportation aid and other forms of categorical aid.

the same for both districts, it is reasonable to conclude, given what is known about incidence of the residential portion of the property tax, that many families in Levittown were paying a greater proportion of their income as school property taxes while at the same time the Levittowners received substantially fewer dollars in revenues for education.

The story of Levittown and Great Neck can be repeated over and over again by comparing other districts throughout the state. Confining our analysis to Long Island, however, we find that big suburban districts lose out and thousands of children get less education than their counterparts in smaller, more affluent districts. Smaller, richer districts have more money to spend on their children for education. For all the small, privileged districts such as Roslyn, Great Neck, Manhasset and Cold Spring Harbor, there are many larger, impecunious districts such as Levittown, Brentwood, Commack, Lindenhurst, Middle Country, West Islip and Smithtown.

FULL STATE FUNDING AS A SOLUTION TO FINANCIAL INEQUALITIES IN EDUCATION

Until a few years ago, the idea of full state funding of public elementary and secondary education was generally considered a radical and impractical concept. In 1968, the concept was revived and given impetus when it became the subject of an insightful memorandum from one great American educator, Dr. James B. Conant, to another, the late Dr. James B. Allen, then New York State Commissioner of Education, which, with Dr. Conant's consent is published here in pertinent part.

MEMORANDUM

Proposed New York Commission to Consider the Feasibility of Shifting the Financing of the Public Schools from a Local-State Basis to a Complete State Basis

It is the belief of the writer of this memorandum that public education in New York State would be greatly improved if educational decisions at the local level could be completely divorced from considerations of local taxes. At present, the fact that some of the money for the elementary and secondary schools is provided through local taxes erects barriers to the solution of the following important problems:

THE ISSUE OF LOCAL CONTROL

It has often been argued that local control would disappear if the state supplied all the funds for the elementary and secondary schools. The writer doubts if such an argument is valid. If all the school districts were large enough to have as many as at least a thousand teachers, the annual turnover would provide flexibility in the staff. As long as the local superintendent is on contract, his tenure is essentially at the pleasure of the board. His freedom for innovation might be even greater than at present if the size and compensation of the teaching staff were determined by state law. A necessary consequence of state financing would be a statewide salary schedule. It would be desirable to have a statewide recognition of the ratio of staff to student body to provide the basic instruction at all levels. Each district would then receive its minimum quota of places to be filled as the board saw fit. In addition, each district might be allowed a 10 per cent increase in the teaching staff for innovations. If the accounting between the state and the local board were in terms of places not dollars, each superintendent would know how many teachers he could hire each year irrespective of a financial budget.

The question of local control of capital expenses would disappear under the scheme here considered. The issue of approval of bonds and budgets would disappear. At present the state must approve all building plans so that there would be no increase in state control if the local board appealed to the state for the funds to build new buildings. The Chief State Officer's accounting staff would, of course have to have an annual budget in terms of dollars to meet the projected capital needs of the state as well as the projected employment of teachers.

The Source of the State Funds

The abolishment of local school taxes would require the state to raise a large sum of money for school purposes. How such a sum could be raised is the main question which should be explored by the Commission proposed in this memorandum. Perhaps a uniform state property tax for schools could be authorized. The collection of such a tax and its relation to other state and local taxes needs to be examined. Also, other ideas should be considered. Particularly, the transition to the new and radically different tax system requires expert thought. With the hopes that the advantages of a drastic shift in financing the public schools may be apparent, this memorandum has been written.

JAMES B. CONANT

March 22, 1968

Today, full state funding has the explicit support of such widely respected organizations as the Advisory Commission on Intergovernmental Relations and the Committee for Economic Development.[2] The public's willingness to consider the idea, however, is probably more closely related to growing local tax burdens than it is to the educational merits of the plan. Nevertheless, this public concern has permitted serious consideration of the advantages and disadvantages of shifting the responsibility for financing education to the state level.

Article XI, Section 1 of the Constitution of the State of New York reads:

> The Legislature shall provide for the maintenance and support of a system of free common schools, wherein all the children of this state may be educated.

Taking account of this constitutional mandate, the equity considerations as described, and other matters yet to be discussed, the Commission recommends that the State of New York undertake full funding of educational costs. By full state funding we mean that the State Government become the governmental entity responsible for raising all or practically all of the money to maintain and support public elementary and secondary schools except for that amount of money which the Federal Government shall contribute.*

General Principles of Full State Funding

—The state shall provide all or nearly all the money for the operation of elementary and secondary schools (with the exception of federal aid). The additional state revenues necessary to meet "full costs" of operating elementary and secondary schools may be obtained by a statewide property tax (as a substitute for local property taxes in support of education) or by more intensive use of state income taxes or sales taxes.

—The state shall eradicate most of the discrepancies in levels of spending for local educational services before full state funding shall be fully operational. This entails raising expenditures of lower spending districts ("leveling up") rather than reducing expenditures of higher spending districts. The leveling-up cost could be spread over several years of the state's budget.

—The state shall determine a defensible basis of distributing money to school districts. Equal sums of money shall be made available for each student, *unless a valid educational reason can be found for spending some different amount.*

—The state's accelerating development of regional educational centers provides a basis for simplifying the process of determining how much money should be spent in individual school districts. Under our proposed plan for expanding Boards of Cooperative Educational Services (BOCES) (outlined in the chapter on Governance), the state would distribute to districts certain *educational services* such as vocational education, programs for the handicapped, remedial programs, programs for the gifted, student transport,

---

* We urge in the next chapter that the federal contribution be increased substantially above current levels.

health services, etc., thus avoiding precise interdistrict budgetary judgments with respect to the cost of these services. This is "aid in kind" rather than aid in money.

The Advisory Commission on Intergovernmental Relations has stated:

> [We] assume that there would be a limited opportunity for local enrichment of the educational program. However, failure to circumscribe the amount of local enrichment—by limiting it to 10 per cent of the state grant, for example—would undermine its . . . objective—[to create] a fiscal environment more conducive to educational opportunity. . . .[3]

However, *this Commission recommends that all local option for supplementary school levies should be terminated.* Such levies would inevitably become a point of bargaining between the state and local governments. Also, existing disparities in per-pupil property valuation would give rich districts an indefensible advantage with respect to their capacity to raise the add-on amount. If the add-on is 10 per cent this year, pressure will be brought to bear upon the Legislature to raise the allowable percentage to 20 in the next, and, rather quickly, the present inequitable system could be recreated. In the process local authorities and the Legislature would be distracted from consideration of serious educational issues.

—Full state funding implies some control over the powers of local school districts to engage in collective bargaining with professional and nonprofessional staff. We anticipate that with full state funding collective bargaining relating to salary schedules and pensions would be conducted on a statewide basis.* This process might well establish a system of regional salary differentials that could be recognized in the state's distribution formula.

Distribution Recommendations

THE COMMISSION'S DISTRIBUTION FORMULA Full state funding consists of a distribution formula for the allocation of money to school districts to meet their educational costs, and a revenue plan, under which the state obtains the funds that are to be distributed. The distribution formula is based on two central considerations:

The first is that full state funding must remove disparities in educational spending that are unrelated to the educational requirements of students or to geographic differences in prices of educational services; the second is that funds must begin to flow according to the educational needs of students.

Removing disparities in spending that are unrelated to educational need or price differentials cannot be done overnight. As a first step, *we propose that expenditures of all districts be brought up to the level of the district*

---

* For details, see the chapter on Education and Educational Policy.

*spending at the 65th percentile in a ranking of districts according to their
Base Expenditures.* ["Base Expenditures" are herein defined as total general fund expenses (which do not include federal funds) *per enrolled pupil* minus the following exclusions: debt service, transportation, lunch, tuition, BOCES operation and urban aid.*] This leveling-up step would assure a minimum expenditure level that is much more realistic with respect to today's educational costs than the existing minimum level. Further, our support plan does not recommend that the development of a full state funding formula be linked to or dependent upon changes in the form or extent of federal aid.**

In order to allocate funds for the support of education it is essential to have a count of students, as students are the primary measure of need to spend funds in schools. At present, the measure used is average daily attendance of students who reside in a given district, weighted as follows: 0.5 for kindergarten, 1.0 for elementary, and 1.25 for secondary. *We propose instead to take a count of enrollment, perhaps several times a year, using no weighting factor by level of education except 0.5 for kindergarten, on the assumption that kindergarten will continue to be a half-day program.*

There are several arguments against the use of weighted average daily attendance:

1. It discriminates unfairly against districts that show high rates of truancy and drop-out. (The rationale for weighted average daily attendance was to encourage districts to reduce their truancy and drop-out rates, but this has simply not occurred.

2. The proportion of elementary vs. high school students is relatively

---

* These particular accounts were excluded because we conceive that these expenditures will continue to be financed separately. In this connection, as described in detail in a subsequent chapter, we recommend that debt service on all new construction be financed by the state through a construction authority. As to outstanding indebtedness for school construction, we recommend that the state reimburse school districts for debt service costs. No new money is required for this proposal, since our proposed statewide property tax was calculated at a level sufficient to defray school districts' costs of debt service, school lunch, student transport and BOCES. The details of our recommendation on school lunch and transportation appear in the chapter on Support Services; those on BOCES are in the chapter on Governance. In all of these cases we recommend full state funding; their distinguishing features are in the proposed distribution of funds for these purposes. It is important to note here that we recommend inclusion of the Big Six cities in the BOCES. In the subsequent table showing the effect in selected districts of leveling up, an adjustment was made to recognize that the Big Six cities are presently excluded from BOCES operations.

Tuition was excluded for a different reason: to avoid double counting since it already appears as part of general per-pupil expenditures in those districts that receive tuition-paying children. Finally, urban aid was excluded because it is replaced by the 0.5 additional weighting for disadvantaged students.

** The chapter on Federal Aid indicates both need and preferred forms for new and expanded federal aid programs for education. However, we do not recommend that implementation of the proposed financing system wait upon possible future increases in such aid.

constant among all school districts; hence, the weighting factor in the current distribution formula has little influence on the distribution of funds among districts.

3. In addition, the pedagogical wisdom of weighting secondary students more heavily than elementary students is questionable: we suspect that in many instances it might be good policy to spend more money per student in the elementary grades than in the secondary, but the present weighting factor has a psychological effect of suggesting that all districts should spend more money on secondary students.

Based on enrollment count, we determined the Base Expenditure in each district and districts were than ranked from low to high in accordance with this measure.

Under our proposal, all districts with a Base Expenditure below that of the district at the 65th percentile point (65 percentage points up from the bottom of the list of school districts or 35 percentage points down from the top) would be provided with funds sufficient to raise their expenditures to the desired statewide level. In 1969–70, the Base Expenditure of that district at the 65th percentile was $1,037. It should be pointed out that this, our recommended expenditure level, is for each child who has no learning problems: our proposed formula adds additional funds for each child who does have learning problems. It is up to the Legislature to establish the Base Expenditure level in the first year of the full-funding program and to adjust the level subsequently.

We propose that districts with Base Expenditures above the district at the 65th percentile point be "saved harmless" on those expenditures—i.e., that they be allowed to continue to spend an amount per student equal to that amount which they were spending in the base year, and that such amount be provided by the state.* After the base year, however, we recommend that their expenditure levels (on a per-student-enrolled basis) not be increased until the statewide level of spending rises to the level of the given saved-harmless district. We estimate the first year amount (1972–73) of this saved-harmless provision to be $230,000,000. It is important to note, however, that *this is not new money; these expenses are already being incurred and are paid for out of present state and local education revenues.* Also, this particular state expenditure account will obviously decrease as the minimum statewide spending level increases.

What of districts that are spending at very low levels? (In 1969–70, one district spent only $436 per student.) It would seem imprudent to more than double the expenditure levels of some districts all at once. We propose

---

* The base year should be determined by the Legislature and will depend upon when full state funding is adopted. In order to prevent high-spending districts from greatly increasing their Base Expenditures forthwith, in anticipation of full state funding, it is suggested that the base year be 1971–72.

that leveling up be accomplished in increments of 15 per cent of the established statewide Base Expenditure level (in 1969–70, 15 per cent of $1,037, or $156). Our calculations indicate that all districts throughout the state except one (Sylvan Beach in Oneida County) would be leveled up by the third year of our plan, the remaining district by the fourth year. Cost of leveling up in 1972–73 is estimated to be $125,000,000 and, unlike the costs of supporting high-spending districts, this would require new money. Sixty-nine per cent of the state's public school students were in the 474 districts that would have received leveling-up assistance in 1969–70. Thirty-one per cent of the state's students were enrolled in the 255 saved-harmless districts.

The second step in our distribution program is to begin to regulate the flow of funds according to the educational needs of the students. We must identify those who have serious learning problems and provide extra funds to help them overcome these problems. *We propose that students who score at a low level in reading and mathematics achievement be weighted at 1.5, as against a weighting of 1.0 for other children, and that the proportion of students so selected be based upon the proportion of third-grade students in each district who obtain marks at or below the third stanine* on third-grade reading and mathematics achievement tests currently being administered in the state Pupil Evaluation Program (PEP).* This mechanism would distribute a share of the state's education budget to schools that are characterized by low rates of student progress and are therefore in greater need.** Use of third-grade achievement scores is a mechanism for distributing educational funds among schools; obviously, the Commission does not intend to restrict these funds to the third-grade level (though we do have a preference for spending the larger portion on elementary school children as described below). Moreover, it is pointed out in following pages that third-grade PEP scores are to be only an interim measure. To avoid chances of manipulation, we recommend that the 1971–72 PEP scores be used as the basis for distribution.

Weighting students who scored poorly on this test at 1.5 of the Base Expenditure amount would have distributed $425 million in 1969–70 and a projected $465 million in 1972–73. This is new money. *We propose that the amount made available for such students be stabilized at 15 per cent of the state's Base Expenditure level multiplied by the number of students enrolled.* This would distribute approximately the amount required by the 0.5 additional weighting factor for disadvantaged children and also lend stability to the state budget should there be any erratic change in test scores.

---

* Approximately the lowest quarter.
** We will recommend, in a later chapter on Children with Special Needs, additional funds for programs to serve children having physical and mental disabilities. The definitional problems created by these distinctions will be resolved in that chapter.

In time, the distribution to districts might be made on the basis of a three-year moving average of test scores.

There is no measure to explain which of the many inputs to the education process (e.g., teachers, books) does the most to increase educational attainment. We cannot assume that the additional money our proposal grants to districts with disadvantaged students should be used to hire more teachers, or more curriculum specialists, or to buy more books for the school library. Perhaps in one school, lowering the pupil/teacher ratio will have a significant effect on student achievement. In another school, money might be spent more profitably on new textbooks. The Commission has no desire to mandate the services for which additional money should be spent. However, *we do recommend that of the money allocated for disadvantaged students, most, perhaps 70 per cent, should go to elementary schools in a district and the remainder to the secondary schools.* We base this recommendation on three findings:

—The process of sorting children into different educational programs according to need and ability begins in the elementary grades and is largely complete by the time a student reaches high school. Money should be concentrated in the early years so that this process does not set restrictive limits on aspirations and achievement when a child is just beginning school.

—Concentrating money on elementary education gets children off to a good start. Remedial programs in later years are more expensive and too often cannot undo the damage of years of bad schooling.*

—Programs of BOCES, to be funded separately by the state, will be directed primarily at high school students.

NEED FOR BETTER DISTRIBUTION MEASURES In suggesting that a substantial part of the state funds for education be directed toward the problem of low achievement, the Commission takes the position that educational priority rather than the artifact of assessed valuation per student should control resource distributions. Once the problem of low achievement, and especially the problem of concentration of low achievement among students of low-income households, is overcome, then resource distributions should properly shift toward promoting the self-development of a broader range of students.

While our preference is for use of the direct approach for measuring need (i.e., test scores rather than household income), this Commission is far

---

* In 1970–71, under its recently instituted open admissions program, CUNY had 7,000 incoming freshmen (of a total of 34,500) who scored below average ninth-grade reading scores and 8,000 who scored below eighth-grade level in mathematics. To do college work successfully, these students require special help, and remedial programs provided at university level are very expensive, relatively speaking. See Benjamin Rosner, "Open Admission at the City University of New York," a paper presented to the American Association for the Advancement of Science, Chicago, December 27, 1970.

from satisfied with the use of third-grade test scores in reading and mathematics as a guide to distribution. We use them only because they are the best available. We urge that "learning readiness" tests that are statistically valid and accurate be introduced as soon as possible into the New York State testing pattern, so that resource distributions to elementary students can be directly related to their capacity to learn as measured when they first enter school. Early testing is essential to see that the resource-distribution mechanism does not operate as an incentive for poor performance or in such a way that districts lose funds as they help their students to perform better. In fact, to distribute funds on the basis of children's scores on tests administered at any point beyond first entry into school runs the risk that schools that are successful in overcoming the problem of low achievement will lose these necessary additional resources just at the time when they will have discovered how to use them effectively.

The Educational Testing Service (ETS), producer of such exams as the Scholastic Aptitude Tests, estimates they will have a good measure of reading and computational preparedness for tests for 5-year-olds and 6-year-olds within the next two years. If their prognosis proves accurate, we would recommend its use in place of the third-grade PEP tests possibly on a carefully designed sample basis. In addition, we strongly suggest that these tests be state-administered and scored to forestall chances of manipulation. Meanwhile, the third-grade PEP tests will serve as an interim measure for a year or two and allow the State Education Department and local school districts to institute statewide a system connecting compensatory aid to test scores that has been developed already in districts served by the Urban Aid program.*

While the use of a state-monitored learning readiness test, administered perhaps by an outside agent, would forestall the problem of test manipulation and avoid the encouragement of failure, there remains the need to insure progress. That responsibility falls mainly on the individual school and its staff, guided by well-informed parents and other citizens. A later chapter on the governance of education in New York contains explicit recommendations on this subject.

It has been noted more than once that there is a persistent, direct correlation between family income and scholastic achievement. Indeed, this is the basis of the federal aid to disadvantaged children grants, under Title I of the Elementary and Secondary Education Act of 1965. It has been suggested, therefore, that a similar standard could be employed to distribute the additional state monies which we believe ought to be directed toward students with special needs.[4] An extra advantage claimed for this proposal is that it is not susceptible of manipulation, whereas superin-

---

* This program provided $39 million in expenditures in 1969–70 based in part on PEP test results.

tendents and principals, it is thought, might be tempted to hold down test scores in order to obtain increased cash flow.

We do not favor this approach. We do not consider the possibility of manipulation a serious one, and in any event we think this danger can be reduced or eliminated by state monitoring of PEP tests.

We do acknowledge, however, that use of third-grade scores might create an incentive for failure, and therefore urge that "learning readiness" tests for entrants into the school system be employed as soon as possible and that they, too, be administered and scored by an outside agency.

Another problem involved in using family income as the need measure is the fact that there exist no compilations of income figures by school districts. Also, the lowest-income groups are not required to file tax returns. It has been suggested that all families could be required by law to file a return for information purposes, even when no tax is due, but we question the degree of compliance possible with any such legislation.

CONSEQUENCES OF THE PROPOSED DISTRIBUTION SCHEME   Table 2.1 shows how *selected* districts in New York State will fare under the distribution plan we have proposed.* We have included the Big Six cities, 13 of the state's 33 enlarged city districts, eight suburban districts within the New York metropolitan area and nine rural school districts. Within each grouping, we have chosen rich and poor districts on the basis of true value assessment per enrolled student in 1969–70. All figures are for 1969–70.

The first column shows school district *enrollment,* with no weighting factor used except 0.5 for kindergarten. Again, this recognizes the fact that most kindergarten programs are half-day, and that, at this time, there is not conclusive evidence to support weighting secondary school more heavily than elementary school.

Column 2 represents the sum of specific school district expenditures which have been excluded from total general fund expenses, hence the heading Major Exclusions. These expenditures include: debt service, school lunch, student transport, tuition and local expenditures for BOCES (an adjustment was made to recognize that the Big Six are presently excluded from BOCES operations). A sixth exclusion—urban aid—is listed separately in Column 3. Note that only 12 of our sample districts received urban aid in 1969–70.

Column 4 lists each district's Base Expenditures for 1969–70. Ranking the districts from low to high by spending, we determine which districts will be granted leveling-up funds. In New York State, there are 729 major

---

* The appendix to Chapter 14, "Schools for Tomorrow: a Summing Up," shows the impact of our proposed revenue raising and distribution plans, updated to 1970-71, on each of the state's 708 operating school districts.

TABLE 2.1

Effect of Leveling up to the 65th Percentile of Expenditures with Save-Harmless Provision and PEP Scores Weighted at .5, on Selected School Districts in New York State (Base Year: 1969–70)

	(1) Enrollment (K = $\frac{1}{2}$)	(2) Major Exclusions	(3) Urban Aid	(4) Base Expend.	(5) Base Expend. & Urban Aid	(6) True Val/Stud. ENR	(7) Effect in First Yr. of Leveling Up to 65th Percentile	(8) Effect with PEP Weighted at .5— at 65th Percentile	(9) Gain at 65th w/PEP Weighting
CITY									
New York City	1,068,502	269	29	1,016	1,045	45,859	1,037	1,273	228
Albany	10,702	310	21	998	1,019	57,498	1,037	1,182	163
Buffalo	68,090	165	34	869	903	28,368	1,024	1,219	316
Rochester	44,290	197	27	1,070	1,097	40,799	1,070	1,260	163
Syracuse	28,668	109	21	946	967	34,737	1,037	1,159	192
Yonkers	29,005	242	29	947	976	46,781	1,037	1,169	193
ENLARGED CITY									
Dunkirk (Chatauqua)	3,258	131		982	982	53,038	1,037	1,133	151
Lockport (Niagara)	6,720	217		899	899	25,081	1,037	1,125	226
Geneva (Ontario)	3,282	144		1,036	1,036	29,044	1,037	1,128	92
Hornell (Steuben)	3,439	198		956	956	14,010	1,037	1,125	169
Elmira (Chemung)	13,358	140	7	957	964	20,359	1,037	1,105	141
Rome (Oneida)	11,646	94	7	895	902	16,877	1,037	1,097	195

Schenectady (Schen.)	12,239	216	23	1,164	1,187	25,535	1,164	1,299	112
Ithaca (Tompkins)	7,871	294		1,095	1,095	31,902	1,095	1,180	85
Oswego (Oswego)	5,166	257		1,024	1,024	47,788	1,037	1,138	114
Beacon (Dutchess)	3,532	181		972	972	27,883	1,037	1,136	164
Hudson (Columbia)	3,461	131	14	934	934	23,416	1,037	1,162	228
Newburgh (Orange)	12,230	217		1,047	1,061	23,118	1,047	1,138	77
Ogdensburg (St. Lawrence)	3,235	169		815	815	13,641	971	1,020	205
SUBURBAN DISTRICT									
Bronxville (Westchester)	1,350	158		1,911	1,911	68,718	1,911	1,911a	0
Great Neck (Nassau)	9,427	254		2,079	2,079	71,413	2,079	2,131	52
Hempstead (Nassau)	5,371	318	23	1,430	1,453	64,752	1,430	1,599	146
Mamaroneck (Westchester)	6,106	211		1,527	1,527	49,410	1,527	1,610	83
Levittown (Nassau)	16,312	201		1,163	1,163	17,995	1,163	1,231	68
Peekskill (Westchester)	3,412	350		1,041	1,041	23,732	1,041	1,140	99
West Islip (Suffolk)	8,961	220		1,037	1,037	17,397	1,037	1,113	76
Mt. Vernon (Westchester)	11,377	210	26	1,123	1,149	35,977	1,123	1,266	117
RURAL DISTRICT									
Indian Lake (Hamilton)	363	287		961	961	48,152	1,037	1,073	112
Red Jacket (Ontario)	1,337	527		833	833	14,854	989	1,074	241
Edwards (St. Lawrence)	407	229		999	999	11,851	1,037	1,130	131
Penn Yan (Yates)	3,141	194		888	888	30,211	1,037	1,086	198
Town of Webb (Herkimer)	483	317		1,505	1,505	78,633	1,505	1,570	65
Carthage (Jefferson)	3,437	175		926	926	14,109	1,037	1,107	181
Malone (Franklin)	3,562	296		867	867	14,617	1,023	1,116	249
Minerva (Essex)	238	541		1,266	1,266	33,951	1,266	1,302	36
Keene (Essex)	171	303		1,459	1,459	42,709	1,459	1,615	156

a AFDC, PEP not available.

districts* to rank, and we find that the Base Expenditure figure of West Islip is at the 65th percentile. The leveling-up figure is the expenditure in this district—$1,037 per enrolled pupil.

Column 5 lists Base Expenditures *plus* urban aid. We include this column because urban aid is not treated as the other major exclusions are in our distribution scheme. The money to finance the Major Exclusions of Column 2 will be returned to districts in grants or programs that are separate from the distribution scheme we are proposing. Urban aid, however, will no longer be granted separately, because its goal—to recognize the special fiscal and educational needs of cities with enrollments over 4,500 and with 1,100 disadvantaged students and high Aid to Dependent Children (ADC) caseloads—is incorporated into our basic distribution plan by the use of PEP test scores. The total urban aid expended in 1969–70 was $39 million; our proposal would provide $425 million in the same year to meet the needs of educationally disadvantaged children throughout the state.

Column 6 gives the true value of property per student enrolled in each district. This serves as our wealth classification: a district with high true value/student, like the Town of Webb ($78,633), can be considered rich; one with low true value/student, like Ogdensburg ($13,641), is poor.

Column 7 represents the effects of leveling up to $1,037. In the first year, 18 of our selected districts are leveled up to this figure. Fourteen other selected districts which were spending more than $1,037 per student before leveling up are saved harmless, and are allowed to spend an amount per student equal to that which they were spending in the base year. Another four districts—Buffalo, Ogdensburg, Red Jacket and Malone—are not leveled up to the $1,037 spending level; they all had very low per-pupil expenditures in the base year and, according to the plan, no district can be leveled up more than 15 per cent of the statewide expenditure level (15 per cent of $1,037 = $156) in any one year. Therefore, these four districts will still be spending less than $1,037 during the first year of leveling up. However, all districts but one throughout the state will be at the $1,037 level by the third year of our plan.

The figures in Column 8 reflect our concern for identifying students with serious learning problems and providing extra funds for their help. Our use of the 1.5 weighting factor adds $519 per low scorer to the distribution scheme, and figures in Column 8 are thus generally greater than figures in Column 7. In one sample district, Bronxville, where PEP score data were not available, the number of students receiving Aid to Dependent Children was substituted and weighted.

Column 9 reveals the net gain for each sample district under the distribution proposal. The gain to each district is computed by subtracting the

---

* Districts employing more than eight teachers.

Base Expenditure plus urban aid figure in Column 5 from the adjusted, leveled-up expenditure in Column 8. As we have noted, urban aid, as a categorical program, is excluded from the Base Expenditure figure used for leveling-up calculations; in this way it is similar to the Major Exclusions listed in Column 2. But it is different from these other exclusions in one important respect: The funds which support debt service, school lunch, student transport, tuition and BOCES operation will still be granted to local districts after leveling up has occurred, either as cash or as aid-in-kind. Urban aid, however, is incorporated into the distribution scheme by using weighted PEP scores, and will not be returned to districts through a separate grant program. We can see from our table that the districts that have been receiving urban aid still gain a great deal in the finance plan we propose. The distribution scheme places money where the problems are, eliminating the necessity of a separate grant program for urban aid.

THE ULTIMATE DISTRIBUTION PLAN   We have thus proposed a formula to guide resource allocation to school districts, a formula that seeks to remove the old wealth-generated inequities, and at the same time recognizes as a priority the problem of educational failure. We acknowledge, however, that any formula in a field as diverse and unpredictable as education is bound to be a crude device at best. Some districts will receive more money than they can well use while others will be deprived of resources necessary to seize important opportunities. We hope soon it will be possible to dispense with the use of statewide allocation formulas altogether; we hope that elementary and secondary education will come to be financed in the same way as the public component of higher education. Under such a system, local authorities would draw up operating and development budgets to reflect the financial needs of short- and long-run objectives, and defend the budgets before an "office of analytical studies" in the State Education Department. In time, a state education budget would be presented and defended in the Budget Division of the Executive Office. A flexible plan for educational finance like this would not only allow assessment of expenditure proposals on the basis of reasonably reliable information about the value of alternative objectives and about the real costs of providing educational services, but also leave a large measure of judgment to local powers to determine how particular objectives might be achieved.

Revenue Recommendations

The following recommendations relating to methods of raising revenues for public education assume that the level of federal funding will remain approximately the same as it is today, that is, 90 to 95 per cent of New York's total education costs will continue to be financed from intra-state sources. Two basic issues are considered:

1. The proper form and scope of a statewide property tax for education finance.
2. The role of existing non-property taxes in education finance. By non-property taxes we mean existing state taxes on personal income, corporate net and gross income, retail sales tax, unincorporated business tax and miscellaneous state taxes.

THE PROPERTY TAX—ITS FUTURE ROLE IN EDUCATIONAL FINANCE   In the 1969–70 school year, $2.28 billion, 47.5 per cent of all revenue for public elementary and secondary education from non-federal sources in New York State, was derived from the local property tax. Although the relative share of all education monies derived from this tax decreased somewhat in the 1960–70 decade (from 56.3 per cent in 1960 to 47.5 per cent in 1969–70), it remains the single most important revenue source in educational finance.

While the property tax is often criticized as being particularly burdensome for low-income households, the massive revenue derived from this tax makes its continuation imperative, at least in the short run. We do not foresee nor do we recommend the immediate abolition of this tax. There are, nonetheless, ways by which the regressivity inherent in property taxation can be ameliorated without sacrificing large amounts of tax revenue. A first step in this direction would be to extend the tax base from local school districts to the state as a whole.

State Property Tax: Establishing a uniform rate for school property tax would be a step toward insuring that educational opportunity would be a function of the wealth of the state as a whole, rather than the wealth of a particular school district. *We recommend that a uniform-rate, statewide tax on the full value of property be levied and earmarked specially for education.* This rate would be set initially at a level sufficient to produce an amount approximately equivalent to current total local contributions to educational revenues. A rate of slightly higher than $2.00 per $100 full value, for example, would generate approximately $2.84 billion in the 1972–73 fiscal year. *We further urge that the movement toward complete uniformity be gradual and take place over a five-year period, during which time high- and low-rate districts would fall or rise to the state average tax rate,* in order to avoid the windfalls and hardships that might devolve from precipitate tax rate changes.

Rate Freeze: We urge that the statewide tax rate be frozen at a point equal to or slightly below the rate prevailing at the time this plan goes into effect. Even frozen at a constant rate, however, our median-range projection for growth in the property tax *base* reveals that *revenues* from a statewide property tax would increase by 4.1 per cent per year in real terms.

Over the 1970–80 decade, we expect the constant dollar revenue from the property tax to increase by 49.5 per cent even if rates are kept constant.

Municipal Overburden: The problem of tax overburden in large cities, generally called municipal overburden, inevitably crops up in a plan such as this. Municipal overburden is the result of two phenomena peculiar to cities: a high population density which requires more and costlier services than those in non-urban localities; and a high percentage of low-income residents necessitating a vast range of additional costs and services. Are we in any way ignoring these unique problems of cities in our requirement that *all* districts below the state average tax rate move up to it?

New York City's school tax rate, for example, was $1.89/100 in the 1970–71 school year—or about $.15 below the proposed statewide property tax rate of $2.04/100.*

In the first year of a five-year plan of phasing into the state average, the city would be obliged to move toward the state rate by one-fifth of the $.15 differential, or $.03/100, which would bring forth an additional $16.0 million in school taxes borne by city property.** In the second year, the city rate would increase by another fifth of the $.15 difference, which would mean another $32.0 million in taxes beyond the base-year revenue. The average annual cost to the city in terms of increased tax liability would be $48.0 million. This estimate assumes that the differential between city and state tax rates, as well as the size of New York City property tax base would remain essentially as it was in 1970–71. The recent trend toward a convergence of city and state average tax rates would, of course, reduce the net cost of a uniform rate to New York City.

Under such a "phasing-in" plan, New York City's tax rate increases seem to ignore the problem of municipal overburden. However, by freezing the state rate at the level of the base year, every district, whether above or below the state average tax rate, should experience a decrease in property taxes relative to what would have been the case had the freeze not been imposed.

Let us consider New York City further. If New York City's school tax rate increases in the next five years at the same average yearly rate as in the

---

* Since 1968, New York City has used a current basis of equalization rate in computing full value of property (Article 12A, Section 1250, Real Property Tax Law). The law increased the City's full value, enabling the imposition of higher taxes and increased indebtedness without violating Constitutional limits. However, in comparison with the rest of the state, which used prior-year full value figures, New York City's tax effort appeared to decline. Using the prior-year full value, New York City's school tax rate in 1970–71 was $1.89. Estimates throughout this chapter of the state's full-value property are based on this prior-year rate for New York City, since we recommend that, for education purposes use of the "current" rate be ended and that full-value in all school districts be computed similarly.

** The $16.0 million first-year cost was derived by multiplying the $.03/100 first-year increase (.0003) by the $53.4 billion taxable full value in New York City in 1970.

1966–71 period (6 per cent), by 1976–77 the city's full-value rate will reach $2.50, or about $0.46 higher than the rate at which we propose to freeze. Recent trends in New York City and New York State property tax rates are shown on Table 2.2.

It might be argued that property taxes for school purposes will in fact not rise at a 6 per cent rate during the next five years but at a lower rate because of anticipated declines in the school population. However, this argument ignores the predicted decline in Catholic school enrollments, which is likely to be substantial no matter what position is taken by the Legislature on aid to these schools.* Our projections suggest that New York City's public school enrollments will, as a result of the influx of Catholic school students, increase by 1980 between 10 per cent and 23 per cent over 1969 enrollments. To varying extents, the enrollments of the other large cities may expect to experience similar increases.

Taking the five-year time span into consideration, we find that with rates frozen at the present state average, no district experiences a larger tax burden than it would have if rates had been allowed to move upward as in the past. The net effect of freezing the average rate would be to decrease the share of property tax revenue in the over-all revenue scheme, and therefore to shift the burden to more progressive and elastic state taxes. Table 2.3 outlines the projected gradual shift from property taxes to more progressive state levies.

The property tax burden should be decreased as rapidly as possible. Assuming economic recovery, the school tax burden should be reduced on the *residential share* of the property levy, for this is where the regressive features of the tax are most clearly apparent. This might be phased so as to cut the residential property tax contribution to schools by 10 per cent a year. Money to replace the consequent loss in yield would be obtained ideally from increased federal contributions, but at least more equitably from the state income tax, a more progressive levy.**

The Impact of a Statewide School Tax on the Municipalities of New York State: With cooperation of the New York State Board of Equalization and Assessment, we have examined the impact of a statewide school tax on municipalities.† Data presented in Table 2.4 refer to municipalities rather than to school districts, because fiscal information about municipalities is more readily available. With small variations the results would apply to

---

 * For more detail on these projected declines, see the chapter on Aid to Nonpublic Schools.
 ** Any tax is likely to produce undesirable side effects; e.g., the progressive income tax may distort investment decisions and may reduce willingness of entrepreneurs and high-salaried executives to take risks. However, such side effects are likely to become of serious concern only when a given tax bears too large a burden. The Commission believes that the high rate of advance of the property tax has placed it in that category.
 † The appendix to Chapter 14, "Schools for Tomorrow: a Summing Up," shows the impact of a $2.04/100 statewide property tax on each of the state's 608 operating school districts.

TABLE 2.2

School District Fiscal Data—Ten-Year Trends,
School Year Ended June 30

Item	1960	1961	1962	1963	1964	1965	1966	1967	1968	1969	1970	1971
FULL VALUE OF TAXABLE PROPERTY ($ BILLIONS)												
New York State	67.5	72.7	80.0	83.1	89.0	92.8	97.9	100.7	103.3	108.3	113.4	124.9
New York City[a]	28.7	30.5	33.9	35.4	38.6	40.6	43.2	44.3	45.4	47.2	49.0	53.4
Upstate	38.8	42.2	46.1	47.7	50.4	52.2	54.7	56.4	57.9	61.1	64.4	71.5
FULL VALUE—PER CENT OF TOTAL												
New York State	100%	100%	100%	100%	100%	100%	100%	100%	100%	100%	100%	100%
New York City[a]	42.5	42.0	42.4	42.6	43.4	43.8	44.1	44.0	44.0	43.6	43.2	42.8
Upstate	57.5	58.0	57.6	57.4	56.6	56.2	55.9	56.0	56.0	56.4	56.8	57.2
SCHOOL PROPERTY TAXES COLLECTED ($ BILLIONS)												
New York State	.938	.978	1.062	1.143	1.264	1.406	1.390	1.602	1.762	1.874	2.173	2.557
New York City[a]	.387	.399	.430	.466	.528	.602	.536	.667	.714	.711	.813	1.009
Upstate (incl. local non-prop. taxes for schools)	.551	.579	.632	.677	.736	.804	.854	.935	1.048	1.163	1.360	1.548
FULL VALUE TAX RATE (PER $100 FV)												
New York State	1.390	1.350	1.328	1.375	1.420	1.515	1.420	1.591	1.706	1.730	1.916	2.047
New York City[a]	1.350	1.308	1.268	1.316	1.368	1.483	1.241	1.506	1.573	1.506	1.659	1.890
Upstate	1.420	1.372	1.371	1.419	1.460	1.540	1.561	1.658	1.810	1.903	2.112	2.165
NYC's Rate as Per Cent of State Average	97.1	96.9	95.5	95.0	96.3	97.9	87.4	94.7	92.2	87.6	86.6	92.3
NYC's Rate as Per Cent of Upstate	95.1	95.3	92.5	92.7	93.7	96.3	79.5	90.8	86.9	79.1	78.6	87.3

[a] Property taxes for support of higher education are not included in the New York City figure.

TABLE 2.3

Percentage Distribution between Property and
Non-Property Taxes for School Support[a]

	1970–71[b]	1974–75[c]	1979–80[c]
Per cent from Property	52.1%	51.0%	49.8%
Per cent from Non-Property	47.9%	49.0%	50.2%

[a] These percentages are derived from the summary table of projected state revenue in Appendix 6.
[b] Property tax levies in 1970–71 school year estimated at $2.5 billion; state aid (non-property levies) estimated at $2.3 billion. Data is from *Analysis of School Finances*, University of the State of New York, The State Education Department, April, 1971, Table 6, p. 26.
[c] Projections based on the following assumptions: (A) No tax rate changes or changes in the proportion of state revenues for public education. (B) Real personal income grows by 3.7% annually. (C) The elasticity of the property tax base is 1.1; the elasticity of the state non-property revenue base is 1.36.

school districts of the areas noted. Also, Table 2.4 shows the effects of *full implementation* of a statewide rate of $2.04; that is, the results shown do not recognize that we recommend a phasing-in of the new plan over a five-year period.

Table 2.4 illustrates that some poor areas and some rich areas would be required to make additional tax contributions for schools (Neversink vs. East Hampton, for example). For this reason, we recommend that increased attention be focused on assessment practices *and* on tax credits for low-income households that are excessively burdened with school tax rates.

It is likewise true that some rich communities, as well as poor communities, benefit from the statewide tax proposal (Scarsdale vs. Montezuma). The statewide tax proposal results in reduced property tax rates for education in any community making a great tax effort, whether it is a destitute town or a wealthy suburban community.

Assessment Practices: It is well known that within a single district there exist great differences in effective property tax rates. Different classes of property are assessed at different ratios of assessed to true or market value. For instance, it has been common practice in New York, as in most other states, to assess residential property at a lower rate than other types of property, and thus effectively to subject such property to a lower tax rate.

We do not believe that rate differentiation among various classes of property is antithetical to the goal of equity sought by a statewide property tax. In fact, a lower rate on residences reduces the inherent regressivity of

TABLE 2.4

School Tax Rates and Change in Levy under Full Implementation of $2.04 Statewide School Property Tax, Selected Municipalities, 1970[a]

	Full Value Per Capita	Residential Full Value Per Capita	Full Value School Tax Rate	Change in Amount of Levy on $10,000 Parcel at $2.04
LOW TAX RATE MUNICIPALITIES				
Scriba	$37,722	$ 3,663	$1.15	$+89
Neversink	33,980	2,572	1.21	+83
West Seneca	6,199	4,573	1.25	+79
Southold	14,590	8,809	1.32	+72
Southampton	16,340	10,242	1.37	+67
Cheektowaga	5,992	3,967	1.38	+66
Greece	8,865	5,912	1.46	+58
Ontario	18,762	8,426	1.52	+52
East Hampton	24,379	15,003	1.55	+49
AVERAGE TAX RATE MUNICIPALITIES				
Schenectady	4,500	2,341	2.04	0
Pittsford	10,196	7,735	2.04	0
HIGH TAX RATE MUNICIPALITIES				
Newburgh	4,392	2,024	2.33	−29
Cortland	4,411	6,530	2.34	−30
Auburn	4,213	2,665	2.41	−37
Mt. Vernon	6,279	2,929	2.48	−44
New Rochelle	8,379	4,947	2.49	−45
Oneonta	3,393	2,154	2.52	−48
Haverstraw	5,530	3,019	2.56	−52
Scarsdale	16,610	14,419	2.58	−54
Hempstead	8,707	6,187	2.61	−57
Montezuma	3,980	653	4.50	−246
BIG SIX CITIES				
Albany	5,611	2,808	1.77	+27
Buffalo	4,087	2,008	1.44	+60
New York City	6,764	3,815	1.89	+15
Syracuse	5,191	2,683	1.66	+38
Rochester	6,954	2,655	1.72	+32
Yonkers	7,507	3,428	1.74	+30
State Average	$ 6,849	$ 4,006	$2.04	0.0

[a] No portions of county sales taxes for education are included in the above calculations (counties having such taxes are Erie, Livingston, Monroe, Sullivan and Wayne). The Commission feels it should be a matter of county choice as to whether a share of these obligations be met by use of non-property levies of county governments.

the over-all tax since it is the tax on residences that is the most regressive part of the over-all property tax. It is important, however, that *within* the classes of property there be a uniformity as to assessment ratios. It is unfair for large one-family houses or estates to be assessed at lower ratios than nearby less valuable housing; it is equally wrong for neighbors living in identical houses to pay significantly different taxes just because one bought the house at a more recent date and therefore has a higher assessed value placed on his residence. Both of these inequities are common in New York State and should be systematically eliminated by improved, more up-to-date local assessment practices, and increased state monitoring.

The technology of the 1970's makes it possible to eliminate this problem. Legislation enacted recently concerning assessment organization, procedures and services (L. 1970, ch. 957—sometimes called the Governor's Assessment Equality Program) is directed toward this end. We estimate that this legislation will require local government expenditures over the next five years of an additional $65 million, more than half of which is already mandated. The State's contribution to the program, however, is not adequately funded, nor does any portion of it set up the necessary mechanisms to direct the local investment into channels which could eliminate inequitable assessments.

Almost all of the local expenditures are directed toward providing the tools (tax maps, property inventories, etc.) that are needed for a good assessment system, and insufficient effort is directed toward providing an environment in which these tools can be used effectively and economically. Without this environment, local expenditures will be fruitless; for example, tax maps in and of themselves do nothing unless they can be used in co-ordination with other records (property inventory, sales, etc.). Indeed, re-valuations conducted in the traditional manner, currently in practice in New York State, result in "appraisals" which (a) rely too heavily on the cost approach to valuation; (b) do not adequately consider the market approach which is the valuation standard in New York State; (c) do not provide the information elements needed for the market approach, such as neighborhood characteristics and other economic data; (d) provide records which are oriented to a (one-time) cost valuation and are unsuited to modern mass appraisal techniques or indeed to any kind of future update. If these local government expenditures are to be protected, the state must provide the necessary information-handling capacity and "mass appraisal" systems. If this is not done, it is virtually impossible for the state to insure that the appraisal systems being purchased by local governments will result in equitable assessment practices. But, if the state were to increase its level of effort to protect and channel the local investments, we estimate that the property tax would still be less expensive to administer than the other major revenue measures.

Specifically, *we recommend developing in the State Board of Equalization and Assessment, the capability to analyze comprehensively the tax*

rolls and assessments of all property-taxing jurisdictions. To begin its de-
velopment, we recommend an allocation of $200,000 to $500,000 in fiscal
1973 for initial planning.

The goal of such a monitoring system is *not* state assessment. The purpose, rather, is to place a check on local assessment practices to keep variations within and among taxing districts within legislatively determined tolerances, to comply with the goals of the 1970 Legislative Program. Without a state monitoring system on assessments, the production of tax maps is a waste of considerable time and money.

For those properties too complex to be accurately assessed by local governments (e.g., utilities and certain industrial properties) the professional guidance of the State Department of Equalization and Assessment is necessary. Toward that end, *we recommend that beginning in 1973, all assessment of utilities be performed for local jurisdictions by teams from the State Board of Equalization and Assessment.*

Uniformity in property taxation should mean uniform full value rates among school districts. That is, the over-all tax levy extracted from District A should bear the same relationship to the full value of property in District A as does the levy extracted in District B to the full value of property in that district. Among different classes of property, however, rates would differ in a pattern that reflects the present *de facto* system. For instance, we would expect to find an over-all reduction in rates on most one- and two-family houses, since these properties are located in districts with higher than average full value taxes.

Tax Credits for Low Income Households: Even at a uniform statewide rate, with lower assessment ratios for residential property, the state property tax would be regressive. Low-income households spend a greater percentage of their incomes on shelter than do the affluent, and as a result their property taxes tend to be higher relative to income than the taxes paid by rich property owners. The regressivity is even worse for poor families living in apartments, since they are not permitted to deduct the property taxes they pay directly in rents from their personal income tax base. This oppressive tax burden on the poor is in no way made acceptable by the use of some of these funds in programs for the poor.

For relief of grossly overburdened homeowners, the Commission recommends the tax credit approach, variations of which are currently used in 10 states, which permits any family paying more than 10 per cent of state taxable income in property taxes for schools to credit the excess against their state income tax bill. In cases where the family pays no income tax, or less income tax than is due the taxpayer from overpayment on the state property tax for education, the state would reimburse the taxpayer for overpayment. A variation of this plan has been in use in Wisconsin since 1963, but the taxable limit there is 7 per cent, and credits are allowed only for the elderly and retired poor.

A special estimation procedure is required for granting relief for apartment dwellers. *We urge that 20 per cent of individual rents be considered state property taxes, and that anyone for whom this 20 per cent figure exceeds the specified per cent of gross income be permitted to credit the excess against income taxes.* A simple numerical example will demonstrate how this would work. If no family is to pay more than 10 per cent of its state taxable income on school property taxes, then in 1971 a family of four with an income of $12,000 a year would be granted a credit for property tax payment above $790 a year (i.e., 10 per cent of $12,000 minus the 13 per cent standard deduction not to exceed $1,500 minus four times the $650 personal exemption). If the family pays $5,000 a year in rent, it is assumed that the family is paying 20 per cent of $5,000, or $1,000 in indirect property taxes. The family would be permitted to deduct the excess of $1,000 over $790, or $210, from its income tax liability. If no income taxes are paid, or if the income tax liability is less than the credit due the household, the family would be reimbursed by the state.

NON-PROPERTY TAXES FOR FINANCING EDUCATION   Non-property taxes levied by the State of New York raised $2.240 billion for public education in 1970–71. This amount represented 47.9 per cent of the entire non-federal portion of educational revenue. The remaining amount was raised by property taxes levied at the local level.

TABLE 2.5

Projected State Revenue, in Billions—1969 Constant Dollars

State Fiscal Year	1971–72	1974–75	1979–80
State Property Tax at $2.04/100[a]	2.542	2.868	3.506
Loss from Tax Credits for Excessive Property Tax Payments[b]	−.125	−.081	−.033
35% of Projected State Non-Property Taxes	2.206	2.501	3.080
Total	4.623	5.288	6.553

[a] Rates frozen at $2.04/100 Full Value throughout the period.
[b] 100 per cent credit given for state property taxes paid in excess of 10 per cent of an individual's state taxable income. We estimate this provision will cost the state about 5 per cent of property revenue in 1970–71, 3 per cent in 1974–75, and only 1 per cent of tax revenue in 1975–79. The percentage loss dwindles over the course of the decade since rates are frozen while income rises.

Historically, 35 per cent of the entire state tax revenue has gone to support public education. A larger percentage than this will probably be required to finance the recommendations made in this report if they are adopted; additional increases might be required in consequence of the fiscal dilemma of the nonpublic schools. On the other hand, the possibility of greatly increased federal aid may assist the state in keeping this percentage constant or, conceivably, even reducing it. We use the historical figure for analyzing the impact of our proposed changes in the taxing system supporting education. Our projections show that if we maintain the ratio of education aid to total revenues at 35 per cent, by 1974–75 such aid will total $2.501 billion, and by 1979–80, over $3 billion in constant (1969) dollars.

IMPACT OF THE COMMISSION'S RECOMMENDED TAX PROPOSALS FOR EDUCATION   Table 2.5 summarizes the projected state revenues for education of the Commission's recommended tax package.

Position of the Cities

There is great concern across the country about the social, political and fiscal health of our great cities. We conclude this part of the chapter with observations on the several ways in which our recommendations—both for obtaining revenues and for distribution of school funds—affect the cities.

—We have noted that the guaranty of an upper limit to school property taxes will accrue to the benefit of the cities. Cities have enjoyed low school tax rates primarily because they have had relatively large private school enrollments. As is documented in the chapter on nonpublic schools, Catholic school enrollments, especially in the large cities, are a shrinking asset for protection of local budgets. As Catholic school populations move steadily into the public schools, it behooves the cities to seek protection for their school budgets by joining a statewide system of financing.

—One of the chief problems of cities has been the limitation of local taxing powers, including constitutional limitation of property tax rates. Our proposal for a new statewide property tax will free considerable property tax revenues for non-school purposes. That is, a property tax for education *imposed by the state* will stand outside the limitations on local taxing powers decreed in Article VIII of the State Constitution.

—The vast majority of poor residents of New York State live in the large central city areas. This population for the first time would be protected from excessive property tax burdens by our proposal for tax credits for low income households. This protection would apply to poor families who are renters as well as to those who are homeowners.

—Our recommendation to shift from an attendance count to an enrollment count of students is obviously of benefit to cities. As demonstrated earlier in this chapter, our distribution formula distributes basic operating funds directly on a count of students. The example of New York City shows that in 1969–70, New York City had 30.97 per cent of the state's total of weighted average daily attendance and 32.87 per cent of enrollment.

—The present state aid formula channels funds toward districts of low full valuation per student and away from localities of high full value. As we have pointed out, the formula does not protect truly impoverished districts well and because of its reliance on the local valuation measure, it does also penalize large cities, because large cities have relatively high full values per student. Our distribution proposal cuts the nexus between local assessed valuation and state school support; hence, cities will be able to make the case that they are subject to high educational *costs* without having to rebut the charge, erroneous as it may be, that they have much available wealth to support schools.

—The leveling-up and the save-harmless provisions protect funds which the cities have previously received under the size-correction adjustment.

—In 1969–70, special urban aid amounted to $39.2 million. Of this, New York City, the locality most severely affected by urban problems, received $31.0 million. We propose that funds to deal with educationally disadvantaged children, chiefly though not exclusively an urban problem, rise to $465.0 million, of which New York City would receive $274 million. The increase for New York City over the 1969–70 amount is thus $243 million. In absolute terms, this is an impressive gain for the city, but the City's *share* of such special aid falls from 79.1 per cent under the 1969–70 plan to 58.9 per cent in our proposal. Hence, the constituency for these funds has been greatly increased, extended, in fact, into the suburbs. One can expect greater stability of political support for such a program.

—As an inclusive kind of measure, let us consider tax cost/benefit ratios for New York City. The city has a concentration of taxable real property and income that is disproportionate to its number of public school students. If taxes and school distributions were neutral, i.e., if taxes were proportional to New York City's share of total state taxable property and income, and school aid proportional to enrollment, New York City would pay $1.41 in taxes for each $1.00 in school support. The actual situation in 1969–70 was $1.21 paid out in taxes for each $1.00 received. Under full implementation of our distribution plan, moving toward a statewide property tax, the ratio improves to $1.14 paid for each $1.00 obtained.

—Though not discussed in this chapter, our complete set of proposals offers additional benefits for urban populations: extension of BOCES services into the cities, additional funds for physically handicapped children, and funds for bilingual instruction.

Relationship of the Proposal to New York's Financial Crisis

Most of the members of this Commission are citizens of New York State. It would be impossible for us to be unmindful of the desperate nature of the budgetary problem with which the state is confronted in the present and next fiscal year at least. The most recent estimate of the budget deficiency for the current year is in the neighborhood of $800 million.

It is clear that the adoption of a state funding system such as we propose means increased over-all spending by the state for education, even before inflationary factors and the cost of improvements in educational quality which we have recommended elsewhere in this report are taken into account. The principal increases in state cost chargeable primarily to the change in system may be identified as follows:

—The cost of leveling up to the 65th percentile, which we have estimated in 1972–73 as $125 million.

—The cost of provisions for the educationally disadvantaged; i.e., the 1.5 weighting: $465 million in 1972–73.

—The over-all loss of revenue from providing property tax credits to overburdened homeowners and renters: $125 million in 1972–73.

We have explained why we have concluded that each one of these cost-increase factors is an essential element to a sound state financing plan. Despite the state's fiscal plight, we consider it proper and responsible for the Commission to recommend this plan for the following reasons:

—Our mission is to recommend the best possible educational plan for the next decade and thereafter. The financial system we propose will surely become feasible in the years ahead, as we show in our analysis of future revenues later in this chapter.

—Some form of federal revenue-sharing seems inevitable in the near future. If this should take the form of federal assumption of all state welfare expenditures, for example, most of the proposals in this report would become feasible in New York, and the state should have a plan ready to be implemented immediately.

—If *Serrano* v. *Priest* becomes the law of the land, New York may be forced to adopt such a plan under judicial mandate. We prefer to adopt the essentials of the plan now, when careful consideration can be given to all its details.

—For obvious reasons, it would be impossible for a state funding system, so far-reaching in its charge, to be put into operation before the fiscal year 1973–74, which means the school year commencing in September, 1973. During the next school year, the state would have to continue to rely on the present financing system. We do urge, however, that the Legislature enact legislation in 1972 which will enable the new system to commence operation the following year.

—The plan is flexible and adaptable to revenue considerations. The weighting of the educationally disadvantaged could start at 1.25 instead of 1.50. And, obviously, the real estate tax relief for low-income families can be reduced or postponed if necessary at the time of enactment. We do not advocate such changes in the plan, but simply note them as possibilities in a time of fiscal crisis.

—Finally, the whole matter of priority determination for public expenditure is essentially a matter for legislative determination. The members of this Commission give education a priority second to none. We prefer added taxation to reduced educational expenditures. With respect to the additional expenditures which we have identified as essential throughout this report, our feeling is the same. The timing and the phasing of all these improvements, however, is clearly a matter to be determined by the arbiters of governmental priorities in this state: the Governor and the Legislature.

CONSIDERATIONS UNDERLYING THE FINANCE RECOMMENDATIONS

Part I of this chapter sets forth in full our recommendations for revising support of public education in New York State and summarizes our reasons therefor. We believe that the material so presented will prove adequate for an informed consideration of the subject by the public generally.

The balance of this chapter consists of a more detailed discussion of some of the most important matters we considered, including alternative proposals, economic analysis, and a historical review that should particularly interest legislators, educators and scholars.

Analysis of Arguments Against Full State Funding

The Commission is mindful that full state funding is, in spite of growing acceptance, still a controversial proposal. We have heard in testimony that full state funding is inimical to local control of schools, and we have been informed that our proposal is inconsistent with the development of innovative programs by high-spending districts that ultimately accrue to the benefit of the system as a whole. The Commission answers these objections as follows.

LOCAL CONTROL   Those who fear that full state funding will mean the end of a long history of local control of schools should look again at the system of educational government now operative. Financed and influenced in varying degrees by at least three levels of government—local, state and federal —there no longer are grounds to argue that any genuinely autonomous units are left in the system. Indeed, the whole governmental system is characterized by interdependency. Recent studies have concluded that centralization and decentralization are not inconsistent concepts and that it is quite possible to have financing at one level and policymaking and other kinds of control at another, with the implication that state financing is not inconsistent with decentralized operating units.[5]

This Commission strongly urges greater powers of decision-making in the *local school*. Specific proposals toward this objective are given in the chapter on Governance. The effective point for expression of citizen and parent-citizen interest in education is the school, not the school district, for the school is the basic operating unit and cost center in the provision of educational services.

As Harold Howe II, former United States Commissioner of Education and now Vice President of the Ford Foundation, has pointed out, "[a] model is Britain's system of publicly-supported schools. Local schools get most of their funds from the Central Ministry of Education, yet they are fiercely independent and operate individual programs. The Ministry maintains an 'Inspectorate,' but inspectors typically play a role that belies their title. They are not authority figures whose business is to check on the minutiae of administrative practice. They are stimulators of change and improvement, communication agents who disseminate good practice by persuasion, and experienced educators and teachers—rather than officious bureaucrats." [6]

Consider the position of the cities. Local control at the city district level is not meaningful when funds to meet educational requirements of students are in limited supply. Non-educational requirements are much greater in urban areas, particularly in central cities, than they are in the suburbs. Accordingly, cities must maintain higher tax levels to support general municipal services than the suburbs. One of the consequences of this situation is that state aid seems to be additive, in large part, to local taxes in the suburbs, while it serves as a replacement for local taxes in central cities.[7] (Apparently, the provision of state aid to education in cities makes it possible for them to transfer a part of their local resources to the support of non-educational services.)

Achieving genuine equality of educational opportunity will require application of different amounts of resources to particular students based on their individual differences in educational need. This fact undoubtedly strengthens the argument for state assumption of financial responsibility. Under a system which would recognize different need levels, it is patently easier to focus resources than under our present fragmented and uncontrollable fiscal arrangement. For the first time, resources would flow in a fashion which would allow decentralization of education to work effectively in large cities.

LIGHTHOUSE DISTRICTS Suburban districts of high residential property values, e.g., Great Neck and Scarsdale, are sometimes referred to as "lighthouse districts," meaning that they spend large sums on educational services in order to conduct innovative programs. It is thought that worthwhile innovations in educational practice flow outward from these districts and influence the rest of the educational system.

However, innovation need not be an accidental by-product of a system of educational finance. There is no reason why state governments could not establish special funds for experimental and innovative programs. Some of these programs should be designed for ghetto schools. As it is now, lighthouse school districts are generally rich ones inhabited by students of rich households. The present system weights innovation and experimentation toward the advantaged. But it is not advantaged schools that have the most serious problems, and it is doubtful that new programs designed for well-off students have much transferability into the ghetto.

District Power Equalizing: an Inadequate Alternative

The Commission is aware that there exists an alternative approach to greater equity in educational finance: district power equalizing. This is a very simple idea that cuts through the long, involved discussions that school finance experts hold about foundation program plans, percentage grants, and the like. Professor John E. Coons of the Law Faculty, University of California, Berkeley, has suggested that there should be a plain relationship between the effort a local school district makes in supporting its schools, as measured by tax rate, and the amount of money that is made available per student for its school programs.[8] This relationship is expressed in Table 2.6.

The figures, of course, are illustrative only, but the essential idea is this: all districts that levied local tax at the same rate would have available equal sums of money per student to spend on their educational programs. Practically speaking, it is certain that the state would wish to establish both minimum and maximum values for school spending. The minimum would be necessary to protect the state against an unduly parsimonious school district. The maximum would be necessary to protect the state budget, as noted below. Both district power equalizing and full state funding imply that an *upper limit* is placed on districts' powers to spend money.

We prefer full state funding to district power equalizing for several

TABLE 2.6

Effort-Local Tax Rate (per $100 of Assessed Valuation)	Dollars Available for Elementary/Secondary Programs per Weighted Student
1.00	800
1.50	1,000
2.00	1,200
2.50	1,400
3.00	1,600
4.00	1,800

reasons. First, assume that wealthy districts are inhabited by wealthy residents and poor districts are populated by the poor. All district power equalizing does then is to assume equity in tax rates vis-à-vis school expenditures. Poor people would have difficulty in meeting the competition of rich people in rich districts, once the latter saw how the finance plan was shaping up and raised their school tax rates to preserve their favored position.

Second, assume (as we do) that there is no absolute standard of education which can be described as "adequate"—that all educational disparities are relative. Then, if one is going to embark on a major revision of educational finance arrangements, why should one not remove "place" inequalities as well as wealth inequalities? [9] The quality of a child's education should, in our view, be no more a function of how highly his neighbors value education than how wealthy they are.

Moreover, we believe that the equal protection clause of the 14th Amendment applies to individual children rather than school districts. If this is so, then the quality of a child's education cannot depend any more on the vote of his neighbors within the confines of a local school district than it can on their aggregate relative wealth vis-à-vis other school districts within the state. The California Supreme Court in *Serrano* v. *Priest* was not explicit on this point, but it did take some pains to argue that territorial uniformity in school finance is constitutionally required. "Where fundamental rights or suspect classifications are at stake," the Court said, "a state's general freedom to discriminate on a geographical basis will be significantly curtailed by the equal protection clause." [10]

To make the point clear, consider two districts, A and B, and let them be of equal wealth. Suppose the residents of district A choose a school program half as costly as the residents of district B. Is it good policy for the state to require the children of A to suffer the lifetime handicap of inferior education, which is to say, should the state exclude these children from the benefits of district B education on the basis of a district boundary line that is itself a historical accident? As we understand the ideals of a democracy, public institutions—and especially the schools—should see to it that personal attributes such as aptitude, talent and energy, play a progressively larger role in an individual's success and development, while parental wealth, on the one hand, and apathy on the other, play a progressively smaller role. We see no way for this ideal to be achieved in the absence of direct state intervention in the allocation of educational resources.

One of the functions of an educational system is to act as a sorting device. Classification of people on grounds of ability and aptitude occurs all the time, and schools often act as a major transmitter of the process. But if primary schooling of some children is of vastly greater quality than that of other children, the sorting process is ineffective and dangerous. Local tastes for basic educational services should not distort the function of the sorting mechanism and possibly undermine students' potential and achievements.

The Rationale of Grants-in-Aid and the Practice of Educational Finance in New York State

This short essay will focus on some important issues regarding the structure of a system of grants-in-aid to local governments. A grant-in-aid is any transfer of resources from a superior level of government (e.g., a state) to one or more governments within its jurisdiction (e.g., school districts). Although the theory can be applied to aid for a variety of purposes, we will concentrate specifically on aid to education.

The possibility of full state funding does not limit the generality of these distributional criteria; the problem of where to put the money remains and is quantitatively more important than before. However, such a state funding arrangement would preclude a system of *matching grants,* since there would no longer be any locally determined expenditure.*

One cannot speak of an optional structure for education grants-in-aid before having clearly in mind the goals which society has set for education. Economists have usually assumed that any distribution scheme must strike a balance between two sometimes conflicting goals: (1) the *economically efficient allocation* of educational investment; and (2) the achievement of *equal opportunity* and *income redistribution* among (a) the present generation of taxpayers and/or (b) the future generation of taxpayers.

Although these goals are analytically separable, in practice, any movement toward the first will influence progress toward the second, and vice versa.

Most state aid formulas have as their explicit goal some form of equalization, with respect to both the ability of the present generation to provide education without undue tax hardships and the future generation's opportunity to compete in the labor market and generally enjoy the benefits of education. Economic efficiency is usually not stated as an explicit goal, although the current movement to attach some sort of performance criterion to aid monies seems to move in that direction. The fact that efficiency considerations are traditionally overlooked in formula distribution schemes may not be as serious as it appears, since movement toward equal opportunity usually enhances the efficiency of the system.

We first describe what is meant by the economically efficient allocation of educational investment, and how a system of grants to school districts should be tailored to achieve it.

EFFICIENT ALLOCATION OF EDUCATIONAL INVESTMENT   Intervention by a superior level of government to achieve an economically efficient quantity

---

* That is the case for a pure state funding scheme, where there is no discretionary spending permitted at the local level.

of educational investment in sub-superior levels is necessitated by two considerations: (1) the desire to maximize educational output, regardless of where the output is located, and (2) the desire to account for spillover benefits which accrue to individuals or to communities other than the ones financing the education.

The first efficiency goal is concerned with where and for what purposes a *given amount* of aid funds should be distributed. The second goal is concerned with the determination of the socially optimal amount of monies to be so distributed.

Maximizing Output: The maximization process first of all requires some measure of output. In practice, test results or retention rates may be used as proxies for educational output. We will merely say here that there are so many units of education being produced at a given time.

A state desiring to maximize its educational output will insure that educational resources are distributed in such a fashion that the marginal yields of outputs are equal in all geographic areas of the state and in all different kinds of programs. This implies that initial distributions of incremental resources at any point in time will be directed toward those places and programs in which marginal yields of output are greatest. To be operational, this principle requires knowledge of the educational production function for each district—the statistical relationship between experience and backgrounds, equipment, textbooks, administrators, guidance counselors, and educational output.

Once uncovered, this functional relationship tells the state administrator exactly what input in what district possesses the greatest marginal educational product (MEP)—i.e., change in output per dollar of input. It also enables the grant administrator to know how the MEP changes as more money is spent on a specific input and how an increase in the quantity of one input affects the MEPs of all other inputs.

Knowing all the relevant MEPs for each district, the maximizing state will give aid earmarked specifically for those inputs in those districts displaying the highest marginal educational products, regardless of the existing level of education output in that district.

To make the problem more concrete, let us assume that there are already school buildings in every district and a certain number of pupils in each building. The buildings are of various sizes and ages, have different plant facilities and differ as to the extent to which they are utilized to capacity. Furthermore, the pupils are of heterogeneous backgrounds, some of very high socio-economic status and strong familial reinforcement for educational attainment. These factors together define a fixed stock of "human capital" which we assume cannot be changed or redistributed in the short run.

The state has an $X billion education budget and wishes to distribute it among the districts in such a way as to maximize the statewide total of education output at lowest cost. It will then scan each school district and each conceivable input until it discovers where the first dollar spent will result in the greatest MEP; it may be for teachers in District 201 or textbooks in District 57 (where the students are so highly motivated they will read even without teacher supervision). The grants will continue solely for this program until its marginal product falls below the next highest input MEP; money will then be shifted to that program. In this manner, distribution of the $X billion continues—care always being taken to channel funds to specific districts. If the state does not know local conditions well enough to specify which educational input is most productive, the grant's purpose should not be narrowly specified.

The obsession with maximizing output may bias funding in favor of the rich districts where, given the existing strength of home investment, a dollar spent by the state may produce the greatest results. Also, these districts may be the ones in which the physical plant is being underutilized, making the introduction of new programs, science labs and new gym equipment more feasible and productive.

This pro-rich bias is suspect, however, when one considers the many non-classroom inputs—nutrition, eye care, dental care, health care—which are properly classed as "education expenditures" and whose marginal educational product may be far higher in poor districts than in rich ones.

A dollar spent on providing breakfasts in poor districts may be such a strong complement to in-school input, at least for some ranges of expenditure, that efficiency dictates expenditure on this first—even before the in-school expenditures are funded. Introduction of this type of "noninstructional" input greatly weakens the argument which equates remedial programs with efficiency.

One can imagine a situation where, given the total dollar amount spent on education, some districts—those notoriously costly or those inefficient in their use of funds—receive no monies at all under the strict efficiency distribution scheme. This could result when district marginal products for the various inputs are so diverse, and when the rate at which productivity declines in the more efficient districts is so slow, that when all the monies are distributed in the manner described above, marginal products of all inputs in some districts are still higher than those inputs in other districts.

Grants to Remedy Educational Spillovers: Educational spillovers occur when benefits from education accrue to individuals other than those being educated, or accrue to regions other than those actually financing education. For example, an educated individual may bring these benefits to the community-at-large:

—Steadier and more informed voter participation.
—Increase in the productivity of his co-workers.

—Reduction in law-enforcement and welfare expenditure.

—Reduction in unemployment compensation.

—Greater tax contributions as a result of increased earning power of the individual.

Similarly, the education financed by community A may benefit community B by the migration of educated workers to B.

In such situations where districts benefit from the educational expenditures of other districts, yet do not pay for their share of the benefits, the total investment in education will be less than socially optimal. Each district will finance education until the marginal cost of the last unit of education just equals the marginal benefit derived by the citizens *of that district* from that unit. The goal of the state should be to tailor its grants to school districts in such a way as to insure that the "correct" amount of education is being produced, i.e., to insure expenditure up to the point where the marginal cost of an additional unit of education in each district equals the marginal benefit derived from it by the entire state.

In a fully state-funded finance system, any spillover benefits accruing to in-state districts are automatically accounted for, since only the state has discretion over spending, and will take these spillovers into account in determining district allocation. In addition, the Federal Government must play a role in remedying the less-than-optimal investment which develops from spillovers between states.

A system of grants designed to remedy spillover inefficiencies would require that each district know what fraction of the total educational benefits accrue to other districts. The grants should then be categorized and matched in a ratio equal to the spillover ratio: e.g., if one-half of the benefits accrue to others, then 50 per cent of district expenditure should be subsidized by the state. This fraction will likely change, since an increase in the quantity of education provided will no doubt affect both the spillover ratio and the marginal benefit of additional units of spillover. The net result may be a reduction in the marginal spillover benefits of education as the quantity of education purchased increases. The donor's share of the cost of the additional units should thereupon decrease; the grant formula would then contain a large number of bracket rates, that is, marginal rates of grant sharing, decreasing as the number of units purchased increased.

The effect of a matching grant is to lower the price of education in a school district by the percentage of subsidy. Ideally, we would hope that a grant would bring no cutback in the district's own expenditure for education, but often the stimulative effect of the grant is countered by movements to lower the school district property levy, or, if the grant is made to a general purpose government, to increase other expenditure and perhaps reduce taxes as well.

Whether or not a matching grant for education actually stimulates expenditure out of the school district's own resources depends on the district's elasticity of demand for education.* If equal to unity, the district will spend the same revenue on education after the grant as before. If the elasticity is less than unity, the categorical matching grant for education becomes a partial general purpose grant which may be used to increase other government services (if a central city district) or to reduce property taxes (if an independent district). And if greater than unity, other services will be reduced, or taxes or borrowing increased.

EQUALITY OF OPPORTUNITY Equality of opportunity is the basic reason for state aid to education. It also underlies much of the current movement toward full state assumption of educational financing. Lumped together under the term "equalization" are two analytically distinct goals: equality for the present generation of taxpayers, and equality for the future generation, i.e., the students.

The Present Generation of Taxpayers: This definition of educational equality requires that equal educational resources be made available for use at a tax rate determined by the statewide ratio of property valuation to the number of students. It does not call for actual equality in the use of educational resources, as does equality among the future generation of taxpayers. Much of the state's role in financing education is motivated by the desire to avoid placing an undue tax burden on low-wealth school districts in providing an adequate measure of education for its children. Within limits, there should be a one-to-one relationship between school property tax rates and revenue per student. The emphasis is on equity among the present generation of school property taxpayers, not on future income distribution.

The use of grants categorically designed for education as a means of redistributing income among adults is indefensible on economic grounds. If the grant results in more educational expenditure, the redistribution is in the form of income-in-kind and creates an excess burden similar to that associated with excise taxation. Income redistribution by means of education expenditure would also discriminate against low-income individuals who have no children or whose children do not attend public schools. It would be more efficient simply to give outright cash grants equal to the cost of the education and to permit grant recipients (local governments) to spend the money as they wish.

If the grant to education results in lower property taxes and more disposable income for poor areas, the excess-burden argument is no longer valid. However, the effect on income distribution would be small and uncertain for two reasons:

---

* Demand elasticity is the percentage change in quantity demanded per each percentage change in price.

—In New York State only $2.4 billion or approximately 3.0 per cent of statewide personal income is distributed by the state in the form of aid to education.

—The grant is to a unit of government within which wealth variations may be greater than variations between such governmental units. Grants differentiated according to school district property valuation per WADA mask this fact. If, for instance, the average per WADA valuation in District A is $4,000 and that of District B is $6,000, and if a few families in A have very high incomes and the rest very low incomes, while those in B have about the same incomes, the taxpaying ability of group A is lower, relative to group B, than the average property values alone might suggest. This conclusion follows if marginal utility is assumed to decrease as income increases (and, of course, if individual's utilities can be compared as is implicit in any distribution formula favoring poor districts).

Equality of Opportunity for Future Generations: Equality among future taxpayers does require grants specifically for education. By investing heavily in the education of low-income children, the state can redress the imbalance in human capital distribution and, by extension, the future distribution of income.

A question arises as to whether investing heavily in low-wealth school districts is the most efficient way of achieving a more equitable future income distribution. Would simple transfers among individuals achieve the same result at less cost to total income growth? The economist's answer would seem to be "no." Studies show the rate of return for investment in primary and secondary expenditures is consistently greater than that obtainable elsewhere. However, there have been no studies of the rate return of that part of total educational investment which represents deliberate redistribution to low-wealth areas. Even if such studies were to show this rate of return to be exceeded elsewhere in the economy, the argument against this sort of redistribution would not be insured. Using the leverage provided by education to change this distribution may be better than money income transfer because of the personal indignities frequently associated with the use of welfare payments.

The Present System of Finance of Education in New York State

Elementary and secondary schools derive their revenues mainly from local taxation and state assistance. We have already described the chief features of property taxation, by far the largest of local levies. Even more complicated is the system of state assistance for local school support, to which we now direct our attention.

STATE ASSISTANCE FOR SCHOOL SUPPORT The New York program of state assistance is estimated to distribute $2.4 billion for public schools in

1971–72. "General aid" represents 93 per cent of the total and eight special aids account for the remainder. Seventy-five per cent of general aid, or $1.672 billion, is distributed under a basic equalization formula. In this particular instance, the basic formula is modified to take account of certain characteristics of districts: extremely small or extremely large size, rate of growth in enrollment, unusually high school tax rates, etc. Under the heading of general aid, the main formula is supplemented by assistance for student transport and debt service (essentially aid for school construction). The nature of the entire system, however, is shaped by the basic equalization formula, which alone determines distribution of $1.672 billion.

The formula in use is of a type called "percentage equalizing grant." [11] A review of the nature of this fiscal device will allow us to see why the system works as it does.*

PERCENTAGE EQUALIZING GRANTS In these grants, first established in England in 1917 and proposed for the state governments of our country by Harlan Updegraff in 1919,[12] the state government shares in the costs of a local program of education; the costs themselves are locally determined and the state's sharing ratio is higher in poor districts than rich. In its complete implementation, the grant assures that any two districts which levy the same local tax rate for schools have precisely the same dollars per student to spend, regardless of their local wealth. For reasons that will become clear, nowhere has this grant system been fully implemented.

The operation of the grant can most easily be described as follows. Let state aid to a given district be determined by the following formula:

$$A_1 = \left[1 - \left(0.5 \times \frac{\text{Assessed valuation per student in the district}}{\text{Assessed valuation per student in the state}} \right) \right]$$
$$\times \text{ Expenditures for the district}$$

Suppose statewide assessed valuation per student is $20,000. Let assessed valuation per student in School District 1, a relatively wealthy district, be $30,000. In School District 2, a poor district, let the corresponding figure be $10,000. Suppose further that both districts, the rich one and the poor one, wish to spend $1,000 per student in their public school programs. Let enrollment in District 1 be 5,000 and in District 2, 10,000. Obviously, total expenditure in District 1 is intended to be $5,000,000 (5,000 students times $1,000 per student) and total expenditure in District 2 is to be $10,000,000. Let us compute state aid and local tax rates as summarized in Table 2.7.

---

* For those interested in even greater detail about educational grant arrangements, Appendix 2C offers observations on the "Strayer-Haig" formula, used in New York State until 1962, and on the views of Henry C. Morrison relative to equalization programs in general.

TABLE 2.7

Comparison of Example Districts

	District 1	**District 2**	**District 3**
Enrollment	5,000	10,000	5,000
Assessed Valuation per Student	$ 30,000	$ 10,000	$ 60,000
Expenditures per Student	$ 1,000	$ 1,000	$ 1,000
Total Assessed Valuation	$150,000,000	$100,000,000	$300,000,000
Total Expenditures	$ 5,000,000	$ 10,000,000	$ 5,000,000
Local Tax Rate (per $100 of Assessed Value)	$2.50	$2.50	$2.50

For District 1

$$A_1 = \left[1 - \left(0.5 \times \frac{30,000}{20,000}\right)\right] \times \$5,000,000 = (1 - 0.75) \times \$5,000,000$$
$$= 0.25 \times \$5,000,000 = \$1,250,000$$

Local Expenditure in District 1 = Total Expenditure − State Aid
$$= \$5,000,000 - \$1,250,000 = \$3,750,000$$

Tax Rate in District 1 = Local Expenditure/Tax Base
$$= \$3,750,000/\$150,000,000 = \$2.50 \text{ per } \$100 \text{ of Assessed Valuation}$$

For District 2

$$A_2 = \left[1 - \left(0.5 \times \frac{10,000}{20,000}\right)\right] \times \$10,000,000 = (1 - 0.25) \times \$10,000,000$$
$$= 0.75 \times \$10,000,000 = \$7,500,000$$

Local Expenditure in District 2 = Total Expenditure − State Aid
$$= \$10,000,000 - \$7,500,000 = \$2,500,000$$

Tax Rate in District 2 = Local Expenditure/Tax Base
$$= \$2,500,000/\$100,000,000 = \$2.50 \text{ per } \$100 \text{ of Assessed Valuation}$$

The local tax rates in Districts 1 and 2 are the same—$2.50 per $100 of assessed valuation—even though District 2 has only one-third the wealth per student as District 1 and even though District 2, the poor district, is twice as large as District 1, the rich district. Under a fully operational percentage equalizing grant system, the rule holds: any set of districts that choose the same expenditure level per student will obtain that expenditure at equal local tax rates, regardless of the wealth of the districts.

This kind of relation between the state and local authorities, a relation under which, in effect, the "price" of educational services stands in a precise one-to-one status with expenditures, has been hailed as an achievement of equity. Surely such a system would be preferable to one under which poor districts must submit to high tax rates to finance meager programs, while rich districts provide themselves with lavish school programs at low tax rates. However, it is extremely difficult to put a percentage equalizing grant into full operation for two reasons:

1. Differences in assessed valuation per student vary in much wider range than shown in our previous example, where District 1 has three times the wealth per student as District 2. It is not uncommon to find that the differences run as high as 10 to 1. (Even among the larger districts of a small geographic region like Long Island, differences are in excess of seven to one.) So suppose we add to our previous example a District 3, having 5,000 students, an expenditure of $1,000 per student, and an assessed valuation per student of $60,000. The formula would read:

For District 3

$$A_3 = \left[1 - \left(0.5 \times \frac{60,000}{20,000}\right)\right] \times \$5,000,000 = (1 - 1.5) \times \$5,000,000$$
$$= -0.5 \times \$5,000,000 = -\$2,500,000$$

Local Expenditure in District 3 = Total Expenditure − State Aid
$$= \$5,000,000 - (-\$2,500,000) = \$5,000,000 + \$2,500,000 = \$7,500,000$$

Tax Rate in District 3 = Local Expenditure/Tax Base
$$= \$7,500,000/\$300,000,000 = \$2.50 \text{ per } \$100 \text{ of Assessed Valuation}$$

The formula produces a negative aid ratio of −.5. This means that District 3 must be expected to pay for its school program in full from its own local taxes *and* make a contribution of $2,500,000 from its own local taxes to the other districts of the state. State governments are not generally inclined to demand such self-sacrifice of rich areas.*

---

* If the coefficient of .5 in the formula were reduced to, say, .1, then the negative grant implied in the original formula would disappear, i.e.,

$$A_3 = \left[1 - \left(0.1 \times \frac{60,000}{20,000}\right)\right] \times \$5,000,000 = (1 - 0.3) \times \$5,000,000$$
$$= 0.7 \times \$5,000,000 = \$3,500,000$$

District 3 now receives state aid for schools in the amount of $3,500,000, instead of (theoretically) being charged $2,500,000. However, as the coefficient is reduced from 0.5 toward 0.1, the state share of total educational spending rises, for the state share is given by $(1 - 0.5) = 0.5$ or $(1 - 0.1) = 0.9$, or, in general, by $(1 - x)$. This last example, where $x - 0.1$ implies 90 per cent state support is in effect, full state assumption. Thus,

Instead, they provide a minimum school aid grant to districts, even the very richest. (In New York, the minimum grant per student in 1971–72 is $310 per student in weighted average daily attendance.)

2. For the percentage equalizing grant to be fully operational, it is implied that one of two conditions must hold: either the state places a ceiling on educational expenditures per student that applies to all districts, or the state shares in educational expenditures with districts at whatever level of spending the local districts choose. The first option is district power equalizing.[13]

Consider the second option: that the state share in locally-chosen expenditure levels without limit. Some state officials see this as giving local districts a blank check. It is a troublesome problem, moreover, because aid ratios can rise to 90 per cent and above, meaning that poor local authorities can buy expensive educational programs with 10¢ per dollar (or less) of local money. Only in Wisconsin and Utah—and only under the constraint of rigid audit procedures—has there been serious experimentation with major open-ended grant programs.

The course commonly chosen by states that have used the percentage equalizing grant—Massachusetts, Pennsylvania, Rhode Island, Vermont, Iowa and New York—is to provide for state sharing of locally-determined expenditures *up to a point* ($860 per student in weighted average daily attendance in New York) but not beyond that point, while at the same time allowing districts to exceed the state-sharing maximum if they wish. The result of this compromise is to make the percentage equalizing grant into a foundation program for all practical purposes, especially when most districts actually do spend beyond the point at which the state stops its contribution, which is the case in New York. In effect, the $860 upper limit of sharing in New York State is the cost of the foundation program per student (Appendix 2C).

Using our simple examples of the three districts, let us assess the effect on local tax rates of the combination of a minimum grant of $300 per student and a ceiling on state sharing of $1,000 per student. Assume all figures as before, *except* that a minimum grant of $300 per student is provided *and except* that all three districts now decide to spend not $1,000 per student but $1,200 (Table 2.8). State ceiling for sharing, as noted, is assumed to be $1,000.

For District 1

$$A_1 = \left[1 - \left(0.5 \times \frac{30,000}{20,000}\right)\right] \times \$5,000,000 = 0.25 \times \$5,000,000 = \$1,250,000$$

This computation reflects the fact that only $1,000 per student is recognized for state sharing; however, the computed amount of aid, $1,250,-

---

the only way the percentage equalizing grant can accommodate extreme ranges in local assessed valuations per student is by establishing state assumption of educational costs.

TABLE 2.8

Comparison of Example Districts with Minimum Grant Provision

	District 1	District 2	District 3
Enrollment	5,000	10,000	5,000
Assessed Valuation per Student	$30,000	$10,000	$60,000
Expenditures per Student	$ 1,200	$ 1,200	$ 1,200
Ceiling on State Sharing	$ 1,000	$ 1,000	$ 1,000
Minimum Grant per Student	$ 300	$ 300	$ 300
Total Assessed Valuation	$150,000,000	$100,000,000	$300,000,000
Total Expenditures	$6,000,000	$12,000,000	$6,000,000
Local Tax Rate (per $100 of Assessed Value)	$3.00	$4.50	$1.50

000, falls short of the district's minimum aid of $300 (5,000 students $\times$ $300 = $1,500,000). So A_1 = $1,500,000, *not* $1,250,000 as the formula suggests.

Local Expenditure in District 1 = $6,000,000 − $1,500,000 = $4,500,000

This computation reflects the fact that the district is not spending $1,200 per student

($1,200 $\times$ 5,000 students = $6,000,000)

Tax Rate in District 1 = $4,500,000/$150,000,000

= $3.00 per $100 of Assessed Valuation

For District 2

$$A_2 = \left[1 - \left(0.5 \times \frac{10,000}{20,000} \right) \right] \times \$10,000,000 = 0.75 \times \$10,000,000 = \$7,500,000$$

Aid remains the same as the previous example.

Local Expenditure in District 2 = $12,000,000 − $7,500,000 = $4,500,000

Tax Rate in District 2 = $4,500,000/$100,000,000 = $4.50

To provide the same quality program, District 2 must now sustain a tax rate 50 per cent higher than District 1.

For District 3

$$A_3 = \left[1 - \left(0.5 \times \frac{60,000}{20,000} \right) \right] \times \$5,000,000 = -0.5 \times \$5,000,000$$

$$= -\$2,500,000$$

However, the minimum grant comes into play and District 3 receives a sum determined as 5,000 students times $300.

$A_3 = \$1,500,000$, *not* $-\$2,500,000$, as the formula suggests

Local Expenditures in District 3 $= \$6,000,000 - \$1,500,000 = \$4,500,000$

Tax Rate in District 3 $= \$4,500,000/\$300,000,000$

$$= \$1.50 \text{ per } \$100 \text{ of Assessed Valuation}$$

Note that the three districts that have equal expenditures per student now have unequal tax rates, and the richer the district, the lower the rate.

Suppose, finally, that District 3 chose to spend $2,000 per student. Its budget would rise to $10 million. Its state aid would hold constant at $1,500,000, and its tax rate would be $8,500,000/$300,000,000—$2.83 per $100 of assessed valuation. Rich District 3 thus spends $800 more per student than poor District 2, but its tax rate is $1.67 per $100 lower. This establishes the inverse relationship between expenditures and tax rates that is characteristic of most state aid systems in the United States.

The formula now in use in New York State for distributing $1,672 million (70 per cent of total state assistance for public elementary and secondary education) is of the form just described. Specifically, aid to a given district is

$$A_1 = \left[1 - \left(0.51 \times \frac{\text{District valuation per student}}{\text{State average valuation per student}} \right) \right] \times E$$

where E = approved operating expenses, subject to an upper limit of $860 per student and subject further to a minimum grant of $310 per student.[14]

Imagine that a state government set out to meet three objectives in its education finance policy: (1) equity, as measured by a plan that would give districts equal spending power per student at equal tax rates; (2) local choice without limit in the amount of educational spending districts wished to undertake; and (3) protection of the state budget (i.e., avoidance of giving away "blank checks"). Reflection will indicate that the three objectives are incompatible, though any two are attainable. One can have equity (fully operational percentage equalizing grant) and full local choice over level of spending, but the state budget will be unprotected. One can have a protected state budget and local freedom to spend (as in New York now), but equity will be sacrificed for the reason that expenditures in excess of the state maximum grant (now $860 per student) will fall with much greater severity on the tax rates of poor districts than of rich. One can have a protected state budget and equity, but local freedom to raise expenditures beyond a state-imposed limit is sacrificed. The Commission holds the right choice to be the last of the three.

Problems in the System of Educational Finance

New York's present finance system must be judged not by the complexity and fine tuning of its formulas but by results achieved. The current system suffers from several deficiencies.

FISCAL INEQUITIES We have already noted the gross (and frequently inverse) disparities between educational spending per student and school tax rates on Long Island. Statewide data are conclusive, moreover, that educational expenditures are indeed a function of local wealth. Consider Table 2.9. The eight richest counties in New York, as ranked by income of house-

TABLE 2.9

High and Low Income Counties and Their Educational Expenditures

	Highest and Lowest Counties by 1969, Personal Income Per Capita		Expenditures in Public Elementary and Secondary Schools for Regular Day Instructional Services per Student in Weighted Average Daily Attendance, 1968–69	
	Dollars	**As % of State Aver. Income, By Counties**	**Dollars**	**As % of State Aver. Expend., By Counties**
HIGH COUNTIES				
Westchester	6759	197	857	131
Nassau	5893	171	813	125
New York City	4738	138	748	115
Monroe	4597	134	702	108
Albany	4380	127	649	99
Dutchess	4015	117	674	103
Schenectady	3881	113	740	113
Erie	3800	111	621	95
State Average	3438	100	653	100
LOW COUNTIES				
Allegany	2897	84	631	97
Lewis	2779	81	632	97
Schuyler	2754	80	553	85
Clinton	2752	80	604	92
Oswego	2675	78	563	86
Saratoga	2653	77	610	93
Franklin	2543	74	600	92
Schoharie	2447	72	586	90

holds, and the eight poorest are compared in terms of educational expenditures per student. The expenditure measure is dollars spent on instructional services, i.e., on teachers' salaries, books, writing paper, and the like. For the issue at hand, it is desirable to concentrate on expenditures to support learning, so that special factors—sparsity-induced student transportation costs on the one hand, and "frills" on the other—do not distort the findings. Note that all but two (Albany and Erie) of the rich counties spend more per student on instructional services than state average expenditure. Not one of the poor counties reaches state average. Between the two groups, there is only a small amount of overlap: Allegany and Lewis Counties spend more than Erie. The relation between wealth and educational expenditures shown in Table 2.9 carries a negligible probability of occurrence by statistical chance. The conclusion is inescapable that wealth is a determinant of instructional expenditures.

In absolute terms, differences in expenditures are larger between school districts than between county averages, for county averages, in the nature of the case, mask the size of inter-district variations. Table 2.10 gives 1969–70 data from New York State school districts, ranked by quartiles, on the basic operating expenditures per student and on full value assessed valuation per student. The relation between district expenditures and wealth is clear; hence, the equalizing grants employed so far by the state fail to remove that invidious relationship.

HANDICAP TO PLANNING   The existing system of educational finance stands in need of change not only because it produces gross inequities but also because present mechanisms for acquiring resources to support school services render planning of education nearly impossible. Schools exist to serve a set of objectives. School boards, parents' associations, teachers' unions, etc.—all parts of the machinery—help us reach consensus in identifying these objectives and in determining priorities to be attached to certain ones.

TABLE 2.10

Operating Expenditures and Assessed Valuation (per Student),
by District Quartiles, 1969–70

Quartile	Expenditure per Student	Average Full Value Property per Student
1	$1,330	$39,836
2	1,041	27,703
3	932	22,389
4	856	17,545

Any important rearrangement of objectives establishes a timed course of action toward fulfillment. This is so whether or not that timed course of action is explicitly recognized. In many cases, attainment of a new—or newly rediscovered—objective in education requires a prolonged period of preparation, another way of saying that educational progress depends fundamentally on planning.

Consider, for example, an objective to "provide each student with a marketable skill." Given high rates of youth unemployment and the concentration of that misfortune on minority groups, this is, let us assume, a commendable objective. It can be "implemented" almost overnight, but in an empty way. That is, the superintendent could notify the principals "to give more attention to vocational education." The principals could see if there was extra space in vocational classes—almost certainly there would be extra places somewhere—the counselors could be directed to channel more students into those courses, and the objective would be declared fulfilled.

Obviously, the steps just described do not represent a serious approach. But a serious approach would require time—five years, say—to work out. What would be involved? An early step would be to identify clients to be served—probably persons who are not going to enter four-year college or university. But one should first decide whether the sorting system is working properly. Are qualified students failing to prepare themselves for four-year college? Are some students who plan to enter four-year college really desirous of entering the work force by some other route? So we need to develop a choice and channeling policy for occupational education.

Another early step would be to discover what are "marketable skills." Surely it is desirable that as high a proportion of students as possible enter levels of work that are not dead ends. But what are the possibilities locally and in the geographically extended labor market? In determining the possibilities, one must do more than read occupational projections; restrictions on entry into certain lines of work may exist. These restrictions, in turn, may or may not be negotiable.

Given knowledge of clients and their future occupations, it would be necessary to define marketable skill, not as such, but in operational terms from the educator's point of view. What does a man need to know to enter a given line of work? What are the basic educational tasks he must have completed in order to learn on the job?

Of these requirements, what ones can the schools serve and with what probabilities of success? At what points in the school career of the student should specific new or revised curricular material be introduced?

Having dealt with clients, training opportunities, requirements and methods, the district might be ready to move toward implementation. Inventories of teachers' capabilities and interests would be required, as well as inventories of instructional space and equipment. Steps to meet needs of teachers, supporting services and plant and equipment could next be started; account should be taken of the degree to which specific training programs might be conducted cooperatively with industry. It would probably be necessary to inaugurate new training programs for staff.

By no means must implementation of the program wait until the whole operation is ready to go into action. It is generally possible to begin pilot projects early. However, putting the whole program into action requires time and consistency of direction. What are the realities? Under the present system of finance, school budgets are unpredictable one year to the next. There are several reasons why this is so, but two are paramount: (1) The local voters frequently decline to pass a budget. (There were 137 school budget defeats in 1969–1970.) (2) Because the state provides only a portion of public school funds (45.7 per cent in 1970–71), it does not feel the ultimate necessity to follow a school finance policy that provides stable, consistent funding in the districts. This year's state aid can be voted up or down from last year's, while the local authorities are expected to take steps to balance their budgets by using their local taxing power.

Where local budgets are unpredictable from one year to the next, planning cannot be taken on as a serious activity. It might seem that the reason is obvious and physical: specific projects would be started up and then shut down for lack of funds, leading to missed deadlines, inability to move to the next stage of implementation, etc. The greater damage, however, may be psychological. Planning and preparation require dedication and willingness to take the long view, i.e., to realize that work satisfactions must be deferred. Too much uncertainty about resources drives school management into short-term programs only, and in too many cases, the appearance of progress, not the reality, is all that is accomplished.

FAILURE TO RECOGNIZE CITY NEEDS   Existing educational finance arrangements were devised during the 1920's, when cities appeared to be rich and had strong, fully developed educational systems. At first, the state's grant programs were intended to redress an imbalance of educational power in that they were to help poor, rural districts improve their primary schools and begin to develop secondary schools. The rural bias in the original state aid formulas has, by this time, become a suburban bias, even though now it is the *cities* which lack educational systems sufficient to the challenge of the day.

The problem in the cities arises because a limited amount of public funds must be used to finance a large number of municipal services. For example, New York City's non-school total per capita expenditures for services related to high population density and large welfare population are much higher than those of other school districts throughout the state (Table 2.11). City costs on a per capita basis for welfare and public safety were each over 2.5 times the average for other school districts, and sanitation and health were each over two times greater.

A look at the tax levy portion of the 1969–70 expense budget for New

TABLE 2.11

Non-School Expenditures Per Capita, 1967–68

	General Government	Safety	High-ways	Sani-tation	Health	Amenities	Other	Total Non-Welfare	Welfare	Total
Big Five Cities	$27	$55	$19	$14	$10	$18	$25	$167	$ 70	$237
Upstate Suburbs	26	33	27	12	11	12	20	139	93	232
Downstate Suburbs	39	61	29	22	10	24	27	212	95	307
Independent Cities	23	34	27	10	6	11	19	130	79	208
Other	25	11	60	3	6	10	20	135	79	214
Total Sample	27	29	42	9	8	13	21	148	83	231
New York City	35	72	7	19	17	11	40	202	216	418

York City shows that 24.1 per cent, or $773 million, of local resources spent on non-school functions went for health and social services, almost all of which provided services for low-income groups. As shown in Table 2.12, a major portion of these funds (over $400 million) was earmarked for public medical assistance under state and federal programs.

In addition to these costly services for the direct aid to low-income groups, the city must provide the normal range of urban services in the areas of criminal justice, fire, sanitation and transportation. Although these services are provided for the total city population, the need for them is often greatest in areas marked by high levels of poverty. For example, three major Presidential crime commissions have noted that most crime can be correlated to substandard socio-economic conditions. Until the conditions are improved, costly police and correction systems must be maintained.

It would be unrealistic to expect other localities to help pay those normal urban expenses related to high population density. Likewise, it would be equally unrealistic to expect city residents to pay for those normal rural costs associated with low population density, such as road construction. However, the responsibility for public and medical assistance to the needy has already been accepted at both the state and federal levels. In fact, local contributions for these programs are effectively mandated on the locality by program matching requirements. It seems logical to assume that any statewide formula for equalizing education costs should, as minimum compensation for those localities burdened with large numbers of needy residents, be adjusted for local expenditures for health and welfare transfer payments.

TABLE 2.12

New York State Expenditures on Public and Medical Assistance, 1969–70 and 1970–71, in $ million

	NEW YORK STATE		NEW YORK CITY	
	1969–70	1970–71	1969–70	1970–71
PUBLIC ASSISTANCE				
Total Expenditures	1,176.7	1,563.6	891.1	1,142.2
Local Tax Levy[a]	340.6	436.5	251.3	318.8
MEDICAL ASSISTANCE				
Total Expenditures	944.4	1,262.4	612.0	843.2
Local Tax Levy[b]	236.1	315.6	153.0	210.8

[a] Estimated as 50 per cent Home Relief and 25 per cent all other expenditures.
[b] Estimated as 25 per cent of total expenditures.

The problems which large cities face extend beyond the issue of municipal overburden. In spite of all their difficulties, it is still the central cities that provide a home for intellectual activities. Only in the cities does one find consistently first-rate museums, libraries, theater, ballet, music and newer forms of folk art. Yet families which offer an intellectually stimulating environment for their children are moving away from the cities, partly in response to educational disparities. The result is a new kind of educational imbalance, relating to municipal overburden but not directly caused by it. Children who have intellectual and artistic interests find themselves in school districts that are unable to make connection with the artistic and intellectual resources of the central city. On the other hand, central city school students lack the opportunity or motivation to develop skills and interests which the resources of the city can greatly enrich. A fiscal imbalance has led to an intellectual and cultural imbalance, and in the process, everyone suffers.

AN UNNECESSARY BARRIER TO SOCIAL CLASS INTEGRATION Because localities are dependent on the property tax for raising educational revenues, they are usually strongly opposed to middle- or low-income housing developments being located in their communities. A local community will not welcome a residential property that cannot yield enough revenue to offset the costs of educating the new students who will enter school once a housing development is built. Since low- or middle-income families, for whom housing is most often planned, usually have at least an average number of school-aged or about-to-be school-aged children, the reliance on the property tax actually creates an incentive to keep lower income people out of wealthier communities. Housing developments planned for these income groups will usually fall below the district average in assessed value of property per student, even though the assessment for new properties is usually higher than the average district rate.

As a result, wealthy districts try to keep out low-income housing. If a housing project is built, school enrollment will increase faster than the revenue from local property taxes; therefore, the school tax rate will have to increase if the expenditure per student is to remain at the level it was before low-income housing was established. State aid should change the situation and make a local tax boost unnecessary. But for those districts so wealthy that even after low-income students arrive they receive money under the "flat grant provision," the state aid formula can do nothing to ameliorate the situation. In these districts, the greater part of increased costs must be met from local tax levies. For other less wealthy districts (those that are not flat grant districts), the state aid matching ratio will increase in response to an influx of lower income students; however, the increase in state aid will probably not be high enough to obviate the need for increase in local taxes on the impact of low- and middle-income housing on school district finance. (See Appendix 2E for a further analysis.)

A local district's reliance on property taxes to finance its educational offering creates a dangerous situation: On one hand, districts try to plan property use to provide a great deal of revenue with few expenses—a large industrial park, for instance—and, at the same time, wealthy districts, which are providing quality educational programs, try to zone out property which is considered "undesirable" for tax reasons—a low-income housing project which does not greatly increase the community's tax base but which signals a need for increased local expenditure. In effect, the property tax dependence is a barrier to effective social class integration. For affluent suburbs, the "cost" of such integration consists in part of a real, measurable tax increase which all residents must bear. Although the economic factor is not the only excuse offered for segregation, it seems safe to say that the elimination of the economic barriers to social-class and racial integration would be at least a first step toward greater equality. Full state assumption of educational costs would work to break down these unnecessary and damaging barriers.

Financial Magnitudes in Public Education Past and Projected

First, some introductory comments. In this section financial magnitudes relating only to the support of public schools are discussed; support of non-public schools is dealt with separately in Chapter 5. Economic data are not always published at the same time, some kinds taking longer to prepare than others; hence, we cannot always be absolutely consistent in the periods of time we are discussing. In general, however, we will be dealing with the decades of the sixties and the seventies.

PERSONAL INCOME   The capacity of a state to finance a public activity like education is most basically a function of its "personal income," which is defined as the sum of wages, salaries, rents, dividends, interest, proprietors' income and net transfer payments earned or received by its inhabitants. No one can pay taxes for schools out of income he does not have, nor can a state undertake to levy taxes at rates which constrict too seriously conventional habits of consumption and savings. Table 2.13 offers a comparison of recent changes in personal income in New York and in the United States as a whole.

During the decade of the sixties, personal income in New York (current dollars) rose at an annual rate of 6.5 per cent. This was a high rate of growth but not as high as that of the United States as a whole during the sixties (7.2 per cent). Per capita income in New York advanced at an annual rate of 5.5 per cent, only slightly below the national rate of 5.8 per cent. That New York more nearly approached the national rate in per capita than in total terms reflects, of course, the fact that population growth in New York, a mature state, occurred at a somewhat lower rate than in the nation as a whole.

TABLE 2.13

**Personal Income, New York and United States, 1960 and 1969,
Current and Constant Dollars**

CURRENT DOLLARS

REGION	TOTAL PERSONAL INCOME			PERSONAL INCOME PER CAPITA		
	Millions of Dollars		Aver. Annual Rate of Change			Aver. Annual Rate of Change
	1960	1969		1960	1969	
New York	46,281	81,384	+6.5%	2,748	4,442	+5.5%
United States	401,000	747,200	+7.2%	2,215	3,680	+5.8%

CONSTANT DOLLARS

REGION	TOTAL PERSONAL INCOME			PERSONAL INCOME PER CAPITA		
	Millions of Dollars		Aver. Annual Rate of Change			Aver. Annual Rate of Change
	1960	1969		1960	1969	
New York	55,559	81,834	4.3%	3,299	4,442	3.4%
United States	481,393	747,200	5.0%	2,659	3,680	3.7%

During the 1970s, personal income is expected to rise at a slower rate than in the 1960s; population growth is also expected to diminish. A conservative estimate of income growth in the state arrived at in studies made for the Commission is 3 per cent per annum in constant (1969) dollars and a more optimistic estimate is 3.7 per cent.[15] Note that both rates, i.e., 3.0 per cent and 3.7 per cent, are lower than the real rate of increase in New York State personal income between 1960 and 1969—4.3 per cent. Personal income in New York (in 1969 dollars) is projected to be $112,655 million in 1980 at the conservative rate and $121,368 million at the more optimistic growth rate. These figures yield projected per capita incomes in 1980 of $5,961 and $6,422 respectively (again, in 1969 dollars).

Two facts are clear from this description of growth rates: (a) even though economic growth in New York failed to match the national rate during the 1960s, the state's personal income per capita is well above national average and (b) even assuming a diminished rate of growth in the 1970s, there will be an ample advance in living standards to support a high quality educational system.

THE STATE'S PUBLIC REVENUES   Revenues of the New York State Government, excluding bond funds and receipts of local governments, have risen considerably more rapidly during the 1960's than personal income. Overall, State Government revenues went up at an average annual rate of 11.5 per cent. The yield of the component, "user taxes and fees," i.e., state sales and use taxes, motor fuel tax, cigarette tax, motor vehicle fees, alcoholic beverage taxes and highway use tax, advanced most rapidly of the major groups of levies (13.8 per cent per annum), followed by the yield of the personal income tax (12.7 per cent). Yields of business taxes, i.e., corporation franchise taxes, corporation and utilities taxes, bank tax, unincorporated business tax and insurance premium tax, went up at a slower rate of 9.2 per cent.

As seen by comparing figures in Tables 2.14 and 2.15, yields of taxes of local governments advanced at a slower pace in the 1960's than yields of state levies.

Nonetheless, yields of local taxes went up more rapidly than personal income. Hence, it necessarily follows that public revenues in New York, state and local combined, came to represent a larger share of personal income during the last decade.

How does the position of personal income paid by New York State residents in taxes compare with that paid by residents of other states? Table

TABLE 2.14

Income of New York State Government, Excluding Bond Funds, 1960 and 1970, Current Dollars (millions)

Class	1960	1970	Average Annual Rate of Change
Total Income	1,998.8	5,907.2	+11.5%
Personal Income Tax	756.6	2,506.4	+12.7%
User Taxes and Fees	554.0	2,025.6	+13.8%
Business Taxes	399.1	962.2	+9.2%
Other Taxes and Receipts	289.1	413.0	+3.6%

TABLE 2.15

Revenues of Local Governments in New York State, Excluding State and
Federal Aid, 1960 and 1968, Current Dollars (millions)

	1960	1968	Average Annual Rate of Change
ALL LOCAL GOVERNMENTS			
Total	3,321.2	5,933.3	+ 7.5%
Property Taxes	2,202.6	3,790.2	+ 7.0%
Non-Property Taxes	617.2	1,204.0	+ 8.7%
Charges and Fees	501.4	939.1	+ 8.2%
NEW YORK CITY			
Total	1,770.8	2,995.2	+ 6.8%
Property Taxes	1,005.9	1,643.9	+ 6.3%
Non-Property Taxes	560.9	1,026.3	+ 7.9%
Charges and Fees	204.0	325.0	+ 6.0%
REST OF STATE			
Total	1,550.4	2,938.1	+ 8.3%
Property Taxes	1,196.7	2,146.3	+ 7.6%
Non-Property Taxes	56.3	177.7	+14.5%
Charges and Fees	297.4	614.1	+ 9.5%

2.16 shows that New York ranked second among the states in combined
state/local taxes as a percentage of personal income in 1961. However, 16
states levy state taxes (as distinct from local) more intensively than New
York. In spite of the fact that state taxes in New York rose more rapidly
than local taxes during the 1960s, New York remains a state that relies
heavily upon *local taxation.*

It is not to be expected, of course, that state and local tax burdens in a
given state fall only on the residents of that state; some, especially those
taxes levied on business, will be "exported" to the residents of other states.
And some taxes levied on other states will, in turn, fall on residents of the
given state. Nor will taxes necessarily come finally to rest on households of
different income with equal severity. Indeed, the majority of public finance
specialists prefer that a tax system be "progressive," i.e., it should take a
larger portion of the income of a rich household than of a poor one; this
has come to be the criterion of a tax based on ability to pay. Generally,
however, local taxes are thought to be "regressive," i.e., to consume a larger
proportion of the incomes of poor households than of rich. State taxes are
thought to bear in roughly equal proportion on the income of households of
different degrees of wealth. Over-all, the state/local tax structure will

likely be tipped to the regressive side because of the heavy reliance placed on local taxation. Table 2.17 offers 1968 state-by-state comparisons of the burden of state/local taxes by income class of household. The state/local tax structure is estimated to be regressive for all the states taken together. In New York, state/local taxes as a proportion of household income *falls* as household income rises up to the income level of $17,500.[16]

REVENUE SOURCES FOR PUBLIC EDUCATION The elementary and secondary schools of New York State draw funds from local taxes (mainly, though not exclusively, from property taxes), state assistance (assistance financed, in turn, by the kinds of state taxes that were noted above), and federal aid. Table 2.18 shows the growth of public school receipts during the 1960s. A comparison of Table 2.18 with Tables 2.13, 2.14 and 2.15 shows that public school receipts grew during the 1960s faster than personal income (Table 2.13), at approximately the same rate as total State Government income (Table 2.14), and at a faster rate than local government receipts, excluding state and federal aid (Table 2.15). Both state assistance and federal aid went up more rapidly than local tax receipts for schools. However, as Table 2.19 shows, federal aid is still a very small proportion of the total elementary-secondary school budget in New York (4.7 per cent in 1969). Local taxes and state assistance now represent approximately equal shares—46.6 per cent and 45.7 per cent, respectively. At the beginning of the decade, local taxes accounted for nearly three-fifths of the education budget, while state assistance provided only about one-third of the total sum made available for education in the state.

REVENUE PROJECTIONS—HOW THE FUTURE LOOKS Let us consider projections of revenue for the coming decade.

State Tax Projections: Future yields of state taxes depend most strongly on the following economic relations: the rate of economic growth in the state; the responsiveness of yields of different taxes to given rates of growth; and the willingness of the people to accept changes in tax rates. Naturally, any single projection of future state revenue is suspect; too many largely unpredictable events may affect yields. Therefore, we must content ourselves with alternative projections.

The projections presented in Table 2.20 are based on two alternative rates of economic growth in the state: 3.0 per cent per annum and 3.7 per cent. (The reader may recall from Table 2.13 that such rates are substantially lower than those experienced in the 1960's.) Three alternative relations of tax yield to economic growth are presented (called "elasticities"): high, low and preferred. Estimates are based on the assumption that there will be *no* increase in state tax rates unless specified to the contrary.

Even the most pessimistic forecast—3.0 growth, low elasticity, constant tax rates—shows an increase in state tax yield by 1980 of $2.21 billion.

TABLE 2.16

State and Local Taxes as a Percentage of Personal Income, by State, Fiscal 1969

State	Taxes (Millions) Total	State	Local	TAXES AS A PERCENTAGE OF PERSONAL INCOME Total %	Rank	State %	Rank	Local %	Rank
United States	$76,711.9	$41,930.7	$34,781.2	11.2	(X)	6.1	(X)	5.1	(X)
Alabama	796.6	575.2	217.5	9.5	43	6.9	21	2.6	47
Alaska	110.1	71.8	38.3	9.7	41	6.3	29	3.4	39
Arizona	654.5	410.7	243.8	13.0	6	8.2	3	4.8	22
Arkansas	440.5	317.6	122.9	9.6	42	6.9	21	2.7	46
California	10,499.1	5,243.5	5,255.6	13.7	3	6.8	23	6.9	2
Colorado	810.2	408.1	402.1	11.9	15	6.0	35	5.9	8
Connecticut	1,176.5	541.6	634.9	9.3	47	4.3	47	5.0	18
Delaware	201.0	157.0	44.0	9.9	36	7.7	10	2.2	49
Florida	2,096.0	1,269.4	826.5	10.7	30	6.5	25	4.2	32
Georgia	1,251.5	828.1	423.4	9.9	36	6.5	25	3.3	42
Hawaii	381.3	289.0	92.3	14.1	1	10.7	1	3.4	39
Idaho	235.5	150.5	84.9	12.6	8	8.0	6	4.5	29
Illinois	4,118.4	1,927.4	2,190.9	9.4	45	4.4	46	5.0	18
Indiana	1,710.4	881.7	828.7	9.9	36	5.1	40	4.8	22
Iowa	1,080.7	588.6	492.1	11.9	15	6.5	25	5.4	13

State									
Kansas	$ 804.0	$ 385.1	$ 418.9	10.6	28	5.1	40	5.5	12
Kentucky	897.0	654.9	242.1	10.5	31	7.7	10	2.8	45
Louisiana	1,115.6	776.7	338.9	11.4	23	7.9	7	3.5	36
Maine	301.3	158.2	143.1	10.9	26	5.7	37	5.2	16
Maryland	1,545.9	862.8	683.1	11.0	25	6.1	33	4.9	20
Massachusetts	2,474.3	1,233.5	1,240.8	11.8	18	5.9	36	5.9	8
Michigan	3,754.1	2,248.8	1,505.4	11.7	20	7.0	19	4.7	26
Minnesota	1,502.8	914.6	588.2	12.3	9	7.5	14	4.8	22
Mississippi	571.0	400.4	170.6	11.7	20	8.2	3	3.5	36
Missouri	1,400.1	711.1	689.0	9.3	47	4.7	44	4.6	28
Montana	243.8	111.8	132.0	12.0	13	5.5	39	6.5	5
Nebraska	524.7	217.3	307.4	11.3	24	4.7	44	6.6	4
Nevada	213.1	125.6	87.6	12.0	13	7.1	17	4.9	20
New Hampshire	214.7	83.2	131.4	9.4	45	3.6	50	5.7	10
New Jersey	2,902.6	1,181.3	1,721.3	10.3	33	4.2	48	6.1	6
New Mexico	321.6	237.4	84.2	12.1	11	8.9	2	3.2	43
New York	10,544.1	5,329.9	5,214.1	14.0	2	7.1	17	6.9	2
North Carolina	1,347.2	1,009.6	337.6	9.9	36	7.4	15	2.5	48
North Dakota	207.9	105.4	102.5	12.1	11	6.2	31	6.0	7
Ohio	3,284.0	1,540.5	1,743.5	8.8	50	4.1	49	4.7	26
Oklahoma	737.1	472.6	264.6	10.2	34	6.5	25	3.6	35
Oregon	786.4	405.8	380.6	11.8	18	6.1	33	5.7	10
Pennsylvania	4,007.4	2,265.8	1,741.6	10.0	35	5.7	37	4.3	31
Rhode Island	345.0	200.1	144.9	10.6	28	6.2	31	4.5	29
South Carolina	605.3	465.1	140.1	9.5	43	7.3	16	2.2	49
South Dakota	232.5	91.9	140.6	12.3	9	4.9	43	7.5	1
Tennessee	1,005.5	645.8	359.7	9.8	40	6.3	29	3.5	36

(Continued)

TABLE 2.16 (Continued)

State	Taxes (Millions)			Total		State		Local	
	Total	State	Local	%	Rank	%	Rank	%	Rank
Texas	$ 3,083.9	$ 1,710.7	$ 1,373.2	9.3	47	5.1	40	4.1	33
Utah	341.9	203.3	138.6	11.9	15	7.0	19	4.8	22
Vermont	168.7	100.9	67.8	12.9	7	7.7	10	5.2	16
Virginia	1,464.7	924.2	540.4	10.4	32	6.6	24	3.8	34
Washington	1,395.3	980.7	414.5	11.5	22	8.1	5	3.4	39
West Virginia	478.1	346.6	131.5	10.7	27	7.8	8	3.0	44
Wisconsin	1,858.5	1,090.8	767.7	13.1	5	7.7	10	5.4	13
Wyoming	132.4	77.9	54.5	13.2	4	7.8	8	5.4	13

TABLE 2.17

Distribution of State-Local Tax Burdens Relative to Family Income Size 50
States and All-State Average, 1968 (Tax Burdens as Percentages of Income[a])

State	$3,500		$5,000		$7,500		$10,000		$17,500	
	%	Rank	%	Rank	%	Rank	%	Rank	%	Rank
United States	12.8		10.9		9.4		8.7		6.5	
Alabama	10.7	42	8.8	44	7.8	40	7.5	39	5.8	36
Alaska	12.1	32	10.5	30	9.2	29	8.5	29	6.4	28
Arizona	14.5	15	12.6	10	10.8	9	9.8	10	7.4	11
Arkansas	10.4	44	8.9	43	7.7	42	7.1	42	5.6	40
California	12.1	33	9.8	34	8.3	37	7.9	35	6.3	30
Colorado	12.7	24	11.1	21	9.8	18	9.3	18	7.2	15
Connecticut	14.6	12	11.7	15	9.5	21	8.2	30	5.9	35
Delaware	10.9	37	9.1	39	8.2	38	8.2	31	7.1	18
Florida	15.0	10	12.2	13	10.0	16	8.7	26	6.0	34
Georgia	13.7	18	11.2	20	9.5	22	8.8	23	7.2	16
Hawaii	9.7	48	9.8	35	9.6	20	9.8	11	7.5	8
Idaho	11.9	34	10.8	27	9.1	31	8.8	24	7.0	21
Illinois	14.6	13	11.7	16	9.5	23	8.2	32	5.6	41
Indiana	15.4	6	13.1	5	11.2	4	10.1	8	7.5	9
Iowa	15.0	11	13.2	4	12.0	3	11.1	3	8.0	6
Kansas	15.5	5	12.7	9	9.3	26	9.6	13	7.3	14
Kentucky	12.4	28	10.9	26	10.6	11	10.4	5	7.9	6
Louisiana	9.7	49	8.3	48	6.7	49	6.3	47	4.5	46
Maine	16.6	1	13.7	2	11.0	7	9.6	14	6.7	25
Maryland	14.6	14	13.0	7	12.5	1	12.6	1	9.4	1
Massachusetts	14.8	16	12.1	14	11.2	5	10.3	6	7.6	7
Michigan	12.9	22	11.1	22	9.5	24	8.9	22	6.9	24
Minnesota	12.2	30	11.3	18	10.8	10	10.7	4	8.4	3
Mississippi	15.2	8	12.3	12	10.4	15	9.8	12	7.4	12
Missouri	12.8	23	11.0	25	9.4	25	.7	27	6.4	29
Montana	10.8	40	9.1	40	8.1	39	7.7	37	6.3	31
Nebraska	15.1	9	12.6	11	10.5	12	9.5	16	7.5	10
Nevada	10.7	43	8.7	46	7.0	47	6.1	48	4.3	49
New Hampshire	13.5	19	10.8	28	8.7	34	7.5	40	5.3	42
New Jersey	16.3	3	13.4	3	10.9	8	9.6	15	6.7	26
New Mexico	12.2	31	10.4	31	9.0	32	8.1	33	5.8	37
New York	13.2	21	11.5	17	10.5	13	10.2	7	8.3	4

(*Continued*)

TABLE 2.17 (*Continued*)

State	$3,500 %	$3,500 Rank	$5,000 %	$5,000 Rank	$7,500 %	$7,500 Rank	$10,000 %	$10,000 Rank	$17,500 %	$17,500 Rank
North Carolina	10.4	45	9.3	38	8.8	33	8.8	25	7.0	22
North Dakota	13.3	20	11.1	23	9.2	30	8.5	29	7.4	13
Ohio	10.9	38	9.1	41	7.6	43	6.8	44	4.3	44
Oklahoma	12.3	29	10.2	33	8.4	35	7.7	38	5.7	33
Oregon	10.9	39	9.7	36	9.3	27	9.2	20	7.1	19
Pennsylvania	15.4	7	13.0	8	11.1	6	9.9	9	7.0	23
Rhode Island	16.4	2	13.1	6	10.5	14	9.1	21	6.5	27
South Carolina	9.8	47	8.3	49	7.4	46	7.1	42	6.1	32
South Dakota	13.9	17	11.3	19	9.3	28	8.1	34	5.7	39
Tennessee	12.5	27	10.3	32	8.4	36	7.4	41	5.0	43
Texas	11.3	36	9.1	42	7.5	44	8.5	46	4.6	45
Utah	12.7	25	10.8	29	9.7	19	9.3	19	7.2	17
Vermont	12.7	26	11.1	24	9.9	17	9.4	17	7.1	20
Virginia	10.1	46	8.8	45	7.8	41	7.8	36	6.1	33
Washington	11.7	35	9.4	37	7.5	45	6.5	46	4.4	47
West Virginia	9.4	50	7.8	50	6.6	50	5.9	50	4.4	48
Wisconsin	15.7	4	13.8	1	12.5	2	12.2	2	9.3	2
Wyoming	10.8	41	8.7	47	7.0	48	7.0	48	4.3	50

[a] Adjusted gross income: family of four, 1968.

TABLE 2.18

**Receipts of Public Schools, by Sources of Receipts,
1960 and 1969 Current Dollars (millions)**

Year	Total Receipts	Local Taxes	State Assistance	Federal Aid	Other
1960	1,611.2	938.0	577.8	46.7	48.7
1969	4,178.0	1,948.5	1,910.4	196.4	122.7
Average Annual Rates of Change	+11.2%	+8.4%	+14.2%	+17.3%	+10.8%

TABLE 2.19

Percentage Shares of Public School Receipts in
New York State, 1960 and 1969

Year	Total Receipts	Local Taxes	State Assistance	Federal Aid	Other
1960	100.0	58.2	35.9	2.9	3.0
1969	100.0	46.6	45.7	4.7	2.9

These estimates, it should be noted, are free of the influence of inflation. Insofar as inflation continues, actual yields should be higher than those projected here.

Methods used in making these projections are shown in Appendix 2F.

Local Tax Projections: Different procedures must be used to read the future of property taxation. Property tax rates are quite diverse in the state and are subject to frequent change. What is of primary interest is the future size of the full value property tax *base.* Estimates for 1980 (in 1969 dollars) are shown in Table 2.21. Projections for land, existing structures and new construction are shown separately. The preferred estimate is an increase in 1980 to a taxable base of $176.1 billion, a rise of $62.2 billion over the 1969 full values. Again, we note that methods used in devising these projections are shown in Appendix 2F.

Federal Revenues: A discussion of federal aid to education is taken up separately in the next chapter.

Projected Expenditures for Elementary and Secondary Education

The anticipated costs of the Commission's finance proposals in 1972–73 as noted earlier in the chapter, are $715 million and are comprised of the following items:

1. Leveling up to the 65th percentile of school districts ranked by base expenditures—$125 million.
2. Additional .5 weighting of students with educational needs—$465 million.
3. Providing tax credits to persons paying more than 10 per cent of their taxable personal income in property taxes—$125 million.

TABLE 2.20

State Tax Projections (billions of 1969 dollars)

3.7% PROJECTIONS

Tax Category	Adjusted Revenue, 1969–70	Revenue, 1971–72	Revenue, 1980[d]	1980[e]	Revenue, 1980[f]	1980[g]
Personal Income	2.506	2.358	3.815	3.983	3.759	4.235
General Business[a]	.962	1.060	1.411	1.441	1.391	2.221
Sales and Use Taxes	1.012	1.447	1.876	1.888	1.839	3.751
Other Consumption Taxes[b]	1.014	.988	1.153	1.170	1.125	1.513
Other Taxes[c] and Misc. Revenue	.413	.449	.545	.560	.529	.640
Total:	5.907	6.302	8.800	9.042	8.631	12.360

3.0% PROJECTIONS

	Adjusted Revenue, 1969–70	Revenue, 1971–72	Revenue, 1980[d]	1980[e]	Revenue, 1980[f]	1980[g]
Personal Income	2.506	2.358	3.537	3.617	3.439	3.927
General Business[a]	.962	1.060	1.336	1.358	1.319	2.101
Sales and Use Taxes	1.012	1.447	1.790	1.795	1.759	3.580
Other Consumption Taxes[b]	1.014	.988	1.114	1.134	1.087	1.460
Other Taxes[c] and Misc. Revenue	.413	.449	.526	.534	.515	.620
Total:	5.907	6.302	8.304	8.438	8.119	11.688

[a] Corporate franchise, bank, unincorporated business, utilities (Article 9), and insurance premium tax.
[b] Motor vehicle, motor fuel, highway use, alcoholic beverage, cigarette tax.
[c] Estate, parimutuel, lottery, real estate transfer, boxing and racing tax, and miscellaneous revenue. Miscellaneous revenue consists mainly of revenues of general departments, refunds and reimbursements, real estate sold, abandoned property receipts, and income from investments and bank deposits.
[d] Preferred elasticities and constant tax rates.
[e] High elasticities and constant tax rates.
[f] Low elasticities and constant tax rates.
[g] Preferred elasticities with rate changes equal to that of last decade (equal percentage increase).

NOTE: The numbers may not add precisely because of errors due to rounding off to the nearest million in revenue.

TABLE 2.21

Tentative Projections of Full Value of Property Taxable for Schools,
New York State, 1980 ($ Billions)

Component	Estimated 1969 Level[a]	Basis For Projection	1980 Projection	
1. Land	$ 39.9	5.3%[b]	$70.4	
2. Existing Structures	74.0			
A. High projection		0.5%[b]	78.17	
B. Low projection		—	74.0	
3. New construction	—			
A. High projection		$3.7[c]	40.7	
B. Low projection		2.5[c]	27.5	
Totals:	$113.9			
1 + 2A + 3A			$189.3	High
1 + 2B + 3B			171.9	Low
1 + 2A + 3B			176.1	Preferred
1 + 2B + 3A			185.1	

[a] Distinction between land and structures estimated.
[b] Average annual rate of increase in excess of general price level.
[c] Average annual level of new construction reflected on tax rolls.

If this magnitude of resource commitment by the state were spread over two years ($358 million per year), it would be well within past annual rates of increase in educational expenditures in the state.

The Fiscal Crisis in the Schools

The widespread talk of a fiscal crisis in schools is shorthand for some deep-seated problems, all very real. First and foremost is the fiscal crisis in the state itself with expenditures currently exceeding revenues. Next is the lack of adequate federal support for education. Fragmentation is another problem; there are simply too many small districts. The imbalance of revenue resources within the state is another; there is an inordinate reliance on the local property tax, which is rapidly reaching the point of diminishing returns. A fifth problem is a crisis in educational fiscal management, graphically illustrated by the inability of districts in their collective bargaining activities during the past decade to achieve increases in productivity in return for substantially higher salaries. Finally, education is the nation's second largest public activity (national defense is the largest), yet in the midst of the fiscal crisis, the problem of balancing the education budget is still left to the local district, the weakest unit of government because of its dependence on an inelastic tax that already bears a disproportionately large share of the over-all tax burden. Of the alternatives available to the people of New York, we believe full state funding offers the best avenue toward a solution of the majority of these problems.

State Aid to Education, 1971–72

INTRODUCTION

State aid to education in New York is a billion-dollar business. More than half of the state's Local Assistance Fund which provides aid to local governments is allocated to education. Over 90 per cent of all education aid goes to the state's public school system. The largest component of aid to public schools is general, unrestricted aid. In 1971–72 the state Education Department estimates that 93 per cent of total aid to public elementary and secondary schools will be in this general aid category.

The rest of the aid program was allocated to help purchase textbooks for public and private schools, support Boards of Cooperative Education Services, County Vocational Education and Extension Boards, Orphan Schools, the Lunch-Breakfast Program, Pre-Kindergarten Program, Educational Television Program and the Urban Education Program.

Table 2A.1 reveals the breakdown of the total education aid program provided by the state this year.

GENERAL AID

General aid is provided for two types of school districts: those employing eight or more teachers and those employing fewer than eight teachers.

General aid for districts employing eight or more teachers is based on six separate formula computations: operating expense aid, growth aid, size correction aid, building expenses aid, transportation expenses aid, and high-tax-rate aid.

To be eligible to receive the maximum general aid to which it otherwise would be entitled, a district must levy local taxes (real property and non-

Components of State Aid to Education, 1971–72 (Estimated)

	Amount in $ Millions	Per Cent of Total Aid
GENERAL AID		
Operating Expense	1,672.00	70
Growth	36.00	
Budget	5.40	
Size Correction	111.98	
Transportation	151.00	
Building	212.80	
Reorganization Incentive	14.00	
High-Tax	25.70	
Total	2,228.88	93
SPECIAL AIDS		
Textbooks	20.00	
BOCES	87.10	
CVEEB	0.10	
Orphans	0.48	
Lunch-Breakfast	11.50	
Pre-Kindergarten	5.00	
Educational Television	.48	
Urban Education	47.00	
Total	171.66	7
TOTAL AID	2,400.54	100

property taxes) at a rate equivalent to the higher of a tax rate of $1·1 per $1000 actual valuation, or a tax rate equivalent to the rate required to meet the local share in the district of average wealth, for the base year approved operating expenses, not exceeding the operating expense ceiling.

General aid is reduced by the amount by which the district's computed tax rate is less than the higher of the two rates above. The difference in tax rate in such cases is applied to the district's actual valuation, and the result deducted from the maximum general aid which it would otherwise receive.

Operating Expense Aid

Of the five major components of general aid, operating expense aid is the largest and most fundamental. In 1971–72 operating expense aid represented 70 per cent of total general aid. Such aid may be used by school districts for teachers' salaries, instructional supplies and equipment maintenance and the operation of the school plant, insurance and administrative expenses.

Under 1971 legislation, basic operating expense aid and its three adjustments, growth aid, size correction, and budgeted operating expense aid (see below), were payable in 1971–72 under either of two basic options. Each district may choose the option which provides the greater amount of aid. The basic features of the two options are:

OPTION I
a. Operating expense aid computed on the basis of approved 1970–71 expenses, or approved budgeted 1971–72 operating expenses, not in excess of $860 per pupil in weighted average daily attendance (that is, per WADA). The minimum, or "flat grant," operating expense aid is $310 per WADA.
b. Growth aid computed on the basis of 1970–71 operating expenses not in excess of $860 per WADA.
c. Size correction aid equal to 50 per cent of the size correction aid received for the 1969–70 school year.
d. *General* urban aid. This aid is *not* available to any district which does not qualify for 1971–72 categorical urban aid. Each qualifying district is informed of the exact amount of its general urban aid allocation by the State Aided Programs Unit of the Division of Educational Finance.

OPTION II
a. Operating expense aid, computed on the basis of approved 1970–71 operating expenses, or approved 1971–72 budgeted operating expenses, not in excess of $760 per WADA. The minimum, or "flat grant," operating expense aid is $274 per WADA.
b. Growth aid computed upon the basis of 1970–71 operating expenses not in excess of $760 per WADA.
c. Size correction aid equal to 100 per cent of the size correction aid received during the 1969–70 school year.
d. An additional amount equal to 10 per cent of the computed basic operating expense aid, and of computed net budgeted operating expense aid, *not* including growth aid.

Operating expense aid is determined by application of a formula. The formula yields an aid ratio which is used to determine the state's share of a district's operating expenses. The formula may be expressed as:

$$\text{Aid Ratio} = 1 - \left[\frac{\text{Actual Valuation per RWADA of district}}{\text{State Average Actual Valuation per State WADA}} \times .51 \right]$$

The aid ratio formula is designed so that in a district with actual valuation per WADA *equal* to the statewide average actual valuation per WADA, the state will share 49 per cent of the appropriate expenditures, and the district the remaining 51 per cent. In districts in which this measure is *below* the state average, the state's share *increases* from 49 per cent; in districts where this measure is *above* the state average, the state's share *becomes less* than 49 per cent.

The local factors used in determining a district's aid ratio are RWADA and the total actual valuation of taxable real property of the district. For the purpose of computing aid payable in the 1971–72 school year, the 1969–70 school year RWADA and 1969 actual valuation of real property are used.

To determine operating expense aid, approved operating expenses are multiplied by the district's aid ratio. However, there are upper and lower limits to such aid, depending on the option chosen. Thus, operating expenses are used only to the extent that they do not exceed $860 per pupil in weighted average daily attendance (per WADA), or are less than $310 per WADA, often referred to as "flat grant aid," under Option I. Under Option II, the ceiling is $760 and the flat grant $274. This flat grant provision assures every district, regardless of wealth, of at least $274 or $310, depending on the option chosen in operating expense aid.

Growth Aid

This is an adjustment in operating expense aid to compensate for the increase in expenditures between the base year and the current year due to an increase in attendance. Growth aid is calculated by applying a percentage to the operating expense aid. This percentage is the percentage of increase in attendance between the base year and the current year. It is measured by determining the percentage (if any) by which attendance during the first attendance period of the current year is greater than attendance during the first period of the base year.

In 1971–72 under Option I growth aid will be computed on the basis of 1970–71 operating expenses not in excess of $860 per WADA; under Option II the computation will not be in excess of $760.

In 1971–72 growth aid represented 2 per cent of general aid.

Size Correction Aid

The second adjustment to operating expense aid is for sparsity or density of population. Size correction is no longer a separate formula aid computation. For 1971–72 size correction is a dollar amount based on the size correction aid paid in 1969–70. However, the amount a district will receive depends on the option chosen. Under Option I, size correction aid will be equal to 50 per cent of the size correction received by the district in 1969–

70. Under Option II, the aid will be equal to 100 per cent of that awarded in 1969–70.

The 1969–70 computation was based on the following criteria:

A district received size correction aid which was not less than 10 per cent of its approved base year operating expenses per WADA or $76, whichever was less, multiplied by its aid ratio, and multiplied by its base year WADA, but not more than 1,500 of such WADA plus 60 per cent of the excess above 8,000 of such WADA.

School districts had three other alternatives to compare the above formula to, and could choose the one which provided the greatest amount of aid. The options were:

a. If the approved base year operating expense per WADA exceeds $760, the size correction aid may consist of such excess but not more than 1,250 of such WADA multiplied by the aid ratio.

b. If the actual valuation per resident pupil in weighted average daily attendance (RWADA) is less than $18,000, the size correction aid may consist of 10 per cent of operating expenses per base year WADA, multiplied by base year WADA but not more than 1,500 of such WADA.

c. If the sum of the approved base year operating expense and the approved base year transportation expense exceeds $760 multiplied by WADA, the size correction aid may consist of whichever of the following is the smallest: (1) such excess multiplied by the aid ratio, (2) the sum of such transportation expense and the approved base year operating expense for pupils enrolled in programs for physically handicapped, mentally handicapped, emotionally disturbed, delinquent, and non-English-speaking children, multiplied by the aid ratio, or (3) $38 multiplied by base year WADA multiplied by the aid ratio.

The Big Six Cities' school districts may receive size correction aid calculated at 17½ per cent of the sum of operating expense aid, growth aid, and budgeted operating expense aid.

Budgeted Operating Expense Aid

An alternative to operating expense aid is budgeted operating expense aid.

If the operating expenses in the base are less than $860 (Option I) or $760 (Option II) per WADA and the district is budgeting to spend at a higher rate in the current year, it may use its budgeted operating expenses for computing operating expense aid. The budgeted operating expenses which are aidable may not exceed the $860 (Option I) or $760 (Option II) per WADA ceiling.

Since budgeted operating expenses per WADA reflect the estimated current year WADA, districts receiving aid on the budget do not also receive growth aid.

Size correction aid in 1969–70 was computed on base year operating expenses except for a Big Six City which could receive size correction aid on budgeted operating expenses if applicable.

One additional calculation is made under Option II which applies to operating aid for 1971–72. Districts which chose that option will receive an additional amount equal to 10 per cent of the computed basic operating expense aid and of the computed net budgeted operating expense aid, *not* including growth aid.

Borough Aid

New York City's aid is calculated on a borough-by-borough basis. In other words, each borough is treated as if it were a separate school district for purposes of the calculations described herein. This results in an amount of state aid for the city greater than if one calculation were made for the entire city.

School Building Expense Aid

General aid is also provided for expenses connected with the construction of new buildings, additions to buildings and renovation of existing district-owned buildings. This component of general aid is computed separately, and no minimum or "flat grant" aid is provided to wealthier districts which would receive little or no aid pursuant to the aid ratio formula.

State aid is available only to districts employing eight or more teachers. Expenses for which this aid is available are:

1. Debt service payments on indebtedness incurred to finance a building project: debt service on bonds, bond anticipation notes, or capital notes.
2. Capital expenditures from budgetary appropriations; aid for debt service is apportioned currently in the same year in which the debt service expense is made. Aid for capital expenditures is apportioned the school year following the year the expenditure is made.

Aid is computed by multiplying the district's aid ratio by the expenses incurred to pay for the approved cost of the school building project. The approved costs and, therefore, the approved expenses, are limited by a cost allowance maximum for each building project based on a per-pupil cost allowance multiplied by the rated capacity of the building. An additional percentage of the construction allowance (20 per cent for K-6 buildings and 25 per cent for 7–12 buildings) is permitted for incidental costs (site acquisition, architect, equipment, etc). The cost allowance maximum for a school bus garage is the approved cost of the garage.

State aid is based upon expenses up to the cost allowance maximum. If a building project is financed through the creation of indebtedness, the ratio (not to exceed 1.0) of the approved cost to the actual cost of the project (bond percentage) is applied to each year's debt services expenses to determine the amount of approved expenses eligible for state aid. This amount is then multiplied by the aid ratio for a given district in any year to determine the state aid for building for that year.

Incidental costs may include the cost of site purchase and improvements, original equipment, furnishings, machinery or apparatus and professional fees and other costs incidental to such construction. The construction cost allowance is adjusted monthly, based upon an index which reflects changes in the cost of labor and materials. The cost allowance maximum for any building project is established for the month the general construction contract is approved. If a project is financed from both indebtedness and capital expenditures, state aid for approved expenses is applied first to the bond indebtedness, and then to capital expenditures for any amount remaining within the cost allowance. Building aid made up 9 per cent of total aid in 1971–72.

Transportation Expense Aid

General aid is also provided for a district's transportation expenditures. For districts employing eight or more teachers, the aid is calculated at 90 per cent of approved expenditures.

Transportation expenses are those incurred in transporting all pupils living over 1.5 miles from school to and from school once daily. They include expenditures for the operation of buses owned by the district, buses leased under contract by the district and public service (common carrier) buses.

Included in approved expenses available for aid are driver's wages, gas, oil, tires, chains, maintenance, repairs, storage, water and sewage charges, insurance premiums, tolls, and capital outlay for buses.

Other Components of General Aid

The other components of general aid accounted for 1 per cent of general aid in 1971–72. They include: save-harmless, reorganization incentive aid, adjustments for prior years, high tax rate, fewer-than-eight teacher districts, and contract districts.

a. The save-harmless provision guarantees that no district would receive less aid in 1971–72 than it received in the 1965–66 school year. (NOTE: A district receiving aid on this basis shall also receive the 10 per cent increase in operating expense aid computed on a $760 ceiling under Option II.)

b.   Reorganization incentive aid is composed of additional operating and building aid for newly reorganized districts. The 1971 Legislature extended the provision of incentive operating expense aid to districts which reorganize before September 1, 1972 (rather than 1971), and which meet all other qualifications for such aid.

c.   High tax aid is additional general aid, payable in 1971–72; it is available to certain eligible districts having high tax rates in the 1970–71 school year. To qualify for high tax rate aid districts must have a 1970–71 tax rate of at least $24 per thousand and a valuation per pupil less than $30,000. Either 1969 equalization rates or the rates for the roll used to collect taxes in 1970–71 may be used. Districts that received high tax rate aid in 1970–71 are guaranteed at least the same amount for 1971–72.

d.   General aid for districts employing fewer than eight teachers is based on operating expenses and transportation expenses only. Operating expenses and operating expense aid are computed just as they are for eight-or-more teacher districts. Approved operating expenses have a ceiling which cannot exceed the sum of (a) $4,500 multiplied by the number of full-time teachers employed during the base year, and (b) the base year WADA multiplied by $60 plus an amount computed by multiplying the base year WADA by $.90. Budgeted operating expenses may not be used by these districts.

Transportation expenses are determined in the same way as for eight-or-more teacher districts. Transportation expenses aid is calculated by multiplying the expenses by the district's aid ratio.

The save-harmless aid for districts employing fewer than eight teachers is the amount of aid such districts received in 1964–65 based upon the 1963–64 school year. This save-harmless amount is reduced in proportion to the decrease in the number of teachers; if a district's aid ratio is less than the 1964–65 aid ratio, the save-harmless is reduced by the difference in aid ratios. In the event the district experienced both a reduction in teachers and a reduction in aid ratio, only the greater of the two deductions is made. If, after adjustment, the save-harmless aid is greater than the sum of the transportation and operating expenses aids, the district is entitled to the greater amount.

When local revenue raised by tax for school purposes is less than $9.00 per $1,000 of actual valuation, the apportionment is reduced by the difference between the local revenue and the amount that would have been raised by the $9.00 tax rate.

In cases where the entire district, or portions thereof, did not have a 180-day total session, adjustments are made according to the same pattern used for eight-or-more districts.

e. General aid for a district not maintaining a school and contracting for the education of its children is based on approved operating expenses and transportation expenses. In this case, tuition is considered an approved operating expense. The aid is calculated by deducting from operating and transportation expenses a local contribution expressed as a tax rate per $1,000 of actual valuation. The tax rate is the higher of (a) the tax rate of the receiving district(s) with the highest rate, or (b) $10 per $1,000 of actual valuation.

SPECIAL AIDS

There are eight programs under this general heading for which state aid is available. They represent 7 per cent of total state aid.

Textbook Aid

Special state aid is provided to public school districts for the reimbursement of the expense of textbooks purchased for loan to children residing in the district and attending grades 7–12 in any public or nonpublic school complying with the compulsory education law. State aid for the school year 1971–72 was equal to the actual expense of textbooks but not to exceed $10 per pupil residing in the district and attending grades 7–12.

Boards of Cooperative Educational Services

BOCES aid is provided through a formula based upon the expenditures made by the BOCES in behalf of each component school district, and is limited to salaries not exceeding $8,500 and administrative expenditures not exceeding 10 per cent of the total expenditures.

The state aid for each component district will be the higher of (1) approved expenditures multiplied by the district's aid ratio or (2) the approved expenditures minus a local share obtained by dividing 6 mills (formerly 5 mills) by the local tax rate times the approved expenditure. Where services are provided to a school district which is included within a central high school district, or to a central high school district, state aid will be computed on the basis of the approved expenditures minus a local share obtained by dividing 3 mills (formerly 2½ mills) by the local tax rate times the approved expenditures. State aid is also provided for debt incurred for acquisition or construction of buildings as well as for the cost of renting facilities on a current basis.

County Vocational Education and Extension Boards

County boards may receive state aid for approved programs of service provided to individual districts, and for the transportation of pupils to the classes or schools operated by the county board. Aid is apportioned directly to the county board. The aid for programs of service is one-half the salary paid each teacher, director, assistant, and supervisor, but not to exceed $3,000 for each. The aid for transportation is one-half the approved expenditures for the transportation of pupils under age 21 to schools and classes maintained by the board.

Orphan School Aid

State aid for schools operated by the incorporated orphan asylum societies in the State of New York, other than those in New York City, is available for approved programs of education provided directly by the schools. The aid is based upon the salary paid to each teacher but is not to exceed $4,000, and if the average daily attendance per teacher is less than 10, then the aid is equal to $400 multiplied by the average daily attendance.

Most of the orphan schools educate a small percentage of the pupils residing at the schools. Generally, the orphan schools educate the atypical child and provide instruction for their other children in the local public or nonpublic schools.

School Lunch and Milk

In 1971–72, state aid in the amount of $11.5 million will be apportioned in addition to federal aid in support of the school lunch and milk programs of the schools.

Pre-Kindergarten

For a program for disadvantaged children, the state pays for 85 per cent of the approved cash expenditures except for transportation, which is aided at 90 per cent of approved cash expenditures.

Educational Television

This program encourages and stimulates the further development and use of educational television in the schools. The state aid is 50 per cent of the approved cash expenditures for the acquisition and installation of equipment, and a sliding scale percentage of the approved cash operating expenditures. The scale varies from 50 per cent to 10 per cent, decreasing 10 per cent in each of the first five years of the project.

Urban Education Aid

School districts with special educational needs associated with poverty receive urban education aid at the rate of 100 per cent of approved expenditures. Approval of projects in eligible districts is subject to these considerations:

1. Proportion of the disadvantaged receiving the expected benefits.
2. The priority the district has placed on educational benefits.
3. The educational feasibility of, and availability of, resources to implement the project.
4. The nature of the special needs the district is trying to meet.
5. Economic rationality of the plan.

The 1971 Legislature continued Urban Education funding for the school year 1971–72 with two basic changes. Although the allocation formula remains the same, the appropriation has been reduced to $47 million and all carry-over of unused funds has been eliminated. Therefore, unexpended funds from the 1970–71 allocation will not be available for use in 1971–72. Each participating district will be allocated the same proportionate share of the $47 million that was computed against the $52 million appropriation for 1970–71.

School Finance Inequities on Long Island

INTRODUCTION

Before examining data on school districts of Long Island, let us first postulate a guiding rule. This rule is found in the branch of economics called public finance and it can be stated as follows: Government should treat equals in equal fashion. As applied to the field of public education, that rule means two things: first, young people of similar interests and abilities should be offered educational programs of equal standard; second, taxpayers should be taxed in direct relation to the quality of educational services provided and in relation to their ability to pay, as measured by their income. The first aspect of the "equal treatment" rule of public finance cannot be applied in absolutely precise ways because the interests and abilities of young people cannot be measured accurately nor can the appropriateness of different educational programs to serve those interests and abilities be determined (neither in the general sense nor in the sense of comparing programs available to students in different localities). However, it is reasonable to say that when the expenditures per-student per-year vary widely from one school district to the next in a small geographic area and when such differences are systematically related to a variable—namely, taxable value of real property in school districts—that has only a remote connection, if any, with the interests and abilities of young people who live in those districts, the rule of equal treatment is being violated.

The second aspect of the equal treatment rule—that taxpayers should be treated fairly—is also difficult to interpret. Schools are supported from levies of the federal, state and local governments. Taxes are paid in the first instance by businesses as well as households. It is an impossible research task to determine precisely who pays how much for any school program. Taxes may be shifted by businesses to households through changes in product prices or through changes in wage rates. Taxes distort consumer buying patterns and, hence, affect opportunities for use of economic assets, including human labor. However, it is possible to isolate inequities in *local taxation*. Within a small geographic region, such inequity exists when there is a markedly imperfect relation between the level of local tax rates on true property value and school expenditures per-student per-year. Suppose that taxpayers in a school district, call it Hard Hit, have a local tax rate of $3.00 per $100 true value and suppose that these taxpayers pay such a rate to provide a public school program costing $1,000 per student per year. Let the taxpayers in the immediately adjacent school district, call it Easy Off, have a local tax rate of $1.00 per $100 of true value to support a program costing $2,000 per student. Most reasonable people would agree that taxpayers of the two school districts are not being treated equally.

In New York State school programs of markedly different quality (as measured by dollar expenditures per student) exist within small geographic areas, for example, Long Island. Furthermore, the tax rate situation described hypothetically in the previous paragraph is a common one. Thus, even though we are unable to make precise judgments about the extent to which the canon of equal treatment is being violated, we can be sure that the reforms under consideration by the Commission can be defended.

LONG ISLAND SCHOOL DISTRICTS

With the exception of New York City, Long Island—that is, Nassau and Suffolk counties—has the largest concentration of public school enrollment in the state. In 1968–69, there were 615,494 students enrolled in the public elementary and secondary schools in the region. This enrollment represented 18.12 per cent of the state's total. (Table 2B.1.) Long Island also contains a large number of school districts. Long Island is not a large geographic area. About three-quarters of it is densely populated. Yet, in 1968–69 the region included 131 school districts of various classifications. Eighty-

Enrollment and Weighted Average Daily Attendance, 1968–69

County	Enrollment	WADA	Ratio of Enrollment to WADA	Per Cent of State Enrollment	Regional Revenues Per Enrollee
New York City	1,116,711	1,036,656	1.08	32.87	1,203.53
Long Island	615,494	625,431		18.12	1,320.59
Nassau	330,845	341,308	.97	9.74	
Suffolk	284,649	284,123	1.00	8.38	
Rockland-Westchester	220,735	222,155		6.50	1,435.85
Rockland	52,769	52,978	1.00	1.55	
Westchester	167,966	169,177	.99	4.94	
Mid-Hudson	167,776	168,788		4.94	1,165.41
Columbia	11,937	12,248	.98	.35	
Dutchess	45,682	45,640	1.00	1.35	
Greene	7,417	7,521	.99	.22	
Orange	49,301	49,897	.99	1.45	
Putnam	11,597	11,428	1.02	.34	
Sullivan	11,203	11,362	.99	.33	
Ulster	30,639	30,692	1.00	.90	
Capital District	168,362	170,268		4.96	1,131.89
Albany	46,981	46,998	1.00	1.38	
Rensselaer	27,760	27,747	1.00	.82	
Saratoga	30,284	30,831	.98	.89	
Schenectady	31,315	31,640	.99	.92	
Schoharie	6,382	6,698	.95	.19	
Warren	12,163	12,360	.98	.36	
Washington	13,477	13,994	.96	.40	
Northern	91,643	94,010		2.70	1,127.28
Clinton	17,985	18,211	.99	.53	
Essex	7,056	7,341	.96	.21	
Franklin	11,514	11,730	.98	.34	
Jefferson	21,436	21,792	.98	.63	
Lewis	6,823	7,078	.96	.20	
St. Lawrence	26,829	27,858	.96	.79	
Mohawk Valley	97,461	99,700		2.87	1,045.33
Fulton	12,176	12,725	.96	.36	
Hamilton	1,101	1,135	.97	.03	
Herkimer	15,045	15,762	.96	.44	
Montgomery	10,829	11,135	.97	.32	
Oneida	58,310	58,943	.99	1.72	

County	Enrollment	WADA	Ratio of Enrollment to WADA	Per Cent of State Enrollment	Regional Revenues Per Enrollee
Binghamton	90,928	92,651		2.68	1,065.46
Broome	54,497	54,443	1.00	1.60	
Chenango	13,606	14,186	.96	.40	
Delaware	11,228	11,764	.95	.33	
Otsego	11,597	12,258	.95	.34	
Syracuse	170,189	171,965		5.01	1,068.22
Cayuga	15,935	16,265	.96	.47	
Cortland	10,378	10,647	.98	.31	
Madison	16,950	17,316	.98	.50	
Onondaga	100,670	101,297	.99	2.96	
Oswego	26,256	26,440	.99	.77	
Rochester	234,286	235,596		6.90	1,142.38
Genesee	14,454	14,804	.98	.43	
Livingston	11,642	12,157	.96	.34	
Monroe	137,644	137,433	1.00	4.05	
Ontario	18,938	19,312	.98	.56	
Orleans	9,993	10,115	.99	.29	
Seneca	7,747	8,005	.97	.23	
Wayne	21,583	21,397	1.01	.64	
Wyoming	7,759	7,793	1.00	.23	
Yates	4,526	4,580	.99	.13	
Elmira	95,632	97,766		2.82	1,079.26
Allegheny	11,641	12,069	.97	.34	
Chemung	23,839	24,185	.99	.70	
Schuyler	3,683	3,767	.98	.11	
Steuben	27,642	28,428	.97	.81	
Tioga	12,960	13,265	.98	.38	
Tompkins	15,867	16,052	.99	.47	
Buffalo	328,196	332,711		9.66	1,057.27
Cattaraugus	21,456	22,324	.96	.63	
Chautauqua	36,279	36,798	.99	1.07	
Erie	213,639	216,078	.99	6.29	
Niagara	56,822	57,511	.99	1.67	
Total	3,397,413	3,347,697	1.02	100.00	

Size of School District Enrollment by Region, 1968–69

Region	Number of Districts With More Than 5000 Enrollment	Districts With 2001–5000 Enrollment	Districts With 1200–2000 Enrollment	Districts With Less Than 1200 Enrollment
New York City	31	0	0	0
Long Island	49	39	9	34
Rockland-Westchester	14	20	10	13
Mid-Hudson	7	22	16	27
Capital District	9	15	19	32
Northern	1	13	14	37
Mohawk Valley	4	10	13	27
Binghamton	3	11	9	26
Syracuse	9	16	13	13
Rochester	10	25	25	11
Elmira	4	8	10	29
Buffalo	17	26	15	16
Total	127	205	143	265

two of these had student enrollment of less than 5,000. (Table 2B.2.) The average regional revenues per student on Long Island in 1968–69 were $1,320.59. This figure was exceeded in the state only by Rockland-Westchester's $1,435.85.

Let us examine the Long Island region under the equity criteria. Table 2B.3 has been constructed for this purpose. Part A presents data on the 92 districts that have enrollment through the elementary and secondary grades. Our discussion will center on these districts. For completeness, Part B of Table 2B.3 offers data on the additional 38 districts that serve only elementary or secondary students. These latter districts are generally small and many are very wealthy.

Consider now Table 2B.3, Part A. Column 1 shows enrollment in the schools of the district. Column 2 indicates the General Fund Revenue of the district on a per-student basis. Column 3 is the divergence, expressed as a percentage, of the actual revenues per student in each district (Column 2) from regional average revenues per student—$1,320.59. Plus signs indicate districts that had above-average revenues, and minus signs indicate districts of below-average revenues. Great Neck had revenues 57.32 per cent above regional average and Massapequa had revenues 18.14 per cent below regional average. By regional standards, both of these two districts are large in enrollment. The absolute dollar difference per student between

TABLE 2B.3 (Part A)

School Revenues and Tax Rates in Long Island, 1968–69
(Districts Offering Elementary *and* Secondary Educational Service)

District Name and Type	(1) Enrollment	(2) Rev./Pupil (by enrollment)	(3) Per Cent Divergence Dist. Rev./Pupil to Req. Rev./Pupil	(4) Local Full Value Tax Rate	(5) Index of Local Tax Rate	(6) Presumptive Educ. Rev. per Pupil	(7) Divergence of Act. Rev. from Presumptive	(8) True Value Assessed Prop. per Pupil	(9) Exp./Pupil WADA	(10) Exp./Pupil WADA for Instruction
Nassau County										
Baldwin (I.U.F.)[a]	8,805	1,283.61	− 2.80	2.46	1.07	1,413.03	− 129.42	28,100.32	1,205.49	729.12
Bethpage (I.U.F.)	6,106	1,350.38	+ 2.26	2.55	1.11	1,465.85	+ 115.47	29,635.88	1,321.66	747.96
Carle Place (I.U.F.)	2,676	1,296.16	− 1.85	2.21	.97	1,280.97	+ 15.19	35,789.17	1,247.43	789.25
East Meadow (I.U.F.)	16,582	1,136.35	− 13.95	2.09	.91	1,201.74	− 65.39	20,054.86	1,093.55	700.18
East Rockaway (I.U.F.)	2,031	1,265.95	− 4.14	2.30	1.00	1,320.59	− 54.64	33,273.84	1,257.53	803.30
East Williston (I.U.F.)	2,170	1,786.05	+ 35.25	2.44	1.07	1,413.03	+ 373.02	52,203.14	1,698.67	1,045.71
Farmingdale (I.U.F.)	12,964	1,335.46	+ 1.13	2.81	1.23	1,624.33	− 288.87	24,881.85	1,314.27	786.58
Freeport (I.U.F.)	7,283	1,269.54	+ 3.87	2.27	.99	1,307.38	− 37.84	39,016.46	1,259.69	765.68
Garden City (I.U.F.)	4,904	1,578.67	+ 19.54	1.81	.79	1,043.27	+ 535.40	67,651.85	1,497.09	935.68
Glen Cove (City)[b]	5,245	1,263.32	− 4.34	2.19	.96	1,267.77	− 4.45	34,342.06	1,270.31	755.89
Great Neck (I.U.F.)	9,869	2,077.52	+ 57.32	2.72	1.19	1,571.50	+ 506.02	64,375.60	1,918.75	1,104.65
Hempstead (I.U.F.)	5,509	1,409.69	+ 6.75	1.73	.76	1,003.65	+ 406.04	59,600.37	1,436.48	873.78
Herricks (I.U.F.)	6,247	1,548.00	+ 17.22	2.72	1.19	1,571.50	− 23.50	30,055.68	1,466.77	825.05
Hicksville (I.U.F.)	11,871	1,372.04	+ 3.90	2.51	1.10	1,452.65	− 80.61	30,727.61	1,339.49	847.01
Island Trees (I.U.F.)	5,604	1,317.12	+ 0.26	2.86	1.25	1,650.74	− 336.62	18,653.96	1,260.34	730.73
Jericho (I.U.F.)	3,918	1,569.56	+ 18.85	2.42	1.06	1,399.83	+ 169.73	47,850.99	1,445.75	858.52
Lawrence (I.U.F.)	7,884	1,603.73	+ 21.44	2.23	.97	1,280.97	+ 322.76	53,105.85	1,551.88	889.41
Levittown (I.U.F.)[c]	17,280	1,189.37	− 9.94	2.72	1.19	1,571.50	− 382.13	16,245.96	1,175.74	733.67
Locust Valley (I.U.F.)	3,139	1,462.65	+ 10.76	1.80	.79	1,043.27	+ 419.38	62,541.72	1,444.44	821.71
Long Beach (City)	6,323	1,422.71	+ 7.73	2.21	.97	1,280.97	+ 141.74	45,064.14	1,466.95	834.59
Lynbrook (I.U.F.)	3,541	1,480.19	+ 12.08	2.17	.95	1,254.56	+ 225.63	49,916.77	1,407.65	891.41
Malverne (I.U.F.)	2,927	1,272.58	+ 3.63	2.08	.91	1,201.74	+ 70.84	40,924.58	1,336.64	824.61
Manhasset (I.U.F.)	2,776	1,759.15	+ 33.21	1.61	.70	924.41	+ 835.05	87,059.41	1,775.11	1,055.53
Massapequa (I.U.F.)	16,772	1,080.99	− 18.14	2.12	.93	1,228.15	− 147.16	22,808.93	1,065.49	659.99
Mineola (I.U.F.)	4,769	1,457.74	+ 10.39	2.17	.95	1,254.56	+ 203.18	46,018.48	1,465.41	889.43
Oceanside (I.U.F.)	10,289	1,226.45	− 7.13	2.24	.98	1,294.18	− 67.73	29,203.49	1,178.43	721.75
Oyster Bay (I.C.)	2,648	1,746.10	− 32.22	2.28	1.00	1,320.59	+ 425.51	60,689.86	1,701.42	1,070.76
Plainedge (I.U.F.)	7,247	1,349.78	+ 2.21	3.04	1.33	1,756.38	− 406.60	18,713.90	1,326.05	777.35
Plainview (I.C.)	11,122	1,438.68	+ 8.94	2.87	1.25	1,650.74	− 212.06	25,578.57	1,390.77	831.07
Port Washington (I.U.F.)	6,752	1,478.68	+ 11.93	2.30	1.00	1,320.59	+ 157.60	47,846.64	1,417.19	829.58
Rockville Center (I.U.F.)	4,343	1,497.43	+ 13.39	2.26	.99	1,307.38	+ 190.05	52,389.18	1,443.83	895.92
Roosevelt (I.U.F.)	3,770	1,245.56	− 5.68	2.29	1.00	1,320.59	− 75.03	23,662.85	1,331.47	863.35
Roslyn (I.U.F.)	4,434	1,869.38	+ 41.56	2.88	1.26	1,663.94	+ 205.44	52,419.28	1,831.84	1,083.72
Sea Cliff (I.C.)	3,525	1,625.56	+ 23.09	1.70	.74	977.24	+ 648.32	76,241.78	1,559.87	934.79

District Name and Type	(1) Enrollment	(2) Rev./Pupil (by enrollment)	(3) Per Cent Divergence Dist. Rev./Pupil to Req. Rev./Pupil	(4) Local Full Value Tax Rate	(5) Index of Local Tax Rate	(6) Presumptive Educ. Rev. per Pupil	(7) Divergence of Act. Rev. From Presumptive	(8) True Value Assessed Prop. Per Pupil	(9) Exp./Pupil WADA	(10) Exp./Pupil WADA for Instruction[a]
Seaford (I.U.F.)	4,742	1,272.59	− 3.63	2.59	1.13	1,492.27	− 219.68	22,931.00	1,201.26	729.58
Syosset (I.C.)	8,745	1,547.43	+17.18	2.54	1.11	1,465.85	+ 81.58	38,813.03	1,382.16	834.45
Uniondale (I.U.F.)	7,430	1,340.54	+ 1.51	2.14	.93	1,228.15	+ 112.39	43,857.67	1,321.43	825.31
Wantagh (I.U.F.)	5,387	1,370.46	+ 3.78	2.80	1.22	1,611.12	− 240.66	26,626.89	1,322.46	811.47
West Hempstead (I.U.F.)	3,673	1,395.07	+ 5.64	2.26	.99	1,307.38	+ 87.69	39,510.12	1,511.34	891.57
Westbury (I.U.F.)	4,724	1,473.21	+11.56	2.49	1.09	1,439.44	+ 33.77	41,730.94	1,585.14	936.54
Woodmere (I.U.F.)	5,765	1,480.66	+12.12	2.58	1.13	1,492.27	− 11.61	44,604.88	1,407.83	815.87
Suffolk County										
Amityville (I.U.F.)	4,531	1,246.21	− 5.63	2.28	1.00	1,320.59	− 74.38	30,868.52	1,241.65	757.87
Babylon (U.F.)d	2,652	1,325.88	+ 0.40	2.45	1.07	1,413.03	− 87.15	31,999.59	1,252.01	770.38
Bayport Blue Point (U.F.)	2,949	909.56	−31.12	2.60	1.14	1,505.47	− 595.91	21,304.00	1,186.57	730.96
Bay Shore (U.F.)	7,326	1,218.15	− 7.76	2.49	1.09	1,439.44	− 221.29	29,440.53	1,259.42	809.04
Bellport (Central)e	4,363	1,199.46	− 9.17	2.50	1.09	1,439.44	− 239.98	19,038.05	1,290.97	800.10
Brentwood (U.F.)	20,903	1,092.02	−17.31	2.38	1.04	1,373.41	− 281.39	12,720.02	1,108.14	655.99
Bridgehampton (U.F.)	377	1,428.94	+ 8.20	1.55	.68	898.00	+ 530.94	60,460.59	1,424.84	907.49
Center Moriches (I.C.)	1,115	1,238.13	− 6.24	1.93	.84	1,109.30	+ 128.83	22,958.31	1,232.20	816.74
Central Islip (I.C.)	6,826	1,129.74	−14.45	2.46	1.07	1,413.03	− 283.29	15,345.71	1,207.48	718.37
Cold Spring Harbor (I.U.F.)	2,170	1,899.54	+43.84	3.05	1.33	1,756.38	+ 143.16	46,816.22	1,757.02	1,036.95
Commack (I.C.)	14,172	1,257.98	− 4.74	2.81	1.23	1,624.33	− 366.35	17,916.13	1,271.62	754.24
Connetquot (I.C.)	6,308	1,459.41	+10.51	2.83	1.24	1,637.53	− 178.12	24,647.84	1,402.24	764.95
Copiague (I.C.)	6,301	1,157.92	−12.32	2.14	.93	1,228.15	− 70.23	19,692.28	1,250.53	683.32
Deer Park (U.F.)	8,164	1,065.09	−19.35	1.81	.79	1,043.27	+ 21.82	18,320.76	1,078.72	632.38
Eastport (U.F.)	592	1,189.63	− 9.92	1.54	.67	884.80	+ 304.83	21,848.54	1,153.68	673.90
East Hampton (U.F.)	1,265	1,752.06	+32.67	1.57	.69	911.21	+ 840.89	67,589.73	1,521.72	893.85
East Islip (I.U.F.)	6,812	1,199.64	− 9.16	2.14	.93	1,228.15	− 28.51	18,138.05	1,185.98	680.79
Elwood (U.F.)	4,140	1,362.64	+ 3.18	2.89	1.26	1,663.94	− 301.30	19,994.38	1,372.41	783.91
Fisher's Island (U.F.)	132	1,555.24	+17.77	.99	.43	567.85	+ 987.39	133,507.10	1,639.84	1,102.10
Greenport (U.F.)	869	1,474.98	+11.69	1.94	.85	1,122.50	+ 352.48	35,947.10	1,339.11	765.22
Half Hollow Hills (I.C.)	9,204	1,388.96	+ 5.18	2.61	1.14	1,505.47	− 116.51	31,748.30	1,341.48	697.75
Hampton Bays (U.F.)	839	1,310.50	− 0.76	1.22	.53	699.91	+ 610.59	73,793.34	1,280.86	745.48
Harborfields (Central)	5,058	1,377.49	+ 4.31	2.83	1.24	1,637.53	− 260.04	24,961.73	1,320.86	804.01
Hauppauge (I.U.F.)	6,145	1,323.25	+ 0.20	2.41	1.05	1,386.62	− 63.37	22,848.92	1,274.22	685.75
Huntington (I.U.F.)	8,542	1,452.86	+10.02	3.11	1.36	1,796.00	− 343.14	29,966.00	1,443.77	890.95
Islip (U.F.)	4,380	1,210.60	− 8.33	2.33	1.02	1,347.00	− 136.40	22,512.85	1,235.36	740.63
Kings Park (Central)	4,859	1,130.93	−14.36	2.13	.93	1,228.15	− 97.22	23,042.54	1,159.57	681.32

District Name and Type	(1) Enrollment	(2) Rev./Pupil (by enrollment)	(3) Per Cent Divergence Dist. Rev./Pupil to Req. Rev./Pupil	(4) Local Full Value Tax Rate	(5) Index of Local Tax Rate	(6) Presumptive Educ. Rev. per Pupil	(7) Divergence of Act. Rev. from Presumptive	(8) True Value Assessed Prop. per Pupil	(9) Exp./Pupil WADA	(10) Exp./Pupil WADA for Instruction
Lindenhurst (I.U.F.)	11,104	1,126.51	−14.70	2.20	.96	1,267.77	− 141.26	17,649.41	1,116.60	641.72
Mastic Beach (U.F.)	2,943	1,372.77	+ 3.95	2.41	1.05	1,386.62	− 13.85	29,662.77	1,453.41	837.96
Mattituck (U.F.)	796	1,073.78	−18.69	1.48	.65	858.39	+ 215.39	38,497.01	1,045.58	582.99
Middle Country (I.C.)	12,304	1,201.96	− 8.98	2.56	1.12	1,479.06	− 277.10	14,028.34	1,136.04	660.83
Middle Island (Central)	2,925	1,437.31	+ 8.84	2.32	1.01	1,333.80	+ 103.51	31,533.25	1,438.81	832.46
Northport (I.U.F.)	9,204	1,413.51	+ 7.04	2.51	1.10	1,452.65	− 39.14	32,356.42	1,359.77	799.41
North Babylon (U.F.)	9,683	1,191.54	− 9.77	2.53	1.10	1,452.65	− 261.11	14,533.35	1,190.48	701.47
Patchogue (I.U.F.)	8,492	1,149.56	−12.95	2.32	1.01	1,333.80	− 184.24	21,901.26	1,174.87	685.37
Port Jefferson (U.F.)	2,606	1,456.62	+10.30	1.40	.61	805.56	+ 651.06	44,505.94	1,402.16	829.99
Port Jefferson Sta. (Comsewogue) (U.F.)	3,996	1,216.63	− 7.87	2.39	1.04	1,373.41	− 156.78	17,798.82	1,246.83	734.67
Riverhead (Central)	4,236	1,154.99	−12.54	1.85	.81	1,069.68	+ 85.31	41,691.32	1,093.87	628.80
Sachem (I.C.)	9,932	1,085.41	−17.81	.91	.40	528.24	+ 557.17	19,337.03	1,063.69	600.84
Sag Harbor (U.F.)	762	1,150.69	−12.86	1.63	.71	937.62	+ 213.07	32,069.58	1,134.20	672.83
Sayville (I.U.F.)	4,290	1,209.76	− 8.39	2.48	1.08	1,426.24	− 216.48	21,511.39	1,170.47	667.27
Shelter Island (U.F.)	247	1,984.69	+50.29	1.13	.49	647.09	+1,337.60	138,222.16	1,806.95	1,037.88
Smithtown (I.C.)	11,576	1,133.60	−14.16	2.13	.93	1,228.15	− 94.55	24,650.99	1,166.29	693.96
Southampton (I.U.F.)	1,776	1,476.48	+11.80	1.13	.49	647.09	+ 829.39	82,275.81	1,427.03	832.12
Southold (U.F.)	950	1,071.53	−18.86	1.07	.47	620.68	+ 450.85	45,242.94	1,029.61	607.51
South Huntington (I.U.F.)	11,837	1,336.94	+ 1.24	2.85	1.24	1,637.53	− 300.59	21,985.65	1,338.36	786.21
Three Village (I.C.)	7,823	1,501.74	+13.72	1.43	.62	818.77	+ 149.00	26,496.02	1,537.34	807.22
Westhampton Beach (U.F.)	1,744	1,357.02	+ 2.76	2.86	1.25	1,650.74	+ 538.25	34,779.57	1,267.02	721.44
West Babylon (I.U.F.)	7,570	1,199.74	− 9.15	2.27	.99	1,307.38	− 107.64	19,718.91	1,162.76	698.32
West Islip (I.U.F.)	9,132	1,138.04	−13.82	2.54	1.11	1,465.85	− 327.81	16,749.15	1,085.82	639.38
Wyandanch (U.F.)	2,315	1,302.06	− 1.40	2.84	1.24	1,637.53	− 335.41	16,678.98	1,577.56	848.78

Independent Union Free School District.
b City School District.
c Independent Central School District.
d Union Free School District.
e Central School District.
Regional Revenue/Pupil Enrolled = $1,320.59.
Regional True Value of Assessed Prop./Pupil Enrolled = $30,517.00.

School Revenues and Tax Rates in Long Island, 1968–69
(District Offering Elementary or Secondary Educational Service)

District Name and Type	(1) Enrollment	(2) Rev./Pupil (by enrollment)	(3) Per Cent Divergence Dist. Rev./Pupil to Req. Rev./Pupil	(4) Local Full Value Tax Rate	(5) Index of Local Tax Rate	(6) Presumptive Educ. Rev. per Pupil	(7) Divergence of Act. Rev. from Presumptive	(8) True Value Assessed Prop. per Pupil	(9) Exp./Pupil WADA	(10) Exp./Pupil WADA for Instruction	(11) Per Cent of Exp. for Instruction
Nassau County											
Bellmore (U.F.)[a]	2,182	1,046.58	− 20.75	2.16	.94	1,241.35	− 194.77	46,075.95	1,171.13	633.12	54.06
Elmont (U.F.)	4,215	1,173.47	− 11.14	2.25	.98	1,294.18	− 120.71	70,465.72	1,332.06	804.48	60.39
Floral Park (U.F.)	1,860	773.65	− 41.42	1.78	.78	1,030.06	− 256.41	84,811.24	919.77	582.18	63.30
Franklin Square (U.F.)	2,484	1,276.34	− 3.35	2.34	1.02	1,347.00	− 70.66	68,539.85	1,420.23	873.40	61.50
Island Park (U.F.)	1,691	1,314.75	+ 0.44	1.20	.52	686.71	+ 628.04	75,079.40	1,865.92	1,122.71	60.17
Mepham (C.H.S.)[b]	10,260	1,368.91	+ 3.66	N.A.	N.A.	N.A.	N.A.	N.A.	1,217.42	743.69	61.09
Merrick (U.F.)	3,372	1,049.91	− 20.50	2.23	.97	1,280.97	− 231.06	50,598.26	1,163.03	670.17	57.62
New Hyde Park (U.F.)	1,838	1,106.80	− 16.19	2.09	.91	1,201.74	− 94.94	95,971.92	1,277.30	774.40	60.63
No. Bellmore (U.F.)	4,005	1,089.53	− 17.50	2.27	.99	1,307.38	− 217.85	42,119.48	1,202.81	698.16	58.04
No. Merrick (U.F.)	1,878	1,161.44	− 12.04	2.18	.95	1,254.56	− 93.12	47,424.81	1,319.53	783.33	59.36
Sanatorium (Common)[c]	9	1,415.11	+ 7.16	N.A.	N.A.	N.A.	N.A.	N.A.	N.A.	N.A.	N.A.
Sewanaka (C.H.S.)	11,826	1,523.88	+ 15.39	N.A.	N.A.	N.A.	N.A.	N.A.	1,283.65	830.25	64.68
Valley Str. Hempstead 13 (U.F.)	2,976	1,181.66	− 10.52	2.26	.99	1,307.38	− 125.72	65,936.16	1,342.88	831.27	61.90
Valley Str. Hempstead 24 (U.F.)	1,473	1,306.39	− 1.07	2.44	1.07	1,413.03	− 106.64	71,651.19	1,583.66	945.14	59.68
Valley Str. Hempstead 30 (U.F.)	1,632	1,254.15	− 5.03	2.12	.93	1,228.15	+ 26.01	94,081.48	1,443.15	917.62	63.59
Valley Stream CHS (C.H.S.)	7,353	1,438.77	+ 8.95	N.A.	N.A.	N.A.	N.A.	N.A.	1,163.16	778.37	66.92
Suffolk County											
Amagansett (Common)	177	1,955.47	+ 48.08	1.01	.44	581.06	+ 1,374.41	168,911.63	2,062.18	1,411.34	68.44
Cutchogue (U.F.)	230	1,747.33	+ 32.31	1.11	.48	633.88	+ 1,113.45	113,273.40	1,694.01	1,097.39	64.78
East Moriches (U.F.)	376	1,236.63	+ 6.36	1.54	.67	884.80	+ 351.53	45,530.25	1,357.90	973.13	71.66
East Quogue (U.F.)	300	1,965.12	+ 48.81	1.56	.68	898.00	+ 1,067.12	87,439.24	1,919.60	1,232.82	64.22
Laurel (Common)	58	2,492.53	+ 88.74	1.26	.55	726.32	+ 1,766.21	178,780.45	3,545.37	2,462.97	69.47
Miller Place (U.F.)	983	1,407.66	+ 6.59	2.07	.90	1,188.53	+ 219.13	39,177.79	1,501.97	933.48	62.15
Montauk (U.F.)	271	1,879.43	+ 42.32	.90	.39	515.03	+ 1,364.40	182,078.83	2,167.53	1,306.81	60.29
Mt. Sinai (Common)	180	2,208.86	+ 67.26	1.75	.76	1,003.65	+ 1,205.21	88,295.49	2,770.79	1,710.83	61.75
New Suffolk (Common)	28	2,043.14	+ 54.71	1.08	.47	620.68	+ 1,422.46	173,651.79	3,337.68	2,731.12	81.83
Ocean Beach (U.F.)	34	5,057.79	+ 283.00	.24	.10	132.06	+ 4,925.73	2,042,950.85	5,957.05	3,161.06	53.06
Orient (Common)	100	2,640.64	+ 99.96	1.19	.52	686.71	+ 1,953.93	177,820.00	2,975.25	1,867.22	62.76
Peconic (U.F.)	27	3,093.41	+ 134.25	1.05	.46	607.47	+ 2,485.94	261,729.78	2,778.17	1,902.03	68.46
Quogue (U.F.)	142	1,891.31	+ 43.22	.81	.35	462.71	+ 1,429.10	172,248.63	2,157.05	1,290.59	59.83

District Name and Type	(1) Enroll-ment	(2) Rev./Pupil (by en-rollment)	(3) Per Cent Divergence Dist. Rev./Pupil to Req. Rev./Pupil	(4) Local Full Value Tax Rate	(5) Index of Local Tax Rate	(6) Presumptive Educ. Rev. per Pupil	(7) Divergence of Act. Rev. from Presumptive	(8) True Value Assessed Prop. per Pupil	(9) Exp./Pupil WADA	(10) Exp./Pupil WADA for Instruction	(11) Per Cent of Exp. for Instruction
Remsenburg (Common)	141	2,814.75	+113.14	1.38	.60	792.35	+2,022.40	144,486.69	2,659.00	1,575.85	59.27
Rocky Point (Common)	1,036	1,427.77	+8.12	1.79	.78	1,030.06	+397.71	53,567.90	1,474.30	937.59	63.60
Sagaponack (Common)	12	3,985.75	+201.82	.61	.27	356.56	+3,629.19	640,263.25	3,516.54	2,755.48	78.36
Shoreham (U.F.)	508	1,988.93	+50.61	2.61	1.14	1,505.47	+483.46	44,020.23	2,073.95	1,385.52	66.81
South Haven (U.F.)	77	1,910.39	+44.66	2.20	.96	1,267.77	+642.62	61,964.69	2,621.09	1,480.20	56.47
South Manor (U.F.)	173	1,800.54	+36.34	1.82	.79	1,043.27	+757.27	63,833.46	1,875.74	1,228.51	65.50
Springs (Common)	306	1,880.42	+42.39	1.63	.71	937.62	+942.80	91,309.67	1,957.55	1,211.27	61.88
Tuckahoe (Common)	191	1,893.97	+43.42	1.34	.59	779.15	+1,114.82	111,189.44	2,035.09	1,375.79	67.60
Wading River (U.F.)	248	1,719.98	+30.24	2.02	.88	1,162.12	+557.86	49,414.55	1,999.70	1,222.38	61.13
Wainscott (Common)	12	7,598.50	+475.39	.97	.42	554.65	+7,043.85	742,577.00	9,488.93	7,993.28	84.24

a Union Free School District.
b Central High School District.
c Common School District.

Regional Revenue/Pupil Enrolled = $1,320.59.
Regional True Value of Assessed Prop./Pupil Enrolled = $30,517.00.
N.A. = Not available

Great Neck and Massapequa was $996.53. This is approximately $20,000 a classroom. There is no clear reason to expect that students in these two districts have such different interests and abilities that a $20,000 per-classroom disadvantage for Massapequa youth can be justified. Assuming these expenditure differentials were allowed to continue, the child entering kindergarten in Great Neck next year would have received, by the time of high school graduation, the benefit of $12,500 worth of educational resources (in real dollars) over those of his Massapequa neighbor.

These two districts present rather extreme examples of revenue differences (though districts listed in Part B of Table 2B.3 show even wider disparities), but the fact is that educational opportunities (measured by revenues available to purchase educational inputs) are markedly uneven on Long Island. Furthermore, the area of Long Island is sufficiently small that one would not expect revenue differences to be offset by differences in costs, i.e., in prices of educational services. For example, the salaries that Great Neck and Massapequa would need to offer in order to hire teachers of a given standard of proficiency would be approximately the same. Probably whatever cost differences exist favor Great Neck because of its reputation as an outstanding school district.

Columns 4 through 8 show to what the expenditure differences are chiefly related. The analysis is based on the standard of one-to-one relation between local tax rates on true value of property and revenues per student. A purist might maintain the following: if the local tax rate in District X is 10 per cent higher than the rate in District Y, then, and only then, should revenues per student in District X be 10 per cent higher than in District Y. For purposes of analysis, we are taking the purist's approach. Basic to this approach is the idea that local tax rates represent prices for local government services. It is a general view that people should pay for what they get, and residents of school districts who want better-than-average school programs can reasonably be expected to tax themselves locally at higher-than-average rates. The only reasonable departure from the purist's rule would be to suggest that districts populated mainly by people of low household income might be subsidized to the extent that any given tax rate in those poor districts yield a higher-than-expected amount of school revenues, thus recognizing educational disadvantage of students. In this discussion, we are not suggesting such an extreme step.

Column 4 shows local school tax rates on full value of property. Column 5 is an index of these local tax rates as compared to a region-wide tax rate of $2.29. For example, the tax rate of Baldwin in Nassau County in 1968–69 was 7 per cent above region-wide average tax rate and that of Carle Place was 3 per cent below. Column 6 is a set of "presumptive" educational revenues in each of the districts. These presumptive revenues were obtained by applying the index of local tax rates to the regional average school revenue of $1,320.59. For example, the presumptive revenue for Baldwin is Baldwin's index of local tax rate, 1.07, times region-wide average school revenues, $1,320.59, which equals $1,413.03. Because Baldwin was willing to tax itself at a rate of 7 per cent above regional average, it is presumed to be entitled to school revenues 7 per cent above regional average revenues. This is simply the result of applying the one-to-one relation between school tax rate and school tax expenditure.

Column 7 divides the school districts of Nassau-Suffolk into "winners" and "losers." Winners, noted by a plus sign, are places that have actual revenues higher than their presumptive revenues. In other words, they are places that have more money to spend on their schools than a strict examination of their local tax rate could justify. The losers, marked by minus signs, are places that have actual revenues below their presumptive revenues. In other words, the losers are districts that do not actually have the amount of money to spend on their schools that their tax rates would indicate they should have.

Winners and losers may profitably be examined against the enrollment data in Column 1 and the true value assessed property per student data in Column 8. Almost without exception winners are districts of high assessed valuations (Garden City, Great Neck, Hempstead, Lawrence, Port Washington), or are both small and rich (East Williston, Locust Valley, Oyster Bay, Sea Cliff, Bridgehampton, East Hampton, Hampton Bays). Similarly, almost without exception, the losers are districts of low assessed valuation per student (Island Trees, Roosevelt, Seaford, Bellport, Wyandanch), or districts which have valuations per student ranging up to moderate levels but which are large in enrollment (Hicksville, Levittown, Plainview, Brentwood, Commack, Lindenhurst). *The evidence appears conclusive that the present system of finance discriminates against low-wealth districts and large districts while favoring the small and rich. These discriminations are contrary to long-established aims of the state to promote equity and, incidentally, to establish efficient organization of school districts, aims which run back a half-century in time.*

The Strayer-Haig Formula and the Morrison Approach to Education Finance

THE FOUNDATION PROGRAM PLAN AND THE COLE ACT

The present approach to state aid for education dates from the work of the Educational Finance Inquiry Commission (1921–1924). The major portion of that Commission's report for New York State was prepared by George D. Strayer and Robert M. Haig; it offered what Professor Paul Mort described as the "conceptual basis" of present day practice in equalization.[17] The basic arrangement of state-local finance is often referred to as either the "Strayer-Haig Formula" or the "Foundation Program Plan." With certain technical modifications, this fiscal formula determines the allocation of school funds to local districts in the majority of states today, including New York.

In describing the situation in New York State in the early 1920's, Strayer and Haig stated:

A precise description of the basis upon which federal and state money is apportioned among the localities is an elaborate undertaking. The present arrangements are the product of a long history of piecemeal legislation. The result is chaos.[18]

The authors did provide, however, the following summary:

Almost all of the state aid is distributed primarily on a per-teacher quota basis which varies with the classification of the school district and, in the case of one of the quotas, with the assessed valuation in the district. Approximately one-half of the state aid is entirely unaffected by the richness of the local economic resources back of the teacher, and the position which is so affected is allocated in a manner which favors both the very rich and the very poor localities at the expense of those which are moderately well off.[19]

In support of their recommendation for a new fiscal arrangement, Strayer and Haig stated:

There exists today and has existed for many years a movement which has come to be known as the "equalization of educational opportunity" or the "equalization of school support." These phrases are interpreted in various ways. In its most extreme form the interpretation is somewhat as follows: The state should insure equal educational facilities to every child within its borders at a uniform effort throughout the state in terms of the burden of taxation; the tax burden of education should, throughout the state, be uniform in relation to taxpaying ability, and the provision of the schools should be uniform in relation to the educable population desiring education.[20]

This has a modern ring as far as the prescription about tax burden goes. However, it is no longer possible to believe that "equal educational facilities" represent "equal educational opportunity." It is now recognized that equality of purchased inputs does not, on the average, produce equality of education outputs among the different groups of our society. That is, the learning requirements of one student may be different from those of another, and an educational program which allows the first to develop his abilities to a high degree may be either more or less expensive than a similarly effective program for the second student.

Strayer and Haig proposed the following state-local system of support:

> To carry into effect the principle of "equalization of educational opportunity" and "equalization of school support" . . . it would be necessary (1) to establish schools or make other arrangements sufficient to furnish the children in every locality within the state with equal educational opportunities *up to some prescribed minimum;* (2) to raise the funds necessary for this purpose by local or state taxation adjusted in such manner as to bear upon the people in all localities at the same rate in relation to their taxpaying ability; and (3) to provide adequately either for the supervision and control of all the schools, or for their direct administration, by a state department of education.[21] [Emphasis added.]

The authors replaced "equal educational facilities" with the notion of "equality up to some prescribed minimum." They also suggested that some schools may be directly administered by the State Department of Education. One of the weakest points about the education system in New York State is that a school which is obviously and grossly failing to meet the needs of its students is allowed to continue under the same local district management year after year. The suggestion of Strayer and Haig which could have helped to rectify the situation has not yet been adequately pursued.

The proposal for the new system of state-local finance was set forth as follows:

> The essentials are that there should be uniformity in the rates of school taxation levied to provide the satisfactory minimum offering and that there should be such a degree of state control over the expenditure of the proceeds of school taxes as may be necessary to insure that the satisfactory minimum offering shall be made at reasonable cost. Since costs vary from place to place in the state, and bear diverse relationships to the taxpaying abilities of the various districts, the achievement of uniformity would involve the following:
>
> 1. A local school tax in support of the satisfactory minimum offering would be levied in each district at a rate which would provide the necessary funds for that purpose in the richest district.
> 2. This richest district then might raise all of its school money by means of the local tax, assuming that a satisfactory tax, capable of being locally administered, could be devised.
> 3. Every other district could be permitted to levy a local tax at the same rate and apply the proceeds toward the cost of schools, but
> 4. Since the rate is uniform, their tax would be sufficient to meet the costs only in the richest districts and the deficiencies would be made up by state subventions.[22]

An example may help clarify this plan. Suppose it is determined (just how remains a problem to this day) that a "satisfactory offering" of educational services costs $1,200 per student per year. Suppose further that the richest district has an assessed valuation of $40,000 per student. Then a levy of $3.00 per hundred of assessed valuation will finance the school program in the richest district. All districts would be expected to tax themselves at the $3.00 per-hundred rate or higher. Every district but the richest would receive some state aid. How much? Just enough to meet the deficiency between the yield of the $3.00 per-hundred levy and the cost of the satisfactory minimum offering. A district with $39,000 of assessed valuation per student would receive $30 per student from the state. Likewise, a district with only $2,000 per student of assessed valuation would receive from the state $1,140 for each of its students. All districts could provide the minimum offering, then, while paying a local tax at no higher rate than would be paid for a $1,200 program in the richest district.

The Strayer-Haig proposal was translated into legislative form by Professor Paul Mort in a report to the Special Joint Committee on Taxation and Retrenchment (the Davenport Report) in 1925. The cost of the "foundation" or basic program was estimated at $70 per student. The local contribution rate was set at 1.5 mills per dollar of the full value of property. It was further provided that no district should receive less state aid than it had formerly received. This proposal, the Cole Law, was adopted by the Legislature in 1925.

Mort's simple proposal was subject to much adjustment. The dollars-per-student measure of local district need was quickly changed into a dollar-per-teacher measure. The local contribution rate was revised periodically. Though Professor Mort had opposed the state's offer of financial incentives to local districts to spend money on schools, an incentive provision was built into the system. Districts would not receive the full amount of equalization money to which they were otherwise entitled unless they spent not 1.5 mills of local tax levy for schools, but 5 mills. Nonetheless, the main features of the plan were those outlined by Professors Strayer and Haig—and they remain in use today.

Imperfections in Application of the Foundation Program Plan

In practice, the Strayer-Haig system of state-local finance has a number of drawbacks.

a. States which use the plan, including New York, do not achieve true equalization among their school districts. That is, some low-wealth districts find it necessary to levy a local tax at a high rate to produce a low expenditure (per student) program, while at the same time rich districts are able to provide themselves with high expenditure (per student) programs at low tax rates. Thus, the relation between the quality of the school programs provided in different districts (as measured by dollar expenditure per student) and local tax effort is inverse, rather than direct. As noted in the beginning of this chapter, a body of legal experts across the country has now raised the question whether such a condition—a condition, essentially, under which the state dispenses public education services according to the wealth of districts it itself has created—is constitutionally suspect under equal protection guarantees of state and federal constitutions.[23]

It might appear strange that a fiscal device whose chief object is "equalization" fails so flagrantly to achieve its purpose. There are at least three reasons for this:

—The dollar value of the minimum educational offering is commonly set too low. Many districts, rich and poor alike, find that they must exceed it in order to provide adequate educational services. Above the value of the minimum offering (or foundation program), the inter-district differences in assessed valuation per student have their full effect. Suppose, for example, that the minimum offering is $1,200 per student and two districts, A and B, each elect to spend $1,600 per student. Let assessed valuation per student in A be $20,000 and in B, $5,000. The extra tax rate effort to advance expenditures from $1,200 to $1,600 per student is $2.00 per hundred in A and $8.00 per hundred in B. Suppose B could advance its rate only by $4.00 per hundred, taking account of local fiscal realities, and legal constraints imposed by tax limitations. B would have half the supplementary program of A at twice the supplementary tax rate.

—The local contribution rate is seldom high enough to pay for the foundation program in even the richest district. Given the very unequal distribution of nonresidential properties, the richest district (on an assessed valuation per student basis) is likely to be very rich indeed, and the mandatory local contribution rate would be very small. The result of a literal reading of the Strayer-Haig formula would mean that the state government would be paying for almost all education services. To avoid this, a higher local contribution rate is set than that which would raise the value of the foundation program in the richest districts.

—Theoretically, then, those rich districts which raise *more* than the value of the foundation program per student at the standard local contribution rate should turn that excess over to the state for redistribution to poorer districts. However, no matter how wealthy districts may be, they are granted "flat grant" per student. The result is anti-equalizing.

b. It is difficult to define differences in costs for different categories of students. For example, the state aid program does little to encourage districts to meet the needs of non-English speaking students. In the common practice of computing aid, high school students are weighted by a factor such as 1.25 and elementary students by 1.00. However, there is a growing feeling that the primary school years, not the secondary, are the points at which extra money should be concentrated. The "sparsity correction" is not really a correction for the extra costs of transport, etc., but a reward for maintaining school districts of uneconomically small size. Such examples are plentiful.

c. The widespread adoption of the so-called equalizing formulas appears to have encouraged state governments to abdicate their responsibility to deal with the hard questions in education to local districts. Much is written in the Education Law about which courses are to be taught in the various grades and about certification of teachers, but nothing definitive is said about the quality of the program offered to different categories of students. Such decisions are left to the local authorities on the grounds that local people have had their fiscal resources "equalized" and, hence, are in a good position to use their knowledge of their students to develop the programs they need. Neither assertion is fully justified. Legislative attention is distracted *from* specifying educational objectives *toward* scrutinizing proposed reforms of the equalization formula to see how many extra dollars might come to one's home district.

THE DISSENT OF A CENTRALIST, HENRY C. MORRISON

It should not be inferred that all educational economists supported the degree of localism implicit in the Strayer-Haig approach to school finance. In his book *School Revenue* (1930) Henry C. Morrison made the following points:

a. Some districts have such an ample source of taxables behind each child that with little effort they can raise abundant school revenue, while other districts can support only meager schools under a burden of taxation that eventually proves destructive to the tax base.[24] Past efforts to devise grant-in-aid schemes represent nothing more than tinkering with the problem, at best, and, at worst, bribery of an arcane type. Morrison went on to say:

> We have a childish faith in "plans." When the inevitable disillusionment comes, we conclude that the plan "did not work" and look for another. In the case of equalization schemes, the disillusionment is prone to come at a time when the original plan has been forgotten and inequality is discovered all over again.[25]

b. Education is set off from other public activities, such as street cleaning, in which the standard of performance in one local district is of relative indifference to the citizens of other neighboring districts.[26] In other words, Morrison recognized the "spillover" of benefits and costs from one local area to the next as characteristic of education (though, as we have noted earlier, local fiscal decisions may fail to recognize such spillover completely).

c. But cannot some substantial revision of the state's fiscal responsibility in education allow the local district structure to be preserved? Morrison says, not so. First, what sum of money is to be redistributed? "If the state attempted to describe equal opportunity in terms of the schools of rich residential suburbs, there would be an early exodus from the state of all movable capital." [27] Thus, it is necessary to define realistically the costs of citizenship education, and *a priori* the cost per pupil will vary from one district to another and, indeed, from one year to the next. Only the state could provide such computations. In Morrison's view, the cost per pupil would be highest in slum schools and in isolated, sparsely populated rural areas; they would be lowest in rich residential towns. As long as the concept of localism is predominant, the citizens of rich residential areas will decline to pay that volume of state taxes necessary to support adequate schools in the slums and rural regions.

> Our people still largely think of public education as a purely individual and local benefit . . . poor school districts are looked upon as poor relations at best, and perhaps sometimes not even the relationship is acknowledged. Tales of destitute townships are assimilated rather to tales of suffering in the Near East. We are sorry—and glad we do not live there.[28]

The local district structure necessarily implies that a large share of taxable income, namely that of the residents of rich towns, is removed from the support of schools of the state. It is thus necessary to place limits on the expenditures of rich districts in order that public funds shall not be diverted into what amounts to "private schools." Having gone this far, we have arrived clearly at a state system of education. Taxes for schools are to be collected where taxable income can be found in the state, and school resources are to be distributed in accordance with local requirements to provide a uniform standard of education.

d. To show that a state system of education would be beneficial, Morrison cited the analogy of a large, progressive city system that has grown large through the process of annexation. Before annexation, the small local districts surrounding the central city would likely have varied in wealth, in the quality of local leadership, and in the quality of educational services they provided. The rich unincorporated areas would maintain handsome schools and have extremely low tax rates, which is to say that taxable resources were being removed from the area-wide support of the educational services. Poor areas might have shockingly inadequate schools, and, in some cases, these inadequacies might truly reflect the educational aspirations of the residents. After

annexation, all taxables of the rich areas—and poor areas as well—
are placed at the disposal of city needs. Standards of education in the
poor areas are raised to the level of those enjoyed by the city residents
generally. Inadequacies in educational services are mitigated, and equity
of contribution is improved. Morrison put it this way:

> Localism grew out of ward lines at least . . . the poorer sections of
> practically all cities get better schools than the inhabitants of those sec-
> tions either could or would vote . . . The city district has thus acted as
> a device for equalizing schools throughout the local community. The
> Board of Education is expected to provide the schools which are needed
> in all parts of the city regardless of regional resources, and it is legally
> able to do so.[29]

The consolidation of local school districts into a state system would
presumably have the same kinds of favorable effects.

Distribution of State Money to School Districts, 1962–70, and the Diefendorf Law

This report will summarize the education finance laws in New York State
prior to 1962 and their subsequent amendments resulting from the work
of the 1962 Diefendorf Commission Report (Charles H. Diefendorf,
Chairman). It also describes changes in the flow of state funds for public
schools since enactment of the law, identifies factors associated with the
changes, and evaluates the operation of the law. It is assumed that readers
will be familiar with the basic features of the law as explained in the State
Education Department's *A Guide to Programs of State Aid for Elementary
and Secondary Education,* which deals with the computation of attendance,
aid ratios, and other factors affecting the amount of state money payable to
a school district.

SUMMARY OF 1962 LAW

The 1962 law contained a number of important technical modifications
(and introduced some new terminology), but it retained the basic features

---

* Written for this Commission by Arvid J. Burke, formerly of the State University of
New York.

Changes in Basic Factors in Public School Support Formula, 1951–70

Legislative Year	Chapters of Laws	Equalization Base (Ceiling) per Weighted Pupil	Full Valuation Tax Rate per/M for Local Share	Flat Grant per Weighted Pupil
1951	758	$220.00[a]	$ 6.20	$ 96.00
1954	142	233.00[a]	6.20	109.00
1956	718	330.00[b]	6.80	125.00
1957	682	330.00[b]	6.80	129.00
1958	930	356.40[b]	7.34	139.00
1960	444	389.40[b]	7.08	152.00
1962	657	500.00[c]	9.59[d]	180.00[c]
1965	83	600.00[c]	10.47[d]	216.03[c]
1966	767	660.00[c]	11.29[d]	238.00[c]
1968	685	760.00[c]	12.34[d]	274.00[c]
1970	122	860.00[c]	13.58[d]	310.00[c]

[a] Weighting for secondary school pupils was fixed at 24.546 by this law.
[b] Weighting for secondary school pupils was fixed at 25% by this law.
[c] Based upon operating expense under this law, no change in weighting.
[d] Based upon aid ratio under this law.

of previous laws for distributing state money to public schools. (Table 2D.1.) The distribution continued to depend largely upon two key factors: a count of pupils derived from average daily attendance and the yield of a specified tax rate applied to the full valuation of taxable real property per pupil. The basic method of determining the number of pupils was retained. As in previous laws, there was a minimum guarantee of state money per pupil as well as a maximum allowable expenditure per pupil for purposes of computing the state money payable.

In preceding laws the maximum allowable expenditure had been applied to total expenses and was referred to as the "equalization base" (often called "foundation program"). Under the Diefendorf proposals separate "ceilings" were to be applied to operating expense, school building expense, and transportation expense. However, no ceiling on the transportation expenses was enacted between 1968 and 1969. The 1962 law replaced a $389.40 maximum on total expense per pupil with a $500 maximum on operating expense for purposes of computing the state share. It replaced a minimum of $152 per pupil of state money for total expense with a minimum of $180 for operating expense purposes only.*

---

* A $200 minimum applying to total expense was retained but few districts found it to their advantage.

Operating expense was defined as the amount remaining after subtracting balances, transfers, school building expense, transportation expense, certain expenses financed by other state or federal funds, expense financed by borrowing or receipts which reduce the amount of the expenditure, or tuition payments to other districts, and certain other disallowed expenditures.

The old law had used a tax rate of $7.08 per thousand on full valuation per pupil in computing the local share. The 1962 law introduced an "aid ratio," but this can be converted into a tax rate. As may be seen in Table 2D.1, the equivalent tax rate in 1962 was $9.59 per thousand.

The reason for shifting to an aid ratio was to eliminate the necessity to revise the tax rate factor in the law whenever the full valuation per pupil was increased due to revisions in the state equalization rates or to changes in the maximum allowable expenditures per pupil. Using the aid ratio, the tax rate used to compute the local share is automatically reduced whenever the state average full valuation per pupil is increased. The rate is increased automatically whenever the maximum (ceiling) expenditure per pupil is increased.

The main policy shift entailed a reduction in the amount of state money distributed for special purposes. Within the formula itself the weightings for kindergarten and secondary school attendance were retained without change but those for adult education, continuation schools, summer schools, night high schools, and central school districts were dropped. The corrections for handicapped pupils and small districts were virtually eliminated but a new 10 per cent correction in attendance was introduced for the six largest cities. An adjustment for attendance growth was incorporated into the law.

Special aids for transportation and school buildings previously not included in the formula and limited largely to central districts, were made available to all districts with eight or more teachers. Incentives for district reorganization were replaced with a denial of size correction and school building money to small districts failing to reorganize. Special aids also were retained for school lunches, boards of cooperative educational services, vocational education and extension boards, experimental programs, educational television, and summer schools for migrants. Special aid laws for New York City, enlarged city school districts, and high tax districts were repealed.

SUBSEQUENT CHANGES

Since 1962 the major changes, other than increases in ceiling or local share (Table 2D.1) made in section 3602, have been these:

1. 1963 restored the 10 per cent size correction for the first 1,250 pupils in districts with less than $18,000 full valuation per pupil.

2. 1965 nullified the penalty provisions for small districts, restored incentives for district reorganization, and raised the size correction for the six largest cities from 10 per cent to 17.5 per cent.
3. 1966 increased incentives for district reorganization; authorized use of current budget instead of expenses of previous year for districts spending below the ceiling; restored the 10 per cent size correction in all districts based upon first 1,500 pupils, and provided additional size correction for districts with over 8,000 (60 per cent of the excess over 8,000).
4. 1967 authorized New York City to compute aid on borough basis.
5. 1968 added special aid for special educational needs associated with poverty; restored high tax rate aid, and changed payment schedule.
6. 1969 reduced amount payable in 1969–70 over the 1968–69 amount by one-eighth of one per cent of full valuation; reduced the state sharing from 49 per cent of ceiling to 46 per cent in a district with average full valuation per pupil; reduced minimum guarantees; repealed the size corrections; cut transportation aid from 90 per cent to aid ratio amount but not less than 30 per cent, all except the first effective for the 1970–71 school year.
7. 1970 avoided the application of the cuts for 1970–71; continued one-half of 1969–70 size correction for districts using new $860 ceiling (option I) and full amount for those using option II (1969–70 basic formula); enacted a ceiling on transportation expense to be reimbursed at 90 per cent, and modified provisions relative to pupil transportation generally effective for the 1971–72 school year.

STATE TRENDS: 1962

The fiscal year of the state is from April 1 through March 31, while that for school districts (with few exceptions) is from July 1 through June 30. For this reason trends will be shown on both bases. Data for the first are derived from Annual Reports of the State Comptroller and data for the second from the Annual Educational Summary of the State Education Department.

Use of the latter source produces data which differ somewhat from those published by the Division of Educational Finance. Its figures reflect the amount paid by June 30 and not the amount received prior to July 1 by a school district. The data also differ from those published by the Department of Audit and Control largely due to differences in handling expenditures from borrowed funds. The 1969–70 data available when this report was written are often based upon unaudited data. They are preliminary and subject to revision, especially those relating to New York City.

Because of the overlap in fiscal years, the impact of an increase in state funds for school districts is spread over two state fiscal years. Under the

Trends in Total School District Expenditures, Taxes
and State Money, 1961–63 and 1967–70

TOTAL AMOUNT (MILLIONS)

School Year	Expenditures	State Money	Local School Taxes[a]	Per Cent State Money Is of Expenditures
1961–62	$1,915.2	$ 800.8	$1,075.0	41.8
1962–63	2,146.3	953.6	1,161.9	44.4
1967–68	3,621.2	1,651.2	1,802.9	45.6
1968–69	4,152.4	2,016.1	1,948.5	48.3
1969–70	4,548.5	2,058.0	2,117.4	45.3
Change, 1961–70	137.3%	157.0%	96.9%	8.4%

[a] Property and nonproperty.

payment schedule in effect since 1968 nearly 42 per cent of the increase falls within the first state fiscal year and over 58 per cent in the second. Prior to that date, the percentage had been about 50 in each year. This shift accounts for the sharp 1968–69 drop in the percentage of total state expenditures going for school district purposes. (Table 2D.4.)

State Money and School District Revenues

During the first year of operation of the 1962 law, state money for school districts rose from nearly $801 million to nearly $954 million or $153 million. (Table 2D.2.) The proportion of public school expenditures financed by the state rose from 41.8 to 44 per cent.

This percentage grew to 48.3 by 1968–69, when the amount of state money exceeded school district tax revenues. The percentage dropped to 45.3 the next year when local taxes again exceeded state funds. In 1969–70 the amount of state money for school districts had increased to over $2 billion—up 157 per cent, or over $1.2 billion over 1961–62. Between 1961–62 and 1969–70, local taxes for school increased by $1.1 billion, or 104 per cent. Since expenditures rose by $2.6 billion, or 137 per cent there was some shift from the local property tax to the state base.

The average school district tax rate (on full valuation) rose steadily after 1961–62. The mean for 1962–63 was higher ($13.93 compared with $13.23 per thousand). By 1969–70 the mean had increased to $19.39— up 46.5 per cent over 1961–62. The rate increase resulted from the fact

Taxable Real Property Full Valuation and School Tax Rates, 1961–63 and 1967–70

School Year	Full Valuation (billions)	Mean Computed Full Valuation Tax Rate per Thousand[a]
1961–62	$ 80.0	$13.28
1962–63	83.3	13.93
1967–68	103.4	17.02
1968–69	108.3	18.08
1969–70	113.3	19.39
Increase, 1961–70	41.5%	46.6%

[a] Based upon total local property and nonproperty taxes (Table 2D.2) and full valuation.

that the real property tax base rose only 41.5 per cent, while expenditures increased by over three times that rate. (Table 2D.2 compared with Table 2D.3.)

Without the over $1.2 billion increase in state funds, the 1969–70 school district expenditures would have required a mean tax rate which would have been over $11.00 higher or about $31.00 per thousand on full valuation.

It is anticipated that state money for school districts will be over $273 million higher in the 1970–71 school year. It is very probable that the total amount received from the state again will exceed the amount of local

State Money for School Districts Relative to Personal Income, State Taxes and State Expenditures, 1961–64 and 1968–70 (State Fiscal Year Basis)

State Fiscal Year	PER CENT STATE MONEY FOR SCHOOLS IS OF			
	Estimated Personal Income	State Tax Revenues	State General Fund Expenditures	Local Assistance Expenditures
1961–62	1.6%	32.7%	32.9%	59.2%
1962–63	1.7	34.7	33.6	62.4
1963–64	1.8	36.4	35.4	63.0
1968–69	2.3	34.2	31.4	52.7
1969–70	2.5	34.8	33.4	55.0

school taxes. It is probable, too, that in 1970–71 the percentage of total expense financed by state money will increase, depending upon how much expenditures will have increased.

Federal money has been a relatively insignificant factor in school district finances during this period. Prior to 1964–65 it amounted to less than $20 million a year. Between then and 1970 it grew from $22 million to over $190 million, but this still amounts to less than 5.0 per cent of total school district expense. Since most of the federal funds have been earmarked for special programs they have not reduced the burden upon state and local tax bases. It is possible that they might have increased them by their demands upon staff time.

State Money for School Districts and the State Budget

The 1962–63 school year increases were not fully reflected in the state budget until state fiscal 1963–64. By then, state money for school districts represented an increased proportion of state tax revenues and general fund expenditures. (Table 2D.4.) The former increased from 32.7 per cent to 36.4 per cent and the latter from 32.9 per cent to 35.4 per cent. State money for school districts also took a higher proportion of all local government assistance from the state—up from 59.2 per cent to 63.0 per cent.

By 1969–70 all of those percentages had dropped again. Indeed, state funds for school districts represented a smaller proportion of the total local government assistance than it had in 1961–62. Its proportion of state general fund expenditures was only slightly higher. Its percentage of state tax revenues remained above the 1961–62 level.

The state in its 1970–71 fiscal year will spend an estimated $140 million more for school district assistance. Nevertheless, it is very possible that the per cent of state revenues, general fund expenditures, and local assistance used for such school districts will be lower than in 1969–70.

The proportion of estimated state personal income represented by state money for school districts has risen steadily since 1962. It grew from 1.6 per cent in 1962 to 2.5 per cent in 1969–70.

State money distributed to other local governments increased at a faster rate, however, between 1962 and 1970. (Table 2D.5.) The former went up by 222 per cent and the latter by 171 per cent. Both increased at a faster rate than state tax revenues and expenditures for state operations—up 154 per cent and 158 per cent respectively. Capital construction had the least gain—up 80 per cent.

If Tables 2D.2 and 2D.5 are compared, it will be seen that state expenditures are increasing at a faster rate than those of school districts. It is possible that this trend will continue into 1970–71, depending upon how much state expenditures fall below the appropriated amounts.

What has been happening since 1962 is a gradual shift of the financing of local government to the state. The rapid growth of local government (other

**State Money for School Districts Compared with Other State Expenditures
and State Tax Revenues, 1961–64 and 1968–70**

TOTAL STATE (MILLIONS)

General Fund Expenditures by Purpose

State Fiscal Year	Tax Revenues	Total	State Operations	School Districts	Other Local Government	Capital Construction
1961–62	$2,292	$2,275	$ 718	$ 749	$ 516	$292
1962–63	2,483	2,556	807	863	520	366
1963–64	2,672	2,743	873	972	570	328
1968–69	5,008	5,418	1,651	1,701	1,528	538
1969–70	5,821	6,067	1,853	2,028	1,660	526
Increase: Amount (millions)	$3,529	$3,792	$1,135	$1,279	$1,144	$234
Per Cent	154	167	158	171	222	80

than school districts) expenditures will continue, especially as a result of
Chapter 142 of the laws of 1970 which, beginning in the 1971–72 state
fiscal year, will share state personal income tax collections with towns,
counties, cities and villages. The fact that state money for schools has been
growing at a faster rate than state spending or school district spending reflects this shift.

Details of other programs of state money for local government in New
York State can be found in the following publication: Department of Audit
and Control, Division of Municipal Affairs, Bureau of Municipal Research
and Statistics, *State Aid to Local Government.*

School Districts and Other Local Governments

Revenues and expenditures for other local governments are published
annually by the Department of Audit and Control in its *Special Report on
Municipal Affairs.* The latest one available (April, 1971) covers the fiscal
year ending in 1968.

Table 2D.6 shows how the expenditure trends for school and non-
school functions have compared between the 1961–62 and the 1967–68
fiscal years. From the table it may be observed that:

1. Local government expenditures exclusive of those for school district
   purposes increased at a faster pace than did school district expenditures both for current operations and for capital purposes.

Local School and Non-School Revenues and Expenditures Compared, 1961–62 and 1967–68

AMOUNTS (MILLIONS)

Revenues or Expenditures[a]	1961–62	1967–68	Increase	Per Cent of Increase
Property Taxes:				
School[b]	$1,045.6	$1,735.1	$ 689.5	65.9
Non-School	1,326.6	1,899.4	572.8	43.2
Non-Property Taxes:				
School	16.7	26.7	10.0	59.9
Non-School	636.3	1,177.3	541.0	85.2
Total Local Taxes:				
School	1,062.3	1,761.8	699.5	65.9
Non-School	1,962.9	3,076.7	1,113.8	56.7
State Funds:				
School	796.3	1,621.6	825.3	103.7
Non-School	512.2	1,578.4	1,066.2	208.2
Federal Funds:				
School	14.1	181.9	167.8	1,190.1
Non-School	238.5	959.4	720.9	302.3
Current Expense:				
School	1,668.4	3,387.4	1,719.0	103.0
Non-School	2,764.9	5,682.7	2,917.8	105.2
Total Expense:				
School	2,285.1	4,247.8	1,962.7	87.2
Non-School	4,017.1	7,601.8	3,584.7	89.2

[a] Amounts differ from those reported by the New York State Education Department because of differences in accounting methods.
[b] School means school district purposes.

2. Local property tax revenues for local governments exclusive of school districts did not increase at so fast a rate as did those of school districts, because:
   a. Other governments increased their local non-property taxes more rapidly.
   b. Although other local governments did not increase tax rates so rapidly as did school districts, the amount of the increase for other purposes was almost double that for school purposes.

c. State funds for other local government were increased at double the rate for school districts.

d. Although federal funds for other local governments increased at a slower rate, the amount of increase was over five times that for school districts.

CHANGES IN THE FLOW OF MONEY

The New York State Education Department, Bureau of Educational Finance Research, has prepared an annual report on the operation of the law since 1962 both by purpose and by types of school districts. The series is now entitled *Analysis of School Finances; New York State School Districts* (for school year specified).

This section is based upon that series plus supplementary data from the original tabulations. The series employs a different definition of general aid and special aid than will be used here. In this report general aid will be identified as "unrestricted." Special aid will mean funds intended for a specific purpose or specific type of school district whether or not incorporated into the basic formula. Certain aspects of the distribution for operating expense have the characteristics of a special aid. Indeed some of them are among the special aids discontinued by the 1962 law.

Purpose Classification

It is difficult to classify state money by purpose in New York State because special purpose grants often have been incorporated into the basic structure of the support law as well as into various special statutes.

The data in Table 2D.7 differ from what has been published by both the Diefendorf Committee and by the Department. Prior to the 1962 law, special aid for central school districts was an integral part of the basic support law as well as in separate laws. Although the Diefendorf law repealed the special aid in the basic support formula, the figures used for 1961–62 were not adjusted for this factor. The table contains such an adjustment. The change increased the proportion distributed for special purposes (from 18.2 to 21.2) in 1961–62. As will be noted in the text, similar adjustments have been made for 1969–70. Thus the proportion of special purpose grants is somewhat higher than shown by official figures.

Another difficulty is that money for equalization purposes and money for local real property tax relief (regardless of property valuation per pupil) are distributed within the same formula. The amount of property tax relief is determined by fixing the tax rate for purposes of computing the local share below what would be required for equalization alone. It is accomplished to a lesser extent by guaranteeing a minimum of state money per pupil. Determining how much of the money distributed on the aid ratio

Purposes of State Money Payable to School Districts, 1961–63, 1969–70[a]

Purpose	AMOUNTS (MILLIONS)			PER CENT OF STATE TOTAL		
	1961–62	1962–63	1969–70	1961–62	1962–63	1969–70
Unrestricted[b]						
Total Expense	631.2	—	—	78.8	—	—
Operating Expenses	—	769.4	1,559.4	—	80.7	75.8
School building	37.9	116.2	192.9	4.7	12.2	9.3
Transportation	37.4	44.6	117.3	4.7	4.7	5.7
Other special purpose[c]	94.3	23.4	188.8	11.8	2.4	9.2
Total	800.8	953.6	2,058.4	100.0	100.0	100.0

[a] Totals will not correspond to amounts reported by school districts.
[b] All adjustments or reductions applying to total aid have been applied to this portion only; also, see text notes on adjustments of figures for 1961–62 and 1969–70.
[c] Includes some funds payable for private school pupils, e.g., transportation and school lunch.

See text for explanations of these totals.

basis for equalization purposes is a problem. It depends upon the definition of equalization applied. At what point on a scale of fiscal capacity is state money required to accomplish equalization?

Unrestricted and Special Purpose Money

One of the major purposes of the 1962 law was to decrease the impact of special aids. In a sense its effect was to eliminate general support entirely. Just as state money earmarked for education is "categorical" or "special" when all state money for local governments is considered, so too is state aid for "approved operating expense."

During the first year in which the 1962 law was effective, nearly 81 per cent of the total amount payable to school districts was for operating expenses. (Table 2D.7.) By 1969–70 that percentage had dropped to under 76. The proportions for other categorical aids have risen, although there was a decline during the first year. As may be seen in the table, the proportion earmarked for school building expense has increased greatly; the proportion for transportation has remained stable, and the proportion designated for other special purposes first dropped sharply and then began to grow again.

Although they continued to be earmarked, money for school building and transportation no longer were provided primarily as incentives for district reorganization. They became available to cities and other major districts.

The largest special aids eliminated in 1962 were those that had been incorporated as weightings or corrections within the basic law, namely:

Type of Adjustment	Amount (millions)
Handicapped Pupils	$28.6
Central School Districts	24.3
Enlarged City School Districts	3.9
Night High and Continuation Schools	1.4
Adult Education	1.4
Summer Schools	1.3
Total	$60.9

The other two special provisions repealed were in order of the amounts involved: high tax ($9.4) and New York City ($5.0), or a total of $14.4 million.

The foregoing total is $75.3 million, but if allowance is made for the increases in the special aids retained in 1962 (school lunch, boards of cooperative educational services, vocational education and extension boards, experimental programs, educational television, and summer schools for migrant children) the net reduction in state aid during the first year of the new law was $70.9 million. (Table 2D.7.)

The effect of many of the amendments enacted since 1962 has been to restore central school district grants which were discontinued in 1962. As in previous laws this was accomplished largely by adjusting certain components of the basic aid formula. The size correction amendment of 1963, the 1965 incentives for district reorganization, the 1966 size correction, and current budget amendments were especially beneficial to central districts as a class.

Table 2D.7 also differs from official reports because the amount of special purpose grants shown in the table has been increased by $23.0 million to reflect the estimated effect of such amendments upon the small, low-valuation central school districts where the correction equals or approximates 10.0 per cent of attendance plus the amount for current budget.

By 1969–70, special-purpose money plus operating expense aid had risen above the 1961–62 level to 24.2 per cent. The proportion for school building expense had nearly doubled.

Money for special programs increased from $23 million in 1962–63 to nearly $189 million in 1969–70. The largest increase (close to $50 million) was for boards of cooperative educational services. The second largest gain (over $39 million) was for special educational needs associated with poverty (so-called urban aid).

Among the other larger increases in special aids were these:

Aid	Amount, 1969–70 (millions)
Text Books	$17.7
High-Tax-Rate Districts	13.9
District Reorganization	13.1
Pre-Kindergarten Programs	6.3
Total	$51.0

In 1969–70 special-purpose grants and operating expense aid amounted to nearly $500 million. There were nearly as many special aid provisions as there had been in 1961–62. In addition to those retained from 1962 and cited above, special monies were appropriated for correcting racial imbalance, for the culturally deprived, for work-study programs, and for the extended school year.

Money for Operating Expense Only

State money for operating expense is distributed according to five different factors: aid ratio, number of pupils, size correction, growth in attendance, and current budget as noted in the first section. The most significant is the aid ratio basis which accounted for over 90 per cent of aid distributed in the first year of operation of the law and dropped to under 84 per cent in 1969–70. (See Table 2D.8.)

The per-pupil minimum had increased over 400 per cent by 1969–70, but still accounted for only 6.6 per cent of the total money for operating expense.

Size correction showed the greatest growth rate (over 450 per cent), but it still accounts for less than 8.0 per cent of the total. Under the law as amended in 1969 and 1970, size correction in the future will be based upon the amount paid in 1969–70, ranging between 50 and 100 per cent of that amount.

The amount distributed for attendance growth declined a little (−8.3 per cent) and it now accounts for less than 2.0 per cent of the total. Current budget was an insignificant factor in 1969–70. However, it had amounted to $31.1 million in 1968–69 due to the fact that ceiling on operating expense had been increased to $760 that year. It is anticipated that it will become more important again in 1970–71 due to the increase in ceiling to $860 per pupil.

After the law first became effective state money financed 44.2 per cent of operating expense. The percentage rose to 48.7 by 1968–69 and dropped to 45.8 per cent by 1969–70. As may be observed in Table 2D.9 state money for operating expense increased by 106 per cent between 1962 and

**Bases of Money Distributed to School Districts for
Approved Operating Expense, 1962–63 and 1969–70**

Formula Base	AMOUNT (MILLIONS)		Per Cent of Change	PER CENT OF STATE TOTAL	
	1962–63	1969–70		1962–63	1969–70
Aid Ratio Amount	$687.6	$1,344.7	+95.6	90.2	83.6
Per-Pupil Minimum Amount[a]	20.9	106.7[c]	+410.5	2.7	6.6
Size Correction	22.7	125.8	+454.2	3.0	7.8
Growth in Attendance	31.2	28.6	−8.3	4.1	1.8
Current Budget	0.0	2.8[d]	—	0.0	0.2
Total	$762.4[b]	$1,608.6[e]	+111.0	100.0	100.0

[a] This amount is the excess payable over the aid ratio amount.

[b] Amount paid (Table 2D.7) will not equal this amount due to certain transition provisions in the 1962 law.

[c] Computed on a borough basis in New York City ($74.9 million); on a city-wide basis the amount would be $61.4 million.

[d] This amount had dropped from $31.7 million in 1968–69.

[e] Amount paid will not equal this amount due to a deduction made in the 1969–70 amounts paid to certain districts.

1970 while operating expense experienced a 99 per cent increase. The proportion of total expense represented by operating expense remained relatively stable until 1968–69, dropping to 76.1 per cent in 1969–70.

According to Table 2D.10, state money for other expenses increased at a much faster rate than did that for operating expense. Between 1962–63 and 1969–70 other expense rose 120 per cent and state money for such expense rose nearly 158 per cent. In 1962–63 the state financed 47.2 per cent of the expense. By 1969–70 the percentage rose to 53.9.

Equalization Funds

The same distribution of state operating expense money to districts would result from a law which gave each district the minimum guarantee for operating expense and then equalized the difference between that amount ($310) and the ceiling ($860) using the same aid ratio or tax rate factor ($13.58). On this basis it can be assumed that at least $1.0 billion or 66 per cent of the 1969–70 amount was distributed for property tax relief

School District Operating Expense and State Money, 1961–63 and 1967–70

AMOUNTS (MILLIONS)

School Year	Expense	State Money for[b]	Per Cent Operating Expense Is of Total Expense	Per Cent Operating Expense from State Money
1961–62	$1,555	—	81.2	—
1962–63	1,739	$ 769	81.0	44.2
1967–68	2,802	1,287	80.9	46.0
1968–69	3,241	1,577	81.0	48.7
1969–70	3,459	1,584[a]	79.4[b]	45.8
Per Cent Increase, 1962–70	100.0	106.0	—	—

[a] Not adjusted as in Table 2D.7; but adjusted by $24 million to reflect its share of the $28.2 million reduction in the 1969–70 normal increase under the law.
[b] Based upon $4,355 total general fund expense.

School District General Fund Expenditures and State Money Exclusive of Operating Expense Amounts, 1961–63 and 1967–70

AMOUNTS (MILLIONS)

School Year	Expense[a]	State Money	Per Cent Expense Is of Total Expense	Per Cent of Expense Financed by State Money
1961–62	$360	—	18.8	—
1962–63	407	$184	19.0	47.2
1967–68	664	364	19.1	54.8
1968–69	761	439	19.0	57.7
1969–70	896	474	20.6	53.9
Per Cent Increase, 1963–70	120.1	157.6	—	—

[a] Based upon $4,355 million general fund expense and Table 2D.9 operating expense.

rather than for equalization purposes. This estimate is based upon multiplying the total weighted average daily attendance (3.35 million) by the minimum guarantee. This method would fix the equalization money at about one-third or about what it was under the law of 1851 when the equalization portion was explicit.

Another way of estimating the amount distributed for equalization purposes would be to determine the amount required to finance the operating expense ceiling in all districts at the tax rate that would have been required to finance it in the district with average full valuation per pupil. Using this criterion would result in the use of a tax rate of over $25.00 per thousand on full valuation. Since a rate of only $13.58 was used, it could be assumed under this method that property tax relief to the extent of nearly $12 per thousand on full valuation is being provided.

Such a rate applied to the over $113 billion full valuation of 1969–70 results in an estimate of over $1.3 billion of property tax relief funds. Under this method of estimation the equalization amount is reduced to less than 20 per cent of the total.

Both of these estimates would have to be increased for that portion of school building and transportation funds not required for equalization.

CHANGES IN THE FLOW BY TYPES OF SCHOOL DISTRICTS

For the purpose of this study school districts were grouped into three classes: (1) large cities in metropolitan areas, (2) suburban counties in metropolitan areas, and (3) non-metropolitan counties. Since school district lines are not always coterminus with county lines, school districts were assigned to counties according to official designation.

New York City and State Remainder

New York City is a consolidation of five counties. These were counties formerly divided into hundreds of school districts comparable to many districts still in existence in the surrounding suburban counties. The city has approximately one million public school pupils or about 30 per cent of the state total enrollment. In the Education Law, the city is treated as if it were a school district. Local support for schools is assumed to derive from property taxation in official state reports, although almost half of local taxes in the city are derived from non-property taxes.

State money for the public schools in New York City (Table 2D.11) was increased by $59 million or about 30 per cent during the first year of the 1962 law. In the remainder of the state, the increase amounted to nearly $93 million or less than 16 per cent.

The increases for the city during the first year resulted from two major

State Money As a Source of School District Revenues,[a] New York City
and State Remainder, 1962, 1963, 1969, and 1970

School Year	NEW YORK CITY Amount (Millions)				STATE REMAINDER Amount (Millions)			
	Total	State	Local	Per Cent from State	Total	State	Local	Per Cent from State
1961–62	$ 649.9	$196.0	$446.5	30.2	$1,270.6	$ 589.5	$ 628.5	46.4
1962–63	765.5	255.1	491.3	33.3	1,411.0	682.2	670.6	48.4
1968–69	1,395.5	549.6	772.6	39.4	2,782.5	1,437.1	1,143.7	51.6
1969–70	1,403.0	557.0	785.1	39.7	3,053.0	1,492.5	1,379.6	48.9
Per Cent Increase, 1962–70	115.9	184.2	75.8	31.4	140.2	138.3	119.5	5.4

[a] Exclusive of school lunch money.

factors: (1) the extension of state money for school buildings and transportation to the city, and (2) the 10 per cent size correction for operating
expense.

Between 1961–62 and 1969–70 the trend continued. Funds to the city
increased by 183 per cent as compared with 138 per cent for the state
remainder. Since expenditures did not go up as fast as they did outside the
city, local taxes for schools increased at a slower rate than they did in the
state remainder—83 per cent and 119 per cent respectively.

The proportion of expense financed by the state in the city grew from
30.2 per cent to 39.4 per cent in 1968–69 and stood at 39.7 per cent in
1969–70. During its first year the law raised the state share of the expenditures in the remainder of the state from 46.4 per cent to 48.4 per cent. By
1968–69 the state share had risen to over half (51.37), remaining at
nearly 49 per cent in 1969–70. (Table 2D.11.)

The increases in various types of state money for New York City are
summarized in Table 2D.12. Nearly $190 million of the increase was for
operating expense. The size correction added nearly $55 million and special
aids exclusive of transportation added another $45 million. The increase
for the latter was nearly $25 million.

Metropolitan and Non-Metropolitan Areas

New York City was granted an increase in its proportion of total state
school money between 1961–62 and 1969–70. Its share grew from less than
25 per cent to over 27 per cent (Table 2D.13). The proportion for other

Changes in State Money for Public Schools in
New York City, 1962–63 to 1969–70

Type of State Funds	AMOUNT (MILLIONS)			Per Cent Change
	1962–63	1969–70	Change	
Operating Expense	$195.6	$383.5	187.9	96.1
Growth	6.3	1.2	5.1	80.9
Building	33.8	34.1	0.3	0.1
Transportation	3.0	27.9	24.9	830.0
Size Correction	13.2	67.7	54.5	412.9
Other Adjustments	+3.6	−1.9	—	—
Special[a]	3.5	48.8	45.3	1,294.3
Total	$259.0	$555.2	296.2	114.4

[a] Exclusive of school lunch.

metropolitan areas remained about the same—about 52 per cent. The non-metropolitan areas received a reduced share—down from 23 to 21 per cent.

In 1969–70 over half (51.5 per cent) of the money was received by the New York City Metropolitan Area. Its percentage had been less than half (49.1 per cent) in 1961–62.

As may be seen in the same table, New York City had the largest percentage increase in state funds for public schools during the eight-year span. The rate of increase for other large cities upstate and for suburban counties was about the same (157 per cent) or under. Other large cities in the New York City Metropolitan Area had a gain of nearly 142 per cent. The percentage of increase in the non-metropolitan areas was 133. The state as a whole experienced a rise of nearly 157 per cent.

When the flow of state money to school districts is compared with the flow of money to other local governments (Table 2D.14) it becomes evident that:

1. The proportion of state money used for school district purposes has declined in New York City and in metropolitan counties, with the sharpest decline in New York City.
2. It has increased only in the non-metropolitan areas from under 73 per cent in 1961–62 to about 75 per cent in 1969–70.

State money for local government purposes other than schools increased by nearly 295 per cent in New York City and by over 258 per cent in its suburban counties. It grew by nearly 169 per cent in upstate metropolitan

Changes in the Amount of State Money Flowing to School Districts, by
Major Areas, 1961–62 to 1969–70 (Exclusive of School Lunch Money)

Area	AMOUNT OF STATE SCHOOL MONEY (MILLIONS)				PER CENT OF STATE TOTAL	
	1961–62	1969–70	Increase	Per Cent Increase	1961–62	1969–70
New York City	$196.0	$557.0	$361.0	184.2	24.8	27.4
Other Large Cities[a]	9.0	21.8	12.8	142.2	1.1	1.1
Suburbs[b]	183.4	466.5	283.1	157.3	23.2	23.0
NYC Met. Area	388.4	1,045.3	650.9	169.1	49.1	51.5
Large Cities[c]	45.1	115.7	70.6	156.5	5.7	5.7
Suburbs[d]	174.6	443.2	268.6	153.8	22.1	21.8
Other Met. Areas	219.7	558.9	339.2	154.4	27.8	27.5
Non-Met.[e]	183.1	426.7	243.6	133.0	23.1	21.0
State Total	$791.2	$2,030.9	$1,239.7	156.7	100.0	100.0

[a] Mount Vernon, New Rochelle and Yonkers.
[b] Nassau, Rockland, Suffolk and Westchester exclusive of large cities.
[c] Albany, Binghamton, Buffalo, Niagara Falls, Rochester, Schenectady, Syracuse, Troy and Utica.
[d] Albany, Broome, Erie, Monroe, Niagara, Oneida, Onondaga, Rensselaer and Schenectady counties exclusive of large cities plus Herkimer, Livingston, Madison, Orleans, Oswego, Saratoga, Tioga and Wayne counties.
[e] Remainder of counties.

counties as contrasted with 161 per cent for school district purposes. In the non-metropolitan countries state school district funds went up nearly 141 per cent, while state funds for other local governments went up less than 118 per cent.

The proportion of state money used for school district purposes varies markedly from a low of 34 per cent in New York City to a high of nearly 75 per cent in the non-metropolitan areas. In suburban counties the percentages are 70 for upstate and nearly 74 for the New York City area.

The data for 1961–62 state money distributed to local governments other than school districts on a state fiscal year basis were not available for large cities other than New York City. The data were not obtainable for the 1969–70 fiscal years of these local governments. However, the differing allocations for services such as health and welfare between the large cities and the counties upstate would make the data difficult to interpret even if they were available.

State Money for School Districts and for Other Local Governments Compared, 1961–62 and 1969–70 (State Fiscal Year Basis)

AMOUNTS (MILLIONS)

Area	School Districts			Other Local Governments			Per Cent of State Total For School Districts	
	1961–62	1969–70	Per Cent Increase	1961–62	1969–70	Per Cent Increase	1961–62	1969–70
New York City	$195.6	$566.9	189.3	$274.3	$1,082.4	294.9	41.6	34.4
Suburban Counties[a]	184.6	481.5	160.3	47.8	172.2	258.4	76.6	73.6
NYC Met. Area	380.2	1,048.4	175.8	322.1	1,254.6	289.8	54.2	45.5
Other Met. Areas[a]	212.1	553.4	161.0	88.0	236.7	168.9	72.6	70.0
Non-Met. Counties[b]	177.0	425.9	140.7	65.6	143.3	117.9	72.8	74.8
State Total	$769.3	$2,027.7	163.7	$475.7	$1,634.6	243.5	61.8	55.4

[a] Same counties as in Table 2D.13.
[b] Will not agree with Table 2D.13 due to differences in fiscal years.

It has been shown that the bulk of state money paid school districts depends upon a combination of two factors—weighted average daily attendance and aid ratio, with the latter being largely dependent upon the former. Special adjustments in the formula and special aids are of relatively minor significance in the state total, although any one of them may be very important as applied to particular districts or classes of districts. Each of these four factors will be examined in this section.

Weighted Average Daily Attendance

Weighted average daily attendance increased over 24 per cent outside New York City from 1961–62 through 1969–70, but less than 2.0 per cent in New York City. (Table 2D.15.) Yet, fall enrollment went up over 11 per cent in the City and about 26 per cent outside.

Other large cities in the New York City Metropolitan area (see Table 2D.16) experienced a small drop in the per cent of fall enrollment represented by weighted average daily attendance. The reverse was true in the suburban counties.

In the large cities of other metropolitan areas average daily attendance registered a decline. The per cent of enrollment reflected in the attendance also dropped. In the suburbs the trends were upward in both.

TABLE 2D.15

Changes in Enrollment and Attendance in New York City and
State Remainder, 1961–64 and 1967–70 (Thousands)

| School Year | ATTENDANCE (WADA) | | FALL ENROLLMENT | | PER CENT WADA IS OF ENROLLMENT | |
	NYC	Remainder	NYC	Remainder	NYC	Remainder
1961–62	982	1,859	1,004	1,852	97.8	100.4
1962–63	1,007	1,940	1,027	1,933	98.1	100.4
1963–64	1,024	2,025	1,046	2,005	97.9	101.0
1967–68	1,028	2,255	1,100	2,225	93.5	101.3
1968–69	1,040	2,311	1,117	2,280	93.0	101.4
1969–70	998	2,358	1,114	2,329	89.6	101.5
Per Cent Change, 1961–70	1.7	24.4	11.3	25.9	−8.4	1.1

Changes in Weighted Average Daily Attendance and Fall Enrollment by Major Areas, 1961–62 and 1969–70 (Thousands)

Area	ATTENDANCE (WADA)			FALL ENROLLMENT			PER CENT ATTENDANCE IS OF ENROLLMENT	
	1961–62	1969–70	Per Cent Increase	Increase, 1961–62	1969–70	Per Cent Increase	1961–62	1969–70
New York City	982	996	1.4	1,004	1,114	11.3	98	90
Other Large Cities	50	53	6.0	50	54	8.0	100	98
Suburbs	596	815	36.1	602	802	33.2	99	101
N.Y.C. Met. Area	1,628	1,864	14.5	1,656	1,970	13.0	99	94
Large Cities	222	216	–2.7	222	222	0	100	97
Suburbs	500	679	35.8	497	666	34.0	101	102
Other Met. Areas	722	895	24.3	719	888	23.5	100	100
Non-Met. counties	491	599	22.0	482	585	21.4	102	102
State Total	2,841	3,358	18.2	2,857	3,443	20.5	99	98

The data for individual large cities show that Albany, Binghamton, Niagara Falls, and Utica account for most of the drop in attendance. Albany had the lowest percentage of enrollment in attendance (86.9). Others with low percentages are Mount Vernon (95) and Yonkers (96). The percentages are below 100 in four other cities: Buffalo (98), Syracuse (98), Troy (97), and Utica (99). The percentages are 100 or higher in another four: Binghamton (100), Mount Vernon (103), New Rochelle (101), and Schenectady (100).

Although the percentage of enrollment reflected in the weighted average daily attendance changed very little in the non-metropolitan counties, it remained high (at 102 per cent).

Aid Ratios

The full valuation of real property per resident per pupil in weighted average daily attendance used to compute aid ratio in New York City registered

TABLE 2D.17

**Trends in Full Valuation per Pupil and Aid Ratings, New York City
and State Remainder, 1962–63 and 1970–71**

| School Year of Apportionment[a] | FULL VALUATION PER PUPIL[b] | | | AID RATIO | |
	New York City	State Remainder	State Total	New York City	State Remainder
1962–63	$31,700	$23,900	$26,600	39.2%	54.2%
1963–64	34,000	25,100	28,200	38.5	54.6
1964–65	35,200	24,700	28,300	36.6	55.5
1965–66	37,900	25,000	29,300	34.0	56.5
1966–67	39,700	25,000	29,800	32.1	57.2
1967–68	42,600	25,700	31,200	30.4	58.0
1968–69	43,300	25,800	31,400	29.7	58.1
1969–70	44,300	25,700	31,500	28.3	58.4
1970–71	45,400	26,400	32,300	28.3	58.3
Per Cent of Change, 1962–71	43.1	10.5	21.4	−27.8	7.6

[a] The full valuation used to compute aid for operating expense is that for two years prior to the year of apportionment.
[b] Based upon full valuation per resident pupil in weighted average daily attendance used to compute aid ratios.

Relative Full Valuation per Pupil[a] New York City and
the State Remainder, 1962–63 and 1970–71

INDEX NUMBER[b] (STATE AVERAGE = 100)

School Year of Apportionment	New York City	State Remainder
1962–63	119	90
1963–64	121	89
1964–65	124	87
1965–66	129	85
1966–67	133	84
1967–68	136	82
1968–69	138	82
1969–70	141	82
1970–71	141	82

[a] See Table 2D.17 for footnotes.
[b] Based upon full valuation per resident pupil.

a 43 per cent gain between 1962–63 and 1970–71. (Table 2D.17.) In the remainder of the state, the figure increased by 10.5 per cent. As a result, the aid ratio of New York City fell from 39.2 to 28.3. That for the rest of the state rose from 54.2 to 58.3.

When the full valuation per pupil figures are converted to index numbers, the City's index was 119 (state average equals 100) in 1962–63, and rose to 141 in 1970–71. The remainder of the state had an index of 90 in 1962–63 and 82 in 1969–70. (Table 2D.18.)

The changes in full valuation per pupil for major areas outside New York City are summarized in Table 2D.19. The second highest increase (after New York City) was in other large cities in the New York City Metropolitan area, up nearly 32 per cent between 1961–62 and 1969–70. The suburbs of the City ranked third with a gain of over 19 per cent, followed closely by the non-metropolitan counties (18.7 per cent). Large cities in upstate metropolitan areas experienced a small increase (two per cent), but their suburban counties showed a drop of over six per cent.

The trends differed widely in individual large cities. The aid ratios decreased between 1962–63 and 1969–70 in five: Albany (−32.5 per cent), Binghamton (−5.9 per cent), Mount Vernon (−27.8 per cent), New Rochelle (−16.2 per cent), and Yonkers (−13.0 per cent). Major gains occurred in three: Buffalo (47.5 per cent), Niagara Falls (36.7 per cent),

Full Valuation per Pupil by Major Areas, 1961–63 and 1969–70[a]

Area	FULL VALUATION PER PUPIL (THOUSANDS)		
	1961–62	1969–70	Per Cent Increase
New York City	$34.4	$49.1	42.8
Other Large Cities	33.9	44.7	31.9
Suburbs	27.7	33.0	19.1
N.Y.C. Met. Area	32.6	41.3	26.7
Large Cities	31.1	31.8	2.2
Suburbs	22.4	21.0	−6.3
Other Met. Areas	25.1	23.7	−5.6
Non-Met.	19.8	23.5	18.7
State	28.1	33.8	20.3

[a] Will not check with full valuation figures used in Table 2D.17 due to difference in method of computing and the year to which they apply. 1969–70 are preliminary.

and Troy (28.1 per cent). The increases in Rochester and Syracuse were 17.3 and 16.3 per cent respectively. The ratio in Utica changed very little.

Impact upon Flow of Funds

The differing rates of growth of attendance account for part of the changes in the flow of money to school districts between 1961–62 and 1969–70. This effect is eliminated by reducing the figures to amounts per pupil. (Table 2D.20.)

New York City experienced the highest percentage of increase (178 per cent) from $200 to $556. The next highest gain (over 166 per cent) occurred in the large cities in the upstate metropolitan areas. The third highest is that for other large cities in the New York City metropolitan area (122 per cent). Suburban counties ranked next, those upstate showing an increase of 90 per cent and those around New York City, nearly 89 per cent. The non-metropolitan areas had a growth of under 80 per cent as compared with the state average increase of nearly 119 per cent.

The table also shows how the average amounts of state aid per pupil within major areas compare with the state average both in 1961–62 and in 1969–70.

For example, the New York City figure was 71.1 per cent of the average

Total State Money per Pupil for Public School Purposes
by Major Areas, 1961–62 and 1969–70[a]

Area	AVERAGE AMOUNT PER PUPIL		PER CENT INCREASE	PER CENT OF STATE AVERAGE	
	1961–62	1969–70	1961–70	1961–62	1969–70
New York City	$200	$556	178.0	71.7	91.1
Other Large Cities	180	400	122.2	64.5	65.6
Suburbs	308	581	88.6	110.4	96.7
NYC Met. Area	239	563	135.6	85.7	92.3
Large Cities	203	541	166.5	72.8	88.7
Suburbs	349	665	90.6	125.1	109.0
Other Met. Areas	304	635	108.9	109.0	104.1
Non-Met.	399	716	79.5	143.4	117.4
State Average	279	610	118.6	100.0	100.0

[a] 1969–70 figures are preliminary.

in 1961–62 as contrasted with 91.1 per cent in 1969–70. Whereas large cities in upstate metropolitan areas received 72.8 per cent of the state average in 1961–62, they were paid 88.7 per cent of it in 1969–70. The change was not so marked for other large cities in the New York City metropolitan areas. Upstate suburban counties retained part of their advantage (109 per cent of the state average), but those adjacent to New York City lost ground, down from over 110 per cent of the average to under 97 per cent. The non-metropolitan areas lost the most ground— from 143 per cent to over 117 per cent in 1969–70. Yet, this was still the highest excess over the average of the various areas.

When districts outside New York City are classified according to full valuation per pupil, the highest percentages of increase in state money per pupil from 1961–62 to 1969–70 are found in districts with above average full valuation per pupil. As shown in Table 2D.21, the highest gain (123 per cent) is in the group with a valuation per pupil between $28,000 and $36,000. The next highest (110.5) is in the group having between $36,000 and $44,000. The third highest percentage, 106.4, is found in the districts having between $20,000 and $28,000 per pupil. The lowest percentage is in the group with $44,000 or over of full valuation per pupil.

The most significant fact revealed by Tables 2D.20 and 2D.21 is that

State Money per Pupil According to Full Valuation per Pupil,
1961–62 and 1969–70 (Exclusive of New York City)

| Full Valuation per Pupil | TOTAL STATE MONEY PER PUPIL | | PER CENT OF INCREASE |
	1961–62	1969–70	1961–70
− $12,000–12,000	$462	$896	93.9
12,000–19,999	399	770	93.0
20,000–27,999	314	648	106.4
28,000–35,999	248	554	123.4
36,000–43,999	211	445	110.5
44,000+	224	391	74.6
State (Except NYC)	320	634	98.1

aid per pupil increased at a more rapid rate than did the increase in ceiling on operating expense between 1962 and 1970.

Between 1962 and the 1969–70 school year the ceiling on operating expense was increased from $500 to $760, or 52 per cent. Thus, the per pupil increase in state money per pupil between 1962–63 and 1969–70 in any district or class of districts would have been 52 per cent assuming no change in the aid ratio or in various special provisions affecting the amount of money distributed per pupil. Any class of districts having increases above 52 per cent experienced higher aid ratio or received enough under other provisions to make up the difference.

The fact that New York City had the highest per cent of increase in spite of its decrease in aid ratio is explained by changes in size correction and other special provisions. State money financed 39.6 per cent of the City's public school outlays in 1969–70 as compared with 30.8 per cent in 1961–62. In the remainder of the state, the percentage rose from 48.3 in 1961–62 to 50.1 in 1969–70.

The decline in aid ratio would have meant a loss of nearly $100 million in state money for school building and operating expenses in the City between 1962–70 if it had not been for the flat grant and the size correction in the law. The potential flat grant was increased by $94 million and the size correction by $54 million. Nevertheless, the aid ratio automatically transferred the $100 million to districts outside the City and made possible the increase in state sharing. (Table 2D.17.)

The provision for use of borough data in computing aid ratios in the City added over $100 million to the aid ratio portion of its state money and over $10 million to its flat grant portion. This provision, along with other changes in the formula, account for over $220 million of the City's increase from 1961–62 to 1969–70. Other special provisions added another $70 million.

Special Provisions

It is obvious from the foregoing that special provisions have greatly affected the flow of money to New York City since 1962. (Tables 2D.22 and 2D.23.)

Special provisions account for over $620 million of the money distributed in 1969–70. New York City received $172 million or 27.6 per cent of this amount. The City was paid nearly 54 per cent of the size correction and 32.3 per cent of the money for special programs, but it received less than 24 per cent of money for transportation and less than 18 per cent of that for school buildings. It was allocated less than two per cent of other special funds or adjustments. (Table 2D.22.)

When the data are analyzed by major areas outside the City (Table 2D.23), it can be seen that other larger cities received a relatively small proportion of such funds. Over 45 per cent was paid to districts in suburban counties and over 21 per cent to those in non-metropolitan counties.

TABLE 2D.22

Additional Funds Payable[a] under Special Provisions, New York City and State Remainder, 1969–70 (Exclusive of School Lunch Money)

AMOUNTS (MILLIONS)

Special Provisions	New York City	State Remainder	Total	Per Cent to City
School Building	$34	$159	$193	17.6
Special Programs[b]	41	86	127	32.3
Size Correction	68	58	126	53.9
Transportation	28	89	117	23.9
Other[c]	1	57	58	1.7
Total	$172	$449	$621	27.6

[a] Will not equal amounts paid due to other factors, particularly the 1969–70 temporary reduction.
[b] Includes boards of cooperative educational services, urban education, textbooks, pre-kindergarten, racial imbalance and other small programs.
[c] Includes corrections for growth, high tax and current budget and incentives for district reorganization.

Additional Funds Payable[a] under Special Provisions by Major Areas, 1969–70 (Exclusive of School Lunch Money)

Area	AMOUNTS (MILLIONS)						Per Cent of State Total
	School Buildings	Special Programs	Size Correction	Transportation	Other	Total	
New York City	$ 34	$ 41	$ 68	$ 28	$ 1	$172	27.6
Other Large Cities	3	2	1	0[b]	0[b]	6	1.0
Suburbs	51	31	11	29	24	146	23.4
N.Y.C. Met. Area	88	74	80	57	25	324	52.1
Large Cities	8	9	8	3	0[b]	28	4.5
Suburbs	50	23	20	30	15	138	22.3
Other Met. Areas	58	32	28	33	15	166	26.8
Non-Met.	47	21	18	27	18	131	21.1
State	$193	$127	$126	$117	$58	$621	100.0

[a] Will not equal the amount actually paid because of other factors.
[b] Under $500,000.

Over half the money for school buildings, transportation, growth, and high tax goes to the suburban group. Over half the size correction goes to the largest six cities.

If Tables 2D.13 and 2D.23 are compared, it can be seen that the distribution of money on the basis of special provisions closely follows the pattern for that distributed upon the basis of pupils and aid ratios by major areas outside New York City. Of course, certain individual districts within these areas deviate from the central tendencies.

OBSERVATIONS ON THE FLOW OF STATE FUNDS SINCE 1961–62

There is no single basis for evaluating as a whole a multi-purpose system of distributing state money to school districts such as the one in New York State. The proper standard for special purpose or special program (categorical) provisions is the attainment of a purpose or a program assuming that either is what public policy demands in terms of conditions at the time.

The problem of appraising the equalization objective is finding a definition of equalization that will be generally acceptable. The law assumes that equalization means giving each district an equal sum of money per pupil and equalizing the property tax rates required to raise this uniform amount. Many question this definition and would not evaluate the objective in terms of such a definition.

Others judge the whole system solely in terms of their definitions of equalization. Yet, the bulk of the funds are not distributed for equalization purposes. The primary objective in this state has been to shift an increasing proportion of the cost of public education from the local property tax base to the state tax base.

This objective, however, has been implemented within the framework of a law designed for the equalization purpose using the same key factors: the number of pupils and the full valuation of taxable real property per pupil. Hence, a critical issue in evaluation is the validity of these two in achieving the intended purposes.

Finding a Criterion

Two criteria often applied in evaluating state distribution of school money are based upon questionable definitions of equalization. These two criteria are the extent of equalization attained in (1) expenditures per pupil and (2) school tax rates.

The relative equality of expenditures per pupil among schools and school systems can be a misleading criterion for a number of reasons: (1) It presumes that equality of expenditures is desirable. Yet, if attention is centered upon results achieved under given conditions, it would be reasonable to assume that it will cost more to attain a specified education result under the most unfavorable social and economic conditions. (2) The special program funds provided by the federal and state governments by their very nature would tend to disequalize expenditures per pupil. (3) As long as districts are given discretionary power over spending and as long as some are willing to impose heavier taxes upon themselves than others, there will be differences in expenditures per pupil. (4) As long as the school district tax system is allowed to exist, there will be resource inequalities which become reflected in expenditure differences.

A criterion based upon school district property tax rates is just as questionable. (1) As long as school districts have any discretion in spending for education, differing wants or standards will be reflected in varying tax rates. (2) School districts have different property tax bases affecting their ability to shift taxes to incomes outside their boundaries which affects the level of school tax rates. (3) Legal restrictions on the property tax rates for school purposes vary considerably within the state, with school districts in certain cities having the least taxing powers. (4) Other demands upon the property tax vary among localities and influence the level of school property tax rates. (5) School district property tax rates reflect both economic and political conditions. Some of the differences are attributable to political factors, such as the age and occupational composition of the population or the degree of public interest or participation in decisions on tax rates.

The tests that will be applied in this section are global. The first test assumes a completely state-supported school system in which the only problem is to predict the budgetary requirements of individual schools or school system in the state. How well does weighted average daily attendance reflect basic essential budgetary requirements (what educators call "needs" and economists refer to as "demands")?

The second test assumes that there is local taxation for schools and that the problem is to predict taxable resources available in one place relative to others. In this test the predictions yielded by aid ratios between 1962 and 1970 will be related to other trends since then. Do the ratios yield estimates of fiscal capacity consistent with what social and economic developments would cause one to anticipate?

The Count of Pupils

According to the attendance factor used in the distribution formula, New York City and most other large cities in the state would appear to have a smaller proportion of the essential school costs to be financed in the state than they had in 1961–62. Yet it has been shown that attendance makes the proportion lower than would enrollment.

Substitution of enrollment for attendance would alleviate somewhat the limitation of the count used, but would not be of sufficient magnitude to correct the real lack of validity of the measure. Test results published by the State Education Department indicate that the difficulties of achieving learning in large cities have been growing and that the most serious difficulties have been concentrated in these cities. In terms of the changing urban environment and the increasing demands upon urban schools, it is unreasonable to assume that their share of state total basic school budgets has declined since 1962. Estimates based upon attendance alone are misleading. The probability is that the share of large cities as determined in 1961–62 was too small. It did not reflect the differing environments or school conditions among neighborhoods existing in 1962. The same unrealistic assumption was applied then as was applied in 1969–70, namely that the education of a pupil required the same financial investment in all neighborhoods regardless of the conditions surrounding the home and school.

The state has adopted two types of corrections for the foregoing probability of error: (1) the size correction and (2) special provisions for urban education. Of the two, size correction is the most inadequate because it treats New York City and five very much smaller cities as if they had the same school conditions and because it does not extend the same treatment to other large cities and urban areas with similar conditions.

The major difficulties with the urban education provision is that it does not apply to smaller districts with acute problems and was designed to distribute a predetermined sum of money rather than assess the total requirements of the school systems involved.

Size correction has been repealed and should not be restored. However, at least the same amount of money should be distributed to large cities and other districts with similar problems as determined by more refined indicators of excess costs than are now contained in the urban education law with due regard to funds available under Title I of the Elementary and Secondary Education Act as well as other federal or state funds provided for the same cost factors.

If attendance or enrollment is retained for purposes of distributing state funds, it might be possible to overcome some of their weaknesses through a refinement of the weightings used—for example, adding a weighting for pupils with serious learning difficulties as revealed by diagnostic test results or socio-economic indicators.

Aid Ratios

The use of the pupil count to determine the ability of localities to support education is probably the greatest weakness in the law. It shows New York City to be very rapidly gaining capacity to support schools at the very time that it has been confronted with mounting welfare costs, out-migration of population and resources, and high and rapidly rising total municipal taxes.

Not only has the aid ratio shown New York City to have had a very large increase in fiscal capacity since 1962, but it also shows the City to be substantially above average relative to the rest of the state in its capacity to impose taxes for school support.

This latter conclusion is very doubtful. On the basis of full valuation per capita New York City is close to the state average in 1970. If allowance is made for the heavy demands made upon its resources arising from poverty and related problems, it probably is below average. In terms of income received by its residents and retail sales to residents, the same relative ranking would tend to hold true.

New York City has the highest average total real property tax rates of all the major areas studied. Including non-property taxes, its local taxes are substantially higher than the average for other cities, suburban areas or non-metropolitan areas. Resources available for school support, according to the aid ratio, really are not available. Services such as highway construction transferred to the state by areas outside the City have not been transferred in New York City. New York cannot transfer health and welfare costs to the counties, as have other large cities. In terms of the allocation of governmental functions and taxing powers, the City is not comparable to any other city or school district in the state. Yet, it is treated as another school district in law.

New York City is a consolidation of five counties (300 square miles) in which school districts of the type found elsewhere in the state were abolished over seventy years ago. Since 1898 the City has had to perform the equalization function assumed by the state in other counties which are still divided into school districts. Its four suburban counties with fewer public school pupils had 186 school districts in 1969–70. Over 70 of these covered areas with fewer than five square miles. About 60 per cent of them were under ten miles square; and over 80 per cent under 15 square miles.

One of the most defensible provisions added to the law is allowing the City to compute aid ratios on a borough basis. It is but a step in the direction of having the state do within the City what it had been doing within counties outside the City—that is to equalize school support in the sub-areas where poverty is concentrated.

When all special provisions are considered, the City has been treated more in accord with its true fiscal capacity than it would have been if the aid ratio provision had been allowed to operate by itself. How equitably it has been treated will depend upon how its additional school costs have been estimated after allowing for federal funds received for the same purposes. Yet, when special provisions are reviewed as a whole, they may prove to be an expensive way of solving the City problem. For example, the flat grant, so essential to the City, also benefits small area, high resource, low tax districts.

The fact that the City in 1969–70 received over 66 per cent of state money distributed for non-school purposes also is relevant in making a judgment on its proper share of the school money.

It is questionable whether New York City, with its five counties and no school districts of the kind found in other counties, should continue to be treated as a school district in school finance laws. It might be well to make the first division of state school funds between New York City and the rest of the state in terms of (1) total demands made on its resources as compared with the rest of the state with due regard to such factors as total federal and state money for other governmental functions and differences in the allocation of functions between the state and local governments and (2) the relative budgetary requirements for public elementary and secondary education within the two large sections.

A major consequence of the aid ratio feature has been to increase the per cent of state sharing outside the City of New York. A major policy shift was made without legislative action. It was accomplished through the mechanics of the law. Another side effect of the change in sharing outside the City was to reduce the impact of rising full valuation per pupil upon aid ratios in other large cities in the state. For example, the state sharing in Buffalo, the next largest city, actually increased. Nevertheless, the pattern has been the same generally throughout the state. The aid ratios tended to show large cities gaining in fiscal capacity at a faster rate than their suburbs. In terms of the out-migration of population and resources to suburbs, this prediction is probably unrealistic.

If trends in fiscal capacity since 1962 revealed by aid ratios are subject to doubt, so too are the proportions of fiscal capacity assigned to cities, suburbs and other areas. If the count of pupils failed to show the relative financial requirements, the aid ratios from the beginning would have failed to show relative fiscal capacities.

The limitations implicit in the use of aid ratios arise from the attempt to separate resources to finance education from resources to finance all local governmental services. What has been happening since 1962 (as well as before) is that younger families with children have been migrating to the suburbs. The cities have tended to attract single persons, the poor (and their children), the older citizens especially those on welfare), and the transients.

Total population is not a good indicator of total public demands upon resources, because a population with a high proportion of poor will have a higher demand than will a population with a high proportion of rich. Yet, in terms of population, large cities tend to have less full valuation per capita than do their suburbs. .

Although it is essential to estimate relative fiscal capacity of local governments in terms of total demands upon their resources, to do so renders evaluation of the laws very complicated. These difficulties include such factors as differences in the allocation of governmental functions among local units (e.g., county and city), federal and state funds for all local functions, differences in taxing and borrowing powers for various purposes, differences in the demands for various services among local units, and public policy differences over what services are to be financed publicly or privately.

Such an undertaking is beyond the scope of this study. The data presented here do indicate that if the law had been allowed to operate without special provisions, the error in the distribution between large cities and suburbs generally would have been much greater than it has been. The study also indicates that any measure of fiscal capacity derived from any pupil count will not produce equity between large cities and their suburbs. Cities and school districts within all metropolitan areas may have to be treated in the same manner as that suggested for New York City.

Impact of Low- and Middle-Income Housing on School District Finance

The dependence on the property tax by both school districts and municipalities has resulted in strenuous efforts by these governments to keep out new construction which is tax exempt or which has a taxable value per occupant considerably below the local average. The introduction of these properties into a locality will result, it is said, in an increase in governmental costs in excess of the tax revenue realized from the new structures. The level of government services per capita or per student will deteriorate unless taxes are increased. Thus, those localities which are rich in property have zoning laws designed to keep out all property which cannot "pay its own way" in property taxes.

Table 2E.1 contains a fiscal model of a school district and a co-linear municipality. While the structure of this model is a drastic simplification of reality, it does indicate the basic direction in which a change in property values will influence the municipal/school district fiscal position. The major conclusion drawn from an examination of this model is that, at least for small influxes of such low tax value properties, tax rate increases are neither inevitable nor necessarily burdensome. The explanation for this deviation from the usual doctrine lies in two general assumptions which we have incorporated in the model.

COSTS

While an influx of low tax value property will not pay its own way and thus will increase total governmental costs because of the need to provide services for the new residents inhabiting that property, the cost of each *additional* resident or student will be less than the existing average cost per resident or pupil. This is so because (by assumption) the increase in numbers to be served by the municipality or school district is small enough and the previously unused capacity great enough that no additional capital costs are incurred. The increase in operating expenditure is limited to those items which directly serve the resident or student: in the school district these items include teachers, equipment and textbooks, but not such items as debt service, Board of Education, central administration and some undistributed costs which will not change with small increases in student population. We have arbitrarily put the marginal costs of education (i.e., the cost of educating an additional student) at 75 per cent of the pre-existing average cost per pupil, which includes all the fixed costs noted above.

For the model municipality we assume that a two-to-one relationship exists between average and marginal costs—in other words, each additional resident imposes a cost just one-half as great as the pre-existing average cost per resident.

The major revenue compensation for the reduction in average property valuation per student is the increased state aid to the school district based on enrollment growth and other factors. The model includes three of the many types of aid for education: general operating aid, high tax aid, and growth aid. Most of these aid monies are made available only one or two years after the change in school district wealth or numbers takes place. The model therefore traces the year-to-year changes in state aid revenues for a period of two years after the initial influx of property and new residents.

Another possible source of revenue comes from in-lieu payments made by the Urban Development Corporation (UDC) for properties it constructs. These properties are tax exempt but the UDC pays an amount equal to 10 per cent of the total annual shelter rental of the property. This total is divided between the school district and municipality in a ratio equal to the ratio of property tax rates of each unit of government. Such in-lieu payments never fully compensate for the loss in taxes due to the tax exempt status of these properties, but they serve to mitigate any tax rate increase.

Any part of total cost which is not covered by state aid or by in-lieu payments from UDC properties must be made up by local property tax revenue.

The model compares the impact on school district or town finances of a UDC-financed project and an apartment house identical to the UDC project in all respects except that it is privately financed. Everything else is identical in the two situations: both apartments contain 125 units which house 500 occupants, of whom half, or 250, are children of school age. While a public project might be expected to have a higher percentage of school-age children than an apartment house, this possibility is overlooked here in order to focus solely on differences arising from the tax exempt status of the former.

Following is a year-by-year analysis of the impact of new property on school district finances. The fiscal model on which this discussion is based as well as data generated by it are presented in Figures 2E.1 and 2E.2.

We start with Year 0, the year before the new apartment is built. For the subsequent three years, the property-induced changes are discussed both under the UDC and private financing assumptions.

YEAR 0 (BEFORE THE NEW PROPERTY IS BUILT)
The town has a population of 10,000, of which 2,000 are students in the

Impact of a Fiscal Model of a School District of the Introduction of an Apartment Building under Public (UDC) and Private Financing

	UDC PROJECT BUILT YEAR 1				APARTMENT HOUSE BUILT YEAR 1			
	Year 0	Year 1	Year 2	Year 3	Year 0	Year 1	Year 2	Year 3
DEMOGRAPHIC DATA								
Population	10,000	10,500	10,500	10,500	10,000	10,500	10,500	10,500
Change in Population from Last Year	0	500	0	0	0	500	0	0
Weighted Average Daily Attendance	2,000	2,250	2,250	2,250	2,000	2,250	2,250	2,250
Change in WADA	0	250	0	0	0	250	0	0
WADA per Capita	.200	.214	.214	.214	.200	.214	.214	.214
FINANCIAL DATA								
Full Value of Taxable Property	$64.000M.	$63.900M.	$63.900M.	$63.900M.	$64.000M.	$65.875M.	$65.875M.	$65.875M.
Full Value per WADA	32,000	28,400	28,400	28,400	32,000	29,278	29,278	29,278
State Aid Ratio	.490	.490	.490	.547	.490	.490	.490	.533
Equilibrium Property Tax Rate	3.993	4.190/100	4.178/100	4.008/100	3.99	4.111	4.096	3.970
School District Rate	2.430	2.600/100	2.587/100	2.416/100	2.43	2.555	2.540	2.414
Municipal Rate	1.563	1.590/100	1.591/100	1.592/100	1.56	1.556	1.556	1.556
SCHOOL DISTRICT OPERATING COSTS								
Average Cost Per WADA	$1,200	$1,167	$1,167	$1,167	$1,200	$1,167	$1,167	$1,167

Marginal Cost Per WADA	900	875.25	875.25	900	875.25	875.25	875.25
Total Cost	2.400M.	2.625M.	2.625M.	2.400M.	2.625M.	2.625M.	2.625M.
SCHOOL DISTRICT REVENUE							
State Aid	$.843M.	$.958M.	$1.067M.	$.843M.	$.948M.	$.952M.	$1.035M.
Operating Expense Aid	.843M.	.948M.	1.058M.	.843M.	.843M.	.948M.	1.031M.
Growth Aid	0	0	0	0	.105M.	0	0
High Tax Aid	0	9,720.00	9,392.40	0	0	3,865.50	3,703.50
Property Tax Revenue	1.557M.	1.653M.	1.544M.	1.577M.	1.677M.	1.673M.	1.590M.
In Lieu Payments (from UDC)	0	13,961.25	13,941.00	0	0	0	0
Total Revenue	2.400M.	2.625M.	2.625M.	2.400M.	2.625M.	2.625M.	2.625M.
MUNICIPAL OPERATING COSTS							
Average Cost Per Capita	$100	$95.24	$95.24	$100	$95.24	$95.24	$95.24
Marginal Cost Per Capita	50	47.62	47.62	50	47.62	47.62	47.62
Total Municipal Cost	1.000M.	1.025M.	1.025M.	1.000M.	1.025M.	1.025M.	1.025M.
MUNICIPAL REVENUES							
Property Tax	$1.000M.	$1.0164M.	$1.0175M.	$1.000M.	$1.025M.	$1.025M.	$1.025M.
In Lieu Payments (from UDC)	0	8,538.75	8,559.00	0	0	0	0
Total Revenue	1.000M.	1.025M.	1.025M.	1.000M.	1.025M.	1.025M.	1.025M.

NOTE: Total in lieu payments from UDC = 10% of shelter rents = 10% of 12 months × 125 families × $150/mo. = 10% of $225,000 = $22,500. This is divided between town and school district in proportion to the relative property tax rates of each unit.

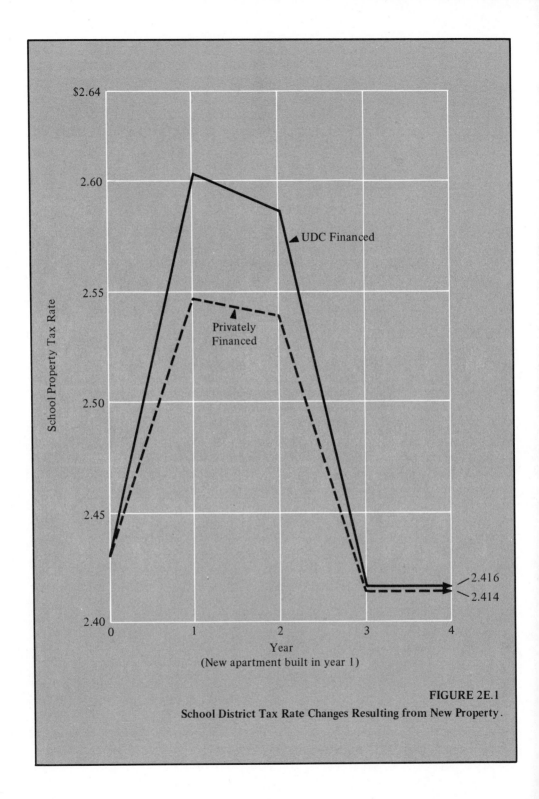

FIGURE 2E.1

School District Tax Rate Changes Resulting from New Property.

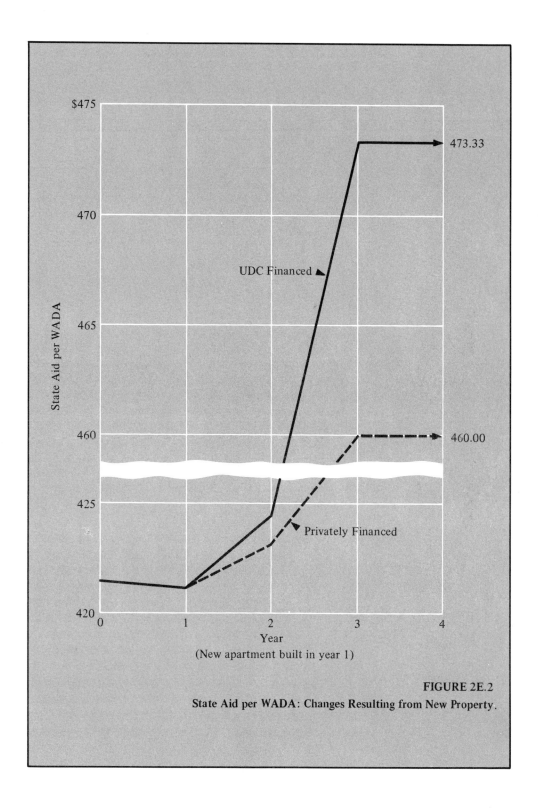

FIGURE 2E.2

State Aid per WADA: Changes Resulting from New Property.

school system. An average of $1,200 per WADA per school year is spent on education—both current and capital expenditure: The total school district budget is therefore $2,400,000, of which $843,000 is financed through state operating-expenses aid, and $1,557,000 via the property tax (lines 16 and 19 on Table 2E.1). The latter gives rise to a $2,43/100 school district tax rate (line 10). Full property value equals $64,000,000 —or about $32,000 per WADA—the statewide average.

YEAR 1 (THE NEW PROPERTY IS BUILT)
UDC—Built January 1
The UDC project brings in 500 additional residents, of whom 250 are children of school age. The additional school district cost is equal to $900 per additional student—or about $25,000 in all. (We assume that these 250 additional students do not constitute a large enough increase to warrant additional capital expenditure—hence their "marginal cost" is less than the previous "average cost per WADA.") Total school district expenditure rises to $2,625,000.

The only increase in state aid during the year of construction is growth aid. This aid is equal to the per cent increase in WADA (in our case 250/100, or 12.5 per cent) multiplied by the previous year's operating-expense aid. Therefore, growth aid in Year 1 equals .125 × $843,000, or $105,000. This is an addition to the operating-expense aid of $843,000 —the same as Year 0's.[30] Hence, total state aid in Year 1 amounts to $105,000 plus $843,000 = $948,000.

In-lieu payments to the school district and town paid by UDC are equal to 10 per cent of the annual shelter rents of the project. We assume that each of the 125 units yields a $150/month rental, hence the total in-lieu payments equal: 10% of 125 units × $150/unit/month × 12 months = 10% of $225,000 = $22,500. This sum is divided between school district and town in proportion to the ratio of the previous year's tax rates; hence, the school district gets (2.43/3.99 = 60.9%) of the $22,500, or $13,702.50.

The remainder of school district costs, $1,663,000 ($2,625,000 minus $948,000 state aid minus $13,702.50 in lieu), is financed via property taxes. The school tax rate is determined by dividing this amount by the full value figure of $63,900,000 ($1,663,000/$63,900,000) which gives us a rate of $2.600/$100 full value. This is $.17/$100 or about 7 per cent higher than in Year 0.

Note that the district full value has actually declined by $100,000 since Year 0: This decline represents the value of the land on which the project is built and which is no longer "taxable for school district purposes."

Private Apartment—Built
The increase in total school district costs and state aid is identical to that under the UDC project.

There are, of course, no in-lieu payments when the apartment is privately financed; the property is fully taxable. To arrive at an appropriate full-value figure for this apartment, the traditional technique of letting capital value equal 100 times total monthly rental is used. In this case, full value becomes 100×125 units $\times \$150$/month $= \$1,875,000$. Total school district full value equals $65,875,000 in Year 1, an increase equal to the value of the apartment.

To calculate the school tax rate, we divide that part of total cost not covered by state aid ($2,625,000 minus $948,000, or $1,677,000) by our full value of $65,875,000; we get a rate of $2.555 per $100 full value. Although this rate is higher than in the previous year, it is less than the rate experienced under a UDC arrangement.

YEAR 2 (THE YEAR AFTER THE NEW PROPERTY IS BUILT)
UDC Financed
There is no growth aid now, but the operating-expenses aid has increased to $948,000, reflecting the 12.5 per cent increase in district WADA (lagged by one year). In addition, the district now receives high tax rate aid in an amount equal to $9,720,000. (See Table 2E.1, line 18.) This aid is given, in our model, to those districts with tax rates exceeding $2.50 in the previous year. The formula for determining exactly how much aid is given to high tax districts is rather complicated, as is seen in the Table.

In-lieu payments increase by about $260 to $13,961.25. This increase reflects the increase in the school district tax rate relative to the municipal rate in Year 1.

The full-value tax rate in Year 2 is found by subtracting from total school costs ($2,625,000) the operating-expenses aid, high tax aid, and the in-lieu payments, and dividing this difference by the $63,900,000 full value figure. We get a rate of $2.587 per $100 in Year 2. This is about $.015 less than Year 1's rate, due mainly to the increase in operating-aid WADA.

Privately Financed
Operating-expenses aid is the same this year as under UDC financing— $948,000. The high tax aid is $3,865.50—or about $6,000 less than under the UDC program. This difference is due to the lower school tax rate in Year 1 under the privately financed arrangement.

Although the school property tax levy, under private financing, $1,673,000, is more than that under UDC financing, the resultant tax rate is $2.54/$100 or almost $.05/$100 less than under the UDC situation.

YEAR 3
UDC Property
This year sees a major increase in operating-expenses aid to $1,058,000 resulting from the increase in the aid ratio to .547. The increase in this

matching ratio is attributable to the decrease in full value per WADA which occurred in the year the UDC apartment was built, but was un-recorded until the Board of Equalization and Assessment's sample survey of this year. As a result of this large increase in state aid, school district tax rates actually drop below the rate which existed in Year 0. The tax rate is now $2.416/$100, about $.015/$100 less than in Year 0.

Privately Financed
The state aid ratio is increased even when the apartment is fully taxable since the apartment's full value per occupant WADA is considerably less than the district average. There are, let us say, industrial and commercial structures in the locality which inflate the full value per WADA signifi-cantly; any residential structure other than a luxury apartment will di-minish full value per WADA. So even when put on the tax rolls, the new apartment will increase the state aid ratio.

The increase in state aid (to $1,035,000) is large enough to permit a reduction in the property tax rate of $2.414 per $100 full value, or $.015 less than in Year 0 when the apartment was built.

Projecting Future New York State Tax Revenue*

METHODOLOGY

To estimate future tax revenue one must assume constants over the pro-jection period. For instance, the number and type of taxes in the year for which the projections are made is assumed to be identical to that which exists in the present (base) year. Any increase or decrease in taxes is considered to be a political phenomenon and therefore beyond systematic prediction. Also kept constant, at least in first approximations, are the rates and structures of the base period taxes: exemption and deduction policy, definition of the legal base, the number and progressivity of income brackets, and the timing of collections.

We are left with two basic elements for analysis and projection:

---

* Much of this analysis is based on the work of Dr. Dick Netzer of New York Univer-sity, a consultant to the Commission.

1. The projection of economic activity to 1980 as reflected in the growth of personal income in constant (1969) dollars, and
2. The sensitivity of tax revenues at constant rates to changes in personal income (i.e., revenue elasticity).

The conventional projection technique used for most studies of regional or statewide economies consists of two distinct steps. The first is to project the size of the national economy in the target year(s). The aggregate dimensions are projected as follows:

(a)   Total Population (projected on the basis of assumed fertility, mortality and net immigration rates)

× (b)   Assumed labor force participation rate

= (c)   Labor force

× (d)   Assumed percent employed

= (e)   Total employment

× (f)   Assumed average hours worked

= (g)   Total employment income-hours

× (h)   Average productivity per hour

= (i)   Total output

Thus, we have projected population, employment, productivity and output. Converting total current output of goods and services to personal income is a simple operation. Essentially, personal income equals GNP minus depreciation allowances, net contributions to social insurance (social security) and undistributed corporate profits.

The second step is to project the size of the regional state or local economy, given the dimension of the national economy. Initially, a region's economy is projected as if each of its export sectors grows at the national rate. Then, on the basis of additional information regarding locational forces and trends, this rate is adjusted for changes in the region's share of the national totals for each of its export sectors. This provides projections of employment and output in export industries. Regional inter-industry matrices and consumption functions (or similar estimating devices) are used to derive projections for non-export sectors. Regional population projections are, in a sense, derived from these economic projections (keeping labor force participation rates and productivity constant).

This two-step method of projecting regional output has an advantage over isolated regional studies in that the entire national output must be accounted for, and thus there cannot be a hidden conservative or optimistic bias—the shares of all regions cannot decline or increase simultaneously.

In recent years, two major sets of nationwide regional projections have been developed. A projection by the Center for Economic Projections of the National Planning Association (NPA), published in 1965, was done on a state-by-state basis. A second projection was completed in 1968 by the Regional Economics Division, Office of Business Economics (OBE), U.S. Department of Commerce, based on groupings of counties.

Two more organizations have developed independent regional projections of the New York State area: The Tri-State Transportation Committee has projected personal income for those counties which account for nearly three-fourths of New York State personal income, but have recently had a growth rate somewhat higher than the rest of the state. Also, The New York State Office of Planning Coordination (OPC) published projections of population and income in 1969. OPC has worked closely with NPA, but its projections are strikingly different from earlier NPA projections.

Table 2F.1 summarizes these four sets of projections. (Note that the projections are for different periods and for different geographical locations, yet all concern New York State.) The first column of the table shows

TABLE 2F.1

Increase in New York Personal Income, 1969–80, under Various Projections
(Dollar amounts in millions of constant 1969 dollars)

Projections and Periods for Which Made	Average Annual Increase[a]	Eleven-Year Increase[b]	1980 Personal Income Implied[c]
OBE, 1970–80	3.7%[d]	49.1%	$121,368
NPA, 1970–75	3.4	44.5	117,559
OPC, 1970–80	4.4	54.5	125,730
1968–80	4.5	55.4	126,503
1967–80	4.8	67.5	136,302
Ti-State, 1963–85	3. 8[e]	50.7	122,670

[a] Average annual growth rate calculated from the actual projections themselves, expressed in constant dollars.

[b] Compounded rate for eleven years, of figures in previous column.

[c] Percentages in previous column applied to 1969 actual, $81,384 million.

[d] Growth rate for an area which does not exactly coincide with New York State boundaries (see text).

[e] Growth rate for New York portion of Tri-State Region: New York City, Nassau, Rockland, Suffolk, Westchester, Dutchess, Putnam, and Orange Counties, accounting for 73 per cent of New York State personal income in 1968.

Increase in U.S., New York State Personal Income

	AVERAGE ANNUAL GROWTH RATES		
	U.S.	N.Y. State	New York ÷ U.S.
Actual, 1962–69 (constant dollars)	5.3%	4.5%	.85
OBE, 1970–80	4.4	3.7	.85
NPA, 1970–75	4.1	3.4	.83
OPC, 1968–80	5.2	4.5	.87

the average annual rates of increase in personal income in constant dollars (for whatever year is used in the projections). The final column indicates what New York State personal income, in constant 1969 dollars, would be if those annual rates in column one prevailed over the 1969–80 period. The full range is nearly $19 billion; the highest figure (OPC projection, 1967–80) is 16 per cent above the lowest (NPA projection, 1970–75).

To estimate 1980 future tax revenues we used two different growth rates for personal income: the 3.7 per cent year rate predicted by OBE, and an arbitrary 3.0 per cent rate which is possible in light of the current economic situation although lower than any of the projected rates.

The OBE annual growth projection of 3.7 per cent is used as our optimistic forecast for three reasons: (1) the methodology used in formulating this projection seems more sound than that used to arrive at the other projections; (2) the projections of national growth rate used in the OBE analysis seems to be more reasonable than the rates used in other projections; and (3) the relationship between New York State's growth rate and the national growth rate used in the OBE formulation seems to be more logical than in the other projections. Table 2F.2 compares three different sets of personal income projections with actual change in personal income between 1962 and 1969.

A rate of growth approaching that experienced from 1962 to 1969, 5.3 per cent, seems most improbable for the 1969–80 period. The latest Census Bureau population projections suggest that average population growth of just 1.1 per cent per year between 1970 and 1980 is likely. While a decline in birth rates does not directly influence the size of the labor force, extremely rapid economic growth does seem inconsistent with low population growth since rapid economic expansion is to some extent dependent on the size of the labor force. The 3.7 per cent figure must be viewed as being optimistic based on the experience of 1970 and the first half of 1971. For the remainder of the 1969–80 period a rate of personal income growth higher than 3.7 per cent per year will be necessary if the 3.7 per cent average rate is to be realized over the entire period.

REVENUE ELASTICITY

Formally defined, the elasticity of a given tax with respect to another variable is the per cent change in tax revenue divided by the per cent change in the other variable. In algebraic terms, elasticity with respect to personal income is defined as follows:

$$E_y = \frac{R_t - R_{t-1}/R_{t-1}}{Y_t - Y_{t-1}/Y_{t-1}}$$

E_y = elasticity with respect to personal income
R_t, R_{t-1} = tax revenue in year T, year $T - 1$ (a year before year T)
Y_t, Y_{t-1} = personal income in year T, year $T - 1$

To be consistent, both per cent changes must be observed over the same length of time, although the exact period can be staggered. For instance, recognizing the time lag between the realization of income and its translation into taxable purchases, it seems logical to define the elasticities of some sales taxes as:

$$E_y = \frac{R_t - R_{t-1}/R_{t-1}}{Y_{t-1} - Y_{t-2}/Y_{t-1}} \qquad \text{or per cent change}$$

in revenue for year T divided by the percentage change in personal income in the preceding year $T - 1$.

If revenue elasticity, E_y, is equal to one, then a 10 per cent increase in personal income would generate a 10 per cent increase in tax revenue. An elasticity greater than 1 would indicate that tax revenues grow at a rate faster than income; thus, if $E_y = 1.2$, a 10 per cent increase in personal income would generate 12 per cent more tax revenue. State expenditures increase at a faster rate than personal income. Therefore, to insure that increasing expenditures are met without rate increases or introduction of new taxes, the revenue elasticity of the total tax system must be greater than 1.

The elasticities of all major New York State taxes were estimated by our consulting economist, Dr. Dick Netzer. They are presented in Table 2F.3, with estimates for similar taxes in all states from an ACIR study.* Some explanation for the range of estimates is the difficulty of treating rate

---

* Advisory Commission on Intergovernmental Relations, *Federal-State Coordination of Personal Income Taxes* (Washington, D.C.: Government Printing Office, 1965).

Elasticity Estimates (Yearly Basis)

Tax	PERSONAL INCOME[a] ELASTICITY (NYS)			GNP[b] ELASTICITY (ALL STATES)		
	Med.	High	Low	Med.	High	Low
Personal Income	1.735	1.830	1.611	1.65	1.8	1.5
Corporate Income	1.122	1.203	1.081	1.2	1.3	1.1
Business Gross Receipts	.641	.735	.595	NA[c]	NA	NA
Retail Sales	.889	.914	.827	.97	1.05	.90
Motor Vehicle Fees	.341	.392	.286	NA	NA	NA
Motor Fuel	.676	.735	.641	.50	.60	.40
Highway Use	1.122	1.203	1.081	NA	NA	
Alcoholic Beverage	.441	.495	.392	.50	.60	.40
Cigarette Tax	.286	.441	.000	.35	.40	.30
Estate Tax	1.000	1.162	.827	NA	NA	NA
Parimutuel	.392	.441	.286	NA	NA	NA
Lottery	.781	1.000	.546	NA	NA	NA
Real Estate Transfer	1.162	1.162	1.162	NA	NA	NA
Boxing and Racing	.370	.370	.370	NA	NA	NA

[a] Extracted from Dick Netzer, "Potential Educational Revenues in the Coming Decade. Final Report to the Fleischmann Commission." The Netzer elasticities are based on changes in personal income — i.e., per cent change in revenue divided by per cent changes in personal income.
[b] Advisory Commission on Intergovernmental Relations, *Federal-State Coordination of Personal Income Taxes* (Washington, D.C.: Government Printing Office, 1965), p. 42.
[c] NA: Not available.

and timing changes during the observation period The effect of such changes on revenues must be "netted out" to obtain true elasticities. Also, the elasticity estimate for the New York State personal income tax is higher than the national average. This fact can be explained by the greater progressivity of this tax in New York, i.e., income brackets, much rate differentiation and high personal exemption levels in this state.

The progressiveness of a tax is a function of the rate at which it increases and the points on the income scale at which it increases. In New York State, tax rates climb steeply, from a bottom marginal rate of 2 per cent to a top marginal rate of 14 per cent, and their rapid climb occurs where most income is, in the middle and upper-middle ranges of income distribution. For example, for a married couple with two children, tax as a percentage of income more than triples between gross income levels of $5,000 and $10,000, nearly doubles again at $20,000, and

Current and Projected State Tax Revenue (Billions of 1969 Dollars)

Tax	REVENUE '69–70	'71–72	REVENUE 1980ᵃ	1980ᵇ	PER CENT RATE CHANGE 1958–69	REVENUE 1980ᶜ	1980ᵈ
PERSONAL INCOME	2.506	2.358	3.815	3.537	+ 11.0	4.235	3.927
SALES AND USE	1.012	1.447	1.876	1.790	+100.0	3.751	3.580
OTHER CONSUMPTION	1.014	.988	1.153	1.114	NAᵉ	1.513	1.460
Motor Fuel	.370	.375	.456	.440	+ 36.6	.624	.600
Cigarette	.257	.241	.273	.257	+138.8	.379	.357
Motor Vehicle	.212	.205	.228	.223	+ 15.9	.264	.258
Alcoholic Bev.	.113	.112	.126	.124	+ 31.4	.166	.163
Alcoholic Lic.	.033	.030	.033	.035	+ 31.4	.043	.046
Highway Use	.029	.025	.037	.035	0	.037	.035
BUSINESS TAXES	.962	1.060	1.411	1.336	NA	2.221	2.101
Corp. Franchise	.529	.567	.788	.741	+ 60.0	1.261	1.185
Corp. Utilities	.248	.299	.362	.348	+ 50.0	.543	.521
Bank	.086	.102	.142	.134	+ 60.0	.228	.214
Unincorporated Business	.078	.061	.078	.074	+ 60.0	.125	.119
Insurance Premium	.022	.030	.041	.039	+ 60.0	.065	.062
OTHER	.322	.336	.412	.397	NA	.484	.469
Parimutuel	.159	.161	.180	.177	+ 40.0	.252	.248
Estate	.128	.136	.181	.172	0	.181	.172
Lottery	.026	.030	.037	.036	0	.037	.036
Real Estate Transfer	.006	.006	.007	.007	0	.007	.007
OTHER	.004	.004	.006	.005	NA	.006	.005
MISCELLANEOUS RECEIPTS	.091	.113	.133	.129	+ 17.4	.156	.151
Total	5.907	6.302	8.800	8.304		12.360	11.688

ᵃ Preferred elasticities, no rate changes, 3.7% annual growth in personal income.
ᵇ Preferred elasticities, no rate changes, 3.0% annual growth in personal income.
ᶜ Preferred elasticities, rate changes equal to that of the preceding decade, 3.7% annual growth to income.
ᵈ Preferred elasticities, rate changes equal to that of the preceding decade, 3.0% growth in income.
ᵉ NA = not available.

NOTE: The numbers may not add precisely because of errors due to rounding off to the nearest million in revenue.

State Tax Projections (Billions of 1969 Dollars)

Tax Category	Adjusted Revenue '69–70	Revenue '71–72	3.7% PROJECTIONS Revenue 1980[d]	Revenue 1980[e]	Revenue 1980[f]	Revenue 1980[g]
Personal Income	2.506	2.358	3.815	3.983	3.759	4.235
General Business[a]	.962	1.060	1.411	1.441	1.391	2.221
Sales and Use Taxes	1.012	1.447	1.876	1.888	1.839	3.751
Other Consumption Taxes[b]	1.014	.988	1.153	1.170	1.125	1.513
Other Taxes & Misc. Revenue[c]	.413	.449	.545	.560	.529	.640
Total	5.907	6.302	8.800	9.042	8.631	12.360

Tax Category	Adjusted Revenue '69–70	Revenue 71–72	3.0% PROJECTIONS Revenue 1980[d]	Revenue 1980[e]	Revenue 1980[f]	Revenue 1980[g]
Personal Income	2.506	2.358	3.537	3.617	3.439	3.927
General Business[a]	.962	1.060	1.336	1.358	1.319	2.101
Sales and Use Taxes	1.012	1.447	1.790	1.795	1.759	3.580
Other Consumption Taxes[b]	1.014	.988	1.114	1.134	1.087	1.460
Other Taxes[c] & Misc. Revenue	.413	.449	.526	.534	.515	.620
Total:	5.907	6.302	8.304	8.438	8.119	11.688

[a] Corporate franchise, bank, unincorporated business, utilities (Article 9), and insurance premium tax.
[b] Motor vehicle, motor fuel, highway use, alcoholic beverage, cigarette tax.
[c] Estate, parimutuel, lottery, real estate transfer, boxing and racing tax, and miscellaneous revenue. Miscellaneous revenue consists mainly of revenues of general departments, refunds and reimbursements, real estate sold, abandoned property receipts and income from investments and bank deposits.
[d] Preferred elasticities and constant tax rates.
[e] High elasticities and constant tax rates.
[f] Low elasticities and constant tax rates.
[g] Preferred elasticities with rate changes equal to that of last decade (equal percentage increase).

NOTE: The numbers may not add precisely because of errors due to rounding off to the nearest million in revenue.

doubles once more at $50,000. As aggregate personal income levels increase, more households exhaust the personal deductions, exemptions and credits, and are therefore subject to income tax liability for the first time, and those who are already paying are exposed to higher marginal rates. Another reason for the observed difference is that New York State elasticities are based on changes in personal income, a closer approximation to the base of the personal income tax than is the GNP base of the ACIR national estimates.

Analysis of the most recent (1970–71) data on personal income tax collections shows the influence of yet another factor, the division between non-taxable items such as social security and welfare transfer payments and other taxable forms of income. During the current recession, these non-taxable transfer payments have increased as a per cent of personal income while taxable income such as wages and salaries has declined. Because of declining stock prices, capital gains have also decreased. Furthermore, capital gains are not included in the Commerce Department's definition of personal income, which again lowers the apparent elasticity of the personal income tax.

Another reason for the small increase in collections relative to personal income was that revenue during the previous year (1969–70) was artificially inflated as a result of the 1968 tax rate increases, the effects of which were felt during the 1969–70 fiscal year. In addition, the 1970–71 revenues reflect the increase in personal deductions from $625 to $650 in accord with the Federal Tax Reform Act of 1969. The revenue loss from this change, however, was almost exactly offset by the gain from postponing refunds until the next fiscal year (i.e., 1971–72).

The slightly lower corporate income tax elasticities in New York State are no doubt attributable to the deletion of undistributed corporate profits from the Commerce Department's definition of personal income. However, the low elasticities of gross receipt taxes—which include such expenditure items as insurance premiums and utility services—is unexpected. These are normally considered to be highly elastic expenditures.

A number of explanations are suggested by Dr. Dick Netzer: the weakness during periods in the past ten years of the transportation sector (which currently accounts for about one-tenth of the revenue from these taxes); a low elasticity for certain types of utility services, such as water supply; and a generally lower-than-national income elasticity for utility services in New York State partly attributable to already high tax rates on such services.

The lower elasticities for retail sales taxation in New York State can be explained by two factors: (1) low disposable income relative to personal income in New York State since New York incomes are higher than average and thus subject to higher tax rates; and (2) different transportation patterns among New Yorkers. New Yorkers spend relatively little on automobile purchase and operation—which are covered by the sales tax—

and relatively large fractions of income on medical care, foreign travel and private education, all of which are not covered by the sales tax. The latter group of expenditures are highly elastic, with regard to income and may be especially so in New York. The lower bias in New York State elasticities is offset somewhat by the very high elasticities exhibited by service establishments—e.g., beauty parlors, taxis, home remodeling and repair.

State Tax Revenue Projections

Projections of 1980 state tax revenues are presented in Tables 2F.4, 2F.5 and 2F.6. These projections are the product of combining the estimated rates of income growth with the estimated elasticities of the various taxes. The methodology behind these projections is explained by the following example:

First, we look at two different estimates of annual growth of real personal income—3.7 per cent and 3.0 per cent. The elasticity estimates of the personal income tax range from high (1.830) to medium (1.735) to low (1.611). We thus have six estimates for the yearly rate of revenue increase for the personal income tax, each corresponding to a different combination of income growth and elasticity. Each, however, assumes that tax rates are held constant over the eight-year period.

Elasticity	3.7%	3.0%
High	$1.830 \times 3.7 = 6.77\%$	$1.830 \times 3.0 = 5.49\%$
Medium	$1.735 \times 3.7 = 6.47$	$1.735 \times 3.0 = 5.20$
Low	$1.611 \times 3.7 = 5.96$	$1.611 \times 3.0 = 4.83$

The projected percentage increase over the eight-year period (fiscal year 1972 to fiscal year 1980) is calculated algebraically from each yearly rate as follows:

Elasticity	3.7%	3.0%
High	$(1.0677)^8 = 68.89\%$	$(1.0549)^8 = 53.35\%$
Medium	$(1.0647)^8 = 65.13\%$	$(1.0520)^8 = 50.01\%$
Low	$(1.0596)^8 = 58.90\%$	$(1.0483)^8 = 45.84\%$

In deriving a projected revenue figure, one must multiply these eight-year growth rates times the adjusted 1971–72 revenue figure for this tax, \$2.358,* and add the resulting product to the \$2.358 base.

---

* The actual and projected revenue figures are all in 1969 dollars.

The range of revenue estimates for this tax thus becomes:

Elasticity	3.7%
High	(68.88% of 2.358) + 2.358 = 3.983
Medium	(61.79% of 2.358) + 2.358 = 3.815
Low	(59.4 % of 2.358) + 2.358 = 3.759

Elasticity	3.0%
High	(53.35% of 2.358) + 2.358 = 3.617
Medium	(50.01% of 2.358) + 2.358 = 3.537
Low	(45.84% of 2.358) + 2.358 = 3.439

TOTAL TAX REVENUE 1980

In Table 2F.4 are projected revenues (to 1980) for each of the present major state taxes.

By repeating the procedure for each tax and summing the results, one can generate six estimates for total state tax revenue, 1980. It must be emphasized again that these first six estimates (the first three of the 1980 columns in Table 2F.5) assume that tax rates are held constant over the 1969–80 period. The estimates range from a high of $9.042 billion in 1980 (the high elasticity, 3.7 per cent of growth-rate combination), to a low estimate of $8.119 billion (the low elasticity, 3.0 per cent growth-rate combination). This is an 11.4 per cent spread and represents an increase over the 1972 adjusted total, ($6.302 billion) of $2.740 billion (43.5 per cent) on the high side to $1.817 (28.8 per cent) on the low side.

It is now possible to speak of the elasticity of the entire state revenue system: the per cent change in total state tax revenue at constant rates divided by the change in personal income.* For this computation we first use the 3.7 per cent medium elasticity projection of 1980 state revenues, $8.800 billion. This figure is 39.6 per cent greater than the fiscal 1972 adjusted total of $6.302 billion. In the same eight-year period, personal income is expected to increase by 33.7 per cent (3.7 per cent compounded annually for eight years). The elasticity of the entire state tax system for this eight-year period is thus (39.6 per cent / 33.7 per cent), or 1.18. Similar computations using high tax elasticity estimates reveal an overall elasticity of 1.28 for the same eight-year period.

It appears that the state government's revenue is, overall, somewhat more elastic than the local real property tax. Roughly two-fifths of state revenue is produced by the highly elastic personal income tax, with a probable elasticity of 1.74 annually. Another two-fifths is derived from taxes of moderate elasticities, business taxes (as a group) with a probable elasticity of 1.00 annually and the sales tax with one of .89. The remaining

Per Cent of Total Revenue From Selected Taxes

Tax	PER CENT OF TOTAL		Change, 1969–80	Preferred Elasticity
	1969 (Adjusted)[a]	1980[b]		
Personal Income	38.2	43.4	+5.2%	1.735
Retail Sales	21.1	21.3	+ .2	.89
Corporate Income	13.5	9.0	−4.5	1.12
Business Gross Receipts	4.8	4.1	− .7	.64
Motor Fuel	5.8	5.2	− .6	.68
Alcoholic Beverage	2.3	1.4	− .9	.44
Cigarette	4.0	3.1	− .9	.29
Parimutuel	2.5	2.0	−2.0	.39

[a] Adjusted to reflect what 1969 revenue would have been had changes as of June 30, 1971 been in effect.
[b] Based on medium elasticity, 3.7% growth projections.

fifth, largely other consumption and use taxes and gambling revenue, is quite inelastic, with the probable average for this group of taxes only .55.

A consoling feature of low-elasticity tax systems is that if tax rates are kept constant, and the number and type of taxes remain the same, over time the elasticity of the system will come to resemble more and more the elasticity of its most sensitive tax. This inevitably is the case since: (1) the elasticity of the entire system is simply the sum of the weighted elasticities of the component taxes, and (2) over time, the weights of the more elastic taxes increase relative to the less elastic taxes. Evidence of these changing weights over time is seen for the 1969–80 period in Table 2F.6.

Juxtaposed against the state revenue system elasticity estimates of 1.18 and 1.28 derived above is the fact that state expenditures have in the past decade moved, vis-à-vis personal income, in a manner indicating an expenditure elasticity of 1.9 to 2.0. Thus it seems that even if high revenue elasticities and the optimistic growth rate prevail tax rate increases might be necessary in order for state services to remain at their present levels.

* This total elasticity will, in fact, be equal to the sum of the individual tax elasticities, each weighted by their share of total revenue.

Summary of Total State Tax Revenue Projections, Fiscal 1980 (1969 Dollars)

1969–70 Revenue (Adjusted): *$6.389B*

TOTAL TAX REVENUE, 1980

	PERSONAL INCOME GROWTH	
	3.7%	**3.0%**
High Elasticities	$9.042	$8.438
Med. Elasticities	8.800	8.304
Low Elasticities	8.631	8.119
Med. Elasticities with Tax Rate Change Equal to Last Decade's	12.420	11.700

CHANGE IN TOTAL TAX REVENUE

	PERSONAL INCOME GROWTH	
	3.7%	**3.0%**
High Elasticities	+$2.653	+$2.049
Med. Elasticities	2.411	1.915
Low Elasticities	2.242	1.730
Med. Elasticities with Tax Rate Change Equal to Last Decade's	6.031	5.311

PER CENT CHANGE IN TOTAL TAX REVENUE

	PERSONAL INCOME GROWTH	
	3.7%	**3.0%**
High Elasticities	+41.5%	+32.10%
Med. Elasticities	+37.7%	+29.9%
Low Elasticities	+35.1%	+27.1%
Med. Elasticities with Tax Rate Change Equal to Last Decade's	+94.4%	+83.1%

In response to this unpleasant possibility, we have shown in the last column of Table 2F.5 what 1980 revenues would be if tax rate changes equal to those of the past decade are repeated in this decade. The assumption of continued tax rate increases for all taxes is illustrative only and is, in fact, extremely unlikely; if there are substantial increases certain taxes will have to bear most of the weight. The only long-run solution is to rely more heavily on centralized revenue collection to avoid the deleterious effects of inter-state competition (see the chapter on Federal Aid). Otherwise the states run a race between invention of new tax instruments and fiscal collapse.

Table 2F.7 contains a summary of all the revenue projections, both under constant rate and the equal percentage rate increase assumptions. Note that these projections seem far more sensitive to tax rate changes than they do to variation in elasticities or economic growth rates. Tax rates affect revenue estimates by a factor of more than 44 per cent: elasticity differences result in, at most, a 5 per cent difference, while growth rates influence revenues by about 7.1 per cent.

DERIVING STATE AID TO EDUCATION PROJECTIONS

The above revenue projections were compiled in a systematic, almost scientific, manner. Unfortunately, this degree of rigor is impossible when one attempts to determine what share of the total revenue will go to education. State aid must be divided among a number of agencies which provide funds for, among other things, mental hospitals, welfare, pollution abatement and the State University system. It is exceedingly difficult to assess the relative strength over the next decade of these rival claims and to include them in the revenue totals we project below.

Two alternative methods of deriving state aid projections from estimated revenues are employed in this report:

1 *Method A:* The division of total tax revenues between aid to public education and all other services is assumed to remain stable—roughly 35 per cent for education vs. 65 per cent for the remainder. With this simplistic technique, we merely multiply the various revenue estimates times .35 to arrive at estimated state aid.
2 *Method B:* Current non-education expenditure is projected independently in accord with certain specified "most-likely" assumptions; the education aid monies are projected as the difference between this non-education expenditure projection and the various total revenue projections.

In the judgment of our consulting economist, Dr. Dick Netzer, the most likely figure for fiscal 1980 nonpublic education expenditure is $6.910 billion (1969 dollars). His model, in general, assumes that state expenditure for most costly activities will increase a good deal less than they did in the past.[31] Specifically, with regard to personnel costs which represent 80 per cent of total non-aid expenditures:

a. Rates of pay will increase from 1970–71 to 1980–81 by an annual average of three per cent above the general price level.
b. The number of full time equivalent state employees will increase far less rapidly than has been the case in the past decade—60 per cent for the State University (versus more than 300 per cent in the past decade) and by 30 per cent for all other expenditures (versus about 45 per cent in the past decade).
c. Employee fringe benefits will increase somewhat more rapidly than payrolls largely because of the rapidly mounting costs of pension systems.

The size of 1980 state welfare aid is sensitive to the form that federal welfare legislation takes. The intermediate range possibility assumes that welfare reform legislation will allow a freeze on state expenditure for this service at $1 billion (1969 dollars), which is marginally above the 1969–70 and 1970–71 expenditure levels.

The amount of general local assistance is fixed by statute as a specified per cent of personal income tax receipts. Our estimate is that the legislature will restore the 21 per cent figure in place of the currently mandated

TABLE 2F.8

Judgment Projections of Non-School Expenditure from State Government Curren Revenue, 1980–81 (Millions of 1969 dollars)

Type of Expenditure	Actual 1969–70	1970–71, in 1969 dollars[a]	Projected 1980–81
State Purposes	1,992	2,190	4,190
Payrolls and Non-Personnel Costs	1,600	1,768	3,130
Employee Fringe Benefits	253	255	560
Debt Service	139	167	500
Local Assistance (Except School Aid)	1,640	1,648	2,915
Social Services	878	826	1,000
General Local Assistance	287	335	1,015[b]
Other	475	487	900
Capital Construction from Current Revenue	222	93	150
Total	3,854	3,931	7,255

[a] Actual 1970–71 expenditure divided by 1.0528, the increase in the GNP implicit price deflator between 1969 and 1970.
[b] 21 per cent of personal income tax receipts assuming current tax rates, a 3.7 per cent average annual growth rate and the preferred elasticity estimate.

18 per cent. This would mean, assuming preferred elasticities and 3.7 per cent rate of growth, a three-fold increase in general local assistance to $1.015 billion by 1980.

The other state programs are much more modest. For higher education and mental health, it is assumed that state aid will increase in proportion to direct state expenditure through state agencies. A large percentage increase in state assistance for local housing programs is assumed, but even doubling this assistance will not involve huge sums of money. For the other aid programs, some of which have not been rising much at all in recent years, various increases averaging only 33 per cent are projected.

A small drain in tax revenue has been capital outlay financed from current tax receipts; recently no more than $100 million or so of capital outlay has been financed from this source. Rather arbitrarily, we project the figure in the target year as $150 million.

Table 2F.8 contains a summary of our expectations regarding the most likely course of state expenditure for all purposes other than aid to education.

AID TO EDUCATION—1980

Sixteen separate projections of state aid to education are presented in Table 2F.9. While this may seem unduly complicated to some, when one considers the literally thousands of additional permutations and combinations of elasticity, tax rate, and growth rate assumptions, this number of projections seems selective indeed. Even so, there is considerable range in the dollar estimates; from a high of $5.510 billion (Method B, 3.7 per cent growth, medium elasticities with tax rate increases assumption) to $1.213 billion (Method B, 3.0 per cent growth, low elasticities—no rate increases).

A quick perusal of Table 2F.9 shows that, as was the case for revenue projection, state aid projections are more sensitive to policy decisions regarding tax rates than they are to the state of the economy or the magnitude of elasticities, at least within the ranges we have postulated. This also applies to policy regarding non-education expenditure, which impinges on state aid in a one-to-one fashion; i.e., one more dollar of non-education expenditure equals one less dollar of state aid to education in Method B projections.

Five of the eight Method B projections indicate a net decline in state aid over the 1970–80 decade. This anomaly is the result of methodological weaknesses inherent in this type of projection when revenues and non-educational expenditure are projected independently, and state aid computed as a residual. The correlation between expenditures and revenues render some Method B combinations extremely improbable.

State Aid to Education, Fiscal 1980 (Billions of 1969 Dollars)

State Aid, 1969–70 = $2.123

PROJECTIONS: 1980

	Method A: 35% of Total Revenue		Method B: Total Revenue Minus $6.910	
	3.7% Growth	*3.0% Growth*	*3.7% Growth*	*3.0% Growth*
High Elasticities	$3.165	$2.953	$2.132	$1.528
Med. Elasticities	3.080	2.906	1.932	1.402
Low Elasticities	3.021	2.842	1.721	1.209
Med. Elasticities plus Tax Rate Change Equal to Last Decade's	4.347	4.095	5.510	4.790

CHANGE: 1969–80

	Method A		Method B	
	3.7%	*3.0%*	*3.7%*	*3.0%*
High Elasticities	$+1.042	$+ .830	$+ .009	$− .595
Med. Elasticities	+ .957	+ .783	− .191	− .721
Low Elasticities	+ .898	+ .719	− .402	− .914
Med. Elasticities plus Tax Rate Change Equal to Last Decade's	+2.224	+1.972	+3.387	+2.667

PER CENT CHANGE: 1969–80

	Method A		Method B	
	3.7%	*3.0%*	*3.7%*	*3.0%*
High Elasticities	+49.1	+39.1	.4	−28.0
Med. Elasticities	+45.1	+36.9	− 9.0	−34.0
Low Elasticities	+42.3	+33.9	−18.9	−43.0
Med. Elasticities plus Tax Rate Change Equal to Last Decade's	+104.8	+92.9	+159.5	+125.6

Federal Aid to Education

In the years ahead, New York State will need increasing amounts of revenue to improve the quality of its schools. Responsibility for generating that revenue cannot fall totally upon the state. If the educational needs of the state are to be met, the Federal Government must contribute far more to the financing of education—in New York and all other states—than it does at present.*

This chapter sets forth the position of the Commission on federal school aid. Specific proposals and recommendations are presented in the last section. These proposals and recommendations are directed not to the President and Congress but to our constituency for this entire report—the Governor, Legislature, Regents, and people of New York. New York State must endorse and actively seek the involvement of the Federal Government in the financing of local education.

WHY FEDERAL GOVERNMENT PARTICIPATION?

It is obvious that all of society benefits from the contributions of an educated citizen; this is the basic rationale behind the maintenance of a free public school system. Similarly, the entire nation suffers the disadvantages

---

* Currently, federal aid to elementary and secondary education in New York State amounts to about 4 per cent of expenditures. The national average is 7 per cent. A summary of New York's current receipt and use of federal school aid funds is included in Appendix 3A.

and social and economic ills which are associated with inadequate education. Thus, education is an issue of national concern. As more fully described below, federal assistance in support of elementary and secondary education should accomplish the fulfillment of national educational priorities, the creation of a more equitable tax system, the encouragement of economies of scale and interstate cooperation, and the efficient use of public resources.

Meeting National Needs

From time to time, wide-scale educational deficiencies become apparent which transcend the boundaries of individual states; in these instances Federal Government financial incentives and assistance are particularly appropriate. For example, the Smith-Hughes Act was passed by Congress in 1917 to provide federal financial assistance in response to the pressure of manpower needs during World War I. Similarly, the National Defense Education Act, passed in 1958, provided assistance for educational progress emphasizing technological training in response to increasing competition in this field from the Soviet Union. Other examples of federal intervention to assist with specific educational problems are the Allied Health Professions Act, the Manpower Development and Training Act, and the establishment of the National Science Foundation. These and other federal educational programs were established to meet national priorities which the states could not afford individually and which required coordination on a national level.

The Elementary and Secondary Education Act of 1965 (ESEA) was also directed principally toward a pressing national problem: the education of children from low-income families. New York State has a larger number of disadvantaged children than any other state. Federal funds under Title I of the Act ($180 million in 1969–70) have helped to improve the quality of New York's schooling and increase educational opportunities.[1] Nevertheless, the programs established by the Act have never been funded up to the levels authorized. Appropriations for the nation generally, and for New York State specifically, have fallen far short of the amounts which are required to deal adequately with the educational problems of disadvantaged children.

Efficient and Equitable Generation of Revenue

The federal tax structure is more progressive and its collection machinery more efficient than that of any state.* In 1968 the Federal Government collected approximately 71 per cent of all United States tax dollars; the remaining 29 per cent was divided between state and local governments.[2]

---

* "Progressive" taxes place a proportionally greater burden on the wealthy. The graduated income tax is an example of a progressive tax.

Moreover, the Federal Government collected 90 per cent of all the nation's personal income taxes, and the federal income tax is the most rapidly growing source of revenues.[3] For a variety of reasons some of which are discussed later, state and local governments cannot rely as heavily as the Federal Government on such an elastic source of funds. Therefore, in order to fund their operations, states and localities have had to increase rates on other more regressive taxes in recent years.* Because of the elasticity of graduated income taxation, however, the Federal Government has been able to maintain constant, or even slightly decreasing, tax rates over the last decade. (The only exception to this has been the anti-inflation surcharge of recent years.)

If public services are to expand, then almost inevitably the revenues for their support must come to a greater extent from increased Federal Government contributions. State and local governments will be hard-pressed to continue to increase their rates of contribution. The reliance on state and local taxes to finance services such as education, which are of national concern, results in unhealthy competition among local governments and states. If a state or local government imposes taxes at a higher rate than its neighbors, it runs a substantial risk of discouraging industrial or commercial development and losing middle- and high-income residents. New York, for instance, is threatened by a large-scale relocation of corporate headquarters to other states, and corporate and personal tax rates have certainly been a factor in these moves.

Interstate Coordination and Efficiency

Research and development in the complex field of "learning" is time-consuming and expensive. Resources far beyond the capacities of most school districts and states are required to undertake adequate studies on the learning process. Moreover, it is not economically advantageous for individual states to undertake such projects on a large scale even if they were financially capable of supporting them. To recommend that New York finance major educational research projects if Illinois and California, for example, did not do so, would be to ask New York citizens to pay unfairly for the education of children residing in other states.

Without some higher level unit to coordinate major research and development operations, there is the risk of unproductive duplication of effort. A coordinating unit is also needed to disseminate the results of research efforts. A local program or state-initiated project might produce significant findings, but the absence of a larger organization responsible for effectively disseminating the research findings might severely limit their impact.

---

* "Regressive" taxes, such as sales and property taxes, place a proportionally greater burden on the poor.

Despite the necessity of federal leadership in large-scale educational research and development, present support levels are disappointing. As a result, the "technology" presently in general use for instructional purposes, for example, is not much different than it was following the invention of the printing press and movable type. Massive amounts of additional federal support are needed if significant improvements in this and other areas are to be achieved.

THE FUTURE FEDERAL ROLE

Improved Categorical Aid

At present, most New York State elementary and secondary school aid is funded under statutes which provide aid for specific or "categorical" purposes. In 1969–70, total federal aid to New York State for elementary and secondary education amounted to $246 million.[4]

Federal statutes provide funds for a variety of programs. For example, the Elementary and Secondary Education Act (ESEA), under which the great bulk of federal aid is provided, authorizes funds for compensatory schooling of children from low-income families, purchase of instructional materials, support of innovative programs, buttressing of the State Education Department's administrative capability, bilingual education and dropout prevention.

While these appropriations have had a substantial impact in New York and other states, they still fall far short of the objectives they were designed to achieve. None of the authorizations has been funded at the rate intended when it was enacted by Congress. For example, the annual appropriation under Title I of ESEA, designed to provide compensatory education for underprivileged children, has been substantially less than the amount authorized by Congress.[5]

Moreover, Congressional appropriations procedures, which do not get underway until late winter, are often not completed until it is too near to the opening of the subsequent school year for plans to be made to spend the funds efficiently. In order to maximize the effectiveness of federal grants for education, a school superintendent must know the amount of money he can expect six or more months in advance of the date in which the programs will become operational. Under present arrangements, he may not know the exact size of his share until after he can employ capable personnel, order appropriate materials or arrange for proper facilities. In 1970, federal funds were not fully appropriated until March, seven months into the school year for which they were intended. In the fiscal years 1971 and 1972, however, federal funds were appropriated in timely fashion, thus permitting more orderly and efficient use.

Another obstacle to the effective use of federal funds is the lack of coordination and resultant duplication of effort in administration of categorical aid. The large number of existing federal programs encourages fragmentation on the part of local and state school authorities. Presently, project proposals must be submitted to five or more existing federal authorities, not all of which are in the United States Office of Education (USOE). Standards for proposal evaluation differ among various divisions of the USOE and differ even more between the USOE and other agencies. Sacrifices of both human labor and financial resources occur in the process. Neither students nor the national interest are well served.

Moreover, when state education systems undertake programs in fields which are also federal educational priorities—such as remedial reading—the federal and state programs often stand in isolation from each other. The same student may be enrolled in two or more special programs, each funded by separate agencies and using conflicting methods of instruction. The concern of the Federal Government that federal categorical funds supplement rather than replace existing state and local expenditures sometimes, in fact, encourages states to maintain separate programs, thus forestalling coordination.

New Categorical Aid

Throughout its investigations, this Commission has been impressed with the potential contribution of technology to elementary and secondary education. Schools have begun to utilize machines more widely for data processing, but they have barely scratched the surface of potential applications for instructional purposes. For example, we are persuaded that some elements of reading, mathematics and foreign language instruction are somewhat mechanical and repetitive in nature, and as such might be taught more efficiently by properly programmed instructional equipment.*

Similarly, cable television could be effectively and economically used for educational purposes. If broadly conceived and efficiently designed, a cable system could allow many different kinds of televised programs to come into schools to supplement the curriculum. Moreover, a cable system allowing two-way communication would permit the student to take an active part in the instructional program. Cable television could also permit direct connection between students and libraries, museums, symphonies, businesses and other institutions insufficiently utilized by our formal education system.

Cable television and other forms of technology tease us with promises of quality improvement at decreased cost, but a substantial amount of development remains to be done before these various technologies can be made adaptable to widespread educational application. Development of educational technology is enormously expensive. The burden of financing

---

* A full discussion of the potential uses of computers and other educational hardware is contained in Chapter 13.

this development rests with the public sector. The private sector, with no assurance that ultimate markets will be sufficiently large to offset development costs, has been reluctant to make large commitments.

Furthermore, within the public sector, because it makes little sense for a financially pressed state government to commit large sums of money for the development of technological applications in education, particularly when the benefits of such an effort would accrue equally to other states, the Federal Government must assume responsibility for the greatest portion of the task. We recommend specifically that the proposed National Institute of Education (NIE) assume as one of its major responsibilities the expenditure of resources necessary for massive educational technology development programs. A sufficiently large federal commitment should be made to assure that substantial cost-effective applications of technology be operational by the end of the decade.

General Aid

While we recommend the continuation and expansion of categorical aid programs through which federal funds are distributed to states and localities to defray costs in areas of identifiable need, more money will be required to meet future general educational needs and improve quality over the next decade. Consequently, we recommend that new federal funds be made available which will assist in the general support of schools.

We have identified five feasible mechanisms through which federal funds might be made available for the general support of education: (1) direct federal subsidization of elementary and secondary education; (2) general revenue sharing; (3) federal incentives for state and local tax reform and intra-state educational expenditure equalization; (4) federal assumption of the costs of welfare; and (5) federal tax credits to individuals for payment of state and local income taxes. While each of these five mechanisms will be discussed hereinafter independently, it is to be understood that they are by no means mutually exclusive; all five could be employed simultaneously in a variety of combinations.

DIRECT FEDERAL SUBSIDIZATION Toward the end of 1971 there was speculation in the press that a federal tax on value-added designed to yield $20 billion in its first year was being given serious consideration by the Nixon Administration.[6] Furthermore, it was also speculated that proceeds from this tax would be used to provide general aid to education under a plan that would provide for local property tax relief. This Commission does not deem it appropriate to comment specifically on such speculative matters other than to say that increased federal aid to general education at the state level is sorely needed. Elsewhere, we have expressed our preference for the graduated income tax as the most progressive form of taxation, but the fiscal crisis of the states is so acute that help would be welcome from federal resources generated in any reasonable manner.

GENERAL REVENUE SHARING The first serious proponent of general revenue sharing was Walter Heller, the late President Kennedy's first chairman of the Council of Economic Advisors. In 1964, when the economy was languishing and unemployment was high, Heller reasoned that the transfer of federal revenues to states and localities would stimulate the economy but, unlike tax reductions, would not create fiscal deficits in the public sector.[7]

To expedite enactment, general revenue sharing was originally proposed in its simplest form: distribution to the states on a simple population basis. This also was the recommendation of a special task force appointed by President Lyndon B. Johnson under the chairmanship of Joseph Pechman.

Revenue sharing was conceived originally as a means to stimulate the economy. Recently, however, it has been proposed as a means to help state and local governments meet their sharply rising costs in the face of slowly growing revenues. The "Growing Fiscal Crisis" is described in President Nixon's message on general revenue sharing:

> In the last quarter-century, state and local expenses have increased twelve-fold, from a mere $11 billion to an estimated $132 billion in 1970. In that same time, our GNP, our personal spending, and even spending by the Federal Government, have not climbed at even one-third that rate. . . . How have the states and localities met these growing demands? They have not met them. . . . Some authorities estimate that normal revenue growth will fall some $10 billion short of outlays in the next year alone.[8]

The reasons for sharing revenue among states and localities from a central federal tax base are rooted both in practicabilities and in theoretical principles underlying our federal system.

The architects of our federal structure were determined that a measure of choice and variety among different states and localities with respect to the delivery of public services should be preserved. This Commission agrees. Accordingly, federal revenue sharing must be devised so that funds are shared among states and localities without undue restrictions on their use.

If public services are to be funded and distributed equitably and according to need, the Federal Government should assume greater responsibility for revenue raising and distribution. To the extent that it does not, interstate wealth disparities are not easily overcome.

Furthermore, regional disparities in rates of taxation tend to influence decisions on the part of both business and individual taxpayers as to where they will locate, at least to the extent that such disparities are not directly reflected in the quality of public services provided the taxpayers. However, the incidence of this phenomenon decreases as the tax base becomes broader. Thus, taxation differentials between two countries are less likely to influence such a decision between them than are taxation differentials between two states. Similarly, taxation differentials between two states are less likely to influence locational decisions than are taxation differentials between two municipalities.

This phenomenon is most pronounced when a narrow-based taxing jurisdiction attempts to institute a progressive levy, such as a graduated income tax. If such a tax is imposed by a locality or state so that wealthy people would bear a greater tax burden than they would if they resided and worked in other nearby localities or states, their decisions as to where to locate are likely to be influenced accordingly. Again, if such a tax is imposed by the Federal Government, the probability is increased that any impulse to locate outside the taxing jurisdiction in order to avoid the tax will be overborne by other considerations.

Under the Nixon Administration's general revenue sharing plan, the amount of general revenue to be shared would be determined by the size of the federal personal income tax base.* Specifically, the plan provides that 1.3 per cent of taxable personal income be earmarked for general revenue sharing.[9] The Nixon proposal would result in a total pool of approximately $5 billion in fiscal 1971–72.[10] Distribution among the states would be on the basis of population adjusted for "fiscal effort"—or the comparative ratios of total state and local taxes to total statewide personal income. Under this formula, New York State would receive approximately 10.6 per cent of the entire pool—or about $534 million in fiscal 1972.[11] This amount is about 20 per cent higher than would be the case if population alone were the criterion for distribution because New York State makes a strong fiscal effort relative to the national average.

If, after discounting inflation, the total revenue sharing pool were to increase at the rate of 5 per cent per year and the state's relative share were to remain the same, by 1980 New York State would receive $789 million in constant 1972 dollars, or $685 million in 1969 dollars.

A pass-through provision in the Administration's plan stipulates that a certain percentage of the state's allotment is to be shared with local general purpose governments. Specifically, the local share is to equal the ratio of local general revenues to the total of state and local general revenues. For New York, in 1980, this provision would require that the state channel 51 per cent of its allotment ($352 million) to the localities, while retaining the remaining 48.5 per cent ($333 million).

School districts are not specifically mentioned as recipients of pass-through monies under the Nixon plan. In view of our recommendation, set forth in Chapter 2, that the state assume the full burden of funding

---

* The plan proposes to earmark a fixed percentage of taxable personal *income* rather than a percentage of personal income *tax receipts*. We prefer the latter because as per capita personal income increases, personal income taxation captures a greater percentage of it. Thus, in an expanding economy income tax receipts grow at a faster rate than income.

elementary and secondary education, we do not advocate that school districts be designated recipients of federal shared funds. However, since full state funding of educational costs would place an increased financial burden on the state, we recommend that the plan be amended to provide that a smaller percentage of federal revenues be passed through to localities.

This Commission supports the general approach of the Administration's plan. If enacted, it would provide a helpful step toward equitable local-state-federal sharing of the nation's educational burdens. As the plan now stands, however, we recommend three principal modifications: (1) that the pass-through provisions be amended, or perhaps eliminated, to conform with this Commission's recommendations relating to full state funding of education as set forth in the preceding chapter, (2) that the amount of revenue to be shared be determined by federal income tax receipts rather than taxable personal income, and (3) that the amount of revenue to be shared be increased substantially over the current proposed amount. In order to make an effective contribution, the proportion of federal revenues set aside for sharing should be at least 10 to 15 per cent of personal income tax receipts.

WELFARE REFORM   At this writing, Congress has before it a welfare reform bill (HR1), which, if enacted, would perhaps relieve some of New York State's heavy welfare costs.

This Commission supports federal assumption of welfare costs. It would make available added revenues for state services such as education. In addition, it would redress many of the present inequities in this nation's treatment of its aged, indigent and handicapped citizens. There are significant disparities in welfare benefits among states. Not only is this unfair to recipients in low-benefit states, but it also motivates these people to move to high-paying states such as New York.

For calendar year 1971, it is estimated that New York State and its localities will have contributed $796 million as their share of the following welfare costs to which HR1 would contribute: Aid to Dependent Children, Old Age Assistance, Aid to the Blind, Aid to the Disabled and Home Relief.[12] Predictions of annual savings to the state if HR1 had been in effect range from $12 million to $48 million.* While even the high figure does not approach the recommended level of federal funding for schools, even a good portion of it would provide a welcome contribution. We urge, however, a far greater assumption of welfare costs by the Federal Government than called for in HR1 to free more state resources for educational use.

FEDERAL INCENTIVE GRANTS TO ENCOURAGE FULL STATE FUNDING
Progress toward more equitable education finance systems on the part of

---

* Based on preliminary low and high estimates made by the Temporary State Commission to Revise the Social Services Law of the State of New York, December 1971.

states has been slow. While this Commission has directed its attention chiefly to expenditure disparities in New York, we are aware that such disparities are even greater in some other states. The Federal Government should provide incentives for all states to assume financial responsibility for public schools.

As a state proceeds toward the full assumption of educational costs, it may be forced, through fiscal necessity, to slight other social welfare activities, such as health, low-cost housing and the more progressive programs of public assistance. Yet, it is clear that the performance of disadvantaged youth in schools is sensitive to poor housing and health conditions, precisely the areas that might suffer as states move toward full state funding. It is even possible that school performance of disadvantaged youth is more strongly related to complementary social services—health care, nutrition, housing—than to educational expenditures *per se*. Hence, if states are left to their own devices and revenue sources to implement full state funding, some of the potential benefits of changing the education finance system might well be temporarily dissipated.

Therefore, this Commission recommends that the Federal Government enact legislation which will provide financial assistance and incentives to states which assume financial responsibility for their public schools. The Federal Government could, for example, establish a schedule of dollar federal aid per public school student enrolled that would increase as the percentage of state—as opposed to local—funding increased.[13] By the same token, legislation should be designed to provide incentives that would encourage states to rely on forms of taxation more progressive than the property tax.

TAX CREDITS   Federal tax credits could be designed to encourage tax reform by providing incentives for increased use of the personal income tax at state and local levels.

There are at least two forms which a tax credits plan might assume:

1. A specified percentage of state and local income taxes paid by an individual might be credited against his federal income tax liability. Such a plan would reduce the individual's federal income tax burden and simultaneously provide states and localities with a potential progressive tax resource. Under a bill introduced in 1971 by Representative John W. Byrnes of Wisconsin (HR8193), a taxpayer, in addition to taking his deduction for state and local taxes as currently provided by law would simply claim a credit on his federal return for 20 per cent of the state and local income taxes he paid. A tax credit is a greater benefit to a taxpayer than a deduction: a credit is applied against final tax liability, whereas a deduction is merely subtracted from taxable income, thus giving a lower figure upon which to calculate tax liability.

Assuming the Byrnes tax credit proposals had been in effect in fiscal 1970, and that there had accordingly been a 25 per cent increase in state and local income tax rates, the total yield from the plan would have been about $2.5 billion in additional state and local revenues; $709 million would have accrued to New York State and local taxing authorities.[14]

New York benefits more from the Byrnes bill than it does from the Nixon Administration's general revenue sharing plan where from the pool of $5 billion, New York received only $534 million.

The Byrnes bill would also increase the federal tax credit for state death taxes to 80 per cent of the tax on the first $150,000 of the taxable estate, and 20 per cent of the remainder. This provision would have created an additional $150 million revenue resource for New York State in fiscal 1970.

2. Full federal tax credits might be extended to a state on its residents' federal income tax liabilities. For example, if a resident of New York State owed $2,000 on his federal income tax in a given year, the Federal Government could allow New York State to have a portion of that payment up to a maximum of, say, 10 per cent by allowing the taxpayer a full credit against his federal tax liability for that amount. Thus, in this example, the Federal Government would receive $1,800 and the state $200. The advantage of this approach is that its incidence would be determined by the federal personal income tax, which is currently more progressive than New York State's. Moreover, no competitive advantage would accrue to a state that did not impose the surtax because the total tax liability of a resident taxpayer would remain the same, the only difference being that the Federal Government would continue to realize the revenues that would have accrued to the state if it had imposed the surcharge.

The surtax would be adjusted to exclude items which a state cannot or might not choose to tax, such as interest on federal bonds, state pensions, and income earned out of state. It could be administered as a separate item at the bottom of the state income tax form.

A 10 per cent state surtax on the 1971 federal income taxes paid by New York State residents would realize additional revenues for New York State estimated at $1.2 billion. If earmarked specifically for education, this amount would make possible an across-the-board 48 per cent reduction in real property taxes for educational purposes.

SUMMARY

The unusually large projected disparity between New York State revenues and expenditures in fiscal year 1972 reflects what is hopefully a temporary economic recession. Nevertheless, if this nation is to continue to improve the quality of its public services, including education, reliance on state and local taxation as presently constituted in this country will continue to place an untenable financial strain on state and local governments in the decade ahead. Only the Federal Government with its broader based revenue resources can provide relief. Mindful that in New York, as in most states, public elementary and secondary education is by far the single largest state expenditure, this Commission has focused its attention on the most productive and feasible methods by which the Federal Government can provide states with financial assistance for public education at a level equal to 25 to 30 per cent of total cost, as compared with a current level of approximately 7 per cent nationwide and 4 per cent in New York. Our recommendations are summarized as follows:

1. Current federal categorical aid programs should be continued and increased for children identified as educationally disadvantaged. In Chapter 9 we consider the special needs of handicapped children and analyze the financial dimensions of the problem of serving them adequately. Attending to the special needs of handicapped children is a problem throughout the nation and should be the object of major federal categorical financial assistance.

    In addition, the Federal Government should make substantial contributions to states and localities for the specific purpose of reducing racial and ethnic segregation in the schools. In this connection, as described in detail in the chapter on integration, we endorse the Senate version of the proposed $1.5 billion Emergency School Assistance Program. The Senate bill, unlike the House version, contains no restrictions on the use, by state and local authorities, of busing—an essential remedial implement to overcome racial and ethnic segregation.

2. While we urge the continuation of current categorical aid programs, we recommend also that many of them be consolidated pursuant to a logical plan to permit more flexible and efficient application for and employment of federal funds by state and local education authorities.

3. We recommend that a massive federally-sponsored research and development effort with special emphasis on the educational applications of technological advances be instituted having as its goal increasing the quality and reducing the cost of education by the end of this decade. The proposed National Institute of Education seems the logical agency to undertake this effort.

4. Finally, we recommend that general federal aid for education be made available to the states by a judicious combination of the following mechanisms:

    a. Outright grants of federal funds to states earmarked for educational purposes but not otherwise restricted; these funds could be raised from existing or new forms of taxation.

b. General revenue sharing distributed in a manner that takes account of state tax effort as well as population.

c. Welfare reform designed to spread the cost of this public service, which unduly burdens some states, particularly New York, more than others, over a broad federal base.

d. Incentive grants to states for providing full state funding of education with concomitant equalization of inter-school district per-pupil expenditure disparities. Direct federal incentives might also be employed to encourage states to substitute more progressive forms of taxation—particularly graduated income taxation—for the property tax.

e. Federal tax credits for state and local income tax. We prefer a state surcharge on federal income tax liability fully credited against federal income tax payments. This method would assure (1) that no state could gain a competitive advantage on the other states by failing to institute the surcharge and (2) that the tax incidence would be determined by the federal personal income tax which is currently considerably more progressive than its New York State counterpart.

Federal Funds for Education in New York State

Since 1960, the amount of federal funds* available for education in New York State has increased significantly. The most dramatic growth occurred in fiscal year 1966 (school year 1965–66), when New York State appropriations were more than two and one-half times those for the previous fiscal year. Most of the increase that year resulted from passage of the

---

* For applicable years, figures include: Elementary and Secondary Education Act, Higher Education Facilities Act, Higher Education Act, Vocational Educational Act, School Lunch Act, School Milk Act, Child Nutrition Act, Federally Affected Areas Act, Manpower Development and Training Act, Vocational Rehabilitation Act, Federal Property and Administrative Services Act, National Defense Education Act, Economic Opportunity Act, Adult Education Act, Library Services and Construction Act, Mental Retardation Facilities Act, Civil Rights Act of 1964, Social Security Act, Civil Defense Act of 1950, Cooperative Research Programs, Vocational Agriculture and Home Economics Fund, National Foundations on the Arts and Humanities Act, Federal Grants to the Board of Regents, and Education Professions Development Act.

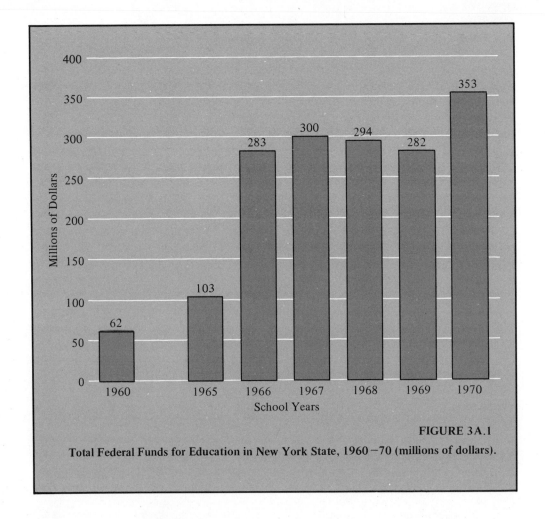

FIGURE 3A.1

Total Federal Funds for Education in New York State, 1960–70 (millions of dollars).

Elementary and Secondary Education Act of 1965. Appropriations for fiscal 1970 were $71 million higher than in 1969. (Figure 3A.1.)

In federal fiscal year 1970, New York State received approximately $353 million under some 26 federal education programs. Twelve of the programs (Elementary and Secondary Education Act, Higher Education Facilities Act, Higher Education Act, Vocational Education Act, School Lunch Act, School Milk Act, Child Nutrition Act, Federally Affected Areas Act, Manpower Development and Training Act, Adult Education Act, Vocational Rehabilitation Act, and the Federal Property and Administrative Services Act) accounted for nearly 97 per cent of the total amount of federal funds received. (Figure 3A.2.)

The first Act listed on Figure 3A.2, the Elementary and Secondary Education Act, provided about $196.3 million dollars to New York State in 1970 and accounted for about 55.7 per cent of all federal funds received.

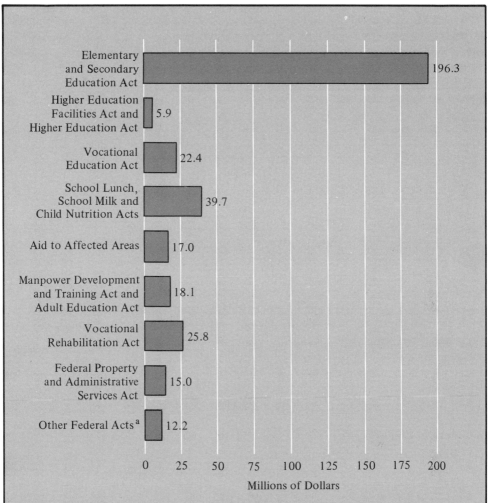

Elementary and Secondary Education Act								196.3	
Higher Education Facilities Act and Higher Education Act	5.9								
Vocational Education Act	22.4								
School Lunch, School Milk and Child Nutrition Acts	39.7								
Aid to Affected Areas	17.0								
Manpower Development and Training Act and Adult Education Act	18.1								
Vocational Rehabilitation Act	25.8								
Federal Property and Administrative Services Act	15.0								
Other Federal Acts[a]	12.2								

0   25   50   75   100   125   150   175   200

Millions of Dollars

[a]"Other Federal Acts" include: National Defense Education Act, Economic Opportunity Act, Library Services and Construction Act, Mental Retardation Facilities Act, Civil Rights Act of 1964, Social Security Act, Civil Defense Act of 1950, Cooperative Research Program, National Foundation on the Arts and Humanities Act, Federal Grants to the Board of Regents, Education Professions Development Act, Highway Safety Act, Social Security Fund and Public Broadcasting Act of 1967.

FIGURE 3A.2

Major Components of Total Federal Aid for Education in New York State, Federal Fiscal Year 1970 (in millions.)

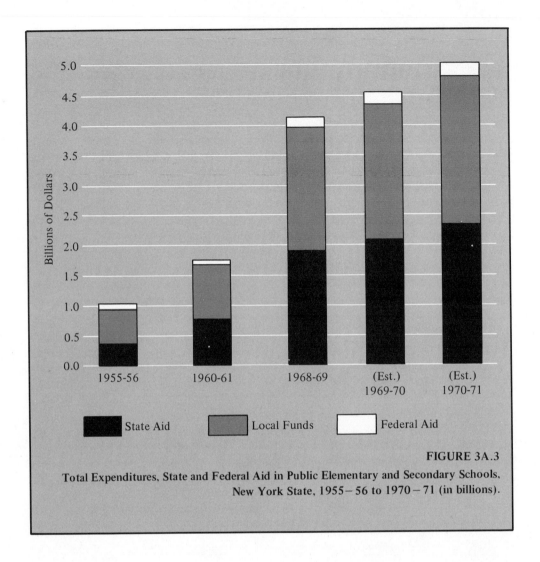

Billions of Dollars

1955-56	1960-61	1968-69	(Est.) 1969-70	(Est.) 1970-71

State Aid   Local Funds   Federal Aid

FIGURE 3A.3

Total Expenditures, State and Federal Aid in Public Elementary and Secondary Schools, New York State, 1955−56 to 1970−71 (in billions).

4

Racial and Ethnic Integration in the Public Schools

The central theme of this report is that the promise of equal educational opportunity must become a reality in this decade. The Commission believes that while equity in the distribution of financial resources is an essential first step toward attainment of this goal, equitable financing is only the beginning. The creation of educational opportunity in which every child's aspirations are checked only by his or her *individual* limitations is the ideal to which we are committed. Certainly discrimination based on racial, ethnic, social class or sexual criteria wherever it exists in the public school system of this state, even in the subtlest of forms, cannot be tolerated, and the resources of the state must be employed to check its development.

Racial, and in some cases ethnic, isolation as it exists in the public schools of New York State, reflects, in the view of this Commission, a monumental societal failure which must be corrected regardless of its cause. Much has been made of the distinction between state sanctioned *de jure* segregation, which has been held to be actionable under the 14th Amendment, and that kind of segregation called *de facto,* thought to be based upon adventitious housing patterns and therefore not a proper subject of constitutional inquiry. Even aside from the fact that this distinction may not be widely applicable, in that very little segregation is purely accidental, this Commission concurs with the conclusion articulated by the Supreme Court in *Brown* v. *Board of Education*: ". . . in the field of public education, the doctrine of 'separate but equal' has no place. Separate educational facilities are inherently unequal." [1]

We are persuaded that regardless of the distribution of financial and other material resources, the educational opportunities afforded segregated blacks and other minorities have not been as great as those afforded whites similarly situated. This finding only reflects the rather obvious general truth that where racial and ethnic isolation exist, better social services, most of which are not susceptible to constitutional measurements, tend to be distributed to the dominant culture. Thus, the Commission believes that the attainment of equal educational opportunity is conditional upon racial and ethnic integration.

For most children, the first experience with the legal and political framework of their society is in the school. They know that the public maintains the schools, and that they are required by law to attend. And quite apart from the reading, writing and arithmetic they learn in their schools, they also receive an unspoken message—their society's concern, or lack of concern, for them, and the seriousness, or lack of seriousness, of the principles the society professes.

The best traditions of our country, those of which we are proudest and which we try, in our explicit teaching, to transmit to our children, envisage a heterogeneous but fraternal society in which individuals are free to identify with and develop their own special cultural heritage if they choose, but in which no hard lines will be drawn separating group from group and citizen from citizen. This Commission believes that a school system, maintained by law, governed by public officials, supported by public revenues, cannot, by acts of commission or omission, permit the young who come into its charge to draw the inference that public authority accepts, encourages, or participates in, the division of our society into first- and second-class citizens. Nor can it permit students to come away from their education with grounds to believe that, despite the Pledge of Allegiance, with its phrase, "one nation, under God, indivisible, with liberty and justice for all," the schools are content to accept as permanent and incurable a state of distrust and hostility between different races, classes, or cultural groups.

Our nation and our state are informed by founding ideals which are admittedly difficult to live by. The only thing that is likely to be more difficult is the acceptance of a status quo departing radically from these ideals. Cynicism, despair, apathy, rebelliousness, hypocrisy, are the price. There can be reasonable disagreement between honest men about the best way to achieve the goal of integration. No one has a monopoly of wisdom with regard to this matter, and different approaches have to be tried in an experimental spirit. On the necessity to act, and on the validity of the goal itself, however, we see little room for disagreement among those who take seriously the promise of this nation. A "good education for our children" means, at the minimum, an education in which they become aware that our society is making a serious effort to practice what it preaches.

Furthermore, the Commission is persuaded that an integrated education carries with it promises of improved quality that cannot be achieved in a segregated environment, and that full interracial and inter-ethnic exposure throughout the educational process enhances each individual's self-aware-ness and social consciousness in ways that redound not only to his own but society's advantage as well. In a pluralistic world that increasingly demands interracial and inter-ethnic cooperation and understanding at all levels, segregated education makes no sense. The notion that the harm of segregation and the concomitant benefit of integration accrues only to minorities is painfully inaccurate; the problem has become increasingly that of the dominant white culture. History is replete with examples of how op-pression is ultimately more of a burden on the guilt-ridden oppressor than on the oppressed. Dr. Kenneth B. Clark puts it succinctly when he says that segregated schools are destroying the human development of sensitive white children more surely than that of black children.

Interracial and inter-ethnic exposure increases understanding and co-operation. Integration in the schools should be given the highest priority because it is clear that such cooperation and understanding are more easily instilled in young people than in adults.

THE MAGNITUDE OF RACIAL ISOLATION IN THE SCHOOLS

The basic conclusion of the *Report of the National Advisory Commission on Civil Disorders* (the Kerner Commission) in 1968 was that this nation is moving toward two societies, one black, one white—separate and un-equal. Six months previously, the United States Civil Rights Commission reported a similar trend in the nation's schools in *Racial Isolation in the Public Schools*. While there are indications that racial polarization at some levels of society has decreased since 1968, all evidence shows that racial isolation in the public schools has increased throughout the country since that time, with the notable exception of public schools in the Southern states.

The second national survey of racial and ethnic enrollments in the public schools conducted by the United States Department of Health, Education and Welfare, indicates that the percentage of Negroes attending schools with 50 per cent or greater Negro population in the 11 Southern states* has decreased from 81.6 per cent to 60.9 per cent between the years 1968 and 1970, while in New York State those percentages have increased from 67.7 per cent to 71.2 per cent.[2] Moreover, in New York State the percent-age of Spanish-surnamed Americans in similarly segregated schools has in-

---

* Alabama, Arkansas, Florida, Georgia, Louisiana, Mississippi, North Carolina, South Carolina, Tennessee, Texas, Virginia.

creased from 82.4 per cent in 1968 to 83.4 per cent in 1970,* and the percentage of all minorities—including Negroes, Spanish-surnamed Americans, Indians and Orientals—attending schools with more than 50 per cent minority enrollment, has increased from 72.1 per cent to 74.7 per cent.[3]

Even more alarming to the Commission is the number of students in the state attending grossly segregated schools: the percentage of minority students attending public schools in which the enrollment of minority students exceeds 90 per cent has increased from 45.5 per cent in 1968 to 49.2 per cent in 1970.[4] Conversely, during the school year 1970–71, 74.4 per cent of the state's white** students attended schools in which the minority population was less than 10 per cent.[5]

By contrast, in the 11 Southern states the percentage of minorities in grossly segregated schools† decreased from 70.4 per cent in 1968 to 33.0 per cent in 1970; the percentage of whites in schools with a minority population of less than 10 per cent decreased from 70.5 per cent to 46.3 per cent over the same period.[6] (Figure 4.1.)

Population migrations have been a contributing factor in the increasing racial isolation in New York State schools. For example, white school enrollments in the state's six largest cities†† have, in all cases except Yonkers, decreased since 1960, and minority-group enrollments have increased.[7] Moreover, while total enrollments in the state increased 5 per cent—from 3.3 to 3.5 million students—over the same period, minority-group children accounted for 97 per cent of that increase.[8] White migration out of the cities combined with the rise in minority-group school-age children within the cities has caused the number of segregated schools to rise significantly: while minority-group enrollments throughout the state increased 22 per cent between 1967 and 1970, the number of minority-group children in schools with minority enrollments exceeding 50 per cent, increased by 43 per cent.[9]

In short, by applying almost any standard, it is clear that racial and ethnic segregation in New York State public schools is a problem of major proportions which continues to grow. That the problem is not insoluble has been demonstrated dramatically in the South, where the trend toward increased school segregation has not only been arrested but reversed.

REMEDIES FOR THE NORTH

It is beyond the compass and ability of this Commission to prescribe for each of the state's racially imbalanced school districts the method it should

---

* In this chapter, references to 1970 data are to information collected in the Fall of 1970, except where otherwise noted.
** Hereinafter synonymous with "non-minority" unless otherwise indicated.
† "Grossly segregated" here refers to schools with over 90 per cent minority enrollment.
†† New York, Buffalo, Rochester, Yonkers, Syracuse, and Albany.

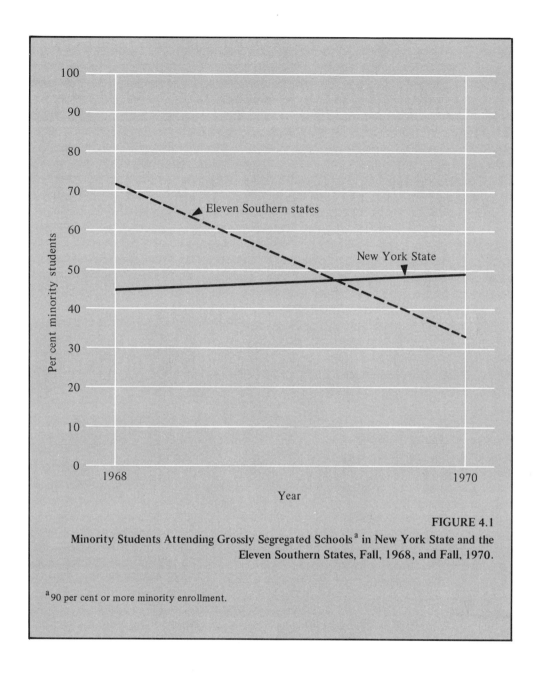

FIGURE 4.1

Minority Students Attending Grossly Segregated Schools[a] in New York State and the Eleven Southern States, Fall, 1968, and Fall, 1970.

[a] 90 per cent or more minority enrollment.

employ to end the isolation of races in its schools. Rather, our recommendations focus on the need to develop statutory tools which will assure that desegregation of the state's segregated school districts receives immediate attention. Every community has its unique personality and we do not suggest that one solution applies to all. Nevertheless, given the segregated housing patterns that do exist in New York State, most desegregation plans will involve the careful placement of schools as well as the transportation of students. With respect to the latter, the effects of busing and the accompanying loss of control over their children's schooling are sources of deep concern to parents. The Commission's positions on these difficult issues follow.

BUSING   The Supreme Court recognized as recently as April, 1971,[10] that student transportation is necessary to accomplish racial and ethnic desegregation. Unfortunately, however, the term "busing" has been invested with fearful connotations. The fact is that 19.6 million of the nation's public school children—approximately 42 per cent of the total—are bused to school every day, in every section of the country.[11] Two million of these children are in New York State alone.* In fact, some 58 per cent of the public school children in the state, excluding New York City, are bused to school.[12] The preponderance of this busing is not compelled by court order; in fact, most of it occurs in predominantly white suburban and rural areas where parents pay handsomely, either directly or indirectly, for what they consider the privilege. Bus transportation has been an integral part of the public education system for years and was perhaps the single most important factor in the transition from the one-room schoolhouse to the consolidated school. Within tolerable limits, busing neither endangers health or safety nor impinges on the educational process. However, the anxiety parents feel at the prospect of sending their young children on buses to schools a distance from their homes is very real, and school administrators must make every effort to show parents that their children are safe and cared for. Parents themselves might be recruited to ride the buses as chaperones. Parents from outside the district might also be hired as liaison workers or in some other capacity in the school to minister to the special needs of children who come from other neighborhoods.

COMMUNITY CONTROL   One of the objections most frequently raised by parents, particularly in large cities, is that they will lose their voice in the administration of their children's schools if their children are bused out of the neighborhood. The Commission shares the view that parent participation and interest are vital to the success of the desegregated school. Community control has been an effective alternative strategy since the 1960's, when the integration movement appeared to be blocked. However, despite its successes, the Commission views community control as a palliative, a powerful transitional device with limited potential when viewed in the context of the much greater social and educational benefits of integration.

School desegregation is likely to be a slow process, but when it is

---

* See Chapter 8 for a discussion of transportation practices in New York State.

achieved, involvement of parents from all the neighborhoods served by the school must be assured.* The Commission's recommendations for the establishment of Parent Advisory Councils** would provide for many levels of parent involvement.

This Commission firmly believes that opposition to busing can be overcome when steps are taken to reassure parents of the well-being of their children. We also believe that if in a particular instance community control and integration cannot be reconciled, the latter must prevail.

In this context, then, the Administration-sponsored amendment to the proposed Emergency School Assistance Act, which would expressly prohibit the use of any of the bill's $1.5 billion to defray the cost of any busing other than that required by law, is very regrettable.[13]

This action by the Federal Government has had the effect of undermining desegregation efforts throughout the country, confusing the American public and eroding the position of those school officials who have extended themselves to discharge their legal and moral responsibilities by attempting to implement desegregation.

The issue of desegregation in general, and busing in particular, became a partisan political matter in the 1972 Presidential election. This complex and agonizing problem must be dealt with at all levels on a bipartisan basis if solutions are to be found. The issue is not whether to bus or not; the issue is the quality of education at the end of the bus ride and indeed, in a larger sense, the quality, tenor and tone of life in this country.

INTEGRATED SCHOOLS

The goal to which the schools must aspire is not merely desegregation but integration. Many schools in this nation and state have been desegregated, few have been integrated. The difference is profound: simply stated, in a desegregated school, students from different racial, ethnic and social class backgrounds are placed together in a building, and expected to co-exist harmoniously; in an integrated school, a full range of programs and safeguards is employed to assure that the highest degree of tolerance, trust, cooperation and understanding between all participants will prevail.[14]

1. *Classroom racial balance.* Sorting systems such as "tracking," to the extent that they have the effect of segregating races and social classes into separate classrooms or units of study, are damaging to all students in educational, psychological and social terms.[15] In an integrated

---

* A three-year study by Educational Testing Service of the recently desegregated elementary schools of Evanston, Illinois, suggests that one result of integration, which involved extensive busing, was increased participation of black parents in parent-teacher association activities and other school-related community projects.
** See Chapter 11.

school, efforts should be made to assure that individual classes reflect the racial balance of the entire grade.[16]

2. *Teacher training.* Racial and ethnic prejudice, at least to the extent that it is a societal norm, exists among teachers as it would among any other group selected at random. Because the great majority of teachers are white, and because of the strong influence the teacher-figure has on a child, racial prejudice on the part of the teacher operates to the severe disadvantage of the minority child. It is also possible that teacher attitudes are communicated to white children as well as black, and thus exacerbate the racial prejudice in a classroom.[17]

   In order to minimize the possibility of a teacher's conscious or unconscious prejudices undermining integration, teacher re-training might be needed. Experimental approaches such as team teaching, which tends to diminish the effect of a prejudiced teacher on children, should also be tried.

3. *An integrated curriculum.* Selection of curricular units and activities related to the minority child's cultural background can obviously do much to increase the white child's respect and regard for him as well as to heighten the minority child's self-image. Presentation of the curricular materials in an appropriate fashion is essential. Such materials should be integrated into the regular curriculum so that children do not perceive them as a fad in the regular course of study. They should be presented by a teacher who is sympathetic to the subject matter and devoid of those prejudices that might cause the children to disdain it.

4. *Participant preparation.* Prior to educational desegregation in a community, there is generally minimal preparation of the direct participants (students, teachers, administrators), and of the indirect participants (parents, community leaders, members of community groups). The process of desegregation is fraught with psychological conflict and tension. Better preparation, including some attention to the emotional processes at work in all participants, is needed both when desegregation begins and as it continues. Local media (radio, newspapers, and television) are also part of the participating community, and they should be prepared and instructed as to how to help constructively.

5. *Development of self-awareness.* It is important for all people, both white and minority, to establish strong personal identities, and part of that process involves the confrontation of their ethnicity. Thus, the desire of minority groups to examine and explore their unique cultural identities and backgrounds is legitimate and constructive. In an integrated school system, opportunities should exist for such examination and exploration to occur for whites as well as minorities. Racial and ethnic studies, in addition to those required of all students, should be included on an elective basis in the formal curriculum as demand re-

quires, and appropriate time and space should be set aside for students to consider the meaning of their ethnicity in more informal fashion.

THE BURDEN OF THE SCHOOLS

Although the question of housing is beyond the scope of the Commission's charge, we are well aware that the separation of racial and ethnic groups in cities and suburbs is attributable to many complex factors, including housing policies and practices by private as well as public agencies. In order for our society to achieve true integration, many institutions, in addition to schools, will have to be involved. However, those in positions of educational leadership must exercise prompt initiative to achieve the goals of integrated education; the schools cannot wait for other social, business and political forces to respond first. They have the best opportunity to make a contribution here and now to the desegregation and integration of our society.

CONCLUSIONS AND RECOMMENDATIONS

Summary of Commission Conclusions

In preparing its recommendations for an intense assault on racial imbalance in New York State schools, the Commission arrived at the following conclusions. They are presented here as the primary presuppositions upon which the Commission's recommendations, which follow, are based.

1. *Racial and ethnic segregation are incompatible with the ideals of this nation.*
2. *In spite of a firm policy promulgated by the Board of Regents and efforts at implementation by the State Education Department, racial and ethnic isolation have increased dramatically in New York State during the last decade.*
3. *Elimination of racial and ethnic isolation in the schools cannot be postponed until discrimination and isolation in areas such as housing and employment are eliminated.*
4. *It is imperative that desegregation occur at the elementary school level since it is at the earliest ages that the possibilities of overcoming racism and other forms of prejudice are greatest.* However, desegregation plans must be developed and carried through at the secondary level as well.
5. *In the absence of federal leadership, the state bears ultimate responsibility for equalizing educational opportunities, and it is the obligation of local school authorities to develop and implement plans in harmony with state policy.*

6. *School integration is not antithetical to the continued cultural, racial and political efforts and achievements of minority groups; indeed, only through the process of full integration can divisive political viewpoints that are based solely on racial and ethnic distinctions be eliminated.*

School integration is a means to create an atmosphere in which our society's remarkable racial and cultural diversity can flourish to the benefit of all.

Commission Recommendations

FEDERAL ACTION   The Federal Government should examine the effects of its laws and regulations on increased geographical racial isolation, particularly in the area of residential segregation. In this connection, the argument has frequently been advanced that residents in suburban school districts suffer a financial hardship when low-cost housing is constructed, because it inevitably increases the number of children to be educated while simultaneously reducing the per-pupil real property tax wealth in the district. Under the Commission's proposed finance formula, which provides for State assumption of the major burden of educational finance and the imposition of a uniform statewide property tax rate, this argument would no longer obtain.

We fully endorse the principle of the Federal Emergency School Assistance Act designed to provide $1.5 billion for purposes of promoting desegregation and integration. We strongly urge, however, that no restrictions be placed on the use of a fair portion of such monies by school systems attempting voluntary desegregation. We strongly urge also that no restriction be placed upon the use of such monies for the purpose of busing children to accomplish desegregation, whether or not such busing be pursuant to court order or voluntary.

STATE ACTION
1. *The Legislature should create a statutory obligation on the part of each local school district to develop a plan designed to promote racial and ethnic understanding and positive interracial and inter-ethnic attitudes in the schools within its jurisdiction. Where applicable, the elements of such a plan shall include the elimination of racial and ethnic imbalance within the schools, the hiring of multi-racial and multi-ethnic administrative and teaching staffs, and the use of multi-racial and multi-ethnic curriculum materials.*

   Such a statute should adopt in preamble form and as legislative findings the educational case for fully integrated schools as previously articulated by the Board of Regents. Whenever the Commissioner shall determine that racial and/or ethnic imbalance exists in a public school, based on information and statistics which are currently received by the Education Department from each district, he shall promptly give notice thereof to the Board of Education having jurisdiction over such schools.

Each Board of Education which is so notified shall thereupon submit to the Commissioner a plan for the elimination of such racial imbalance and a timetable (not to exceed a total of three years) for implementation, which plan and timetable shall be acceptable to the Commissioner. Elements of each such plan shall include changes or revisions of school attendance zones, transportation of pupils, closing of schools, construction of new schools, pairing and grouping of schools, teacher recruitment and reassignment, and combinations of these elements and any other elements which the Board of Education may deem feasible, and which the Commissioner approves, provided, however, that any such plan shall:

a. Not place an undue share of the burden of reassignment or transportation on any one racial or ethnic group.
b. Avoid transportation of pupils for lengths of time or distance that risk their health or significantly impinge on the educational process, provided further, however, that if the result of this stipulation is that racial imbalance will not be corrected in all schools in a given district, such result must be justified to the satisfaction of the Commissioner. Where transportation of young children is required, efforts should be made to recruit parents to serve as chaperones on the buses.

Each such plan shall also include:

a. The beginning and completion dates for each desegregation step together with the projected desegregation results of each step including the identity of the schools and the number and percentages of pupils to be affected thereby.
b. Establishment of practices for recruitment, hiring and assignment of teachers and administrators which will effectively promote racial and ethnic balance and equalize staff competence and experience among all schools in the district. Efforts should be made to have the staff reflect the racial and ethnic balance of the community.
c. Provision for the avoidance of tracking systems or other educational techniques or innovations without provision for safeguards against racial segregation within school buildings as a consequence.
d. Provision for either teacher attitude training or for deployment of teachers in a way that will increase their sensitivity and ability to cope with situations and problems in a desegregated context as well as to exploit integration to provide a richer educational experience.
e. Provisions to assure that no loss in student achievement results from desegregation. Such provisions might include, for example, increasing the number of adults who work in the schools, particu-

larly as remedial specialists, and specially appointed teachers from the neighborhoods of the students attending a particular school. Both males and females should be hired in these capacities, many working part-time where appropriate.

f. Special care should be taken to integrate the professional staff which makes decisions for the district regarding special classes and schools for children with learning disabilities based on physical, emotional or behavioral problems.

The statute should also provide that no school facility or addition to any existing school shall be opened unless the opening of such school or addition has been approved by the Commissioner as consistent with the racial balance plans of the district and the region.

Finally, enforcement of the provisions of this proposed statute should be within the jurisdiction of the New York State Supreme Court upon the complaint of the Commissioner or of any parent or parents of a child attending a school which is racially imbalanced. No such parent or parents shall be required to appeal or petition to the Commissioner pursuant to Section 310 of the Education Law prior to seeking judicial relief.

The passage of such legislation would advance the cause of desegregation and integration immeasurably. First, it would demonstrate commitment and leadership on the part of the Legislature, which would lead local school authorities toward accomplishment of those goals. Moreover, it would create statutory duties on the part of local school authorities that could be enforced by the State Supreme Court. This, we believe, is the single most important recommendation of this chapter. The gradual but impressive desegregation of the schools in the South is a result primarily of firm leadership from the executive branch of the Federal Government together with the sanction applied by the federal courts, i.e., the threat of contempt action against defiant and recalcitrant state and local officials. The same result can and must be attained in New York.

Community participation in the formulation of the foregoing plans should be required, including the preparation of alternative plans by interested groups. However, situations must be avoided such as the one in Mount Vernon, New York, where the school board's insistence on implementation of a plan requiring exorbitant expenditures has impeded any meaningful desegregation for the past seven years. Local boards must defer to the Commissioner's legal power to substitute his judgment, where necessary, for that of the local board.

2. *The Legislature should, at the very least, not only restore the Racial Imbalance Fund to the Education Department's fiscal 1973 appropriation but increase it. An allocation of $10 million in fiscal 1973 would provide monies for such things as pupil transportation and temporary school space and defray other costs related to integration efforts.*

3. *The Division of Intercultural Relations of the State Education Department should be greatly expanded and carefully staffed with representatives of all minority groups and both sexes to assist local boards in preparing, up-dating and implementing integration plans.*
4. *The Legislature should, by statute, facilitate consolidation of school districts to achieve desegregation as well as eliminate statutory obstacles to cross-busing of children across district lines for the same purpose.* (See, e.g., pp. 279–80.)
5. *Pending such legislative corrections, the Commissioner of Education, through the Department's Division of Intercultural Relations, should begin to examine segregation as a regional problem and work out regional solutions where needed.*
6. Submission and implementation of complete desegregation and integration plans, as outlined above, would be required only in districts such as those designated "Target Districts" in this analysis. However, *all districts*—those that are desegregated and those 622 that have less than 4 per cent minority or white enrollments—*should be required to submit to the Intercultural Relations Division a description of the use and presentation of multiracial and multiethnic materials in their curriculum.* Textbooks should be free of historical error and ethnic bias, and positive contributions of ethnic groups to American and other societies should be stressed. In short, the curriculum should be integrated even if the student body is not.

LOCAL ACTION   The goal of integration will only be achieved with the full cooperation and involvement of every school district in New York State. While federal and state authorities may provide direction and guidance, the real momentum for this effort must come from the local districts, each of which should view equality and integration as essential goals of their educational system.

1. *Plans for community participation in desegregation must be developed and put into action so that civic leaders, school administrators, teachers, parents and students are prepared for full integration to take place.*
2. *Even where desegregation has occurred, continued effort should be made to assure that full integration is accomplished.*

In most cases this involves an ongoing effort; most segregated schools in New York State are segregated because neighborhoods are. For most people interracial or inter-ethnic contact is minimal throughout their lives; suspicion and fear are the consequences. This situation cannot be changed overnight; conflict should be expected between civic leaders, parents, administrators, teachers and students when desegregation is effected. Conflict is normal and integration has a better chance to succeed if it is exploited as a learning device to produce greater self-awareness and understanding of others. In order to be prepared for such conflict, however, local school authorities must take active steps to educate themselves and the community at large. Trust and respect must be established at all levels; teachers must be retrained, if necessary, to teach in an interracial and inter-ethnic environment, and students should be encouraged to explore openly the nature of racism and prejudice, not only in society at large but among themselves.

3. *The Report of Annual Performance, required of each school, as described in the chapter on Governance, should include a comprehensive assessment of interracial and inter-ethnic relations to which representatives of each racial and ethnic group would contribute.*
4. *Each district—white, black and desegregated—should seek ways to improve racial balance throughout its schools. Cooperative arrangements with adjoining school districts and opportunities for regional consolidation should be pursued; such plans should be submitted to the Commissioner of Education.*

REGIONAL ACTION   Our recommendations relating to regional governance are set forth in detail in the chapter on Governance. It is contemplated, however, that many services to facilitate desegregation and integration could be accomplished at the regional level. *Region-wide desegregation planning should occur in order to facilitate inter-district cooperation generally. Specifically, regional coordination of transportation and school construction should take place with a view toward encouraging integration. The Division . of Intercultural Relations should operate, at least in part, on the regional level to provide planning and implementation assistance to local school authorities.*

Similarly, efforts to recruit minority-group teachers should be coordinated regionally, as should in-service training of experienced teachers to help them adjust to integrated classrooms.

Furthermore, the Commission recommends that large regional "exemplary schools" be constructed, with either federal or state financing, to provide alternative and imaginative approaches to education. Located on the outskirts of cities, these schools would enroll students from many different racial, ethnic and socio-economic backgrounds. Specialized facilities and instruction would attract talented students from a broad geographic area. These schools would serve as centers for applied educational research and teacher training and would function in the field of education as teaching hospitals do in the field of medicine. Moreover, these schools could serve the serious cultural and academic interests of students, as well as other members of the community, in after-school and weekend hours. Thus, they would be well equipped with laboratories, libraries, studios, shops, auditoriums, rehearsal space, athletic facilities and a wide variety of other equipment which would encourage many stimulating activities in a racially and ethnically integrated environment.

A Model for Family Choice

This Commission believes that alternative types of public education should be available to students and parents. Our recommendations relating to school assessment, which are set forth elsewhere, are designed, in large part, to encourage individual schools to establish identities and styles of their own and to publicize information relating to their individual characteristics as well as their performance so that families might make a rational choice among several schools. However, family choice plans in segregated areas might result in increased segregation; therefore, we insist that safeguards against this eventuality be incorporated into any such plan. The model we advocate is fully developed in the chapter on Governance.

MAJOR FINDINGS

If the Commission's recommendations for immediate action against racial isolation and discrimination in the schools convey a sense of urgency, that is the intention. These recommendations were developed after analysis of grim statistics. As a Commission studying the proper role and responsibilities of public education, we feel it is no less imperative that our children be taught in school how to live in an integrated world than that they be taught how to read.

The statistics which follow show that for the most part the schools of our state reflect all too accurately the ghettos—black and white—in which we live.

In the state's three largest cities, New York, Buffalo and Rochester, we have looked beyond the numbers to the actions of officials and found that only in Rochester is a comprehensive attack on school segregation being made. Summaries of these urban case studies are included here.

We have examined present federal and state resources and policies with regard to school desegregation and tried to point out their strengths and weaknesses. And finally we have reviewed the powerful role of the law.

The figures speak for themselves; the critical question is, can we find the strength and the means to reverse the destruction, the fear and the waste that they represent?

Racial and Ethnic Segregation in New York State

According to 1970 data, the state's minority populations are increasingly concentrated in large urban centers and the areas immediately surrounding them:

—77 per cent of New York State's non-white population (Indians, Orientals and blacks) lives in New York City. (Blacks account for 90 per cent of the non-white population.)[18]

—86 per cent of the non-white population lives in the New York City Standard Metropolitan Statistical Area.[19]

—96.5 per cent of the non-white population in the state lives in the SMSA's of the Big Six* cities.[20]

—95 per cent of the Puerto Rican population in the state lives in New York City (based on 1969 estimates.)[21]

Further, these urban-centered minority populations are growing larger as whites migrate to the suburbs:

—Statewide, the proportion of non-whites to total population has increased from 4.4 per cent in 1940 to 13.2 per cent in 1970. This represents an increase from 600,000 non-whites (nearly all black) in 1940 in a total population of 13.5 million, to 2,400,433 non-whites in 1970 in a total population of 18,190,740.[22]

—The number of Puerto Ricans (who did not constitute a significant portion of the state population in 1940) has increased 59 per cent from 1960 to 1969. The statewide population of Puerto Ricans is approximately 1,000,000 (5.8 per cent of the total state population), 960,000 of whom live in New York City.[23]

Segregation in the Schools

In recent years the percentage of minority-group enrollments in the public schools has risen more dramatically than the percentage of minority group increases in overall population:

—Between 1967 and 1970, the statewide public school enrollment increased from 3,336,678 to 3,500,592—an increase of 4.9 per cent. Blacks and Spanish-surnamed students (most of whom are Puerto Rican) accounted for 97 per cent of that increase. That is, of the 163,914 total student enrollment increase, 159,528 were black or Spanish-surnamed Americans.[24]

—From 1967–1970, the enrollment of Spanish-surnamed students increased from 256,094 to 317,211 (an increase of 23.9 per cent in four

---

* So called because they were the only cities in the state with populations exceeding 125,000. The school districts in such cities share tax and debt limitations with their respective cities; the 1970 Census revealed that Albany's population had slipped below 125,000 and therefore, pursuant to the State Constitution, the Albany school district was no longer fiscally dependent. As a result, the Big Six cities are now, technically, the Big Five. For purposes of this analysis, however, we continue to treat Albany together with New York, Buffalo, Rochester, Yonkers and Syracuse and refer to the group as the Big Six.

years). The Spanish-surnamed portion of the total enrollment increased from 7.7 per cent to 9.1 per cent.[25]
—Between 1967 and 1970 the white public school enrollment increased by only 4,386 (0.2 per cent).[26]

DISCRIMINATION IN HIRING Minority-group representation among professional staff has never been adequate. However, as the minority-group student population increases and the minority-group representation among professionals fails to keep pace, the problem becomes more acute. (Table 4.1.)

—While minority students represent 25.3 per cent of the state's public school enrollment, only 5.1 per cent of the total staff are minority-group members.[27]
—Between 1967 and 1970 minority student enrollment increased by 21.9 per cent. In that same four-year period minority staff increased by only 13.6 per cent.[28]

TABLE 4.1

Summary of Ethnic Census of Students and Staff in New York State, 1967–70

STUDENTS

	Total	White (No.)	(%)	Black (No.)	(%)	Spanish-Surnamed Americans (No.)	(%)	Other Minority (No.)	(%)
1967	3,336,678	2,609,236	78.2	462,992	13.9	256,094	7.7	8,356	.3
1968	3,406,658	2,606,956	76.5	494,919	14.5	280,275	8.2	24,508	.7
1969	3,453,987	2,615,535	75.7	520,487	15.1	291,610	8.4	26,355	.8
1970	3,500,592	2,613,622	74.7	542,855	15.5	317,211	9.1	26,904	.8

STAFF

	Total	White (No.)	(%)	Black (No.)	(%)	Spanish-Surnamed Americans (No.)	(%)	Other Minority (No.)	(%)
1967	181,209	172,285	95.1	7,549	4.2	432	.2	943	.5
1968	210,868	195,970	92.9	12,501	5.9	1,980	.9	417	.2
1969	190,432	181,098	95.1	7,869	4.1	1,083	.6	382	.2
1970	199,617	189,480	94.9	8,309	4.2	1,345	.7	483	.2

Segregation and Desegregation in New York State School Districts

In order to assess the extent of segregation throughout the state, the Commission examined the racial and ethnic composition in the schools of each of the 760 school districts. Based on this analysis each school district was determined to be either segregated or desegregated. The results of that analysis, summarized in Table 4.2, follow:

RACIALLY ISOLATED DISTRICTS—WHITE   Based on criteria given below, 621 of the state's 760 school districts are white isolated. These school districts do not enroll enough minority students to enable them to be considered racially balanced. Such isolation may not be due to explicit acts or policies adopted by the local governing or school authorities, but may instead reflect historical segregated housing patterns of the community. Nevertheless, it is a fact and we believe an unfortunate one, that 45.2 per cent of the state's public school children—a total of 1,582,900 students—attend schools in districts which are 98.6 per cent white.

RACIALLY ISOLATED DISTRICTS—MINORITY   One district in the state, Wyandanch, is minority isolated: 96.3 per cent of this district's enrollment is minority.

TARGET DISTRICTS   Fifty-four school districts are designated "Target Districts." These districts, unlike the "Racially Isolated" districts, have sufficient numbers of white and minority students to achieve racial balance in their schools. Schools within these districts, however, are not racially balanced. The Target Districts include all of the Big Six cities as well as many other large districts. In total, 1,683,000 children—nearly 50 per cent of the total public school population—are being educated in these Target Districts.* Table 4.3 is a complete list of the Target Districts.

DESEGREGATED DISTRICTS   Eighty-four districts, which are shown in Table 4.4, were considered desegregated according to our criteria. These 84 districts enroll a total of 234,771 students, only 6.7 per cent of the state's public school enrollment.

CRITERIA FOR DETERMINING RACIAL ISOLATION OR SEGREGATION   For the purposes of this analysis, a school district was considered "Racially Isolated" when neither its minority enrollment on the one hand, nor its white enrollment on the other, exceeded 4 per cent of the total school dis-

---

* Appendix 4B contains profiles of each Target District except New York, Buffalo and Rochester which, as the state's three largest cities, are given more detailed consideration hereinafter. The profiles include information relating to the ethnic composition of pupil enrollment, minority-group representation among professional staff and deviation of individual schools from district-wide ethnic enrollment proportions.

TABLE 4.2

Distribution of New York State Students in Racially Isolated, Segregated and Desegregated Districts

	No. of Districts	Total Enroll-ment	% of State Total Students	White Enrollment (No.)	(%)	% of State Total	Minority Enrollment (No.)	(%)	% of State Total
DESEGREGATED DISTRICTS	84	234,771	6.7	198,940	84.7	7.6	35,831	15.3	4.0
RACIALLY ISOLATED DISTRICTS									
White "	621	1,582,900	45.2	1,560,950	98.6	59.7	21,948	1.4	2.5
Minority " (Wyandanch)	1	2,499	0.1	92	3.4	—	2,409	96.3	0.3
TARGET DISTRICTS									
Big Six Cities	(5 + 31)a	1,327,197	37.9	559,952	42.2	21.4	767,245	57.8	86.5
Other	48	353,225	10.1	293,688	83.1	11.2	59,537	16.9	6.7
Total Racially Isolated and Segregated Districts	706	3,265,821	93.3	2,414,682	73.9	92.4	851,139	26.1	96.0
Total State	790a	3,500,592	100.0	2,613,622	74.7	100.0	886,970	25.3	100.0

a Includes New York City's 31 decentralized districts.

TABLE 4.3

Target Segregated Districts (Districts with Greater than 4% White and 4% Minority Enrollments Which Are Segregated)

Albany	New Rochelle
Amsterdam	New York City
Auburn	Niagara Falls
Bay Shore	Niagara Wheatfield
Beacon	North Babylon
Brentwood	North Rockland
Buffalo	Ossining
Catskill	Patchogue
Deer Park	Peekskill
Dunkirk	Peru
Elmira	Port Chester
Elmont	Poughkeepsie
Gowanda	Riverhead
Great Neck	Rochester
Hempstead	Salamanca
Hudson	Salmon River
Huntington	Schenectady
Ithaca	Spring Valley
Kingston	Syracuse
Lackawanna	Troy
La Fayette	Uniondale
Lawrence	Utica
Lockport	Valhalla
Mamaroneck	Wallkill
Monticello	Warwick Valley
Mt. Vernon	White Plains
Newburgh	Yonkers

trict enrollment. (A list of such districts is included in Appendix A to this chapter.) A school district was considered a "target" segregated district when it was not Racially Isolated and schools within the district were found to be racially imbalanced. The racial balance of individual schools was measured against the district-wide percentage of minority students. Districts were designated as racially imbalanced when:

1. Minority enrollment in one or more schools in the district varied from the district-wide minority percentage by more than 10 per cent, or
2. When the minority enrollment in two or more schools exceeded the district-wide minority percentage by more than 5 per cent.

TABLE 4.4

Desegregated Districts (Districts with Greater than
4% White and 4% Minority Enrollments)

Akron	Freeport	Pawling
Albion	Geneva	Pocantico Hills
Amityville	Glen Cove	Port Jervis
Arkport	Goshen	Prattsburg
Avoca	Greenburgh	Red Creek
Babylon	Greenport	Rockville Centre
Barker	Hawthorne Knolls	Roosevelt
Batavia	Highland Falls	Rome
Bedford (Mt. Kisco)	Holley	Roslyn
Bellport	Island Park	Rye
Binghamton	Letchworth	Rye Neck
Bridgehampton	Liberty	S. S. Seward Institute
Caledonia Mumford	Livingston Manor	Sag Harbor
Center Moriches	Long Beach	Saratoga Springs
Central Islip	Lyndonville	Silver Creek
Charlotte Valley	Lyons	Sodus
Clyde	Malverne	Southampton
Cohocton	Manhasset	South Huntington
Copiague	Marlborough	Spackenkill
Corning	Mattituck	Tarrytown
Coxsackie Athens	Medina	Tuckahoe
Dover Plains	Middle Island	Washingtonville
East Moriches	Middletown	Wayland
Eastport	Millbrook	West Babylon
Elba	North Rose Wolcott	Westhampton Beach
Ellenville	Nyack	West Valley
Elmsford	Onondaga	Westbury
Fallsburgh Central	Pavilion	Williamson

Desegregation of schools cannot be determined solely on the basis of fixed statistical criteria; therefore, each district not Racially Isolated was examined for extent of racial imbalance and exceptions were made based on considerations such as the following:

1. When a large minority enrollment of preschool children caused a school to exceed the district-wide minority average by more than 10 per cent, the district was not considered segregated for that reason, but
2. When only one school exceeded the district-wide minority enrollment percentage by 5 per cent, but also enrolled more than half the district's minority children, the district was considered segregated.

TABLE 4.5

Distribution of Public School Students in the Big Six Cities in New York State, Fall, 1970

	Total Enrollment	Per Cent of State Total	White Enrollment (No.)	(%)	Per Cent of State Total	Minority Enrollment (No.)	(%)	Per Cent of State Total
Albany	10,999	0.3	7,214	65.6	0.3	3,785	34.4	0.4
Syracuse	29,402	0.8	21,991	74.8	0.8	7,411	25.2	0.8
Yonkers	30,632	0.9	24,859	81.2	1.0	5,773	18.8	0.7
Rochester	45,500	1.3	28,410	62.4	1.1	17,090	37.6	1.9
Buffalo	70,305	2.0	41,021	58.4	1.6	29,284	41.6	3.3
New York City	1,140,359	32.6	436,457	38.5	16.7	703,902	61.5	79.4
Total:	1,327,197	37.9	559,952	42.2	21.4	767,245	57.8	86.5
State Total:	3,500,592	100.0	2,613,622	74.7	100.0	886,970	25.3	100.0

SUMMARY   Of the state's 3,500,592 public school students, 3,205,900—or 93.3 per cent of the total enrollment—are going to schools in either "racially isolated" or segregated districts; only 234,771, 6.7 per cent of the total, attend schools in desegregated districts. Further, 92.4 per cent of the white children and 96.0 per cent of the minority children in public schools in New York State are in "racially isolated" or segregated districts.

The Big Six Cities

The absolute size of the problem of racial and ethnic segregation in the New York City public schools, which enroll 1.14 million students, is greater than in any other single district in the state; nonetheless, segregation in other districts is also serious, particularly in urban areas. The other five cities which comprise the Big Six—Buffalo, Rochester, Yonkers, Syracuse and Albany—together enroll 187,000 students in their public schools; segregation of both students and staff is acute in all of them. (Table 4.5.)

Analysis of the extent and effectiveness of integration efforts in the state's three largest cities follow.

CASE STUDY OF NEW YORK CITY

New York City,* the largest city in the nation, contains 43.3 per cent of the entire population of New York State in an area of 300 square miles, with a city-wide population density of over 26,000 people per square mile. From 1950 to 1960 the city population declined from 7,891,957 to 7,781,984. However, it increased during the next 10 years by 86,000 to a total of 7,867,760 in 1970.[29] (Table 4.6.)

The population of the New York City Standard Metropolitan Statistical Area (SMSA)[30] has increased from 10,694,633 in 1960 to 11,528,695 in 1970. During this same decade, the black population of the New York SMSA increased from 1,227,625 to 1,883,292. These blacks represent 86.9 per cent of the black population of the state; 76.9 per cent of such population is in New York City alone. Similarly, the New York SMSA Puerto Rican population increased from 629,430 in 1960 to approximately 998,000 in 1969. Ninety-eight per cent of the state's Puerto Rican population resides in the New York SMSA, with 95 per cent in New York City alone. Thus, in 10 years the New York SMSA black and Puerto Rican populations together increased by some 1,000,000 people. By contrast, the white population in the New York SMSA increased by only 42,000. Within New York City, the minority populations increased during the last decade by 936,000; the city's white population during that period decreased by some 617,000.[31]

---

* The special problems of New York City schools are discussed in more detail in a separate chapter.

TABLE 4.6

Population of New York City and Its Boroughs, 1950–1960–1970

	1950	1960		1970	
	No.	No.	Per Cent Change	No.	Per Cent Change
New York Total	7,891,957	7,781,984	− 1.4	7,867,760	+ 1.1
Bronx	1,451,277	1,424,815	− 1.8	1,472,216	+ 3.3
Brooklyn	2,738,175	2,627,319	− 4.0	2,601,852	− 1.0
Manhattan	1,960,101	1,698,281	−13.4	1,524,541	−10.2
Queens	1,550,849	1,809,578	+16.7	1,973,708	+ 9.1
Richmond (Staten Island)	191,555	221,991	+15.9	295,443	+33.1

SCHOOL ENROLLMENT   New York City's schools enrolled 32.6 per cent of New York State's public school children in 1970. In addition to its public school enrollment, a considerable though declining number of New York City children attend nonpublic schools. According to 1969 data, these nonpublic school students comprise 27.5 per cent of the city's total school enrollment and 51.5 per cent of the nonpublic school enrollment in the state.[32] Nineteen per cent of the students enrolled in nonpublic schools in New York City are from minority groups (7.3 per cent are Negro, 10.6 per cent are Spanish-surnamed Americans, and the remainder are American Indian and Oriental) compared with 4.2 per cent statewide, excluding New York City.[33]

During the past four years, the city's public schools have shown a fairly steady increase in total enrollment. Reflecting the trend of white migration from the city, however, white enrollment has declined; it is significant that the rate of decline in white enrollments has decreased over the past three years, indicating that this trend is subsiding. (See Table 4.7.)

A closer examination of racial and ethnic distribution of students among New York City's schools shows that isolation of minorities by both county and decentralized district is severe. (See Table 4.8.) County-wide, public school enrollment of whites ranges from a low of 15.5 per cent in Manhattan (where whites represent approximately 60 per cent of the borough's population)* to a maximum of 86.3 per cent in Staten Island (where 94.0 per cent of the population is white).[34]

---

* U.S. Census data do not isolate Puerto Rican as a racial category. While Census information does isolate numbers of Puerto Ricans, it does not permit accurate comparisons with Anglo-white and Negroes. Puerto Ricans are racially categorized as white or Negro.

TABLE 4.7

Number and Per Cent of New York City Public School Students by Ethnic Group, 1967–1970

	WHITE		NEGRO		SPANISH-SPEAKING AMERICAN		OTHER MINORITY (INDIAN, ORIENTAL)		TOTAL	
	No.	%	No.	%	No.	%	No.	%	No.	%
1967	529,930	47.9	332,192	30.0	243,427	22.0	—	—	1,105,549	100
1968	467,365	43.9	334,641	31.5	244,302	23.0	17,279	1.6	1,063,787	100
1969	452,957	40.5	376,322	33.7	270,215	24.2	17,680	1.6	1,117,174	100
1970	436,457	38.3	393,516	34.5	292,664	25.7	17,115	1.5	1,140,359	100

Staten Island and Queens (where 62.5 per cent of the enrollment is white) have sizable white enrollments; Brooklyn (the most populous county), Bronx and Manhattan are dominated by minority students. Also, Brooklyn's three predominantly white districts are located in the southern sector of the county, reflecting the tendency of white population concentrations to gather on the city's boundaries; similarly, Districts 10 and 11, which have the largest white enrollments in the Bronx, both border Westchester County on the city's northern boundary.

Not only are public school enrollments by counties within New York City and by districts within the counties racially and ethnically imbalanced, the individual schools are as well. Indeed, as Table 4.9 indicates, 88.7 per cent of the city's schools deviate from the city racial/ethnic average by more than 10 percentage points.

Fall, 1970, data on ethnic enrollments, which have been compiled district by district within the city, allow examination of the ethnic balance in schools within each district. As Table 4.8 indicates, the districts with medium and low concentrations of minority students—those with the greatest potential for balance within districts—tend to have the greatest number of racially imbalanced schools. (For example, District 2 in Manhattan, District 10 in the Bronx, Districts 15, 18, 19 and 21 in Brooklyn, and every district in Queens and Staten Island.)

Table 4.8 also indicates that 60 of the city's 65 academic high schools and 23 of its vocational schools are racially/ethnically imbalanced in that minority enrollments in them deviate by more than 10 percentage points from the citywide average at grade level. It is noteworthy that enrollment in New York City's four prestigious specialized high schools is 75.7 per cent white.

TABLE 4.8

Isolation of Minority Students in Schools Within Grade Levels in Districts in New York City, 1970

District	Grade Level	Percentage of Minority Students	Number of Schools	Number of Schools deviating ±10 Percentage Points from Grade Level Minority Average
MANHATTAN				
1	Elementary	90.6	16	4
	Junior H.S.	93.2	4	0
2	Elementary	63.7	21	18
	Junior H.S.	71.2	5	3
3	Elementary	86.0	19	15
	Junior H.S.	90.2	4	1
4	Elementary	98.0	18	0
	Junior H.S.	99.1	4	0
5	Elementary	98.8	19	1
	Junior H.S.	99.4	5	0
6	Elementary	82.1	11	10
	Junior H.S.	82.4	3	1
BRONX				
7	Elementary	98.4	18	0
	Junior H.S.	98.2	4	0
8	Elementary	77.6	19	17
	Junior H.S.	76.8	6	4
9	Elementary	92.2	20	4
	Junior H.S.	90.7	5	1
10	Elementary	49.2	17	13
	Junior H.S.	57.4	7	5
11	Elementary	52.1	19	9
	Junior H.S.	48.0	6	4
12	Elementary	96.2	17	1
	Junior H.S.	99.3	4	0
BROOKLYN				
13	Elementary	95.7	18	2
	Junior H.S.	97.8	4	0
14	Elementary	91.0	21	4
	Junior H.S.	90.7	6	1
15	Elementary	67.8	20	15
	Junior H.S.	78.4	5	2
16	Elementary	93.2	23	2
	Junior H.S.	93.1	4	1
17	Elementary	90.5	13	2
	Junior H.S.	91.5	4	1
18	Elementary	37.4	13	11
	Junior H.S.	52.4	5	4
19	Elementary	87.8	22	17
	Junior H.S.	85.5	7	3
20	Elementary	24.4	24	12
	Junior H.S.	27.7	6	2

District	Grade Level	Percentage of Minority Students	Number of Schools	Number of Schools deviating ±10 Percentage Points from Grade Level Minority Average
BROOKLYN (*Continued*)				
21	Elementary	27.5	23	16
	Junior H.S.	24.0	6	4
22	Elementary	17.9	22	9
	Junior H.S.	18.3	5	2
23	Elementary	99.4	19	0
	Junior H.S.	99.6	4	0
QUEENS				
24	Elementary	34.2	19	13
	Junior H.S.	36.0	5	3
25	Elementary	21.1	22	14
	Junior H.S.	18.8	6	2
26	Elementary	19.8	24	5
	Junior H.S.	18.7	5	0
27	Elementary	39.0	27	25
	Junior H.S.	32.1	4	0
28	Elementary	54.9	22	20
	Junior H.S.	61.7	6	6
29	Elementary	69.1	22	19
	Junior H.S.	68.5	4	4
30	Elementary	41.9	20	13
	Junior H.S.	39.4	5	4
RICHMOND (S.I.)				
31	Elementary	14.4	37	24
	Junior H.S.	11.6	6	2
HIGH SCHOOLS[a]	Academic H.S.	49.2	65	60
	Vocational H.S.	68.5	27	23
SPECIAL SCHOOLS	Hospital, Handicapped	61.6	11	8
	Elem. Deaf	82.4	2	0
	JHS Deaf	69.3	1	0
	Spec. Ed. (Delinquent)	80.6	36	22
SCHOOLS FOR PREGNANT WOMEN	(Manhattan)	97.5	2	0
	(Bronx)	100.0	1	0
	(Brooklyn)	98.9	2	0
	(Queens)	95.2	1	0

[a] Included in this category are the city's four specialized high schools. The percentage of minority students in each of these schools is: Bronx High School of Science, 18.7; High School of Music and Art, 37.1; Peter Stuyvesant High School, 20.7; Brooklyn Technical High School, 33.4.

TABLE 4.9

Deviation of New York City Schools from
City Racial/Ethnic Average, Fall, 1969

Deviation from Racial Balance[a]	Number of Schools	Per Cent of Schools
0–10%	102	11.3
10.1–30	206	22.7
30.1–Totally Segregated	598	66.0
Total	906	100.0

[a] Balance = 59.4% minority.

CLASSROOM SEGREGATION   In addition to racial and ethnic isolation in counties, districts and schools, "tracking," which results in further isolation of students *within* schools, is an acknowledged practice in New York City. While the educational merits of ability grouping for all children must be carefully weighed, authorities familiar with New York City schools assert that ability grouping is highly correlated with race and ethnicity.

More than four years ago, Judge Skelly Wright found tracking as practiced in the Washington, D.C., school system to be unconstitutional. His finding was based, in part, on the following observation:

Even in concept the track system is undemocratic and discriminatory. Its creator admits that it is designed to prepare some children for white-collar, and other children for blue-collar jobs. Considering the tests used to determine which children should receive the blue-collar special and which the white, the danger of children completing their education wearing the wrong collar is far too great for this democracy to tolerate.[35]

Despite Judge Wright's ruling, however, New York and other cities continue to track and minority students appear to be victimized. In New York City children are sorted into tracks as early as the first grade based on inadequate, if not discriminatory, achievement tests. That ability grouping is common as early as the elementary school is evidenced by the 1969 United Federation of Teachers (UFT) contractual agreement with the Board of Education which is still in force.[36]

Thereafter, psychological damage of tracking is profound. The children in the "stupid" classes find it hard even in adulthood to shake the fear that the school was right and that they are really stupid. They, in turn, reject the school and seek other ways of regaining self-esteem. The self-fulfilling prophecy is realized: a child is identified as having a learning deficiency, teachers accept the diagnosis and treat the child as deficient; the child lives up to their negative expectation, whether or not the deficiency, in fact, existed in the first place.

DISCRIMINATION IN HIRING   While minority student enrollments in New York City were 61.5 per cent of the total in 1970, minority professionals have had nowhere near proportionate access to staff positions. In fact, in 1970 only 6,619 or 9.9 per cent of the 67,757 professional staff positions in New York City schools were occupied by minority-group members. Three years earlier minority-group members occupied 10.8 per cent of these positions. The shortage of minority teachers is so acute that 56 of the 148 public schools in New York City with a minority enrollment greater than 99 per cent have fewer than 15 per cent minority teachers.[37]

Most of New York's teachers are graduates of city colleges which, until 1970 at least, were almost all white; their students were selected from among the highest achieving students in heavily white academic high schools. A further screening process discriminating against minorities is the examination administered by the Board of Examiners, which New York City teachers must take in addition to meeting state certification requirements.* That the Board of Examiners has perpetuated discrimination against minorities has been the conclusion of nearly every formal school study during the past 20 years.[38]

Indeed, a recent federal court decision found that the examinations administered by the Board of Examiners to supervisory personnel violated the equal protection clause of the Federal Constitution in that they did, in fact, discriminate against minorities and had no rational justification as a measure of future job performance.[39] As a result, the Court has ordered that no similar examination for supervisory personnel be administered, that no future appointments be made from existing lists of people deemed qualified by virtue of success on previously administered examinations and that no new lists be established based upon successful performance on previously administered examinations.[40] Based on this decision and other considerations outlined in the chapter on Educators and Educational Policy, we recommend abolition of all examinations currently in use by the Board of Examiners as a basis for selection of teachers and other personnel for the New York City public schools.

Desegregation Efforts in New York City Since 1954

Long before most Northern cities had become aware of racial imbalance, New York City was generating plans and programs aimed at correcting it. Integrationist community groups, inspired by the 1954 *Brown* v. *Board of*

---

* Buffalo and New York City are the only cities in the state with examination procedures.

Education of Topeka decision, focused their attention on demands for open enrollment, rezoning, and construction of new schools on sites that would promote integration. These and other remedies were tested in New York City, but tested cautiously and without commitment by education authorities. The impotence of integration plans adopted by the Board of Education is illustrated by the fact that from 1954 to 1965 the number of segregated black and Puerto Rican schools in New York City increased 290 per cent, from 52 in 1954 to 201 in 1965.[41]

The tactic of the school boycott was widely used by parents.[42] In fact, it was the threat of such an action in March of 1964 that sent the Board of Education to then Commissioner James E. Allen with the request that he evaluate the city's integration programs. The Allen Report, a stinging indictment of the Board's efforts, was released in May 1964.[43] The following are comments from that report:

On open enrollment:

Open enrollment has had no significant effect on the extent of segregation. It cannot have, as it depends wholly upon voluntary choice among Negro and Puerto Rican parents. In September, 1964, for example, when the program was revised and enlarged, about 110,000 elementary pupils were offered the opportunity to transfer. Of this number, about 2,000 applied, and some 1,800 were, in fact, transferred—an impact of less than 2 per cent of those given the option. [Page 4.]

On free choice transfer:

In our judgment, the Free Choice Transfer Policy, whatever its other merits, and we think it has some, will probably have no citywide effect on the level of segregation. It is an optional, not a required program. It puts the burden for desegregation entirely on the voluntary and individual decisions of Negro and Puerto Rican parents. [Page 7.]

On the pairing plan:

In 1958, 12 per cent of all elementary schools were Negro-Puerto Rican segregated, compared with 22 per cent in 1963. If all 21 of the pairings proposed by the Board were to be introduced at once in 1964–65, this fraction of 22 per cent would drop to 21 per cent. The pairing proposal thus would reduce minority school segregation in the city by 1 per cent, if introduced all at once. Not only have many of the proposed sites been withdrawn following local opposition, however, but the Board proposed to make only four such pairings in September, 1964. [Page 8.]

On the 1964–70 school building program:

The school building program as presently set forth reinforces substantially the historic pattern of building on sites within the most segregated areas. This is the case chiefly in Negro residential areas, but it is also true in some mainly white neighborhoods, and thus helps to intensify both forms of segregation.

To date, desegregation has not been a main factor in the programming of construction and physical renovation. Building plans have developed in response to population increase, age and quality of existing plant, transport conditions, and site availability. If the purpose to desegregate was a consideration at all, it apparently was ranked in importance below these other considerations. [Page 6.]

On the junior high school feeder pattern changes:

The Board of Education plans to change the pattern of elementary schools feeding into junior high schools. Specifically, the Board proposed 10 such changes and then reduced this number to six, out of a total of 132 regular junior high schools.

If a great effort were made to desegregate the 25 junior high schools which are now Negro-Puerto Rican type schools, the new policy could make a difference within a single decade. Such an effort is not proposed by the Board of Education. [Page 7.]

The Allen Report concluded:

We must conclude that nothing undertaken by the New York City Board of Education since 1954, and nothing proposed since 1963, has contributed or will contribute in any meaningful degree to desegregating the public schools of the city. Each past effort, each current plan, and each projected proposal is either not aimed at reducing segregation or is developed in too limited a fashion to stimulate even slight progress toward desegregation. [Page 8.]

In recommending steps for corrective action, the Allen Report called for four major reforms: (1) combining the academic and vocational high schools to create unified and integrated comprehensive high schools, (2) eliminating the three-year junior high and the three-year senior high schools by substituting a 4-4-4 plan with the purpose of bringing children out of segregated neighborhood elementary schools into integrated middle schools a year earlier, that is, in the fifth grade, (3) planning a network of educational parks that would bring all children into integrated, well equipped centers, and (4) establishing educational complexes, clusters of elementary schools around intermediate middle schools.

It took the Board of Education a full year to issue a policy statement endorsing the Allen Report, and that delay accurately predicted the fate of the report's recommendations.

Creation of comprehensive high schools involved costly construction, and a time-consuming capital construction process. Gradually whatever momentum the recommendation had was drained. By 1967, when several sites finally had been chosen, the Board effectively abandoned the comprehensive high school notion.

The 4-4-4 plan also went unfulfilled. A few middle schools, most of them segregated, have been built, but the Board was either unwilling or unable to build enough new middle schools to make the plan viable. Thus the large majority of children in the system still move through the traditional and still segregated 6-3-3 organization.

Educational parks suffered similarly. Three were planned. Only one of them, Linear City, a huge education complex for south central Brooklyn, would have resulted in significant desegregation; it died in the early planning stages. The other two, both in the largely white northern Bronx, are under construction.

There are now a few educational complexes in the city. When the first, I.S. 201 in Manhattan, opened in September, 1966, it was 99.2 per cent black and Puerto Rican.

The blame for the failure of desegregation efforts in New York City is most frequently leveled at the Board of Education on grounds that, at the very least, it failed to exert initiative and leadership. David Rogers makes the following charges regarding the Board's culpability:

> The Board did not take initiative in informing the public (about its open enrollment program). It did little to prepare parents, students, staff and communities participating in the program. And when people were informed, it turned out that local school officials and many headquarters personnel were by and large opposed to the plan. There is no available evidence to suggest, for example, that the Board and school officials had pointed out with much conviction the possible advantages of participating in open enrollment. And there is evidence to suggest otherwise. . . .
>
> Extensive records and files . . . suggest a widespread pattern of sabotage by principals, teachers, and field superintendents and a very limited publicity campaign from headquarters. The practice of not informing Negro parents in ghetto schools of the new opportunities open to them to send their children to underutilized white schools was so widespread, in fact, that headquarters took over more and more of this function. The further practice of lecturing to Negro parents on the many "costs" of transferring their children out, engaged in by many principals and teachers, and the rather strong urging that parents keep their children in their local schools undoubtedly contributed to the low percentage who participated in open enrollment.[44]

Policy priorities with respect to integration are still not clear and present practices continue to be confused.

Desegregating New York City: a Feasibility Study

In the years since the Allen Report, it has become a widely held assumption that the dimensions of racial and ethnic segregation in New York City's school system are so broad that desegregation is physically impossible. To test this notion the Commission asked Professor Dan W. Dodson of New York University to prepare a feasibility study on the desegregation of elementary and junior high schools in New York City. His findings are startling. "The more one examines the matter," Professor Dodson asserts, "the more convinced one is that the physical aspects of correcting imbalance in New York City are not the determining ones. They are matters of emotion, of prejudice and of politics." [45]

Because of limited time and resources, Dr. Dodson was unable to prescribe specific student assignments necessary to accomplish the desegregation of each school in New York City. His efforts were concentrated instead on the feasibility of desegregating the 30 districts in Manhattan, the Bronx, Brooklyn and Queens on the assumption that school assignments within the individual districts could be worked out later. Because of its geographic isolation, Staten Island was excluded from the desegregation plan; nonetheless, if a citywide desegregation plan were adopted, all schools on Staten Island would be expected to reflect the district-wide enrollment of minority groups.

Dodson rejects the middle school plan recommended in the 1964 Allen Report because it requires large additional expenditures to relieve the congested conditions that now exist in junior and senior high schools. The combination of a projected decline in over-all school enrollment with the present surplus of space in elementary schools makes these expenditures hard to justify.[46]

Central to the Dodson Plan is abandonment of the notion that neighborhood schools constitute the only legitimate approach to elementary education. As long as residential segregation remains, desegregation cannot be accomplished by continued insistence on neighborhood schools; therefore, in those places where racial and ethnic isolation exist, adherence to the neighborhood school concept must yield to the more important value of desegregation.

Furthermore, Dodson contends that an inviolate neighborhood school policy is financially unsound in a period of declining birth rates and emigration from the city. Because the neighborhood school plan is necessarily inflexible, many districts would quickly find their schools underutilized; other districts would become overcrowded. Dodson cites as an example of the financial waste imposed by adherence to the neighborhood school policy the case of Stuyvesant Town on the east side of Manhattan. When the housing development was built in 1947, the Board of Education, under substantial pressure, erected P. S. 40 and P. S. 19 to meet the demand created by the influx of young families with children. Initially the schools were overcrowded. Today the school buildings are used at 64 per cent capacity and further declines in enrollment are anticipated.

In the Commission's view, Dr. Dodson's work is extremely provocative. His study is summarized here in the interest of (a) demonstrating that New York City schools *can* be desegregated, and (b) stimulating official action against racial isolation in the city's school system. It is not endorsed as a recommendation by the Commission because we believe that any specific integration proposal should emanate in the first instance from the district to be affected.

The Dodson Plan

The plan begins with the desegregation of elementary schools, or grades 1–6. Kindergarten is excluded because attendance there is not compulsory and it typically lasts for one-half day only.

Dodson's first procedural step was to conduct an inventory of the total space available in New York City for elementary education.

By examining the Board of Education data Dodson identified those schools in 14 outlying districts in Queens, Bronx and Brooklyn where 85 per cent or less of the space was being used. He calculated the number of vacant seats in such schools to be 34,303. In the desegregation model, those seats were the first to be filled, taking advantage of favorable traffic flow during the morning rush hour. (An additional benefit of filling schools outside the center would be the possibility of phasing out the equivalent of 50 obsolete, inefficient elementary schools in the city with capacities of 600 students each.)

The racial and ethnic composition of the total New York City elementary school population is as follows:

Black	216,832	37.5%
Spanish-Surnamed	177,324	30.7
Other	184,150	31.8
Total	578,306	100.0%

Dodson suggests that ideally every school in the city would reflect this racial and ethnic balance, but concedes that, logistically, perfect balance would be difficult to accomplish. Consequently, in making district assignments it was arbitrarily decided to allow a tolerance of 5 per cent above or below the citywide enrollment percentage for each group. Thus, black enrollment in any district could vary from 32.5 per cent to 42.5 per cent, Spanish-surnamed enrollment from 25.7 per cent to 35.7 per cent, and Others from 26.8 per cent to 36.8 per cent.

Dodson has developed a plan to accomplish inter-district desegregation allowing for the above deviation, which would require transportation of 155,648 elementary school students—27 per cent of the total—from their district of residence to another district where they would attend school. The number of students to be bused, broken down by ethnic group, is as follows:

Black	50,700
Spanish-Surnamed	52,612
Other	52,336
Total	155,648

Dodson uses similar procedures to effect inter-district desegregation of junior high school students. In this case, 59,355 out of a total of 218,931 seventh, eighth and ninth grade students—or 27 per cent—would be transported out of their districts of residence.

It has been difficult to estimate the cost of desegregating elementary and junior high schools in accordance with Professor Dodson's model. For example, the Dodson model accomplishes only inter-district racial and ethnic balance; undoubtedly some further intra-district busing would be required to achieve racial and ethnic balance school by school. However, Dodson's model represents the maximum amount of inter-district reassignment that would be necessary.

The Dodson desegregation plan would require that a total of 215,000 elementary and junior high school students be assigned to schools out of their home districts. The city currently buses 116,000 students to school daily at an annual cost of $34 million. Of these students, 15,000 are physically handicapped, and the Bureau of Budget estimates that $18 million is spent on the transportation of these pupils alone.

According to these figures the annual cost of busing the remaining 101,000 non-handicapped children (30,000 to nonpublic schools, 71,000 to public schools) is $16 million, or approximately $158 per child. Based on this per-pupil cost, busing of 215,000 children could be accomplished for approximately $34 million. It must be conceded that in some cases the plan calls for busing long distances which might inflate the per-pupil cost. This might be partially offset by allowing roughly half the junior high students to use existing public transportation. Also, it is assumed that many of the 71,000 non-handicapped public school children currently being bused could be subsumed under the plan and the amount of new money required for transportation would be reduced accordingly.

The plan suggests further benefits. It is believed that better space would be provided since current and projected enrollment declines would permit abandonment of outmoded schools. Also, the city would be relieved of the burden of constructing new buildings for a considerable period of time. If the 34,000 vacant seats found in the 14 districts analyzed by Dodson were matched by similar vacancies in the remaining 16 districts, it is possible that many elementary schools could be taken out of service.

At the junior high school level, chronic overcrowding could be alleviated by abandonment of the middle school plan and the return of the fifth and sixth grades to the elementary schools where space is available. This in turn would make it possible to return the ninth grade to the junior high schools, thereby relieving congestion in the high schools.

Thus, the Dodson model would reduce the costs of education, and such cost reductions would, in part, if not completely, balance the cost of operating additional buses.

CASE STUDY OF BUFFALO

With a population of 457,814 in 1970, Buffalo is the state's second largest city. Because of its substantially smaller size, Buffalo's failure to alleviate racial imbalance in its public schools is even more disheartening than New York City's. Racial imbalance in Buffalo's schools is grave: almost nothing concrete has been done to overcome such imbalance, and, given current community attitudes and lack of leadership, there is very little reason to expect that anything will be done voluntarily.

Population Trends

Since 1950, Buffalo's population and wealth have declined, while its minority-group numbers have increased; this trend is typical of most Northern and Western cities. Buffalo is exceptional, however, in the clustering of its people of similar ethnic origins (Polish and Italian in particular) in separate communities, and in the high percentage of its school-age children in nonpublic schools (33 per cent).[47] Also, its surrounding suburbs are severely segregated.[48] Of the 30 Erie County school districts, only six have over 1 per cent nonwhite students. Of these six, the only two districts with significant nonwhite student populations are Buffalo (46.6 per cent) and Lackawanna (19.2 per cent).[49] Akron, with a sizable Indian population, has the third highest nonwhite population, representing 16 per cent of the total.[50]

SCHOOL POPULATION   Between 1960 and 1970, Buffalo's population decreased 14.1 per cent, and both its public and nonpublic school enrollments declined: public to 70,305 from 73,200; nonpublic to approximately 35,000 from 40,000.[51] The increase in the proportion of minority-group population to white enrollment in the schools has been slow, averaging about 1.4 per cent per year. The number of black children in the school system has remained stable; therefore, the change in racial composition has been caused by the movement of white families out of Buffalo. Population projections, moreover, indicate that nonwhites are not expected to exceed 48 per cent of the public school enrollment even if nonpublic enrollments do not decline.[52] (Table 4.10.)

Table 4.11 describes the problem of segregation in Buffalo public schools from the perspective of the deviation in enrollments from district-wide racial balance. A balanced school in 1967–68 had a 37.5%:62.5% minority to majority student ratio. In 1970–71, that ratio was 41.6%:58.4%.

PERSONNEL   The total number of administrators, teachers and other personnel has decreased slightly since 1967 in Buffalo's schools, while the number of minority personnel has remained constant. As a result, the proportion of minority personnel to the total has increased from 9.8 per cent to 9.9 per cent, or 364 out of 3,682.[53] Furthermore, the few minority-group teachers in the school system tend to be concentrated in a few schools.

With respect to supervisory personnel, in 1970–71 only four out of 77 elementary school principals and one out of 20 secondary school principals

TABLE 4.10

Buffalo Public School Enrollments and Ethnic Proportions, 1967–70

	White		Black		Spanish-Surnamed		Indian & Oriental		Total	
	No.	*%*	*No.*	*%*	*No.*	*%*	*No.*	*%*	*No.*	*%*
1967	45,430	62.5	25,641	35.3	1,136	1.6	485	.7	72,692	100
1968	43,942	60.9	26,381	36.6	1,278	1.8	514	.8	72,115	100
1969	42,546	59.6	26,940	37.7	1,393	1.9	562	.8	71,441	100
1970	41,021	58.4	27,069	38.5	1,620	2.3	595	.8	70,305	100

were from minority groups; out of a total of 105 assistant principals, only seven were from minority groups.

A History of Desegregation Efforts in Buffalo

There is, and has been for many years, considerable segregation of white and minority-group pupils in Buffalo's public schools. In February, 1965, the Buffalo Board of Education was ordered by the State Commissioner of Education to desegregate its schools.[54] At that time, 15 elementary schools,

TABLE 4.11

Deviation of Buffalo Public Schools from District Racial Balance, 1967 and 1970

	NUMBER OF SCHOOLS	
Deviation from Racial Balance	1967 Balance = 37.5% Minority	1970 Balance = 41.6% Minority
0–10%	11	10
11–30%	36	34
31–Totally Segregated	52	51
Total	99	95

two junior high schools, and one senior high school had concentrations of black students exceeding 90 per cent of their total enrollments. Six years later, in 1970–71, each of the same schools had a concentration of minority students not less than 98 per cent.[55] In addition, since 1965, two more elementary schools have moved into the 90 per cent category, and another high school has a concentration of 85 per cent black students.[56]

The Board submitted a plan for desegregation to the Commissioner of Education in May, 1965; it was not accepted. The following year, under the auspices of the Commissioner, the Center for Urban Education (CUE) prepared a plan for desegregating Buffalo's public schools. The heart of the plan was reorganization of the grades from a 6-3-3 grouping (elementary, junior high, high school) to a 4-4-4 grouping (elementary K–4; middle school 5–8; high school 9–12). The plan was a compromise, trading desegregation in grades 5–12 for continued segregation in grades K–4, and it required major new construction.[57]

Since 1966, with one exception, the Buffalo Board of Education has relied solely on the CUE plan to accomplish racial desegregation and the focus has been on the creation of new middle schools. In 1968, the Board raised the cost of this approach substantially by amending the CUE plan to include 12 new middle schools on the grounds that the six new schools originally contemplated would have to be too large. The single alternative approach has been a one-way busing program that was implemented in 1967 and that in 1971 sent 3,200 black students out of the inner city to 29 predominantly white schools. While this program may have had some influence in reducing the number of all-white schools in Buffalo from 42 to 20 in 1966, it has had no impact on segregation in the black schools.

The Board's almost total reliance on the middle school plan has not been warranted. A junior high school was converted to a middle school in the fall of 1966. One new middle school was opened in September, 1969. The Common Council (Buffalo's 15-member elected city council) tried to halt construction of that new school in 1968 when it was two-thirds complete by withholding additional funds. The Council relented after a five-month struggle, and the school was finally completed. The only other action taken by the Board on its middle school plan was to reject, under public pressure, a site for a third school selected by the Board's staff in 1970.

School officials claim that their middle school program, which they continue to see as the answer to the problem of segregation, has not progressed since 1968 because of the Common Council's continued and consistent opposition to desegregation of schools. While Common Council intransigence on the issue is well established, the Board has nevertheless been unwilling to develop other alternatives for desegregating its schools, despite the three-year impasse on its plan, and its inability to find or approve sites for middle schools ($1.5 million already approved for this purpose remains unspent).

Voluntary desegregation of Buffalo's public schools thus appears unlikely. Six years after being ordered by the Commissioner to begin desegregation, the situation remains basically the same as it was at the time of the order, if not worse. This order is still in force, and the Commissioner has retained jurisdiction.

An urban-suburban transfer program, similar to the one in Rochester, also appears doomed. Bitterness and divisiveness engulfed two suburban districts, Cleveland Hill and Williamsville, when their school boards attempted unsuccessfully to gain support for the importation of inner-city black students.[58]

In short, substantial racial imbalance exists in the schools of both Buffalo and its surrounding Erie County communities and very little progress has been made in recent years to redress the situation.

CASE STUDY OF ROCHESTER

In March, 1971, the Board of Education of Rochester, the third largest city in the state, adopted a reorganization plan designed to effect complete desegregation of its public schools by 1974, using only available resources. Rochester's achievement so far has been impressive; however, success is still only tentative. The next three years will be crucially important.

Population and Housing in Rochester

While the total population of Monroe County, in which Rochester is located, increased from 586,387 to 711,917 between 1960 and 1970, the total population of Rochester declined from 318,611 to 296,233 over the same period. Indeed, Rochester's population has been declining steadily since 1950, when it reached a peak of 332,488.[59]

The total number of white residents in Rochester declined between 1960 and 1970 by nearly 50,000, while the number of blacks increased from less than 24,000 to nearly 50,000.[60] In 1970, Rochester accounted for only 41.6 per cent of Monroe County's total population, but 95.1 per cent of the county's black population.[61]

Segregated housing patterns in Rochester were described by the U.S. Commission on Civil Rights in its 1966 Staff Report:[62]

> Over the years, Negroes have been concentrated in nine census tracts located on both sides of the Genesee River, which bisects Rochester's downtown district. In 1964, these tracts housed six out of every 10 Rochester Negroes, and all were at least 50 per cent or more Negro in racial composition. Well over half of the increase in Negro population since 1950 has been absorbed by these tracts.
>
> And almost all of the remainder went into seven additional tracts which bordered them. All seven of the border tracts were between 30 and 50 per cent Negro in racial composition. Taking all 16 tracts together, fully 84 per cent of all Rochester Negroes resided two years ago within an area representing not more than 7 per cent of the city's total land acreage.

Negroes who lived in Rochester's suburbs of Monroe County in 1964, unlike those who lived in the city, were not heavily concentrated in only a handful of localities. Although only 808 Negroes lived in these suburbs in 1964, an increase of 210 persons since 1960, the 1964 Census Survey found at least a few Negroes in each of the 19 suburban towns of the county; in only five cases did they number more than 1 per cent of the suburb's total population. The largest percentage of suburban Negroes, about 5 per cent, was located in the town of Rush.

As in other American cities, the Negro population of Rochester is housed less adequately than its white population. At the time of the 1960 Census, close to half (46 per cent) of Rochester's nonwhite households occupied dwellings classified as either deteriorating or dilapidated. Only 13 per cent of all white households in the city were this poorly housed.

School Population

Enrollment trends in the schools are just beginning to reflect population trends. Since the high of 47,372 reached in 1968, the total enrollment in Rochester schools has declined to 45,500 in 1970.[63] Meanwhile, since 1962, the minority enrollment for elementary and secondary schools has shown a steady increase. In the five-year period 1966–70, the total number of students from ethnic minority groups (including Negro, Spanish-surnamed American, Indian, Oriental) has increased from 13,015 to 17,090 and the proportion of minorities to total enrollment has increased from 28.7 per cent to 37.6 per cent. (See Tables 4.12 and 4.13.)

TABLE 4.12

Minority Enrollment in Rochester

	1962	1963	1964	1965	1966	1967[a]	1968[a]	1969[a]	1970[a]
ELEMENTARY									
Total	5,862	6,577	7,412	8,103	9,878	10,111	10,392	11,205	11,171
Per Cent	24.0	26.6	29.1	31.3	33.2	35.6	36.8	39.1	40.4
SECONDARY									
Total	1,591	2,052	2,388	2,745	3,137	4,089	4,964	5,286	5,919
Per Cent	9.2	11.6	13.8	16.2	20.1	22.4	26.0	29.1	33.1
TOTAL CITY	7,453	8,629	9,800	10,848	13,015	14,200	15,356	16,491	17,090
CITY PER CENT	17.8	20.3	22.9	25.3	28.7	30.5	32.4	35.2	37.6
TOTAL CITY ENROLLMENT	44,146	44,845	45,152	45,220	45,358	46,570	47,372	46,843	45,500

[a] B.E.D.S. data.

TABLE 4.13

Number and Per Cent of Public School Students,
by Ethnic Group in Rochester, 1967–70

| | White | | Black | | Spanish-Surnamed | | Indian & Oriental | | Total |
	No.	%	No.	%	No.	%	No.	%	100%
1967	32,370	69.5	12,781	27.4	1,280	2.7	139	.3	46,570
1968	32,016	67.6	13,679	28.9	1,553	3.3	124	.2	47,372
1969	30,352	64.8	14,586	31.1	1,739	3.7	166	.4	46,843
1970	28,410	62.4	15,082	33.2	1,853	4.1	155	.4	45,500

Further, in 1970, the percentage of minority pupils was highest at grade one (44.6 per cent) and declined to a low of 20.4 per cent of the students enrolled at grade 12. In 1969, these percentages were 40.9 per cent and 19.1 per cent respectively.[64] Thus, the Rochester City School Board of Education projects that by 1974, when reorganization will have been completed, the minority enrollment will be 45.6 per cent.[65]

A History of Desegregation Efforts

The most recent, but by no means final, chapter in Rochester's long effort to desegregate its school system began in September, 1971. All the high schools and junior high schools and a limited number of elementary schools opened in the fall with redrawn attendance patterns designed to promote racial balance—part of the phased implementation of a total school reorganization plan. This massive reorganization required elaborate preparation and planning involving all segments of the Rochester community.

This courageous decision by the Rochester school board was taken on March 5, 1971, when the Board of Education voted by 3–2 to reorganize the district feeder patterns so as to eliminate racial imbalance in all schools by the fall of 1974. During the month of February and the first days of March, the Board resolved to desegregate all nine secondary schools and five of the 43 elementary schools by September, 1971, and to desegregate the remaining elementary schools in stages. (Eight schools had been reorganized prior to the March, 1971 decision.) "By 1973, only one racially imbalanced school will remain in the City School District and the replacement of that school with a new primary and intermediate combination will correct that imbalance." [66]

REORGANIZATION PLAN   The elementary school reorganization plan separates the 43 existing elementary schools into 11 "enlarged home zones."

Each such zone will include one intermediate school (grades 4–6) and two or more elementary schools. Three zones with a total of 12 schools had been reorganized by the fall of 1971. In all but four of the 11 home zones racial balance will be achieved while maintaining contiguous school groupings within a single enclosed zone boundary. (See Figure 4.2.)

The reorganization plan has as its goal complete racial balance in all schools, meaning that in no school will the percentage of minority students vary from the citywide average by more than 5 per cent. Thus, each school will have a minority enrollment ranging from 30 per cent to 45 per cent, depending on the grade level. Further objectives of the plan are minimal busing, minimal new construction, and the creation of zone boundaries which would absorb anticipated minority enrollment increases while maintaining racial balance district-wide. For elementary school reorganization there was an additional concern that every child be within walking distance of either the primary or the intermediate school he was to attend so that no child would require transportation to both.

TEACHERS   The reorganization plan for Rochester calls for the racial balance of students in schools throughout the district. There are no provisions, however, for racial balance of staff. The plan makes mention of recruitment, reassignment, and in-service training of staff as steps in its implementation, but as yet no plan exists for minority teacher recruitment or the achievement of staff desegregation. This represents a problem, since in 1969 only 185 out of a total of 2,126 teachers—8.7 per cent—were from minority groups.[67]

REACTION TO REORGANIZATION   Although the Board has passed the reorganization plan, many community groups have raised objections that remain to be resolved. One issue of concern to many integration-minded citizens is the decision to reorganize the secondary schools first. They suggest that the increasing number of racial incidents in the secondary schools is the result, in part, of the sudden confrontation in high school of white and black students whose emotions are heightened by the polarization of the larger community. The argument is that elementary school reorganization would lead more naturally to the elimination of prejudice in integrated secondary schools.

Others argue the reverse: integration and busing may be acceptable for secondary students, who are old enough to take care of themselves, but not for elementary school children. Anti-reorganization whites, who consistently disavow any notion of personal prejudice against blacks, argue for neighborhood schools and oppose busing for the following reasons:

1. Children learn best in a familiar environment where they feel secure. To bus the child to a different area places undue physical and psychological strain on the child and inhibits his learning in two ways: first, the bus ride in both directions is tedious, and, second, a foreign environment is disorienting to the child.

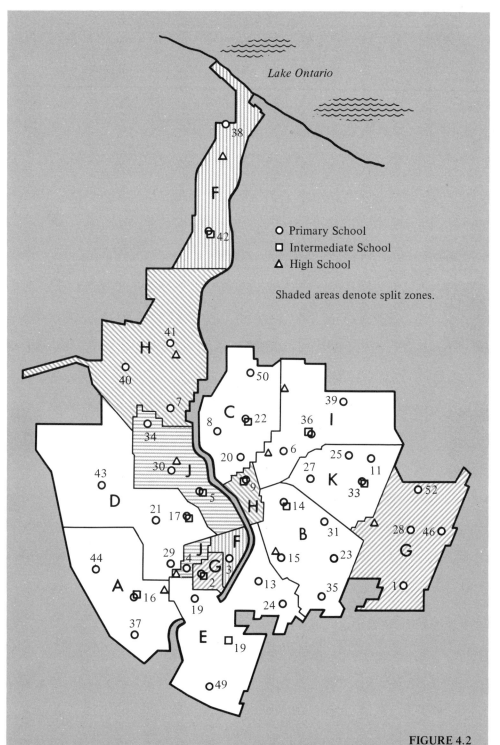

Lake Ontario

○ Primary School
□ Intermediate School
△ High School

Shaded areas denote split zones.

FIGURE 4.2

Rochester Elementary Schools—Enlarged Home Zone Plan (K-3; 4-6); Boundaries of
Reorganization of Elementary Level Zones.

2. Busing is a costly and unnecessary expense.
3. If the child becomes ill during the school day, and parents work, do not drive, or for some other reason cannot cross town to pick him up, a predicament arises. Presumably, the school will not send the child home alone on a school bus. If the child lives close to the school—within walking distance—this problem, it is felt, is less serious.
4. Heavy snows may bar travel and thereby cause the child to miss school. Also, buses can break down and bus drivers may go on strike.

Others express fears for their children's health, welfare, safety and ethical values if they are bused to deteriorating, high-crime, inner-city areas.

Some black and Puerto Rican inner-city parents, especially those on the Community School Councils (parent groups organized to work with the nine inner-city schools) are opposed to elementary school reorganization for some of the same and some different reasons. Some are against busing and raise similar concerns about distance. Other objections include the following:

1. Community School Councils feel they have gained a certain amount of control over the nine inner-city elementary schools, and they feel this control, coupled with the Reading Mobilization Year—an intensive remedial reading program—and the expanded bilingual education program have tightened up these schools and improved the quality of education in them immeasurably. The parents are reluctant to give up this opportunity to oversee the schools. Reorganization will mean that their children will be scattered all over the city. For all parents, but parents with large families especially, it will be impossible to maintain the same familiarity with the child's school and learning experience.
2. There is fear that the minority children will be discriminated against, in subtle and not-so-subtle ways, in the hostile, white, outer-city enclaves. While learning achievement may or may not increase, the psychological damage of such discrimination is less easily measured.
3. Many parents have gained a large measure of pride in their inner-city schools, which they feel have improved in recent months through parental pressure. This pride is at odds with the popular notion of integration, that its primary value is to the lower social class child who can benefit from the example of his better-off white peers.

The reorganization plan was preceded by many years of experimentation with small-scale integration programs. Some of them, such as the Pupil Transfer Program, have been quite successful.

Pupil Transfer Programs

In February, 1964, the Rochester school administration implemented a program which bused 515 children from six predominantly black inner-city elementary schools to 18 predominantly white schools on the city's outer rim.[68] By the fall of 1970, 1,040 elementary school children were being bused under the program to an expanded number of schools on the outer rim. Additionally, by 1970, an estimated 320 inner-city secondary school students were being transported to secondary schools on the city's boundaries.[69] (Table 4.14.)

URBAN-SUBURBAN TRANSFER The success of this experiment led some suburban districts where the schools had few if any blacks to open their facilities to children from the inner city with the announced purpose of overcoming the isolation of white children. This urban-suburban transfer program was initiated by the West Irondequoit school district in 1965 with the acceptance of 24 inner-city children. By 1970, the program had grown to include 616 inner-city children who traveled to five suburban districts. The city provides transportation and pays tuition for the inner-city children who attend these suburban schools.[70]

REVERSE OPEN ENROLLMENT In 1967, a reverse open enrollment program was instituted by the Rochester school administration under which 140 white children from 30 elementary schools in the outer rim and in the

TABLE 4.14

Pupil Transfer Programs, 1963–71, Summary

	'63–64	'64–65	'65–66	'66–67	'67–68	'68–69	'69–70	'70–71
OPEN ENROLLMENT (Elementary)	459	480	675	727	1,374	1,237	1,200	1,040
OPEN ENROLLMENT (Secondary)				233	183	256	321	320[a]
REVERSE OPEN ENROLLMENT					140	215	248	185
URBAN-SUBURBAN TRANSFERS			24	144	351	590	555	616
TOTAL SCHOOL YEAR	459	480	699	1,104	2,048	2,298	2,324	2,161
SUMMER SCHOOL PROGRAMS	25	35	147	425	707	62	45	
GRAND TOTAL	520	515	846	1,529	2,755	2,360	2,369	

[a] Estimated.

suburbs were bused into the inner city to attend two newly integrated experimental schools—the World of Inquiry School and the Clara Barton School. By 1970, 185 children were being bused into these two schools; several thousand children applied.

Impediments to Expanding Transfer Programs

While the transfer of 616 pupils from city schools to the suburbs and the busing of 185 students into the inner city are not significant in terms of the total county school enrollment of over 142,000,[71] these programs are a notable beginning. But clearly the program must be substantially expanded if it is to have any value either for the increasing minority school populations of Rochester or the white suburban students. Rochester's location in the center of Monroe County is particularly conducive to expanded transfer programs, and interest in such programs is evident:

> . . . the districts now involved in the Urban-Suburban Transfer Program have indicated a willingness to increase the number of children to be accepted from the City of Rochester during 1971–72, and additional districts have indicated interest in accepting City of Rochester students for 1971–72.
>
> Some districts that will be accepting City of Rochester students in 1971–72 are considering . . . providing two-way interchange of students—from the City of Rochester to their districts, and from their districts to the City of Rochester, on a voluntary basis.[72]

Several factors, however, inhibit the expansion of these programs. The main barrier to the voluntary expansion of these programs is a legal one involving the cost of tuition and transportation. State law prohibits a board of education of a central school district from paying tuition to another school district on its own authority. Rather, the voters of a district must approve such transfers and tuition payments by referendum before the board may enter into such an agreement with another district. Because the dimensions of the demand for pupil transfer are still very small, such a referendum is thought to have little chance of passage.

This has meant that the City of Rochester, a fiscally dependent city school district which does not have to submit proposed pupil transfers to a referendum, has had to bear the brunt of the financial burden for the pupil transfer programs. Rochester must pay part of the cost of tuition (that part which is not covered by state and federal aid programs) to the suburban districts for the inner-city children sent to their schools under the Urban-Suburban Transfer Program. The city also bears the cost of transportation. However, the suburban parents, not the district, must pay tuition for their children enrolled in Rochester's two inner-city experimental schools. These programs appear to be financially profitable to the suburban district. A small number of their children are being educated free in Rochester, and Rochester pays tuition to these districts for its children who are filling otherwise empty spaces in the suburban schools.

These programs have been made possible by state assistance. In 1970–71, for example, the State Education Department contributed $280,000 from its Racial Imbalance Fund and $215,000 in Urban Education Aid. Rochester contributed $51,000. In a proposal for a "Prototype Urban-Suburban Transfer Program for Rochester–Monroe County Schools," jointly sponsored by the City School District of Rochester and five suburban central school districts, a total of $707,375 has been requested to serve 716 students in the program for 1971–72. A federal grant for $300,000 has been approved.[73] The remaining portion was to have been funded by state racial imbalance funds, which were categorically eliminated from the Education Department's fiscal 1972 appropriation.

Some suburbs have been eager to cooperate with Rochester in significant ways. Brighton, for example, in addition to participating in the Urban-Suburban Transfer Program since 1966, has had its Equal Educational Opportunity Committee pass the following resolution:

. . . We urge the Board of Education of the Brighton Central Schools to halt plans for a middle school until a full study of the feasibility of a joint Brighton-Rochester district can be completed. In this way, the possibility of this means of obtaining quality integrated education will not be precluded.[74]

Conclusion

The polarization of groups and opinions suggests that, while reorganization in Rochester has the force of law, its implementation will not be easy. Some argue that it came too late; others are angry that it came at all. The deep-seated resistance was expressed in the November, 1971, election of five School Board members who ran on an anti-busing platform and who assumed office January 1, 1972.*

Any attempt to rescind the reorganization plan at this time might, in fact, be the basis for a legal suit, particularly in view of recent judicial interpretations of what constitutes *de jure* segregation.

In any case, the decision of the Rochester board sets a commendable precedent for many school districts in the state, including the other Big Six cities. We are encouraged by Rochester's reorganization efforts and hope that the new Rochester school board will endorse and continue to implement them. Other communities throughout the state are also encouraged to look to Rochester's actions and take steps in the same direction.

---

* The school board was expanded to 7 members by leglislative action in 1971.

New York State, through the Board of Regents, entrusted by law with the responsibility of determining the educational policies of the state, has articulated as strong a policy as any state in the nation to eliminate racial imbalance in its public schools; yet racial isolation in the state has increased over the past decade. The following is an anlysis of the various federal and state government resources that have been brought to bear on the problem and indicates why, for the most part, they have been unsuccessful.

Federal Resources

To a certain extent New York State may be viewed within the larger context of national efforts to bring about school desegregation. While it is true that New York State has acted, and surely will continue to act, independently of the Federal Government, attitudes expressed by a given administration and current federal programs of categorical aid can be an important influence on policy formation. Attitudes of national leaders influence state policy-makers as well as their common constituency, and thereby affect receptivity to programs. These attitudes are expressed through program priorities, through decisions on which programs to fund and the level to which such programs are funded.

The effectiveness of the federal effort in the North has been marginal at best, demoralizing and dysfunctional at worst. There are three federal programs affecting desegregation: Title IV, Civil Rights Act of 1964; Title VI, Civil Rights Act of 1964; and the Emergency School Assistance Program of 1970–71.

TITLE IV, CIVIL RIGHTS ACT   Title IV of the Civil Rights Act of 1964 (P.L. 88–352) is designed to provide assistance where problems occur as a result of school desegregation. Sections 403 through 405 authorize three discrete types of federal assistance for the desegregation of public education —technical assistance, training institutes, and grants to local school boards. This Title has provided the bulk of federal assistance to New York State in its efforts to bring about school desegregation. (Table 4.15.)

However, while there are no adequate evaluative studies on the use of Title IV money in New York State, clearly these funds have not had much impact. Over a period of six years (1965–1970) only $1.7 million has been allocated for all of New York State; it has been used primarily as seed money, financing a technical assistance staff to advise local districts.

TITLE VI, CIVIL RIGHTS ACT   The Regional Title VI office, located in New York City, has jurisdiction over New York, New Jersey, the Virgin Islands, and Puerto Rico. Its purpose is to enforce compliance with the

TABLE 4.15

Federal Outlays Under Title IV, Civil Rights Act,
1964, and Outlays in New York, 1965–71

	Total Expended Nationally	Total Expended, New York State	New York State % of U.S. Total
1965	$ 5,942,203	$163,691	2.75
1966	6,206,129	494,995	7.98
1967	6,577,859	219,589	3.34
1968	8,467,956	314,094	3.71
1969	9,238,032	213,880	2.32
1970	19,000,000	304,214	1.60
1971	19,000,000	610,654[a]	3.21

[a] Allocation rather than expenditure.

Civil Rights Act of 1964. The focus is discrimination in hiring practices and so on, not racial imbalance.

The Regional Title VI education office in New York City consists of an investigating team of 11 people and a clerical staff of four. This office investigates school districts, basing its inquiry partly upon racial and ethnic data which all school districts are obliged to submit.

When discrimination in violation of the Civil Rights Act is discovered, the procedure is to negotiate a remedy with appropriate authorities. The office has been reluctant to withhold funds because already poor areas would be likely to suffer the most.[75] If a violation is not corrected, it is reported to the Title VI General Counsel's office in Washington which issues a complaint or refers it to the Justice Department for legal action.

EMERGENCY SCHOOL ASSISTANCE PROGRAM On April 26, 1971, the United States Senate, by a vote of 74 to 8, approved its version of the Emergency School Aid and Quality Integrated Education Act of 1971,[76] which would provide $1.5 billion, primarily for desegregation purposes. In early October, 1971, the House Committee on Education and Labor sent its version[77] to the floor with the possibility of its being voted upon by the end of the current session. While the House version is almost certain to contain more constraints than the Senate bill on the use of funds by local school districts to overcome racial imbalance voluntarily, if finally approved, this legislation may provide the first substantial federal financial assistance to New York State districts seeking to redress racial and ethnic segregation.

The Senate bill, as passed, authorizes appropriation of $1.5 billion between the date of enactment and July 1, 1973—$500 million the first year,

TABLE 4.16

Allocation of Funds under Emergency School Aid and Quality Integrated Education Act of 1971 (S.1557)

	Approx. % Total Funds	Approx. Amount
Funds Apportioned to States for Programs to Establish and Maintain Quality Integrated Schools; Aid Desegregation; and Eliminate, Reduce and Prevent Isolation of Minority Groups	69	$1,035,000,000
Metropolitan Area Programs for Cooperative Integrated Schools, Educational Parks and Planning for the Elimination of Minority Group Isolation	15	225,000,000
Commissioner's Discretionary Fund	8	120,000,000
Children's Educational Television	3	45,000,000
Bilingual Bicultural Programs	4	60,000,000
Evaluation of Programs	1	15,000,000
Total	100	$1,500,000,000

$1 billion the second year. As Table 4.16 indicates, 69 per cent of the funds would be apportioned to the states for programs to establish and maintain stable, quality integrated schools, and to reduce and eliminate minority-group isolation. Of these funds New York State would be eligible for $26 million the first year and $61.6 million the second year—a total of $87.8 million. The remaining 31 per cent of the funds is reserved for special purposes. (Table 4.16.)

In order to qualify for funds, a school district must have a comprehensive plan for eliminating segregation. In addition, a portion of the money must be used to create at least one "stable, quality, integrated school" although school districts under federal court order to desegregate can be exempted from this requirement. Once these assurances are established, grants can be used to eliminate, reduce or prevent racial isolation.

State Resources

In general, the Board of Regents of the University of the State of New York has been consistently firm in its resolve to eliminate racial imbalance in the schools, as has the State Education Department. Closer to popular attitudes, however, the Legislature has been less resolute.

REGENTS' POLICY   Over a decade ago, the Board of Regents formally recognized the adverse effects of racial imbalance:

Modern psychological knowledge indicates that schools enrolling students largely of homogeneous ethnic origin may damage the personality of minority group children. Such schools decrease their motivation and thus impair the ability to learn. Public education in such a setting is socially unrealistic, blocks the attainment of the goals of democratic education, and is wasteful of manpower and talent whether this situation exists by law or by fact.[78]

In a letter dated June 14, 1963, to all local superintendents and presidents of boards of education, the late Commissioner James E. Allen asserted that the position of the State Education Department, based on the policy of the Regents, was that gross racial imbalance must be eliminated from the schools of New York State. In order that the Department might know what plans each school district had for carrying out its responsibility in this connection, the letter requested submission, by September 1, 1963, of the following information:

1. A statement indicating the situation in your district with regard to any problem of racial imbalance, regardless of the number of Negro children enrolled, or to the actual existence of or trend toward racial imbalance. At this time, and *for the purpose of this report,* a racially imbalanced school is defined as one having 50 per cent or more Negro pupils enrolled.
2. A statement of policy by your Board of Education with respect to the maintenance of racial imbalance in your schools.
3. In districts where racial imbalance exists, or is a problem, a report of progress made toward eliminating it.
4. In such districts, your plan for further action, including estimates of the additional cost, if any, and of the time required for carrying out your plan.

In January, 1968, the Regents issued a statement of policy and recommendations entitled *Integration and the Schools,* in which they took the position that the Regents and all others in positions of educational leadership cannot be satisfied to wait for other social, business and political forces to remedy social ills, but must take the initiative in overcoming the ignorance which is at the root of those ills. Toward that end they made the following recommendations:

1. The establishment of school attendance areas that make possible, wherever feasible, a student body that represents a cross-section of the population of the entire school district.
2. Action by school boards to develop and keep up-to-date a district plan for achieving and maintaining racially integrated schools. This plan should be developed with the assistance of a citizens' advisory committee broadly representative of the community. Appropriate and

effective participation in the formation of educational policies is the right of every parent, and special effort should be made to provide opportunity for the involvement of minority-group parents in school affairs that affect their children.

3. A continuing emphasis upon racially comprehensive enrollment policies in nonpublic schools and an active effort on the part of public school authorities to bring nonpublic schools into the total community effort to eliminate racial segregation in education.

4. Initiative by school boards in seeking cooperation and assistance of other local agencies, public and private, in the development of plans and programs for integration. Although the schools bear the major responsibility for the provision of quality integrated education for all, other community agencies dealing with welfare, housing, transportation, health, and community development or planning also have vital responsibilities which are an essential part of the effort to achieve the ultimate goal.

5. The exploration by school boards of the possibilities of improving racial balance in their schools through cooperative action with neighboring districts.

6. The establishment and modification of school district boundaries so as to eliminate and avoid those which result in racial segregation.

7. The revision and simplification of legislation authorizing school district reorganization and the substantial increase of existing financial incentives for reorganization.

8. The modification of constitutional tax and debt limits on real property affecting city school districts in order to permit greater flexibility for the organization, administration, and financing of school systems which involve the city and its neighboring districts.

9. Increased state appropriations to stimulate school desegregation and to help school districts finance the additional costs incurred in carrying out programs for achieving integration.

10. An accelerated effort to have, in all our classrooms, textbooks and other teaching materials that reflect in their content and presentation the ethnic and cultural diversity of our world, and in particular of American life. The curriculum should provide for all children an understanding of the contribution of the Negro, Puerto Rican and other minority groups, and the background and nature of the present struggle for justice and equality of opportunity.

11. A broader and more intensive program of workshops for school board members and administrators, sponsored by the State Education Department, designed to promote a fuller understanding of both their local and statewide responsibilities for integration.

12. The provision throughout the state of more extensive and stronger in-service programs for teachers and administrators to increase their

understanding and competence in dealing with new situations and requirements of integrated schools.

13. The broadening of the programs in our colleges and universities for the training of teachers and administrators to include preparation for the special requirements of integration. This preparation should include such experiences as student teaching, internships, seminars and workshops involving minority-group children and adults.

LEGISLATIVE REACTION   As desegregation efforts proceeded around the state, resistance began to set in. The enactment of Education Law Section 3201(2) in the spring of 1969 reflected an effort on the part of the Legislature to slow the process of school desegregation at least insofar as pupil assignment and busing were to be used as remedial implements.

Education Law Section 3201(2) has subsequently been declared repugnant to the equal protection clause of the Federal Constitution on the grounds that the statute involves "an explicitly racial classification" by creating an exception, in matters involving racial criteria, to the broad supervisory powers that the State Commissioner of Education exercises over public education.[79] However, even prior to these legal determinations, the Regents had expressed their opposition to this "anti-busing" statute, asserting that:

> The Act denies the State the power, through the State Commissioner of Education, to execute the State's ultimate responsibility for providing equal educational opportunity through the elimination of racial segregation where a school district fails or refuses to act.[80]

RACIAL IMBALANCE FUND   Over the six-year period 1965 through 1970, the Legislature appropriated a total of $13 million to the State Education Department to provide assistance to school districts seeking to overcome racial imbalance. (Table 4.17 gives the yearly appropriation.) Although by no means sufficient to make any substantial impact on segregation statewide, this Racial Imbalance Fund, which amounted to $3 million for the fiscal year ending March 31, 1971, has provided valuable assistance both to districts attempting to desegregate voluntarily and to those which have been ordered to desegregate by the Commissioner of Education. Upon application by a local district, money has been granted for the following diverse desegregation and integration purposes:

Desegregation: (1) Rental or relocatable classrooms. (2) Transportation. (3) Minor alterations of school buildings. (4) Planning and other studies; demographic studies. (5) Establishment of an office of school integration and planning (to plan and coordinate school districts' efforts).

TABLE 4.17

State Aid for Correcting Racial Imbalance, 1966–71

Fiscal Year	Appropriation	Total Districts' Programs Approved	Total Approved State Contribution
1966–67	$ 1,000,000	$ 2,460,010	$ 999,930
1967–68	3,000,000	5,643,037	3,104,349
1968–69	3,000,000	5,309,287	3,144,095
1969–70	3,000,000	6,153,950	3,203,194
1970–71	3,000,000	4,481,385	3,092,004
1971–72	Discontinued		
Totals	$13,000,000	$24,047,669	$13,543,572

Integration: (1) School-community relations. (2) Urban-suburban action exchange programs (metropolitan concept in education). (3) Maintenance of an integrated transitional school. (4) In-service training programs and workshops for teachers and staffs. (5) Development of integrated curriculum materials. (6) Reduction of class size. (7) Use of teacher aides. (8) Tutorial and pupil enrichment programs.

The requests for aid from districts have been prompted in part by an annual letter from the Commissioner to all districts reiterating the policy of the Regents, explaining the fund's existence and purposes, and inviting proposals and applications. In the six years of program funding, 43 different school districts have received aid, 15 of which are presently desegregated. Of those 15 desegregated districts, about half received assistance for programs designed to integrate schools previously desegregated. In addition to those 15 districts, five additional white suburban districts have received funding to underwrite tuition costs in urban-suburban transfer programs.

By any standard the $3 million annual allocation by the Legislature for State Aid to Correct Racial Imbalance has been insufficient to achieve the purposes for which the fund was created. In 1970, for example, budget requests submitted to the state totaling $8.2 million were reduced to $4.5 million, of which the state share was less than $3.1 million. Further, the total staff of the State Education Department's Division of Inter-Cultural Relations, the office that administers both the Federal Title IV money and the State Aid Fund for Correcting Racial Imbalance, consists of only eight professionals, hardly enough to administer two categorical funds, to survey —for policy purposes—the degree of racial imbalance in the state, to offer technical planning and implementation assistance, to monitor program efforts and to provide leadership and guidance to nearly 100 separate school districts throughout the state.

Given this background, the Legislature's categorical deletion of the fund from the fiscal year 1972 appropriation to the Education Department is a particularly harsh blow.

Commissioner's Efforts to Implement State Policy

Section 310 of the New York State Education Law provides that any person conceiving himself aggrieved in consequence of any action by local school authorities may take an appeal or petition to the Commissioner of Education. Decisions and orders of the Commissioner under §310 are to be implemented unless purely arbitrary.[81] Furthermore, upon proper showing of disobedience by a school official or school district regarding any decision, order, rule or regulation of the Regents or the Commissioner, the Commissioner is empowered to remove such official from office or withhold such district's share of state funds.[82] Many such appeals have been heard by the Commissioner based upon complaints of racial imbalance.

In theory, then, given the firm policy of the Regents and the apparent resolve of Commissioners Allen and Ewald B. Nyquist over the past decade to achieve integration, racial imbalance should no longer be a problem of large proportions. In fact, however, because of such factors as the continuing trend toward geographical concentration of the nonwhite population in urban centers, concomitant migration of the white population to the suburbs and beyond, recalcitrant local school authorities (usually bolstered by community sentiment on behalf of "neighborhood schools"), the enactment of the "anti-busing law" [83] and inadequate funding by the Legislature for correction of racial imbalance, the progress toward racial balance in the schools of New York State has been less than satisfactory. Even where orders have been issued to desegregate, recalcitrant local officials have been able to make the process interminable. Illustrative of this is the situation in Mount Vernon, where an endless array of delaying tactics has kept desegregation at a standstill since 1963, while the black population of the district has increased from less than 20 per cent to more than 60 per cent.

Desegregation is also impeded by district organization as presently constituted. Illustrative of a case where current state law prohibited an effort to desegregate is *Matter of McCoy et al.*[84] In the fall of 1967, the school population of Union Free School District #9 (Wyandanch) was 85 per cent black (the percentage has since risen to 93 per cent).[85] It was felt by a group of parents that for pupils residing in such a district to receive an integrated education, total dissolution of the district would be required, followed by annexation of parts of the former district to a number of surrounding districts. When the district superintendent refused to initiate such dissolution and annexation, an appeal was taken to the Commissioner.

The Commissioner ruled that the proposed dissolution and annexation would be "impracticable." The law regarding such a course of action—unlike that regarding the centralization of a district or districts, or dissolution and annexation of a district in its entirety to another district—is deficient in two important respects: no provision is made for the property and indebtedness of a dissolved district to be allocated to the other districts to which the parts would be annexed, and no provision is made for the tenure and seniority of teaching and supervisory staff to be protected if such staff were transferred to such other districts.

The Commissioner directed his staff to prepare legislation to remedy these deficiencies. Bills were accordingly introduced in the Assembly and Senate in February, 1970, where they have since languished in committees.

Recent Developments in the Federal Courts

In *Brown* v. *Board of Education of Topeka*[86] the Supreme Court struck down school segregation imposed or expressly permitted by state law. In so doing, the Court found that segregation generates among children "a feeling of inferiority as to their status in the community that may affect their hearts and minds in a way unlikely ever to be undone." [87] Moreover, the Court concluded that regardless of the quality of facilities and other tangible factors, "separate educational facilities are inherently unequal." [88] Despite these judicial findings as to the effects of segregation irrespective of the cause, the *Brown* decision has been interpreted as applying only to *de jure* segregation, or that imposed by law, but not to *de facto* segregation, or that which results from purely adventitious housing patterns. Furthermore, for many years after *Brown, de jure* segregation was thought, for the most part, to be limited to the Southern states; only rarely was it found to exist in the North.

Some exceptions to this pattern, however, are worthy of note. For example, in *Taylor* v. *Board of Education of New Rochelle*[89] the New Rochelle Board was found to have gerrymandered the attendance lines of a predominantly black elementary school in 1930, and in ensuing years, as the black population expanded, extended the lines to contain that black population. The school board offered no evidence to refute the evidence of gerrymandering but maintained that the school in question was not a component of a dual school system such as that condemned in *Brown,* since it was only 94 per cent black. Finding that *Brown* "was premised on the factual conclusion that a segregated education created and maintained by official acts had a detrimental and deleterious effect on the education and mental development of minority-group children," the Court concluded that there was no difference "between segregation established by the formality of a dual system of education, as in *Brown,* and that created by gerrymandering of school district lines and transferring of white children as in the instant case." [90] The fact that the school was six per cent white did not, in the Court's view, divest it of its segregated character. The Court ordered the schools to desegregate.

In *Taylor* there was unrefuted evidence of purposeful segregation. However, it is a rare case, particularly in the North, where the facts unmistakably demonstrate deliberate segregation of the minority school population. This problem was recognized by the United States Commission on Civil Rights in its 1967 report, *Racial Isolation in the Public Schools*:

> In a large urban city . . . it is difficult to find a set pattern sufficiently uncomplicated that the motive emerges with clarity. With the school board necessarily making a great number of decisions—some complex—over the relevant period of time, the search for the real motive becomes frustrating. If the school district fails to redraw boundary lines, and absorbs excess capacity in existing classrooms and through use of temporary classrooms on school property or in adjacent rented sites, it may be impossible as a practical matter to disentangle the legal search for motive from the multi-faceted issues of educational administration which face the school board.[91]

The issues of whether the equal protection clause forbids adventitious school segregation has been litigated frequently but remains an open question. The Supreme Court of the United States has not yet confronted it, and the lower federal courts and the state courts are in disagreement. However, at least two cases in lower federal courts in New York State lend support to the notion that there is some constitutional duty to overcome adventitious segregation in public schools.

In *Branche* v. *Board of Education of Hempstead* [92] the plaintiff, charging that the Hempstead Board had been maintaining racially segregated schools, sought an injunction prohibiting this practice and restraining the enlargement of two predominantly black schools. The attendance lines had been drawn in 1949 when the two schools were 16.5 per cent and 14.0 per cent black respectively, but by 1961 the schools had become 67 per cent and 68 per cent black respectively. The Court accepted the contention of the school board that segregation in the schools was the result of residential patterns rather than gerrymandering or any other deliberately discriminatory action. Denying the school board's motion for summary judgment, however, the Court said:

> The educational system that is . . . compulsory and publicly afforded must deal with the inadequacy arising from adventitious segregation; it cannot accept and indurate segregation on the ground that it is not coerced or planned but accepted.[93]

The Court, however, went on to say:

> How far that duty extends is not answerable perhaps in terms of an unqualified obligation to integrate public education without regard to circum-

stance, and it is certainly primarily the responsibility of the educational authorities and not the Courts to formulate the educational system.[94]

Also, in *Blocker* v. *Board of Education of Manhasset,*[95] the same Court was confronted with a school district in which the attendance lines were drawn in 1929 and had not been changed since. Ninety-nine per cent of the white children attended two all-white schools while 100 per cent of the black children attended a separate school. A rigid no-transfer policy was enforced. The Court noted that, "the facts in the instant case present a situation that goes beyond mere racial imbalance" [96] and stated:

> Viewed in this context then, can it be said that one type of segregation, having its basis in state law or evasive schemes to defeat desegregation, is to be proscribed, while another having the same effect but another cause, is to be condoned? Surely, the Constitution is made of sturdier stuff.[97]

Ordering the Board to present a desegregation plan, the Court held that "In a publicly supported, mandatory state educational system, the plaintiffs have the civil right not to be segregated, not to be compelled to attend a school in which all of the Negro children are educated separate and apart from over 99 per cent of their white contemporaries." [98]

In the course of its opinion, the Court maintained that the plaintiffs had to show that they were injured by the segregation and found, on the evidence, that they were damaged psychologically just as the plaintiffs in *Brown* had been damaged by formal segregation. Pointing out that a remedy was available, the Court observed that there were "[not] present here the complicated problems present in . . . large metropolitan areas—New York City for example. There are, no doubt, situations in which no alternative may be feasible. No such insurmountable obstacle appears to be present here." [99]

Despite some exceptions, like *Taylor, Branche* and *Blocker,* until quite recently the general rule still prevailed that the courts were unwilling to attack Northern* school segregation as violative of the 14th Amendment. Examination of Northern school segregation decisions in the past three years, however, and of the proof underlying them, suggests that the issue has been revisited with far greater sophistication. Courts are coming to understand, for example, that for many years school authorities in almost every community have assigned pupils and teachers to particular schools. School segregation, therefore, is not totally adventitious but has resulted

---

* "Northern" here is meant to describe places where racial dual school systems were not mandated by explicit statements of public law or policy as was the case in places with "Southern" school segregation, as that term is herein used.

from the actions of public officials. In such circumstances it is not surprising that school segregation in the North, as well as the South, is coming to be viewed as state-imposed and therefore unconstitutional under the 14th Amendment.

In 1968 in *Green* v. *County School Board of New Kent County* (Virginia),[100] the Supreme Court for the first time imposed an affirmative obligation on a defendant school board to desegregate its schools, finding an open-enrollment system which did not, in fact, end school segregation, inadequate under the 14th Amendment. After that decision a line of Federal Court decisions has emerged in which Northern school segregation has been held actionable.

Although confronted with a case of Southern segregation, the Supreme Court, in its recent *Swann* v. *Charlotte-Mecklenburg Board of Education* and *North Carolina State Board of Education* v. *Swann*[101] opinions lent support to such decisions. There the Court emphasized that existing policy and practice with regard to such things as faculty assignment, school construction, transportation of students and the quality of school buildings and equipment were important signs of a segregated school system. In the new Northern cases, proof of a pattern of school segregation has been most important as a basis for judicial review. This proof usually begins with statistics showing the extent of pupil segregation: the number and percentage of all or predominantly black and white schools, and the number and percentage of black and white pupils attending racially separated schools. In many school systems, however, the racial separation of pupils is far from complete. Where the statistics on pupil segregation do not speak so distinctly, other proof may show a constitutional violation just as clearly. School authorities have considerable discretion in assigning teachers and pupils to schools, constructing and locating schools and attendance boundaries, choosing initial student assignments, and setting transfer policies and enforcing them. Careful examination often reveals choices and practices, and their effects, which operate to segregate schools on a racial and ethnic basis.

As an illustration, in *Davis* v. *School District of the City of Pontiac,*[102] the Court acknowledged the options available to school authorities for pupil and teacher assignment and for location of school facilities. The Court concluded that the school authorities had chosen locations for school facilities that led to greater racial segregation. This resulting segregation was then held to be unconstitutional. On appeal, the Sixth Circuit Court of Appeals reached the following conclusion:

> Although . . . each decision considered alone might not compel the conclusion that the Board of Education intended to foster segregation, taken together, they support the conclusion that a purposeful pattern of racial discrimination has existed in the Pontiac school system for at least 15 years.[103]

As a result of this decision the City of Pontiac is currently undergoing school desegregation pursuant to a Court-ordered plan which involves substantial busing of pupils and teacher reassignment.

Similarly, in *Johnson* v. *San Francisco Unified School District,* decided one week after *Swann,* the Court found that "neither the logic nor the force of [*Swann*] is limited by any North-South boundary lines." [104] In determining that San Francisco elementary schools were unconstitutionally segregated, the Court relied on the following findings of fact:

1. That public elementary schools in the San Francisco Unified School District are racially segregated.
2. That while only 28.7 per cent of all the children enrolled in the elementary schools are black, 80 per cent of the black children are concentrated in 27 schools out of a total of more than 100. The student bodies of these 27 schools range from 47.3 per cent black to 96.8 per cent black. In only two of them are black children even slightly in the minority and in only four are the student bodies less than 72 per cent black.
3. That acts and omissions of the San Francisco Board of Education are proximate causes of the racial segregation.
4. That such acts include:
    a. Construction of new schools and additions to old schools in a manner which perpetuated and exacerbated existing racial imbalance.
    b. Drawing attendance zones so that racial mixture has been minimized; modification and adjustment of attendance zones so that racial separation is maintained.
    c. Allocating a highly disproportionate number of inexperienced and less qualified teachers to schools with student bodies composed predominantly of black children.
5. That such omissions include:
    a. Failure to accept suggestions offered by school officials regarding the placement of new schools so as to minimize segregation.
    b. Failure to adopt a policy of consulting with the Director of Human Relations of the School District as to the predictable racial composition of new schools.
    c. Prolonged failure to pursue a policy of hiring teachers and administrators of minority races.
    d. Failure to take steps to bring the racial balances in elementary schools within the guidelines set by the State Board of Education.
    e. Failure to adopt sufficient measures to improve the education of children in predominantly black schools despite the Board's knowledge that education in these schools was inferior to that provided in predominantly white schools.
    f. Failure to respond to recommendations regarding integration made

at the Board's request by the Stanford Research Institute and by the Report of the Citizens' Advisory Committee to the Superintendent's Task Force Studying Educational Equality/Quality and Other Proposals.[105]

Having found unconstitutional segregation to exist, the Court ordered a plan to be submitted that would accomplish the following minimum objectives by the start of the 1971 school year:

1. Full integration of all public elementary schools so that the ratio of black children to white children will then be and thereafter continue to be substantially the same in each school. To accomplish this objective, the plans may include provisions for:
    a. Use of non-discriminatory busing, if, as appears now to be clear, at least some busing will be necessary for compliance with the law.
    b. Changing attendance zones whenever and wherever necessary to eliminate or head off racial segregation.
2. Assurance that school construction programs will not promote racial segregation whether by enlargement of existing facilities or location of new ones or otherwise.
3. Establishment of practices for the hiring of teachers and administrators which will effectively promote racial balance in the respective staffs.
4. Establishment of practices for the assignment of teachers and administrators which will effectively promote racial balance of the respective staffs in each school.
5. Establishment of practices for the assignment of teachers and administrators which will effectively promote equalization of competence in teaching and administration at all schools.
6. Avoidance of use of tracking systems or other educational techniques or innovations without provision for safeguards against racial segregation as a consequence.[106]

San Francisco's elementary schools, like Pontiac's, began the process of desegregating in the fall of 1971. Although there has been substantial resistance from many quarters based on espousal of the virtues of neighborhood schools, there is evidence that in time desegregation and, we hope, full integration will prevail.

Another recent decision involving Northern segregation is *Bradley* v. *Milliken*.[107] There, the Court held that Detroit's public school system, which is the fourth largest in the nation and in which nearly two-thirds of the students are black, had been deliberately segregated. The Court found that government action and inaction at all levels—federal, state and local—combined with the action and inaction of private organizations such as loan institutions, real estate associations and brokerage firms, had caused *housing* segregation.

Moreover, the Court found that state and local government actions have played a substantial role in promoting racial isolation in the schools. It was noted that the state Legislature had declined to pay for transportation of pupils in the Detroit school system regardless of their poverty or distance from school, although it paid for transportation of students in the generally white suburban and rural school districts. It was also noted that the Legislature had struck down a plan drawn by the Detroit Board of Education in April, 1971, that would have spread white pupils throughout the city's high schools.

The Court concluded further that the Detroit Board of Education had encouraged segregation in the following ways:

1. By creating optional school zones in changing neighborhoods allowing pupils to choose between identifiable "black" and "white" schools.
2. By busing black students past or away from closer white schools to black schools and failing to bus whites into black schools.
3. By creating and maintaining school attendance zones in such a way as to encourage segregated schools.
4. By constructing new school facilities and creating attendance zones for new facilities in such a way as to contain black students.

On October 4, 1971, Judge Roth ordered that the State of Michigan develop within four months an integration plan involving both Detroit and its suburbs, the net effect of which would be racial integration of predominantly white school districts ringing the city.[108] The implication is clearly that because the power of the state was used to promote segregation, the state is responsible for devising a plan involving many school districts throughout the metropolitan region to eliminate such segregation.

As the foregoing three cases indicate, when the factors underlying school segregation and the alternatives available to school authorities are subjected to scrutiny, the rights of Northern as well as Southern minority school-children no longer depend upon the ill-will or the caprice of school authorities, and the much-heralded distinction between *de facto* and *de jure* segregation loses significance. Those labels are essentially conclusions in any case; neither is very descriptive or analytic. By definition, *de jure* means actionable under the 14th Amendment; *de facto,* not actionable. The point is not that *de facto* school segregation is unconstitutional, but that the overwhelming majority of public school segregation is *de jure.*

A new approach to overcoming racial segregation, which in the context of the foregoing decisions is more evolutionary than revolutionary, is incorporated in a decision by Judge Robert R. Mehrige of the Eastern District Court of Virginia handed down in January, 1972. In *Bradley* v. *City School Board of Richmond,*[109] Judge Mehrige ordered the consolidation of the city school district of Richmond, Virginia (nearly 70 per cent black), with the suburban school systems of Chesterfield and Henrico counties (91 per cent white) to create a metropolitan system (66 per cent white and 33 per cent black) in which each of the schools is to be racially balanced at something close to the over-all ratio.[110] If this decision survives appeal, it will have far-reaching practical impact because school district boundaries reflecting racial residential housing patterns will no longer be permitted to define the racial composition of the schools.

Judge Mehrige reasoned substantially as follows: that education is the responsibility of the state, that school district boundaries are creatures of the state, and therefore, that these boundaries have to yield when they create or perpetuate an unconstitutional situation. As to the definition of an unconstitutional situation, Judge Mehrige concluded that "school authorities may not constitutionally arrange an attendance-zone system which serves only to reproduce in school facilities the prevalent pattern of housing segregation, be it publicly or privately enforced. To do so is only to endorse with official approval the product of private racism." Therefore, he reasoned, "when a school board, having demonstrated concern for problems of segregation, and operating in an area where segregated housing patterns prevail and are continuing, builds its facilities and arranges its zones so that school attendance is governed by housing segregation, it is operating in violation of the Constitution. These conclusions apply in a case where no history of other past intentional segregation was relied on in order to establish an affirmative duty to desegregate." [111]

This decision appears clearly to hold that the state's responsibility for education extends to the *effect* of state action, rather than limiting it to some specified *intent*. As such, if affirmed, it should have substantial impact on racial imbalance in New York and throughout the North. For one thing, it should create greater stability in individual urban schools by curtailing the incidence of white migration to the suburbs in search of racially segregated schools. Judge Mehrige's definition of unconstitutional segregation is consistent with the conclusion of the Supreme Court in *Brown*:

. . . that in the field of public education the doctrine of a "separate but equal" has no place. Separate educational facilities are inherently unequal.[112]

The inherent inequality in segregation has nothing to do with achievement test scores or any implication that minority children make minority schools inferior. It is based on the fact that segregation in the public schools, Northern and Southern, is imposed on racial and ethnic minorities by a dominant white majority which is intent on containing minorities in separate neighborhoods and schools. When that intent is fulfilled in the public schools that most people are compelled by law to attend for a decade of their lives, the minimum objective must be, as the Supreme Court said in *Swann*:

to eliminate from the public schools all vestiges of state-imposed segregation.[113]

One conclusion seems inescapable to this Commission: The factual bases which established the existence of unconstitutional segregation in Pontiac, San Francisco and Detroit, and those which violate the Civil Rights Act of 1964 in Boston, are surely no more compelling than those that could be found to exist in many school systems in New York State. Rather than waiting to be required to do so by judicial mandate, it would seem much more sound, as a matter of public policy, for those in positions of leadership and authority to bring about desegregation voluntarily.

The Commission is of course aware that overcoming negative popular attitudes to achieve integration is fraught with political danger. However, we are encouraged in this connection by accumulating evidence of increased popular acceptance of integration goals.[114] In any event, the following observation of Edmund Burke seems applicable:

Your representative owes you not his industry only, but his judgment, and he betrays instead of serving you if he sacrifices it to your opinion.[115]

SEPARATE VIEWS OF COMMISSIONERS

A PLEA FOR MODERATION AND OBJECTIVITY IN THE NEW YORK STATE PROGRAM FOR RACIAL AND ETHNIC INTEGRATION IN THE PUBLIC SCHOOLS

A Statement by Commissioner Thomas Laverne

This statement constitutes a separate opinion concerning the subject matter of Chapter 4 of the Fleischmann Report, "Racial and Ethnic Integration in the Public Schools." I concur with that part of the opening statement in the report which states "On the necessity to act, and on the validity of the goal itself, however, we see little room for disagreement." [116]

There is no question that efforts toward integration are essential. The schools must bear a fair share of the burden of achieving the goal of an integrated society. Desegregated housing and equal economic and job opportunity are all vital in the creation of a truly integrated society. The schools cannot be expected to bear the entire burden. For an integration program to be workable, timing, scope and pace are vital factors. Cooperation at the local level is basic.

It is quite possible to achieve integration in the purely physical sense and at the same time create a situation which may well be more like "disintegration." The following quotation from the book, *Desegregation Research: An Appraisal,* pages 259–60, is apropos the fact that integration must be carried out sympathetically and scientifically:

> ". . . unhappily, however, the research literature does support the proposition that desegregation may be harmful to the Negro child. As Katz indicated, a prerequisite for a truly integrated school is an atmosphere of acceptance and mutual respect. In the absence of such support desegregation may lose a good part of its favorable impact." [117]

Thus, in an intense, sincere desire to mix majority with minority, it may harm those we desire to help.

What we need is methodical planning commencing at the state level. We must establish priorities in terms of immediate and future goals, within the limits of the availability of funds.

Some of the proposals and recommendations of the Fleischmann Report are, in these respects, so theoretical that they can in fact be dangerous. The chapter shows a lack of comprehension of the pragmatic and political overtones which could be created.

It is not the intention of this paper to deny the Commission's intention to convey a "sense of urgency." [118] Rather the intention is to emphasize the fact that in our haste to correct the situation we must consider the danger of overreaction and creating a counterproductive situation.

The Commission states:

> . . . we have looked beyond the numbers to the actions of officials (New York, Buffalo and Rochester) and found that only in Rochester is a comprehensive attack on school *segregation being made.*[119] [Emphasis added.]

What has been described as a comprehensive attack has now ended in what might be termed a debacle, to the extent that integration in Rochester has suffered a setback.

Disagreement and conflict may arise from individual or small group action on the part of parents fearful for the safety of their children. The report states, "This Commission firmly believes that opposition to busing can be overcome when steps are taken to reassure parents of the well-being of their children." [120]

All parents and children from the inner city have equal concerns with those from suburbia. They want the schools, which their children are being asked to attend, to have a safe, friendly environment. They want schools where teachers and students are responsive to the social and cultural differences.

The chapter of the Report concerning the status of education states the following concerning drug abuse:

Studies conducted for the Commission reveal that one high school student in four in New York State routinely takes some form of psychoactive drug. In New York city, the figure is one high school student in two.[121]

We must recognize that the heaviest addiction will be found in the high population concentrations of our inner cities. One does not need to cite the by-products of drug addiction. Certainly there can be no reassurance of well-being for adults or children in any setting involving a high incidence of drug addiction. Thus, an all-out declaration of war on the drug traffic must precede any massive integration efforts.

The quality of inner-city schools, plant and personnel must be substantially improved. We cannot wait for integration. As Dr. Kenneth B. Clark has stated in his book *Dark Ghetto,*

> One thing is clear and that is that meaningful desegregation of urban ghetto schools can occur only if all of the schools in the system are raised to the highest standards. The goals of integration and quality education must be sought together.[122]

According to 1970 data, the state's minority populations are increasingly concentrated in large urban centers and the areas immediately surrounding them:

> 77 per cent of New York State's non-white population (Indians, Orientals, and blacks) lives in New York City. (Blacks account for 90 per cent of the non-white population.)[123]

On the basis of these figures, the Report asks this rhetorical question: "Can we find the strength and the means to reverse the destruction, the fear and the waste that they represent?" [124]

That question should be answered in this way: We do have the strength and the means, provided that we use both wisely and cooperatively and, with carefully considered priorities, not waste our strength or means in artificially engendered conflicts.

Despite the discouraging reports concerning the situation in New York City, we must continue to make every effort to improve these schools. We emphasize that the improvement of such schools would not be considered as a step toward a "separate but equal" system. It is an urgent prerequisite for implementing the goal of integration while proper approaches are worked out to prepare these children and families for integration.

Following the Report's proposal that the Legislature create a statutory obligation requiring each district to prepare a detailed plan for integration, which can be enforced by the Supreme Court, this statement is found:

> This situation can not be changed overnight; conflict should be expected between civic leaders, parents, administrators, teachers and students when

desegregation is effected. Conflict is normal and integration has a better chance to succeed if it is exploited as a learning device.[125]

The exercise of any legal or administrative sanctions to impose integration may or may not succeed. If they succeed, it could be a pyrrhic victory, but the social losses might well outweigh the gains. Charles E. Silberman states in his book *Crisis in Black and White*:

> . . . integration is a moral imperative—the greatest moral imperative of our time. But integration should not be confused with the mere mixing of Negroes and whites in the same classroom, or in the same school, or in the same neighborhood. To throw white and black youngsters into a classroom in the name of integration, without regard to what one may reasonably expect to happen, is to violate the Commandment which prohibits the worship of false gods; it is to sacrifice the children for the sake of an abstract principle.[126]

The leaders of the Legislature should support all financial proposals to improve the quality of individual schools with particular emphasis on urban areas, to assist in community planning and in the functioning of regional educational centers, to finance voluntary busing between urban and suburban areas, to encourage a system of open enrollment and the total involvement of the community in its school system.

The majority of the Legislature has demonstrated its resistance to compulsory busing and other efforts for the sole purpose of attaining the proportionate racial mix. Such efforts are counterproductive to the real needs of the children and society as a whole.

Desegregation is a physical act quite simple to achieve if one does not worry about the consequence. *Integration* is a social and spiritual achievement which comes slowly and sometimes painfully. It is seldom, if ever, the result of compulsion.

The following is quoted from a book entitled *Integration and Education* in the chapter entitled "Moderation and Common Sense Applied to Desegregation":

> Decisions relating to desegregation must be both right and wise. It may be easier, in fact, to be right than to be wise. The wise person realizes that, unless desegregation secures better education, it may produce—as it has, in fact, already produced—even greater desegregation* and disappointment. As desegregation is accepted by more and more school systems and boards of education, the system-wide desegregation may take place within a period of one to three years. This system-wide desegregation, however, must be guided and controlled so that transfer[s] of Negroes to all-white schools meet the usual criteria for successful transfers before desegregation takes place. By

---

* So in original. The author obviously intended the word to be "segregation."

transferring those Negro students whose records forecast successful work under desegregated conditions, the educational advantages of desegregation will be realized and accepted more readily.[127]

This is the type of moderation and common sense that should be the foundation of a state integration plan. Notice that in the quotation it is stated that, if some desegregation takes place, a system-wide plan may be put into effect within a period of one to three years. We urge this type of approach—careful selection and encouragement of districts where desegregation and integration can work. This, in and of itself, will take several years. This long range and practical approach will be successful.

The Regents have taken a strong stand on integration. The Commissioner has been responding to petitions for integration with decisions favorable to desegregation and integration. The report states:

In theory, then, given the firm policy of the Regents and the apparent resolve of Commissioners Allen and Ewald B. Nyquist over the past decade to achieve integration, racial imbalance should no longer be a problem of large proportions. In fact, however, because of such factors as the continuing trend toward geographical concentration of the nonwhite population in urban centers, concomitant migration of the white population to the suburbs and beyond, recalcitrant local school authorities (usually bolstered by community sentiment on behalf of "neighborhood schools"), the enactment of the "anti-busing law" and inadequate funding by the Legislature for correction of racial imbalance, the progress toward racial balance in the schools of New York State has been less than satisfactory. Even where orders have been issued to desegregate, recalcitrant local officials have been able to make the process interminable.[128]

How then can the Commission proposals for legislation to force integration be accepted as practicable?

The conflict, which the report considers normal, has proven to be counterproductive to the point that it disrupts the educational process as well as detracts from the quality of education. The element of coercion always brings a counterreaction. Then, too, the most reactionary elements in our communities ride the crest of disaffection, overturn the leadership of educators, legislators, teachers and community leaders and set back progressive educational services for years. Current events are proof of the truth of this position. We do not have so many forward-thinking and active leaders that we can afford to make martyrs of any of them. However, some of them may be expendable if it is justified in the cause of education priorities. No child, however, should be required to be made a martyr nor should any child be expendable.

If one ponders the problem and views current events, it becomes more and more evident that in addition to moving forward on a program basis, planning must be conducted and be led at the state level. All of us agree that "the promise of equal educational opportunity must become a reality in this decade." [129] If such a promise is to be kept, the establishment of priorities and over-all planning must be geared to the various regions of the state as well as to the funds available. We are familiar with the over-all problem. It needs to be dissected and examined at the state level, not parcelled out to various school districts as is presently being done. The Commission Report uses the phrase "target districts" [130] to designate fifty-four districts that must be integrated within three years. Rather than creating "targets of hostility," let us select those that may properly be termed "targets of opportunity." We can then concentrate on the "targets of opportunity" and abandon the shotgun and noncooperative approach which is proposed.

The philosophy of requiring each school district to prepare its own plan has been in vogue for several years. It has not worked. The Report says so. Leadership in planning for integration should be strengthened at the state level. Studies of all of the possibilities can be conducted with existing state department personnel preparing the data and alternative proposals. A plan and this information would help people understand the scope of the problem. It will be a basis for the Legislature to provide funds. It will strengthen school board's positions.

The Master Plan for reorganization established in 1947 and still in effect[131] called for consolidation of districts. Where possible, reorganization for the purpose of accomplishing integration should continue to be urged. Even more important are the potentialities for reorganization of schools by grade. Where reorganization is presented after combined state-multi-district study, it will constitute a major step in the right direction. It should be conceived initially on a short-distance basis or without compulsory busing. The state should furnish incentive aid as a "carrot" to provide supportive services and to assist the districts in the direct expense involved just as is done for major reorganizations. By furnishing personnel to work with school districts and community groups to develop a comprehensive understanding of the problems and resultant solutions, the department will be showing real leadership.

As varied approaches are attempted and community acceptance gains, a new order of integration will emerge.

The Report recommends the following:

STATE ACTION:
1. *The Legislature should create a statutory obligation on the part of each local school district to develop a plan. . . .*[132]

To require the preparation of half-a-hundred little master plans from all over the state is an artificial and futile attempt to delegate state responsibility.

2. *The Legislature should . . . defray other costs related to integration efforts.*[133]

With this we concur. The school districts willing to cooperate in integration planning and implementation should be fully reimbursed. Incentive funds must be made available.

> 3. *The Division of Intercultural Relations of the State Education Department should be greatly expanded . . . to assist local boards in preparing, updating and implementing integration plans.*[134]

We concur but emphasize that planning for integration is a task to be borne by the department as a whole as a coordinated effort.

> 4. *The Legislature should, by statute, facilitate consolidation of school districts to achieve desegregation as well as eliminate statutory obstacles to cross-busing of children across district lines for the same purpose.*[135]

This suggestion is entirely impracticable and could not be achieved under existing conditions.

> 5. *Pending such legislative corrections, the Commissioner of Education, through the Department's Division of Intercultural Relations, should begin to examine segregation as a regional problem and work out regional solutions where needed.*[136]

There is a need for regional solutions and it is a department responsibility to lead in working out these regional solutions.

Before any successful attack on integration can be carried out, there are many positive programs which must be created and initiated by the state on a statewide basis. A Regents' position paper, *Integration in the Schools* (January, 1968), is quoted in the Report on page 275. Several examples are worthy of particular attention as positive, necessitating acceptance of state responsibility.

1. TEACHER PROGRAMS With respect to teachers, the Regents' Report recommended:

> The provision throughout the state of more extensive and stronger in-service programs for teachers and administrators to increase their understanding and competence in dealing with new situations and requirements of integrated schools.
>
> The broadening of the programs in our colleges and universities for the training of teachers and administrators to include preparation for the special requirements of integration. This preparation should include such experience as student teaching, internships, seminars and workshops involving minority-group children and adults.[137]

The area of teacher training, for both veteran teachers and new teachers, is particularly important. I do not believe that the responsibility for retraining can be left solely to the cities and supervisory districts. Courses should be conducted on a regional basis in conjunction with the state university. Instructional staffs should be recruited who can move into areas to conduct well-organized and interesting courses. Within city school districts, particular attention should be given to the evaluation of teachers working with minority groups to assure their understanding of their students and that there is proper communication with them.

2. STUDENTS   The Regents' Report also contained the following recommendation:

> An accelerated effort to have, in all our classrooms, textbooks and other teaching materials that reflect in their content and presentation the ethnic and cultural diversity of our world, and in particular of American life. The curriculum should provide for all children an understanding of the contributions of the Negro, Puerto Rican and other minority groups, and the background and nature of the present struggle for justice and equality of opportunity.[138]

In addition, greater training for student leadership and student understanding of minority problems and cultures is an essential prerequisite to successful integration.

3. COMMUNITY   The Regents' Report also calls for:

> A broader and more intensive program of workshops for school board members and administrators, sponsored by the State Education Department, designed to promote a fuller understanding of both their local and state-wide responsibilities for integration.[139]

In addition, we must expand these programs into the communities. We should also seek greater utilization of school buildings. The attitude that schools are educational plants to be used solely as classroom complexes is outmoded. Principals and teachers are community leaders. Recreational facilities must be made available to the community in the evenings. Cafeterias should be utilized to a far greater extent. Such programs bring the people to the schools and will insure the total community involvement. That will strengthen the entire structure.

All these 1968 programs should be substantially implemented; some can be accomplished without additional funds.

Establishment of Priorities

Obviously, the job of integration cannot be done in a short time. To attempt to do it on an unplanned basis by requiring the same action in the fifty-four "target districts" is futile if they cannot be funded, cannot be implemented and might well be outmoded by shifts in population. Therefore, areas must be chosen for integration on a selective basis. Generally speaking, those areas would be first where an integration program can be successful and where some of the programs cited had been accomplished, to a reasonable extent, by the time a priority becomes effective.

Some of the priorities which should be emphasized for a successful integration plan are:

1. *Control of Drugs and Elimination of Lawlessness* Programs are already under way in this field. Provision must be made within the schools for adequate medical examinations. There can be no assurance of well-being for parents or children in any setting where drugs are in use.

> When the school is a place where children find that they can be successful and then experience just treatment, they develop respect for law and for habits in harmony with the regulations of their society. But when the school is a place where children fail or where they experience unjust treatment, they become frustrated, they reject society's values, and they are more likely to resort to violence in an effort to solve their problems.[140]

2. *Teaching Training* When areas are to be selected for integration, the teachers in that area should have top state priority in the retraining or refresher programs.

3. *There Must Be Immediate Substantial Improvement in the Inner-City Schools* As we have said before, the children in these areas cannot wait for integration. The quality of education in these schools must equal or better that of the suburban areas. This will assure the parents of these areas, as well as suburban areas, that when transfers are made the receiving school will sustain the educational needs of the child.

4. *Construction of New Schools* Priority in the allocation of the limited state funds available for new construction should be established on a first-come basis to areas in the process of integrating.

5. *Incentive Funds* In addition to racial imbalance funds, incentive funds should be reestablished and increased. These should include funds and legal authority:
   a. To allow tuition payments where voluntary placement takes place,
   b. To assist in open enrollment programs,
   c. To expand voluntary interchange programs, and
   d. To fund: (1) Community meetings to discuss integration problems. (2) Community utilization of schools.

Conclusion

My position is best stated by quoting Dr. Urie Bronfenbrenner, professor of psychology at Cornell University and forum chairman for the 1970

White House Conference on Children and Youth, who recently observed that children should not be used as pawns no matter how righteous the cause. In this context he stated:

> Busing poses a great dilemma. We have two great injustices. However, where busing is forced and the parents disapprove, the effect upon the children is counterproductive. We should not use children to end the evils of segregation.[141]

I believe my plea for moderation and objectivity in implementing the objectives of racial and ethnic integration in the public schools is based on a realistic appraisal of the interaction of the forces in our society. This plea must be heeded!

Separate Statement of Commissioner Dorothy Levitt

I believe very strongly in the validity of the goal of integration and in the necessity to act in order to achieve that goal.

Based on my experience as a teacher and community coordinator in New York City I am especially concerned that minorities be involved in the governance of inner-city schools.

On the very troublesome issue of compulsory busing to achieve integration, I wish to be recorded as believing that busing is an unhappy—though in some cases perhaps necessary—device to overcome a major societal problem. Mindful of the definitional problems involved, I am instinctively opposed to the busing of advantaged children to inferior schools solely for the purpose of achieving racial and ethnic integration. However, where disadvantaged children can be bused into advantaged neighborhoods with superior schools, I believe such busing should occur.

Racially Isolated Public School Districts in New York State, by County of Location

ALBANY
*Albany
Berne Knox
Bethlehem
Cooksburg
Cohoes
Green Island
Guilderland
Maplewood
Menands
North Colonie
Potter Hollow
Ravena Coeymans
South Colonie
Voorheesville
Watervliet

ALLEGANY
Alfred Almond
Andover
Angelica
Belfast
Belmont
Bolivar
Canaseraga
Cuba
Fillmore
Friendship
Richburg
Rushford
Scio
Wellsville
Whitesville

BROOME
Chenango Forks
Chenango Valley

Deposit
Endicott
Harpursville
Johnson City
Maine Endwell
Sanitaria Springs
Sunrise Terrace
Susquehanna Valley
Vestal
Whitney Point
Windsor

CATTARAUGUS
Allegany
Cattaraugus
Childrens Home
Ellicottville
Franklinville
**Gowanda
Hinsdale
Limestone
Little Valley
Olean
Pioneer
Portville
Randolph
**Salamanca

CAYUGA
*Auburn
Cato Meridian
Moravia
Port Byron
Southern Cayuga
Union Springs
Weedsport

* Segregated "target" districts.
** Segregated "target" districts with Indian children (see p. 376).

CHAUTAUQUA
Bemus Point
Brocton
Cassadaga Valley
Chautauqua
Clymer
*Dunkirk
Falconer
Fredonia
Frewsburg
Forestville
Jamestown
Mayville
Panama
Pine Valley
Ripley
Sherman
Southwestern
Westfield

CHEMUNG
*Elmira
Elmira Heights
Horseheads

CHENANGO
Afton
Bainbridge Guilford
Greene
Mount Upton
New Berlin
Norwich
Oxford
Sherburne-Earlville
South New Berlin
South Otselic

CLINTON
Beekmantown
Champlain
Chazy
Dannemora
Keesville
North Adirondack
*Peru
Plattsburgh
Saranac

COLUMBIA
Berkshire Farm Boys
Chatham
Germantown
*Hudson
Ichabod Crane
New Lebanon
Taconic Hills

CORTLAND
Cincinnatus
Cortland
Homer
Marathon
McGraw

DELAWARE
Andes
Delaware
Downsville
Franklin
Grand Gorge
Hancock
Margaretville
Roxbury
Sidney
South Kortright
Stamford
Walton

DUTCHESS
Arlington
*Beacon
Greer School
Hyde Park
Pine Plains
*Poughkeepsie
Red Hook
Rhinebeck
Wappingers Falls
Webutuck

ERIE
Alden
Amherst Central High School
*Buffalo

Cheektowaga
Clarence
Cleveland Hill
Depew
East Aurora
Eden
Eggertsville
Frontier
Grand Island
Griffith Institute
Hamburg
Holland
Iroquois
Kenmore
*Lackawanna
Lake Shore
Lancaster
Maryvale
North Collins
Orchard Park
Sloan
Snyder
Sweet Home
Tonawanda
West Seneca
Williamsville

ESSEX
Crown Point
Elizabethtown
Keene
Minerva
Moriah
Newcomb
Lake Placid
Schroon Lake
Ticonderoga
Westport
Willsboro

FRANKLIN
Brushton Moira
Chateaugay
Malone
**Salmon River

Saranac Lake
St. Regis Falls
Tupper Lake

FULTON
Broadalbin
Caroga
Gloversville
Johnstown
Mayfield
North Main Street Extension
Northville
Oppenheim Ephratah
Perth
Rockwood
Stratford
Washburn
Wheelerville

GENESEE
Alexander
Byron
Corfu E. Pembroke
Le Roy
Oakfield Alabama

GREENE
Cairo
*Catskill
Durham
Greenville
Hunter Tannersville
Windham Ashland

HAMILTON
Indian Lake
Inlet
Lake Pleasant
Long Lake
Mountain Home
Piseco
Raquette Lake
Wells

HERKIMER
Dolgeville
Frankfort
Herkimer
Ilion
Little Falls
Mohawk
Mount Markham
North Lake
Owen D. Young
Poland
Town of Webb
West Canada Valley

JEFFERSON
Alexandria I
Alexandria Bay
Belleville
Carthage
General Brown
Henderson
Hounsfield
Indian River
La Fargeville
Lyme
South Jefferson
Thousand Islands
Watertown

LEWIS
Beaver River
Copenhagen
Harrisville
Lowville
South Lewis

LIVINGSTON
Avon
Dansville
Geneseo
Keshequa
Livonia
Mount Morris
York

MADISON
Brookfield
Canastota
Cazenovia
Chittenango
De Ruyter
Hamilton
Madison
Morrisville Eaton
Oneida
Stockbridge Valley

MONROE
Brighton 1
Brighton 5
Brockport
Churchville Chili
East Irondequoit
East Rochester
Fairport
Gates Chili
Greece
Greece 4
Greece 8
Greece 10
Hilton
Honeoye Falls
Irondequoit
Penfield
Pittsford
*Rochester
Rush Henrietta
Spencerport
Webster
Wheatland Chili

MONTGOMERY
*Amsterdam
Canajoharie
Collins Corners
Fonda Fultonville
Fort Plain
Lutheran Church
St. Johnsville

NASSAU
Baldwin
Bellmore
Bethpage
Carle Place
East Meadow
East Rockaway
East Williston
*Elmont
Farmingdale
Floral Park
Franklin Square
Garden City
*Great Neck
*Hempstead
Herricks
Hicksville
Island Trees
Jericho
*Lawrence
Levittown
Locust Valley
Lynbrook
Massapequa
Mepham
Merrick
Mineola
New Hyde Park
North Bellmore
North Merrick
Oceanside
Oyster Bay
Plainedge
Plainview
Port Washington
Sanatorium
Sea Cliff–North Shore
Seaford
Sewanhaka
Syosset
*Uniondale
Valley Stream–
  Hempstead 13
Valley Stream–
  Hempstead 24

Valley Stream–
  Hempstead 30
Valley Stream Central
  High School
Wantagh
West Hempstead
Woodmere

NEW YORK CITY
*New York City

NIAGARA
Lewiston Porter
*Lockport
Newfane
*Niagara Falls
**Niagara–Wheatfield
North Tonawanda
Royalton–Hartland
Star Point
Wilson

ONEIDA
Adirondack
Augusta 6
Camden
Chadwicks
Clinton
Holland Patent
New Hartford
New York Mills
Oriskany
Oriskany Falls
Remsen
Sauquoit Valley
Sherrill
Sylvan Beach
*Utica
Waterville
Westmoreland
Whitesboro

ONONDAGA
Baldwinsville
Camillus

Dewitt
East Syracuse
Fabius
Jordon Elbridge
**La Fayette
Liverpool
Lyncourt
Manlius
Marcellus
North Syracuse
Skaneateles
Solvay
*Syracuse
Tully
Westhill

ONTARIO
Bloomfield
Canandaigua
Honeoye
Marcus Whitman
Naples
Phelps–Clifton Springs
Red Jacket
Victor

ORANGE
Chester
Cornwall
Greenwood Lake
Minisink Valley
Monroe Woodbury
Montgomery
*Newburgh
Otisville
Pine Bush
Tuxedo
*Warwick Valley

ORLEANS
Kendall

OSWEGO
Altmar Parish
Central Square

Fulton
Hannibal
Mexico
Oswego
Phoenix
Pulaski
Sandy Creek

OTSEGO
Andrew S. Draper
Cherry Valley
Cooperstown
Edmeston
Gilbertsville
Laurens
Milford
Morris
Oneonta
Richfield Springs
Springfield
Unatego
Worcester

PUTNAM
Brewster
Carmel
Garrison
Haldane
Mahopac
Manitou
Putnam Valley

RENSSELAER
Averill Park
Berlin
Brittonkill
East Greenbush
George Washington
Hoosic Valley
Hoosick Falls
Lansingburg
Rensselaer
Sanatorium
Schodack
*Troy

Williams
Wyantskill

ROCKLAND
Lakeside
Nanuet
New City
*North Rockland
Pearl River
South Orangetown
*Spring Valley
Suffern

ST. LAWRENCE
Canton
Clifton Fine
Colton Pierrepont
Edwards
Gouverneur
Hammond
Hermon Dekalb
Heuvelton
Knox Memorial
Lisbon
Madrid Waddington
Massena
Morristown
Norwood Norfolk
Ogdensburg
Parishville Hopkinton
Potsdam
St. Lawrence

SARATOGA
Ballston Spa
Burnt Hills
Corinth
Edinburg
Galway
Mechanicville
Schuylerville
Shenendehowa
South Glens Falls
Stillwater
Waterford

SCHENECTADY
Draper
Duanesburg
Mohonasen
Niskayuna
Sanatorium
Schalmont
*Schenectady
Scotia Glenville

SCHOHARIE
Cobleskill
Gilboa Conesville
Jefferson
Middleburgh
Richmondville
Schoharie
Sharon Springs

SCHUYLER
Odessa Montour
Watkins Glen

SENECA
Border City
Romulus
Seneca Falls
South Seneca
Waterloo

STEUBEN
Addison
Bradford
Campbell
Canisteo
Greenwood
Hammondsport
Haverling
Hornell
Jasper
Savona
Troupsburg

SUFFOLK
Amagansett
Bayport Blue Point

*Bay Shore
*Brentwood
Cold Spring Harbor
Commack
Comsewogue
Connetquot
Cutchogue
*Deer Park
East Hampton
East Islip
East Manor
East Quogue
Elwood
Fishers Island
Half Hollow Hills
Hampton Bays
Harborfields
Hauppauge
*Huntington
Islip
Kings Park
Laurel
Lindenhurst
Mastic Beach
Middle Country
Miller Place
Montauk
Mount Sinai
New Suffolk
Northport
*North Babylon
Ocean Beach
Orient
*Patchogue
Peconic
Port Jefferson
Quogue
Remsenburg
*Riverhead
Rocky Point
Sachem
Sagaponack
Sayville
Shelter Island
Shoreham

Smithtown
South Haven
Southold
South Manor
Springs
Three Village
Tuckahoe
Wading River
Wainscott
West Islip
West Manor
Wyandanch

SULLIVAN
Delaware Valley
Eldred
Jefferson Youngsville
*Monticello
Narrowsburg
Roscoe
Tri Valley

TIOGA
Candor
Newark Valley
Owego–Apalachin
Spencer Van Etten
Tioga
Waverly

TOMPKINS
Dryden
George Jr. Republic
Groton
*Ithaca
Lansing
Newfield
Trumansburg

ULSTER
Highland
*Kingston
New Paltz
Onteora
Rondout Valley

Saugerties
*Wallkill

WARREN
Abraham Wing
Bolton
Chestertown
Glens Falls
Hadley Luzerne
Hague
Horicon
Johnsburg
Lake George
Pottersville
Queensbury
Warrensburg

WASHINGTON
Argyle
Cambridge
Fort Ann
Fort Edward
Granville
Greenwich
Hartford
Hudson Falls
Putnam
Salem
Whitehall

WAYNE
Marion
Newark
Palmyra
Wayne

WESTCHESTER
Ardsley
Briarcliff Manor
Bronxville
Byram Hills
Chappaqua

Cottage
Croton Harmon
Dobbs Ferry
Eastchester
Echo Hills
Edgemont
Graham Home for Children
Harrison
Hastings on Hudson
Hendrick Hudson
Irvington
Katonah Lewisboro
Lakeland
*Mamaroneck
Mount Pleasant
*Mount Vernon
*New Rochelle
North Salem
*Ossining
*Peekskill
Pelham
Pleasantville
*Port Chester
Ridge Street
Scarsdale
Somers
St. Christopher's
*Valhalla
*White Plains
Wiltwyck
*Yonkers
Yorktown Heights

WYOMING
Attica
Perry
Warsaw
Wyoming

YATES
Dundee
Penn Yan

Profiles of Target Segregated Districts Other Than New York City, Buffalo and Rochester*

Albany's nonpublic school enrollment (12,368) exceeds its public school enrollment (10,999). Both enrollments declined between 1967 and 1970–71. Minority enrollment, fairly constant since 1967, is 34.4% of total enrollment of public schools and 6.5% of total enrollment of nonpublic schools (in 1969–70).

I. ALBANY PUBLIC SCHOOL ENROLLMENT & ETHNIC PROPORTIONS, 1967–68 TO 1970–71

	White	%	Black	%	Spanish-Surnamed	%	Indian & Oriental	%	Total	%
1967–68	8,959	70.7	3,684	29.0	10	0.1	21	0.2	12,674	100
1968–69	8,272	68.9	3,685	30.7	30	0.2	23	0.2	12,010	100
1969–70	7,545	66.7	3,701	32.7	39	0.3	29	0.3	11,314	100
1970–71	7,214	65.6	3,734	34.0	23	0.2	28	0.2	10,999	100

* Data sources for profiles: B.E.D.S., Ethnic Census for Public Schools, 1967–68, 1969–70, 1970–71, and for Nonpublic Schools, 1967–68, and 1969–70. United States Dept. of Health, Education and Welfare, Office of Civil Rights, *Directory of Public Elementary and Secondary Schools in Selected Districts, Fall, 1968.* Interviews with school district personnel and community members in each of the target districts. New York State Education Department, Division of Intercultural Relations, documents and discussions with staff.

The number of minority teachers and administrators has increased slightly from 1967–68 to 1970–71, but minority-group members constitute only 6.1% of the staff. The number of total staff has decreased since 1967.

II. ALBANY PUBLIC EDUCATION STAFF & MINORITY-GROUP PROPORTIONS, 1967–68 & 1970–71

	White	%	Minority	%	Total	%
1967–68	743	95.7	33	4.3	776	100
1970–71	634	93.9	41	6.1	675	100

Albany's total population is declining while minority population has increased 31.7% since 1960. Twenty-two of Albany's 25 public schools vary by at least five percentage points from the district's average black population. Despite the degree of racial imbalance, there is no immediate official integration plan nor is integration a specific public issue. An open enrollment option for students is little used. Albany High suffered racial disturbances in 1970–71 (issues: black studies program and cultural dress) and relations between the police department and the black community are strained. Extensive tracking of black students is also a grievance of the black community.

III. DEVIATION OF ALBANY PUBLIC SCHOOLS FROM DISTRICT RACIAL BALANCE, 1967–68 & 1970–71

	NUMBER OF SCHOOLS	
Deviation from Racial Balance	1967–68 Balance = 29.3% Minority	1970–71 Balance = 34.4% Minority
0–5%	5	3
5.1–10%	1	4
10.1–30%	15	13
30.1–Totally Segregated	4	5
Total Schools	25	25

Amsterdam's public school enrollment was 5,363 in 1970–71. Of this, 6.0% (323) were minority-group children. Nonpublic schools enrolled 1,428 children in 1969–70, 1.1% from minority groups.

The white public school enrollment is decreasing while the minority-group enrollment has more than doubled since 1967–68.

I. AMSTERDAM PUBLIC SCHOOL ENROLLMENT & ETHNIC PROPORTIONS, 1967–68 TO 1970–71

School Year	White	%	Black	%	Spanish-Surnamed	%	Indian & Oriental	%	Total	%[a]
1967–68	5,338	96.5	49	0.9	141	2.5	6	0.1	5,534	100
1968–69	5,247	96.3	43	0.8	159	2.9	0	—	5,449	100
1969–70	5,174	95.3	44	0.8	210	3.9	0	—	5,428	100
1970–71	5,040	94.0	36	0.7	279	5.2	8	0.1	5,363	100

[a] May not total 100% because of rounding.

The total size of the public school staff has increased since 1967, but the minority staff has remained at one.

II. AMSTERDAM PUBLIC EDUCATION STAFF & MINORITY-GROUP PROPORTIONS, 1967–68 & 1970–71

	White	%	Minority	%	Total	%
1967–68	300	99.4	2	0.6	302	100
1970–71	328	99.7	1	0.3	329	100

Amsterdam has 12 elementary schools, nine of which are very small— 291 or *fewer* children each—and six of these are 100% white. Most of the Spanish-surnamed children are concentrated in two schools. The most imbalanced school has a Spanish-speaking assistant principal who has taught the rest of the staff conversational Spanish. The board is trying to find replacements for two Spanish-speaking teachers recruited two years ago who left. Apparently there are no racial incidents, no community pressures to desegregate, no plans to do so, and no money being spent on other than remedial services.

III. Deviation of Amsterdam Public Schools from District
Racial Balance, 1967–68 & 1970–71

Deviation from Racial Balance	NUMBER OF SCHOOLS	
	1967–68 Balance = 3.5% Minority	1970–71 Balance = 6.0% Minority
0–5%	12	3
5.1–10%	1	9
10.1–30%	1	2
30.1–Totally Segregated	—	—
Total Schools	14	14

Auburn's public school enrollment was 7,680 in 1970–71. Of this number, 4.1% (318) were minority-group children. Another 2,634 children were in non-public schools, 0.9% of them from minority groups (in 1969–70).

Total public school enrollment is increasing; proportional white and minority enrollments have remained constant.

I. AUBURN PUBLIC SCHOOL ENROLLMENT & ETHNIC PROPORTIONS, 1967–68 TO 1970–71

	White	%	Black	%	Spanish-Surnamed	%	Indian & Oriental	%	Total	%
1967–68	6,228	95.8	271	4.2	0	—	2	—[a]	6,501	100
1968–69	6,427	95.7	286	4.3	2	—	0	—	6,715	100
1969–70	6,823	95.7	308	4.3	0	—	1	—[a]	7,132	100
1970–71	7,362	95.9	305	4.0	5	—	8	0.1	7,680	100

[a] Less than 0.1%.

The number of teachers and administrators has increased since 1967, as has the proportion of minority group staff—but the number of minority group staff is still small.

II. AUBURN PUBLIC EDUCATION STAFF & MINORITY-GROUP PROPORTIONS, 1967–68 & 1970–71

	White	%	Minority	%	Total	%
1967–68	313	99.1	3	0.9	316	100
1970–71	380	97.9	8	2.1	388	100

Consolidation of the district's high school population from three buildings into one, and creation of a new middle school has not eliminated segregation of white and minority group students in Auburn. Although the middle schools have had some degree of tension, it is apparently due to social class rather than racial disparities, and the schools which present the major segregation problem in Auburn are not being attended to. Three schools, which deviate from the district minority enrollment average by more than five percentage points, are all elementary schools.

III. Deviation of Auburn Public Schools from District
Racial Balance, 1967–68 & 1970–71

Deviation from Racial Balance	NUMBER OF SCHOOLS	
	1967–68 Balance = 4.2% Minority	1970–71 Balance = 4.1% Minority
0–5%	9	8
5.1–10%	1	2
10.1–30%	1	1
30.1–Totally Segregated	—	—
Total Schools	11	11

Bay Shore's public school enrollment was 7,462 in 1970–71, of which 906 (12.1%) were minority children. Another 1,147 children were in non-public schools; 3.9% of them were from minority groups (1969–70).

Both the number and percentage of minority students in the public schools are increasing slowly.

I. Bay Shore Public School Enrollment & Ethnic Proportions, 1967–68 to 1970–71

	White	%	Black	%	Spanish-Surnamed	%	Indian & Oriental	%	Total	%
1967–68	6,164	89.5	629	10.2	78	1.1	17	0.2	6,888	100
1968–69	6,539	89.3	639	8.7	128	1.7	18	0.2	7,324	100
1969–70	6,572	88.3	730	9.8	126	1.7	16	0.2	7,444	100
1970–71	6,556	87.9	768	10.3	117	1.6	21	0.3	7,462	100

The number of teachers and administrators has increased since 1967. The proportion of minority-group staff has risen slightly.

II. Bay Shore Public Education Staff & Minority-Group Proportions, 1967–68 & 1970–71

	White	%	Minority	%	Total	%
1967–68	365	97.9	8	2.1	373	100
1970–71	407	96.2	16	3.8	423	100

Bay Shore is in a state of controversy over a proposed plan to reassign pupils and grades and use busing to desegregate two heavily white and two heavily black schools. Integration is a key issue in school board elections.

Bay Shore has two elementary schools which are more than 96% white and two which are 24% and 32% minority.

III. Deviation of Bay Shore Public Schools from District Racial Balance, 1967–68 & 1970–71

	NUMBER OF SCHOOLS	
Deviation from Racial Balance	1967–68 Balance = 10.5% Minority	1970–71 Balance = 12.1% Minority
0–5%	3	3
5.1–10%	1	1
10.1–30%	3	3
30.1–Totally Segregated	—	—
Total Schools	7	7

Beacon's public school enrollment was 3,593 in 1970–71, of which 25.9% (929) were minority children. Another 681 were in nonpublic schools, 2.2% of them from minority groups (in 1969–70).

Total school enrollment has been increasing; proportional white enrollment is declining and proportional minority-group enrollment has been increasing.

I. BEACON PUBLIC SCHOOL ENROLLMENT & ETHNIC PROPORTIONS, 1967–68 TO 1970–71

	White	%	Black	%	Spanish-Surnamed	%	Indian & Oriental	%	Total	%[a]
1967–68	2,463	76.3	619	19.2	137	4.2	8	0.2	3,227	100
1968–69	2,624	77.3	598	17.6	162	4.8	9	0.3	3,393	100
1969–70	2,629	74.4	676	19.1	216	6.1	14	0.4	3,535	100
1970–71	2,664	74.1	678	18.9	232	6.5	19	0.5	3,593	100

[a] May not be 100% because of rounding.

The number of teachers and administrators has increased slightly since 1967. The proportion of minority-group staff has also increased.

II. BEACON PUBLIC EDUCATION STAFF & MINORITY-GROUP PROPORTIONS, 1967–68 & 1970–71

	White	%	Minority	%	Total	%
1967–68	171	94.0	11	6.0	182	100
1970–71	169	89.4	20	10.6	189	100

Five out of six of the Beacon public schools have minority populations that deviate 6 percentage points or more from the district average. One school whose minority population is 51.4% deviates more than 25 percentage points from the district average.

There have been few active efforts to desegregate the four racially imbalanced schools in Beacon, although efforts have been made to hire minority-group teachers. The superintendent of schools claims that the high minority enrollment in the most segregated school will decrease naturally next year as a result of population shifts in town, due to an urban renewal project. He claims that black parents of children attending this school (the South Ave. school) are unenthusiastic about busing their children to distant sections of Beacon.

III. DEVIATION OF BEACON PUBLIC SCHOOLS FROM DISTRICT
RACIAL BALANCE, 1967–68 & 1970–71

Deviation from Racial Balance	NUMBER OF SCHOOLS	
	1967–68 Balance = 23.7% Minority	1970–71 Balance = 25.9% Minority
0–5%	2	1
5.1–10%	1	4
10.1–30%	2	1
30.1–Totally Segregated	—	—
Total Schools	5	6

Brentwood, the 9th largest district in the state (public school enrollment 22,004 in 1970–71), has a minority student enrollment of 3,723, representing 16.9% of the public school student population. Another 1,800 children are in nonpublic schools, 4.7% of them from minority groups (in 1969–70).

Both white and minority enrollments in the public schools are increasing.

I. BRENTWOOD PUBLIC SCHOOL ENROLLMENT & ETHNIC PROPORTIONS, 1967–68 TO 1970–71

	White	%	Black	%	Spanish-Surnamed	%	Indian & Oriental	%	Total	%
1967–68	17,157	86.1	912	4.6	1,776	8.9	79	0.4	19,924	100
1968–69	17,760	85.2	1,022	4.9	2,041	9.8	24	0.1	20,847	100
1969–70	17,805	83.4	1,028	4.8	2,446	11.5	64	0.3	21,343	100
1970–71	18,281	83.1	1,030	4.7	2,645	12.0	48	0.2	22,004	100

The number of teachers and administrators has increased since 1967, but the proportion of minority-group staff has decreased slightly.

II. BRENTWOOD PUBLIC EDUCATION STAFF & MINORITY-GROUP PROPORTIONS, 1967–68 & 1970–71

	White	%	Minority	%	Total	%
1967–68	910	90.4	97	9.6	1,007	100
1970–71	1,034	91.2	100	8.8	1,134	100

Though there has never been a statement by the Board of Education on desegregation, there has been some busing of students in an attempt to reduce racial imbalance in two elementary schools. An attempt to bus about 30 black children to an almost all white school failed last year because of opposition from both black and white parents (the blacks opposed the plan because the busing was only one way). There is a new black history course in the high school and a Spanish culture course in one of the junior high schools.

There have been several incidents of racially inspired violence in the high school since 1968.

There is considerable segregation of white and minority group students.

III. Deviation of Brentwood Public Schools from District
Racial Balance, 1967–68 & 1970–71

| Deviation from Racial Balance | NUMBER OF SCHOOLS | |
	1967–68 Balance = 13.9% Minority	1970–71 Balance = 16.9% Minority
0–5%	4	4
5.1–10%	10	9
10.1–30%	6	5
30.1–Totally Segregated	—	1
Total Schools	20	19

Catskill's public school enrollment was 2,358 in 1970–71, of which 9.6% (227) were minority children. Another 548 children were in nonpublic schools, 0.2% of them from minority groups (in 1969–70).

White enrollment is decreasing while minority enrollment is increasing in the public schools.

I. CATSKILL PUBLIC SCHOOL ENROLLMENT & ETHNIC PROPORTIONS, 1967–68 TO 1970–71

	White	%	Black	%	Spanish-Surnamed	%	Indian & Oriental	%	Total	%[b]
1967–68	2,422	91.9	197	7.5	15	0.6	1	—[a]	2,635	100
1968–69	1,999	90.6	181	8.2	24	1.1	3	0.1	2,207	100
1969–70	2,077	92.6	149	6.6	16	0.7	2	0.1	2,244	100
1970–71	2,131	90.4	190	8.1	33	1.4	4	0.1	2,358	100

[a] Less than 0.1%.
[b] May not total 100% because of rounding.

The number of teachers and administrators has increased since 1967, but the proportion of minority-group staff has remained almost constant.

II. CATSKILL PUBLIC EDUCATION STAFF & MINORITY-GROUP PROPORTIONS, 1967–68 & 1970–71

	White	%	Minority	%	Total	%
1967–68	114	99.1	1	0.9	115	100
1970–71	116	98.3	2	1.7	118	100

There is definite movement toward bringing in students from two small, rural, isolated, all-white elementary schools and placing them in with other students in the two larger elementary schools. However, the minority population is clearly concentrated in one of these larger schools—19.2% in one versus 2.9% in the other.

III. DEVIATION OF CATSKILL PUBLIC SCHOOLS FROM DISTRICT RACIAL BALANCE, 1967–68 & 1970–71

NUMBER OF SCHOOLS

Deviation from Racial Balance	1967–68 Balance = 8.1% Minority	1970–71 Balance = 9.6% Minority
0–5%	3	3
5.1–10%	3	2
10.1–30%	1	1
30.1–Totally Segregated	—	—
Total Schools	7	6

The public school enrollment in Deer Park was 8,669 in 1970–71, of which 6.9% (599) were minority children. Only 0.5% of the 1,092 nonpublic school students were non-white (in 1969–70).

Both white and minority enrollments have been gradually increasing, but the proportions of each group have remained about the same.

I. Deer Park Public School Enrollment & Ethnic Proportions, 1967–68 to 1970–71

	White	%	Black	%	Spanish-Surnamed	%	Indian & Oriental	%	Total	%[a]
1967–68	7,497	94.1	371	4.7	71	0.9	30	0.4	7,969	100
1968–69	7,705	93.3	395	4.8	120	1.5	41	0.5	8,261	100
1969–70	7,956	93.4	411	4.8	121	1.4	34	0.4	8,522	100
1970–71	8,070	93.1	412	4.8	155	1.8	32	0.3	8,669	100

[a] May not total 100% because of rounding.

The number of teachers and administrators has increased since 1967, but the number and percentage of minority staff has increased only slightly.

II. Deer Park Public Education Staff & Minority-Group Proportions, 1967–68 & 1970–71

	White	%	Minority	%	Total	%
1967–68	401	97.8	9	2.2	410	100
1970–71	448	97.6	11	2.4	459	100

The percentage of non-white students in the five elementary schools ranges from 1.0% to 23.9%. Deer Park's geographical location, adjoining the nearly all-black Wyndanch district, has made many residents hesitant to take any action regarding racial imbalance, fearing that such steps might lead to large-scale inter-district busing or district reorganization.

III. Deviation of Deer Park Public Schools from District Racial Balance, 1967–68 & 1970–71

	NUMBER OF SCHOOLS	
	1967–68	1970–71
Deviation from Racial Balance	Balance = 5.9% Minority	Balance = 6.9% Minority
0–5%	7	4
5.1–10%	0	3
10.1–30%	1	1
30.1–Totally Segregated	—	—
Total Schools	8	8

Dunkirk's public school enrollment was 3,376 in 1970–71, of which 12.5% were minority children (422). Another 1,482 children were in nonpublic schools, 5.6% of them from minority groups (in 1969–70).

White enrollment fluctuates slightly while minority enrollment is increasing.

I. DUNKIRK PUBLIC SCHOOL ENROLLMENT & ETHNIC PROPORTIONS, 1967–68 TO 1970–71

	White	%	Black	%	Spanish-Surnamed	%	Indian & Oriental	%	Total	%[b]
1967–68	3,015	90.1	124	3.7	207	6.2	2	—[a]	3,348	100
1968–69	2,938	88.7	137	4.1	229	6.9	8	0.2	3,312	100
1969–70	3,400	88.2	157	4.6	245	7.2	1	—[a]	3,407	100
1970–71	2,954	87.5	151	4.5	268	7.9	3	0.1	3,376	100

[a] Less than 0.1%.
[b] May not total 100% because of rounding.

The number of teachers and administrators has increased since 1967; there is no minority staff as of 1970–71.

II. DUNKIRK PUBLIC EDUCATION STAFF & MINORITY-GROUP PROPORTIONS, 1967–68 & 1970–71

	White	%	Minority	%	Total	%
1967–68	155	100	0	—	155	100
1970–71	161	100	0	—	161	100

Dunkirk has a very active Puerto Rican community. The last racial incident occurred in 1969 and centered around the issue of busing and free hot lunches for disadvantaged children. In response to pressure, the boundaries of the town were redistricted. There are no plans to institute a busing program.

One school (elementary) has approximately one-third of the Spanish-surnamed students of the district; a low-income project is located across the street.

III. Deviation of Dunkirk Public Schools from District
Racial Balance, 1967–68 & 1970–71

Deviation from Racial Balance	NUMBER OF SCHOOLS	
	1967–68 Balance = 9.9% Minority	1970–71 Balance = 12.5% Minority
0–5%	4	5
5.1–10%	2	1
10.1–30%	1	1
30.1–Totally Segregated	—	—
Total Schools	7	7

Elmira's public school enrollment was 13,753 in 1970–71, of which 7% (906) are minority children. Another 2,179 children were in nonpublic schools, 1% of them from minority groups (in 1969–70).

White enrollment in the public schools has declined slightly; black enrollment has remained stable.

I. ELMIRA PUBLIC SCHOOL ENROLLMENT & ETHNIC PROPORTIONS, 1967–68 TO 1970–71

	White	%	Black	%	Spanish-Surnamed	%	Indian & Oriental	%	Total	%[b]
1967–68	13,244	93.6	891	6.3	3	—[a]	13	0.1	14,151	100
1968–69	13,213	93.5	902	6.4	5	—[a]	6	—[a]	14,126	100
1969–70	13,041	93.5	896	6.4	6	—[a]	7	0.1	13,950	100
1970–71	12,847	93.4	884	6.4	12	0.1	10	0.1	13,753	100

[a] Less than 0.1%.
[b] May not total 100% because of rounding.

The number of teachers and administrators has increased slightly since 1967, as has the proportion of minority staff.

II. ELMIRA PUBLIC EDUCATION STAFF & MINORITY-GROUP PROPORTIONS, 1967–68 & 1970–71

	White	%	Minority	%	Total	%
1967–68	720	98.0	15	2.0	735	100
1970–71	725	97.3	20	2.7	745	100

Despite a desegregation plan implemented in fall 1968, there remain four schools with less than 1% minority enrollment. Some of these schools are rural. (There is also a handful with substantial minority enrollment.) "Follow-through" guidelines have resegregated some schools that had been desegregated. The plan includes two-way busing, which State Racial Imbalance Funds helped pay for. (Parochial schools cooperated; they refused to become white havens.) Extensive attitude studies of parents and children show great improvements since integration. There was substantial community involvement and communication in planning.

There has been only one major incident since then, although police-minority youth relations were bad for a long time.

III. Deviation of Elmira Public Schools from District
Racial Balance, 1967–68 & 1970–71

| Deviation from Racial Balance | NUMBER OF SCHOOLS | |
	1967–68 Balance = 6.4% Minority	1970–71 Balance = 7.0% Minority
0–5%	8	11
5.1–10%	11	7
10.1–30%	—	3
30.1–Totally Segregated	2	—
Total Schools	21	21

Elmont's public school enrollment in its elementary Union Free District was 4,168 in 1970–71. Of this number 7.5% (314) were minority group children. Another 1,490 children were in nonpublic schools, 0.9% of them from minority groups (in 1969–70).

The white school population of Elmont has been gradually decreasing, while the minority enrollment has increased slightly.

I. ELMONT PUBLIC SCHOOL ENROLLMENT & ETHNIC PROPORTIONS, 1967–68 TO 1970–71

	White	%	Black	%	Spanish-Surnamed	%	Indian & Oriental	%	Total	%[a]
1967–68	4,158	94.4	185	4.2	38	0.9	24	0.5	4,405	100
1968–69	4,042	94.3	186	4.3	45	1.0	13	0.3	4,286	100
1969–70	3,986	94.1	201	4.7	37	0.9	11	0.3	4,235	100
1970–71	3,854	92.5	231	5.5	72	1.7	11	0.3	4,168	100

[a] May not total 100% because of rounding.

The number of teachers and administrators has decreased slightly since 1967; the number of minority-group staff has also decreased.

II. ELMONT PUBLIC EDUCATION STAFF & MINORITY-GROUP PROPORTIONS, 1967–68 & 1970–71

	White	%	Minority	%	Total	%
1967–68	220	97.3	6	2.7	226	100
1970–71	208	97.7	5	2.3	213	100

The Elmont Union Free School District pursues a neighborhood school policy and has made no moves toward desegregating its two all-white schools. One highly racially imbalanced school, the Elmont Road School, was closed since 1967, but the motives reflected economic concerns more than the desire to correct a racially imbalanced situation. There has been little push from the black community for further desegregation of the schools.

Three of the six elementary schools in the district have enrollments that deviate more than five percentage points from the district average; two of these schools have white enrollments over 97%.

III. Deviation of Elmont Public Schools from District
Racial Balance, 1967–68 & 1970–71

| Deviation from Racial Balance | NUMBER OF SCHOOLS | |
	1967–68 Balance = 5.6% Minority	1970–71 Balance = 7.5% Minority
0–5%	5	3
5.1–10%	1	2
10.1–30%	—	1
30.1–Totally Segregated	1	—
Total Schools	7	6

Great Neck's public school enrollment was 9,271 in 1970–71. Of this, 6.8% (633) are minority children. Another 1,023 are in nonpublic schools, 24 of them (2.3%) from minority groups (in 1969–70).

The white enrollment has decreased substantially while the minority enrollment has nearly doubled in the past four years.

I. GREAT NECK PUBLIC SCHOOL ENROLLMENT & ETHNIC PROPORTIONS, 1967–68 TO 1970–71

	White	%	Black	%	Spanish-Surnamed	%	Indian & Oriental	%	Total	%[a]
1967–68	9,728	96.2	316	3.1	29	0.3	42	0.4	10,115	100
1968–69	9,426	95.3	404	4.1	30	0.3	36	0.4	9,896	100
1969–70	9,211	94.8	385	4.0	73	0.8	49	0.5	9,718	100
1970–71	8,638	93.2	476	5.1	100	1.1	58	0.6	9,272	100

[a] May not total 100% because of rounding.

The number of teachers and administrators has decreased since 1967, while the number of minority-group staff has increased slightly.

II. GREAT NECK PUBLIC EDUCATION STAFF & MINORITY-GROUP PROPORTIONS, 1967–68 & 1970–71

	White	%	Minority	%	Total	%
1967–68	689	98.4	11	1.6	700	100
1970–71	648	97.7	15	2.3	663	100

The secondary schools are balanced and have apparently been free from incident. However, of the 11 elementary schools two represent a nadir of minority enrollment (2.9% and 0.7%) and three a zenith of minority enrollment (13.8%, 15.1% and 25.9%). The remaining six range between 4.8% and 9.8%. Statistically the situation has worsened in the last four years. In 1967–68 only one school was imbalanced, albeit dramatically; now four are.

The administration contends that the imbalance is only in K-3 schools that feed into balanced schools afterwards; but actually only two of the four are K-3. There are no plans for change at present; an attempt to bus in inner-city kids failed; and a minority-staff recruiting drive has not been successful.

III. Deviation of Great Neck Public Schools from District
Racial Balance, 1967–68 & 1970–71

Deviation from Racial Balance	NUMBER OF SCHOOLS	
	1967–68 Balance = 3.8% Minority	1970–71 Balance = 6.8% Minority
0–5%	14	11
5.1–10%	—	3
10.1–30%	1	1
30.1–Totally Segregated	—	—
Total Schools	15	15

Hempstead's public school enrollment was 5,665 in 1970–71. Of this, 81.3% (4,607) were minority children. Nonpublic schools enrolled 1,679 children in 1969–70, 9.1% from minority groups.

Minority enrollment is increasing while white enrollment is decreasing.

I. HEMPSTEAD PUBLIC SCHOOL ENROLLMENT & ETHNIC PROPORTIONS, 1967–68 TO 1970–71

	White	%	Black	%	Spanish-Surnamed	%	Indian & Oriental	%	Total	%
1967–68	1,561	28.4	3,833	69.7	76	1.4	27	0.5	5,497	100
1968–69	1,546	26.5	4,159	71.4	102	1.8	21	0.3	5,828	100
1969–70	1,265	22.4	4,196	74.2	159	2.8	35	0.6	5,655	100
1970–71	1,058	18.7	4,330	76.4	242	4.3	35	0.6	5,665	100

The number of minority administrators and staff has increased substantially since 1967, but it is still well below the proportion of minority students in the district.

II. HEMPSTEAD PUBLIC EDUCATION STAFF & MINORITY-GROUP PROPORTIONS, 1967–68 & 1970–71

	White	%	Minority	%	Total	%
1967–68	291	86.4	46	13.6	337	100
1970–71	243	69.4	107	30.6	350	100

Despite its small geographic area and a court decision ordering integration, there is considerable racial imbalance in Hempstead.

Five schools have a minority enrollment that exceeds 96%. Half of the white students in the district are concentrated in two schools. Hempstead, with one of the highest percentages of minority population in the state, is a school system in which the small number of whites are segregated away from the overwhelmingly black schools.

III. DEVIATION OF HEMPSTEAD PUBLIC SCHOOLS FROM DISTRICT RACIAL BALANCE, 1967–68 & 1970–71

	NUMBER OF SCHOOLS	
Deviation from Racial Balance	1967–68 Balance = 71.6% Minority	1970–71 Balance = 81.3% Minority
0–5%	—	2
5.1–10%	1	—
10.1–30%	6	6
30.1–Totally Segregated	2	1
Total Schools	9	9

The Hudson public school enrollment was 3,667 in 1970–71. Of this number, 9.7% (357) were minority-group children. The 571 nonpublic school students include 6.5% from minority groups (1969–70 data).

The white school enrollment has increased while the minority enrollment has fluctuated, but most recently decreased.

I. HUDSON PUBLIC SCHOOL ENROLLMENT & ETHNIC PROPORTIONS, 1967–68 TO 1970–71

	White	%	Black	%	Spanish-Surnamed	%	Indian & Oriental	%	Total	%[b]
1967–68	3,085	89.2	371	10.7	0	—	1	—[a]	3,457	100
1968–69	3,146	89.2	375	10.6	5	0.1	1	—[a]	3,527	100
1969–70	3,151	87.9	422	11.8	6	0.2	4	0.1	3,583	100
1970–71	3,310	90.3	352	9.6	3	0.1	2	0.1	3,667	100

[a] Less than 0.1%.
[b] May not total 100% because of rounding.

The total size of the public school staff has increased since 1967, but the proportion of minority staff members has remained constant.

II. HUDSON PUBLIC EDUCATION STAFF & MINORITY-GROUP PROPORTIONS, 1967–68 & 1970–71

	White	%	Minority	%	Total	%
1967–68	179	97.8	4	2.2	183	100
1970–71	195	97.5	5	2.5	200	100

Hudson is an enlarged city school district; three of its five elementary schools are old buildings in outlying rural communities. They are imbalanced, although they have been cut back from K-8 to K-6.

The district has not requested imbalance aid because it is felt the area is not segregated. The board president has taken a stand against busing to achieve racial integration. There has been some discussion of redistricting, including a possible annexing of a wealthy fringe district, protested by those parents for fear of violence. (There was a minor knifing incident.) Federal monies have been spent on a drum and bugle corps for disadvantaged children.

III. DEVIATION OF HUDSON PUBLIC SCHOOLS FROM DISTRICT
RACIAL BALANCE, 1967–68 & 1970–71

Deviation from Racial Balance	NUMBER OF SCHOOLS	
	1967–68 Balance = 10.8% Minority	**1970–71** Balance = 9.7% Minority
0–5%	2	2
5.1–10%	2	4
10.1–30%	3	1
30.1–Totally Segregated	—	—
Total Schools	7	7

Huntington's public school enrollment was 8,454 in 1970–71. Of this, 11.1% (939) were minority children. Another 1,790 were in nonpublic schools, 4.1% of them from minority groups (in 1969–70).

Minority enrollment has been increasing and white enrollment decreasing.

I. HUNTINGTON PUBLIC SCHOOL ENROLLMENT & ETHNIC PROPORTIONS, 1967–68 & 1970–71

	White	%	Black	%	Spanish-Surnamed	%	Indian & Oriental	%	Total	%
1967–68	7,848	92.8	492	5.8	89	1.1	27	0.3	8,456	100
1968–69	7,859	92.4	521	6.1	113	1.3	17	0.2	8,510	100
1969–70	7,807	90.5	543	6.3	256	3.0	24	0.3	8,630	100
1970–71	7,515	88.9	599	7.1	316	3.7	24	0.3	8,454	100

The number of teachers and administrators has declined, as has the number of minority-group staff.

II. HUNTINGTON PUBLIC EDUCATION STAFF & MINORITY-GROUP PROPORTIONS, 1967–68 & 1970–71

	White	%	Minority	%	Total	%
1967–68	498	97.6	12	2.4	510	100
1970–71	482	97.8	11	2.2	493	100

Huntington has been the scene of severe racial tensions which have necessitated school closings. A district plan to reduce imbalance by closing three elementary schools and sending the children to a larger school in an urban renewal area is being opposed by white parents.

Out of fourteen schools there are five that have white enrollments of 96% or more, and three schools that have a minority enrollment 11 percentage points greater than the district average.

III. DEVIATION OF HUNTINGTON PUBLIC SCHOOLS FROM DISTRICT RACIAL BALANCE, 1967–68 & 1970–71

	NUMBER OF SCHOOLS	
Deviation from Racial Balance	1967–68 Balance = 7.2% Minority	1970–71 Balance = 11.7% Minority
0–5%	7	5
5.1–10%	5	5
10.1–30%	2	4
30.1–Totally Segregated	—	—
Total Schools	14	14

Ithaca's public school enrollment was 8,174 in 1970–71. Of this, 6.1% (496) were minority children. There were 516 children in nonpublic schools in 1969–70, of whom 9.5% were from minority groups.

Minority enrollment in the public schools has increased slightly and white enrollment has declined slightly.

I. ITHACA PUBLIC SCHOOL ENROLLMENT & ETHNIC PROPORTIONS, 1967–68 TO 1970–71

	White	%	Black	%	Spanish-Surnamed	%	Indian & Oriental	%	Total	%[a]
1967–68	7,775	95.1	335	4.1	0	—	62	0.8	8,172	100
1968–69	7,784	94.6	360	4.4	44	0.5	38	0.5	8,226	100
1969–70	7,814	94.1	399	4.8	27	0.3	62	0.7	8,302	100
1970–71	7,678	93.9	410	5.0	32	0.4	54	0.7	8,174	100

[a] May not total 100% because of rounding.

The number of minority staff has increased so that it is now slightly higher than the district average of minority pupils, and the number of white staff has decreased.

II. ITHACA PUBLIC EDUCATION STAFF & MINORITY-GROUP PROPORTIONS, 1967–68 & 1970–71

	White	%	Minority	%	Total	%
1967–68	409	99.3	3	0.7	412	100
1970–71	365	93.6	25	6.4	390	100

Because Ithaca does not bus on the elementary school level, there are two schools which are 100% white and two which have minority enrollments of 30% and 41%, respectively. There has been racial unrest on the junior high school and high school level.

III. DEVIATION OF ITHACA PUBLIC SCHOOLS FROM DISTRICT RACIAL BALANCE, 1967–68 & 1970–71

	NUMBER OF SCHOOLS	
Deviation from Racial Balance	1967–68 Balance = 4.9% Minority	1970–71 Balance = 6.1% Minority
0–5%	13	12
5.1–10%	1	3
10.1–30%	2	1
30.1–Totally Segregated	—	1
Total Schools	16	17

Kingston's public school enrollment was 11,430 in 1970–71. Of this number, 7.1% (813) were minority children. Another 1,845 children were in nonpublic schools, 2.2% of them from minority groups (in 1969–70).

Both white and minority enrollments in the public schools are increasing.

I. KINGSTON PUBLIC SCHOOL ENROLLMENT & ETHNIC PROPORTIONS, 1967–68 TO 1970–71

	White	%	Black	%	Spanish-Surnamed	%	Indian & Oriental	%	Total	%
1967–68	9,880	94.1	559	5.3	32	0.3	24	0.2	10,495	100
1968–69	10,248	93.8	583	5.3	62	0.6	33	0.3	10,926	100
1969–70	10,373	93.5	644	5.8	65	0.6	18	0.2	11,100	100
1970–71	10,617	92.9	714	6.2	66	0.6	33	0.3	11,430	100

The number of teachers and administrators has increased since 1967, but the number of minority-group staff has decreased.

II. KINGSTON PUBLIC EDUCATION STAFF & MINORITY-GROUP PROPORTIONS, 1967–68 & 1970–71

	White	%	Minority	%	Total	%
1967–68	549	97.0	17	3.0	566	100
1970–71	584	98.5	9	1.5	593	100

Kingston buses 80% of its elementary school pupils under state mandate. There was some dissension at the junior high school. Subsequently, black studies programs in both junior and senior high schools were introduced.

Two elementary schools have minority enrollments of more than 35%; four others have white enrollments of more than 98%.

III. DEVIATION OF KINGSTON PUBLIC SCHOOLS FROM DISTRICT RACIAL BALANCE, 1967–68 & 1970–71

	NUMBER OF SCHOOLS	
Deviation from Racial Balance	1967–68 Balance = 5.9% Minority	1970–71 Balance = 7.2% Minority
0–5%	15	12
5.1–10%	1	5
10.1–30%	2	1
30.1–Totally Segregated	—	1
Total Schools	18	19

Lackawanna's public school enrollment in 1970–71 was 5,736. Of this number, 19.2% (1,100) were minority group children. Another 1,812 children attended nonpublic schools in 1969–70, 13.6% of them from minority groups.

Public school enrollment has remained stable over the past four years. The proportional white enrollment has remained the same; the black population has decreased slightly and the Spanish-surnamed population has slightly increased.

I. LACKAWANNA PUBLIC SCHOOL ENROLLMENT & ETHNIC PROPORTIONS, 1967–68 TO 1970–71

	White	%	Black	%	Spanish-Surnamed	%	Indian & Oriental	%	Total	%
1967–68	4,625	80.5	963	16.8	123	2.1	31	0.6	5,742	100
1968–69	4,754	81.1	951	16.2	155	2.6	5	0.1	5,865	100
1969–70	4,743	81.3	932	16.0	152	2.6	7	0.1	5,834	100
1970–71	4,636	80.8	901	15.7	192	3.4	7	0.1	5,736	100

The number of teachers and administrators has increased since 1967, as has the number of minority staff.

II. LACKAWANNA PUBLIC EDUCATION STAFF & MINORITY-GROUP PROPORTIONS, 1967–68 & 1970–71

	White	%	Minority	%	Total	%
1967–68	294	98.7	4	1.3	298	100
1970–71	325	97.3	9	2.7	334	100

Political corruption in Lackawanna, as evidenced by grand jury indictments against one school board member, a former member, a school administrator, an employee, and others, affects the educational system and other aspects of city life. In addition a strong segregationist bloc makes its voice heard in matters regarding education as well as housing. There has been no effort to desegregate the highly racially imbalanced schools. Tentative plans to acquire land to build a middle school which would indirectly help balance the school system have been around for a number of years but have not been pursued.

Five of the eight schools deviating by more than five percentage points from the district minority average have white enrollments over 95%, including four elementary schools and one junior high school. Three schools have minority enrollments higher than 99%, and two elementary schools and another junior high school have minority enrollments higher than 60%.

III. DEVIATION OF LACKAWANNA PUBLIC SCHOOLS FROM DISTRICT
RACIAL BALANCE, 1967–68 & 1970–71

NUMBER OF SCHOOLS

Deviation from Racial Balance	1967–68 Balance = 19.5% Minority	1970–71 Balance = 19.2% Minority
0–5%	1	—
5.1–10%	1	2
10.1–30%	5	5
30.1–Totally Segregated	3	3
Total Schools	10	10

Lawrence's public school enrollment was 7,741 in 1970–71. Of this, 8.5% (658) were minority-group children. Another 2,039 children were in non-public schools, 3.6% of them from minority groups (in 1969–70).

The total public school enrollment has been decreasing, as has the proportional white enrollment. The proportional minority enrollment has been slowly increasing.

I. LAWRENCE PUBLIC SCHOOL ENROLLMENT & ETHNIC PROPORTIONS, 1967–68 TO 1970–71

	White	%	Black	%	Spanish-Surnamed	%	Indian & Oriental	%	Total	%
1967–68	7,361	92.8	545	6.9	14	0.2	13	0.2	7,933	100
1968–69	7,388	92.5	541	6.8	38	0.5	22	0.3	7,989	100
1969–70	7,251	92.2	573	7.3	25	0.3	15	0.2	7,864	100
1970–71	7,083	91.5	590	7.6	53	0.7	15	0.2	7,741	100

The number of teachers and administrators has remained constant. The number of minority staff has increased since 1967, though it is still lower than the proportion of minority students.

II. LAWRENCE PUBLIC EDUCATION STAFF & MINORITY-GROUP PROPORTIONS, 1967–68 & 1970–71

	White	%	Minority	%	Total	%
1967–68	451	97.4	12	2.6	463	100
1970–71	440	95.2	22	4.8	462	100

There have been few efforts to desegregate the Lawrence school system. Sporadic tension has occurred in the high school between whites and blacks and at least one walk-out by black students has taken place. In response to the demands made by the black students at the walk-out, an aggressive campaign of minority hiring was mounted. Although minority staff has doubled since 1967, it still amounts to only 22 out of 462 teachers and administrators.

Six schools in Lawrence have minority enrollments which deviate from the district average by more than 5 percentage points. All of these are elementary schools. Two of the schools have white enrollments which are higher than 99%.

III. Deviation of Lawrence Public Schools from District Racial Balance, 1967–68 & 1970–71

Deviation from Racial Balance	NUMBER OF SCHOOLS	
	1967–68 Balance = 7.3% Minority	1970–71 Balance = 8.5% Minority
0–5%	3	2
5.1–10%	4	5
10.1–30%	1	1
30.1–Totally Segregated	—	—
Total Schools	8	8

The public school enrollment in Lockport was 6,937 in 1970–71, of which 5.4% (378) were minority-group children. This percentage has been constant for several years. Only one of the 975 nonpublic school children was non-white in 1969–70. The number and percentage of enrolled minority students has gradually increased while the white enrollment has fluctuated slightly.

I. LOCKPORT PUBLIC SCHOOL ENROLLMENT & ETHNIC PROPORTIONS, 1967–68 TO 1970–71

	White	%	Black	%	Spanish-Surnamed	%	Indian & Oriental	%	Total	%[b]
1967–68	6,434	95.2	294	4.4	19	0.3	6	0.1	6,753	100
1968–69	6,566	95.2	302	4.4	18	0.3	9	0.1	6,895	100
1969–70	6,686	94.8	319	4.5	33	0.5	12	0.2	7,050	100
1970–71	6,564	94.6	328	4.7	43	0.6	2	—[a]	6,937	100

[a] Less than 0.1%.
[b] May not total 100% due to rounding.

The percentage of minority-group teachers is less than 1%. The number of teachers and administrators has remained practically constant since 1967.

II. LOCKPORT PUBLIC EDUCATION STAFF & MINORITY-GROUP PROPORTIONS, 1967–68 & 1970–71

	White	%	Minority	%	Total	%
1967–68	347	99.1	3	0.9	350	100
1970–71	346	99.4	2	0.6	348	100

In the eight elementary schools, minority-group enrollment ranges from 0.2% to 20.5%. No action has been taken regarding this imbalance. A limited number of children (60 to 70 this year, both black and white) are bused beyond the school closest to them in order to balance class sizes, but no major busing has taken place for desegregation purposes.

III. DEVIATION OF LOCKPORT PUBLIC SCHOOLS FROM DISTRICT RACIAL BALANCE, 1967–68 & 1970–71

	NUMBER OF SCHOOLS	
Deviation from Racial Balance	1967–68 Balance = 4.8% Minority	1970–71 Balance = 5.4% Minority
0–5%	10	9
5.1–10%	—	1
10.1–30%	1	1
30.1–Totally Segregated	—	—
Total Schools	11	11

In 1970–71, the public school enrollment in Mamaroneck, a relatively wealthy community, was 6,281, of which 5.9% (369) were minority-group children. Of the 1,437 nonpublic school students, 4.7% were from minority groups.

The ethnic proportions have been stable over recent years, as has the total enrollment.

I. MAMARONECK PUBLIC SCHOOL ENROLLMENT & ETHNIC PROPORTIONS, 1967–68 TO 1970–71

	White	%	Black	%	Spanish-Surnamed	%	Indian & Oriental	%	Total	%
1967–68	5,816	94.2	283	4.6	27	0.4	48	0.8	6,174	100
1968–69	5,937	94.7	248	4.0	53	0.8	34	0.5	6,272	100
1969–70	6,064	94.7	242	3.8	64	1.0	33	0.5	6,403	100
1970–71	5,912	94.1	262	4.2	74	1.2	33	0.5	6,281	100

The number and percentage of minority-group staff members has increased since 1967.

II. MAMARONECK PUBLIC EDUCATION STAFF & MINORITY-GROUP PROPORTIONS, 1967–68 & 1970–71

	White	%	Minority	%	Total	%
1967–68	382	97.9	8	2.1	390	100
1970–71	393	96.3	15	3.7	408	100

Of the five elementary schools, one is 20.3% non-white, while the non-white percentage in no other elementary school exceeds 3.5%. No action has been taken by school authorities to alleviate this situation.

III. DEVIATION OF MAMARONECK PUBLIC SCHOOLS FROM DISTRICT RACIAL BALANCE, 1967–68 & 1970–71

	NUMBER OF SCHOOLS	
Deviation from Racial Balance	1967–68 Balance = 5.8% Minority	1970–71 Balance = 5.9% Minority
0–5%	5	4
5.1–10%	—	1
10.1–30%	1	1
30.1–Totally Segregated	—	—
Total Schools	6	6

Monticello's public school enrollment was 3,485 in 1970–71, of which 19.2% (671) were minority-group children. Another 699 children were in nonpublic schools, 5.6% of them from minority groups (in 1969–70).

Total public school enrollment has been increasing, as has the number of both white and minority students, except for a slight decrease in 1968–69.

I. MONTICELLO PUBLIC SCHOOL ENROLLMENT & ETHNIC PROPORTIONS, 1967–68 TO 1970–71

	White	%	Black	%	Spanish-Surnamed	%	Indian & Oriental	%	Total	%
1967–68	2,611	83.9	421	13.5	49	1.6	30	1.0	3,111	100
1968–69	2,239	78.8	492	17.3	88	3.1	24	0.8	2,843	100
1969–70	2,750	81.9	518	15.4	68	2.0	23	0.7	3,359	100
1970–71	2,814	80.8	559	16.0	95	2.7	17	0.5	3,485	100

The number of teachers and administrators is basically the same as in 1967–68. The number of minority-group staff has increased.

II. MONTICELLO PUBLIC EDUCATION STAFF & MINORITY-GROUP PROPORTIONS, 1967–68 & 1970–71

	White	%	Minority	%	Total	%
1967–68	179	98.9	2	1.1	181	100
1970–71	174	94.1	11	5.9	185	100

Five or six years ago, on its own initiative, the board divided two elementary schools located in the town itself into K-2 and 3-6 respectively to alleviate an accelerating racial imbalance. Apparently, this move was not generated by community pressure and there was no community reaction to it.

There remain three racially imbalanced elementary schools in Monticello. Two of these have white enrollments of 92.4% and 96.9%. These two schools are located four and seven miles out of town, and there has been no discussion of balancing them racially via busing. The third imbalanced school has a minority enrollment of 31.5%.

III. Deviation of Monticello Public Schools from District
Racial Balance, 1967–68 & 1970–71

| Deviation from Racial Balance | NUMBER OF SCHOOLS | |
	1967–68 Balance = 16.1% Minority	1970–71 Balance = 19.2% Minority
0–5%	4	3
5.1–10%	2	—
10.1–30%	—	3
30.1–Totally Segregated	—	—
Total Schools	6	6

Mount Vernon's public school enrollment was 11,938 in 1970–71, of which 59% (6,984) were minority children. Another 2,467 children were in non-public schools during the 1969–70 school year; 13.7% of them were from minority groups.

White enrollment in public schools is decreasing; minority enrollment is increasing.

I. MOUNT VERNON PUBLIC SCHOOL ENROLLMENT & ETHNIC PROPORTIONS, 1967–68 TO 1970–71

	White	%	Black	%	Spanish-Surnamed	%	Indian & Oriental	%	Total	%
1967–68	6,594	50.9	6,244	48.2	71	0.5	55	0.4	12,964	100
1968–69	5,770	46.8	6,336	51.4	173	1.4	53	0.4	12,332	100
1969–70	6,584	52.5	5,749	45.8	174	1.4	43	0.3	12,550	100
1970–71	4,890	41.0	6,725	56.3	259	2.2	64	0.5	11,938	100

The number of teachers and administrators has decreased since 1967, while minority-group staff has decreased slightly.

II. MOUNT VERNON PUBLIC EDUCATION STAFF & MINORITY-GROUP PROPORTIONS, 1967–68 & 1970–71

	White	%	Minority	%	Total	%
1967–68	640	87.4	92	12.6	732	100
1970–71	539	82.8	112	17.2	651	100

Five elementary schools have over 67% white enrollment; five others have over 89% black enrollment. A constant struggle between the community and the Board of Education regarding desegregating the schools has resulted in court action, still unresolved. (The Black Community Planning Board issued a plan which was counteracted by a plan submitted by the Board of Education.) No funds have been used for correcting racial imbalance since 1967.

III. DEVIATION OF MOUNT VERNON PUBLIC SCHOOLS FROM DISTRICT RACIAL BALANCE, 1967–68 & 1970–71

NUMBER OF SCHOOLS

Deviation from Racial Balance	1967–68 Balance = 49.1% Minority	1970–71 Balance = 59.0% Minority
0–5%	1	1
5.1–10%	2	1
10.1–30%	8	4
30.1–Totally Segregated	8	10
Total Schools	19	16

Newburgh's public school enrollment was 13,077 in 1970–71, of which 27.8% (3,635) were minority children. Another 1,750 children, 9.3% from minority groups, were in eight nonpublic schools as of 1969–70.

The number and proportion of minority students in the public schools are gradually increasing. White enrollment has changed more erratically, increasing for three years and then decreasing.

I. Newburgh Public School Enrollment & Ethnic Proportions, 1967–68 to 1970–71

	White	%	Black	%	Spanish-Surnamed	%	Indian & Oriental	%	Total	%
1967–68	9,229	75.6	2,647	21.7	301	2.5	27	0.2	12,204	100
1968–69	9,348	73.5	2,925	23.0	374	2.9	73	0.6	12,720	100
1969–70	9,635	73.6	3,001	22.9	432	3.3	19	0.1	13,087	100
1970–71	9,442	72.2	3,156	24.1	460	3.5	19	0.1	13,077	100

The number of teachers and administrators has increased somewhat since 1967 as has the number of minority-group staff. There are two black principals.

II. Newburgh Public Education Staff & Minority-Group Proportions, 1967–68 & 1970–71

	White	%	Minority	%	Total	%
1967–68	623	95.0	33	5.0	656	100
1970–71	694	94.2	43	5.8	737	100

Racial isolation in Newburgh schools is extreme. In an enlarged district of 19 schools, 16 are imbalanced, with five schools over 90% white and three schools over 70% black and Puerto Rican.

No integration plans have been proposed, although about 500 inner-city youngsters are being bused without incident to two new middle schools outside the city; emphasis has been on alleviation of overcrowding rather than on integration.

In 1969, following an NAACP suit, Commissioner Allen ordered the school board to produce an integration plan. Since any plan, including the NAACP's, would demand busing, the anti-busing law wiped out the movement. Integration action may be revived now that the law has been overturned.

The consensus is that Newburgh will not integrate voluntarily.

III. DEVIATION OF NEWBURGH PUBLIC SCHOOLS FROM DISTRICT
RACIAL BALANCE, 1967–68 & 1970–71

NUMBER OF SCHOOLS

Deviation from Racial Balance	1967–68 Balance = 24.4% Minority	1970–71 Balance = 27.8% Minority
0–5%	2	3
5.1–10%	3	3
10.1–30%	8	9
30.1–Totally Segregated	4	4
Total Schools	17	19

New Rochelle's public school enrollment was 11,976 in 1970–71, of which 25.0% (2,991) were minority children. Another 6,356 children were in nonpublic schools, 5.9% of them from minority groups (in 1969–70).

White enrollment in the public schools has been decreasing while minority enrollment has been on the rise.

I. New Rochelle Public School Enrollment & Ethnic Proportions, 1967–68 to 1970–71

	White	%	Black	%	Spanish-Surnamed	%	Indian & Oriental	%	Total	%
1967–68	9,961	79.2	2,429	19.3	48	0.4	143	1.1	12,581	100
1968–69	9,580	77.7	2,569	20.8	85	0.7	97	0.8	12,331	100
1969–70	9,300	76.4	2,627	21.6	113	0.9	135	1.1	12,175	100
1970–71	8,985	75.0	2,675	22.3	176	1.5	140	1.2	11,976	100

The number of teachers and administrators has increased since 1967, as has the proportion of minority-group staff.

II. New Rochelle Public Education Staff & Minority-Group Proportions, 1967–68 & 1970–71

	White	%	Minority	%	Total	%
1967–68	590	90.4	63	9.6	653	100
1970–71	613	88.7	78	11.3	691	100

Controversy over school sites, out-busing, racial confrontations, open enrollment, and severe fiscal problems have made New Rochelle a troubled district.

Racial balance is a particular problem at the elementary school level. One elementary school is 92% white. Three others have over a 40% minority enrollment. Nine of the district's 13 schools deviate by more than five percentage points from the district's average minority population.

III. Deviation of New Rochelle Public Schools from District Racial Balance, 1967–68 & 1970–71

	NUMBER OF SCHOOLS	
Deviation from Racial Balance	1967–68 Balance = 20.8% Minority	1970–71 Balance = 25.0% Minority
0–5%	3	4
5.1–10%	4	3
10.1–30%	7	6
30.1–Totally Segregated	—	—
Total Schools	14	13

Niagara Falls' public school enrollment was 17,247 in 1970–71, of which 18.8% (3,244) were minority children. Another 4,251 children were in nonpublic schools, 4.1% of them from minority groups (in 1969–70).

While white enrollment in the public schools has been decreasing (as has the total public school enrollment), the minority enrollment has increased slightly.

I. NIAGARA FALLS PUBLIC SCHOOL ENROLLMENT & ETHNIC PROPORTIONS, 1967–68 TO 1970–71

	White	%	Black	%	Spanish-Surnamed	%	Indian & Oriental	%	Total	%
1967–68	15,760	83.6	2,973	15.8	11	—[a]	116	0.6	18,860	100
1968–69	15,312	83.1	2,986	16.2	24	0.1	104	0.6	18,426	100
1969–70	14,838	82.5	3,004	16.7	23	0.1	122	0.7	17,987	100
1970–71	14,003	81.2	3,077	17.8	29	0.2	138	0.8	17,247	100

[a] Less than 0.1%.

The number of teachers and administrators has increased since 1967, but the number of minority staff has been rather stable.

II. NIAGARA FALLS PUBLIC EDUCATION STAFF & MINORITY-GROUP PROPORTIONS, 1967–68 & 1970–71

	White	%	Minority	%	Total	%
1967–68	917	96.1	37	3.9	954	100
1970–71	945	96.2	37	3.8	982	100

Niagara Falls has exerted considerable energy and funds to encourage racial balance. The district is in the process of implementing Plan 21, a two-way busing plan to achieve integration.

Still problems of racial imbalance remain. Five schools over-enroll blacks by more than nine percentage points. One junior high and one high school are more than 95% white.

III. DEVIATION OF NIAGARA FALLS PUBLIC SCHOOLS FROM DISTRICT RACIAL BALANCE, 1967–68 & 1970–71

NUMBER OF SCHOOLS

Deviation from Racial Balance	1967–68 Balance = 16.4% Minority	1970–71 Balance = 18.8% Minority
0–5%	8	16
5.1–10%	6	7
10.1–30%	13	5
30.1–Totally Segregated	2	—
Total Schools	29	28

The 1970–71 public school enrollment in North Babylon was 9,956, of which 13.2% (1,316) were minority-group children. The 996 nonpublic school enrollment (in 1969–70) included 3.3% minority-group children.

The white public school population is decreasing while the minority school enrollment is increasing. The total school district enrollment is also increasing.

I. North Babylon Public School Enrollment & Ethnic Proportions, 1967–68 to 1970–71

	White	%	Black	%	Spanish-Surnamed	%	Indian & Oriental	%	Total	%
1967–68	8,680	90.4	872	9.1	45	0.5	6	—a	9,603	100
1968–69	8,506	87.7	1,018	10.5	167	1.7	10	0.1	9,701	100
1969–70	8,600	87.6	1,096	11.2	102	1.0	16	0.2	9,814	100
1970–71	8,640	86.8	1,124	11.3	173	1.7	19	0.2	9,956	100

a Less than 0.1%.

The total size of the public school staff has increased slightly since 1967, as has the number of minority staff.

II. North Babylon Public Education Staff & Minority-Group Proportions, 1967–68 & 1970–71

	White	%	Minority	%	Total	%
1967–68	487	97.2	14	2.8	501	100
1970–71	517	95.9	22	4.1	539	100

In 1970, a major incident, growing out of white resentment over a high school assembly honoring black achievements led to establishment of a Black-White Student Committee to deal with in-school conflicts. No federal money has been spent on integration; there is a special recruiting policy for minority staff.

An all-white elementary school was eliminated between 1967 and 1970. Four of the remaining seven elementary schools each received a fraction of black students bused (one-way) from the predominantly black quadrant of the city. (This section has no elementary schools.) Three elementary schools are still imbalanced.

III. Deviation of North Babylon Public Schools from District
Racial Balance, 1967–68 & 1970–71

Deviation from Racial Balance	NUMBER OF SCHOOLS	
	1967–68 Balance = 9.6% Minority	1970–71 Balance = 13.2% Minority
0–5%	5	4
5.1–10%	4	3
10.1–30%	2	3
30.1–Totally Segregated	—	—
Total Schools	11	10

North Rockland's public school enrollment was 7,515 in 1970–71, of which 14.2% (1,070) were minority children. Another 1,457 children were in nonpublic schools, 5.8% of them from minority groups (in 1969–70).

Both white and minority enrollments in the public schools are increasing substantially. The proportion of minority enrollment is increasing gradually.

I. NORTH ROCKLAND PUBLIC SCHOOL ENROLLMENT & ETHNIC PROPORTIONS, 1967–68 TO 1970–71

	White	%	Black	%	Spanish-Surnamed	%	Indian & Oriental	%	Total	%
1967–68	5,149	88.0	170	2.9	512	8.8	19	0.3	5,850	100
1968–69	5,625	87.7	149	2.3	632	9.9	10	0.1	6,416	100
1969–70	6,084	86.4	165	2.3	783	11.1	10	0.1	7,042	100
1970–71	6,445	85.8	184	2.5	875	11.6	11	0.1	7,515	100

The number of teachers and administrators has increased since 1967. The number and proportion of minority-group staff has increased only slightly.

II. NORTH ROCKLAND PUBLIC EDUCATION STAFF & MINORITY-GROUP PROPORTIONS, 1967–68 & 1970–71

	White	%	Minority	%	Total	%
1967–68	280	96.9	9	3.1	289	100
1970–71	378	96.2	15	3.8	393	100

Three of the elementary schools are 96.9% to 98.8% white, while one is 45.0% minority; one of the middle schools is 94.9% white, while the other is 75.3% white. There is a definite segregation of minority children in the two middle schools. In fact, two years ago there was only one middle school, so the situation has deteriorated. On the other hand, the opening of two new elementary schools next fall will mean new districting so the imbalanced elementary school should drop from 45% to 35% minority, while one of the new elementary schools will be about 30% minority and the other predominantly white. The two most imbalanced schools are the oldest in the district. There have been minor incidents, mostly in the imbalanced middle school. But the racial imbalance efforts over-all have been rather minimal.

III. Deviation of North Rockland Public Schools from District Racial Balance, 1967–68 & 1970–71

NUMBER OF SCHOOLS

Deviation from Racial Balance	1967–68 Balance = 12.0% Minority	1970–71 Balance = 14.2% Minority
0–5%	4	2
5.1–10%	—	2
10.1–30%	4	4
30.1–Totally Segregated	—	1
Total Schools	8	9

Ossining's 1970–71 public school enrollment was 5,528, of which 18.8% (1,040) were minority children. Another 1,418 children were in nonpublic schools, 4% of them from minority groups (in 1969–70).

The number of minority students has been increasing while the white enrollment has decreased at a fairly steady rate.

I. Ossining Public School Enrollment & Ethnic Proportions, 1967–68 to 1970–71

	White	%	Black	%	Spanish-Surnamed	%	Indian & Oriental	%	Total	%[a]
1967–68	4,682	84.7	809	14.6	24	0.4	10	0.2	5,525	100
1968–69	4,536	82.9	845	15.4	85	1.6	7	0.1	5,473	100
1969–70	4,466	81.5	896	16.4	111	2.0	6	0.1	5,479	100
1970–71	4,488	81.2	896	16.2	135	2.4	9	0.2	5,528	100

[a] May not total 100% because of rounding.

The number of teachers and administrators is the same as in 1967, but the number of minority-group staff has increased slightly.

II. Ossining Public Education Staff & Minority-Group Proportions, 1967–68 & 1970–71

	White	%	Minority	%	Total	%
1967–68	302	95.3	15	4.7	317	100
1970–71	294	93.0	22	7.0	316	100

The two secondary schools and one of the five elementary schools are well balanced, but the other four elementary schools are badly imbalanced: two have a high imbalance of minority students, the other two nearly all white.

A serious incident in 1969 brought in the SED, which set up an interracial grievance committee; discipline was "tightened." There has been no visible movement by the school board toward integration.

III. Deviation of Ossining Public Schools from District Racial Balance, 1967–68 & 1970–71

	NUMBER OF SCHOOLS	
Deviation from Racial Balance	1967–68 Balance = 15.2% Minority	1970–71 Balance = 18.8% Minority
0–5%	2	2
5.1–10%	1	1
10.1–30%	4	4
30.1–Totally Segregated	1	—
Total Schools	8	7

Patchogue's public school enrollment was 9,300 in 1970–71, of which 6.9% (644) were minority children, mostly Spanish-surnamed. Another 202 children were in nonpublic schools, 1.5% of them from minority groups (in 1969–70).

Both white and minority enrollments in the public schools increased from 1967–68 to 1970–71, as has the total public school enrollment.

I. PATCHOGUE PUBLIC SCHOOL ENROLLMENT & ETHNIC PROPORTIONS, 1967–68 TO 1970–71

	White	%	Black	%	Spanish-Surnamed	%	Indian & Oriental	%	Total	%
1967–68	7,721	95.6	102	1.3	231	2.9	20	0.2	8,074	100
1968–69	7,271	94.5	116	1.5	293	3.8	12	0.2	7,692	100
1969–70	8,605	94.5	121	1.3	371	4.1	13	0.1	9,110	100
1970–71	8,656	93.1	135	1.5	497	5.3	12	0.1	9,300	100

The number of teachers and administrators has increased since 1967, but the number of minority-group staff has declined.

II. PATCHOGUE PUBLIC EDUCATION STAFF & MINORITY-GROUP PROPORTIONS, 1967–68 & 1970–71

	White	%	Minority	%	Total	%
1967–68	442	96.5	16	3.5	458	100
1970–71	506	97.9	11	2.1	517	100

Redistricting in the fall of 1970 reduced the number of minority children in the River Avenue elementary school by nearly 10 percentage points, from 23.1% in 1969–70 to 14.7% in 1970–71.

The River Avenue school and one other elementary school have a Spanish-surnamed enrollment of over 10%. Three other schools in the district are more than 98% white.

III. DEVIATION OF PATCHOGUE PUBLIC SCHOOLS FROM DISTRICT RACIAL BALANCE, 1967–68 & 1970–71

Deviation from Racial Balance	NUMBER OF SCHOOLS	
	1967–68 Balance = 4.4% Minority	1970–71 Balance = 6.9% Minority
0–5%	7	7
5.1–10%	1	3
10.1–30%	1	1
30.1–Totally Segregated	—	—
Total Schools	9	11

Peekskill's public school enrollment was 3,509 in 1970–71, of which 31.9% (1,119) were minority children. Another 1,066 children were in nonpublic schools, 18.8% of them from minority groups (in 1969–70).

Public school enrollment has increased since 1967. White enrollment seems to be decreasing and minority enrollment increasing, but at a very slight and uneven rate.

I. PEEKSKILL PUBLIC SCHOOL ENROLLMENT & ETHNIC PROPORTIONS, 1967–68 TO 1970–71

	White	%	Black	%	Spanish-Surnamed	%	Indian & Oriental	%	Total	%[b]
1967–68	2,328	70.1	863	26.0	129	3.9	2	—[a]	3,322	100
1968–69	2,216	66.3	967	29.0	153	4.6	4	0.1	3,340	100
1969–70	2,430	66.3	1,054	28.8	175	4.8	6	0.2	3,665	100
1970–71	2,390	68.1	952	27.1	162	4.6	5	0.1	3,509	100

[a] Less than 0.1%.
[b] May not total 100% because of rounding.

The number of teachers and administrators has decreased. Minority-group staff has stayed at the same level—far lower than the proportional minority student enrollment of the district.

II. PEEKSKILL PUBLIC EDUCATION STAFF & MINORITY-GROUP PROPORTIONS, 1967–68 & 1970–71

	White	%	Minority	%	Total	%
1967–68	187	94.9	10	5.1	197	100
1970–71	173	95.1	9	4.9	182	100

At least one school in Peekskill has been closed for reasons related to racial imbalance, but this effort has not been enough to achieve desegregation in the schools. No direct effort has been made to increase the number of minority-group teachers.

Five out of six of the Peekskill public schools have minority enrollments which deviate more than five percentage points from the district average, which is 31.9%. The two most segregated schools have a minority enrollment of 58.8% and a white enrollment of 86.2%, respectively.

III. DEVIATION OF PEEKSKILL PUBLIC SCHOOLS FROM DISTRICT
RACIAL BALANCE, 1967–68 & 1970–71

	NUMBER OF SCHOOLS	
Deviation from Racial Balance	1967–68 Balance = 29.9% Minority	1970–71 Balance = 31.9% Minority
0–5%	—	1
5.1–10%	3	2
10.1–30%	5	3
30.1–Totally Segregated	—	—
Total Schools	8	6

Peru's public school enrollment was 4,370 in 1970–71, of which 9.0% (392) were minority children. Another 103 were in nonpublic schools; none was from a minority group (1969–70).

Both white and minority enrollments in the public schools have increased from 1967–68 to 1970–71.

I. Peru Public School Enrollment & Ethnic Proportions, 1967–68 to 1970–71

	White	%	Black	%	Spanish-Surnamed	%	Indian & Oriental	%	Total	%
1967–68	3,363	93.0	186	5.1	6	0.2	63	1.7	3,618	100
1968–69	3,505	93.1	222	5.9	13	0.3	25	0.7	3,765	100
1969–70	3,610	92.7	249	6.4	27	0.7	10	0.3	3,896	100
1970–71	3,978	91.0	330	7.6	40	0.9	22	0.5	4,370	100

The number of teachers and administrators has increased considerably—83% since 1967–68—but there have never been more than three minority-group members on the staff.

II. Peru Public Education Staff & Minority-Group Proportions, 1967–68 & 1970–71

	White	%	Minority	%	Total	%
1967–68	199	99.0	2	1.0	201	100
1970–71	240	98.8	3	1.2	243	100

About 42% of the students in the district are from the local Air Force base. (Of the district's 330 black children, 232 attend the two elementary schools located on the base.) Of Peru's five schools, four have problems of racial imbalance. One elementary school enrolls nearly half the district's population of blacks. Two other elementary schools are 99% white.

III. Deviation of Peru Public Schools from District Racial Balance, 1967–68 & 1970–71

	NUMBER OF SCHOOLS	
Deviation from Racial Balance	1967–68 Balance = 7.0% Minority	1970–71 Balance = 9.0% Minority
0–5%	1	1
5.1–10%	3	3
10.1–30%	1	1
30.1–Totally Segregated	—	—
Total Schools	5	5

Port Chester's 1970–71 public school enrollment was 4,900, of which 30.2% (1,478) were minority-group children. There were 1,463 children in nonpublic schools, of whom 17.2%, mostly Cubans, were from minority groups.

The white public school enrollment is decreasing while the minority-group proportion is rising.

I. PORT CHESTER PUBLIC SCHOOL ENROLLMENT & ETHNIC PROPORTIONS, 1967–68 TO 1970–71

	White	%	Black	%	Spanish-Surnamed	%	Indian & Oriental	%	Total	%
1967–68	3,736	77.0	1,050	21.6	49	1.0	18	0.4	4,853	100
1968–69	3,603	72.6	1,101	22.2	246	5.0	16	0.3	4,968	100
1969–70	3,480	70.2	1,143	23.0	319	6.4	18	0.4	4,960	100
1970–71	3,422	69.8	1,147	23.4	312	6.4	19	0.4	4,900	100

The total size of public school staff has increased. Both the number and proportion of minority staff have also increased since 1967.

II. PORT CHESTER PUBLIC EDUCATION STAFF & MINORITY-GROUP PROPORTIONS, 1967–68 & 1970–71

	White	%	Minority	%	Total	%
1967–68	256	97.7	6	2.3	262	100
1970–71	273	94.1	17	5.9	290	100

Port Chester is one of the more segregated districts in the state. Only the smallest of the seven elementary schools escapes being badly imbalanced. Two are considerably imbalanced on the white side and two on the minority side.

There is admitted tension in the community. Black studies were begun in 1969–70, but no desegregation plan has been formulated and no state racial imbalance funds have been applied for.

III. DEVIATION OF PORT CHESTER PUBLIC SCHOOLS FROM DISTRICT RACIAL BALANCE, 1967–68 & 1970–71

NUMBER OF SCHOOLS

Deviation from Racial Balance	1967–68 Balance = 23.0% Minority	1970–71 Balance = 30.2% Minority
0–5%	1	2
5.1–10%	2	—
10.1–30%	3	6
30.1–Totally Segregated	3	1
Total Schools	9	9

Poughkeepsie's public school enrollment was 5,659 in 1970–71, of which 34.0% (1,927) were minority children. Another 2,022 children were in nonpublic schools as of 1969–70, of whom 2.4% were from minority groups.

The total school population has been decreasing since 1968–69, with the number of white students declining gradually as the percentage of minority students fluctuates.

I. POUGHKEEPSIE PUBLIC SCHOOL ENROLLMENT & ETHNIC PROPORTIONS, 1967–68 TO 1970–71

	White	%	Black	%	Spanish-Surnamed	%	Indian & Oriental	%	Total	%[a]
1967–68	4,132	71.1	1,648	28.4	4	0.1	25	0.4	5,809	100
1968–69	3,973	66.9	1,940	32.7	11	0.2	13	0.2	5,937	100
1969–70	3,880	66.1	1,969	33.5	8	0.1	12	0.2	5,869	100
1970–71	3,732	66.0	1,910	33.8	7	0.1	10	0.2	5,659	100

[a] May not total 100% because of rounding.

The number of minority teachers and administrators out of a total of 331 has increased since 1967; however, the percentage of minority staff (7.3%) is well below the minority enrollment (34.0%).

II. POUGHKEEPSIE PUBLIC EDUCATION STAFF & MINORITY-GROUP PROPORTIONS, 1967–68 & 1970–71

	White	%	Minority	%	Total	%
1967–68	277	94.9	15	5.1	292	100
1970–71	307	92.7	24	7.3	331	100

In 1969 Poughkeepsie implemented a "total" desegregation plan. It revolved around a new middle school and one-way busing to two white elementary schools. Because the board has shifted from a 1–4 to 4–1 majority against integration, it is doubtful that further efforts will be made in the immediate future. Indeed, the new 1970–71 preliminary budget does not include money for busing. (Model Cities supplied $60,000 for the first year of busing; the second year the city paid for busing from November to April.) There is now talk of going back to a 6-3-3 plan instead of keeping the new 4-4-4 arrangement.

There are incidents at all grade levels. State Racial Imbalance Funds helped equip a new cafeteria in a previously white school.

III. Deviation of Poughkeepsie Public Schools from District
Racial Balance, 1967–68 & 1970–71

NUMBER OF SCHOOLS

Deviation from Racial Balance	1967–68 Balance = 29.9% Minority	1970–71 Balance = 34.0% Minority
0–5%	1	3
5.1–10%	4	1
10.1–30%	2	4
30.1–Totally Segregated	3	—
Total Schools	10	8

Riverhead's public school enrollment was 4,401 in 1970–71, of which 31.2% (1,371) were minority children. Another 1,752 children were in nonpublic schools as of 1969–70, 1.2% of them from minority groups.

The total public school population is gradually increasing but the proportions of white and minority enrollments remain stable.

I. Riverhead Public School Enrollment & Ethnic Proportions, 1967–68 to 1970–71

	White	%	Black	%	Spanish-Surnamed	%	Indian & Oriental	%	Total	%
1967–68	2,926	69.5	1,245	29.6	17	0.4	23	0.5	4,211	100
1968–69	2,921	68.9	1,260	29.7	37	0.9	22	0.5	4,240	100
1969–70	2,925	69.1	1,258	29.7	23	0.5	30	0.7	4,236	100
1970–71	3,030	68.8	1,315	29.9	38	0.9	18	0.4	4,401	100

The number of teachers and administrators has increased since 1967, as has the proportion of minority-group staff.

II. Riverhead Public Education Staff & Minority-Group Proportions, 1967–68 & 1970–71

	White	%	Minority	%	Total	%
1967–68	208	99.0	2	1.0	210	100
1970–71	225	95.3	11	4.7	236	100

There have been no efforts taken in Riverhead to reduce the racial imbalance of the schools. The high school has experienced incidents reflecting racial tension, but no school closings have occurred.

Two elementary schools with minority enrollments of 44.2% and 14.4%, respectively, deviate the most from the district average. The high school minority enrollment, 23.6%, also deviates by more than five percentage points from the district average.

III. Deviation of Riverhead Public Schools from District Racial Balance, 1967–68 & 1970–71

	NUMBER OF SCHOOLS	
Deviation from Racial Balance	1967–68 Balance = 30.5% Minority	1970–71 Balance = 31.2% Minority
0–5%	1	1
5.1–10%	5	3
10.1–30%	1	3
30.1–Totally Segregated	—	—
Total Schools	7	7

Schenectady's public school enrollment was 12,987 in 1970–71, of which 8.6% (1,114) were minority children. Another 4,113 are in nonpublic schools as of 1969–70, 2% of them from minority groups.

Both white and minority enrollment in the public schools have increased very slightly.

I. SCHENECTADY PUBLIC SCHOOL ENROLLMENT & ETHNIC PROPORTIONS, 1967–68 TO 1970–71

	White	%	Black	%	Spanish-Surnamed	%	Indian & Oriental	%	Total	%
1967–68	11,687	92.6	896	7.1	26	0.2	15	0.1	12,624	100
1968–69	11,924	92.2	950	7.3	44	0.3	10	0.1	12,928	100
1969–70	11,868	91.8	992	7.7	41	0.3	24	0.2	12,925	100
1970–71	11,873	91.4	1,053	8.1	27	0.2	34	0.3	12,987	100

The number of staff members has decreased markedly, but the number and proportion of minority staff have increased slightly.

II. SCHENECTADY PUBLIC EDUCATION STAFF & MINORITY-GROUP PROPORTIONS, 1967–68 & 1970–71

	White	%	Minority	%	Total	%
1967–68	905	98.0	18	2.0	923	100
1970–71	712	96.3	27	3.7	739	100

In the fall of 1969, two junior high schools were merged to correct racial imbalance. The new school is now 17.3% minority. Attendance lines have been restructured to improve integration, but some white students have begun to use an open enrollment policy to escape its impact.

There are eight schools that have white enrollments greater than 97% and there are three schools that are more than 17% minority enrolled. The highest minority enrollments, in two elementary schools, are 29.0% and 38.7%.

III. DEVIATION OF SCHENECTADY PUBLIC SCHOOLS FROM DISTRICT RACIAL BALANCE, 1967–68 & 1970–71

NUMBER OF SCHOOLS

Deviation from Racial Balance	1967–68 Balance = 7.4% Minority	1970–71 Balance = 8.6% Minority
0–5%	11	11
5.1–10%	11	12
10.1–30%	3	2
30.1–Totally Segregated	1	—
Total Schools	26	25

Spring Valley's public school enrollment was 16,583 in 1970–71, of which 10.6% (1,759) were minority children. Another 2,600 children were in nonpublic schools, 1.2% of them from minority groups as of 1969–70.

Both white and minority enrollments in the public schools are increasing.

I. Spring Valley Public School Enrollment & Ethnic Proportions, 1967–68 to 1970–71

	White	%	Black	%	Spanish-Surnamed	%	Indian & Oriental	%	Total	%
1967–68	13,072	91.2	1,165	8.1	43	0.3	47	0.3	14,327	100
1968–69	13,886	90.9	1,264	8.3	101	0.7	32	0.2	15,283	100
1969–70	14,559	90.5	1,359	8.5	126	0.8	36	0.2	16,080	100
1970–71	14,824	89.4	1,554	9.4	158	1.0	47	0.2	16,583	100

The number of teachers and administrators has increased since 1967, as has the proportion of minority-group staff.

II. Spring Valley Public Education Staff & Minority-Group Proportions, 1967–68 & 1970–71

	White	%	Minority	%	Total	%
1967–68	838	95.6	39	4.4	877	100
1970–71	945	94.0	60	6.0	1,005	100

Redistricting and a one-way busing program begun in 1967 on the elementary level have not eliminated segregation of white and minority students in Spring Valley.

There are four elementary schools that have white enrollment greater than 97%, and there are three other elementary schools that are more than 20% minority enrolled. The highest minority enrollment is 24.9% in the central city school.

III. Deviation of Spring Valley Public Schools from District Racial Balance, 1967–68 & 1970–71

Deviation from Racial Balance	NUMBER OF SCHOOLS	
	1967–68 Balance = 8.8% Minority	1970–71 Balance = 10.6% Minority
0–5%	9	12
5.1–10%	9	5
10.1–30%	—	3
30.1–Totally Segregated	—	—
Total Schools	18	20

There were 29,402 pupils enrolled in the public schools of Syracuse during the 1970–71 school year; 25.2% were from minority groups. In 1969–70 there were 10,184 nonpublic school children, 5.0% of whom were non-white.

Total enrollment has been declining, while non-white enrollment has been increasing.

I. SYRACUSE PUBLIC SCHOOL ENROLLMENT & ETHNIC PROPORTIONS, 1967–68 TO 1970–71

	White	%	Black	%	Spanish-Surnamed	%	Indian & Oriental	%	Total	%[a]
1967–68	24,779	80.3	5,946	19.3	41	0.1	96	0.3	30,862	100
1968-69	23,873	78.5	6,365	20.9	62	0.2	128	0.4	30,428	100
1969–70	23,118	76.5	6,773	22.5	80	0.3	143	0.5	30,114	100
1970–71	21,991	74.8	7,056	24.0	120	0.4	235	0.8	29,402	100

[a] May not total 100% because of rounding.

Although the minority staffs of the schools have increased, minority teachers make up only 124 of 1,485 teachers (8.4%).

II. SYRACUSE PUBLIC EDUCATION STAFF & MINORITY-GROUP PROPORTIONS, 1967–68 & 1970–71

	White	%	Minority	%	Total	%
1967–68	1,496	95.3	73	4.7	1,569	100
1970–71	1,361	91.7	124	8.3	1,485	100

Syracuse's black population increased 90.7% since 1960, while the total population declined 8.7%. The surrounding suburban communities' population has increased 42.2%. Thirty-six of Syracuse's 45 schools vary by more than five percentage points from district average minority enrollment. Syracuse has been experiencing much civil rights agitation since 1960, the most recent occurring in October, 1968; April, 1969; and May, 1970. Efforts to eliminate racial imbalance include: boundary changes; compulsory busing (blacks); voluntary busing (whites); proposed redistricting (defeated). Most large-scale attempts to mandate integration (such as four educational park plans) have been killed by public resistance, and at present there are no long-range plans. However, it is hoped that the addition of a new high school and a rezoning of attendance areas will somewhat alleviate the present situation.

III. Deviation of Syracuse Public Schools from District Racial Balance, 1967–68 & 1970–71

Deviation from Racial Balance	NUMBER OF SCHOOLS	
	1967–68 Balance = 19.7% Minority	1970–71 Balance = 25.2% Minority
0–5%	10	9
5.1–10%	10	9
10.1–30%	19	21
30.1–Totally Segregated	4	6
Total Schools	43	45

Troy's 1970–71 public school enrollment was 6,849, of which 12.5% (855) were minority children. There were 12 nonpublic schools with an enrollment of 3,813 as of 1969–70; 4.2% of them were children from minority groups.

The minority enrollment has increased slightly and the white has decreased slightly.

I. TROY PUBLIC SCHOOL ENROLLMENT & ETHNIC PROPORTIONS, 1967–68 TO 1970–71

	White	%	Black	%	Spanish-Surnamed	%	Indian & Oriental	%	Total	%[a]
1967–68	6,035	87.9	809	11.8	5	0.1	16	0.2	6,865	100
1968–69	6,369	87.3	899	12.3	9	0.1	15	0.2	7,292	100
1969–70	6,044	87.6	824	11.9	8	0.1	24	0.3	6,900	100
1970–71	5,994	87.5	826	12.1	9	0.1	20	0.3	6,849	100

[a] May not total 100% because of rounding.

The number of teachers and administrators has increased slightly since 1967, as has the proportion of minority-group staff. Troy has attempted to assist some local minority high school students to enter teaching and get through college; a very few have returned to teach in their home town.

II. TROY PUBLIC EDUCATION STAFF & MINORITY-GROUP PROPORTIONS, 1967–68 & 1970–71

	White	%	Minority	%	Total	%
1967–68	364	99.2	3	0.8	367	100
1970–71	372	98.7	5	1.3	377	100

Of 13 schools, nine are imbalanced. Two schools have significantly disproportionate minority enrollments (47.5% and 31.3%), and three schools have white enrollments greater than 96%. Correction of overcrowded classrooms and phasing out of dilapidated buildings led to some population redistribution. A middle school for *all* students will be completed in 1974.

No State Racial Imbalance Funds have been sought. There was one serious incident last year: 67 blacks walked out of the high school, protesting three plain-clothes policemen (called "monitors") on duty in the lunchroom.

III. Deviation of Troy Public Schools from District Racial
Balance, 1967–68 & 1970–71

Deviation from Racial Balance	NUMBER OF SCHOOLS	
	1967–68 Balance = 12.0% Minority	1970–71 Balance = 12.5% Minority
0–5%	4	4
5.1–10%	5	6
10.1–30%	2	2
30.1–Totally Segregated	2	1
Total Schools	13	13

Uniondale's public school enrollment in 1970–71 was 7,407, of which 16.1% (1,195) were minority children. Another 1,106 children were in nonpublic schools, 1.5% of them from minority groups as of 1969–70.

Minority enrollment is increasing while white enrollment is decreasing.

I. UNIONDALE PUBLIC SCHOOL ENROLLMENT & ETHNIC PROPORTIONS, 1967–68 TO 1970–71

	White	%	Black	%	Spanish-Surnamed	%	Indian & Oriental	%	Total	%[a]
1967–68	6,259	87.6	850	11.9	12	0.2	22	0.3	7,143	100
1968–69	6,467	87.2	875	11.8	57	0.8	19	0.3	7,418	100
1969–70	6,429	85.9	986	13.2	60	0.8	12	0.2	7,485	100
1970–71	6,212	83.9	1,092	14.7	83	1.1	20	0.3	7,487	100

[a] May not total 100% because of rounding.

There has been a small increase in the number of teachers and administrators and in the proportion of minority staff since 1967.

II. UNIONDALE PUBLIC EDUCATION STAFF & MINORITY-GROUP PROPORTIONS, 1967–68 & 1970–71

	White	%	Minority	%	Total	%
1967–68	409	96.0	17	4.0	426	100
1970–71	411	94.7	23	5.3	434	100

Five years ago, some whites in Uniondale reacted against a shift in attendance boundaries to improve racial balance. Not since then has integration been a public issue. There have been scattered incidents over implementing black studies courses.

Uniondale's nonpublic school enrollment in 1969–70 was less than half of what it had been in 1967–68. About 55% of Uniondale's black elementary school population is concentrated in two schools; another elementary school has three minority students out of an enrollment of 251.

III. DEVIATION OF UNIONDALE PUBLIC SCHOOLS FROM DISTRICT RACIAL BALANCE, 1967–68 & 1970–71

NUMBER OF SCHOOLS

Deviation from Racial Balance	1967–68 Balance = 12.4% Minority	1970–71 Balance = 16.1% Minority
0–5%	6	5
5.1–10%	1	2
10.1–30%	3	2
30.1–Totally Segregated	—	1
Total Schools	10	10

Utica's 1970–71 public school enrollment was 14,475, of which 14.2% (2,058) were minority children. Utica's 15 nonpublic schools enrolled 5,845 children as of 1969–70, 1% (57) of whom were from minority groups.

White enrollment has been decreasing slightly, while minority enrollment has been rising.

I. Utica Public School Enrollment & Ethnic Proportions, 1967–68 to 1970–71

	White	%	Black	%	Spanish-Surnamed	%	Indian & Oriental	%	Total	%[a]
1967–68	13,151	88.4	1,573	10.6	133	0.9	12	0.1	14,869	100
1968–69	12,697	87.1	1,715	11.8	155	1.1	14	0.1	14,581	100
1969–70	12,520	86.5	1,763	12.2	172	1.2	16	0.1	14,471	100
1970–71	13,417	85.8	1,839	12.7	203	1.4	16	0.1	14,475	100

[a] May not total 100% because of rounding.

The number of teachers and administrators is virtually the same now as in 1967; the proportion of minority-group staff has increased by two.

II. Utica Public Education Staff & Minority-Group Proportions, 1967–68 & 1970–71

	White	%	Minority	%	Total	%
1967–68	771	98.6	11	1.4	782	100
1970–71	776	98.4	13	1.6	789	100

Seventeen of Utica's schools are imbalanced. These 17 schools enroll more than half of the city's students. In August, 1970, the school board passed a resolution endorsing racial balance and designated two board members to organize and direct two community committees assigned the task of devising an acceptable desegregation plan to be implemented in the fall of 1971. However, the board asserted its right to accept or reject the final plan.

There have been no incidents in the schools, though for election to the community school board, candidates have a one-plank platform: opposition to busing. The Teachers' Association has endorsed a voluntary teacher exchange program to help prepare for integration, and has provided interim funds for busing a group of students from an elementary school that was closed when a dispute about "free rides" arose. Originally, $7,000 in State Racial Imbalance money helped pay for busing, but the absence of a comprehensive plan precluded additional money. ESEA Title IV money has been applied for. A 310 grievance filed this spring from citizens alleging inequality of opportunity is to be ruled on by the Commissioner of Education.

III. Deviation of Utica Public Schools from District Racial Balance, 1967–68 & 1970–71

Deviation from Racial Balance	NUMBER OF SCHOOLS	
	1967–68 Balance = 11.5% Minority	1970–71 Balance = 14.2% Minority
0–5%	5	5
5.1–10%	7	4
10.1–30%	8	10
30.1–Totally Segregated	2	3
Total Schools	22	22

Valhalla's public school enrollment in 1970–71 was 2,264, of which 11.2% were non-white. As of 1969–70, 1% of the 287 nonpublic school students were non-white. The ethnic balance has remained constant for several years, as the total enrollment has increased slightly.

I. VALHALLA PUBLIC SCHOOL ENROLLMENT & ETHNIC PROPORTIONS, 1967–68 TO 1970–71

	White	%	Black	%	Spanish-Surnamed	%	Indian & Oriental	%	Total	%
1967–68	1,944	89.0	230	10.5	3	0.1	8	0.4	2,185	100
1968–69	1,930	88.1	241	11.0	8	0.4	11	0.5	2,190	100
1969–70	2,003	88.8	230	10.2	6	0.3	16	0.7	2,255	100
1970–71	2,011	88.8	236	10.4	6	0.3	11	0.5	2,264	100

The percentage of minority-group teachers is small, but has increased since 1967–68. The total staff, according to the data, has increased two and one-half times since 1967. We have not been able to ascertain the reason for this tremendous increase.

II. VALHALLA PUBLIC EDUCATION STAFF & MINORITY-GROUP PROPORTIONS, 1967–68 & 1970–71

	White	%	Minority	%	Total	%
1967–68	60	98.4	1	1.6	61	100
1970–71	148	96.1	6	3.9	154	100

There are only three elementary schools in the district, and parents may send their children to the school of their choice; no request has yet been denied. The school with the heaviest black enrollment (11.1%) is regarded as the best school in the district, and has a large number of children from affluent families. This appears to account for the blacks' willingness to tolerate the imbalance that exists.

III. DEVIATION OF VALHALLA PUBLIC SCHOOLS FROM DISTRICT RACIAL BALANCE, 1967–68 & 1970–71

	NUMBER OF SCHOOLS	
Deviation from Racial Balance	1967–68 Balance = 11.0% Minority	1970–71 Balance = 11.2% Minority
0–5%	2	2
5.1–10%	1	1
10.1–30%	1	1
30.1–Totally Segregated	—	—
Total Schools	4	4

Wallkill's public school enrollment was 2,325 in 1970–71, of which 14.4% (335) were minority children. Another 26 children were in nonpublic schools, none of them from minority groups, as of 1969–70.

Both white and minority enrollments in the public schools are increasing, the latter at a higher rate.

I. WALLKILL PUBLIC SCHOOL ENROLLMENT & ETHNIC PROPORTIONS, 1967–68 TO 1970–71

	White	%	Black	%	Spanish-Surnamed	%	Indian & Oriental	%	Total	%[a]
1967–68	1,878	88.5	36	1.7	200	9.4	7	0.3	2,121	100
1968–69	1,874	86.0	55	2.5	246	11.3	3	0.1	2,178	100
1969–70	1,970	86.1	44	1.9	261	11.4	12	0.5	2,287	100
1970–71	1,990	85.6	41	1.8	287	12.3	7	0.3	2,235	100

[a] May not total 100% because of rounding.

The number of teachers and administrators has increased since 1967, and the number of minority-group staff has doubled, from one to two.

II. WALLKILL PUBLIC EDUCATION STAFF & MINORITY-GROUP PROPORTIONS, 1967–68 & 1970–71

	White	%	Minority	%	Total	%
1967–68	116	99.1	1	0.9	117	100
1970–71	132	98.5	2	1.5	134	100

There have been no incidents in the secondary schools, which are balanced. But the majority of Spanish-surnamed elementary children are centered in one school: it has a 38.6% minority population contrasted with 6.7% and 4.6% in the other two elementary schools. There have been several formal protests to the Commissioner of Education about the prejudicial treatment of minority children, but there is no official effort to integrate the schools.

III. DEVIATION OF WALLKILL PUBLIC SCHOOLS FROM DISTRICT RACIAL BALANCE, 1967–68 & 1970–71

	NUMBER OF SCHOOLS	
Deviation from Racial Balance	1967–68 Balance = 11.4% Minority	1970–71 Balance = 14.4% Minority
0–5%	2	2
5.1–10%	1	2
10.1–30%	1	1
30.1–Totally Segregated	—	—
Total Schools	4	5

Warwick Valley's 1970–71 public school enrollment was 2,802, of which 7.5% (210) were minority children. Another 615 children were in non-public schools, 28.1% of them from minority groups, as of 1969–70.

The white enrollment is increasing while the minority enrollment is decreasing.

I. WARWICK VALLEY PUBLIC SCHOOL ENROLLMENT & ETHNIC PROPORTIONS, 1967–68 TO 1970–71

	White	%	Black	%	Spanish-Surnamed	%	Indian & Oriental	%	Total	%
1967–68	2,257	90.1	176	7.0	54	2.2	18	0.7	2,505	100
1968–69	2,471	90.3	194	7.1	68	2.5	3	0.1	2,736	100
1969–70	2,533	91.1	167	6.0	72	2.6	7	0.3	2,779	100
1970–71	2,592	92.5	155	5.5	52	1.9	3	0.1	2,802	100

The number of teachers and administrators has decreased since 1967, as has the proportion of minority-group staff.

II. WARWICK VALLEY PUBLIC EDUCATION STAFF & MINORITY-GROUP PROPORTIONS, 1967–68 & 1970–71

	White	%	Minority	%	Total	%
1967–68	154	97.5	4	2.5	158	100
1970–71	144	98.6	2	1.4	146	100

This is a rural migrant area, with three levels of minority representation in the schools, depending on the season: 150–200 children from very late spring through very early fall (as measured in data above); about 30–50 in October and April; and fewer throughout the winter and early spring. In the one imbalanced school, attendance drops from 49 to 10 or 12 during the school year.

A private Catholic school shelters some 90 teen-age black and Puerto Rican boys who attend the high school but whose parents are not in the town. There was some talk of busing white 6th graders to relieve over-crowding, but parents objected.

III. DEVIATION OF WARWICK VALLEY PUBLIC SCHOOLS FROM DISTRICT RACIAL BALANCE, 1967–68 & 1970–71

Deviation from Racial Balance	NUMBER OF SCHOOLS	
	1967–68 Balance = 9.9% Minority	1970–71 Balance = 7.5% Minority
0–5%	5	4
5.1–10%	—	—
10.1–30%	1	1
30.1–Totally Segregated	—	—
Total Schools	6	5

White Plains' 1970–71 public school enrollment was 8,493, of which 23.6% (2,002) were minority children. Another 3,303 children were in nonpublic schools as of 1969–70, 5.2% of them from minority groups.

White enrollment is decreasing; minority enrollment is increasing slowly.

I. WHITE PLAINS PUBLIC SCHOOL ENROLLMENT & ETHNIC PROPORTIONS, 1967–68 TO 1970–71

	White	%	Black	%	Spanish-Surnamed	%	Indian & Oriental	%	Total	%
1967–68	7,289	82.2	1,499	16.9	62	0.7	17	0.2	8,867	100
1968–69	7,063	78.8	1,637	18.3	224	2.5	40	0.4	8,964	100
1969–70	6,823	79.3	1,629	18.9	141	1.6	14	0.2	8,607	100
1970–71	6,491	76.4	1,727	20.3	244	2.9	31	0.4	8,493	100

The number of teachers and administrators has decreased since 1967. The proportion of minority-group staff has increased slightly.

II. WHITE PLAINS PUBLIC EDUCATION STAFF & MINORITY-GROUP PROPORTIONS, 1967–68 & 1970–71

	White	%	Minority	%	Total	%
1967–68	476	91.9	42	8.1	518	100
1970–71	458	91.1	45	8.9	503	100

White Plains has a Racial Balance Plan which keeps the black (but not total minority) enrollment in all schools within a range of 20%. After extensive community meetings, the plan was updated in 1970. Of the children who are bused, 90% are black. It is alleged that extensive tracking within schools further isolates children along racial lines.

Black student unrest, a boycott in 1968, and other intermittent disturbances have not led to the resolution of racial issues, which include demands for more black teachers, black subjects, etc.

One school has a minority enrollment of 37%.

III. DEVIATION OF WHITE PLAINS PUBLIC SCHOOLS FROM DISTRICT RACIAL BALANCE, 1967–68 & 1970–71

	NUMBER OF SCHOOLS	
Deviation from Racial Balance	1967–68 Balance = 17.8% Minority	1970–71 Balance = 24.6% Minority
0–5%	8	6
5.1–10%	2	3
10.1–30%	1	2
30.1–Totally Segregated	—	—
Total Schools	11	11

Yonkers, the largest city in Westchester County, and the fourth largest in the state, had 30,632 pupils enrolled in its public schools in 1970–71, 18.8% (5,773) of whom were from minority groups. While white enrollment is steadily decreasing, minority enrollment increases every year. Nearly one-third of the school-age pupils attend nonpublic schools (10,623 in 1969–70); approximately 94% of them are white.

I. YONKERS PUBLIC SCHOOL ENROLLMENT & ETHNIC PROPORTIONS, 1967–68 TO 1970–71

	White	%	Black	%	Spanish-Surnamed	%	Indian & Oriental	%	Total	%[a]
1967–68	25,617	84.6	3,486	11.5	935	3.1	258	0.9	30,296	100
1968–69	25,599	83.1	3,698	12.0	1,323	4.3	174	0.6	30,794	100
1969–70	25,006	82.0	4,003	13.1	1,328	4.4	167	0.5	30,504	100
1970–71	24,859	81.2	4,128	13.5	1,455	4.7	190	0.6	30,632	100

[a] May not total 100% because of rounding.

Out of 1,743 teachers, 150, or 8.6%, are from minority groups. There are four Spanish-surnamed teachers for 1,455 Spanish-surnamed students. There are no bilingual programs.

II. YONKERS PUBLIC EDUCATION STAFF & MINORITY-GROUP PROPORTIONS, 1967–68 & 1970–71

	White	%	Minority	%	Total	%
1967–68	1,313	92.7	103	7.3	1,416	100
1970–71	1,593	91.4	150	8.6	1,743	100

Yonkers' population is increasing steadily; whites increased slightly while blacks skyrocketed 69.7% since 1960. There is little current effort to correct segregation in the schools, although there has been considerable racial turmoil in recent years over grievances such as achieving increases in minority staff members and establishment of bilingual programs. The black militant community seems to be moving away from integration as a goal, in favor of decent schools in their own communities. In May 1970, the Commissioner of Education requested integration plans from all racially imbalanced school districts. Of 42 public schools, 26 deviate from the district average of 18.8% minority enrollment by more than 10 percentage points; 19 are over 90% white, six are over 40% minority. There are no current hopes for elimination of de facto segregation of housing, which would aid integration.

III. DEVIATION OF YONKERS PUBLIC SCHOOLS FROM DISTRICT
RACIAL BALANCE, 1967–68 & 1970–71

NUMBER OF SCHOOLS

Deviation from Racial Balance	1967–68 Balance = 15.4% Minority	1970–71 Balance = 18.8% Minority
0–5%	6	5
5.1–10%	7	5
10.1–30%	23	26
30.1–Totally Segregated	4	6
Total Schools	40	42

The segregation of Indians differs from the segregation of other minority groups in several important ways:

1. *The state has direct responsibility for the education of Indians on the reservations from kindergarten through college;* at least 27 separate sections of the Education Law support this. Today the Commissioner carries out this responsibility by contracting with 13 school districts and four BOCES. Five of these school districts have imbalanced schools: Salmon River, La Fayette, Gowanda, Salamanca, and Niagara-Wheatfield.

2. *The state pays the total per-pupil cost* to the district of educating each of these children: busing, construction, and tuition/overhead. After deducting payment already made to the districts through regular state aid, the state pays the balance of costs. These funds are not earmarked. During 1969–70 the five districts received a total of $2,003,492, as follows: Salmon River, $850,756; La Fayette, $774,428; Gowanda, $192,250; Salamanca, $60,287; and Niagara-Wheatfield, $125,771.

3. *Indians have little voice in how this money is to be spent.* The extra aid is based on old treaty arrangements, but the pattern of decision making at state and local levels is such that it virtually excludes them. In fact, except in Salamanca, Indians could not even vote in local school board elections until just three years ago.

4. *Indians are not only a minority group; they constitute virtually separate nations.* The state counsel's ruling that reservations were separate entities was reversed only in 1968. As one Indian said, "We did not seek to enter the mainstream." To preserve Indian cultures and languages while moving into the twentieth century is a most serious matter to most Indians.

Gowanda and Salamanca, Cattaraugus County

PREFACE   The Kinzua Dam construction, which flooded 10,000 acres of Seneca land in the mid-60's, obliterated a reservation school. Currently, Seneca children are split between Silver Creek, Salamanca, and Gowanda districts. The latter two, Salamanca and Gowanda, have imbalanced schools that are *not* reservation schools.

Although the Senecas protested the dam, it did bring $1.8 million for education and rehabilitation to them, administered now by the Seneca Education Foundation. The Foundation's board includes the Silver Creek,

Salamanca, and Gowanda superintendents. The Foundation helps with orientation programs for new teachers at both Salamanca and Gowanda, and maintains close liaison with the three districts. In addition, the National Americans for Indian Opportunity have set up a regional office in the area and are helping to establish Indian social/tutorial clubs in Salamanca and Gowanda High Schools.

Gowanda's 1970–71 public school enrollment was 2,450. Of these, 19.6% (481) were Indian children. Of the 185 children in nonpublic schools as of 1969–70, only six (3.1%) were minority children. White enrollment has increased slightly; Indian enrollment has decreased slightly.

I. GOWANDA PUBLIC SCHOOL ENROLLMENT & ETHNIC PROPORTIONS, 1967–68 TO 1970–71

	White	%	Black	%	Spanish-Surnamed	%	Indian & Oriental	%	Total	%
1967–68	1,905	79.3	0	—	0	—	496	20.7	2,401	100
1968–69	1,887	79.0	0	—	0	—	501	21.0	2,388	100
1969–70	1,937	79.2	1	—a	0	—	507	20.7	2,445	100
1970–71	1,969	80.4	0	—	0	—	481	19.6	2,450	100

a Less than 0.1%.

The number of teachers and administrators has decreased since 1967; the minority staff has grown from one to two; both are Indian.

II. GOWANDA PUBLIC EDUCATION STAFF & MINORITY–GROUP PROPORTIONS, 1967–68 & 1970–71

	White	%	Minority	%	Total	%
1967–68	143	99.3	1	0.7	144	100
1970–71	125	98.4	2	1.6	127	100

Gowanda is closing down its most imbalanced school next year. Since 1967 it has shut down two similarly imbalanced schools and built a larger school. Gowanda has an Indian on the school board and is adding Indian culture to the curriculum.

Gowanda's superintendent, however, regards the Indian money as "in lieu of taxes," to be spent on all children equally.

III. DEVIATION OF GOWANDA PUBLIC SCHOOLS FROM DISTRICT RACIAL BALANCE, 1967–68 & 1970–71

	NUMBER OF SCHOOLS	
Deviation from Racial Balance	1967–68 Balance = 20.7% Minority	1970–71 Balance = 19.6% Minority
0–5%	1	2
5.1–10%	2	2
10.1–30%	3	1
30.1–Totally Segregated	—	—
Total Schools	6	5

Salamanca's 1970–71 public school enrollment was 2,392, of which 11.0% (264) were minority-group children. All of the 298 children enrolled in nonpublic schools as of 1969–70 were white. Both white and Indian public school enrollments have increased slightly.

I. Salamanca Public School Enrollment & Ethnic Proportions, 1967–68 to 1970–71

	White	%	Black	%	Spanish-Surnamed	%	Indian & Oriental	%	Total	%
1967–68	2,063	89.3	0	---	0	—	248	10.7	2,311	100
1968–69	2,102	90.2	0	—	0	—	228	9.8	2,330	100
1969–70	2,121	89.2	0	—	0	—	258	10.8	2,379	100
1970–71	2,128	89.0	1	—[a]	0	—	263	11.0	2,392	100

[a] Less than 0.1%.

The number of teachers and administrators is practically the same now as in 1967; the minority-group staff has grown from one to two; both are Indian.

II. Salamanca Public Education Staff & Minority-Group Proportions, 1967–68 & 1970–71

	White	%	Minority	%	Total	%
1967–68	127	99.2	1	0.8	128	100
1970–71	122	98.4	2	1.6	124	100

Two-thirds of the school district's elementary school Indian children attend one school.

III. Deviation of Salamanca Public Schools from District Racial Balance, 1967–68 & 1970–71

	NUMBER OF SCHOOLS	
Deviation from Racial Balance	1967–68 Balance = 10.7% Minority	1970–71 Balance = 11.0% Minority
0–5%	2	2
5.1–10%	2	2
10.1–30%	1	1
30.1–Totally Segregated	---	---
Total Schools	5	5

La Fayette's 1970–71 public school enrollment was 1,654, of which 21.5% (356) were minority children. There is no nonpublic enrollment. Both white and minority enrollments in the public schools are increasing.

I. La Fayette Public School Enrollment & Ethnic Proportions, 1967–68 to 1970–71

	White	%	Black	%	Spanish-Surnamed	%	Indian & Oriental	%	Total	%
1967–68	1,219	79.6	1	—	0	—	311	20.3	1,531	100
1968–69	1,194	79.2	2	0.1	0	—	312	20.7	1,508	100
1969–70	1,218	78.2	4	0.3	0	—	335	21.5	1,557	100
1970–71	1,298	78.5	1	—a	0	—	355	21.5	1,654	100

a Less than 0.1%.

The number of teachers and administrators has increased 50% since 1967; minority-group staff has grown from none to one; that staff member is an Indian.

II. La Fayette Public Education Staff & Minority-Group Proportions, 1967–68 & 1970–71

	White	%	Minority	%	Total	%
1967–68	61	100.0	0	0.0	61	100
1970–71	95	99.0	1	1.0	96	100

La Fayette is the center of the current state controversy over possession of wampum belts. (Teachers there have campaigned for the belts' return from the State Education Department's museum.) In this spirit, two La Fayette area Indian chiefs have recently been to Washington, seeking funds for a separate Indian high school. Indians have not been even informally represented in decision-making since the La Fayette school board insulted the advisory delegate by suggesting he should be democratically elected, contrary to Indian custom.

There is evidence that the central school's curriculum includes some attention to Indian culture. A teacher poll requested by a state legislator, now being conducted, is to show the teachers' position on integration. Of the two elementary schools, one is nearly all white; the other is a reservation school that is 100% Indian. There is no move to desegregate the Indian reservation school, except that voluntary transfer out is allowed.

III. Deviation of La Fayette Public Schools from District Racial Balance, 1967–68 & 1970–71

Deviation from Racial Balance	NUMBER OF SCHOOLS	
	1967–68 Balance = 20.4% Minority	1970–71 Balance = 21.5% Minority
0–5%	1	1
5.1–10%	0	0
10.1–30%	1	1
30.1–Totally Segregated	1	1
Total Schools	3	3

Niagara-Wheatfield's 1970–71 public school enrollment was 5,919, of which 8.5% (387) were minority children. Of 204 children enrolled in nonpublic schools as of 1969–70, 202 (99.0%) were white. Both white and minority enrollments have risen slightly.

I. NIAGARA-WHEATFIELD PUBLIC SCHOOL ENROLLMENT & ETHNIC PROPORTIONS, 1967–68 TO 1970–71

	White	%	Black	%	Spanish-Surnamed	%	Indian & Oriental	%	Total	%
1967–68	5,149	92.2	83	1.5	0	—	355	6.4	5,587	100
1968–69	5,329	92.0	97	1.7	6	0.1	359	6.2	5,791	100
1969–70	5,339	92.1	93	1.6	2	—a	360	6.2	5,794	100
1970–71	5,414	91.5	118	2.0	11	0.2	376	6.3	5,919	100

a Less than 0.1%.

The number of teachers and administrators has increased slightly since 1967, but the number of minority-group staff has decreased. Both of the minority teachers in 1970–71 were Indian.

II. NIAGARA-WHEATFIELD PUBLIC EDUCATION STAFF & MINORITY-GROUP PROPORTIONS, 1967–68 & 1970–71

	White	%	Minority	%	Total	%
1967–68	289	98.3	5	1.7	294	100
1970–71	308	99.4	2	0.6	310	100

Of the dozen schools here, six are small (95–155 pupils), and these six are also totally imbalanced: five are 100% white and one is 100% Indian. Of the remaining six larger schools, five are well-balanced and the sixth is only slightly imbalanced. There is no busing, and no plan to integrate beyond probable school consolidation for space reasons.

There is evidence of the schools' effort to direct attention to Indian culture and identity. The reservation school is used as a community center. Indians have pride in this school; apparently many would like to extend it to fifth grade. On the other hand, the district has talked about busing white fifth graders *in* because of space shortages. A new superintendent has not yet indicated his position on this.

III. Deviation of Niagara-Wheatfield Public Schools from District Racial Balance, 1967–68 & 1970–71

| Deviation from Racial Balance | NUMBER OF SCHOOLS | |
	1967–68 Balance = 7.8% Minority	1970–71 Balance = 8.5% Minority
0–5%	7	5
5.1–10%	4	6
10.1–30%	—	—
30.1–Totally Segregated	1	1
Total Schools	12	12

Salmon River's 1970–71 public school enrollment was 1,981, of which 36.9% (731) were Indian. All of the 105 children enrolled in nonpublic schools as of 1969–70 were white. Both white and minority enrollments in the public schools are increasing.

I. SALMON RIVER PUBLIC SCHOOL ENROLLMENT & ETHNIC PROPORTIONS, 1967–68 TO 1970–71

	White	%	Black	%	Spanish-Surnamed	%	Indian & Oriental	%	Total	%
1967–68	1,174	63.3	0	—	2	0.1	679	36.6	1,855	100
1968–69	1,185	62.3	0	—	0	—	717	37.7	1,902	100
1969–70	1,177	63.8	0	—	0	—	669	36.2	1,846	100
1970–71	1,250	63.1	0	—	0	—	731	36.9	1,981	100

The number of teachers and administrators, including minority-group staff, has been constant since 1967. The four minority staff members are Indian.

II. SALMON RIVER PUBLIC EDUCATION STAFF & MINORITY-GROUP PROPORTIONS, 1967–68 & 1970–71

	White	%	Minority	%	Total	%
1967–68	116	97.5	3	2.5	119	100
1970–71	116	96.7	4	3.3	120	100

A planetarium and a swimming pool are features of the modern central school, which is actually two schools under one roof. It houses a portion of the K-3 population and all children in grades 4-12. The separate, 277-pupil reservation school is all Indian except for 30 white children attending the town's only pre-K program there. Reservation children will, upon request, be bused into the central school 10 miles away. Few have done so.

In 1968, Indians boycotted the Salmon River schools and, as one of the consequences, gained the right for all New York State Indians to vote in school board elections. There is no apparent movement to integrate the reservation school.

III. Deviation of Salmon River Public Schools from District
Racial Balance, 1967–68 & 1970–71

Deviation from Racial Balance	NUMBER OF SCHOOLS	
	1967–68 Balance = 36.7% Minority	1970–71 Balance = 36.9% Minority
0–5%	1	1
5.1–10%	—	—
10.1–30%	—	1
30.1–Totally Segregated	2	1
Total Schools	3	3

5

Aid to Nonpublic Schools

It was perhaps inevitable that Commission members would come to different conclusions with respect to this highly controversial subject. Not surprisingly, then, intensive study and discussion in this area have not resulted in unanimity of opinion. The chapter begins with the views of a majority of Commission members. A separate statement representing the views of other Commissioners follows.

INTRODUCTION

In announcing the appointment of this Commission, Governor Rockefeller and the Board of Regents called attention to some of the matters which they considered to be within the purview of the proposed study. This charge to us included the following item:

> What should be the proper role of the state regarding the financial needs of nonpublic schools, particularly those serving disadvantaged neighborhoods?

Obviously, the most difficult part of this particular charge has to do with aid to church-connected, sectarian schools. Since the creation of the Commission, this subject, highly controversial throughout the life of the nation, has become even more so, if that is possible. This is a result of at least four factors:

1. The financial situation of most nonpublic schools in this state has worsened.
2. The New York State Legislature enacted the Mandated Services Act of 1970, which has made approximately $28 million per year available to nonpublic schools for examination, inspection and record-keeping functions. This aid was increased by enactment in 1971 of the Secular Education Services Act (SESA), through which an additional $33 million was appropriated to nonpublic schools to provide secular educational services. The great bulk of these appropriations would benefit sectarian schools, since students in nonsectarian schools account for only 6.5 per cent of all children attending nonpublic schools in New York.
3. The Supreme Court of the United States on June 28, 1971, in the case of *Lemon* v. *Kurtzman*,[1] ruled that direct state aid to sectarian schools for teachers' salaries, textbooks and instructional materials is in violation of the prohibition of the Federal Constitution against laws "respecting an establishment of religion." In January 1972, in *Committee for Public Education and Religious Liberty et al.* v. *Levitt et al.*, a three-judge federal panel, relying on the *Lemon* case, ruled that SESA is unconstitutional. It has been announced that the state will not appeal this decision. A suit in a federal court challenging the Mandated Services Act is still pending.*
4. President Nixon, Governor Rockefeller and high officials of the Roman Catholic Church have expressed the view that public support of nonpublic schools is in the public interest, and that a way must be found to provide aid despite the recent court decisions.

Recognizing the importance and complexity of this problem, the Commission authorized a full study of the subject by a committee of consultants headed by Louis R. Gary. These consultants included Rev. Ernest Bartell, Ph.D., President of Stonehill College and former chairman of the Department of Economics of the University of Notre Dame; Rev. Msgr. George A. Kelly, Ph.D., John A. Flynn Professor of Contemporary Catholic Problems at St. John's University and former Secretary for Education to Terence Cardinal Cooke and Francis Cardinal Spellman; George R. LaNoue, Ph.D.,

---

* In April, 1972, the Mandated Services Act was also ruled unconstitutional by a three-judge panel whose decision will be appealed to the U.S. Supreme Court. Another recent bill enacted by the New York legislature (L. 1972, ch. 414) authorizes (1) state aid for maintenance and repair of nonpublic school buildings; (2) tuition reimbursement payments by the state to low-income parents of children attending nonpublic schools; (3) tax deductions for other parents who send their children to nonpublic schools; (4) special aid for public school districts experiencing increased enrollments as a result of nonpublic school closings; and (5) acquisition by public school districts of closed nonpublic school buildings. Suit has been brought challenging the first three of these provisions, and in its initial decision a federal panel held unconstitutional the maintenance and repair aspect of the bill. A ruling on the other two challenged provisions is pending.

Associate Professor of Government and Education at Columbia University Teacher's College and member of the Church-State Committee of the American Civil Liberties Union; André L. Daniere, Ph.D., Associate Research Professor of Economics at Boston College; George F. Madeus, Ed.D., Associate Professor of Education at Boston College; Rev. Patrick S. Duffy, J.D., Ph.D., at the University of California, Berkeley; Leo Pfeffer, J.D., Professor of Constitutional Law and Chairman of the Department of Political Science at Long Island University and Special Counsel to the American Jewish Congress; Kenneth M. Brown, Ph.D., Assistant Professor of Economics at the University of Notre Dame; and Donald A. Erickson, Ph.D., Associate Professor of Education at the University of Chicago.

The findings and recommendations of the so-called Gary Report, "The Collapse of Nonpublic Education: Rumor or Reality?" * have already been publicized in the press. The report, like this chapter, focuses on Catholic schools because enrollment in these schools constitutes 85 per cent of all nonpublic school enrollment in New York. The report's figures on enrollment, past and present costs and current methods of financing are relied upon in the balance of this chapter. The projections of future enrollment and costs, together with the analysis of the effect on the public school system of a continued decrease in enrollment in Catholic schools, are inherently less authoritative. They are, at most, indicative of trends which are subject to a variety of factors not susceptible of exact estimate. For this reason we neither accept nor reject these projections as such. We do believe that the Gary Report correctly appraises current trends in nonpublic education and that its estimates of the financial consequences of the acceptance or rejection of our recommendations represent a reasonable analysis of a most complex subject. The recommendations made in this chapter, however, are those of this Commission and not necessarily those which may be gleaned from the Gary Report.

CONCLUSIONS AND RECOMMENDATIONS

1. *The principle of separation of church and state should not be abrogated: public funds or tax revenues ought not to be used in support of the attendance of students at sectarian schools.*
2. *The decision of the United States Supreme Court in the* Lemon *case is controlling and binding on the states.* The decision concerned the payment of a portion of salaries of teachers in nonpublic schools in Rhode Island, and the "purchase" of certain educational services from nonpublic schools in Pennsylvania. As noted above, the decision appears to preclude any amount of direct aid, large or small, to sectarian schools other than for incidental services such as transportation; we do

---

* The Gary Report is available through the Education Section, New York State Library, in Albany.

not believe that any Commission members disagree on this precise point. In our view, the principles on which the *Lemon* case was decided would also prohibit any amount of public aid to sectarian schools either by way of direct grants or by voucher or other provision of financial assistance to students in religious schools or to their parents. *Any plan for such aid in that view would be held to violate the United States and New York State Constitutions; it follows that it would be improper and inappropriate for a public commission such as this to recommend to the Legislature that it increase aid to sectarian schools, directly or indirectly, in the face of these controlling constitutional proscriptions.* *

It should be added that plans for shared time and dual enrollment of pupils in both public and nonpublic schools seem permissible under the Federal and State Constitutions, and we recommend that the right of a local district to experiment with such plans be clarified, by legislation if necessary. The constitutionality of such arrangements is also discussed in Appendix 5A, as is the special case of aid to sectarian schools for children with special needs.

3. *The preceding conclusions are the controlling ones, although the economic interests of the state seem, in the short term, to dictate increases in the current level of support of nonpublic education.* Our conclusions as to the economics of the situation are these:
   A. Since per-pupil expenditure in the public schools is higher than in Catholic schools and in most other sectarian schools, it would be to the short-term economic advantage of the state to help keep these schools open rather than to have large numbers of children transfer into the public school system.
   B. The expenditure differential, however, will rapidly disappear because of (a) substitution of lay teachers for religious-order teachers in Catholic schools; (b) steadily increasing wage demands, principally but not exclusively on the part of the lay faculty; and (c) the upward spiral of other educational costs, from which sectarian schools are not exempt. This trend will certainly accelerate if Catholic teaching personnel come to rely on public aid in support of their wage demands. Meanwhile, Catholic school enrollment will continue to decline for a variety of reasons, even if state aid were provided at a level which would eliminate the need for all tuition payments. Increased expenditure per pupil

---

* A detailed legal analysis supporting these conclusions appears in Appendix 5A. Among the Commission members comprising the majority on this issue, Commissioner Frankel agrees with this interpretation of the *Lemon* case but wishes to emphasize that he is not a lawyer, and Commissioners Levitt and Williams prefer to express no opinion on this legal question. A contrary legal view is set forth in Appendix 5B.

will result, to the point where the difference between public and nonpublic in this regard becomes small or nonexistent, and nonpublic schools will require increasing amounts of money in order to educate their students. Thus, over a period of years, the savings which now accrue to the state because of the existence of nonpublic school systems will greatly diminish as increased amounts of state aid are required to maintain those systems.

C. If the State Government, despite our recommendations, elects to continue aid to sectarian schools on an increasing scale, such aid should be conditioned upon greater self-help, including increased tuition and parish-church support, redistribution of parish-church resources and the kind of school consolidation specified in the Gary Report and outlined below.

D. Assuming that aid is held at the present level or decreased, transfers of children from nonpublic to public schools will unquestionably accelerate, although we do not expect an early or total demise of the Catholic or other nonpublic school system. On the contrary, we think that large numbers of students will continue to attend such schools, both primary and secondary, for the foreseeable future. Support will be provided, we think, by a combination of increased gifts, tuition, and in the case of sectarian schools, church funds.

E. Thus, the people of this state are faced with inevitable increases in the total education bill, either by increases in aid to nonpublic schools, or by the additional cost of educating those nonpublic school students who transfer, for one reason or another, to the public school system. As such transfers take place, special grants should be made to those public school districts where unusual expenses are encountered because of rapid increases in enrollment, expenses which are not fully met by the distribution formula discussed in the Finance chapter of this report. Also, a policy of state purchase or lease of nonpublic school facilities should be adopted in preference to construction of new public school facilities wherever this is possible. Any abandonment of usable school structures is not justifiable.

4. Statistics compiled in the Gary Report reveal that in New York the extent of racial segregation in sectarian schools on the whole exceeds that which prevails in the public schools. Elsewhere in this report we have decried the magnitude and growth of such *de facto* segregation in the state, and have recommended positive and immediate steps designed to alleviate this segregation. These recommendations will, of course, cost money. *We do not feel that we can advocate increased aid to nonpublic schools where the degree of segregation is so acute, while at the same time we would have the public school system devote its attention and resources to relieving the inequities caused by racial*

imbalance. This would amount to advocating public support to two school systems, one to be ultimately integrated and the other possibly to remain segregated, a morally unjustifiable position. Any aid which the state might determine to provide to sectarian schools, despite the recommendations we make here, ought, therefore, to be conditioned on these schools making intensive affirmative efforts to overcome segregation.

We would also require nonpublic schools, as a condition to receipt of any state funds, to accept all students regardless of religious affiliation. We stress, however, that "open admissions" does not suffice as a means of desegregating these—or any—schools, and that integration must be accomplished through means similar to those we have advocated for the public schools.

5. Our recommendation against additional aid to sectarian schools obviously applies to schools maintained by any denomination. The same constitutional restrictions would not apply to an attempt to aid nonsectarian nonpublic schools. We believe, however, that the fiscal restraints under which the public school system now operates, when coupled with the increasing financial need arising from projected student transfers out of the Catholic school system, forbid serious consideration of a plan which would benefit only a chosen handful. *We therefore recommend against public support of nonsectarian nonpublic schools.* Minor exceptions to our recommendations regarding orphanages and other institutions—both sectarian and nonsectarian—are discussed in our chapter on Children with Special Needs.

SCOPE OF NONPUBLIC EDUCATION

Prior to an exposition of the reasons behind the Commission's recommendations, an account of the extent of nonpublic education in New York and of current state aid to nonpublic schools will serve as essential background to the rest of this chapter. The figures in this section, unless otherwise noted, are for the 1969–70 school year. In that year, 841,378 children were educated in 1,967 nonpublic elementary and secondary schools in New York State. For every four children in the public schools, one child is studying

---

* Under present law, "religious educational institutions" are permitted to select students exclusively from members of the sponsoring religion, but may not discriminate on the basis of race, color or national origin. (Ed. Law Sec. 313.) This law applies by its terms only to institutions of post-secondary grade, but elementary and secondary schools receiving funds under the Mandated Services Act or SESA are also subject to its provisions.

TABLE 5.1

Public and Nonpublic School Enrollment, 1969–70

	Elementary (K–8)	Secondary (9–12)	Total (K–12)	Per Cent of State Total
Nonpublic	650,699	190,679	841,378	19.6
Public	2,468,672	974,137	3,442,809	80.4
Total	3,119,371	1,164,816	4,284,187	100.0

in a nonpublic school. (Table 5.1.) The nonpublic school enrollment in New York is greater than that of the combined public and nonpublic enrollment in each of 30 other states. The Catholic school system of New York City alone is the fourth largest city school system, public or nonpublic, in the country.

In other states with high nonpublic school enrollments, schools sponsored by the Catholic Church usually account for over 95 per cent of the students in nonpublic schools. While Catholic school enrollment is also dominant in New York, accounting for 84.5 per cent of the nonpublic students, there are other significant school groups.

The Jewish-sponsored schools account for 6.3 per cent of the nonpublic enrollment. Other sectarian schools account for 2.7 per cent of the enrollment, divided among nine dominations, and nonsectarian schools accommodate 6.5 per cent. (Table 5.2.) Thus, the nonpublic sector of New York's educational market is vast and the sponsorship diverse.

There are great differences among the four groups of nonpublic schools. Pupil-teacher ratios range from 12 to 1, to 33 to 1. (Table 5.3.)

Average teacher salaries range from $3,746 for Catholic elementary schools to $12,774 for nonsectarian secondary schools. (Table 5.4.) Within Catholic schools there are further differences in salary between religious-order teachers and lay teachers.

The cost of educating a student in a nonpublic elementary school ranges from $194 in the Catholic group to $1,768 in the nonsectarian group. (Table 5.5.)

Tuitions and fees vary similarly. A Catholic parent paid an average of only $50 in tuition in 1969–70 to educate his child in a Catholic elementary school, whereas nonsectarian schools charged an average of $1,388.

A comparison of the percentage of school costs covered by tuition shows that among nonpublic schools, Catholic schools cover the lowest proportion of their costs through tuition. The nonsectarian group covers the highest in this manner.

TABLE 5.2

Nonpublic School Enrollment by Affiliation, 1969–70

	Elementary (K–8)	Secondary (9–12)	Total (K–12)	Per Cent of State Total
CATHOLIC	557,470	153,643	711,113	84.5
JEWISH	39,109	13,752	52,861	6.3
OTHER SECTARIAN				
Lutheran	8,840	1,294	10,134	
Episcopal	4,468	1,632	6,100	
Seventh Day Adventist	1,583	574	2,157	
Greek Orthodox	1,951	67	2,018	
Society of Friends	857	764	1,621	
Baptist	168	—	168	
Methodist	37	9	46	
Russian Orthodox	6	38	44	
Mennonite	33	5	38	
TOTAL OTHER SECTARIAN	(17,943)	(4,383)	(22,326)	2.7
NONSECTARIAN	36,177	18,901	55,078	6.5
TOTAL	650,699	190,679	841,378	100.0

The range of school size for each of the groups also varies. (Table 5.6.) Within each group, there are significant variations depending upon the location of the schools. Schools in New York City tend to be significantly larger than the statewide average, and those in rural areas smaller.

Nonpublic enrollment is concentrated in urban areas; 51 per cent of nonpublic enrollment in the state is in New York City alone. (Table 5.7.)

TABLE 5.3

Public and Nonpublic Full-Time Elementary and Secondary Classroom Teachers and Pupil-Teacher Ratios, 1969–70

	Full-Time Classroom Teachers	Pupils per Teacher
NONPUBLIC		
Catholic	21,834	32.6
Jewish	2,502	21.1
Other Sectarian	1,283	17.4
Nonsectarian	4,654	11.8
PUBLIC	174,303	19.8

TABLE 5.4

Elementary and Secondary School Teacher Salaries by Group, 1969–70

	Average Elementary School Salaries	Average Secondary School Salaries
Catholic	$ 3,746[a]	$ 4,937[a]
Jewish	6,450	7,168
Other Sectarian	7,221	9,979
Nonsectarian	10,123	12,774

[a] Catholic figures include religious order and lay teachers.

NOTE: The State Education Department reports the median salary for New York State Public School elementary and secondary teachers in 1969–70 was $9,800.

CURRENT AID TO NONPUBLIC SCHOOLS IN NEW YORK STATE

Aid to nonpublic education in New York State has traditionally been defined narrowly as categorical aid given in the form of services to nonpublic schools and their students. The most extensive service provided by the state is the busing of students to and from nonpublic schools. Most districts in the state are required to provide certain health services for children in

TABLE 5.5

Total Tuition and Operating Costs per Pupil,[a] 1969–70

	ELEMENTARY (K–8)		SECONDARY (9–12)	
	Tuition	Costs	Tuition	Costs
Catholic	50	194	317	435
Jewish	391	701	502	845
Other Sectarian	567	639	1,394	1,472
Nonsectarian	1,388	1,768	1,993	2,234

[a] Tuition averages are derived from tuition actually collected, not from the tuition scale in effect at a particular school, so that full or partial scholarships that are given as tuition rebates or decreases are reflected in these figures.

NOTE: The State Education Department estimates total expenditures for public elementary and secondary students in 1969–70 at $1,255 per pupil.

TABLE 5.6

Average Enrollment in Elementary and Secondary Nonpublic Schools, 1969–70

	Average Elementary (K–8) Enrollment	Average Secondary (9–12) Enrollment
Catholic	518	743
Jewish	272	289
Other Sectarian	205	295
Nonsectarian	267	242

nonpublic schools to the extent that they are provided in the public schools and are requested by the nonpublic schools. The state also provides for the free loan of textbooks for the use of high school students. Additional state funds are available for school lunch programs and attendance and testing services. (Table 5.8.)

The amount of aid currently provided is substantial. The total dollar value is difficult to compute, since it involves dividing amounts between direct grants and cost of services. However, the total for 1971–72 will be approximately $70 million.

Only recently has legislation been passed which provides broad general aid through direct money grants to nonpublic schools. The Mandated Services Act, enacted in 1970, provides up to $28 million to nonpublic schools for services for examination and inspection in connection with administering tests and examinations and maintaining enrollment, health and other records. (Table 5.9.) The Secular Educational Services Act, (SESA),

TABLE 5.7

Nonpublic School Enrollment by Location and Group, 1969–70

	New York City	Other Urban	Suburban	Rural
Catholic	365,185	91,327	208,244	46,377
Jewish	31,328	12,571	8,273	689
Other Sectarian	9,487	5,243	7,366	230
Nonsectarian	26,658	10,299	13,732	4,389
Total	432,658	119,440	237,595	51,685
	(51.4%)	(14.2%)	(28.2%)	(6.1%)

TABLE 5.8

State Expenditures for Aid to Public and Nonpublic Education, 1967–68

	Total	Public	Nonpublic
Transportation	$157,142,119	$134,142,119	$23,000,000
Health Service	41,458,601	32,458,601	9,000,000
Textbooks (Secondary Schools)	18,500,000	13,500,000	5,000,000
School Lunch	11,109,355	10,294,518	814,837
Attendance	10,852,470	N.A.	N.A.
Census	791,480	N.A.	N.A.
Testing Services to Schools	966,000	784,300	181,700
Handicapped—Section 4407	8,000,000	—	8,000,000
Orphan Asylum Schools— Section 4001	190,537	—	190,537
Home Instruction	N.A.	N.A.	N.A.
Summer School	N.A.	N.A.	N.A.

NOTE: N.A. = Not available.

enacted in 1971 and recently ruled unconstitutional, appropriated $33 million to nonpublic schools for "secular educational services." *

POLICY CONSIDERATIONS

Despite the legal prohibitions we have summarized above, the Commission could nonetheless, if it were convinced that such a course is in the public interest, recommend increased aid to sectarian schools pending judicial determination of the constitutionality of the particular program of aid which might be advocated. Indeed, the Commission could also recommend repeal of constitutional prohibitions against state aid to religious schools. However, we consider that the same persuasive principles of public policy that dictated the incorporation of such prohibitions in the federal and in virtually every state constitution require that no change be made in the historic doctrine of the separation of church and state under the American system of government.

* The Mandated Services Act has initially been ruled unconstitutional, but L. 1972, ch. 414 authorizes substantial additional funds for nonpublic schools and for parents of children attending such schools. See footnote, page 388.

TABLE 5.9

Nonpublic School Eligibility for Funds Under Mandated Services Act, 1970–71 and 1971–72 (in Millions)

	1970–71	1971–72
Catholic	$20.8	$20.8
Other Nonpublic	4.1	4.1
Total	$24.9	$24.9

We recognize the existence of honest differences of opinion on this subject; we know that many nations and societies of the free world function harmoniously despite governmental support of religion and religious schools, while in other countries competition for public funds between public and religious schools has been a continuous source of divisiveness and disorder. We believe, however, that in the United States the draftsmen and enactors of constitutional provisions designed to maintain the separation of church and state acted wisely for the future of the nation.

The value of, and rationale for, church-state separation has, of course, been discussed and written about extensively throughout the course of American history. We do not propose at this point to set forth a lengthy essay on the subject. We do propose, however, to express briefly our basic thoughts on this matter, and to quote a few additional statements of this national policy.* These statements are intended to explain further why we are philosophically opposed to state support of religious schools, or state support of pupils' attendance at such schools, and why we would be so opposed even if such support were legally permissible.

The Purpose of Religious Schools

We begin with the premise that the very existence of sectarian schools is based on a desire to propagate a religious faith. Moreover, religious instruction is a matter of general atmosphere and value orientation. If a sectarian school is performing its function, it does its teaching, wherever it can, from a religious point of view. We do not object to this practice or to the goals which are thereby sought; we recognize the right of every parent to provide a religiously oriented education for his children. But no parent should ask

---

* We point out also that legal decisions concerning the "establishment of religion" are themselves expressive of the philosophy underlying the doctrine of church-state separation. The analysis of the *Lemon* case, set forth in Appendix 5A, involves considerations of principle and philosophy which are basic to the position adopted in this chapter.

other citizens to pay for this education and thus to help promulgate particular religious teachings through compulsory taxation. Religion, in a house of worship or in a school, must be a private matter. Religious liberty in America, it seems to us, means not only the right to free exercise of one's religious beliefs, but freedom from compulsion to help foster the religious beliefs of others.

To those who assert that sectarian schools can and do separate secular and religious teaching, we respond that the government must assure itself, for the sake of the religious liberty of its citizens, that such separation is in fact maintained. And any steps which the government may take in this regard to determine just what it is that sectarian schools are doing with money derived from public revenues involve surveillance that is likely to generate rancor and ill-will between church and state.*

Separation of Church and State

Moreover, whether it is proposed that state aid be given directly to sectarian schools or to parents for use in such schools, problems persist in defining what religions shall be permitted to sponsor eligible schools, and how much aid shall be provided. The potential for recurrent political and public conflict revolving around an issue based on religious preference is great, and the prospect is not a happy one.[2] The state has too many divisive problems to deal with as things are. It is also clear that the independence of various religions and their schools is threatened by conditions attached to receipt of public funds; church interests as well as governmental interests are best served, we think, by as great a separation of their respective realms as possible. In sum, in a pluralistic society such as ours, civic tranquillity is best maintained by having the state remain apart from the sphere of religion and religious institutions.

We include in expressing our position on this subject quotations from two men who served as Presidents of the United States. One of the most eloquent statements of principle in our nation's history declaring opposition to public taxation for religious purposes was made by James Madison in an essay against a bill that would have provided tax support for teachers of the Christian religion in Virginia.[3] A basic fault of the bill was that it would have favored one religion above others, but much of what Madison wrote is applicable to any legislation which would help to foster the teaching of all religions equally. Portions of his statement follow:

> . . . The Religion then of every man must be left to the conviction and conscience of every man; and it is the right of every man to exercise it as these may dictate. . . . We maintain therefore that in matters of Religion,

---

* This is the "entanglement" issue which the Supreme Court discussed at length in the *Lemon* case.

no man's right is abridged by the institution of Civil Society, and that Religion is wholly exempt from its cognizance. True it is, that no other rule exists, by which any question which may divide a Society, can be ultimately determined, but the will of the majority; but it is also true, that the majority may trespass on the rights of the minority.

. . . if religion be exempt from the authority of the Society at large, still less can it be subject to that of the Legislative Body. The latter are but the creatures and viceregents of the former. Their jurisdiction is both derivative and limited; it is limited with regard to the co-ordinate departments, more necessarily it is limited with regard to the constituents. The preservation of a free government requires not merely, that the metes and bounds which separate each department of power may be invariably maintained; but more especially, that neither of them be suffered to overlap the great Barrier which defends the rights of the people. . . .

. . . Who does not see that . . . the same authority which can force a citizen to contribute three pence only of his property for the support of any one establishment, may force him to conform to any other establishment in all cases whatsoever?

. . . a [just] government will be best supported by protecting every citizen in the enjoyment of his Religion with the same equal hand which protects his person and his property; by neither invading the equal rights of any Sect, nor suffering any Sect to invade those of another.

. . . [the bill] will destroy that moderation and harmony which the forbearance of our laws to intermeddle with Religion, has produced amongst its several sects. . . .

Also, familiar to all Americans is the ringing declaration of John F. Kennedy, when he was a candidate for the Presidency:

I believe in an America where the separation of church and state is absolute . . . where no church or church school is granted any public funds or political preference.[4]

The Desirability of Pluralism

Another aspect of this issue which deserves mention is the emphasis which many proponents of aid to nonpublic schools place on the desirability of pluralism. This is of course an attractive concept. The fact of the matter is, however, that, by and large, public and nonpublic schools are very similar with respect to methods of teaching and the substance of what is taught. There is no convincing evidence of the superiority of one or the other. What is different is, first, sectarian training in sectarian schools and, second, a stronger code of discipline that is maintained in some sectarian schools. Neither of these is to us a distinction which justifies expenditures of the tax money of all on behalf of a favored few who choose not to have their children attend public schools.

Support of pluralism has often been based on the argument that nonpublic schools will compete with public schools, and a higher level of educational quality will result in all sectors. Moreover, it is contended that new techniques, if established in nonpublic education, should be a model for the public sector. In this way, the public schools can adapt the effective new procedures to their curricula and thus improve the quality of education.

No studies, however, can be cited to demonstrate the effectiveness of a "free market" concept between public and nonpublic sectors. There are no effective links between the public and nonpublic sectors to allow for the dissemination of information on innovative techniques, so that to consider nonpublic schools as models for public schools is not valid. In addition, the public school system itself does not comprise a monolithic institution, but a pluralistic one, providing diversity of educational programs and approaches within its scope. Most important, this pluralism does not involve sectarian components or divisions; its varied resources are available to all children.

THE FUTURE OF NONPUBLIC SCHOOLS IN NEW YORK STATE

Since the majority of the Commission recommends against additional state aid to nonpublic schools, we considered carefully whether it would be appropriate for us to advance suggestions which might be deemed by some an officious attempt to tell the churches supporting such schools how the management of sectarian education might be improved. We concluded, however, that we had an obligation to go into this subject further for two reasons:

1. The Gary Report contains findings based upon extensive research into the economic and financial situation of nonpublic schools in this state, as well as the racial composition of their enrollment. These data and findings, particularly with respect to the Catholic schools, have not previously been assembled in such depth. We think they will be of interest to nonpublic school authorities, as well as to taxpayers who would bear the cost of the increased aid sought by nonpublic school spokesmen.
2. As realists, we cannot ignore the fact that the Legislature has granted increased aid to nonpublic schools in two successive years. Thus, we must consider the possibility that increased aid to nonpublic schools will continue to be an issue, despite the doubts expressed in this report as to the public interest aspects and the constitutionality of such aid. In that event, these data and findings may well prove of value to the Legislature in fashioning the form and measure of any such assistance, including particularly the determination of appropriate conditions which should be attached thereto.

TABLE 5.10

School Enrollment Forecast by Group, 1966–80

	1966–67	1969–70	Per Cent Change	1975–76	Per Cent Change	1980–81	Per Cent Change
Catholic	784,650	711,113	−9.4	438,000	−38.4	321,000	−26.7
Jewish	38,166	52,861	+38.5	55,000	+4.0	57,000	+3.6
Other Sectarian	19,227	22,326	+16.1	20,000	−10.4	18,000	−10.0
Nonsectarian	49,103	55,078	+12.2	53,000	−3.8	50,000	−5.7
Total	891,146	841,378	−5.6	566,000	−32.7	446,000	−21.2

Accordingly, we proceed to a discussion of enrollment and cost trends in nonpublic schools. This brings us to an analysis of financial considerations affecting the future of these schools. We then abstract the material in the Gary Report concerning the racial and ethnic composition of nonpublic school enrollment.*

Enrollment Trends

During the period 1970–80, based on present trends, enrollment in all non-public schools will decline by 47 per cent and in Catholic schools by 55 per cent. (Table 5.10.) Projections indicate that the Catholic population in the state will remain roughly constant; that the numbers of Catholic school-age children will significantly decrease, and that there is a continuing and increasing movement on the part of Catholic families away from enrolling children in Catholic elementary schools. It is not surprising that enrollment declines of such magnitude have become a major issue in the controversy surrounding the question of state aid to nonpublic schools.

Catholic school spokesmen often blame declining school enrollments on tuition increases. Their contention is that Catholic families cannot afford to pay more; and that only state aid can ease the financial squeeze which is forcing these families to transfer their children to public schools. They argue that state aid will not only "save" the Catholic schools, but will save the taxpayers the cost of absorbing Catholic school students into the public school system.

There is no evidence, however, that tuition increases have significantly affected enrollment. Catholic school enrollments are sharply declining in the elementary schools. Yet, while the tuition in these schools has risen 100

---

* All statistics in this portion of Chapter 5 are derived from the Gary Report and refer to the 1969–70 school year unless otherwise specified.

TABLE 5.11

Catholic Elementary and Secondary School Tuitions by Location, 1969–70

	Elementary (K–8)	Secondary (9–12)
New York City	$65	$355
Other Urban	24	308
Suburban	40	294
Rural	25	166
Average	$50	$317

per cent since 1965, it averaged only $50 statewide in 1969–70. This is an exceedingly small portion of most Catholic school family incomes.*

Enrollment declines are occurring in affluent suburbs as well as in deprived neighborhoods. While New York City has an average Catholic elementary school tuition of $65, the average in the suburbs is only $40; yet the suburbs have experienced a proportionately higher decline in enrollments. (Tables 5.11 and 5.12.)

Recent school closings have been cited as evidence of excessively high tuitions forcing enrollments down. But of the 76 elementary schools which have closed in the state between 1965 and 1969, 25 charged no tuition at all.

Past enrollment declines in New York City can be partially explained by the migration of city Catholics to the suburbs, where they often place their children in public schools.

Enrollments in Catholic schools are based on two major factors: the number of Catholic school-age children and the preference of Catholic families. The potential pool of Catholic school students is decreasing rapidly, and Catholic families are choosing to send their children to public schools in even greater numbers.

CATHOLIC SCHOOL-AGE POPULATION   The Catholic school-age population in New York State is expected to decrease from 1,575,000 in 1970 to 1,396,000 in 1975. The declining number of infant baptisms since 1955 supports this projection: infant baptisms per 1,000 New York Catholics numbered 37 in 1955, 27 in 1967, and only 25 per 1,000 in 1970. Infant baptism rates show a steady increase in the number of Catholic school-age children until 1965, and then a sharp and continued decrease in enrollments

---

* The actual average cost per Catholic family included another $21 per pupil which represents book rental charges, uniform costs and other miscellaneous charges and school fund-raising proceeds. Tuition for a family's second or third child in an elementary school is often minimal or nonexistent.

TABLE 5.12

Catholic School Enrollments by Location, Projected to 1975–76 and 1980–81

	1963–64	1969–70	1975–76	1980–81
New York City	388,800	365,137	232,100	170,200
Other Urban	115,600	91,526	49,600	36,300
Suburban	224,800	208,144	133,100	97,500
Rural	63,300	46,306	23,200	17,000
Total	792,500	711,113	438,000	321,000

begins. The effect of the large 1966 drop in baptisms will not be felt in schools until 1972–73.

In recent years, high school enrollments have not declined in proportion to elementary school enrollments. Nevertheless, there should be a strong though delayed relationship between the two. More than 90 per cent of Catholic high school applicants come from Catholic elementary schools. Therefore, in the 1975 to 1980 period, the high schools will begin to suffer heavily from the continuing drop in elementary enrollments. (Table 5.13.)

The decline in baptisms is attributable primarily to a falling birthrate among Catholics. Birthrate declines are a new controlling factor that will be influential during the balance of this decade.

PARENTAL PREFERENCE   Parental choice has had and will continue to have the most substantial effect on enrollments. Even when Catholic school enrollment was at its highest, less than half of the Catholic children were enrolled in Catholic elementary and secondary schools of the state. In the period from 1967 to 1970 when Catholic school enrollments in the state were already in a 4 to 5 per cent annual decline at the elementary level, the school-age population decline for Catholics had not yet taken place, indicating that nearly all of the loss was due to parental decisions to enroll

TABLE 5.13

Catholic School Enrollment Forecast, 1969–80

	1969–70	1975–76	1980–81
Elementary (K–8)	557,470	330,000	242,000
Secondary (9–12)	153,643	108,000	79,000
Total (K–12)	711,113	438,000	321,000

their children in public schools. The Catholic enrollment in Catholic schools per 1,000 school-age children is projected to decline from 334 per 1,000 in 1970 to 237 per 1,000 in 1975.

Professors Kenneth M. Brown and Ernest J. Bartell, in a paper published by the University of Notre Dame and cited in the Gary Report, have elaborated on the complexity of the concept of parental choice:

> . . . perceived quality differences may have to do with differences in physical facilities, special programs and school location. These differences would be very expensive to eliminate and it is most doubtful that state aid would be sufficient to pay for such changes.
>
> It is possible that changes and tastes are working against the religious aspects of Catholic schools. If parents actually prefer the nonsectarian atmosphere of public schools, then no conceivable policy change, however extravagant, could halt the enrollment decline.

Parental preferences vary significantly between city and suburb. In New York City, where Catholic elementary schools charge 62.5 per cent more tuition than those in the suburbs, and where the poor are more heavily concentrated, a proportionately greater number of Catholic families choose Catholic schools for their children than in the suburbs.

The desire for quality education in the suburbs is renowned. If Catholic families perceived suburban Catholic schools to be significantly superior to the local public schools, it is reasonable to assume that a $40 per year tuition would not be a stumbling block. But enrollments have declined in the suburbs by 8.4 per cent since 1963. Projections show that suburban and rural enrollment will continue to decline.

Essentially, when the average Catholic elementary school family maintains that it cannot afford a higher tuition level, particularly in suburban areas, it means that, after all other priorities, education in a Catholic elementary school is regarded as worthy of little financial sacrifice. The "breaking point" is a psychological not an economic one. Catholic families contribute less than two per cent of their incomes to their parish churches, and the rich contribute far less proportionately than the poor.

Only if the state chooses to adopt an aid policy that is explicitly aimed at substantially upgrading the perceived quality of the Catholic schools to a level higher than the neighboring public schools, might the enrollment trend be halted or reversed by state action. We do not suppose that such an extensive program could gain acceptance.

Rising Costs

All education is subject to rising costs in our economy. Costs of services appear to be rising more rapidly than the revenues currently available to pay for them. The nonpublic sector is not exempt from these general eco-

TABLE 5.14

Religious-Order Teachers in Catholic Elementary and Secondary Schools,
Projected to 1975–76 and 1980–81

	1969–70	1975–76	1980–81
Elementary (K–8)	8,777	4,939	889
Secondary (9–12)	3,765	2,835	486
Total	12,542	7,774	1,375

nomic pressures. However, only the Catholic schools are confronting the
question of their very survival.

Religious-order teachers take subsistence cash stipends and room and
board amounting to a statewide average of $2,186 in lieu of the average of
$5,335 salaries paid to laymen for teaching in Catholic schools. This
enormous subsidy by religious-order teachers will virtually come to an end
by 1980. Projections show that instead of the 12,542 religious-order teachers in New York State Catholic schools today, there will not be more than
1,375 by 1980. (Table 5.14.)

The availability of religious-order teachers began to decline in the sixties.
Over 50 per cent of the teachers in the Catholic schools of the prime
survey area* are lay teachers. For instance, the number of teaching sisters
declined from a high of 14,814 in 1966 to 12,177 in 1969. Since the
average difference between salaries of religious-order and lay teachers is
$3,167, each replacement is expensive.

The diminishing supply of religious-order teachers reflects a sharp drop
in applicants for membership in religious orders, particularly women's
orders of nuns. In the Catholic high schools of New York City's boroughs of
Brooklyn and Queens in 1969, only two girls out of a mixed enrollment of
38,102 applied to begin the process of becoming a nun. Not all applicants
complete the process. And while some nuns are resigning from their orders,
others are taking advantage of the modernization of many orders which
permit them to choose vocations other than teaching, such as nursing or
social work.

Orders seem to have been keeping their members in service as long as
possible to compensate for the lack of new members. Soon, a large number
of teaching nuns must retire, and this will create a situation similar to an
inverted pyramid: with few entrants, there is an upward shift in the age

---

* The "prime survey area" refers to the 10 counties in the Catholic Archdiocese of New
York. These counties include school districts in all four locational categories: New York
City, Other Urban, Suburban, and Rural.

composition of the orders, placing a greater burden on the still active members to receive higher compensation in order to maintain the solvency of the order and care for ill and retired members.

Cost-of-living increases will also be necessary to keep pace with inflationary trends over the decade. It is estimated that the annual salaries for religious-order teachers in Catholic elementary schools will rise from $2,186 to $5,000 by 1975 and $5,796 by 1980 (including an allocation for convent room and board). Thus, not only will higher-salaried lay teachers continue to replace lower-salaried religious-order teachers, but the remaining religious-order teachers will be paid more.

Catholic lay teachers have also in the past received substantially lower salaries than public school teachers. In the last few years the gap has been narrowing. Catholic lay teachers' salary schedules are rising at a more rapid rate than are public school salary schedules. This escalation will probably continue until parity with the public school salary schedules is reached or closely approached. Presently, the differential in median salaries is 33 per cent.

As long as lay teachers remained a small minority in Catholic schools, their bargaining power was small. A strike or a threat of a strike was meaningless. A local of the American Federation of Teachers (AFT) is the bargaining agent for all lay teachers in the prime survey area. Unions or teachers' associations not connected with the AFT exist in all other counties. It is reasonable to assume that all lay teachers will be in some form of collective bargaining association within the next five years. In certain areas labor representation elections are being conducted through the State Labor Relations Board, which may bring more teachers into AFT locals.

Catholic schools seeking to improve educational quality are demanding more years of experience and higher degree qualification for their teachers. These quality-motivated changes will raise average teachers' salaries to an even higher point. The statewide average for lay teachers' salaries at the elementary level is $5,335; by 1980 it is projected that it will rise to $15,346, or 86 per cent of the estimated public school salaries for 1980. This is a 288 per cent increase by the end of the decade. (Table 5.15.) These skyrocketing costs must be viewed in the context of the ability of the Catholic Church and the Catholic people to match rising costs with revenues.

Declining Revenues

There are two principal revenue sources for Catholic schools: tuition and general church revenues. Over three-fourths of the Catholic schools in the state are elementary parochial schools. Each is attached to a parish church which serves as its basic economic unit. Tuition provides 26 per cent of school costs and parishes contribute the difference. This difference is de-

TABLE 5.15

Catholic School Teachers' Salaries, Projected to 1975–76 and 1980–81

	1969–70	1975–76	1980–81
RELIGIOUS-ORDER TEACHERS			
Elementary (K–8)	$2,186	$ 5,000	$ 5,796
Secondary (9–12)	2,932	5,000	5,796
LAY TEACHERS			
Elementary (K–8)	5,335	9,867	15,346
Secondary (9–12)	7,634	10,639	16,515

rived from Sunday collections and fund-raising events to which both Catholic school families and Catholics without children in the parochial schools contribute.

The few private Catholic elementary schools owned by religious orders depend to a far greater extent on tuition to cover costs, as do all Catholic high schools. The bishops of the state must cover any deficit in their regional (diocesan) high schools from central church funds. The high schools owned by religious orders have access to only limited subsidies and must keep raising tuitions to cover costs.

In affluent suburbs, parish contributions are sufficiently high that few suburban schools are forced to increase tuitions rapidly to cover educational costs. The poorer city parishes, however, have comparatively lower parish revenues and must pass on a greater burden in tuition to the Catholic school family.

While tuitions could be raised in a number of schools, strong psychological and institutional barriers exist which render tuition increases an unlikely source from which to draw additional revenues. For example, Catholic schoolmen fear that attempts to raise tuition will be offset by lower giving rates at Sunday collections. However, studies have found no significant differences in giving rates between parish churches with schools and parish churches without schools.

As noted above, Catholic elementary school tuitions are quite low, and any "breaking point" Catholic families have reached is more psychological than financial. Catholic spokesmen contend, however, that additional funds cannot be obtained through tuition increases, because Catholic families are unable to pay more. This remains a firmly imbedded belief, and no trend toward obtaining greater revenues from significantly higher tuitions is yet apparent.

Each parish is an autonomous economic unit. If its school has a deficit, but the parish does not, the bishop's office does not become involved. When the parish as a unit does experience a deficit, it is placed on an austerity budget by the local bishop. The local bishop must ask more affluent parishes within his region (diocese) to make funds available for distribution to the parishes in deficit. Since the Catholic financial system is wholly voluntary, parishioners might refuse such a request unless it were modest. There are no adequate distribution mechanisms in the Catholic Church for moving funds from wealthy parish churches to poorer ones or even for adjusting tuitions within a parish church school according to ability to pay.

Parish church contributions have leveled off to a point at which, in the very near future, they will lag behind inflationary trends in the economy, estimated to be approximately six per cent per year. Only slight increases in parish-church revenue collections are projected: 102 per cent of 1970 collections in 1975, and 105 per cent of 1970 collections in 1980. Despite the steady growth in revenues in the past, and despite the growth in Catholic family incomes, this leveling off of revenues has been a clear trend in the prime survey area for the last three years.*

Trends suggest that prospects of obtaining increased funds for Catholic schools from parish church revenues are not bright. Over 55 per cent of parish church revenues is going into parish schools now. This leaves little for other parish social services, the costs of which are also rising. Moreover, forecasts of enrollment declines mean that an increasingly smaller number of Catholic children will benefit from funds channeled to the schools.

While the elements contributing to rising costs are clear, no compensating trends are evident to suggest that revenues will increase.

CAN CATHOLIC SCHOOLS SURVIVE?

The Catholic school enrollment is projected to decline by 55 per cent by 1980. The Catholic Church leadership does not have control over the falling birthrate and the changes in Catholic tastes which are causing the decline. Decisions of the Catholic Church leadership cannot change the inflationary spiral in the national economy, nor the increases in Catholic lay teachers' salaries which are contributing to the rapid rise in the costs of education. The decreasing supply of religious-order teachers and the generally low level of contributions to parish-church collections are also, at least in the short run, trends beyond the Church's control. However, the Church leadership can still influence their schools through their responses to these enrollment and cost trends. Decisions as to future school size, class size, and pupil/teacher ratios are still theirs to make, and will have considerable effect on the solvency of the school system in the future.

Until last year, school policies of the Catholic leadership took little ac-

---

* Current revenue data since 1967 were available for all parish churches in the prime survey area. Churches with schools and churches without schools were included.

count of the enrollment decline which began in the mid-sixties. In an effort to improve the quality of Catholic education, teaching staffs were augmented in order to reduce pupil/teacher ratios. Suburban schools were built to serve the Catholic population which was shifting out of the cities, even though Catholic suburban families are increasingly enrolling their children in public schools. Few schools were closed. Only this year has construction come to a halt, hiring of teachers leveled off, and school closings accelerated slightly.

If the present policy were to be continued, the result could be a cumulative deficit, for the schools, of $2.1 billion projected from 1971–72 through 1980–81 for operating expenses at the elementary level and secondary level.

In 1969–70, the deficit for Catholic elementary and secondary schools in New York State was approximately $72 million. Fifty-five per cent of all parish-church revenues were required to cover this deficit. By 1975–76, the schools are projected to incur a deficit of $170 million. In that year, 125 per cent of projected parish-church revenues would be required in the absence of state or federal aid. Considering the maximum amount of parish-church revenues which could realistically be applied to the school deficits through 1980 (55 per cent), that would leave almost $1.4 billion, or $1,375 million, to be made up by either tuition increases, or state aid, or a combination of both cumulatively through 1980.

Strategies for Survival

In order to make estimates of the comparative costs to the public of aid to Catholic schools and the consequence of accelerated transfers of Catholic children into the public school system, three possible strategies which the Catholic school leadership might adopt will be examined here: the present High Cost Strategy, a Moderate Cost Strategy, and a Low Cost Strategy. The cost projection model utilizes a variety of assumptions under the three strategies. For the High Cost Strategy, it is assumed that no consolidation of schools is attempted and that all schools are kept open despite projected enrollment declines and despite the corresponding declines in pupil/teacher ratios. The Low Cost Strategy, at the other extreme, assumes full consolidation of schools and classes to the extent that pupil/teacher ratios can be maintained at 1970 levels despite projected enrollment declines. The Moderate Cost Strategy presumes some school consolidation and some reduction in class size. Pupil/teacher ratios in this strategy are midway between those for the High and Low Cost Strategies. Only elementary schools are included in the description of the three strategies since they comprise 78 per cent of the total Catholic enrollment.

The Low Cost Strategy is as unrealistic and as difficult to implement successfully as the present High Cost Strategy is impractical. For purposes of analysis, the High and Low Cost Strategies are being described to frame

TABLE 5.16

A Range of Planning Options for Catholic Elementary Schools under Alternative Consolidation Strategies

	High Cost Strategy (No Consolidation)	Moderate Cost Strategy (Partial Consolidation)	Low Cost Strategy (Full Consolidation)
1975–76			
Schools	1,112	809	665
Teachers	15,469	12,147	10,000
Pupils per Teacher	21	27	33
1980–81			
Schools	1,112	656	488
Teachers	15,467	9,949	7,334
Pupils per Teacher	15	24	33

NOTE: In 1969–70 there were 1,112 elementary schools, 15,469 teachers, and 33 pupils per teacher.

the Moderate Cost Strategy. While acknowledging the reality of the projected enrollment decline, the Moderate Cost Strategy would take into account institutional barriers within the Catholic Church to consolidation, traveling distance to school, and parental preferences, and would to some extent accommodate the pressures for smaller class size.

CONSOLIDATION   The critical issues involved under each strategy are the number of schools kept open and the number of teachers employed. The latter factor is represented by the pupil/teacher ratio. The range of options for the Catholic school system under each strategy is shown in Table 5.16.

Nothing contained in the model described should be considered a detailed planning prescription for optimum school size. Instead, the potential extent of consolidation is illustrated. Traveling distances, and the condition and size of specific buildings, would all be involved in any actual consolidation. Projections of Catholic school costs and revenues through 1980–81 under the three strategies are shown in Table 5.17. The amounts of state aid required to meet possible deficits are shown in Tables 5.18–5.21.

PUPIL/TEACHER RATIOS   The pupil/teacher ratios chosen for the strategies determine the reduction in teacher staffs which would have to be accomplished through attrition, retirements and staff cutback. Optimum economic efficiency would call for staff reductions exclusively among the higher-salaried lay teachers, providing full employment to the lower-salaried

TABLE 5.17

Catholic Elementary School Costs and Revenues, Projected to 1980–81 for Alternative Consolidation Strategies

ASSUMING 6% ANNUAL TUITION RISE TO MATCH INCOME GROWTH

	High Cost Strategy (No Consolidation)	Moderate Cost Strategy (Partial Consolidation)	Low Cost Strategy (Full Consolidation)
Enrollment	242,000	242,000	242,000
Total Cost per Pupil	$1,120.40	$732.96	$542.81
Tuition per Pupil	$ 134.78	$134.78	$134.78
Deficit per Pupil	$ 985.62	$598.18	$408.03

ASSUMING 12% ANNUAL TUITION RISE

	High Cost Strategy (No Consolidation)	Moderate Cost Strategy (Partial Consolidation)	Low Cost Strategy (Full Consolidation)
Enrollment	242,000	242,000	242,000
Total Cost per Pupil	$1,120.40	$732.96	$542.81
Tuition per Pupil	$ 246.98	$246.98	$246.98
Deficit per Pupil	$ 873.42	$485.98	$295.83

Catholic Secondary School Costs and Revenues, Projected to 1980–81 for Alternative Consolidation Strategies

ASSUMING 6% ANNUAL TUITION RISE TO MATCH INCOME GROWTH

	High Cost Strategy (No Consolidation)	Moderate Cost Strategy (Partial Consolidation)	Low Cost Strategy (Full Consolidation)
Enrollment	79,000	79,000	79,000
Total Cost per Pupil	$1,582.16	$1,209.50	$1,040.67
Tuition per Pupil	$ 687.18	$ 687.18	$ 687.18
Deficit per Pupil	$ 894.98	$ 522.32	$ 353.49

ASSUMING 12% ANNUAL TUITION RISE

	High Cost Strategy (No Consolidation)	Moderate Cost Strategy (Partial Consolidation)	Low Cost Strategy (Full Consolidation)
Enrollment	79,000	79,000	79,000
Total Cost per Pupil	$1,582.16	$1,209.50	$1,040.67
Tuition per Pupil	$1,259.23	$1,259.23	$1,259.23
Deficit per Pupil	$ 322.93	$ 49.73[a]	$ 218.56[a]

[a] Surplus

TABLE 5.18

Required State Aid for Catholic Elementary Schools, Projected to 1975–76
for Alternative Consolidation Strategies, Assuming 6% Annual
Tuition Rise to Match Income Growth and Maintenance
of 1969–70 Parish Church Level of Effort

	High Cost Strategy (No Consolidation)	Moderate Cost Strategy (Partial Consolidation)	Low Cost Strategy (Full Consolidation)
Deficit per Pupil	$439.55	$307.91	$222.81
Parish Church Subsidy per Pupil	$194.07	$194.07	$194.07
Required State Aid per Pupil	$245.48	$113.84	$ 28.74
If No State Aid Is Provided: Per Cent of Parish Church Revenue Required for Subsidy	125%	87%	68%

NOTE: Parish church subsidy at 55% of revenues ($116,438,968.00).

TABLE 5.19

Required State Aid for Catholic Elementary Schools, Projected to 1980–81
for Alternative Consolidation Strategies, Assuming 6% Annual
Tuition Rise to Match Income Growth and Maintenance
of 1969–70 Parish Church Level of Effort

	High Cost Strategy (No Consolidation)	Moderate Cost Strategy (Partial Consolidation)	Low Cost Strategy (Full Consolidation)
Deficit per Pupil	$985.62	$598.18	$408.03
Parish Church Subsidy per Pupil	$272.42	$272.42	$272.42
Required State Aid per Pupil	$713.20	$325.76	$135.61
If No State Aid Is Provided: Per Cent of Parish Church Revenue Required for Subsidy	199%	121%	82%

NOTE: Parish church subsidy at 55% of revenues ($119,863,644.00).

TABLE 5.20

Required State Aid for Catholic Secondary Schools, Projected to 1975–76
for Alternative Consolidation Strategies, Assuming 6% Annual
Tuition Rise to Match Income Growth and Maintenance
of 1969–70 Central Church Level of Effort

	High Cost Strategy (No Consolidation)	Moderate Cost Strategy (Partial Consolidation)	Low Cost Strategy (Full Consolidation)
Deficit per Pupil	$222.51	$183.24	$103.21
Central Church Subsidy per Pupil	$ 74.46	$ 74.46	$ 74.46
Required State Aid per Pupil	$148.05	$108.78	$ 28.75

NOTE: Since parish churches do not serve as the economic base for Catholic high schools, higher tuitions would have to make up the deficit in the event of no state aid.

TABLE 5.21

Required State Aid for Catholic Secondary Schools, Projected to 1980–81
for Alternative Consolidation Strategies, Assuming 6% Annual
Tuition Rise to Match Income Growth and Maintenance
of 1969–70 Central Church Level of Effort

	High Cost Strategy (No Consolidation)	Moderate Cost Strategy (Partial Consolidation)	Low Cost Strategy (Full Consolidation)
Deficit per Pupil	$894.98	$522.32	$353.49
Central Church Subsidy per Pupil	$ 76.65	$ 76.65	$ 76.65
Required State Aid per Pupil	$818.33	$445.67	$276.84

NOTE: Since parish churches do not serve as the economic base for Catholic high schools, higher tuitions would have to make up the deficit in the event of no state aid.

TABLE 5.22

Required State Aid for Catholic Elementary Schools, Projected to 1975–76 for Alternative Consolidation Strategies, Assuming 12% Annual Tuition Rise and Maintenance of 1969–70 Parish Church Level of Effort

	High Cost Strategy (No Consolidation)	Moderate Cost Strategy (Partial Consolidation)	Low Cost Strategy (Full Consolidation)
Deficit per Pupil	$400.12	$268.48	$183.38
Parish Church Subsidy per Pupil	$194.07	$194.07	$194.07
Required State Aid per Pupil	$206.05	$ 74.41	$ 0.00
If No State Aid is Provided: Per cent of Parish Church Revenue Required for Subsidy	113%	76%	52%

NOTE: Parish church subsidy at 55% of revenues ($116,438,968.00).

TABLE 5.23

Required State Aid for Catholic Elementary Schools, Projected to 1980–81 for Alternative Consolidation Strategies, Assuming 12% Annual Tuition Rise and Maintenance of 1969–70 Parish Church Level of Support

	High Cost Strategy (No Consolidation)	Moderate Cost Strategy (Partial Consolidation)	Low Cost Strategy (Full Consolidation)
Deficit per Pupil	$873.42	$485.98	$295.83
Parish Church Subsidy per Pupil	$272.42	$272.42	$272.42
Required State Aid per Pupil	$601.00	$213.56	$ 23.41
If no State Aid is Provided: Per cent of Parish Church Revenue Required for Subsidy	176%	98%	60%

NOTE: Parish church subsidy at 55% of revenues ($119,863,644.00).

religious-order teachers. This optimum economic situation was used in all cost projections which entail staff reductions, although obviously it may be unattainable in many cases.

Considering the potential declines in enrollment, an attempt to keep all

TABLE 5.24

Required State Aid for Catholic Secondary Schools Projected to 1975–76 for
Alternative Consolidation Strategies, Assuming 12% Annual Tuition Rise
and Maintenance of 1969–70 Central Church Level of Effort

	High Cost Strategy (No Consolidation)	Moderate Cost Strategy (Partial Consolidation)	Low Cost Strategy (Full Consolidation)
Deficit per Pupil	$21.49	$17.78[a]	$97.81[a]
Central Church Subsidy per Pupil	$74.46	$ 0.00	$ 0.00
Required State Aid per Pupil	$ 0.00	$ 0.00	$ 0.00

[a] Surplus

schools open would cause an uneconomic lowering of pupil/teacher ratios.
Without school consolidation, it is impossible to maintain current pupil/
teacher ratios because of limitations within each school. This is particularly true of elementary schools where one teacher teaches the same class
all day and where, often, only one class exists for each grade level. In the
face of enrollment declines, school consolidations would permit the main-

TABLE 5.25

Required State Aid for Catholic Secondary Schools Projected to 1980–81 for
Alternative Consolidation Strategies, Assuming 12% Annual Tuition Rise
and Maintenance of 1969–70 Central Church Level of Effort

	High Cost Strategy (No Consolidation)	Moderate Cost Strategy (Partial Consolidation)	Low Cost Strategy (Full Consolidation)
Deficit per Pupil	$322.93	$49.73[a]	$218.56[a]
Central Church Subsidy per Pupil	$ 76.65	$ 0.00	$ 0.00
Required State Aid per Pupil	$246.28	$ 0.00	$ 0.00

[a] Surplus
NOTE: Since parish churches do not serve as the economic base for Catholic high schools,
higher tuitions would have to make up for the deficit in the event of no state aid under the
high cost strategy.

tenance at each grade level of at least one class of present size so that the size of the faculty can be reduced.

REVENUES   Data on parish church finances show that prime survey area revenues have begun to level off. At present the parish church devotes 55 per cent of its revenues to subsidizing its elementary school, and it is assumed that no larger proportion of church revenues would be devoted to the schools. The decision to hold parish church subsidies at a constant level of effort was based on the contention of the Catholic leaders that rising costs for other services provided by churches will not permit higher levels of church subsidy for the schools.*

Two sets of assumptions are used in projecting tuitions. The first holds the level of effort constant on tuitions, increasing them at six per cent per year compounded annually to match the assumed growth in family income.** The second increases the level of effort by compounding tuition annually by 12 per cent.

The decision to hold levels of tuition constant for one set of projections was based on the contention of Catholic Church leaders that families cannot afford to pay more and that tuition increases will drive even more children out of the schools than forecast in this chapter.

The alternate projection, which assumes an increased level of tuition effort, would naturally reduce the size of the deficit. This assumption has been tested to determine what deficits might be under a requirement imposed either by state action or by church action to increase tuition.

Expenses not covered by tuition income are supplemented by the projected amounts contributed by as parish church subsidies in each of the models. The remaining deficit would have to be made up by state aid, additional increases in tuitions, an increase in the percentage of parish church revenues devoted to school subsidy, or any combination thereof.

Assuming a constant level of tuition effort first, an examination of the size of the deficits for the three strategies clarifies the impact of alternative policies. Deficits could be reduced or, in some cases, eliminated by imposing a higher tuition scale, as Table 5.17 demonstrates.

STATE AID   The amount of aid necessary to cover school deficits would obviously vary with the strategy selected. The projections in Tables 5.18–5.25 should be examined with special attention to the potential burden that could be imposed upon the state by the choices of the Catholic Church leadership.

---

* Parish-church revenues for 1975 were projected at 102 per cent of 1970 and for 1980 at 105 per cent of 1970 revenues.
** This figure is derived from the Gary Report and is more optimistic than would be the projections of family income based upon total state personal income estimates shown in Chapter 2 and Appendix 2F.

The required state aid noted in the projections is for cash payments and does not include the more than $50 million now provided in state categorical aid such as busing and textbook loans.

If no additional state aid were forthcoming, that amount designated as required state aid in each projection would probably be shifted to the school family in the form of higher tuition. There would be no alternative to raising tuitions under the High Cost Strategy because sufficient parish-church revenues would simply not be available. By 1975, 125 per cent of the projected parish-church revenues would be needed to meet the deficits under the High Cost Strategy. Even under the Moderate Cost Strategy, assuming no state aid or compensating increases in tuition, all parish church revenues would go to the schools by 1980, leaving nothing for other church activities.

A policy of keeping all schools open would make the schools extraordinarily dependent on ever increasing amounts of state aid. The state would become the guarantor of solvency. The High Cost Strategy could stretch Catholic school resources so thin that the capital expenditures required to adapt to population shifts might not be available. School and class size could decline to such uneconomic levels that tuitions would skyrocket if there were any unexpected expenditures not covered by state aid or parish church subsidies.

The calculations of the actual cost to the state of aid to nonpublic schools use the Catholic schools as a standard. But any aid provided would probably be distributed to all nonpublic schools. The cost of aid then becomes the per-pupil aid allotment, multiplied by the predicted total nonpublic enrollment.

Moreover, none of these projections has taken account of capital costs. Only operating costs have been included in the calculations. A strategy that would seek to keep all existing schools open would require an estimated $480 million through 1980 for replacement of buildings and major renovations. Although capital costs would be incurred under the Moderate and Low Cost Strategies, use of most of the schools built before 1920—approximately 270 in number—would presumably be phased out and only limited new construction and renovation would be required. Without knowing which schools would be kept open and which closed, we cannot estimate capital expenditures required under the other strategies. If the assumptions on limitations of parish church revenues and the ability to pay tuitions are granted, the ability of the New York Catholic Church to carry out the High Cost Strategy is made even more doubtful by the attendant capital expenditures.

A tragic waste of educational resources could occur if the state provides aid at the level of the Moderate Cost Strategy, while Catholic Church action incurs costs at the level of the High Cost Strategy. None of the consequences that the aid sought to forestall would be affected. In fact, it would be less expensive for the state to absorb Catholic school transfers into the public school system in a transition operation than to provide aid at the level required by the High Cost Strategy.

BARRIERS TO CHANGE   For 1971–72, the state allocated $20.8 million for direct payments to Catholic schools under Mandated Services Act programs. Of course, state aid, assuming its constitutionality, would have to increase annually to keep pace with rising costs. But even assuming that such a level of aid could be sustained by the state, the likelihood that the Catholic Church leadership could successfully implement a consolidation of schools is remote.

Attempts to implement an alternative policy to the present High Cost Strategy may appear to some as defeatism and retrenchment. Public knowledge of the projected enrollment declines and financial deficits in the Catholic schools may lead to a fear of a collapse. Accelerated school closings, even for reasons of consolidation, might seem to confirm these fears. If not properly prepared, discouraged parents might hesitate to enroll their children in schools whose chances of survival seem dim.

As long as enrollment declines are blamed primarily upon tuition increases, and additional state aid is considered to be the only solution, school closings will be viewed with extreme distaste. If this perspective is not altered, all flexibility could be lost. A breaking point could arrive when massive school closings would be required within a short span of time without adequate planning or preparation.

There are also genuine institutional barriers to change within the Catholic Church which will make the task of consolidation quite difficult. The Catholic school group is fiscally and administratively decentralized, and bound by strong traditions of local parish-church autonomy. The overwhelming majority of Catholic schools are totally dependent on the voluntary support of the parishioners of each parish church.

Often the Catholic Church, and consequently the Catholic schools, are thought to be part of a monolithic structure in which the Cardinal Archbishop of New York can issue an order throughout the state and have it executed by priests, nuns, brothers and the Catholic laity. Such a view is a staggering misconception.

The religious orders which staff the schools are financially independent and are not subject to control by the local bishop. His only leverage is to ask the order to stop teaching in his diocese. With an increasing scarcity of religious-order teachers, this is not a request that is often made. Tradition gives the pastor of a local parish great autonomy.

If the Legislature decides to authorize additional dollar aid from the state, we suggest that such aid should be conditioned on the adoption of policies which will render Catholic schools economically viable. First and foremost, this requires a master plan for consolidation of schools to curb the decline in pupil/teacher ratios and consequent escalation of costs. Secondly, while the percentage of parish-church revenues now channeled to finance the schools (55 per cent) is probably stretched to its limit, rates of voluntary parish church contributions might be raised. Thirdly, redistribution mechanisms might be introduced to facilitate the transfer of funds from rich parishes to poor ones. No such mechanisms currently exist. Finally, tuitions ought to be raised in a number of schools. This is especially true at the high school level where there are more applicants than there are spaces available.

Other Nonpublic Schools

The levels of tuitions in other nonpublic schools are already relatively high. Elementary school tuitions average $381 for Jewish, $567 for other sectarian and $1,388 for nonsectarian schools. Some of these school groups may draw from families of higher socio-economic brackets who may have a greater ability to pay. Without adequate family income and attitudinal data, we are not able to calculate the point at which tuition levels might become an operative barrier to growth.

There appears to be no present threat to the survival of these schools. Enrollment forecasts show a 7.8 per cent growth in Jewish Day Schools and 12.1 per cent decline in other sectarian and nonsectarian schools. The rises in cost which will occur are subject primarily to the general inflationary trends of the economy. This has been projected over the decade to be six per cent compounded annually. Tuitions were also projected to increase at six per cent compounded annually, which would match increases in family income. If the same level of parental effort to cover costs is maintained, tuitions for these other nonpublic school groups will be extremely high. They are undoubtedly already a burden for many families. (Table 5.26.)

TABLE 5.26

Jewish, Other Sectarian and Nonsectarian School Operating Costs and Tuitions per Pupil Projected to 1980–81

	1969–70		1980–81	
	Cost	Tuition	Cost	Tuition
JEWISH				
Elementary (K–8)	$ 701	$ 391	$1,331	$ 742
Secondary (9–12)	845	502	1,604	953
OTHER SECTARIAN				
Elementary (K–8)	639	567	1,213	1,076
Secondary (9–12)	1,472	1,394	2,794	2,646
NONSECTARIAN				
Elementary (K–8)	1,768	1,388	3,356	2,635
Secondary (9–12)	2,234	1,993	4,241	3,783

If the state should choose to grant substantial additional aid to nonpublic schools, changes in population trends and in educational choices of Catholic parents will nonetheless mean unavoidable costs to the state. Even state aid at a level that would eliminate all tuitions in Catholic schools would probably not halt the 55 per cent enrollment decline forecast for Catholic schools.

If, however, the recommendations of this report are adopted and the state does not choose to grant substantial dollar aid to nonpublic schools, or if such aid should be constitutionally barred, the number of transfer students to the public schools is likely to increase. If tuitions are increased at an extraordinarily high rate, enrollment declines would exceed the 55 per cent that is forecast.* The state will, in any event, have to provide funds to meet the expenses of local public school districts faced with an additional influx of nonpublic school students. "Influx aid" would include funds for hiring teachers, new construction and rental of temporary facilities.

Under a policy of no direct aid to nonpublic schools or to parents, student influx aid would amount to an additional $960 million above unavoidable costs for operating expenses and $352 million for construction for the period through 1980. This influx aid would be approximately $415 million less than the amount of money necessary to aid the Catholic schools under present strategies of no consolidation. The influx aid would be $372 million more than aid to Catholic schools over the decade under a policy of reasonable consolidation.

These estimates include costs at the state level for interest and principal on school building bonds and for state aid to local school districts for operating expenses. They also include the local school district costs for interest and principal on school building bonds. The operating costs at each level will be far more substantial than the construction costs. Estimates of capital costs, however, do not take into account the possible purchase or lease of nonpublic school facilities by the state, as opposed to construction of new facilities.

As pointed out above, even a clear-cut decision by the Catholic Church leadership to close a major portion of Catholic schools will not mean in the foreseeable future a total, 100 per cent collapse of the Catholic educational system. Some parishioners, particularly the affluent, would probably not allow this to happen. They would sustain whatever increases in tuition were necessary, or reopen some schools under their own auspices.

Some Catholic schools, such as those operated independently by religious orders, would not be affected by a decision to phase down. A de-

---

* It should be noted, however, that the closing of a Catholic school does not automatically mean the transfer of all its pupils to public schools. In Buffalo recently, ten Catholic schools were closed down; at the same time it was announced that all pupils could be accommodated in other diocesan schools.

cision to close schools would affect 1,027 parish, interparish and regional (diocesan) elementary schools and the 122 regional (diocesan) high schools. There are 110 high schools owned and operated independently by religious orders and only 41 independently owned and Catholic-operated elementary schools. Thus, a 70 per cent effective phase-down at the elementary school level and a 50 per cent effective phase-down at the secondary level have been assumed. These students would then have to be absorbed into the public school system. As few as 154,500 elementary school students might be enrolled in Catholic schools by 1980–81 under the phase-down projection.

It is highly unlikely that massive school closings would take place in one year. In calculating the costs to the state of absorbing Catholic school students, these transfers have been spread over an eight-year period to the end of the decade. The costs to the state under these projections should be considered at a minimal level. It is assumed that a residual interest in Catholic schools, particularly at the high school level, will remain. If a panic response occurs, the costs to the state could escalate and turn a phase-down effort into a collapse. While this would not constitute a 100 per cent collapse, it might approach it.

Also incorporated into phase-down projections is the general enrollment decline which the public system will be experiencing as a result of falling birthrates. This will affect the public elementary enrollment throughout the decade and public high school enrollment toward the end of the decade.

TABLE 5.27

Racial/Ethnic Characteristics of Students (K–12) in Public, Nonpublic, Catholic and Total State Enrollment, 1969–70

	Public		Nonpublic		Catholic		Total State	
	Number	%	Number	%	Number	%	Number	%
Black	520,487	15.1	41,723	5.1	30,238	4.4	562,210	13.2
Spanish-Surnamed	291,610	8.4	50,235	6.1	47,446	6.9	341,845	8.0
Other Minority[a]	26,355	0.8	4,111	0.5	1,538[b]	0.2	30,466	0.7
White	2,615,535	75.7	725,294	88.3	608,883	88.5	3,340,829	78.1
Total	3,453,987	100.0	821,363	100.0	688,105	100.0	4,275,350	100.0

[a] Includes American Indian and Oriental American, unless otherwise specified.
[b] Catholic figures in this table do not include Oriental American.

In a majority of districts, Catholic school transfers could be absorbed with-out enrollment ever reaching the point where new public school construction would be required.

RACIAL AND ETHNIC COMPOSITION

On a statewide basis, nonpublic school enrollment does not include minority groups in proportion to their numbers in the state. The nonpublic sector has an 11.7 per cent minority-group enrollment compared to 21.9 per cent in the total public and nonpublic enrollment. (Table 5.27.) We suggest that steps by all nonpublic schools to correct this imbalance ought in any event to be a condition of any increased state aid which may be granted.

Since there is a great variation among Catholic, Jewish day schools, other sectarian schools and nonsectarian schools, each category is reviewed separately to determine where minority students—black, Spanish-surnamed and Other Minority*—are enrolled.

CATHOLIC SCHOOLS Catholic elementary and secondary enrollment is composed of 4.4 per cent black, 6.9 per cent Spanish-surnamed, 0.2 per cent American Indian and 88.5 per cent white. (Table 5.23.)

Obviously, the proportion of any given minority group which is Catholic will have a direct effect on minority enrollment in Catholic schools. Black Catholics are not numerous; less than 2 per cent of American Catholics are black. Non-Catholics in Catholic elementary schools in New York State represent 2.5 per cent of the enrollment, and of these, 68.8 per cent are black. Also, one-third of the blacks enrolled in Catholic schools are non-Catholics.

In contrast to the black category, the Spanish-surnamed category includes families from Puerto Rico, Cuba and Central and South America, where Catholicism is the major religion. Only 1.2 per cent of the Spanish-surnamed students in Catholic schools are non-Catholic. One possible explanation for the relative scarcity of Spanish-surnamed students in Catholic schools is that more families with Spanish surnames are represented among the lower economic strata than are other minorities and they cannot afford even modest tuitions.

Aggregate integration figures on Catholic schools can be misleading. Catholic high schools enroll significantly fewer minority students than do the elementary schools: 6.1 per cent in the high schools compared to 13.0 per cent in the elementary schools. Aggregate minority enrollment in the high schools is about 150,000, and in the elementary schools 535,000.

Two factors help to explain the lower minority-group enrollment in the secondary schools: relatively high tuition and academic selectivity. The

---

* Other Minority includes American Indian and Oriental American, unless otherwise specified.

average tuition for secondary schools, $317, is more than six times the average for elementary schools. Moreover, in general, "private" Catholic schools—those owned and operated entirely by religious orders and unrelated to a local parish church—draw from higher-income-level families and often charge tuition of $1,500 annually. Most of these schools are high schools.

Admission to the high schools is selective. There are about five applications for each place at the less expensive regional (diocesan) high schools. For all private Catholic high schools (those operated by a religious order) in 1971, some 16,187 students took the qualifying admission exam in the New York City area, and 80 per cent were admitted. Since minority-group members frequently come from economically and educationally disadvantaged backgrounds, the tuition and the academic selectivity screen out many potential minority-group candidates. Because Catholic elementary schools are the primary feeders for the high schools, the pool of minority-group students is low to begin with. No recruiting takes place in the public schools.

In New York City, minorities make up 48.2 per cent of the total enrollment and 22.9 per cent of the Catholic school enrollment. Blacks comprise 26.4 per cent of the city's total enrollment, and 7.4 per cent of the Catholic school enrollment. For Spanish-surnamed students, the figures are 20.5 per cent for New York City and 14.5 per cent for the Catholic schools. (Table 5.28.)

Integration within Catholic Schools: About one-half of the students in Catholic schools attend all-white schools—that is, schools 99–100 per cent white. About one-half of the black and Spanish-surnamed students enrolled in Catholic schools are in schools with a nearly equal balance between minority and white students. Over 80 per cent of elementary and secondary students attend Catholic schools that are 80–100 per cent white; 50.7 per

TABLE 5.28

Racial/Ethnic Characteristics of New York City Catholic School Enrollments (K–12), 1969–70

	Catholic		Total Public and Nonpublic	
	Number	*%*	*Number*	*%*
Black	20,123	7.4	407,431	26.4
Spanish-Surnamed	39,348	14.5	315,186	20.5
Other Minority	1,288	0.5	20,792	1.3
White	211,203	77.7	797,114	51.7
Total	271,962	100.1	1,540,523	99.9

cent of elementary and 37.8 per cent of secondary school students attend all-white schools.

State educational policy concerns itself with staff integration as well as integration in the student body. The characteristics of the teacher population are an integral part of the educational environment. The percentage of minority-group teachers is important in the education process, especially as it affects the self-image of minority-group students. Fewer than one per cent of classroom teachers in Catholic schools are black. Public schools are also minimally integrated at the staff level, but Catholic schools have even a smaller percentage of black and Spanish-surnamed teachers.

OTHER NONPUBLIC SCHOOLS   With the exception of Jewish schools, other sectarian schools appear to be well integrated, particularly with respect to black students. However, since there is no breakdown for the racial and ethnic compositions of individual denominations, it is possible that some denominations with extraordinarily high concentrations of black members still maintain racially isolated schools. (Table 5.29.)

In Jewish Day Schools, minority-group students account for less than one per cent of the enrollment. However, it is important to place such statistics in the context of the very special religious orientation of these schools. The Orthodox Jewish community, which sponsors 93 per cent of the Jewish Day Schools, is a small minority of the Jewish community at large. An applicant must be Jewish to be admitted to a Jewish Day School.

Nonsectarian schools as a group have a minority-group enrollment of 14 per cent. The 98 nonsectarian schools which are members of the New York State Association of Independent Schools (NYSAIS) and come closest to the image of the Eastern preparatory school, have only 4.5 per cent minority enrollment. Since these schools by definition do not exercise religious preferences, religious affiliation is not a constraint against fuller integration.

TABLE 5.29

Racial/Ethnic Characteristics of Students in Jewish, Other Sectarian and Nonsectarian Schools (K–12), 1969–70

	Total Jewish	Total Other Sectarian	Total Nonsectarian
Black	0.2%	18.8%	10.7%
Spanish-Surnamed	0.1	2.2	2.3
Other Minority	0.1	1.1	1.0
White	99.6	77.9	85.9
Total	100.0%	100.0%	99.9%

A majority of this Commission have come to the conclusion, based on our economic analysis, that because of rising costs in nonpublic schools an increase in public spending for education is inevitable, whether large amounts, moderate amounts or no amounts of state aid are provided. This increase will be required in order to help pay for the education of children in nonpublic schools or to pay for their absorption into the public school system. We repeat that a gradual but steady decline in nonpublic school enrollment is forecast, whether or not large amounts of state aid are provided. That is, in addition to any state aid that might help to maintain the nonpublic schools, additional public expenditures will be required to educate children who will either transfer from, or not enroll in, nonpublic schools.

We have stated why we believe that increased public funds should not be used in support of nonpublic education. Consistent with this recommendation, we endorse appropriate legislative efforts to cushion the impact of any enrollment transitions from nonpublic to public schools. Special provision should be made for districts which may be suddenly burdened as a result of nonpublic school closings. Any available nonpublic school facilities should, where feasible, be bought or leased in preference to construction of new schools, and usable equipment no longer needed in nonpublic schools should be acquired. These and similar measures, as a part of an over-all and consistent program to deal with declining nonpublic school enrollments, would serve to ensure that the public school system could cope with this occurrence in an orderly manner and emerge strengthened, rather than weakened, as a result of the enrollment influx.

CONSTANCE E. COOK
D. CLINTON DOMINICK III
ALAN A. FLANS
CHARLES FRANKEL
MANLY FLEISCHMANN
PHYLLIS A. HARRISON
H. THOMAS JAMES
FRANCIS KEPPEL
DOROTHY LEVITT
LLOYD N. MORRISETT
JAMES F. OATES, JR.
ARTHUR E. SUTHERLAND
FRANKLIN H. WILLIAMS

Quality Education for All Children: The Case for Continued Aid to Nonpublic Education

PREAMBLE

Approximately two years ago this Commission was given the responsibility by Governor Rockefeller and the Board of Regents to explore the relationship between the state and its nonpublic school pupils. Specifically, that charge stated:

> What should be the proper role of the state regarding the financial needs of nonpublic schools, particularly those serving disadvantaged neighborhoods?

This charge has not been fulfilled. The authors of the no-aid statement never really explored or responded to the specific charge to the Commission. In fact, they entirely ignored the latter part of that directive regarding disadvantaged neighborhoods. The recommendations of Commissioners Cook, Dominick, Flans, Frankel, Fleischmann, Harrison, James, Keppel, Levitt, Morrisett, Oates, Sutherland and Williams clearly oppose any *additional* aid to nonpublic education. On the basis of their arguments it would follow that they are equally opposed to existing apportionment programs or whatever substitutes might be enacted by the Legislature. The no-aid advocates may feel comfortable in saying that they make no recommendation on existing nonpublic aid programs, but it is clear from their presentation that they would prefer their elimination. Therefore, the real question is: Should government provide aid to nonpublic education? Our response is yes.

The opposition opinion would preclude aid payments to nonpublic education because, in their language, "The decision of the United States Supreme Court in the *Lemon* case is controlling and binding on the states." However, in a more sweeping statement which reflects more of an intransigent attitude than a constitutional interpretation, the no-aid advocates state:

The principle of separation of church and state should not be abrogated: public funds or tax revenues ought not to be used in support of the attendance of students at sectarian schools. This would be our view even if the First and Fourteenth Amendments to the United States Constitution and Article XI, Section 3 of the New York State Constitution (the "Blaine Amendment") were to be repealed, modified or judicially construed so as to permit such support.*

In substance this argument attempts to superimpose the aura of a constitutional interpretation on what is really a tenaciously held private opinion. *We, Commissioners Raymond R. Corbett, Virginia M. Kopp, Thomas L. Laverne, George S. Moore and Edward J. Mortola, wish to disassociate ourselves from this statement and reaffirm publicly our support for the proposition that financial aid can be rendered by New York State to the children in nonpublic schools in a constitutional and legal manner.*

We believe our opinions are shared by a majority of the general population. We believe that the financial support of nonpublic education is vital if we are to protect the cherished concepts of individual rights and quality public education. We shall present evidence to sustain our position and we shall rely for support upon the research contained in the document officially authorized by this Commission to study this matter: Louis R. Gary, *The Collapse of Nonpublic Education: Rumor or Reality?* (the "Gary Report"). We believe that the authors of the opposition report have misinterpreted the facts contained in the Gary Report. In our judgment the following fundamental premises unmistakably emerge from that report:

1. It is in the public interest that nonpublic education survive.
2. Unless financial aid from government sources is continued, enrollment in the nonpublic sector will precipitously decline and jeopardize quality education for all children.

Therefore, we must conclude that the goal of quality education for all children can be best pursued by continuing financial aid to nonpublic education.

To those who would sincerely challenge our position on constitutional grounds, we reply only that it is our belief as lawyers, educators, labor leaders and business executives that the Constitutions of the State of New York and the United States of America do permit aid to nonpublic education in one form or another. The constitutionality of vouchers,** parent-aid payments, tax credits, and other tuition relief programs has yet to be deter-

---

* The second sentence of this paragraph was in all previous drafts but was deleted in the final copy. (See page 389.)
** Vouchers may be defined as forms presented by the parent to a public or nonpublic school; they represent a commitment of a government to pay its share of the cost of the pupil's education.

mined and we are convinced that at least one of these, if not all, will be upheld by the Supreme Court of the United States. We find strong precedent for governmental support of secular activities of religious organizations in such areas as higher education, social welfare, hospital care, and the treatment and education of handicapped pupils.

We also find it highly unusual that the authors of the opposition report, who were given the specific responsibility to explore all viewpoints on aid to nonpublic schools, have chosen to support their recommendation against any such aid with a legal brief (Appendix 5A). Accordingly, we now find it necessary to submit a legal brief, attached as Appendix 5B to this chapter, in support of such aid.

The reader will note in the pages that follow a significant number of references to Catholic schools and Catholic education. Again, we believe it unfortunate that the no-aid proponents gave so little attention to the total spectrum of nonpublic education and instead concentrated on Catholic schools when responding to the Governor's mandate to explore the needs of all nonpublic education. Thus, if we are to present a meaningful analysis, we must confront these arguments even when they are narrowly based.

It is our intention to comment only on major issues, philosophy and questions, though we realize many points of lesser significance could be added.

PUBLIC SUPPORT FOR POSITION OF AID

Our conviction that aid can be constitutionally offered to meet the needs of nonpublic education has substantial and renowned support.

The President of the United States, Richard M. Nixon, recognizing the crisis in nonpublic education, has affirmed the necessity for governmental assistance on many occasions and as recently as August, 1971.[5] His predecessor, of a different political affiliation, President Lyndon B. Johnson, pioneered governmental aid for children in nonpublic schools by signing into law the monumental Elementary and Secondary Education Act of 1965.

In addition, elected representatives of the people of New York State have overwhelmingly supported nonpublic aid. Once again this support has always been bi-partisan. Governor Nelson A. Rockefeller has supported aid measures designed to provide financial assistance to nonpublic education. In his State of the State Message on January 18, 1972, the Governor re-affirmed his support by saying:

> . . . the Federal courts have just struck down last year's legislation to provide aid for secular teaching in the nonpublic schools. I am confident, however, that we can find a constitutionally acceptable way to provide the badly needed assistance. Without it the nonpublic school system could collapse, adding up to 700,000 students to the public school system.

Among legislative leadership, Senate Majority Leader Earl W. Brydges and Assembly Speaker Perry B. Duryea were joined in support of aid measures by the minority leaders in both Houses, Senator Joseph Zaretzki and Assemblyman Stanley Steingut. Furthermore, the aid proposals, which passed both Houses with overwhelming majorities, cut across political party lines.

National surveys indicate that the people of the United States are more in favor of such aid to nonpublic education than against it. The Second Annual Survey of Public Schools 1970, sponsored by CFK Ltd. (Charles F. Kettering) and Gallup International, showed that 48 per cent of those polled were in favor of aid to nonpublic schools, 44 per cent were against, and the remainder were undecided. Even more significant is that young people, high school juniors and seniors, ran up a convincing 56 per cent in favor of aid.

In addition, we find our position consistent with the highest educational policy-making board in New York State—the Board of Regents. We note an absence of any reference by those opposing aid to the position adopted by a vote of 11–3 on May 27, 1971, by the Board of Regents of the University of the State of New York. The no-aid advocates have totally ignored one of the clearest and most responsible expressions of government's relationship to nonpublic schools on the matter of aid; we feel that the following excerpt from the Regents' statement must be included within the body of this report:

The private and parochial schools now find themselves in a critical fiscal plight and have turned to public sources for support beyond that already available.

The advantages of diversity in the educational enterprise of the State must be reconciled with the goal of equal educational opportunity and this constitutes a major consideration in the enactment of legislation to aid secular instruction in nonpublic schools.

The question is thus presented: to what extent, and under what conditions, should the State contribute funds to protect diversity and make viable the right of parents to choose nonpublic schools for the education of their children?

The Regents believe that for these purposes additional financial aid is required and will support legislative proposals in harmony with the following principles: such legislation should not jeopardize the welfare, stability, and adequate support of the public schools.

Such legislation should be effective in providing meaningful opportunities to children of lower income families, who, of all groups, have the least options in determining when and where their children are to be educated, as well as to middle-income families who are feeling the economic pinch of higher tuition cost.

The support of nonpublic education must be sufficient to maintain a pluralistic system adequate in quality and economical in operation but not so extensive as to jeopardize the independence of the nonpublic school or dry up sources of private and philanthropic support or encourage organization of new schools with the purpose or effect of increasing racial separatism.

Such legislation should require accountability for public funds received, should contain safeguards against increasing racial and social class isolation in the nonpublic schools, should insure against use of public funds for any sectarian purpose or function and that admission policies be nondiscriminatory except where permitted by law on the basis of creed.

All nonpublic schools receiving public funds must be required to meet standards of quality prescribed by public authority but the State should be involved as little as possible in the operation of nonpublic schools.

Finally such legislation must conform to the principles of constitutionality already enunciated by the courts or have reasonable prospect of being approved by the courts in the event of a challenge to its constitutional validity.[6]

We fully support the position and the principles of aid formally adopted by the Board of Regents and assert that their resolution should provide the guidelines for determining educational policy.

After an extensive and scholarly study on nonpublic schools, financed by the Commission, Louis R. Gary, the author, concludes:

The Governor and the Legislature, by their enactment of major programs of aid, have demonstrated their support for nonpublic education. The Regents have consistently and emphatically endorsed the value of nonpublic schools in the State's educational system. *This Report has found no evidence that would undermine the high value placed on nonpublic education by the Regents.*[7] [Emphasis ours.]

EMPIRICAL JUSTIFICATION FOR STATE ASSISTANCE

The validity of aid for the education of children in nonpublic institutions does not and should not rest simply on support from public, political and educational authorities for its justification. We believe the protection of individual rights and the pursuit of a policy consistent with the public good are the fundamental responsibilities of a democratic society. We, therefore, wish to present a development of the principles which support our position.

Protection of Parental and Individual Rights

According to the no-aid advocates, government's relationship with nonpublic education should be circumscribed by the constitutional prohibition of direct aid of any type, by restriction of all state educational resources to public school children only, and by sufferance solely of those programs previously declared legitimate by the courts (transportation, textbooks, etc.).

This view totally overlooks parental rights in the education of their children and indeed the individual rights of those children.

In the well-known U.S. Supreme Court *Pierce* decision, the rights of parents in the education of their children were constitutionally recognized and guaranteed.[8] The Court held that the state could not pass a law which would deny parents the right to send their children to schools of their choice other than public. Government cannot, therefore, pass a law which would directly abrogate or hinder the right and freedom of paternal choice in the education of children. But should government do so indirectly? Should government contribute to hindering that right by failing to act? Would a person really possess that right if it became impossible to exercise it freely?

As the cost of education continues to rise, the opportunity of exercising that right will become diminished and eventually restricted to the affluent and elite. Indeed the Gary Report states:

> But if tuitions experience extraordinarily high rates of increase, enrollments could fall far beyond the 55% decline forecast for Catholic schools in 1980. Such increases in tuitions would undoubtedly influence the socio-economic composition of the student body and could turn a mass system into an elitist system.[9]

It is interesting to note that those opposing aid recognize the future necessity of increasing tuitions if the nonpublic schools are to remain in existence. In assigning a low priority to the levels of tuition, as a significant factor in parental choice, we can only wonder whether the authors of the no-aid chapter were aware that the tuition level in the Brooklyn diocesan high schools has already reached $700 per pupil.*

It is our view that the state cannot remain neutral where non-action, no funding, would diminish the reasonable availabilities of freedom of choice in education. Those opposing aid indicated that the right of freedom of choice is not being diminished. They state that parents are simply unwilling to pay for nonpublic education and are in fact opting for the secular environment of the public school. According to this view, tuition increases are supposedly not an economic factor, but rather a psychological one.

We believe that such a viewpoint is a misreading of the Gary Report which notes that tuition, although not a significant factor in the past, could become a controlling factor due to skyrocketing costs. In fact, the Gary Report notes that even under the most *optimistic* conditions elementary tuition levels will exceed $250 per pupil by the end of this decade if state aid is withheld.[10]

Granting that declining birthrates will diminish the total school-age population, and even granting that many parents will select schools other than religious schools, we cannot accept the claim of only a casual relationship between enrollments and tuitions. Indeed, we read in the opposition report itself:

---

* Lower tuition cited in the Gary Report was for 1969–70 and as noted in the Report tuitions have already begun to escalate sharply.

Assuming that aid is held at the present level or decreased, transfers of children from nonpublic to public schools will unquestionably be accelerated, although we do not expect an early or total demise of the Catholic or other nonpublic school system.

Therefore, we are forced by both research and reason to conclude that the absence of financial assistance will increase the tuition impact and accelerate enrollment decline.

Further, it should be apparent that tuition costs are assessed against the marginal income of parents. This means that tuition is paid from whatever remains after the basic necessities of food, shelter, clothing and utilities are paid. Moreover, as taxes for the support of public education and other services escalate, and as inflation continues, the wage earner's income is seriously reduced. This is particularly true with regard to the blue collar and lower income white collar workers who comprise the majority constituency in nonpublic schools.

It is most significant that the Gary Report indicates that these families cannot afford the massive tuition increases that will be required if state aid is discontinued:

> The limited information available shows that Catholic school families are not generally from high socio-economic levels. The latest data available (1967) showed that Catholic elementary school families in New York City had a median income of approximately $7,200. The median income for all city families for that year was estimated at $7,468. It might also be noted that tuition in New York City averages about 30% higher than the state-wide average.[11]

We believe that current social and economic factors will cause the cost of education to increase; tuition costs will increase accordingly and, failing any type of aid program, will increase most evidently and drastically. The resulting effects would decimate nonpublic school enrollment.

The impact of rising tuition levels, spiraling inflation and the threatened cut-off of state aid on parental decision-making should not be minimized. We submit that there are limitations on the quality and quantity of hope. State aid to nonpublic education is the last great expectation of supporters of nonpublic schools. To the extent that that expectation is diminished or made less viable, parental decision-making will be adversely affected. Decision-making cannot be sustained on empty promises. Again we summarize with a quote from the Gary Report:

> Discouraging trends in enrollment and tuitions, coupled with the knowledge that state dollar aid may be barred, could accelerate the school closings and enrollment declines.[12]

Regrettably, we must conclude that if aid is withdrawn, adverse parental reaction, motivated by the inability to pay, will be swift, and the resulting decline in nonpublic enrollment will be immediate and precipitous. *We view any change of this nature as detrimental to the quality of all education in New York State.*

Public Benefits of Nonpublic Education

The opposition statement has failed to assess in any comprehensive manner the significance of nonpublic education for the general welfare or public good of New York State. Attention and study should have been given to this fundamental question: *Are the existence and operation of nonpublic schools beneficial or detrimental to the best interests of the people of the state?*

We believe them to be beneficial. We believe the following positive findings and assertions to be verification of nonpublic education's immense contribution to our society.

1. *The disadvantaged or inner-city neighborhoods of the larger urban areas of the state have benefited from the presence of nonpublic schools, particularly those related to church or synagogue communities.*

National representatives of six major city, county and state government associations subscribed to the following statement to the President of the United States and the Domestic Affairs Council on December 6, 1971:

> It is important to keep in mind that this aid would almost of necessity have to get to parochial school children because in many cases the parochial schools offer the only haven for stability and order in the inner city.

The Mayor of the City of New York, the Honorable John V. Lindsay, has affirmed in a communication that the parochial schools of New York City "have contributed to the stability of various neighborhoods." [13]

This is also the case for schools of all religious faiths, nonsectarian private schools, independent community schools and store-front academies, which are serving the educationally and economically disadvantaged in special programs.

In the effort to overcome educational and cultural deprivation, nonpublic schools generally make greater contributions of services and resources to their inner-city schools than to their more affluent schools serving the middle class. In the Gary Report, the following observations are recorded:

> The one startling contrast between designated "poverty area" schools and schools not so classified is the ratio of religious order teachers to students. The "poverty area" students have more religious order teachers per students than other schools. Since these teachers are lower-salaried than lay teachers, there is an apparently greater resource allocation to the "poverty area"

schools in non-monetary form, even though expenditures appear equal in dollar amounts. . . .

Religious teachers on the average have higher degree qualifications and longer years of teaching experience than lay teachers. If these teacher characteristics can be said to be an addition to school quality, Catholic schools are allocating greater resources to "poverty area" schools than is apparent from explicit expenditure data.[14]

2. *The existence of nonpublic schools has saved New York taxpayers literally billions of dollars.*

During 1970–71 the 784,058 children in nonpublic schools represented public school expenses exceeding $1.1 billion on the basis of the public school statewide average of $1500 per pupil total expenditures. Estimated state expenditures during the current year of some $100 million including direct and indirect aid for nonpublic school pupils appear a rather small investment for a return of over 1100 per cent. The amount and impact of capital expenditures would be equally significant.

3. *The attendance of children at nonpublic schools at minimal expense to the state has contributed to quality education in the public schools.*

The enrollments in nonpublic schools have reduced the number of children in the public schools, allowing available educational resources to be expended for fewer children. The presumption here is that tax dollars will always be limited to some extent; thus, the fewer the pupils, the more that can be spent on a per-pupil basis in public education. Indeed, in city school districts, property tax revenues are limited by the New York State Constitution. Most of these school districts have little tax margin remaining. Table 5.30 demonstrates the relationship between remaining property tax leeway, the number of nonpublic school children and the local amount that would be available to support an influx of nonpublic students into the public schools.

The Board of Regents in its 1972 Legislative Recommendations discusses the impact of the state's current fiscal crisis on public school education by stating:

The deep fiscal trouble this year and in the coming years puts in grave jeopardy the educational quality we now have. Consider these examples. The City of Poughkeepsie has reached its constitutional tax limit. This school year that district has been forced to cut 83 of the 330 educational professionals. New Rochelle has likewise reached its constitutional tax limit. It has had to cut $1.2 million from its budget this year because of no additional state assistance.[15]

It seems to us appropriate to suggest that the infusion of more than 600 nonpublic students in New Rochelle and nearly 1,800 students in Pough-

TABLE 5.30

Property Tax Revenue Remaining under Constitutional Limits for the Support of Education in Selected Cities[a]

City	1971–72 Property Tax Margin Remaining	1970–71 Nonpublic Enrollment	Amount Available per Pupil at Local Level if All Nonpublic Pupils Were Transferred to Public Schools
Auburn	$ 254,122	1,809	$140.47
Binghamton	175,826	2,770	63.47
Buffalo[b]	5,528,877	33,886	163.16
Jamestown	36,826	703	52.38
New York[b]	1,400,187	411,227	3.40
Niagara Falls	1,118	3,915	.28
Rochester[b]	2,835,858	15,440	183.66
Syracuse[b]	3,798	9,757	.38
Troy	896,628	3,548	252.71
Utica	664,116	5,501	120.72
Yonkers[b]	0	9,997	0

[a] The above city school districts have within their geographic boundaries more than 60 per cent of all nonpublic school pupils in New York State. It is readily demonstrated from the above table that the ability of those school districts to finance even the local share of education costs (average of $750 per pupil) would be well-nigh impossible if these students should transfer in any substantial numbers. In fact, the table demonstrates that even a small number of transfers in certain cities—New York City, Niagara Falls, Syracuse and Yonkers—could constitute financial disaster for these areas.

[b] Tax revenues in Big Five cities are not separated by object of expenditure and such revenue could be used for purposes other than education.

keepsie would aggravate seriously an already difficult situation. If, as the Regents suggest, the quality of public education is inhibited by the current fiscal dilemma, we feel certain that the already threatened quality would be further diluted by even a small infusion of nonpublic school students.

4. *Nonpublic education contributes at a proportionate level with public schools to the development of an educated society.*

Nonpublic schools provide a quality education more than sufficient to meet the state's standards of achievement; and that quality is comparable to the public school results on every measurement instrument or procedure in common use. The Gary Report concluded:

There is not a great difference between the over-all quality of public and non-public education in the State. Those standardized measures that do exist illustrate that the nonpublic sector provides an education which is, at the least, equivalent to that given in public schools. Classroom techniques, curricula and the quality of teachers are, on the average, very similar. There are highly visible experimental and innovative programs in some nonpublic schools, although the over-all system is no more nor less traditional than the public sector.[16]

At the high school level nonpublic schools have an equal or better record on a proportionate basis than public schools in Regents' scholarships, Regents' examinations, and in graduates pursuing post-secondary educational programs.

At the elementary level the Gary Report notes that the Pupil Evaluation Program (PEP) tests in reading and math for grades three and six, administered by the State Education Department, show that:

> Results in the most general form from 1969 show that median scores of students in Roman Catholic schools were somewhat higher in reading and math achievement at grades 3 and 6 than the public school median scores. Children in all other nonpublic schools scored higher in reading and math than Catholic or public school children.[17]

5. *Nonpublic schools can provide "relevant" education for individual student needs.*

Nonpublic schools offer alternative systems to public schools and to one another. Reflecting the value systems of students and parents alike, the nonpublic schools respond to the desires and needs of youth. This is manifest in the recommendations of the 1970 White House Conference on Youth. On page 87 of the Conference report, it is stated:

> During the past few years students have protested the present curriculum in schools and colleges and have cried out for a "relevant" education. For these students a "relevant" education means one which will suit their specific needs. Thus, instruction must become individualized and a large variety of alternative systems of education and forms of presentation, materials, etc. within these systems must be made available. . . .
>
> Implementation: A. Local, state, and Federal governments should significantly increase and continue to fund research and development programs, as well as alternative systems, materials, and such techniques as performance contracting, the voucher system, deferred tuition programs, independent study programs, the Parkway Progress Program and work-study programs, etc. . . . .

6. *Nonpublic schools reflect a pluralistic society.*

We believe the strength of America is found in its unity and that the vitality of this nation springs from its diversity. The blending of this unity and diversity over the last two centuries evidences the success of the

American experiment in democracy. We view nonpublic education as an example of pluralism and we perceive its continuance to be vital to that principle. Again we turn to the Gary Report for an illustration:

> Pluralism is one of the oldest and most cherished values in American society. In education, pluralism exists to provide parental options, models for experimentation and innovation, and competition among schools for students. The constitutional right of a parent to choose the kind of school his child will attend may not be abridged so long as that choice does not exclude other children from equally rich educational opportunities. Pluralism has often been distorted to promote elitism and segregation. In a more positive sense, it has supported efforts to maintain cultural identity for minority groups. No studies indicate that the major groups of nonpublic schools considered in this Report contribute to divisiveness in American life. In fact, the Greeley and Rossi study indicates that if we examine the education of Catholics in Catholic schools:
>
>> "We will find no trace of a 'divisive' effect of Catholic education, nor will control variables produce any such trace. On the contrary, there will be some indication that among the youngest graduates of Catholic schools there is more tolerance rather than less."[18]

A diminution or elimination of aid to nonpublic schools will seriously compromise the principle of pluralism since rising tuition levels would become even more unreachable for all except the wealthy. Again, Gary points out:

> Thus, pluralism is an integral part of the educational system in New York State in that alternatives do exist. The public school system does not have a monopoly on education. However, tuitions for all but the Catholic elementary schools exclude many families from the benefits of the pluralistic system. Poor families, in particular, are limited in their options not only by financial barriers, but by lack of information, access, and availability of alternative educational opportunities. The vast potential which pluralism holds for creating new school types and for offering real parental options has hardly been tapped.[19]

REFUTATION OF MAJOR POINTS OF OPPOSITION REPORT

While it is tempting to engage in a point-by-point rebuttal, it seems best to us to avoid that kind of detailed discussion in this document. Instead we will focus on three major, glaring misinterpretations: the charge of segregation; the charge that the cost of state support for nonpublic education will increase so as to be virtually equal to the level of per-pupil expenditures in the public schools; and the charge that religious favoritism by the state could influence eligibility for education aid.

Opposition recommendation 4 states:

> . . . that in New York the extent of racial segregation in sectarian schools on the whole exceeds that which prevails in the public schools. . . . *We do not feel that we can advocate increased aid to nonpublic schools where the degree of segregation is so acute, while at the same time we would have the public school system devote its attention and resources to relieving the inequities caused by racial imbalance.*

The implication here, and again in a later section of the no-aid chapter, entitled "Racial and Ethnic Composition," is that nonpublic education is segregationist either by intent or omission. Therefore, in comparison with public schools, the conclusion offered appears to be that nonpublic schools are more guilty of segregation.

We cannot believe that it is the intent of the no-aid proponents to imply that the church-related schools are intentionally pursuing a general policy of segregation. The question, then, is: Are nonpublic schools, particularly the Catholic ones, segregating students or actually improving integration in the education of minority groups?

The bare comparison of the percentages of enrollments between nonpublic and public schools is misleading. Additional analysis is necessary and proves more revealing.

First of all, what is the general trend regarding the number of minority students enrolled in nonpublic schools? According to the State Education Department data, in the 1966–67 school year, out of a total population of 771,169 students in Catholic elementary and secondary schools, 3.5 per cent (27,293) were black and 3.5 per cent (26,923) were Spanish-surnamed. According to the same source, in the school year 1970–71, out of the total enrollment of 661,082, 4.6 per cent (30,524) were black and 7.5 per cent (49,598) were Spanish-surnamed. This comparison of enrollment trends is more revealing than the percentage of total enrollments in any one given year. In the period between the school years 1966–67 and 1970–71 total enrollment *declined* by 14.3 per cent. In that same period, however, black enrollment *increased* 11.9 per cent and Spanish-surnamed 45.7 per cent. In that same five-year period in the Catholic schools of the Archdiocese of New York,* the total enrollments declined some 12.6 per cent, with a large portion of this occurring in the suburban and rural counties outside New York City. However, during that same period black enrollments increased 12.8 per cent and Spanish-surnamed 32.6 per cent.

It must be remembered, as the opposition report itself points out, that of

---

* Includes the counties of Bronx, Richmond, New York, Dutchess, Orange, Putnam, Rockland, Sullivan, Ulster and Westchester. This group was used as a prime survey area in the Gary Report.

the black population only some 2 per cent are Catholic. The Gary Report states that of the blacks enrolled in Catholic schools more than one-third are non-Catholic and these non-Catholic families make no contribution to Sunday collections which provide 55 per cent of the total revenue necessary to operate the schools. Therefore, within a tuition-paying system, reinforced from church contributions, the increasing enrollments of minority groups, on first examination, might well be judged liabilities: the enrollments do not bring proportionate revenues either through tuition or through church donations; in addition, the population served is increasingly non-Catholic, and does not advance so-called religious indoctrination objectives. *Yet,* these schools have shown a marked increase in the enrollment of blacks during the five-year period 1966–71. These factors can only reinforce our judgment that Catholic schools are pursuing successful integration policies.

The opposition report points out from the Gary Report, "about one-half of the students in Catholic schools attend all-white schools; that is, schools 99–100 per cent white." No judgment is made as to whether or not this compares significantly with public school desegregation efforts. The State Education Department report entitled *Racial and Ethnic Distribution of Public School Students and Staff in New York State, 1970–71* contains no comparable 99–100 per cent grouping. It was necessary for us to examine individual school district enrollment percentages on a district-by-district basis.

From this research we find some 114 are listed at 100.0 per cent white; 275 more are in the 99.0 to 99.9 per cent range. Thus, more than 50 per cent of the total of 720 major public school districts are either entirely white or over 99 per cent white.

In addition to having failed to analyze adequately the integration efforts on the part of nonpublic schools, the opposition position presents no evidence as to the quality of the education provided to minority groups in the nonpublic schools. Enrollment numbers themselves are insignificant; the degree of integration within the classroom and the school is more indicative of integration; the achievement of the minority pupils must ultimately be the measure of the success or failure of those integration efforts.

OPPOSITION CHARGE—TWO: *The cost of state support for nonpublic education will eventually increase so as to be virtually equal to the level of per-pupil expenditures in the public schools*

Conclusion 3 in the non-aid chapter states:

> Meanwhile, Catholic school enrollment will continue to decline for a variety of reasons, even if state aid were provided at a level which would eliminate the need for all tuition payments. Increased expenditure per pupil will result,

to the point where the difference between public and nonpublic in this regard becomes small or nonexistent, and nonpublic schools will require increasing amounts of money in order to educate their students. Thus, over a period of years, the savings which now accrue to the state because of the existence of nonpublic school systems will greatly diminish as increased amounts of state aid are required to maintain those systems.

The underlying reasoning leading to this conclusion contains certain erroneous assumptions and overlooks other very significant factors:

1. It should be pointed out that even if expenditures in the public and nonpublic sector were to become identical, the cost to the government measured on any basis would not be identical unless one assumes a complete government takeover of *all* education costs in nonpublic schools including those financed from tuition and church contributions. Such an assumption is repudiated by even the Gary Report's most *pessimistic* high cost projection of required state aid per pupil to nonpublic schools. In fact, the Gary Report projects that figure at $713.20 for 1980–81 and this is approximately one-half of the cost of educating one public school child in 1971–72.[20]

2. The opposition charge disregards the vast contribution of the churches and parents to their schools. In the case of the Catholic Church, the Gary Report tells us that "the parish church devotes 55 per cent of its revenues to subsidizing its elementary school. . . ."[21] The no-aid advocates further disregard tuition payments by parents which even if held constant at 1969–70 levels would, as the Gary Report data show, constitute anywhere from 11 to 24 per cent of the total cost of Catholic elementary education by the beginning of the next decade.[22] The current combination of church support and tuition payments aggregated to more than $300,000,000, or more than $400 per pupil in the Catholic schools alone.[23]

We believe the state, by setting a fair limit on its fiscal contributions to nonpublic education, can assure the continued maintenance of such church support and personal tuition payments. We note that neither the Gary Report nor any other significant research has suggested that there be a substitution of public funds for private ones.

OPPOSITION CHARGE—THREE: *Religious favoritism by the state could influence eligibility for education aid*

Perhaps one of the more difficult statements to comprehend is the one made by the authors of the opposition opinion in which they state:

Moreover, whether it is proposed that state aid be given directly to sectarian schools or to parents for use in such schools, problems persist in defining what religions shall be permitted to sponsor eligible schools, and how much aid shall be provided.

There appears here to be an unfounded proposition that state aid to nonpublic education places the state in the position of favoring one religion over another. Such a situation does not exist, and it is unthinkable that such a connotation should be introduced. The current aid program makes no judgment about the nature or kind of religious school* providing education services to students. The aid is paid only to those schools which comply with the academic requirements as contained in the Education Law and promulgated by the Commissioner of Education. There is no reason to believe that any form of aid introduced in New York State would favor one religion over another, and we find it entirely inappropriate that the opposition should even suggest that such a decision might be called for.

CONCLUSION

While we have found this Commission industrious and diligent and while we can share with our fellow members just pride in other accomplishments of our total work, we must acknowledge publicly our dismay and deep disappointment concerning the recommendations on nonpublic education by those opposing aid. Lacking in objectivity and sensitivity to the needs of nonpublic school children, the opposition report stands as a symbol of philosophical aloofness at a critical time in the history of our state.

Inherent in the attitude of the no-aid position is a preconceived judgment unaffected by research or reality. We found no openness to examine the quality and contributions of nonpublic education. We found no willingness to explore positively the legal and constitutional potential of various types of aid programs in order to guarantee the requirements of law and the courts. The basic intent of those opposing aid is to prevent all but minimal assistance to children in nonpublic schools. Unfortunately, the basic thrust of this opinion is all too clear in the report.

In contrast, we have presented a cogent and logical case for continuing state financial assistance to nonpublic education. We believe that we have a responsibility to those children who now attend and will in the future seek to attend nonpublic schools—a responsibility which in no way conflicts with our obligations to other sound principles of good government. Indeed, any program of assistance to nonpublic education must be consistent with those principles.

---

* State Education Department records show that schools under the auspices of the following religious groups have received aid under the Mandated Services Program: Baptist, Episcopal, Greek Orthodox, Jewish, Lutheran, Quaker, Roman Catholic and Seventh Day Adventist.

Affirming the necessity of assuring the excellence of public schools, we can find no real threat to them in espousing the educational needs of nonpublic school children. If the wealth of this state and nation can alter the surface of the earth, reach the moon, and create unimaginable power for both peace and war, certainly we can afford to help children attend school without depriving one group at the expense of the other. Any program of aid must be examined and evaluated for its impact on public schools, and proper safeguards against any harm to the public system must be included.

Nonpublic education has a long history of economy which has derived the finest of results from the most limited resources. With diminishing fiscal and personnel resources, schools and systems are exploring and instituting programs of cooperation and consolidation. In order to derive optimum results from any state program of assistance, we would expect and recommend, where practical and feasible, productive consolidation of programs and institutions.

We recognize without qualification that state assistance to nonpublic education should be limited to meet only a part of total cost. Any program of aid must be so geared that the continuance of private support through tuition and other contributions is guaranteed, that increases in such aid would be related only to a reasonable rise in general educational cost, and that the essential thrust of aid would be to maintain viability of parental choice, particularly for the economically disadvantaged, and not to underwrite it totally.

Finally, the research authorized by this Commission, the Gary Report, clearly testifies that government financial assistance should be aimed at helping to preserve nonpublic education. We view with alarm the possibility of the collapse of nonpublic education. Such an eventuality would be destructive of the diversity which is vital to our democracy as well as an impairment of the ability of local school districts and state government to sustain the quality education for which the Empire State has long been noted.

We consider our position on this most difficult of issues as demonstrating a genuine concern for both the present and the future of all elementary and secondary students and as one that is both practical and moderate. We are not talking of enormous expenditures; aid amounts would and should always be comparatively small. We are not talking of assumption of total costs; we propose partial support.

We urge consideration of these recommendations as ones which more realistically respond to the needs of our society, to the integrity of our statewide education system, to the will of a majority of the citizens of New York State and to the practical fiscal needs of a strained economy.

THE LAW OF THE LAND AND
THE LAW OF NEW YORK STATE

Before New York State could legislate a broad plan of support to nonpublic schools which included denominational schools, it would have to resolve constitutional problems posed by (1) the prohibitions found in the First and Fourteenth Amendments to the Constitution of the United States, and (2) the prohibitions found in the "Blaine Amendment" to the New York State Constitution (Article XI, Section 3). These problems are reviewed at length in the Gary Report. In addition, they have been the subject of endless analysis and debate by legal scholars over the years. We do not propose in this report to add one more law review article on this difficult and controversial subject. We believe, however, that the United States and state constitutions forbid grants of state or federal aid to students in sectarian schools or to their families for the purpose of paying any or all of the cost of such schooling. We shall content ourselves here with a brief description of the nature of the constitutional problems; a review of the areas of agreement; and an explanation of the majority's belief that no general public aid to students in sectarian schools or their families can survive inevitable constitutional challenges.

We first set forth the pertinent constitutional provisions.

United States Constitution

First Amendment:

Congress shall make no law respecting an establishment of religion, or prohibiting the free exercise thereof. . . .

Fourteenth Amendment:

. . . No state shall make or enforce any law which shall abridge the privileges or immunities of citizens of the United States; nor shall any state deprive any person of life, liberty, or property, without due process of law; nor deny to any person within its jurisdiction the equal protection of the laws.

The Establishment and Free Exercise clauses of the First Amendment were prohibitions directly addressed to Congress, not to the states. The Supreme Court, however, has held that the Fourteenth Amendment applied the religious clauses of the First Amendment to state action. The Court held that free exercise and nonestablishment belong to that core category of right "of the very essence of a scheme of ordered liberty" [24] encompassed within the Fourteenth Amendment. Accordingly, the prohibitions of the First Amendment apply with equal force to both federal and state legislation.

Constitution of the State of New York

Article XI, Section 3 (the "Blaine Amendment"):

Neither the state nor any subdivision thereof shall use its property or credit or any public money, or authorize or permit either to be used, directly or indirectly, in aid or maintenance, other than for examination or inspection, of any school or institution of learning wholly or in part under the control or direction of any religious denomination, or in which any denominational tenet or doctrine is taught, but the legislature may provide for the transportation of children to and from any school or institution of learning.

Initially, it must be observed that for our purposes it does not seem necessary to make fine distinctions between the Federal and State Constitutions. The "Blaine Amendment" appears on its face to be more comprehensive and specific in prohibiting state aid than do the First and Fourteenth Amendments to the Federal Constitution. The Court of Appeals, however, has upheld the furnishing of textbooks to students in sectarian schools at public expense, in a decision which appears to have reduced the restrictiveness of the constitutional prohibition.[25] Thus, it is conceivable that a particular tuition grant or parent-aid plan might survive a test of constitutionality under the First and Fourteenth Amendments and yet be held violative of our State Constitution, or vice versa. However, any suit brought in New York State courts on this matter is likely to be based on both the New York and United States Constitutions, and thus will be subject to appeal to the Supreme Court. In addition, the constitutionality of any such aid may be challenged in the federal courts initially, as has occurred with the Mandated Services Act and SESA. Therefore, we shall devote the principal part of this discussion to a consideration of the law of the land rather than the law of New York.

Pertinent Decisions

The following is a summary of the current state of the law regarding application of the provisions of the United States Constitution to education in sectarian schools.

(1) No state may constitutionally deny to parents the right to send their children to nonpublic schools, including sectarian schools. The Supreme Court held in the 1925 *Pierce* decision that parents may, despite a state's statutory prohibition, discharge their duty under state compulsory education

laws by sending their children to a nonpublic rather than a public school if the school otherwise meets with the secular educational requirements which the state has power to impose.[26] Subsequent opinions on state aid to nonpublic schools have acknowledged the landmark *Pierce* decision and accompanied it with an endorsement of nonpublic education. For example, in the *Lemon* case, while voiding state statutes granting direct aid to sectarian schools, the Court wrote:

> Finally, nothing we have said can be construed to disparage the role of church-related elementary and secondary schools in our national life. Their contribution has been and is enormous. Nor do we ignore their economic plight in a period of rising costs and expanding need.[27]

(2)   The *Lemon* case also restated the accepted doctrine that the United States Constitution does not forbid every type of relationship between church and state:

> Our prior holdings do not call for total separation between church and state; total separation is not possible in an absolute sense. Some relationship between government and religious organizations is inevitable. *Zorach* v. *Clauson,* 343 U.S. 306, 312 (1952); *Sherbert* v. *Verner,* 374 U.S. 398, 422 (1963) (Harlan, J., dissenting). Fire inspections, building and zoning regulations, and state requirements under compulsory school attendance laws are examples of necessary and permissible contracts. Indeed, under the statutory exemption before us in *Walz,* 397 U.S. 664 (1970), the State had a continuing burden to ascertain that the exempt property was in fact being used for religious worship. Judicial caveats against entanglements must recognize that the line of separation, far from being a "wall," is a blurred, indistinct, and variable barrier depending on all the circumstances of a particular relationship.[28]

(3)   To illustrate the last point, the *Lemon* majority opinion lists most of the kinds of aid which have been held permissible:

> Our decisions from *Everson* to *Allen* have permitted the states to provide church-related schools with secular, neutral, or nonideological services, facilities, or materials. Bus transportation, school lunches, public health services, and secular textbooks supplied in common to all students were not thought to offend the Establishment Clause.[29]

It is equally clear that the furnishing by New York State of such secular, neutral, or nonideological services, facilities, or materials would not violate Article XI, Section 3 of the State Constitution.

(4)   The rules with respect to religious instruction in public schools, "released time" and "dual enrollment" also seem to be reasonably clear. They may be stated thus:

(a)   Teaching of religion in the sense of inculcating religious values in the public schools is forbidden. This extends to the reading of the Bible and the saying of prayers.[30]

(b)   Study of the Bible or of religion for literary or historic content may be "presented objectively as part of a secular program of education" in public schools.[31]

(c)   Public schools may, at the request of parents, release students from class during the regular school day so that they may attend religious classes or devotional services on premises outside the public school.[32]

(d)   "Dual enrollment" also seems free from constitutional attack. Certain dual-enrollment arrangements would seem questionable. Examples are those arrangements under which school districts lease classrooms from sectarian schools and send public school teachers into these schools to teach students enrolled in the sectarian school. However, it has been established that a student may receive all his education in a sectarian school rather than a public school (*Pierce, supra*), and that he may receive religious education in a sectarian school and all other education in a public school through a "released time" arrangement (*Zorach, supra*). It would clearly follow that he may enroll in a number of courses in a sectarian school and a number of other courses in a public school. It is difficult to see, therefore, how either the United States or New York Constitutions could forbid the state through its school districts from accepting children for part-time rather than full-time instruction. Indeed, a district's refusal to accept a student for a chemistry course, for instance, simply because he studies his other subjects in a sectarian school, raises serious questions regarding the prohibition of free exercise of religion.

(e)   Since the decision in *Lemon,* it is quite clear that the financing by the state of instruction in secular subjects in sectarian schools (i.e., payment of all or any part of the salaries of teachers of secular subjects in denominational schools), when payments are made either to the schools or to the teachers, is forbidden, because (1) legislation to that end is a law "respecting" the establishment of religion "in the sense of being a step that could lead to such establishment and hence offends the First Amendment," [33] and (2) the inevitable control by the state over the providing of such instruction would foster "an excessive government entanglement with religion." [34]

Vouchers, Tuition Grants, and Student- or Parent-Aid Plans

This brings us to a consideration of the principal question not yet squarely addressed by the Supreme Court in the realm of public aid to sectarian schools—whether the Constitution permits payments or credits directly to students in sectarian schools or to their parents, as distinct from aid paid to the schools. The most common plan of this sort involves a paper ordering the state to pay only on two signatures—the parent's and that of the officer who signs on behalf of the school. The school officer will sign only when he is sure the school will get the money. After this complex ritual the state pays the school. An alternative proposal would require the state to pay a parent after the parent has paid or become legally obliged to pay tuition to the school.

What are the elements in the *Lemon* opinion that lead us to conclude that no voucher or parent-aid plan which would financially benefit sectarian schools through public revenues can escape a judicial finding of constitutional violation?

In the *Lemon* opinion, the Supreme Court discussed the reasons for the enactment and maintenance of the Establishment Clause, and tests for its application to the states through the Fourteenth Amendment. This discussion may be summarized as follows:

(1) As discussed above, the Court points out that the Establishment Clause not only forbids a law which "establishes" a state religon, but also forbids a law "respecting" such establishment.

(2) The Court repeats the three main evils against which the Establishment Clause was designed to afford protection, quoting from *Walz, supra* at p. 688: "sponsorship, financial support and active involvement of the sovereign and religious activity." The Court then called attention to three tests from former cases:

First, the statute must have a secular legislative purpose; second, its principal or primary effect must be one that neither advances nor inhibits religion; . . . finally, the statute must not foster an excessive government entanglement with religion.[35]

It should be said that the third test—entanglement—predominates throughout the opinion. The criteria used by the Court to measure the degree of entanglement in the cases before it were:

the character and purposes of the institutions that are benefited, the nature of the aid that the state provides, and the resulting relationship between the government and the religious authority.[36]

(3) In the context of religious neutrality (which is required), a distinction is made between textbooks and teachers on the ground that "a textbook's content is ascertainable but a teacher's handling of a subject is not." [37] Salaries for teachers of secular subjects in sectarian schools cannot be provided

on the basis of a mere assumption that secular teachers under religious discipline can avoid conflicts. The State must be certain, given the Religious

Clauses, that subsidized teachers do not inculcate religion—indeed, the State here has undertaken to do so.[38]

The opinion continues:

Unlike a book, a teacher cannot be inspected once so as to determine the extent and intent of his or her personal beliefs and subjective acceptance of the limitations imposed by the First Amendment.[39]

(4) The opinion then pointed out—and this is perhaps the most significant restriction by reason of its continued emphasis—that the very precautions taken by the state to ensure that teachers play a strictly non-ideological role become themselves "the sort of entanglement that the Constitution forbids." [40]

(5) In an entirely separate treatment, the Court expanded the base of entanglement to include "the divisive political potential of these state programs," [41] thereby raising political divisiveness to the level of a constitutional criterion. The Court referred to the history of many countries attesting to "the hazards of religion intruding into the political arena. . . ." [42]

(6) Finally, the Court pointed out that state aid programs "have self-perpetuating and self-expanding propensities," [43] indicating that a program initially not involving governmental entanglement might quickly become subject to this constitutional defect.

Regulated and Unregulated Aid

What, then, will be the fate of any state-supported student- or parent-aid program, or voucher system by whatever name? Here it is important to distinguish between two basic types of plan for direct payment to parents or students, which we designate as regulated and unregulated.

A regulated plan forbids discrimination of every kind; it would not permit any school involved in the plan to exercise preference in admissions to adherents of any religion, and would restrict the use of public funds to secular instruction. An unregulated plan, on the other hand, would permit religious discrimination in admissions policy and, more important, would either not establish any regulatory mechanisms to ensure that funds received from students were used by schools for religious purposes, or would not prohibit any such use of the funds in the first place.

We also include in the category of unregulated plans a tax credit plan under which a taxpayer would be credited against his state income tax with an amount equal to the tuition he had paid to a nonpublic school for his children or equal to some other stated amount not in excess of such tuition. Such a plan is the same in effect as if the amount in question were paid to the state in taxes, and later returned to the taxpayer in the form of a voucher or direct payment in cash. Accordingly, the constitutional questions raised by such a plan are the same as those raised by an unrestricted voucher or parent-aid plan.

Our conclusions are these:

1. A regulated plan of aid by means of vouchers or cash payments which mandates no discrimination or preferences of a religious nature and seeks, by regulatory actions, to restrict the use of public funds to secular purposes would be held unconstitutional when applied to sectarian schools because, as pointed out in *Lemon,* this "kind of state inspection and evaluation of the religious content of a religious organization is fraught with the sort of entanglement which the Constitution forbids. It is a relationship pregnant with dangers of excessive government direction of church schools and hence of churches." [44]

2. An unregulated voucher or parent-aid plan which places no restrictions on priority in enrollment for members of the faith which sponsored the school, or fails to place or enforce restrictions on religious instruction in the classrooms, would appear to be unconstitutional on its face, according to the *Lemon* case. This is because without such restrictions, there would be no guarantee of separation between secular and religious educational functions and no assurance that state financial aid supported only the former. We stress that state support of religion would result and would be equally unacceptable whether public funds were provided for religious education indirectly, through a tuition grant or voucher payment to a parent who pays the money over to a sectarian school, or directly through state payments to the school. Justice Douglas' assertion regarding purported distinctions between the secular and religious parts of a sectarian school's education program applies as well to the alleged distinction between direct and indirect payments to sectarian schools: it would make "a grave constitutional question turn merely on cost accounting and bookkeeping entries." [45]

The crux of the matter is that whether a sectarian school receives state money from the state or state money earmarked for the school from a parent, a "comprehensive, discriminating and continuing state surveillance will inevitably be required to ensure that . . . the First Amendment [be] otherwise respected." [46] Later, the Court reiterates that "the very restrictions and surveillance *necessary* to ensure that teachers play a strictly non-ideological role give rise to entanglements between church and state" [47] (emphasis added). The situation which is thus created by the necessity for such restrictions and surveillance has been succinctly set forth by the sole dissenter to the *Lemon* decision, Justice White:

The Court thus creates an insoluble paradox for the state and the parochial schools. The state cannot finance secular instruction if it permits religion to be taught in the same classroom; but if it extracts a promise that religion not be so taught—a promise the school and its teachers are quite willing and on this record able to give—and enforces it, it is then entangled in the 'no entanglement' aspect of the Court's Establishment Clause jurisprudence." [48]

Or, as stated by Justice Douglas in his concurrence:

If the government closed its eyes to the manner in which these grants are actually used it would be allowing public funds to promote sectarian education. If it did not close its eyes but undertook the surveillance needed, it would, I fear, intermeddle in parochial affairs in a way that would breed only rancor and dissension.[49]

In addition to this "insoluble paradox," there are other constitutional problems presented by an unregulated voucher or parent-aid plan. First, the divisive political potential of such a program is apparent and presents "a broader base of entanglement of yet a different character." [50] As stated in *Lemon,* "political division along religious lines was one of the principal evils against which the First Amendment was intended to protect," [51] and the presence of this "evil" in the Rhode Island and Pennsylvania aid programs was one of the bases on which the respective statutes were struck down. Providing aid to sectarian schools indirectly through a voucher or parent-aid plan—of either the regulated or unregulated type—as opposed to directly, would in no way reduce the "potential for political divisiveness related to religious belief and practice" which the Court has decried.[52]

Secondly, there remains to be determined the whole issue of whether the principal or primary effect of a voucher or parent-aid plan would be the advancement of religion. The importance of this constitutional criterion should not be overlooked, despite the stress placed on the "entanglement" test in *Lemon.* In assessing the Rhode Island and Pennsylvania statutes, the Court did not even analyze their principal or primary effect, because unconstitutional entanglement was so pervasive. But even if, or especially if, there were no entanglement, a statute would still have to pass the "effect" test. Without statutory restrictions designed to guarantee the separation between secular and religious educational functions, a voucher or "parent-aid" plan would likely be found to have the principal effect of advancing religion.

Thirdly, and finally, there is the issue of the legislative purpose of a voucher or parent-aid statute. In *Lemon,* the Court accepted the stated legislative intents of both the Rhode Island and Pennsylvania statutes in question, namely, to enhance the quality of secular education in all schools covered by the compulsory attendance laws. However, in the context of legislative attempts to avoid constitutional prohibitions against state support of racially segregated schools, the courts have consistently disregarded assertions of legislative intent and struck down aid to private schools as well as grants to students attending such schools.

For instance, in 1962 the Louisiana legislature authorized a Financial Assistance Commission to provide "tuition grants" to pupils attending private schools in that state. Payments were made "by check to the parent or guardian of, or the person standing *in loco parentis* to, the applicant." Payments were limited to an amount not to exceed the tuition obligation actually incurred by the applicant. A federal three-judge court declared the scheme unconstitutional as a segregation device, stating, "The United States Constitution does not permit the State to perform acts indirectly through private persons which it is forbidden to do directly." The Court forbade enforcement of the legislation by any means,[53] and the United States Supreme Court affirmed the judgment below in a *per curiam* order.[54]

In other cases, "grants to students in the context of the problems of desegregated public schools have without exception been stricken down as tools of the forbidden discrimination," on the grounds that states were attempting to accomplish unlawful ends—the maintenance of segregated school systems—through otherwise lawful means, namely tuition grants.[55]

It is likely that any state would face the same obstacle in sectarian school matters if it attempted to reimburse parents for tuition. Such an arrangement appears only a specious device to channel the state's credit to the sectarian school and would fall under the rule of the *Poindexter* case. A device that cannot evade the Fourteenth Amendment in a desegregation case cannot evade the Fourteenth Amendment in a sectarian school case.

Exceptional Children and Institutional Schools

A final word needs to be said concerning aid to sectarian institutions in certain special circumstances. No child is exactly like any other, but many students in New York State schools differ so drastically from the average that in fairness they require educational treatment which is specially adapted to their exceptional needs. (The education of such pupils is the subject of a chapter on Children with Special Needs.)

However, education of such pupils raises a question germane to the general question of church-connected institutions with which this chapter deals. For generations, the law in New York State has authorized the public authorities, at public expense, to utilize the services of church-connected orphanages and church-connected schools for the deaf, the blind, and children otherwise handicapped, where such private institutions are available and public facilities are not accessible.

Section 4407 of the Education Law, relating to instruction of certain handicapped children; Article 85 of the Education Law, which makes provision for instruction of the deaf and blind; and various provisions for state aid in various ways indirectly authorize use of church-connected institutions at some public expense. How do such institutions escape the impact of the Blaine Amendment?

One answer to this inquiry emerges from two provisions of the New York State Constitution. Article VIII, Section 1 reads, in pertinent part:

Subject to the limitations on indebtedness and taxation applying to any county, city, town or village nothing in this constitution contained shall prevent a county, city or town from making such provision for the aid, care and support of the needy as may be authorized by law, nor prevent any such county, city or town from providing for the care, support, maintenance and secular education of inmates of orphan asylums, homes for dependent children or correctional institutions and of children placed in family homes by authorized agencies, whether under public or private control, or from providing health and welfare services for all children. . . .

Article VII, Section 8 reads, in pertinent part:

Subject to the limitations on indebtedness and taxation, nothing in this constitution contained shall prevent the legislature from providing for the aid, care and support of the needy directly or through subdivisions of the state . . . or for the education and support of the blind, the deaf, the dumb, the physically handicapped, the mentally ill, the emotionally disturbed, the mentally retarded or juvenile delinquents as it may deem proper; or for health and welfare services for all children, either directly or through subdivisions of the state, including school districts; or for the aid, care and support of neglected and dependent children and of the needy sick, through agencies and institutions authorized by the state board of social welfare or other state department having the power of inspection thereof, by payments made on a per capita basis directly or through the subdivisions of the state. . . .

In 1904 the New York Court of Appeals decided *Sargent* v. *Board of Education,* 177 N.Y. 317, which remains a leading case in 1971. The Court held that St. Mary's Boys' Orphan Asylum of the City of Rochester, incorporated under Chapter 319 of the Laws of 1848, was neither a school nor an institution of learning within the meaning of the Blaine Amendment, and that payment from public funds of nuns teaching in the asylum was permitted by the predecessor of Article VIII, Section 1, above. Hence, no State Constitutional provision would impede payment of public funds to such a denominational orphanage.

Legislative and judicial practice and construction thus find an exception to the Blaine Amendment and its underlying policy. Legislative construction, and the scanty judicial precedent available suggest that no Fourteenth Amendment obstacle exists either, even in light of *Lemon,* to state support of sectarian schools for exceptional children.

The federal court cases legitimate such results under various formulae. In 1898 in *Bradfield* v. *Roberts,* 175 U.S. 291, the Supreme Court upheld federal aid for a hospital maintained by a District of Columbia corporation, all of whose members belonged to Roman Catholic monastic orders or sisterhoods. The Court's reasoning was based on the difference between the corporation, which the Court found religiously neutral, and its human members, who were all clerical. The result was government support for a needed hospital.

Another example is *Quick Bear* v. *Leupp,* 210 U.S. 50 (1908). Mr. Leupp, the United States Commissioner of Indian Affairs, contracted with the Bureau of Catholic Indian Missions to conduct a school for Indian children on a reservation. Despite a suit brought by Quick Bear which challenged the statutory lawfulness of the payment, the Court upheld the arrangement. Its stated reason was that the money was paid, not out of general government funds, but out of treaty funds, of which the government was trustee. The court also declared that the payment could not be deemed unconstitutional, citing *Bradfield, supra.*

Probably the underlying explanation of cases involving hospitals, Indian schools, and other institutions for exceptional children, rests simply on the situation of the human beings affected. Handicapped children, orphans, the sick in hospitals, and children on reservations all have in common various degrees of inability to utilize the ordinary institutions of society. Courts seem to have concluded that neither the First Amendment establishment clause, the provisions of the Fourteenth Amendment nor the Blaine Amendment were intended to prevent adjustment of governmental arrangements to provide for such exceptional human situations.

APPENDIX 5B

The Case for Aid: a Legal Analysis

INTRODUCTION

We have come to basic differences with the Commission's no-aid proponents over the question of constitutional permissibility in part because we have viewed the role of the Commission differently.

We do not view ourselves as the law court of last resort, charged with a final and binding judgment on constitutional questions. We leave those responsibilities to the United States Supreme Court and the New York State Court of Appeals.

The Supreme Court itself has recently emphasized the difficulty of its role of interpretation when it said in *Lemon* v. *Kurtzman*:

Candor compels acknowledgement, moreover, that we can only dimly perceive the lines of demarcation in this extraordinarily sensitive area of constitutional law.[56]

We see the charge to the Commission as one requiring the exploration of all possible avenues of assistance to nonpublic education with emphasis on those serving disadvantaged neighborhoods, and to develop means of assistance which would be useful and desirable and not clearly foreclosed by Court rulings.

In contrast, the no-aid proponents begin their analysis with a statement of personal conviction which says, in effect, that they would not propose programs of aid even if there were no constitutional restrictions imposed by the First Amendment and/or the Blaine Amendment. We reject this approach as not consistent with the charge to our Commission and our acceptance of that charge.

Thus, we see the constitutional question before our Commission as a simple one: *Are there programs of assistance to children attending schools under religious auspices which are not clearly prohibited?*

The correlative public policy question for us is "which of these programs do we recommend to meet the terms of our charge?"

Point 1

The United States Constitution does not prevent the state from providing meaningful aid to nonpublic education under religious auspices.

Until *Everson* v. *Board of Education*,[57] the prohibitions of the religion clause of the Federal First Amendment as they apply to state action had not received Supreme Court review.

As a consequence, it is necessary only to review the limited number of Supreme Court decisions involving education aid programs to develop an outline of the kinds of meaningful aid to nonpublic education which have not been found to violate the Federal First Amendment.

There are three principal decisions of the Supreme Court from which the present position of the Court may be deduced.

In *Everson, supra,* the Court sustained a state-financed program of bus transportation for students attending all schools, including church-related schools. In its opinion the Court emphasized the public purpose which was being performed, saying:

It is much too late to argue that legislation intended to facilitate the opportunity of children to get a secular education serves no public purpose.[58]

Twenty years later in *Board of Education* v. *Allen,* the Court sustained a state-financed program of loan of secular textbooks to students in all schools, including those that are church-related.[59] In the majority opinion,

Justice White suggested some of the guidelines for judging constitutional permissibility of other programs, saying:

> Thus, no funds or books are furnished to parochial schools, and the financial benefit is to parents and children, not to schools.[60]

The third case to deal with the issue of education aid was *Lemon* v. *Kurtzman, supra,* decided in an opinion which also determined the related cases of *Earley* v. *DiCenso* and *Robinson* v. *DiCenso,* and on the same day as *Tilton* v. *Richardson,*[61] which dealt with aid to church-related colleges.

Unlike the two prior decisions upholding aid, the *Lemon* decision held the two programs to fund teachers' salaries to be unconstitutional as to teachers in church-related schools.

Just as we have said that *Everson* and *Allen* was limited to permitting buses and textbooks, respectively, so do we find that *Lemon* is limited to outlawing direct payment of teachers' salaries. These are the narrow Court holdings for which we must account carefully in any analysis.

Lemon did not deal with other programs, yet unfashioned, which take the form of scholar awards, parent grants, vouchers, tuition grants, tax credits, tax deductions, and so on. The Court has given strong indication that any program in which direct payments are made to the school and are supervised directly for secularity will be found to be impermissible. This we accept. But we do not find that such conclusion must foreclose us from the consideration of other possible routes of programming. Certainly it is the task of the Court, not ourselves, to evolve the boundaries of constitutional permissibility.

Because of the currency of the *Lemon* decision, the breadth of its treatment, and the virtual unanimity of the Court, we believe that a detailed summary of the Court's indications of permissibility in the case provide a framework for New York to propose meaningful programs of assistance to church-related and other nonpublic education.

FRAMEWORK I *"Secular, Neutral or Non-ideological Services, facilities or materials."*

In the majority opinion in *Lemon,* Chief Justice Burger suggests in this language that there are significant areas of assistance which are permissible under the First Amendment. He states:

> Our decisions from *Everson* to *Allen* have permitted the State to provide church-related schools with secular, neutral or non-ideological services, facilities or materials.[62]

It is of special significance that the same Justice paraphrases this language in *Tilton,* decided the same day, in which grants for building costs at church-related colleges were upheld. There the Court said:

The entanglement between church and State is also lessened here by the non-ideological character of the aid which the government provides. Our cases from *Everson* to *Allen* have permitted church-related schools to receive government aid in the form of secular, neutral, or non-ideological services, facilities or materials that are supplied to all students regardless of the affiliation of the school which they attend.[63]

The language used by the Court, and repeated, is a broadly descriptive characterization which includes a whole range of programs.

We do not urge any specific program among the many suggested. We urge, however, that these areas of constitutional permissibility were ignored by the no-aid proponents.

Recently the Supreme Court of Ohio unanimously upheld a program of special educational services to children in church-related schools, even though it was argued vehemently that the *Lemon* decision foreclosed such programs. In that decision the Ohio Court, dealing with the federal constitutional issue, said:

> We have applied those tests [*Lemon* v. *Kurtzman*] to the Ohio plan, as it existed in 1967, and have found it not violative of the Establishment Clause of the First Amendment. As was stated in *Lemon, supra* at page 758 . . . "our decisions from *Everson* to *Allen* have permitted the State to provide church-related schools with secular, neutral or non-ideological services, facilities or materials." [64]

We feel deeply that this challenging language of the Supreme Court should have been used by the Commission as a base from which meaningful programs are developed.

FRAMEWORK II   *"State aid provided to the student and his parents—not to the church-related school."*

In the majority opinion in *Lemon* the Court made a fundamental distinction between direct money grants and programs of so-called secular and neutral services, as are discussed above.

With respect to direct money grants the Court emphasized that payment to a church-related school was impermissible where excessive entanglement was required. In so stating, the Court went on to say:

> This factor distinguishes both *Everson* and *Allen,* for in both those cases the Court was careful to point out that State aid was provided to the student and his parents—not to the church-related school.[65]

It was this criterion which was expressed by Mr. Justice White in *Allen, supra,* when he emphasized that in that case no funds or books were furnished to parochial schools, and the financial benefit provided is to the parents and children, not to the schools.

Programs which may fall under this broad category of probable permissibility include scholarships, student grants, parent grants, tuition grants, voucher certificates and similar programs.

Here again we find a significant area of exploration for the development of meaningful programs. In fact, three major states have enacted programs in the last four months which are predicated upon their responsible reading of this portion of the *Lemon* opinion.

Illinois has enacted a program to provide tuition grants to students from families receiving public assistance, or with family incomes below $3,000.

Ohio has enacted a program to provide very modest tuition grants to the parents of all nonpublic school pupils in the state.

Pennsylvania has also enacted a program of tuition grants for the parents of all nonpublic school pupils.

This prompt action following the *Lemon* decision indicates there is substantial legal opinion across the country that this portion of the *Lemon* opinion provides a firm basis for sound legislative action.

In the legal memorandum of the no-aid proponents a detailed argument is related to support the contention that all programs of parent or student aid are unconstitutional under *Lemon*. Unfortunately this argument fails to recognize important characteristics of different programs of parent or student assistance which affect measurably their constitutional viability.

Furthermore, this jumping to a constitutional conclusion substitutes the no-aid proponents for the Supreme Court and this is beyond the scope of this Commission's responsibility. We reject such an approach to so vital a question.

Without recounting the fallacies in the legal analysis, we set forth certain postulates for a program of parent or student aid that would meet those contentions:

a. That the aid be predicated on the need of the parent or student and flow to him, just as public funds for medical and hospital care do today. The school only receives the collateral effect as the direct benefit accrues to the student.

b. That appropriate regulation of nonpublic schools would assure that a parent or student may claim a credit or refund only for expenditures made to a school which meets state regulatory requirements.

c. That irrespective of the aid plan, all schools be prohibited clearly by law from any form of discrimination in admission or employment.

In conclusion, we do not accept the distinction of regulated and unregulated aid. We are convinced that the expenditure of all public funds must be subject to regulation. We are satisfied that a skilled and dedicated effort of legal and educational technicians could readily develop the legal and administrative techniques to overcome the administrative obstacles to helping parents and students which are raised in the no-aid proponents' legal memorandum.

FRAMEWORK III *Tax Credits and Tax Deductions.*

It is appropriate to comment briefly upon the legal foundation for programs of tax credit and tax deduction to assist taxpayers in meeting expenditures which contribute to the common good.

While no constitutional challenges of such programs have involved First Amendment questions, the recent opinion of the Supreme Court in *Walz* v. *Tax Commission*[66] suggests affirmatively that the Supreme Court is reluctant to interfere with judgments made by a state in determining classes of tax exemption. This same reluctance is expected to prevail with respect to tax deductions or tax credits.

For example, the deductibility of religious contributions for income tax purposes is an accepted and unchallenged principle of federal and state income tax determination. The use of tax credits for tuition expenditures made to church-related schools comes clearly within the over-all scope of this substantial income tax precedent.

Thus, tax credits or tax deductions for expenditures for elementary and secondary education, of any kind, at both public and nonpublic schools are viable alternatives under the federal and state constitutions.

Point 2

The state constitution does not prevent the state from providing meaningful aid to nonpublic education under religious auspices.

In our opinion the fundamental constitutional issue affecting aid to church-related education will be resolved at the federal level under the Federal First Amendment, as interpreted by the Supreme Court.

Any program of aid must survive the federal constitutional test. We expect the interpretation by the New York Court of Appeals of the state constitutional limitations to follow such principles and guides established under the First Amendment.

While the language of the two constitutions differs substantially, the recent decision of the Court of Appeals in *Board of Education* v. *Allen*[67] laid the foundation for an identification of interpretation. In that case, the Court uses the judicial criteria developed by the Supreme Court in the *Schempp* case[68] to find that the state textbook loan law does not violate Article XI, Section 3 of the state constitution. This analysis is:

> Since there is no intention to assist parochial schools as such, any benefit accruing to those schools is a collateral effect of the statute, and therefore, cannot be properly classified as giving of aid directly or indirectly.[69]

This sentence has been properly called the crux of the Court of Appeals interpretation of the state constitution by consultant Leo Pfeffer in his paper for the Commission which is set forth as part of the Gary Report.

It is significant that Mr. Pfeffer, a known opponent of aid programs, sees the interpretation of the state constitution as broadly permissive under *Allen*. In his paper he says:

> Yet it might not be unfair to suggest that in seeking an explanation for the decision one should look more to the Court's attitude than to its reasoning. The heart of the decision is to be found in the following sentence:
> ". . . unless certain types of aid can be made available to *all* children, we run the risk of creating an educational lag between children in public and private schools." [70]

Therefore, it would seem appropriate to concentrate on the federally permissible areas of assistance and examine whether in those specific areas there are any problems of state constitutional impermissibility. We say that there is not.

With respect to "secular, neutral, non-ideological services, facilities and materials," the Court of Appeals has indicated that it will look to the secular benefit to the child from the program rather than the fact the child is attending a church-related school. The Court said this:

> Certainly not every state action which might entail some ultimate benefit to parochial schools is proscribed. [71]

Then, in developing further its analysis of the state constitution, the Court said:

> It is our view that the words "direct" and "indirect" relate solely to the means of attaining the prohibited end of aiding religion *as such*. [72] [Emphasis added.]

This part of the Court's opinion is particularly important when we relate it to a subsequent paragraph quoted above in which it says:

> Since there is no intention to assist parochial schools *as such*. [Emphasis added.]

With respect to state aid provided to the student and his parents—not to the church-related school—the Court of Appeals decision in *Allen* establishes the guidelines from which the state constitution issue is reviewed. As stated in the Gary Report:

> Moreover, while the language used by the Court in *Allen* in its one-sentence rationale of its decision is quite broad and perhaps almost unlimited in its implications, the holding itself is quite narrow. [73]

Of course, in judging areas of possible permissibility, in probing the frontiers of viable programming, we can expect to look to the rationale and the implications rather than the narrow holding. Further, the Gary Report indicates that the questions of tuition grants and tax credits are open legal questions:

> The crux of the matter lies in the answers to two questions: (1) did the Court in *Allen* establish a new rule for the application of Article XI Section 3 based not on the objective effect of the Legislature's action but upon its intention (i.e., if there was no intention to assist parochial schools as such the aid is necessarily only collateral no matter what form it takes) and (2) if so, are the courts bound by the Legislature's declaration of intention and precluded thereby from further inquiry. If the answer to both questions is yes, *tuition grants and voucher plans may meet the acceptance* of the Court of Appeals. . . .[74] [Emphasis added.]

Point 3

CONCLUSION   In view of the above, we submit that the legality of many types of aid is an open constitutional question. Aid systems that have not been tested in the courts include: tuition grants, voucher plans, parent-aid formulas, tax credits, tax deductions, dual enrollment and the assignment of public school teachers to the nonpublic institutions.

Not wishing to place ourselves in the position of the Supreme Court, we will refrain from commenting on the eventual legality of such proposals. However, it is clear that all avenues of aid have not been closed. Therefore, the Legislature should not be deterred from enacting new programs to aid nonpublic education. It is only through such aid that nonpublic schools will survive, and their survival saves New York State taxpayers millions of dollars annually and, at the same time, makes possible a higher level of education in the public schools.

Notes

[1] New York State Education Department, Information Center on Education, *Annual Education Summary, 1968–69,* and *Education Statistics Estimates, Fall, 1971.*

[2] *Ibid.*

[3] Projections were computed by George B. Kleindorfer, Paul M. Goldfinger and Stephen M. Rhoads. *A Model for Educational Planning in the State of New York,* a report to the Commission, 1971.

[4] Nicholas DeWitt, *Education, Manpower and Employment,* 1971, a report prepared for the Commission:

> . . . It is to be noted that in 1960, for population with 12 or more years of schooling completed, New York State *lagged* behind the national distribution. This is mainly due to the fact that although the proportion of college graduates (with four or more years of college education) was higher in New York State than the national average, the percentage of persons with less than high school education (particularly persons with 8–11 years of education, i.e., school dropouts) was higher in the state than the national distribution [p. 29].

[5] Averages taken from a report prepared for the Commission by Louis R. Gary, *The Collapse of Nonpublic Education: Rumor or Reality?* (1971).

[6] The specific figures for this middle projection are:

Rural Areas: 1970–75: K–8, 9 per cent decrease each year; 9–12, 6.3 per cent decrease each year. 1976–80: K–12, 5.4 per cent decrease each year.

Urban Areas (exclusive of New York City): 1970–75: K–8, 5.5 per cent decrease each year; 9–12, 4.55 per cent decrease each year. 1976–80: K–12, 5.4 per cent decrease each year.

New York City: 1970–75: K–8, 6.3 per cent decrease each year; 9–12, 5.3

per cent decrease each year. 1976–80: K–12, 5.4 per cent decrease each year.

A more complete explanation of the procedures involved in making these forecasts is contained in the report to the Commission by George B. Kleindorfer, *op. cit.* (note 3).

[7] New York State Education Department, Information Center on Education.

[8] New York State Education Department, Information Center on Education, *Education Statistics Estimates, Fall, 1971.*

[9] New York State Education Department, Information Center on Education.

[10] National Education Association, Research Division, *Rankings of the States, 1971. Research Report 1971-R1* (N.E.A.: 1971), p. 20.

[11] National Education Association, *op. cit.,* p. 23.

[12] New York State Division of the Budget, Office of Statistical Coordination, *New York State Statistical Yearbook, 1971* (Albany, 1971), p. 204.

[13] *Ibid.,* p. 211.

[14] *Ibid.,* p. 212.

[15] General fund expenditures per pupil in average daily attendance in public schools are deflated in constant 1958 dollars, using an implicit price deflator for state and local government purchases: *Survey of Current Business,* August, 1965 and 1970.

[16] *New York State Statistical Yearbook, op. cit.* (note 12), p. 209.

[17] New York State Education Department, Bureau of Educational Finance Research.

[18] K. A. Simon and W. V. Grant, *Digest of Educational Statistics, 1970* (Washington, D.C.: Government Printing Office, 1970), p. 55.

[19] *New York State Statistical Yearbook, 1971, op. cit.* (note 12), p. 46.

[20] K. A. Simon and W. V. Grant, *op. cit.* (note 18), p. 55.

[21] *Ibid.,* pp. 26, 38, 42.

[22] New York State Education Department, *Educational Expenditures, Interstate Comparisons* (Albany, 1969), p. 27.

[23] *Ibid.,* p. 25.

[24] K. A. Simon and W. V. Grant, *op. cit.* (note 18), pp. 24, 59.

[25] W. I. Garms, *An Approach to the Measurement of Educational Need,* a report to the Commission, 1971.

[26] New York State Education Department, Office of Planning in Higher Education, *A Longitudinal Study of the Barriers Affecting the Pursuit of a Higher Education by New York State High School Seniors, Phase I* (Albany, August, 1969).

[27] Nicholas DeWitt, *op. cit.* (note 4), p. 170.

[28] New York State Education Department, *Distribution of High School Graduates and College-Going Rate, Fall, 1970* (Albany, 1971).

[29] Data obtained under contract from the American Council on Education, 1971. This study reanalyzed data originally collected for John Creager *et al., National Norms for Entering College Freshmen—Fall, 1969,* American Council on Education, *Research Reports,* Vol. 4, No. 7, 1969.

[30] Ruth E. Eckert and Thomas O. Marshall, *When Youth Leave School,* Regents' Inquiry (New York: McGraw-Hill, 1938), p. 79.

[31] *Ibid.*

[32] State University of New York, *Crucial Questions about Higher Education* (Albany, 1955).

[33] *Ibid.,* p. 23.

[34] Alan E. Guskin, *et al., High Schools in Crisis,* report prepared for the Commission by Community Resources Limited, Ann Arbor, Michigan, 1971.

Sources of Tables

1.1 New York State Education Department, Information Center on Education.

1.2 *Ibid.*

1.3 George B. Kleindorfer *et al., A Model for Educational Planning in the State of New York,* a report to the Commission, 1971.

1.4 Based on data from the New York State Education Department, Information Center on Education.

1.5 New York State Division of the Budget, Office of Statistical Coordination, *New York State Statistical Yearbook, 1971* (Albany, 1971), p. 212; and New York State Education Department, Information Center on Education.

1.6 Unadjusted expenditure figures are from *New York State Statistical Yearbook, 1971, op. cit.* (note for Table 1.5), p. 212; and New York State Education Department, Information Center on Education.

1.7 New York State Education Department, Bureau of Educational Finance Research.

1.8 K. A. Simon and W. V. Grant, *Digest of Educational Statistics, 1970* (Washington, D.C.: Government Printing Office, 1970), p. 55.

1.9 *Ibid.,* pp. 26, 38, 42.

1.10 *Ibid.,* pp. 24, 59.

1.11 Data from College Entrance Examination Board, May, 1971.

1.12 NMSQT Program on New York State Students, May, 1971.

1.13 New York State Education Department, Bureau of Pupil Testing and Advisory Services.

1.14 *Ibid.*

1.15 New York State Education Department, Information Center on Education, *Education Statistics, New York State, January, 1971,* p. 13.

1.16 New York State Education Department, Office of Planning in Higher Education, *A Longitudinal Study of the Barriers Affecting the Pursuit of Higher Education by New York State High School Seniors, Phase I* (Albany, August, 1969).

1.17 *Ibid.*

1.18 New York State Division of the Budget, Office of Statistical Coordination, *New York State Statistical Yearbook, 1971* (Albany, 1971), p. 216.

1.19 See note for Table, 1.1, *op. cit.*

1.20 See note for Table 1.16, *op. cit.*

1.21 New York State Education Department, Information Center on Education, *Distribution of High School Graduates and College-Going Rate, New York State, Fall, 1970.*

1.22 American Council on Education, data supplied to the Commission.

1.23 *Ibid.*

1.24 State University of New York, *Crucial Questions about Higher Education* (Albany, 1955), p. 23.

1.25 United States Department of Labor, Bureau of Labor Statistics, *Characteristics of Workers in Large States and SMSA's 1970* (Washington, D.C.: Government Printing Office, 1971), p. 6.

1.26 Community Resources Limited, *High Schools in Crisis* (Ann Arbor, Michigan, 1971).

Sources of Figures

1.1 New York State Education Department, Information Center on Education, and George B. Kleindorfer *et al., A Model for Educational Planning in the State of New York,* a report to the Commission, 1971.

1.2 *Ibid.*

1.3 *Ibid.*

1.4 New York State Division of the Budget, Office of Statistical Coordination, *New York State Statistical Yearbook, 1971* (Albany, 1971), p. 207.

1.5 *Ibid.,* p. 204.

1.6 *Ibid.,* p. 211, and New York State Education Department, Information Center on Education.

1.7 *New York State Statistical Yearbook, 1971, op. cit.,* p. 209.

1.8 *Ibid.*

1.9 New York State Education Department, Information Center on Education.

CHAPTER 2 (PAGES 53–208)

[1] These figures are computed from State Education Department, *Statistical and Financial Summary of Education in New York State* (Albany, State Education Department, 1970).

[2] Advisory Commission on Intergovernmental Relations, *State Aid to Local Governments* (Washington, D.C.: Government Printing Office, 1969). Committee for Economic Development, *Educating the Disadvantaged* (New York: The Committee, 1970).

[3] Advisory Commission on Intergovernmental Relations, *Urban America and the Federal System* (Washington, D.C.: Government Printing Office, 1969), p. 23.

[4] Henry Levin: "Aspects of Educational Finance and Equal Opportunity," Part III of a report prepared for this Commission, August, 1971.

[5] Committee for Economic Development, *Reshaping Government in Metropolitan Areas* (New York; The Committee, 1970).

[6] Harold Howe II, "Anatomy of a Revolution," *Saturday Review,* November 20, 1971, p. 95.

[7] Alan K. Campbell and Seymour Sacke, *Metropolitan America: Fiscal Patterns and Governmental Systems* (New York: Free Press, 1967).

[8] John E. Coons, *et al., Private Wealth and Public Education* (Cambridge, Mass.: Belknap Press of Harvard University Press, 1970.

[9] Frank I. Michelman, "The Supreme Court, 1968 Term—Foreword: On Pro-

tecting the Poor through the Fourteenth Amendment," *Harvard Law Review,* Vol. 83, No. 1, p. 56.

10 *Serrano* v. *Priest* 5 Cal. 3d 584, 487 P. 2d 1241 (Cal. Sup. Ct., 1971).

11 R. L. Johns and K. Alexander, *Alternative Programs for Financing Education* (Gainesville, Fla.: National Educational Finance Project, 1971), p. 235.

12 Harlan Updegraff, *Application of State Funds to the Aid of Local Schools* (Philadelphia: University of Pennsylvania Press, 1949).

13 John E. Coons, William H. Clune II and Stephen D. Sugarman, *Private Wealth and Public Education* (Cambridge, Mass.: Harvard University Press, 1970).

14 Further details of this formula and of the set of special aids are shown in Appendix 2A to this Chapter. Appendix 2D provides information on the flow of funds from the time (1962) that the present system was established.

15 Dean Dick Netzer of New York University was consultant to the Commission on economic and revenue projections. For analysis of methods used, see Appendix 2F to this Chapter.

16 In earlier years, economists held that distribution of tax burden should be considered separately from distribution of benefits of public expenditures. More recently, it has become common to examine burdens and benefits simultaneously. A regressive tax structure might, for example, be defended on the grounds that the resources it provided were used for purposes that substantially benefited the poor. Even so, it remains to be asked who really benefits most from public expenditure? Work on this question is now well under way, but preliminary results are not heartening—a regressive tax structure may support programs that are progressive, i.e., pro-rich, in benefits. A study of educational expenditures reported, ". . . benefits per student for grades one through 12 are slightly progressive over-all, with some regressivity over the middle-income range; i.e., children of rich parents benefit more than children of the poor. (Progressive benefits are 'pro-rich'; regressive benefits are 'pro-rich.') The additional benefits per person of higher education are strongly progressive, so that benefits per person of the entire system of public education are progressive over the whole income range." (W. Norton Grubb, "The Distribution of Costs and Benefits in an Urban Public School System," *National Tax Journal,* March, 1971, p. 8.)

Appendix 2C

17 See George D. Strayer and Robert M. Haig, *Financing of Education in the State of New York,* a report reviewed and presented by the Educational Finance Inquiry Commission under the auspices of the American Council on Education (New York: Macmillan, 1923). The statement of Professor Mort appears in Paul R. Mort, Walter C. Reusser, and John W. Polley, *Public School Finance* (New York: McGraw Hill, 3rd ed., 1960), p. 203.

18 G. D. Strayer and R. M. Haig, *op. cit.* (note 1), p. 94.

19 *Ibid.,* p. 162.

20 *Ibid.,* p. 173.

21 *Ibid.,* pp. 174–175.

22 *Ibid.*

23 Frank I. Michelman, "The Supreme Court, 1968 Term—Foreword: On Pro-

tecting the Poor through the Fourteenth Amendment," *Harvard Law Review,* Vol. 83, No. 1, pp. 33–59.

24 Henry C. Morrison, *School Revenue* (Chicago: University of Chicago, 1930), p. 164.

25 *Ibid.,* p. 194.

26 *Ibid.*

27 *Ibid.,* p. 196.

28 *Ibid.,* p. 164.

29 *Ibid.,* p. 205.

Appendix 2E

30 This is in spite of the fact that full value per WADA has declined to $28,400 from Year 0's $32,000, and WADA has increased by 250 to 2,250. This decline in full value will affect the state aid ratio after a lag of two years—the time necessary for the Department of Equalization and Assessment to provide the State Education Department with new full value figures for each district.

The new WADA figure will influence state aid allocations after a lag of one year.

Appendix 2F

31 Dick Netzer, "Potential Educational Revenues in the Coming Decade: Final Report to the Fleischmann Commission."

Sources of Tables

2.1 Computations based on data provided by the New York State Education Department, September, 1971.

2.2 New York State Department of Audit and Control, *Financial Data for School Districts, Year Ending June 30, 1969,* Tables F, G and H, pp. 8, 9, 10. University of the State of New York, *Analysis of School Finances,* April, 1971, Tables 6 and 7 (mimeographed), New York State Board of Equalization and Assessment.

2.4 New York State Board of Equalization and Assessment.

2.9 New York State Education Department, *Annual Educational Summary, 1968–69* (Albany, 1971), pp. 142–45. New York State Division of the Budget, Office of Statistical Coordination, *New York State Statistical Yearbook, 1971* (Albany, 1971), p. 96.

2.10 New York State Education Department.

2.11 Based on 104 school district sample in Harvey Brazer, *Fiscal Needs and Resources: A Report to the New York State Commission on Education,* November, 1971, Chapter 3, p. 27.

2.12 Adapted from *Social Statistics* monthly summaries, New York State Department of Social Services.

2.13 United States Department of Commerce, Bureau of the Census, *Statistical Abstract of the United States, 1970* (Washington, D.C.: Government Printing Office, 1970), pp. 315, 320. New York State Division of the Budget, Office of Statistical Coordination, *New York State Statistical Yearbook, 1971* (Albany, 1971), pp. 95, 96.

2.14 *New York State Statistical Yearbook, 1971, op. cit.* (note for Table 2.13), p. 158.

2.15 *Ibid.,* p. 195.

2.16 *Ibid.,* p. 156.

2.17 Minnesota State Planning Agency, *Report to Governor's Minnesota Property Tax Study Advisory Committee.*

2.18 University of the State of New York, State Education Department, *Annual Educational Summary, 1968–69* (Albany, 1971), p. 22.

2.19 *Ibid.*

2.20 "Adjusted Revenue 1969–70" from *State of New York Executive Budget for the Fiscal Year 1972,* p. A3.

2.21 Adapted from Dick Netzer, "Second Interim Report to the Commission on Potential Educational Revenues in the Coming Decade," February, 1971, Table 4, p. 28.

2A.1 New York State Education Department, Bureau of Educational Finance Research, October, 1971.

2B.1 Computed from New York State Education Department, *Annual Educational Summary, 1968–69,* Table 45, pp. 72–73; and State of New York Department of Audit and Control, *Financial Data for School Districts, Year Ending June 30, 1969,* Table 1, pp. 32–33.

2B.2 Computed from New York State Department of Audit and Control, *Financial Data for School Districts, Year Ending June 30, 1969,* Table 3, pp. 38–85.

2B.3 *Ibid.*

2D.2 New York State Education Department data.

2D.3 *Ibid.*

2D.4 New York State Comptroller.

2D.5 *Ibid.*

2D.6 State Comptroller data.

2D.11 New York State Education Department data.

2D.14 New York State Comptroller.

2D.15 New York State Education Department data.

2F.1 Dick Netzer, "First Interim Report to the Fleischmann Commission," p. 5.

2F.2 *Ibid.,* p. 6.

2F.4 Computed from data in *State of New York Executive Budget for the Fiscal Year 1972,* p. A3.

2F.5 See note for Table 2.20, *op. cit.*

2F.6 Based on Table 2F.4.

2F.7 Based on Table 2F.5.

2F.8 Dick Netzer, "Potential Educational Revenues in the Coming Decade: Final Report to the Fleischmann Commission," p. 56.

CHAPTER 3 (PAGES 209–224)

[1] New York State Education Department, *Federal Legislation and Education in New York State* (Albany, January, 1971), p. 76.

2 United States Bureau of the Census, *Statistical Abstract of the United States: 1970 (91st Edition)* (Washington, D.C.: Government Printing Office, 1970), p. 408.

3 United States Chamber of Commerce, Bureau of the Census, *Governmental Finances in 1969–70* (Washington, D.C.: Government Printing Office), p. 5.

4 New York State Education Department, Office of the Associate Commissioner of Finance, December, 1971.

5 For other examples see Advisory Commission on Intergovernmental Relations (ACIR), *The Gap Between Federal Aid Authorizations and Appropriations, Fiscal Years 1966–1970,* Report M-52 (Washington, D.C.: Government Printing Office, June, 1970), pp. 15–17.

6 See, e.g., *Newsweek,* December 20, 1971, pp. 71–72.

7 See Walter Heller, *New Dimensions of Political Economy* (Cambridge, Mass.: Harvard University Press, 1966).

8 United States Department of the Treasury, *General Revenue Sharing: The President's Message,* February, 1971, p. 8.

9 General Revenue Sharing Act of 1971 (S680) Sec. 301(b).

10 Committee on Ways and Means, United States House of Representatives, *Statistical Background Information Related to General Revenue Sharing* (Washington, D.C.: Government Printing Office, June, 1971).

11 *The President's Message, op. cit.,* p. 323.

12 Temporary State Commission to Revise the Social Services Law of the State of New York.

13 See HR6521, 92nd Congress, First Session, introduced by Congressman Dow, New York State, on March 23, 1971, which includes provisions to provide incentives for state responsibility in financing education.

14 Remarks of Congressman Byrnes in the *Congressional Record,* Volume 117, #67, May 10, 1971.

Sources of Figures

3A.1 New York State Education Department, *Federal Legislation and Education in New York State* (Albany, January, 1971).

3A.2 *Ibid.*

3A.3 *Ibid.*

CHAPTER 4 (PAGES 225–385)

1 *Brown* v. *Board of Education of Topeka,* 347 U.S. 483 (1954) at 495.

2 United States Department of Health, Education and Welfare, *HEW News,* June, 1971.

3 *Ibid.*

4 *Ibid.*

5 *Ibid.*

6 *Ibid.*

7 Based on data from New York State Education Department, Information Center for Education, Basic Education Data System (hereinafter B.E.D.S. data).

[8] *Ibid.*

[9] *Ibid.*

[10] We likewise conclude that an absolute prohibition against transportation of students assigned on the basis of race, "or for the purpose of creating a balance or ratio," will similarly hamper the ability of local authorities to effectively remedy constitutional violations. As noted in *Charlotte-Mecklenburg Board of Education* v. Swann, at 402 U.S. 1, 29 (1971), bus transportation has long been an integral part of all public educational systems, and it is unlikely that a truly effective remedy could be devised without continued reliance upon it. See *North Carolina State Board of Education* v. *Swann et al.,* 402 U.S. 43, 46 (1971).

[11] See *New York Times,* January 10, 1972, p. E5.

[12] Based on 1969–70 data from New York State Education Department, Division of Educational Finance.

[13] As passed by the House, the anti-busing provisions of the Act are even more damaging to the cause of equal educational opportunity. Amendments added by the House would (1) prohibit the use of any federal money to pay for buses, drivers or any other cost of transporting schoolchildren out of their neighborhoods because of their race, (2) forbid education officials from requiring, or even encouraging, communities to institute busing plans, and (3) prohibit federal court orders requiring busing to go into effect until all appeals had been exhausted or until the time for appeal had passed.

[14] For a more complete discussion see Mark A. Chesler, *Desegregation and Integration Within the School.* (Ann Arbor, Michigan: Unpublished report for Community Resources Limited, July, 1971).

[15] For the reader who is interested, extensive research has been done in an attempt to assess the effects of desegregation on students. Compilations and critical reviews of this research may be found in: M. I. Berkowitz, *Studies of School Desegregation and Achievement: A Summary* (Pittsburgh, Pa.: Commission on Human Relations, 1967). M. W. Carithers, "School Desegregation and Racial Cleavage, 1954–70: A Review of the Literature," *Journal of Social Issues,* Vol. 24, No. 6, 1970, pp. 25–47. I. Katz, "Review of Evidence Relative to Effects of Desegregation on the Intellectual Performance of Negroes," *American Psychologist,* 1964, Vol. 19, Number 6, pp. 381–399. Robert P. O'Reilly (ed.), *Racial and Social Class Isolation in the Schools* (New York: Praeger, 1970). H. H. Smythe and M. M. Smythe, *Some Benefits of Mixed Schools* (a report developed under contract for this Commission, New York, April, 1971). Meyer Weinberg, *Desegregation Research: An Appraisal* (Bloomington: Phi Delta Kappa, 1970, 2nd ed. Frank A. Petroni, Ernest A. Hirsch, and Lillian C. Petroni, *Two, Four, Six, Eight, When You Gonna Integrate?* (New York: Behavioral Publications, 1970).

[16] A study on the social effects of desegregation by the team of Koslin, Koslin, Pargament and Waxman at the Riverside Research Institute (*Classroom Racial Balance and Students' Interracial Attitudes,* 1971) came to the following conclusions concerning classroom segregation:

> . . . it is likely that in a school where all classes at any given grade level are similar in racial composition, children experience a very different "integration" from that experienced by children in a school where some classes in the grade are all white or predominantly white while others are all black or predominantly black. However "reasonable" the apparent motive for the administrative manipu-

lation (e.g., school lunch versus home lunch, short distance versus long distance busing, low versus high reading scores, etc.), the grouping practice nevertheless helps to create a social environment in which race is salient as a criterion for categorizing people and in which the opportunities for varied interracial contacts are sharply constrained for the majority of students. Hence one possible index of the quality of school integration is the *evenness* with which minority students are assigned to the available classes at their grade level.

[17] Some preliminary findings from the analysis currently being conducted by Koslin *et al.* (op. cit.) are relevant here. In the course of their school study, the researchers noted that white children with negative attitudes toward black children tended to come from specific classrooms; similarly, positive attitudes seemed to be engendered in other specific classrooms. The researchers tested matched groups of children in 12 classrooms one year, and the following year tested new groups of children in the same classroom, that is with the same teacher. Their hypothesis was verified: the majority of certain teachers' white students held positive racial attitudes toward their Negro classmates, and a majority of other teachers' students held more negative ones.

[18] Based on New York State Division of Human Rights, *Population and Housing in New York State, 1970.*

[19] *Ibid.*

[20] *Ibid.*

[21] Based on New York State Division of Human Rights, *Total Non-White and Puerto Rican Population in Counties of New York State: 1960 and 1969.*

[22] Based on "Population and Housing . . . 1970," and New York State Education Department, Bureau of School and Cultural Research, *Racial and Social Class Isolation in the Public Schools,* 1970, pp. 46–48.

[23] Based on New York State Education Department, *Racial and Social Class Isolation in the Public Schools, 1970,* pp. 46–48, and New York State Division of Human Rights, *Total Non-White and Puerto Rican Population in Counties of New York State: 1960 and 1969.*

[24] *Ibid.*

[25] Based on B.E.D.S. data.

[26] *Ibid.*

[27] *Ibid.*

[28] *Ibid.*

[29] *Statistical Abstract of the United States, 1970,* p. 21, and *Population and Housing in New York State, 1970,* New York State Division of Human Rights.

[30] The New York City Standard Metropolitan Statistical Area includes the five counties of New York City (Bronx, Kings, Queens, Richmond and New York) and Nassau, Suffolk, Westchester and Rockland Counties.

[31] Based on United States Census and New York State Division of Human Rights, *Total Non-White and Puerto Rican Population in Counties of New York State: 1960 and 1969.*

[32] B.E.D.S. data.

[33] *Ibid.*

[34] Based on B.E.D.S. data and United States Census.

[35] *Hobson* v. *Hansen,* 269 F. Supp. 401, 442–492, 511–514 (DCDC, 1967).

[36] Article V Section 1 of the "Agreement Between the Board of Education of

the City of New York and the United Federation of Teachers . . ." for 1969–1972, in part, reads as follows:

C. Elementary School Division

1. Teacher Assignments

    b. . . . teachers should be given an opportunity to fill out "preference sheets" indicating three preferences in order of priority of grade level and type of class on that level, with the understanding that, where advisable and possible, such preferences will be honored . . .

    d. In order to make certain that teachers are not frozen into positions which are relatively easy or difficult, the following procedures should be adopted in making class assignments (other than special assignments, such as RIT, IGC) on a particular grade level:

    (1) On each grade level, classes should be divided into two categories, "difficult" and "less difficult" in terms of reading achievement. In general, a teacher who has been assigned to a class in the one category for a period of one year should be assigned to the other category for the next year. . . .

    (2) In the case of IGC classes the policy of rotation every three years of qualified teachers should be followed. [Pages 64–65.]

(It is interesting to note that the contract not only requires ability grouping, but, further, defines these groups on a deficiency basis, as if all children are difficult to teach, but some may be less difficult.)

[37] Based on B.E.D.S. data.

[38] David Rogers, *110 Livingston Street* (New York: Random House, 1969), pp. 285, 288–89.

[39] *Chance* v. *Board of Examiners and Board of Education of the City of New York,* 330 F. Supp. 203 (SDNY, 1971).

[40] *Ibid.*

[41] Annie Stein, "Strategies for Failure," *Harvard Educational Review,* Vol. 41, No. 2, May, 1971, p. 161.

[42] In a noteworthy case (*Matter of Skipwith,* 14 Misc. 2d 325, New York Dom. Rel. Ct., 1958), Judge Justine Wise Polier held that Harlem parents who had held their children out of two public junior high schools on the demonstrated grounds that the schools were segregated and their facilities were inferior, were not guilty of neglecting their children. Judge Polier wrote: "These parents have the constitutionally guaranteed right to elect no education for their children rather than to subject them to discriminatorily inferior education."

[43] The New York State Education Commission's Advisory Committee on Human Relations and Community Tensions, *Desegregating the Public Schools of New York City,* prepared with the assistance of the Institute of Urban Studies, Teachers College of Columbia University, May 12, 1964.

[44] David Rogers, "Obstacles to School Desegregation in New York City: A Benchmark Case," in M. Gotlieb and Alan G. Hevesi, *The Politics of Urban Education* (New York: Praeger, 1969).

45 D. W. Dodson, "Desegregation of New York City Public Schools: A Feasibility Study" (report prepared for the New York State Commission on Education, 1971), p. 40.

46 While public school facilities, at least in some parts of the city, will probably have to accommodate an influx of students resulting from projected declines in nonpublic school enrollments, it is expected that where closings of nonpublic school facilities occur, such facilities could be purchased for public school purposes.

47 B.E.D.S. data.

48 Mary Ellen Warshauer and Robert Dentler, "Public School Segregation and Related Population Characteristics," unpublished paper for the New York State Education Department prepared by the Center for Urban Education, 1967, p. 3.

49 B.E.D.S. data.

50 Ibid.

51 Ibid.

52 Western New York School Development Council, "Project 1990—The Future of Education on the Niagara Frontier, Report #1, Status & Projections, 1970," p. 12.

53 B.E.D.S. data.

54 Matter of Dixon, 4 Ed. Dept. Rep. 115 (1965).

55 B.E.D.S. data.

56 Ibid.

57 This plan has subsequently been modified by the Center for Urban Education in cooperation with Project 1990. See Max Wolff and Annie Stein, A Plan for Middle Schools, Final Report, March, 1970.

58 For a well-documented history of these events, see A Report on Efforts of Suburban Groups to Promote Cooperation among City and Suburban School Districts in the Buffalo, New York, Metropolitan Area; testimony prepared by Austin Swanson and others for the New York State Commission on the Quality, Cost and Financing of Elementary and Secondary Education, March 19, 1971.

59 From United States Census of Population and Housing for Rochester, New York, in 1950, 1960, and 1964 in United States Commission on Civil Rights, "Staff Report on Issues Related to Racial Imbalance in the Public Schools of Rochester and Syracuse, New York," in Racial Isolation in the Public Schools, 1966; and United States Department of Commerce, Bureau of the Census, "1970 Census of Population," Advance Report, New York, February, 1971.

60 Ibid.

61 United States Department of Commerce, Bureau of the Census, "1970 Census of Population," Advance Report, New York, February, 1971.

62 Study for Racial Isolation in the Public Schools, 1966 (note 59).

63 These and following enrollment figures are based on: Annual Ethnic Census: 1970–71, Rochester City School District, Division of Planning and Research, December, 1970; Summary of Annual Enrollment Data, 1959–69, and Projected Annual Enrollments, 1970–71, 1974–75, Rochester City School District, Division of Planning and Research, June, 1970; and B.E.D.S. data.

64 Rochester City School District, Annual Ethnic Census: 1970–71, p. 2.

65 Summary of Annual Enrollment Data, 1959–69, and Projected Annual En-

rollments, 1970–71, 1974–75, Rochester City School District, Division of Planning and Research, June, 1970.

[66] From testimony of David R. Branch, Vice President of the Rochester Board of Education, before the Commission, March 19, 1971.

[67] B.E.D.S. data.

[68] For a more complete discussion of the history of this program, see Norman N. Gross, "Reaching for a Dream: An Experiment in Two-Way Busing," *Children,* Volume 17, No. 4, July–August, 1970, pp. 133 *et seq.*

[69] Norman N. Gross, Administrator, Title I, "ESEA and Urban-Suburban Transfers," Rochester City Board of Education, February 1, 1971.

[70] Gross, "Reaching for a Dream . . . ," *op. cit.,* pp. 133–34.

[71] *Survey of Enrollment, Staff and School Housing, Fall, 1969,* New York State Education Department.

[72] Application to the Commissioner of Education, requesting Special State Aid for Correcting Racial Imbalance in a proposal entitled *Coordinated Prototype Urban-Suburban Transfer Program for Rochester and Monroe County Schools,* February, 1971.

[73] Norman N. Gross, member of Rochester City Board of Education, in conversation with the Commission staff.

[74] Quoted from a draft of a proposal by the Rochester City Board of Education for Title III, ESEA funds for the establishment of a *Coordinated Prototype Urban-Suburban Transfer Program for Rochester and Monroe County Schools,* February, 1971.

[75] In December, 1971, the United States Department of Health, Education and Welfare announced that it would move against the Boston public school system for official actions that have led to a segregated school system. HEW notified Boston school officials that the system violates the 1964 Civil Rights Act and that it could face court action and a loss of federal school funds unless the city designs an acceptable plan for desegregating the 93,000-student system.

[76] United States Senate Bill S 1557.

[77] United States House of Representatives Bill HR 2266.

[78] Regents' Statement on Inter-Cultural Relations in Education, January 28, 1960.

[79] *Lee v. Nyquist,* 318 F. Supp. 710 (W.D.N.Y. 1970), aff'd. 402 U.S. 935 (1971).

[80] Board of Regents, *Integration and the Schools,* December, 1969.

[81] *Board of Education of City of New York v. Allen,* 6 N.Y. 2d 127 (1959).

[82] New York State Education Law, Section 306.

[83] New York State Education Law, Section 3201 (2).

[84] *Matter of McCoy et al.* (8 Education Dept. Rep. 22, 1968).

[85] B.E.D.S. data.

[86] 347 U.S. 483 (1954).

[87] *Ibid.,* 494.

[88] *Ibid.,* 495.

[89] 191 F. Supp. 181 (S.D.N.Y., 1961), aff'd. 294 F. 2d 36 (2d Cid., 1961), cert. den., 368 U.S. 940 (1961).

[90] *Ibid.,* p. 192.

[91] *Op. cit.,* pp. 222–23 (note 59).

[92] 204 F. Supp. 50 (E.D.N.Y. 1962).

[93] *Ibid.,* p. 153.

[94] *Ibid.*

[95] 226 F. Supp. 208 (E.D.N.Y. 1964).

[96] *Ibid.,* p. 225.

[97] *Ibid.,* p. 223.

[98] *Ibid.,* p. 227.

[99] *Ibid.,* p. 229.

[100] 391 U.S. 430 (1968).

[101] 402 U.S. 1 (1971), and 402 U.S. 43 (1971).

[102] 309 F. Supp. 734 (E.D. Mich. 1970) aff'd. 443 F. 2d 573 (6th Cir., 1971).

[103] 443 F. 2d at 576.

[104] *Johnson* v. *San Francisco Unified School District* Slip Op., p. 5 (N.D. Cal., April 28, 1971).

[105] Ibid., at footnote pp. 1–3.

[106] *Ibid.,* pp. 4, 5.

[107] U.S.D.C., E.D. Mich., September 27, 1971, 40 United States Law Week 2192.

[108] *Bradley* v. *Milliken supra,* transcript of proceedings (October 4, 1971).

[109] 338 F. Supp. 67 (D.C. Va., 1972).

[110] As reported in *New York Times,* January 11, 1972, p. 1.

[111] As qoted in *New York Times,* January 13, 1972, 41:1–2.

[112] 347 U.S. at p. 495.

[113] 402 U.S. 1 at p. 15 (1971).

[114] See, for example, a study by National Opinion Research Center, University of Chicago, as reported in *New York Times,* December 8, 1971, p. 33.

[115] Speech to the Electors of Bristol, England, November 3, 1774.

Separate Views of Commissioners

[116] Page 226, this volume.

[117] Meyer Weinberg, *Desegregation Research: An Appraisal* (Bloomington, Ind.: Phi Delta Kappa, 1970), pp. 259–60.

[118] Page 239.

[119] *Ibid.*

[120] Page 231.

[121] Pages 50–51.

[122] Kenneth B. Clark, *Dark Ghetto* (New York: Harper, 1965); and Donald H. Bouma and James Hoffman, *The Dynamics of School Integration: Problems and Approaches in a Northern City* (Grand Rapids, Mich.: Eerdmans, 1968), p. 23.

[123] Page 240.

[124] Page 239.

[125] Pages 237–38.

[126] Charles E. Silberman, *Crisis in Black and White* (New York: Random House, 1964), p. 304.

[127] Henry Hill, "Moderation and Common Sense Applied to Desegregation," *Integration and Education,* ed. by David W. Beggs (Chicago: Rand McNally, 1969), p. 17.

[128] Page 279.

[129] Page 225.
[130] Page 242.
[131] New York State Education Law, Section 314, Subdivision 1.
[132] Page 234.
[133] Page 236.
[134] Page 237.
[135] *Ibid.*
[136] *Ibid.*
[137] Pages 276–77.
[138] Page 276.
[139] *Ibid.*
[140] James S. Campbell, Joseph R. Sahid and David P. Stang, *Law and Order Reconsidered: Report of the Task Force on Law and Law Enforcement to the National Commission on the Causes and Prevention of Violence* (New York: Bantam, 1970), p. 214.
[141] Quoted in a letter from a Rochester constituent, Mrs. Dorothy Phillips, February 15, 1972.

Sources of Tables

4.1 Based on data from New York State Education Department, Information Center for Education, Basic Education Data System (hereinafter B.E.D.S. data).

4.2 *Ibid.*

4.5 *Ibid.*

4.6 United States Chamber of Commerce, Bureau of the Census, *Statistical Abstract of the United States, 1970,* p. 21; and "Population and Housing in New York State, 1970," New York State Division of Human Rights.

4.7 Based on B.E.D.S. data.

4.8 New York City Board of Education, *Racial Census 1970–71.*

4.9 Based on data supplied by United States Department of Health, Education and Welfare, Office of Civil Rights.

4.10 B.E.D.S. data.

4.11 *Ibid.*

4.12 *Annual Ethnic Census: 1970–71,* Rochester City School District; and B.E.D.S. data.

4.13 B.E.D.S. data.

4.14 Norman N. Gross, Administrator, Title I, "ESEA and Urban-Suburban Transfers," Rochester City Board of Education, February 1, 1971.

4.15 Compiled from Equal Educational Opportunities, Annual Report, Fiscal Year 1969, United States Office of Education; and from figures supplied by United States Office of Education, Title IV Office.

4.17 New York State Education Department, Division of Intercultural Relations.

Sources of Figures

4.1 United States Department of Health, Education and Welfare, *HEW News,* June 18, 1971.

4.2 Rochester City Board of Education.

1 403 U.S. 602 (1971).

2 For an account of the struggle for public funds by and among sectarian schools in New York City in the nineteenth century, see B. Congrey, *Secularism in American Education: Its History* (1931) pp. 127–31, cited by Justice Brennan in his concurring opinion in *Lemon* at p. 645.

3 "Memorial and Remonstrance against Religious Assessments," as reproduced in the Appendix to the dissenting opinion of J. Rutledge in *Everson* v. *Board of Education,* 330 U.S. 1, 63 [2 *The Writings of James Madison,* pp. 183–91 (G. Hunt, ed., 1901)].

4 Speech to Ministerial Association, Houston, Texas, September 12, 1960.

Separate Views of Commissioners

5 Speech before Knights of Columbus Convention, New York City.

6 Journal of Meeting of the Board of Regents, May 27–28, 1971, pp. 616–17.

7 Gary Report, Vol. I, p. VI–1.

8 *Pierce* v. *Society of Sisters,* 268 U.S. 510 (1925).

9 Gary Report, p. II–8.

10 *Ibid.,* Tables III–2, III–3, III–4.

11 *Ibid.,* p. IV–12.

12 *Ibid.,* p. VI–3.

13 Letter to Michael Dempsey, Nov. 19, 1971.

14 Gary Report, p. IV–14, 15.

15 Major Recommendations of the Regents for Legislative Action 1972, The State Education Department, 1971, p. 12.

16 Gary Report, p. IV–30.

17 *Ibid.,* p. IV–26.

18 *Ibid.,* p. IV–22.

19 *Ibid.,* p. IV–25.

20 *Ibid.,* Table III–2.

21 *Ibid.,* p. III–5.

22 *Ibid.,* Table III–2.

23 *Ibid.,* "Special Views," p. 63.

Appendix 5A

24 The quoted phrase comes from *Palko* v. *Connecticut,* 302 U.S. 319 (1937) at p. 325. *Palko,* however, dealt with double jeopardy. In *Cantwell* v. *Connecticut,* 310 U.S. 296 (1940) at 303–304, Justice Roberts wrote:

> The First Amendment declares that Congress shall make no law respecting an establishment of religion or prohibiting the free exercise thereof. The Fourteenth Amendment has rendered the legislatures of the states as incompetent as Congress to enact such laws.

[25] *Board of Education* v. *Allen,* 20 N.Y. 22 109 (1967), aff'd, 392 U.S. 236 (1968).

[26] *Pierce* v. *Society of Sisters,* 268 U.S. 510 (1925).

[27] *Lemon* v. *Kurtzman,* 403 U.S. 602, 625 (1971).

[28] *Ibid.,* p. 614.

[29] *Ibid.,* p. 616.

[30] *Illinois ex rel. McCollum* v. *Board of Education,* 333 U.S. 203 (1948); *Engel* v. *Vitale,* 370 U.S. 421 (1962); *School District of Abington Township, Pennsylvania* v. *Schempp et al.,* 374 U.S. 203 (1963).

[31] *Schempp* at 205.

[32] *Zorach* v. *Clausen,* 303 N.Y. 161 (1951), aff'd, 343 U.S. 306 (1952).

[33] *Lemon* at 612.

[34] See *Walz* v. *Tax Commission,* 397 U.S. 644, 674.

[35] *Lemon* at 612–13.

[36] *Ibid.,* p. 615.

[37] *Ibid.,* p. 617.

[38] *Ibid.,* p. 619.

[39] *Ibid.,* p. 619.

[40] *Ibid.,* p. 620.

[41] *Ibid.,* p. 622.

[42] *Ibid.,* p. 623.

[43] *Ibid.,* p. 624.

[44] *Ibid.,* p. 620.

[45] *Ibid.,* p. 641.

[46] *Ibid.,* p. 619.

[47] *Ibid.,* pp. 620–21.

[48] *Ibid.,* p. 668.

[49] *Ibid.,* p. 640.

[50] *Ibid.,* p. 622.

[51] *Ibid.,* p. 622.

[52] *Ibid.,* p. 623.

[53] *Poindexter* v. *Louisiana Financial Assistance Commission,* 275 F. Supp. 813 (D.C.E.D. La. 1967); see pp. 836 and 835 for the quotations above. The payment to the applicant's parent is explained at p. 836.

[54] *Poindexter* v. *Louisiana Financial Assistance Commission,* 389 U.S. 571 (1968).

[55] *Lemon* at p. 632, footnote 17, and cases cited therein.

Appendix 5B

[56] 403 U.S. 602, 612 (1971).

[57] 330 U.S. 1 (1947).

[58] *Ibid.,* p. 7.

[59] 392 U.S. 236 (1968).

[60] *Ibid.,* p. 243.

[61] 403 U.S. 672 (1971).

[62] *Lemon* at 616.

[63] *Tilton* at 687.

[64] *Protestants and Other Americans United for Separation of Church and State et al.* v. *Essex et al.,* 28 O.S. 2d 79, 87 (1971).

[65] *Lemon* at 621.

[66] 397 U.S. 664 (1970).

[67] 20 N.Y. 2d 109 (1967).

[68] *School District of Abington Township, Pennsylvania* v. *Schempp et al.,* 374 U.S. 203 (1963).

[69] *Allen* at 116.

[70] Gary Report, pp. V–49, 50.

[71] *Allen* at 115–16.

[72] *Ibid.,* p. 116.

[73] Gary Report, p. V–55.

[74] *Ibid.,* p. V–67.

Sources of Tables

5.1 Computations based on New York State Education Department data.

5.2 *Ibid.*

5.3 *Ibid.*

5.4 Computations based on Catholic School financial statements and Gary Report's Nonpublic School Questionnaire.

5.5 *Ibid.*

5.6 *Ibid.*

5.7 See note for Table 5.1.

5.8 "Financial Support, Nonpublic Schools, New York State," New York State Education Department, October, 1969.

5.9 See note for Table 5.1.

5.10 Forecast based on National Catholic Education Association Data Bank, 1970–71, the Official Catholic Directory, and New York State Education Department data.

5.11 Computations based on Catholic school financial statements.

5.12 Computations based on Catholic school financial statements, the Official Catholic Directory, and New York State Education Department data.

5.13 See note for Table 5.10.

5.14 Computations based on Gary Report's Catholic Religious Order Questionnaire, the Official Catholic Directory, and National Catholic Education Association Data Bank, 1970–71.

5.15 See note for Table 5.11.

5.16 Computations based on Catholic school financial statements, New York State Education Department data, and National Catholic Education Association Data Bank, 1970–71.

5.17–5.25 *Ibid.*

5.26 Computations based on Gary Report's Nonpublic School Questionnaire.

5.27 Computations based on New York State Education Department data and Diocesan Summary Reports.

5.28 *Ibid.*

5.29 Computations based on New York State Education Department data.

5.30 New York State Office of Audit and Control, and New York State Education Department.

Members of the New York State Commission on the Quality, Cost and Financing of Elementary and Secondary Education*

Manly Fleischmann, Chairman
Partner, Jaeckle, Fleischmann & Mugel—Buffalo
Partner, Webster Sheffield Fleischmann Hitchcock & Brookfield—New York

Constance E. Cook
Member, New York State Assembly

Raymond R. Corbett
President, New York State AFL-CIO

D. Clinton Dominick
Partner, Dominick & Fogarty

Alan A. Flans
President, Kraft Corrugated Containers Corporation

Charles Frankel
Professor, Columbia University

Phyllis A. Harrison, M.D.
Physician, New York City

---

* All Commission members served as individuals, and the contents of this report do not
  reflect the views of their organizations.

Acknowledgments

As in any public endeavor of similar magnitude, literally hundreds of individuals contributed their time, energy and ideas to the shaping of this report. Space limitations have permitted us to acknowledge by name only those persons and organizations who served the Commission in a formal, contractual consulting capacity. We regret that we are unable to acknowledge similarly those many people who lent their assistance and expertise to this venture and who did so without compensation; their contributions were invaluable and we are deeply grateful for their support in this enormous undertaking.

COMMISSION STAFF

Staff Director
  Charles S. Benson
Acting Director—Temporary
  (March–June 1970)
  Stephen D. Sugarman
Deputy Staff Director
  James W. Guthrie
Associate Director/Counsel
  Roger W. Hooker
Associate Director/Research
  Will Riggan

Associate Director/Liaison (May
  1970–August 1971)
  Frank Brown
Co-Counsel
  Carl D. Jaffee
Executive Assistant
  Mary E. Sughrue
Director of Public Information
  Michaela Williams
Editorial Assistant
  Karen C. Cole

Director of Production and Design
  Albert P. Sibley
Secretary to the Chairman
  Genevieve Wagner
Research Associates
  Patricia R. Allen
  James P. Meier
  Joan D. Meskin
  Jessica S. Pers
  Edwin S. Rubenstein
  M. Tracy Sillerman
  Phillip R. Wheeler
Research Assistant
  Lawrence Lieberman
Special Assistants and Secretaries
  Brenda M. Archibald
  Barbara Barnett
  Gwendolyn V. Bright
  Joan Campbell

Valerie C. Gilmore
Margaret A. Holt
Teri Rudinsky

Special Assignments
  Sharon R. Armann
  Betsy L. Bliss
  Deborah D. Burde
  Robert S. Ellenport
  Max C. Evers
  Paul M. Goldfinger
  Ann Greenberg
  Jacqueline Janzen
  Lynda Lippstreu
  Kenneth Miller
  Paul S. Phillips
  Stephen Rhoads
  Carlton M. Smith
  Sabahat Toraby

OUTSIDE CONSULTANTS

Norman Adler
  Hunter College
  New York, N.Y.
John S. Akin
  The University of Michigan
  Ann Arbor, Michigan
American Council on Education
  Washington, D.C.
Architectural Programming and Re-
  search Associates
  Princeton, New Jersey
  Anthony Vidler
Gerald T. Auten
  The University of Michigan
  Ann Arbor, Michigan

Lawrence H. Benjamin
  Bronx Children's Psychiatric
    Hospital
  New York, N.Y.
Harriett Blank
  Syracuse University
  Syracuse, New York
Burton Blatt
  Syracuse University
  Syracuse, New York

Harvey E. Brazer
  The University of Michigan
  Ann Arbor, Michigan
John Broughton
  Lewiston, New York
Clifford H. Browder
  New York, N.Y.
Michele C. Brown
  New York, N.Y.
Roscoe C. Brown, Jr.
  Institute of Afro-American
    Affairs
  New York, N.Y.
Arvid J. Burke
  State University of New York
    at Albany
  Albany, New York
Robert Burkhart
  State University of New York at
    Buffalo
  Buffalo, New York
Building Science, Inc.
  Buffalo, N.Y.
  John P. Eberhart

Jeanne S. Chall

Harvard University
Cambridge, Massachusetts
Chermayeff & Geismar Associates,
Inc.
New York, N.Y.
Thomas H. Geismar
Mark Chesler
The University of Michigan
Ann Arbor, Michigan
William H. Clune III
Northwestern University
Evanston, Illinois
Thomas Cochran
New York, N.Y.
Murray Cohen
Louis D. Brandeis High School
New York, N.Y.
Community Resources Ltd.
Ann Arbor, Michigan
Alan E. Guskin
Judith T. Guskin
Perry Cunningham
Maryann K. Hoff
James Crowfoot
John E. Coons
University of California
Berkeley, California
Joseph M. Cronin
Secretary of Education
Commonwealth of Massachusetts
Boston, Massachusetts
Cynthia S. Cross
The University of Michigan
Ann Arbor, Michigan

Allison Davis
The University of Chicago
Chicago, Illinois
Nicholas DeWitt
Indiana University
Bloomington, Indiana
Dan W. Dodson
New York University
New York, N.Y.
Robert E. Doherty
Cornell University
Ithaca, New York
Joseph Downey

Mamaroneck High School
Mamaroneck, N.Y.
Norman B. Drachler
Washington Institute of Education
Washington, D.C.
Rita S. Dunn
St. John's University
Jamaica, New York

Christopher Edley
New Rochelle High School
New Rochelle, New York
Educational Testing Service
Princeton, New Jersey
Sheldon S. Myers

Free Lance Associates, Inc.
Yonkers, N.Y.
Barbara Carter
Gloria Dapper
Marcia Freedman
Columbia University
New York, N.Y.

Robert M. Gagné
Florida State University
Tallahassee, Florida
Alan P. Gartner
New York University
New York, N.Y.
Stanley L. Gibson
University of California
Berkeley, California
Robert Goodfellow
Syracuse University
Syracuse, New York
Stephanie Green
Ripon College
Ripon, Wisconsin
Richard Greenspan
New York, N.Y.
Richard Guttenberg
Columbia University
New York, N.Y.

Richard Hammer
New York, N.Y.

Willis Harmon
  Stanford Research Institute
  Menlo Park, California
Charles Harrington
  Columbia University
  New York, N.Y.
Ruth N. Hartley
  University of California
  Santa Barbara, California
Kenneth W. Haskins
  Harvard University
  Cambridge, Massachusetts
Frederick O'R. Hayes
  New York, N.Y.
Harold L. Hodgkinson
  University of California
  Berkeley, California
Peter P. Horoschak
  Harvard University
  Cambridge, Massachusetts
Human Affairs Research Center
  New York, N.Y.
  George D. Blair
  Lloyd Hogan

Laurence Iannaccone
  Ontario Institute for Studies in
    Education
  Toronto, Ontario, Canada
Implications Research, Inc.
  New York, N.Y.
  Louis R. Gary, President
  Consultants:
  K. Michael Burke
    Columbia University
    New York, N.Y.
  Ernest J. Bartell
    Stone Hill College
    Stone Hill, Massachusetts
  Kenneth M. Brown
    University of Notre Dame
    Notre Dame, Indiana
  Andre L. Daniere
    Boston College
    Boston, Massachusetts
  Patrick S. Duffy
    University of California
    Berkeley, California

Donald A. Erickson
  University of Chicago
  Chicago, Illinois
George A. Kelly
  St. John's University
  Jamaica, New York
Otto F. Kraushaar
  Harvard University
  Cambridge, Massachusetts
George R. LaNoue
  Columbia University
  New York, N.Y.
George F. Madaus
  Boston College
  Boston, Massachusetts
Leo Pfeffer
  Long Island University
  New York, N.Y.
Institute for Community Studies
  Queens College of the City
    University of New York
  Flushing, N.Y.
  Marilyn Gittell
  Frances Gottfried
Institute for the Advancement of
    Urban Education
  New York, N.Y.
  Lloyd B. Hunter, President
  Consultant:
  Mario Fantini
    State University of New York
      at New Paltz
    New Paltz, New York

Bennett Jaffee
  New York, N.Y.
Adelbert H. Jenkins
  New York University
  New York, N.Y.
Mauritz Johnson
  State University of New York
    at Albany
  Albany, New York
Bruce Joyce
  Columbia University
  New York, N.Y.
Ralph Kaminsky
  New York University
  New York, N.Y.

John F. Kane
  Alexandria, Virginia
Martin T. Katzman
  Harvard University
  Cambridge, Massachusetts
Bel Kaufman
  New York, N.Y.
James F. King
  Alexandria, Virginia
George B. Kleindorfer
  University of California
  Riverside, California
Dennis Krieger
  Strasser, Spiegelberg,
    Fried & Frank
  New York, N.Y.

Dale G. Lake
  State University of New York at
    Albany
  Albany, New York
Fred Landis
  New York University
  New York, N.Y.
Todd Lee
  Caudill Rowlett Scott
  New York, N.Y.
Henry M. Levin
  Stanford University
  Stanford, California
Donald M. Levine
  Columbia University
  New York, N.Y.
Harold Levy
  Bronx High School of Science
  Bronx, New York
Myron Lieberman
  City University of New York
  New York, N.Y.
Roy Loe
  Peekskill, N.Y.

E. L. Mayer
  New York, N.Y.
Nancy G. McNulty
  Montclair, New Jersey
Elissa Meyer
  Buffalo, New York
LaMar P. Miller

New York University
  New York, N.Y.

Robert Neidich
  Union Free School District #5
  Hempstead, New York
Dick Netzer
  New York University
  New York, N.Y.
Wade J. Newhouse
  State University of New York
    Law School
  Buffalo, N.Y.

Anthony G. Oettinger
  Harvard University
  Cambridge, Massachusetts
Penelope Orth
  New York, N.Y.
J. W. Osman
  San Francisco State College
  San Francisco, California

Peat, Marwick, Mitchell & Co.
  New York, N.Y.
  Harold I. Steinberg
  Stanley Schoenfeld
Lewis J. Perl
  Cornell University
  Ithaca, New York
Richard D. Pfister
  State University of New York at
    Albany
  Albany, New York
Bradford Piggery
  Buffalo, New York
Poli-Systems, Inc.
  New York, New York
  Dale Mann
Public Relations Aids, Inc.
  New York, N.Y.
  Michael Smith
Puerto Rican Educators' Association,
    Inc.
  New York, N.Y.
  Awilda Orta
  Hernán La Fontaine
  Carmen Pérez

Dennis L. Roberts II
  New York, N.Y.
Francis J. Roberts
  Three Village Central School
    District #1
  Setauket, N.Y.
Constance Rogers
  Harlem Hospital Center
  Columbia University
  New York, N.Y.
David Rogers
  New York, N.Y.
Helen Rowan
  San Francisco, California

Arthur R. Satz
  Queens College
  City University of New York
  New York, N.Y.
Robert H. Schaffer & Associates
  Stamford, Connecticut
  Robert A. Neiman
  Robert H. Schaffer
Donna Shalala
  City University of New York
  New York, N.Y.
Richard Slitor
  Bethesda, Maryland
Hugh H. Smythe
  City University of New York
  New York, N.Y.
Mabel M. Smythe
  City University of New York
  New York, N.Y.

Annie Stein
  New York, N.Y.
Syracuse University Research Corp.
  Syracuse, New York
  Alan K. Campbell
  Joel S. Berke
  Walter I. Garms
  Robert J. Goettel

Teacher Drop Out Center
  Amherst, Massachusetts

Esther Unger
  New York, N.Y.

Melvin Webber
  University of California
  Berkeley, California
Elizabeth H. Weinstock
  New York, N.Y.
Westat Research, Inc.
  Rockville, Maryland
  Thomas McKenna
David E. Wilder
  Columbia University
  New York, N.Y.
Stephen Willoughby
  New York University
  New York, N.Y.
Mark Wrightman
  New Rochelle High School
  New Rochelle, N.Y.

Jerome Zukosky
  New York, N.Y.

REPORTS OF CONSULTANTS TO THE COMMISSION

Administrator/Community/School Relationships in New York State—A Final Report
  Poli-Systems, Inc.
Affective Concerns in Education
  Dale Lake
Alternative Methods for School Delivery in New York State
  Building Science, Inc.
Analyzing Education Budgets
  Frederick O'R. Hayes
  Michele Brown

Aspects of Educational Finance and Equal Opportunity
   Henry M. Levin
A Model for Educational Planning in the State of New York
   George B. Kleindorfer
   Paul M. Goldfinger
   Stephen M. Rhoads
A Study of the Educational Technologies of Computer-Assisted Instructional Television and Classroom Films Based on a Tour of Sites
   Sheldon S. Myers
Borrowing for Public School Purposes in New York State
   Arvid J. Burke
   Richard D. Pfister
BUILD Academy Report
   Bradford Piggery
Characteristics of College Freshmen from New York State, Fall 1970
   American Council on Education
Children with Special Needs in New York State
   Burton Blatt
   Harriett Blank
   Robert Goodfellow
Community School Health Services to Children
   Constance Rogers
Contraries: A Report and Recommendations on Selected Aspects of New York State Secondary Schools and Their Relation to Higher Education
   Francis Roberts
Curriculum and Humanistic Education: Monolism versus Pluralism
   Bruce Joyce
Decentralization of New York City Schools—Some Important Issues
   Roscoe C. Brown, Jr.
Desegregation of New York City Public Schools: a Feasibility Study
   Dan W. Dodson
Distribution of State Money to School Districts, 1962–70, with Particular Reference to the Diefendorf Law
   Arvid J. Burke
   Richard D. Pfister
Education Manpower and Employment—a Study of Manpower Requirements and Youth Employment Determinants
   Nicholas DeWitt
Educational Objectives and Their Measurement
   Robert M. Gagné
Educational Production Functions and Their Relevance to Education in New York State
   E. L. Mayer
Ethnic Modification of the Curriculum
   LaMar Miller
Family Choice Systems
   John E. Coons
   William H. Clune III
   Stanley Gibson

Dennis Krieger
J. W. Osman

Fiscal Needs and Resources: a Report to the New York State Commission on the Quality, Cost and Financing of Elementary and Secondary Education
Harvey E. Brazer
John S. Akin
Gerald T. Auten
Cynthia S. Cross

High Schools in Crisis: a Study of Organizational Crisis in New York State High Schools
Community Resources Limited
Human Affairs Research Center

Individualization of Instruction
Mauritz Johnson

Impact of the Taylor Law upon the Governance and Administration of Elementary and Secondary Education
Myron Lieberman

Impact of the Taylor Law on the Operation of the Public Schools: a School Board Point of View
Fred Landis

I.S. 201 (film)
Roy Loe

Learning Disorders in Children
Lawrence H. Benjamin

Mathematics Education in New York State
Stephen Willoughby

New York City Teachers' Retirement System
Frederick O'R. Hayes
Donna Shalala

Non-Instructional Services: a Study of Alternatives
Peat, Marwick, Mitchell & Company

Notes on Terminology: "Curriculum," "Instruction," and "Evaluation"
Mauritz Johnson

Organizing and Governing Public Education in New York
Joseph M. Cronin
Peter P. Horoschak
Laurence Iannaccone
Donald M. Levine

Paraprofessionals and the Schools
Alan P. Gartner

Performance Contracting: a Systems Approach to Management in Education
Richard Guttenberg

Performance Contracting in Elementary and Secondary Education
Martin M. Katzman

Political Socialization Implications of Grade School Social Studies Textbooks in New York State
Norman Adler
Charles Harrington

Potential Educational Revenues in the Coming Decade
  Dick Netzer
  Ralph Kaminsky
Public School Facility Cost Studies in New York State Since 1950
  Arvid J. Burke
  Richard D. Pfister
Rationality and the "Humanization" of Education
  Mauritz Johnson
Reorganizing School Government
  Jerome Zukosky
Revising School Finance in New York State
  Syracuse University Research Corporation
School Decentralization and School Policy in New York City
  Institute for Community Studies
Selected Data on Education Personnel and Handicapped Children in New York State from the United States Office of Education School Staff Survey, 1970
  Westat Research, Inc.
Social Utility, Equal Educational Opportunity and Educational Investment Policy
  Henry M. Levin
Some Benefits of Mixed Schools
  Hugh H. Smythe
  Mabel M. Smythe
Spaces for Learning—Environmental Quality and the Educational Program
  Architectural Programming & Research Associates
Stating Educational Goals: Some Problems and a Proposal
  Mauritz Johnson
Statutory Provisions Concerning Curriculum: an Analysis and a Proposal
  Mauritz Johnson
Student Flow, Teacher Costing and Budget Simulation Models: a Brief Description and Sample Analyses
  George B. Kleindorfer
  Paul M. Goldfinger
  Stephen M. Rhoads
Teacher Characteristics: Their Level and Distribution in New York State
  Lewis J. Perl
The Collapse of Nonpublic Education: Rumor or Reality?
  Implications Research, Inc.
The Education of the Puerto Rican Child in New York
  Puerto Rican Educators' Association, Inc.
  Richard Greenspan
The Human Capital Approach to Financing Equality of Educational Opportunity
  Henry M. Levin
The Nature and Extent of the Drug Problem among Students in New York State Public Schools, with a Proposed Model for Workable Drug Education Programs
  Arthur R. Satz

List of Abbreviations

ACIR (Advisory Commission on Intergovernmental Relations) A permanent, national bipartisan body established by Act of Congress in 1959 to give continuing study to the relationships among local, state and national levels of government.

ADA (Average Daily Attendance) The aggregate number of attendance days of pupils in a school district divided by the number of days of actual session.

ADC (Aid to Dependent Children)

AFT (American Federation of Teachers) Bargaining agent for teachers in most New York State school districts outside of New York City.

BEDS (Basic Education Data Systems) Statewide, computerized information system for all New York State school districts containing personnel data, ethnic census information, student achievement profiles, etc.

BOCES (Boards of Cooperative Educational Services) Presently some 47 boards, each representing a number of local school districts, which act as a middle tier of government between the local district and the state. By sharing certain costs and facilities through BOCES, local districts can provide specialized services in a more efficient manner. These now include music and art teachers, programs for handicapped children, vocational education programs and non-instructional services such as data processing and teacher recruitment.

CUE (Center for Urban Education) Federally funded center for education research and innovation serving New York State.

CUNY (City University of New York)

CVEEB (County Vocational Education and Extension Boards)

ESEA (Elementary and Secondary Education Act) Legislation passed in 1965 aimed at providing funds to states for the education of children from low-income families.

ETS (Educational Testing Service) Private corporation based in Princeton, New Jersey, that prepares standard tests such as the SAT.

FV (Full Value) This is determined by dividing the assessed valuation of taxable real property by the equalization rate assigned to the district by the State Board of Equalization and Assessment. Assuming that the equalization rates have been accurately established, real property of identical value in separate but similar communities of the state, which had been assessed by diverse local standards, would have the same full value.

HR 1 Proposed federal welfare reform bill.

K (Kindergarten)

NIE (National Institute of Education) Proposed national research center for education.

NMSQT (National Merit Scholarship Qualifying Tests) National test for college-bound students, some of whom qualify for financial aid.

OPS (Office of Planning Services) Principal planning and forecasting unit of the state government.

PEP (Pupil Evaluation Program) Standardized tests in reading and mathematics given statewide to all students at the third, sixth and ninth grades.

RSCQT (Regents Scholarship and College Qualification Test) Statewide test for college-bound seniors who elect to take it.

RWADA (Resident Weighted Average Daily Attendance) This is calculated by subtracting the WADA of non-resident pupils attending public school in the district from the district's WADA and adding the WADA of pupils resident in the district but attending full-time a school operated by a BOCES or a CVEEB.

SAT (Scholastic Aptitude Tests) National tests administered to college-bound seniors (or in some cases juniors).

SED (State Education Department)

SES (Socio-Economic Status)

SESA (Secular Education Services Act) Legislation enacted by the State in 1971 to provide funds to nonpublic schools for secular services.

SMSA (Standard Metropolitan Statistical Area)

SSA (Spanish-Surnamed American)

UDC (Urban Development Corporation) A state agency and public benefit corporation created by the State Legislature in 1968 to develop and finance housing for low-, moderate- and middle-income families, to assist industrial and commercial development and to provide needed educational, cultural and other civic facilities.

UFT (United Federation of Teachers) Bargaining agent for New York City public school teachers.

USOE (United States Office of Education)

WADA (Weighted Average Daily Attendance) This is determined by applying the following weightings to the average daily attendance: half-day kindergarten, .50; full-day kindergarten and grades 1–6, 1.00; grades 7–12, 1.25.